JFK, Oswald and Ruby

JFK, Oswald and Ruby

Politics, Prejudice and Truth

Burt W. Griffin
Warren Commission Assistant Counsel

McFarland & Company, Inc., Publishers
Jefferson, North Carolina

ISBN (print) 978-1-4766-8776-6
ISBN (ebook) 978-1-4766-4992-4

Library of Congress and British Library
cataloguing data are available

Library of Congress Control Number 2023016969

Front cover: (top left) Lee Harvey Oswald reacts as he is shot by Jack Ruby on November 24, 1963 (photograph by Bob Jackson); (bottom right) John F. Kennedy rides in the presidential limousine in Dallas, Texas, minutes before his assassination (photograph by Walt Cisco)

Printed in the United States of America

McFarland & Company, Inc., Publishers
Box 611, Jefferson, North Carolina 28640
www.mcfarlandpub.com

Table of Contents

Acknowledgments

My judicial colleague C. Ellen Connally prompted this book. Two years before my retirement as an Ohio trial judge, Judge Connally urged me to write a book about the Warren Commission. My answer then was no. Enough JFK assassination books existed.

I wanted to write, instead, about the political consequences of the four presidential assassinations—Lincoln, Garfield, McKinley, and Kennedy. We pride ourselves on being a model democracy. But four presidential assassinations in 98 years is not matched even by the troubled states.

Assassinations have brought major changes in our country. Lincoln's assassination was followed by the 13th, 14th, and 15th Amendments to the U.S. Constitution. Garfield's killing produced Civil Service reform. McKinley's enabled Theodore Roosevelt to launch an era of domestic economic reform. And Kennedy's death was followed by civil rights reform and the Vietnam war. I thought it might be important to examine the motives of each assassin and the political impact of each assassination.

With Ellen Connally's help, I began that quest. In addition to being a trial judge, Ellen was a PhD candidate in American history and loved John Kennedy. She led me to scholarly works about Lincoln, Garfield, and McKinley. She combed the Warren Commission records for relevant testimony. Without Ellen, this book would not have been started.

Ultimately, I began to write about what I knew best: Lee Oswald, Jack Ruby, and the murders of President Kennedy, Officer J.D. Tippit, and Oswald.

After a few months my writing stopped. My computer swallowed my chapters on Oswald's life and wouldn't give them back.

Meanwhile, various groups asked me to talk about the JFK assassination. One talk to a breakfast group brought me to my second inspirer: Todd Kwait. Todd had been a summer intern for me when he was a law student. His father attended the breakfast talk. I asked what Todd was doing. He said that Todd was making documentary movies.

I didn't know the difference between producing a documentary and producing a feature film. I hoped Todd could lead me to someone who could produce a feature film to combat Oliver Stone's *JFK.* Instead, Todd brought to our first luncheon a pile of papers and a plan for a documentary about how the Warren Commission did its work.

He wanted me to recruit Warren Commission staffers for him to interview. That I did. Five years later, in 2020, Todd completed for viewing on Amazon Prime the documentary *The Only Client Is the Truth.* In those five years, Todd created a sequence of new relationships for me. Authors Priscilla McMillan, Vincent Bugliosi, Max Holland, and Gus Russon became friends who helped me with research. I met and interviewed Ruth Paine and Bernard Weissman for the first time. My friendship with Bob Blakey led to an interview about why he thought that Oswald and Ruby were part of a conspiracy. I thank all of them for their time and candor.

Throughout the production process, I renewed Commission friendships from 1964: Mel Eisenberg, Al Goldberg, Murray Laulicht, Dick Mosk, Stuart Pollak, David Slawson, Sam Stern, and, of course, Howard Willens. Each has talked with me or read portions of this book. I thank them for refreshing my memory. Special thanks go to Howard Willens. He read early drafts, clarified facts, and offered helpful suggestions.

When *Truth Is the Only Client* was nearing release, I decided to begin writing again. It was to be a typed 50-page pamphlet that would set forth the essential facts of the assassination and accompany the documentary film. When viewing time arrived, the pamphlet exceeded 400 pages. It was a book quite different from what I conceived when Ellen Connally and Todd Kwait inspired my writing and research.

Rather than begin with a biography of Oswald, I decided to open the assassination story with an account of the evidence gathered by the Dallas Police Department on November 22, 23, and 24, 1963. The Dallas police secured the initial evidence: Oswald, his rifle, cartridges, fingerprints, boxes in the sixth-floor window, and eyewitnesses. Thanks for the idea putting the Dallas police work first go to another judicial friend—Judge Brendan Sheehan.

Even before Todd Kwait joined the scene, Brendan had decided to host monthly discussion groups in his jury room for Cleveland area lawyers interested in the assassination. That led to continuing legal education programs for Ohio lawyers which Brendan, Ellen, and I conducted. We also made presentations to high school students. What became clear was that both lawyers and high school students had little knowledge of the facts of the two murders by Oswald on November 22, 1963—facts that had been developed by the time Oswald was murdered by Ruby, were the basis for indicting Oswald for the Kennedy and Tippit's murders, and were never contradicted by subsequent public investigations. Thus, this book begins with the facts of JFK's assassination, Tippit's murder, and Oswald's arrest.

It made sense to me that the murder of Oswald should come next and that the Ruby portion of the book should begin with the Jack Ruby trial. For help with accounts of that trial, I owe special thanks to Steve Bucha. Steve was my law clerk for many years when I served as an Ohio trial judge. He later became the Chief Referee for our court. Steve spent many volunteer hours reading the Ruby trial chapter and providing research. He thinks that his fellow referees should read the chapters dealing with the Oswald and Ruby witnesses for lesson in judging credibility. Thanks, Steve.

Special thanks are also owed to Gus Russo. Through his book, *Live by the Sword*, Gus provided me the evidence and insight that President Kennedy's allowing the CIA to attempt to assassinate Fidel Castro probably was a major contributor to Oswald's decision to kill Kennedy. No one has looked more closely than Gus Russo at witnesses rejected by the Warren Commission. Gus's reliance on some caused me to evaluate them anew. Through that process, Gus became an important source of information. Although we have ultimately disagreed on some matters of credibility, Gus has become a good friend and helper—one whose integrity, hard work, and intelligence I treasure.

Finding a publisher for this book has not been easy. I was correct when I told Ellen Connally that there were already too many books about the JFK assassination. My law school classmate, Vic Navasky (former editor of the *Nation* magazine), and my Cleveland friend, lawyer and author Jim Robenalt, referred me without success to their book publishers. Thanks, Vic and Jim, for the leads and your suggestions on how to do it.

In the end, of course, McFarland took the risk. To get me there, I owe special thanks to my private editor Judith Keeling and Carole Young, Judith's dearest friend when both were active in academic publishing. Judith has edited and re-edited numerous drafts for content, accuracy, and clarity. She has been an important source of ideas. Carole has not only source-checked many of the citations for accuracy but has become a researcher and constructive critic. Many, many thanks, Judith and Carole.

As the book neared readiness for a publisher, Steve Fagin, Paul Hoch, Max Holland, John McAdams, Gerald Posner, and Richard Reiman were of special importance. All are experts on the JFK assassination. Each read a complete draft as the text neared final form. Fagin located numerous Sixth Floor Museum sources. Hoch volunteered many hours in locating other needed sources. Reiman found valuable newspaper items about Fidel Castro's threat to retaliate against Kennedy. Holland, McAdams, and Posner encouraged me as I worried that another JFK assassination book was not justified. Steve, Paul, John, Max, Gerald, and Rick—many thanks.

In twenty-first-century publishing, computer skills are ones that a twentieth-century author may not have. I am one of those. Thanks to Angie Mcicinnelo and Jennifer Apt for bridging the divide.

Someone suggested to me that getting a book to the public is like managing a political campaign. Family and close friends become volunteers in the publication campaign. Here are some to whom I owe thanks—my sister-in-law, Terese Deboo; my daughter-in law, Desire Roman; and my cousin, Virginia Albrecht. They were each asked to read a draft and tell me when they got bored. They claim they did so, and boredom did not arrive.

My grandson, Andrew Griffin, has been especially helpful. A high school and college student at the time, he source-checked and brought me into the 21st century when I needed word processing advice. His sister, Caitlin, and father, Mark, filled in when college studies kept Andrew away.

Thanks also to my friends Don Freedheim and Frank O'Grady. Both tried to persuade the National Archives to open their records during the pandemic. Frank deserves special praise. He ultimately coordinated assembling all photographs and maps. Credit for crucial touches on the book's title and cover goes to him.

But the greatest thanks go to my son, Bruce Griffin, and my wife, Beatrice. They were contributors even before Ellen Connally. Bruce became an assassination addict shortly after I finished working at the Commission in 1964. He knows more about the evidence and literature than I do. Now a college professor, he has been an editor, researcher, and analyst as this book has developed. My wife, Beatrice (she has been known as Bunny from birth), is a child and adult psychoanalyst. I do not claim to be unaffected by her ideas as to how people like Lee Oswald and Jack Ruby evolve from childhood to adults. Most importantly, she endured hours of isolation as I was absorbed in thinking and writing about the JFK assassination. She has listened for many hours and made suggestions as I have read chapters to her.

Preface

JFK, Oswald and Ruby: Politics, Prejudice and Truth is about finding truth in a political world. It aims to assist the serious reader in his or her search for truth about the weekend of November 22, 1963. Hopefully, in searching for truth about the John Kennedy assassination, the reader will be helped in finding truth in other serious political events.

The lives of President Kennedy, Lee Harvey Oswald, and Jack Ruby are central to our search. The three men interacted in a political world of prejudice and violence remembered as the Cold War and the civil rights movement. The result: three murders in three days. On Friday, November 22, 1963, Oswald killed Kennedy and Dallas police officer J.D. Tippit. Two days later, Ruby killed Oswald in full view of police officers and the TV world.

Ruby's murder of Oswald precluded a trial of Kennedy's death. The world needed to know why. Normally, the question of why would have been pursued by a thorough examination of Oswald's life in the days and months before Kennedy died. But Ruby's action diverted public attention to a search for conspirators. The long-term consequence has been decades of public doubt as to whether the truth has been found.

I was one of the early searchers. Less than two months after President Kennedy's death, I became a lawyer for the President's Commission on the Assassination of President Kennedy (popularly known as the Warren Commission). Ultimately, I had primary responsibility for presenting to the Commission the evidence of whether Jack Ruby was part of a conspiracy to assassinate President Kennedy, Lee Oswald, or both. I made every effort to find evidence of Ruby's involvement in a conspiracy. I found none.

I found, however, considerable evidence of a motive that conspiracy theorists prefer to ignore—that Ruby, who was Jewish, killed Oswald because he feared that Jews would be blamed for Kennedy's death. He hoped that if a Jew killed Oswald, Jews would not be blamed for the Kennedy assassination. The relevant details are crucial to *JFK, Oswald and Ruby: Politics, Prejudice and Truth.*

While I was certain of Ruby's motive for killing Oswald when we finished our work for the Warren Commission in September 1964, I was uncertain of why Oswald killed Kennedy. In a 40-year career as a civil trial attorney, prosecutor, legal aid executive, and trial judge, I have followed closely the debate over who killed President Kennedy and why. I am much more certain now. The answers, I believe, lie in a close examination of Oswald's life and the politics that surrounded him. Helping students of history master those facts is the purpose of *JFK, Oswald and Ruby: Politics, Prejudice and Truth.*

The book has five major parts: Politics One, Two, Three, Four, and Five. Politics One, entitled "Investigators Find a Suspect," addresses the initial investigation by the

Dallas Police Department. By the time Ruby killed Oswald, the Dallas police were certain that Oswald was President Kennedy's assassin. They had no evidence of likely conspirators. That decision might not satisfy the public, however. To obtain a publicly credible decision, President Lyndon Johnson appointed a Commission headed by U.S. Chief Justice Earl Warren. That creation of the Warren Commission and its staff concludes Politics One of this book.

Politics Two, "Prejudice and Truth," deals with Jack Ruby. It begins with his trial, continues to his testimony before the Warren Commission, and ends with the investigation that my colleague, Leon Hubert, and I conducted. The chapters in Politics Two describe a high-profile criminal trial in which publicity for defense lawyers and the trial judge were as important as justice or truth. They show also how Hubert and I conducted our investigation and what we found. The final chapter details how Ruby came to fear that Jews would be blamed for President Kennedy's death and how he became the first private conspiracy investigator.

Politics Three is entitled "Determining Credibility." It highlights five categories of credibility that the Warren Commission faced: (1) those who withheld evidence from the Commission to protect what they believed was national security; (2) those who withheld or distorted evidence to protect their employment; (3) testimony of scientific or forensic experts; (4) honest witnesses who may have been mistaken about what they had seen; and (5) private citizens who deliberately lied to promote a self-interest. Examples include the CIA's failing to tell the Warren Commission about its efforts to assassinate Fidel Castro; FBI Agent James Hosty destroying a note from Oswald; police Sergeant Patrick Dean becoming a premeditation witness against Jack Ruby; disputes related to autopsy and acoustics evidence; Sylvia Odio's honest belief that she had been visited by Lee Oswald; and lawyer Mark Lane deliberately making false claims to the Commission.

Politics One, Two, and Three recount that all official investigations concluded that Lee Harvey Oswald killed President Kennedy, that no credible evidence of a conspiracy has been found, and that no official investigation has determined Oswald's motive.

Politics Four is entitled "Ambition, Failure, and Assassination." It addresses the evidence of Oswald's motive. In twenty-eight chapters, Politics Four sets forth Oswald's early life, his Marine Corps experiences from 1956 to 1959, his defection to the Soviet Union in 1959, his marriage there to Marina Prusakova, his return to the United States in 1962, his political writings, his attempt to kill former General Edwin Walker in April 1963, his flight to New Orleans in May of 1963, his failure to gain admission to Cuba in September 1963, and the weeks in October and November that resulted in his assassinating President Kennedy.

The evolution of the Cold War and the civil rights movement in 1962 and 1963 are presented as they would have been perceived by Oswald from the shortwave radio to which he listened, the newspapers and books he read, and the events he attended. Politics Four recounts the civil rights violence that mounted after Oswald returned to the United States and culminates in September 1963 with the murder of four children at the Sixteenth Street Baptist Church in Birmingham, Alabama.

Politics Four relates also Dallas public officials' worry that followers of General Walker would disrupt President Kennedy's visit to Dallas in November. In October 1963, Walker held a rally in Dallas attended by more than a thousand people. The purpose was to disrupt a Dallas speech the next evening by U.S. Ambassador Adlai Stevenson extolling the United Nations. Oswald attended the Walker rally as an observer.

The next night Oswald did not attend the Stevenson speech. Walker's supporters did and succeeded in disrupting the speech. After the speech, a Walker supporter struck Stevenson with a sign. Dallas officials, the media, and others feared that Kennedy would suffer a similar fate in November. He was urged to remove Dallas from his list of cities to be visited.

Politics Four ends by describing how the Stevenson event, local Dallas fears, the Cold War, the atmosphere of violence in the civil rights movement, and the deterioration of Oswald's personal life resulted in the assassination of President Kennedy. The conclusion of Politics Four is that Oswald killed Kennedy because his own life had collapsed, he had a long-time desire to produce political change of historic magnitude, he believed that Walker and his followers might be blamed, and he hoped that such blame would save Fidel Castro's regime in Cuba. The plan was his own, and he acted alone.

Politics Five, "Coping with Truth in Assassinations," deals with the aftermath of the assassinations. When Marina Oswald testified before the Warren Commission, she believed that her husband was guilty. Thirty years later she thought he was innocent. Within weeks of the assassinations, the Soviet Union began a disinformation campaign suggesting that President Kennedy was assassinated by an undiscovered coalition of business leaders and Kennedy opponents in the government. The movies *JFK* and *Executive Action* incorporate that message. A majority of Americans continue to believe that President Kennedy was probably the victim of an undiscovered conspiracy.

JFK, Oswald and Ruby: Politics, Prejudice and Truth sends this message: Oswald and Ruby were lone killers. There is no evidence of a conspirator. Historians and students of history should cease being criminal investigators. They should focus on the super-abundance of evidence as to why Oswald and Ruby committed political murders, the political and social environment as they saw it, and how the public's knowledge of the lives of Oswald and Ruby may prevent history from repeating itself. They should ignore the political world that fascinates conspiracy theorists.

Armed with that insight, a student of America's history may conclude, as I have, that the deaths of President Kennedy and Lee Oswald and the nation's reaction to those events were turning points in the Cold War and the civil rights movement caused by politically impotent, isolated men acting on the world stage to abet their own insecurities and desires to be important.

May I begin my accounting?

Introduction

As I returned from lunch to my Cleveland, Ohio, office on November 22, 1963, someone in our elevator said, "The president's been shot."

"Those damned segregationists," I thought.

Two months previously, a bombing had killed four Black children at a Birmingham, Alabama, church. In June 1963, Medgar Evers had been murdered in Mississippi for urging African Americans to vote. I knew that many in Dallas hated John Kennedy. He supported the mounting civil rights revolution. Southern segregationists were my logical suspects.

When I reached my office, the receptionist in our eight-lawyer office turned on the radio. A few minutes later, we learned that the president had died. Our office—six Republicans and two Democrats—closed immediately.

At home I watched the investigation unfold on television. For us—my wife, our three-year-old son, and his two-month-old brother—life paused. To this day, our older son remembers the atmosphere.

Soon we heard that Lee Oswald—a Marxist defector to the Soviet Union—had been arrested. My suspicions were aroused. The arrest was too quick. It might be a frame-up. Dallas was a center for right-wing anti-Communists. The chief of the Federal Bureau of Investigation was obsessed with the domestic danger of Communists. Could those investigators be trusted?

Then the unthinkable happened. Two days later, in the basement of the Dallas police station, Jack Ruby, operator of a Dallas striptease club, shot Oswald. Scores of news media personnel in the basement and millions of television viewers saw it. Within an hour, Oswald was dead.

Dallas and America were ashamed. I was ashamed. The City of Dallas and the FBI had every reason to solve these crimes swiftly.

Yet I had reasons myself for distrusting their speedy conclusion. Before entering the private practice of law, I had been an assistant United States attorney in Cleveland prosecuting criminal cases. I had worked with the Secret Service and the FBI. I admired the Secret Service. They were dedicated risk takers. They took pride in their agents' ability to infiltrate counterfeiting rings by posing as criminals.

FBI agents, by contrast, were cautious bureaucrats. Nice people. Dedicated people. Well educated. But thoroughly intimidated by their agency's director, J. Edgar Hoover. When an FBI agent conferred with me about a criminal case, the agency director was not referred to as Hoover or the boss or any other short form. It was always *Mr.* Hoover—as if a supervisor in Washington might overhear the agent in Cleveland.

I was also unimpressed with the FBI's ability to solve well-planned crimes. The FBI had a superb press agency, but it had not been especially effective in catching spies. For example, in 1957 one Soviet spy, a man named Rudolph Abel, was arrested after having been in the U.S. for over eight years, all the while sending information back to Russia without being discovered.[1]

So, like many in the public, I was not ready to accept the FBI's conclusion that Lee Harvey Oswald had killed President Kennedy or that he had acted alone. I was comforted, later, however, to learn that a commission headed by Chief Justice Earl Warren had been appointed to get the facts.

By late December 1963, the assassination of the president and the resulting Commission were not foremost in my mind. My focus was on Christmas, our two young sons, and my relatively new job. Shortly before New Year's, I received a phone call from David Filvaroff, a young lawyer from Cleveland who was now working in the office of Attorney General Robert Kennedy. David was a casual acquaintance. I knew him mainly from cocktail parties. Not expecting to see him again when he moved to Washington, we had dropped him from our Christmas card list.

He was not calling, however, about an overlooked Christmas card. "Would you be interested in working on the Warren Commission?" he asked. Had he dialed the wrong number, I wondered. My caller was not making an offer. He simply wanted to refer my name to Howard Willens, a Justice Department lawyer who had been delegated from the department's Criminal Division to assist the Commission's general counsel, J. Lee Rankin, in assembling a Warren Commission staff.

My caller believed I met Willens' criteria. The Commission wanted geographic diversity. I was from the Midwest. I was the right age—early thirties. My experience was right—former prosecutor. It didn't hurt that I had attended Yale Law School—from which Willens had graduated a few years before me. I had been an officer of the law review there and had clerked for a U.S. Circuit Court of Appeals judge in Washington, D.C.

I sent Willens my resume. A week later a job offer came. So, we packed our bags. On January 10, 1964, my wife, our two young sons, and I were in Washington, D.C. I was to be one of a fifteen-lawyer staff hired to determine who killed President Kennedy and why. My assignment was to learn whether Jack Ruby was part of a conspiracy to assassinate the president, Lee Harvey Oswald, or both.

Thus, my quest began nearly sixty years ago. In many senses, it has never ended. It has been a search for truth in a political world—a world driven by personal ambitions, insecurities, and frustrations. A world tainted by religious and racial prejudice. Here is the story as I perceive it.

POLITICS ONE

Investigators Find a Suspect

1

The Most Extensive Criminal Investigation in History

The murder of President Kennedy may be the most extensively investigated crime in U.S. history.[1] More than twenty thousand individuals were interrogated in the ten months that followed his death. Over the next twenty years, more than a dozen forensic pathologists examined autopsy photographs of the president. In that same period, repeated examinations were made of ballistics, fingerprint, photographic, and audio evidence.

Official bodies twice reviewed the totality of the evidence—the Warren Commission in 1964 and the House Select Committee on Assassinations from 1977 to 1979.[2] Each took testimony from eyewitnesses and experts. Both concluded that Lee Harvey Oswald shot President Kennedy from the sixth floor of the Texas School Book Depository as Kennedy rode in a motorcade through Dealey Plaza in Dallas. Neither the Warren Commission nor the Select Committee identified a conspirator. The Warren Commission concluded that there was no evidence of a conspiracy.

A majority of the House Select Committee believed, however, that acoustics evidence—impulses from static on a dictabelt that were projected onto a graph but were not distinguishable to the human ear[3]—indicated a second shooter. But they found no visible or physical signs of a second shooter: no eyewitnesses of a shooter, no firearm, no bullet marks, no bullet fragments or cartridges, no fingerprints.[4] The Select Committee's majority[5] also could not identify a possible shooter other than Oswald or a link from Oswald to a suspected conspirator or a particular person or group interested in killing the president. Its conclusion—that President Kennedy "was probably assassinated as a result of a conspiracy"—rested entirely on the validity of the acoustics evidence.[6]

The Select Committee requested the U.S. Department of Justice to continue to receive further evidence. In August 1980, the Justice Department contracted with the National Academy of Sciences to review the acoustics evidence and conduct its own research.[7] The National Academy assigned the task to a twelve-member Committee on Ballistics Acoustics headed by Prof. Norman I. Ramsey, Physics Department of Harvard University.[8] It included the eminent physicist Luis Alvarez. After two years of research, the Committee on Ballistics Acoustics concluded in 1982 that the methodology relied on by the Select Committee's specialists could not distinguish between gunshot sounds and sounds coming from other sources and that the dictabelt impulses relied on by the House Select Committee were probably not generated from Dealey Plaza and had occurred at a time different from the assassination.[9] In short, the Ballistic Acoustics

Committee deemed the conclusion of the majority of the House Assassinations Committee invalid.

Thereafter, in March of 1988, the Justice Department closed its role in seeking further participants in the JFK assassination. In a letter to Rep. Peter Rodino, chairman of the Judiciary Committee of the U.S. House of Representatives, the Justice Department said, "all investigative leads which are known to the Department have been exhaustively pursued.... Accordingly, the Department of Justice has concluded that no persuasive evidence can be identified to support the theory of a conspiracy in ... the assassination of President Kennedy.... No further investigation appears to be warranted ... unless new information which is sufficient to support additional investigative activity becomes available. While this report is intended to 'close' the Department's formal response to the Select Committee final report, it is the Department's intention to continue to review all correspondence and to investigate, as appropriate, any potentially productive information."[10] In the more than thirty years since those words were written, no information has surfaced to cause the Department of Justice to re-open the case.

Although governmental authorities considered the investigation closed, private researchers and writers did not. Pressure from those sources—especially Oliver Stone's movie, *JFK*—brought about the *President John F. Kennedy Records Collection Act of 1992* and the Assassination Records Review Board.[11]

From 1994 to 1998, the Assassination Records Review Board gathered and reviewed all known public and private documents, photographs, audio recordings, and physical evidence related to the JFK assassination.[12] The Assassination Records Review Board was not empowered to reach conclusions about the assassination, only to collect relevant evidence.

The Board defined *assassination records* as "all records, public and private, regardless of how labeled or identified, that document, describe, report on, analyze, or interpret activities, persons, or events reasonably related to the assassination of President John F. Kennedy and investigations of or inquiries into the assassination."[13] It was a broad definition, encompassing evidence, innuendoes, rumors, and speculations. The result is that the Board collected many documents that provide no evidence about Oswald, Ruby, or anyone with whom they had contact.

Those documents—without evidentiary value as to the conduct of Oswald or Ruby—have been a source of continuing controversy because of Section 5(g)(2)(D) of the JFK records act. Section 5(g)(2)(D) allows a government agency to withhold or redact a document if the president "certifies ... that a continued postponement is made necessary by an identifiable harm to the military defense, intelligence operations, law enforcement, or conduct of foreign affairs; and the identifiable harm is of such gravity that it outweighs the public interest in disclosure." There is no evidence that any of the withheld or redacted documents hold any information about Oswald or Ruby that is not already available in the documents, photographs, and recordings already available to the public at the National Archives.[14]

Anyone, then, may review the evidence in the most famous criminal case of the 20th century.

Will you join with me in that inquiry?

2

Police and Sheriffs at Work

The starting point is the initial investigation of President Kennedy's and Lee Oswald's deaths conducted by the Dallas Police Department. In 1963, the murder of President Kennedy was a state crime. No federal crime of murder existed unless the killing occurred on federal property. Since President Kennedy's assassination occurred in Texas, his murder could be prosecuted only under the laws of the State of Texas. Consequently, initial responsibility for the investigation began with the Dallas Police Department and the Dallas County Sheriff. Federal investigators were present or available to assist, but they did not have power to prosecute for that murder.

Dallas police and sheriffs had a strong incentive to find the shooter. Not only had the president of the United States been murdered, but the City of Dallas had been disgraced. Blame for the death of the president might fall upon them. Their professional reputations were at stake.

Initially, federal investigators were bystanders, but they could not be passive observers. The safety of the nation seemed threatened. A foreign or domestic conspiracy might be involved. Having far greater investigative resources than Dallas authorities, Federal investigators were essential partners in the crime's investigation.

Seeing the Shooter

Knowledge of the Dallas authorities began with two eyewitnesses: Howard Brennan and Amos Euins. Both said they saw a man shooting at the president from the sixth floor of the Texas School Book Depository in Dealey Plaza.

On November 22, 1963, Brennan, a forty-five-year-old steamfitter, had gone to Dealey Plaza on his lunch break to watch President Kennedy's motorcade. About noon, he joined the assembling crowd and found a place to sit on a short plaza wall. As he waited, he faced the Texas School Book Depository. Before the motorcade arrived, he saw a man leave and return to a window in the building's sixth floor southeast corner.

Almost immediately as the president's car passed him, Brennan heard what he thought was the backfire of a motorcycle or the explosion of a firecracker. He looked up toward the Book Depository. The man he had previously observed was "aiming for his last shot." The man "drew the gun back from the window … and maybe paused for another second as if to assure hisself that he hit his mark, and then he disappeared."[1]

Fifteen-year-old Amos Euins' experience was similar: "As the motorcade turned the corner, I was facing looking dead at the building. So I seen this pipe thing sticking out the window. I wasn't paying too much attention to it. Then when the first shot was

1. TEXAS SCHOOL BOOK DEPOSITORY
2. DAL-TEX BUILDING
3. DALLAS COUNTY RECORDS BUILDING
4. DALLAS COUNTY CRIMINAL COURTS BUILDING
5. OLD COURT HOUSE
6. NEELEY BRYAN HOUSE
7. DALLAS COUNTY GOVERNMENT CENTER (UNDER CONSTRUCTION)
8. UNITED STATES POST OFFICE BUILDING
9. PERGOLAS
10. PERISTYLES AND REFLECTING POOLS
11. RAILROAD OVERPASS (TRIPLE UNDERPASS)

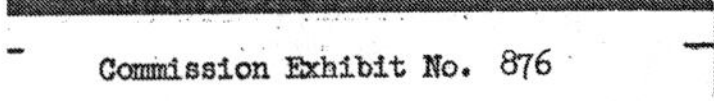
Commission Exhibit No. 876

Dealey Plaza (National Archives. Warren Commission Exhibit CE 876).

fired, I started looking around, thinking it was a backfire.... Then I looked up at the window, and he shot again."[2]

Once sure of their own safety, Brennan and Euins sought nearby police officers.[3] At the west end of Elm Street in Dealey Plaza, Euins found Sergeant D.V. Harkness. Sgt. Harkness was seeking eyewitnesses. Upon hearing Euins, Harkness took immediate steps to seal off the Book Depository building.[4] Brennan's description of the shooter led to an all-cars alert by Dallas police radio for a suspect—"white male, 30, slender build, 5 feet 10 inches, 165 pounds, armed with a 30-caliber rifle."[5]

At a police line-up containing Oswald, Brennan declined to make a full-throated identification of Oswald.[6] To the Warren Commission, he was definite.[7] In his own book, published twenty-four years later, Brennan explained that he had been reticent at the line-up because he didn't trust a particular Dallas police detective to keep his identification secret. Brennan feared greatly the possibility that Oswald had collaborators, and that, as a witness against Oswald, his life was in danger.[8]

Eyewitness Howard Brennan, in black jacket, photographed later on the wall from which he saw the shooter. Brennan circled on the photograph A) the window where he saw the shooter; and B) where he saw other Texas School Book Depository employees (National Archives. Warren Commission Exhibit CE 47).

After they heard shots fired, four other witnesses—Robert H. Jackson, a staff photographer for the *Dallas Times-Herald;* Malcolm Couch, a television news cameraman; Mrs. Earle Cabell, wife of the Dallas mayor; and James Crawford—saw either a rifle or a man moving in the Depository's sixth floor window.[9] Among the many people in Dealey Plaza that day, no one saw at any other location a gun, a person shooting, or an object that might look like a gun. Official attention focused quickly on the Texas School Book Depository.

Some local officers thought at first that the shots might have come from elsewhere. They had not seen the shooter in the window. Deputy Sheriff Luke Mooney, for example, ran from where he had been standing a block southeast of the School Book Depository. Mooney crossed Elm Street in front of the Depository, went up a grassy embankment to the northwest of the building, and jumped a fence into a railroad yard. He had not seen a shooter, but he believed the sounds came from that direction. Behind the fence and in the railroad yard, he and others found nothing unusual.[10]

Finding Physical Evidence

Quickly Deputy Mooney and others were directed by Sheriff Bill Decker to assist in searching the Book Depository. Mooney took a building elevator to the sixth floor—as

Photograph of the boxes set up in Texas School Book Depository sixth-floor window. Oswald's finger and palm prints were found on the boxes (National Archives. Warren Commission Exhibit CE 130).

high as it would go. He began searching the floor by himself. At the southeast window, he saw three boxes piled up as if they could "be a rest for a rifle." Three empty bullet cartridges were nearby. Mooney leaned out the window. He called to Sheriff Bill Decker and Homicide Captain Will Fritz standing on the ground below.[11] Mooney believed he had found the spot from which the shots had been fired.

Soon Sheriff Decker, Captain Fritz, and a multitude of other officers arrived on the sixth floor. Mooney and others began searching for a gun and other evidence. Among the searchers was Deputy Sheriff Eugene Boone. Boone had initially been with Mooney watching the motorcade. He too ran up the embankment into the freight yard behind the book depository—and found nothing unusual there. In the freight yard, he called to a man, Lee Bowers, a railroad employee in a railroad watch tower.[12]

Bowers had been watching the motorcade from the time it reached Houston and Main streets until after shots were fired. Before the shooting, he saw two men, about 10 or 15 feet apart, standing in front of a wooden fence near the top of what has come to be called "the grassy knoll." One was middle aged, dressed in a business suit. The other seemed younger and had a white shirt. Almost immediately after the shots were fired, Bowers saw motorcycle policeman Clyde A. Haygood ride his motorcycle up the knoll from Elm Street, drop the cycle near the top of the knoll, and run into the freight yard. Bowers saw no one with a gun or anything suspicious prior to or after the shooting. In the freight yard after the shooting, no one saw any movement except that of police officers and spectators who had fled the shooting.[13]

Police and sheriff deputies found nothing of importance in the freight yard. Both Officer Haygood and Deputy Boone proceeded to the sixth floor of the School Book Depository. By then Deputy Mooney had found the cartridges on the floor and the boxes by the window. The search for a weapon was underway. Deputy

Circles indicating the three cartridges found near the Texas School Book Depository sixth-floor window. Experts link the cartridges to the rifle found elsewhere on the sixth floor (National Archives. Warren Commission Exhibit CE 510).

The Mannlicher-Carcano rifle found between boxes on the Texas School Book Depository sixth floor (National Archives. Warren Commission Exhibit CE 514).

Boone squeezed through two rows of boxes that stood slightly apart from the west wall of the building. Between the two rows he spotted a rifle, a 6.5-mm Mannlicher-Carcano, with some other boxes pulled over it. The rifle was about three feet from a stairwell.[14] The initial evidence seemed strong to Dallas investigators that President Kennedy had been shot with a rifle by a gunman from the sixth floor of the Texas School Book Depository.

Looking for the Gunman

But where was the gunman? Might he still be in the building? Was he, perhaps, an employee or other worker at the Texas School Book Depository? Dallas police officers inside the building began taking names and interviewing employees. Depository superintendent Roy Truly had seen employee Lee Harvey Oswald inside the building a few minutes after the shooting. Later as he was assembling employees, Truly noticed that Oswald was not among them. He then retrieved Oswald's address from company files and went to the sixth floor, where he notified Captain Fritz of Oswald's absence, and gave him an address: 2515 West Fifth Street in the Dallas suburb of Irving.[15]

It was the most reliable address that Truly had, but it was not Oswald's. It was the address of Oswald's wife, Marina, and their two children. Marina was living with a friend, Ruth Paine, while Oswald stayed, instead, in a rooming house on North Beckley Street in Dallas.

Where Was Oswald?

Where then was Lee Oswald when Dallas police were looking for the shooter of President Kennedy? The story of Oswald's whereabouts begins with Dallas motorcycle Patrolman M.L. Baker. Baker was riding his motorcycle in the motorcade immediately behind the last press car when he heard shots fired at the president. Believing they had come from the Texas School Book Depository, Baker parked his motorcycle, ran to the building, and encountered Roy Truly. Together, they entered the lobby and ran up a flight of stairs, enroute to the top of the building.[16] As Baker reached the second floor, he saw Lee Oswald walking in the lunchroom.[17]

Baker pulled his revolver, entered the lunchroom, and yelled to Oswald, "Come here!"[18]

Empty-handed, Oswald turned and calmly walked toward Baker. Truly, Oswald's supervisor, assured Baker that Oswald was a Depository employee. The two then continued further upstairs to the seventh floor where they searched for a few minutes.[19]

Shortly after Truly and Baker left Oswald, a clerical supervisor on the second floor, Mrs. J.A. Reid, saw Oswald. With a soft drink bottle in hand, he walked through her office area toward a door leading to the front stairway. As he passed her, Mrs. Reid said, "Oh, the president has been shot, but maybe they didn't hit him." Oswald mumbled something that was inaudible and left the Texas School Book Depository. The Warren Commission estimated that Oswald "could have gone down the stairs and out the front door by 12:33 p.m.—3 minutes after the shooting." He wore a T-shirt but no jacket or sweater. A blue jacket that he had worn to work that day was left at the Book Depository.[20]

As Oswald was leaving the building, a young news reporter, possibly Robert MacNeil (of the eventual *MacNeil/Lehrer NewsHour* on the Public Broadcasting Service), entered the building and asked where he could find a telephone. Oswald pointed to another man; said, "Better ask him"; and continued on.[21]

After leaving the Texas School Book Depository, for the next forty minutes, Oswald's activities have been carefully documented.[22] A bus transfer found in his shirt pocket when he was arrested showed that "he probably walked east on Elm Street for seven blocks to the corner of Elm and Murphy where, at approximately 12:40 p.m., he boarded a bus that was heading back in the direction of the Depository building."[23] Although traveling to the Oak Cliff section of Dallas, that bus would not have taken him closest to where he stayed in Oak Cliff.[24] He would have had to wait for another bus, although it was probably close behind.[25]

Dallas Transit Company bus driver Cecil J. McWatters told investigators that a man who was probably Oswald entered his bus at Murphy and Elm streets, seven blocks from the School Book Depository. Mary Bledsoe, the landlady in a rooming house where Oswald once lived, recognized him on the bus.[26] Approximately four minutes later, he left the bus when it was delayed in traffic.[27] As he left, he secured a bus transfer.[28]

From the transit bus, Oswald walked two blocks to a Greyhound bus station at Lamar and Commerce streets. There Oswald secured a cab. He told the driver, William Whaley, to take him to 500 North Beckley. In normal traffic, it was a drive of less than six minutes. As the cab left the bus station, sirens from police cars were blaring. The driver remarked, "I wonder what the hell is the uproar." Oswald said nothing in reply.[29]

As the cab driver headed toward the destination Oswald had given him, 500 North Beckley, he went past Oswald's rooming house at 1026 North Beckley. Perhaps because the coast seemed clear as he passed his rooming house, Oswald had the driver let him off in the 700 block. Walking at a normal pace from there would have taken Oswald, at most, five or six minutes to reach his rooming house.[30]

Earlene Roberts, the housekeeper there, remembered that he arrived at approximately 1:00 p.m.—after she had heard that the president had been shot. She recalled that Oswald entered the house hurriedly.[31]

Oswald would remain there only long enough to secure his revolver, at least fifteen rounds of ammunition, and a jacket. A few seconds after leaving the rooming house, Ms. Roberts saw him standing at a bus stop across the street on North Beckley.[32] He soon left the bus stop, however, and began walking in the residential area, out of sight of through traffic.[33] His destination is unclear.[34]

Meanwhile, Dallas police officer J.D. Tippit was in his police car, patrolling the central Oak Cliff area as part of an all-cars alert. At 12:45 p.m., 12:48 p.m., and 12:55 p.m., Tippit would have heard the description of a wanted suspect: "white male, 30, slender build, 5 feet 10 inches, 165...."[35] Not too different from Oswald.

Sometime between approximately 1:10 p.m. and 1:15 p.m., while driving no more than fifteen miles per hour on 10th Street near Patton Avenue, Tippit saw a man walking with his back to him.[36] The man was Lee Harvey Oswald.[37]

Tippit got out of the car and walked toward the front. Oswald pulled his revolver and fired three shots. Tippit was killed almost instantly. Then Oswald walked to the officer's prostrate body and fired one more shot. He may have said, "Poor dumb cop," and began walking in the opposite direction from where he had been headed.[38] At least four people either saw the shooting or the gunman walking away from the shooting.[39] As he walked away, Oswald unloaded the empty cartridges from his revolver and reloaded. He then began to run. Fleeing, he discarded the jacket he had secured from his room. When he got to a used-car lot at the corner of Patton and Jefferson, he slowed to a fast walk.[40]

Meanwhile, witnesses at the site of the shooting were able to use Tippit's police radio. Police cars were dispatched. Radio news was quickly broadcasting that a police

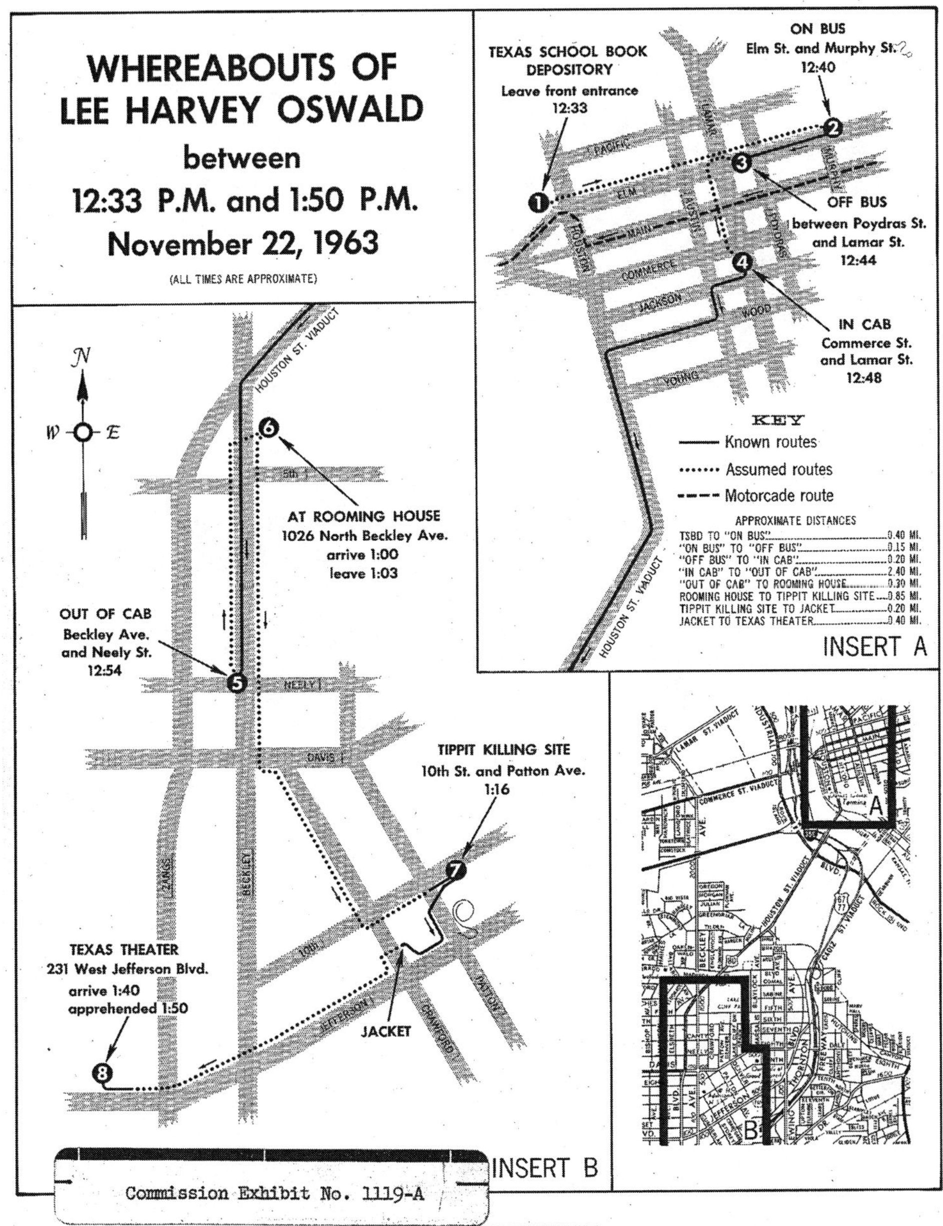

Insert A shows the route of the motorcade and Oswald's flight from the Texas School Book Depository to obtaining a cab. Insert B shows the route to his boarding house, leaving the boarding house to the Tippit murder, and his flight to the Texas Theater (National Archives. Warren Commission Exhibit CE 1119-A).

officer had been shot. When Oswald reached Jefferson Boulevard, police sirens were blaring again. Eight blocks from the shooting, he entered the outside lobby of a shoe store, keeping his back to the street.

Johnny Brewer, the manager of the shoe store, observed Oswald as he stood with his back to the street. "He just looked funny to me," Brewer later told the Warren Commission. "His hair was sort of messed up and looked like he'd been running, and he looked scared, and he looked funny."[41]

When the police sirens eased, Oswald turned toward the street and walked a few store lengths to the Texas Theater. Brewer was suspicious. He had already heard radio reports that a police officer had been shot nearby. He watched Oswald leave the lobby of his store and turn into the theater.

Brewer decided to investigate. He asked Julia Postal, the box office ticket seller, if she had seen the man and whether he had paid. Attracted by the sounds of police cars, Ms. Postal had walked to the curb. She had been looking at the action on the street as Oswald passed and had not seen him enter the theater.[42]

Brewer next went inside to the theater's concession stand where Warren Burroughs had been busy stocking candy. He hadn't seen anyone either. Together, Brewer and Burroughs checked theater doors and determined that no one had exited the theater.

Without turning on the lights, Brewer and Burroughs walked twice to the front of the theater and to the balcony to view the audience. Twenty-four patrons were in the theater.

Recognizing no one in the darkened theater, Brewer and Burroughs returned to the box office. Meanwhile, Julia Postal had called the police. She told Brewer and Burroughs to stand at the exit doors.[43]

Events then proceeded rapidly. At 1:45 p.m., police radio announced, "A suspect just went into the Texas Theater on West Jefferson."[44] Almost simultaneously police cars carrying at least fifteen officers arrived, surrounded the theater, and blocked all exits.[45]

Brewer met Officer M.N. McDonald and four others at the alley exit door. Detective Paul Bentley rushed to the balcony. He told the projectionist to turn up the house lights.[46] Standing on the stage, Brewer pointed out Oswald in a seat near the rear of the theater. McDonald, perhaps as a ruse, first searched two patrons closer to the stage.[47]

When McDonald got to Oswald, he ordered Oswald to stand. Oswald raised both hands, and McDonald started a pat-down. Oswald threw a left jab between McDonald's eyes and reached with his right hand for his own pistol. McDonald swung back with his right hand and grabbed the gun with his left. The gun clicked but did not fire. Three other officers quickly subdued Oswald from all sides. At 1:51 p.m., police car Number 2 reported by radio that it was headed to headquarters with the suspect for the Tippit shooting in custody.[48]

The rapid apprehension of Oswald can be credited to alert, conscientious citizens. If Johnny Brewer and Julia Postal had not acted promptly, Oswald might never have been caught.

3

Lee Harvey Oswald Faces Captain Will Fritz

At about 2:15 p.m., the Dallas Police Department's homicide chief, Captain Will Fritz, returned to police headquarters from the Texas School Book Depository.[1] Waiting for Fritz was Detective Gerald Hill. Hill had come from the Texas Theater in Car Number 2 with Oswald.

As the Warren Commission reported, "Fritz told the detective to get a search warrant, go to an address on Fifth Street in Irving, and pick up a man named Lee Oswald. When Hill asked why Oswald was wanted, Fritz replied, 'Well he was employed down at the Book Depository and he had not been present for a roll call of the employees.' Hill said, 'Captain, we will save you a trip … there he sits."[2]

Less than two hours after the assassination of President Kennedy, Will Fritz had before him the prime suspect in two murders committed within an hour of each other—the president's and Officer J.D. Tippit's. In eight sessions totaling approximately twelve hours over the next two days, Fritz, FBI agents, Secret Service agents, and a U.S Postal inspector questioned Oswald.[3] Oswald's fingerprints were taken; ballistics examinations were conducted; and Oswald was identified in four separate line-ups.

Dallas Police Detectives Richard Sims and Elmer Boyd were with Oswald through all of the interrogations. Sims said that Oswald "conducted himself … better than anyone I have ever seen…. He was calm and wasn't nervous."[4] Boyd observed, "[J]ust as soon as you asked him a question, he would just give you the answer right back—he didn't hesitate about his answers."[5] Oswald lost composure only once—in the first few minutes of Fritz's interrogation, when Dallas FBI Agent James Hosty entered the room and addressed him:

> I said, "Special Agent Jim Hosty with the FBI. I'm here to participate in the interview with the police. I want to advise you of some things. You have a right to remain silent. Anything you may say may be used against you in court. You also have the right to an attorney…." I was interrupted by Oswald. His face had turned ugly, and his whole body jerked in my direction, as if touched by a hot wire. "Oh, so you're Hosty, the agent who's been harassing my wife!" he exploded.[6]

Hosty's assignment had been to keep watch on Oswald, the returned defector, but he had never seen him. The closest he'd come to establishing contact was meeting Oswald's Russian wife, Marina. On November 1, less than two weeks after Oswald's second child was born, Hosty had visited Marina in Irving looking for Lee, who wasn't there. Hosty visited Marina four days later. Again, Lee was not there. These visits angered Oswald—partly because they worried Marina and affected their relationship.

Perhaps, also, because they seemed insensitive, coming so soon after Marina had given birth.

What Hosty never told Fritz or the Warren Commission was that Oswald himself had tried to confront Hosty shortly after Hosty had seen Marina. Within a few days of November 8, Oswald went to the FBI office in Dallas. Not finding Hosty there, Oswald left an angry note—a note that Hosty destroyed on November 24 at the command of his supervisor, an act that was not revealed for more than a decade.[7]

Throughout Fritz's interrogation, Oswald denied shooting either President Kennedy or Officer Tippit. He told news media, "They've taken me in because of the fact I lived in the Soviet Union. I'm just a Patsy."[8] He admitted to Captain Fritz, however, that he had left the Book Depository almost immediately after the shooting, taken a bus and then a cab to his rooming house, had obtained a pistol there, and had gone to the movie theater.[9]

For Captain Fritz, the evidence against Oswald for both murders was convincing. The case for killing Officer Tippit seemed particularly strong. Ballistics evidence later showed that the cartridge cases found near the scene of the Tippit shooting came from the pistol found on Oswald. One witness, Helen Markham, identified Oswald as the shooter.[10] Two others, Barbara Jeanette Davis and Virginia Davis, identified him as running from the scene.[11] Johnny Brewer, a store clerk, saw him hide from the police when cars came near on Jefferson and then duck into the Texas Theater a few doors away. When police confronted Oswald in the theater, he pulled his pistol and tried to shoot.

Circumstantial evidence informed Fritz's belief that Oswald had shot the president. First, Oswald's flight from the Book Depository and murder of Officer Tippit were evidence of guilt in the presidential assassination. The rifle found on the Depository's sixth floor was also material. It had been purchased in the name of A. Hidell. The full name, Alek J. Hidell was on a forged Selective Service card bearing Oswald's photo that was found in Oswald's billfold when he was arrested. The Hidell name was also used on a post office box rented by Oswald. Finally, Oswald's fingerprints were found on boxes mounted at the Book Depository window from which shots were fired, and his palm print was found on the barrel of the 6.5-mm Mannlicher-Carcano.

Equally important to Fritz were Oswald's obfuscations and lies during interrogation. On Sunday morning, November 24, for example, Oswald denied that he knew A.J. Hidell. He said that Hidell was a representative of the Fair Play for Cuba Committee in New York from whom he had received a letter. He said that he had never seen or talked to Hidell.[12] When Fritz confronted Oswald with the Selective Service card, Oswald became angry and said, "Now I've told you all I'm going to tell you about that card in my billfold—you have the card yourself and you know as much about it as I do."[13]

Oswald denied repeatedly that he possessed a rifle, but on November 22 Marina told deputy sheriffs that he owned one. Not only did Fritz have evidence that the rifle was purchased in the name of A. Hidell and mailed to a post office box rented by Oswald, but Fritz was also able to confront Oswald with a photo of him holding a rifle. Marina told police that she had taken the photo. Nonetheless, Oswald, continued to deny ownership of the rifle and claimed that the photo was a forgery.[14]

Evidence was mounting that Oswald had taken the weapon to work on Friday morning from Marina's residence in the Dallas suburb of Irving. Unexpectedly, he had ridden the night before to Irving with a coworker, Buell Wesley Frazier. Frazier said Oswald had explained that he was going to Irving to secure curtain rods for his room in

Dallas. The next morning, when Oswald put a long paper bag in the rear seat of Frazier's car, he told Frazier that it contained curtain rods.

A large paper bag was found on the sixth floor of the Book Depository. It was long enough to have held a disassembled Mannlicher-Carcano rifle. No curtain rods were found at the Depository. Moreover, Oswald's room on Beckley Street already had curtain rods and curtains. Oswald denied he had told Frazier anything about curtain rods. He said the long bag contained his lunch.[15]

Political Candor

Although Oswald was evasive and deceitful regarding matters related to November 22, he was surprisingly frank in expressing his political views. When asked about his religious and political beliefs, Oswald said, "Karl Marx is my religion.... I am a Marxist.... Not a Communist ... or a Marxist-Leninist."[16]

When asked how U.S. policy would be affected by Kennedy's death, Oswald responded, "So far as I know, Johnson's views and President Kennedy's views are the same, so I don't think the attitude of the U.S. government will change toward Cuba."[17]

Oswald's conduct during Fritz's interrogation suggests that he viewed his arrest and future trial through the lens of politics. Protesting his lack of counsel, Oswald was nonetheless selective in whom he wanted to represent him. On Saturday, he declined the help of the Dallas Bar Association, saying his first preference was John Abt and his second preference the American Civil Liberties Union.[18] His multiple attempts to contact John Abt, a New York lawyer, were unsuccessful. Oswald did not know Abt personally but was aware that he had defended Communist Party leaders in criminal prosecutions under the Smith Act, a federal statute intended to deal with Communist Party members.[19] Abt later told the Warren Commission that neither Oswald nor anyone connected to Oswald had ever made contact with him and that he probably could not have represented Oswald because of "[his] commitments to other clients."[20]

Oswald and the Media

As the Dallas police investigation proceeded, the media swarmed the very floor where Oswald was being interrogated by Captain Fritz. Television cameras, live broadcasters, and reporters jammed the hallway outside Fritz's office. The press could watch (but not hear) Fritz's interrogation through a glass window. Oswald could not be moved from the interrogation room to his cell without running a gauntlet of news reporters barraging him with questions.

At 12:10 a.m. on Saturday, Dallas County Prosecutor Henry Wade and Police Chief Jesse Curry brought Oswald before assembled reporters. Only a few feet separated Oswald from the reporters, who launched questions and to whom Oswald responded:

> "Did you kill the president?"
>
> "No, I haven't been charged with that. In fact, nobody has said that to me yet. The first thing I heard about it was when the newspaper reporters in the hall ... asked me that question."
>
> "You *have* been charged," a reporter said.[21]

Oswald (center, not wearing an hat) being questioned by news media on Dallas Police Department third floor when being moved between an interrogation room and holding cell (National Archives. Warren Commission Exhibit CE 2631).

Oswald (center) being questioned by media at the Friday night press conference (National Archives. Warren Commission Exhibit CE 2965).

Oswald had been arraigned five hours earlier for the murder of Officer Tippit. The reporters knew, but Oswald did not, that charges had also been filed against him for the assassination of President Kennedy.[22] At 1:35 a.m., he was arraigned on that charge and returned to his cell.[23]

Transferring Oswald to the County Jail

By Saturday evening, Fritz was satisfied that Oswald would not confess to either crime. Fritz had been a police officer since 1921 and Dallas homicide chief since 1934. He was regarded as the finest interrogator in the Dallas Police Department—perhaps even in all of Texas.[24] He knew when a man was likely to confess. Oswald was not.

Fritz was satisfied that holding Oswald at the Dallas police headquarters for further questioning was unnecessary. On Saturday night, Chief Curry announced that Oswald would be moved to the Dallas County jail the next morning, but not before 10:00 a.m.[25]

Protecting Oswald in the Transfer to Dallas County Jail

By Sunday morning, November 24, anger toward Oswald was widespread. The media and Dallas investigators had made it clear that Oswald was the killer of both the president and Officer Tippit. Chief Curry and Sheriff Decker feared violence to Oswald. Curry even worried that a Dallas police officer might assassinate Oswald over the murder of Officer Tippit.[26]

At about 2:30 a.m., both the FBI in Dallas and Sheriff Decker received phone calls threatening to kill Oswald. To the FBI, a caller said, "I represent a committee that is neither right nor left wing … and tonight, tomorrow morning, or tomorrow night we are going to kill the man that killed the president. There will be no excitement and we will kill him. We wanted to be sure to tell the FBI, police department, and sheriff's office."[27]

A flurry of phone calls among police agencies followed. The police and sheriff thought carefully about safeguards in transporting Oswald. But preventing the media from covering the transfer was not one of them. By 11:00 a.m. television cameras and reporters from every medium filled the garage area where three police vehicles were positioned to receive Oswald and effect the transfer.[28]

Jack Ruby Leaves Home

At the same time, Jack Ruby, a Dallas striptease club owner, was on his way to a downtown Western Union office. That morning one of his strippers, Karen Carlin, had phoned him needing money. As Ruby had closed his clubs upon learning of the president's death, Ms. Carlin had not been paid.

Ruby told her he was going downtown anyhow, and he would wire her a money order. With his favorite dog, Sheba, he drove to the Western Union office—only one block east of the Dallas police station, on the north side of Main Street.

Parking in a lot on Main, Ruby put his billfold and most of his keys in the trunk, put the trunk key in the unlocked glove compartment, and left Sheba in the unlocked car. In his pockets, he had $2,000 cash and a pistol. At Western Union, he waited in line while another patron sent a money order, then sent his own in the amount of twenty-five dollars to Ms. Carlin. It was time-stamped 11:17.[29]

Walking out of the Western Union office, Ruby saw a crowd of people across Main outside police headquarters. They were facing what was normally the entrance ramp of the police garage. Police Officer Roy E. Vaughn stood at the top of the ramp, trying to keep an eye on the crowd as well as activity inside the garage. Just as Ruby reached the ramp, an exiting police car arrived at the top.[30] It was about 11:20 a.m.[31] Vaughn, his back to Ruby, acknowledged the officers inside the car, and Ruby slipped by, walking down the ramp as if he belonged there.[32]

Police vehicles, one of which was to carry Oswald, were in place at the bottom of the ramp. Police officers and newsmen crowded at both ends of the row of vehicles. At 11:21 a.m., Oswald, handcuffed to Detective James R. Leavelle, emerged through the jail office door. Newsmen thrust their microphones toward Oswald. Out of the waiting crowd burst Jack Ruby, .38 caliber revolver in hand, and fired one shot into Oswald's abdomen.[33]

An ambulance arrived quickly, but Oswald was fading rapidly. Detective Billy H. Combest testified to the Warren Commission that he bent over Oswald, lifted his sweater, and saw a bullet hole. Combest claimed he said to Oswald, "Is there anything you want to tell me?" According to Combest, Oswald shook his head slightly and raised his hand very slightly in the nature of a clenched fist salute—a socialist gesture of the

Ruby shooting Oswald in the basement garage of the Dallas Police Department as he was about to be transferred to the Dallas County Jail (Bob Jackson).

Spanish Civil War during the 1930s.[34] It was, if true, Oswald's last statement. At 1:07 p.m., Oswald was pronounced dead at Parkland Hospital, the same hospital where the president had been taken.[35]

Ruby's Explanation

In the garage, Jack Ruby had been wrestled to the floor. Police Detective T.D. McMillon recalled Ruby saying as he shot Oswald, "You rat son-of-a-bitch. You shot the president." And then, as he held Ruby to the floor, "I hope I killed the son-of-a-bitch."[36]

Quickly disarmed, Ruby was taken to the fifth floor. Captain Fritz now had his third murder to investigate in two days. For this one, the issue was not who but why. Efforts to answer the question became the dominating subject of Jack Ruby's trial for murdering Lee Harvey Oswald.

Secret Service Agent Forrest Sorrels was the first to put that question to Ruby. Within twenty minutes of Ruby's shooting of Oswald, Sorrels asked, "Jack—why?" As Sorrels would recount to the Warren Commission, Ruby answered that he just had "to show the world a Jew has guts."[37]

Detective James R. Leavelle would recall saying to Ruby as he was being transferred to the Dallas County Jail the next day, "Jack, … you didn't do us any favor when you shot Oswald. You've really put the pressure on us." According to Leavelle, Ruby replied, "That's the last thing in the world I wanted to do. I just wanted to be a damned hero, and all I've done is foul things up."[38]

4

The Warren Commission Begins Its Work

President Johnson Appoints a Commission

The death of Lee Oswald without a trial meant no witnesses would be publicly examined; the accused would give no public explanation of his alleged actions. Jack Ruby had created a field day for speculators. The nation and the world wanted answers: who killed President Kennedy, how, and why?

The first to offer an explanation was FBI Director J. Edgar Hoover. From the very first minutes of the president being shot, Hoover had been in close contact with the president's brother, Attorney General Robert Kennedy, and the new president, Lyndon B. Johnson. Hoover saw it as his responsibility to find the answers.[1] In addition, he had his own reputation and an agency to protect. Marina and Lee Oswald had been on the FBI's watch list, but his agency had not warned either the Secret Service or the Dallas police of Oswald's presence in Dallas.

Within two days of Oswald's death, Hoover was satisfied that Lee Harvey Oswald had killed the president and that he had acted alone. He wanted to issue a report and close the case.[2] It soon became clear to many, however, that the FBI's conclusions would not satisfy the public. Oswald had not received a public trial. He had been denied justice.

Moreover, there had been immediate fears of a conspiracy with international dimensions. Within minutes of the assassination, all military had been put on alert, and the Mexican border had been sealed to prevent possible conspirators from escaping.[3]

President Kennedy had a myriad of enemies—the Soviet Union, Cuba, Cuban expatriates in the United States, U.S. militants who believed that Kennedy's foreign policy was too timid, Southern segregationists who hated the president for supporting racial integration, and organized crime figures who were feeling pressured by the president's brother, U.S. Attorney General Robert Kennedy. Any among those might have had a motive to kill the president.

Through intense media coverage, the public had already learned that Oswald was an avowed Marxist who had defected to the Soviet Union in 1959 and returned to the United States with a Russian wife in 1962. On his return, he'd distributed pamphlets in support of Cuban President Fidel Castro. It seemed plausible that he could be a tool of the Soviet Union or the Cuban government.

Although subsequent events did not confirm any military threat from abroad, there had nevertheless been a dramatic failure of the nation's security system. How had it failed, and who was at fault? Why had Oswald, an ex-Marine who had defected to the

Soviet Union, been allowed by the State Department to return to the United States? And with a Russian wife. Why hadn't the FBI kept a closer eye on him when he returned? Why hadn't the Secret Service or the Dallas police been watching buildings as the Kennedy motorcade drove past them? Was the evidence against Oswald really as compelling as the FBI claimed? Were there other shooters? How had Jack Ruby been able to gain access to the police garage when Oswald was about to be transported to the Dallas County jail? Had a police officer helped him? Was Ruby connected to organized crime? Those questions merely scratched the surface. A public investigation was inevitable.

The Decision to Appoint a Presidential Commission

Waggoner Carr, the attorney general of Texas, announced that he would appoint a Texas Court of Inquiry.[4] Senator James Eastland of Mississippi, a Democrat, opponent of racial integration, and supporter of those who wanted the United States to invade Cuba, chaired the U.S. Senate Judiciary Committee. He was prepared to conduct an investigation through that committee. U.S. Representative Hale Boggs of Louisiana, a Democrat, called for a joint congressional investigation. He was his party's whip. And, of course, perhaps hundreds of journalists and political activists were ready to conduct their own investigations.

President Lyndon Johnson was inclined initially to allow the State of Texas to conduct the public inquiry.[5] By the simple fact of locale, it remained a state offense. Too, as a Texan, Johnson felt keenly the stain on Texas's reputation.

But an investigation conducted by a commission of the State of Texas was unlikely to engender either certainty or public confidence. Nor could such a commission amass the needed investigatory resources or be structured so as to have widespread credibility. Moreover, a Texas inquiry would not stem Congress's interest in conducting their own investigation. Hoping to forestall state and congressional investigations and maximize public confidence, Johnson's advisors urged a presidential commission.[6]

Appointing the Commissioners

From the U.S. Senate, Johnson appointed his friend and mentor, Democrat Richard Russell of Georgia, and Republican John Sherman Cooper of Kentucky. Russell was especially important. Among the most respected members of the Senate, he was currently leading conservative forces in the Senate in raging opposition to pending civil rights legislation. Senator Russell was also chairman of the Senate Armed Services Committee. That committee oversaw the Central Intelligence Agency.[7] Southern senators—Senator James Eastland in particular—were unlikely to question a determination concurred with by Russell.

From the House of Representatives, President Johnson selected Republican Gerald Ford of Michigan and Democrat Hale Boggs of Louisiana. Both were leaders in their parties. Because Oswald had lived in New Orleans as a child and again during the summer of 1963, Boggs brought not only political credibility but also knowledge of the community where Oswald might have relationships. Through these bipartisan Congressional appointments, Johnson and his advisors believed they were ensuring Congress's abandonment of any competing investigations—provided that the four concurred with the Commission's decision.

From the private sector, President Johnson chose Allen Dulles, former head of the Central Intelligence Agency under both President Eisenhower and President Kennedy, as well as John McCloy, U.S. high commissioner to Germany after World War II. Both were Republicans. Both had knowledge of the Soviet Union, international relations, and espionage. Under President Eisenhower, Dulles had overseen CIA efforts to unseat Fidel Castro in Cuba. The ill-fated Bay of Pigs invasion in March 1961 had occurred during his tenure. He had intimate knowledge of the nation's enemies and enjoyed the confidence of the CIA. Dulles had great affection for the Kennedy family. His appointment to the Commission was recommended by Attorney General Robert Kennedy.[8]

McCloy brought experience not only in foreign affairs but also in investigating an international conspiracy to commit a crime in the United States. As a lawyer in the 1930s, McCloy enabled the Lehigh Valley Railroad to secure damages from the German government for sabotaging a munitions depot in New Jersey during World War I.

Lyndon Johnson named Earl Warren, Chief Justice of the United States, as chairman of the President's Commission on the Assassination of President Kennedy. Persuading Warren was not easy. At first Warren declined. It was not appropriate, Warren demurred, for members of the Supreme Court to engage in extrajudicial public activities.[9] Moreover, the prosecution of Jack Ruby for killing Lee Oswald might command review by the Supreme Court. In addition, this was not a summer recess, and Warren was fully engaged in considering cases whose outcomes would greatly affect the future of the country.

Reminding the Chief Justice of his service in the First World War, Johnson stressed that only an honest, accurate, and trusted investigation might keep the United States

Warren Commission members (left to right): U.S. Representative Gerald R. Ford; U.S. Representative Hale Boggs; U.S. Senator Richard Russell; Chief Justice Earl Warren; U.S. Senator John Sherman Cooper; former World Bank president John J. McCloy; former CIA director Allen Dulles; General Counsel to the Commission J. Lee Rankin (National Archives).

out of a third world war—this time thermonuclear. Warren, Johnson insisted, was the most trusted and revered judge in America.[10]

But for many that was not true. Warren had been the primary architect of *Brown v. Board of Education*—the Supreme Court case that laid the foundation for ending racial segregation. That decision rendered Warren despicable to Georgia's Senator Russell. When Johnson told Russell that he had appointed Warren to the Commission, Russell said he would not serve with Warren. Johnson replied that Russell could not relent as the appointments had already been made public.[11]

Warren brought to the Commission an extensive background in criminal investigation. He understood homicide cases. He had been the chief prosecutor in Alameda County, California, for more than a decade—once being found in a national survey of law enforcement officers to be the "most intelligent and politically independent district attorney in the United States."[12] After that, he had been attorney general of California. Yet, as a Supreme Court justice, his reputation was as a staunch defender of rights of the criminally accused. Even the most diehard segregationists would be hard pressed to challenge his credentials for overseeing the Commission.

The Commission Selects a Staff

The commissioners were not the investigators. For that they hired a staff. The commissioners, in the end, were equivalent to a jury who hears evidence and renders a decision.

The charges to the investigative staff and the Commission were set forth in these instructions from President Johnson:

> [T]o examine the evidence developed by the Federal Bureau of Investigation and any additional evidence that may hereafter come to light or be uncovered by federal or state authorities; to make such further investigation as the Commission finds desirable; to evaluate all the facts and circumstances surrounding such assassination, including the subsequent violent death of the man charged with the assassination, and to report to me its findings and conclusions.[13]

To implement that charge, the Commission established six primary areas of inquiry:

> Area 1. Everything that transpired from the planning of the President's trip to Dallas on November 22, 1963, through the shooting, the events at Parkland Hospital, the return to Washington, and the autopsy at Bethesda Hospital;
> Area 2. the identity of the assassin;
> Area 3. the assassin's motive;
> Area 4. whether the assassin was involved in a conspiracy, foreign or domestic;
> Area 5. whether Jack Ruby was involved in a conspiracy with Lee Harvey Oswald or anyone else to kill President Kennedy or in a conspiracy to kill Oswald; and
> Area 6. how the security system for presidential protection failed to protect the President and what changes were necessary.[14]

The Commission appointed a General Counsel, fourteen assistant counsel, and twelve staff assistants to carry out those inquiries. Only three were employees of a federal executive branch agency. One assistant counsel, Arlen Spector, was an assistant county prosecutor in Philadelphia. The remainder were on short-term leaves of absence from the private sector. This was to ensure that the principal staff members were not dependent on the federal government for future employment. Some worked only part time for the Commission. Three to four months was the expected completion time.

The staff's initial function was not to find witnesses, conduct forensic evaluations, or be photographers. That work had already been done by federal or state agencies. The staff's initial function was to review the evidence that had been accumulated. After that review, it would make further investigatory assignments to available agencies. Those agencies included the FBI, Secret Service, State Department, Central Intelligence Agency, U.S. Post Office Department, U.S. Army, and even state agencies willing to help.

All of the Commission's professional staff, except one, were lawyers. The exception was Alfred Goldberg, Ph.D. Goldberg was an historian on loan from the Department of Defense. His role was to help the legal staff write the ultimate report, critique their analyses, and ensure that the evidence was properly indexed and preserved. The Commission instructed the staff that no evidence was to be destroyed and that all that was relevant was to be reported.

The Commission's selected chief of staff, J. Lee Rankin, had been solicitor general of the United States in the administration of President Dwight D. Eisenhower. As solicitor general, he had represented the United States in arguments before the Supreme Court. Chief Justice Warren knew Rankin well. He had argued the government's case in *Brown v. Board of Education* to declare school segregation unconstitutional.[15] Rankin had grown up in Nebraska and attended law school there.

The Commission wanted a diversified staff of high professional competency and trial, preferably criminal practice, experience. In 1963, *diversity* meant diversity by age and geography. No women. Only one African American, William T. Coleman, Jr, a Republican. No inquiry was made of political philosophy. Many were veterans of World War II or other military service.

Seven of the assistant counsel were forty-two to fifty-five years old. The other seven were twenty-nine to forty.[16] We came from California, Colorado, Illinois, Iowa, Louisiana, New York, North Dakota, Ohio, and Pennsylvania. None had previously worked together. Only a few of us had prior acquaintance.

Our political views and backgrounds were, as it turned out, diverse as well. Assistant Counsel Wesley J. Liebeler (known to us all as Jim) had grown up on a North Dakota farm. He was a Barry Goldwater and Milton Friedman conservative—a libertarian before the country had heard of libertarianism. Assistant Counsel Norman Redlich, a Yale Law School graduate, had worked in his father's manufacturing business for ten years while earning a graduate degree in tax law at night. His politics were at the opposite end of the spectrum from Liebeler's. Redlich had been a member of the Emergency Civil Liberties Council, which—among other causes—vigorously opposed the work of the House Committee on Un-American Activities and Senator Joseph McCarthy. In the political middle were people like David Belin, a Republican from Des Moines; Albert Jenner, another Republican from Chicago; Leon Hubert, a Democrat from New Orleans; David Slawson, a Kennedy supporter from a Denver law firm; Arlen Specter, a Republican prosecutor from Philadelphia; and me, a Kennedy Democrat from Cleveland, Ohio.

As diverse and barely acquainted as we were—and not beholden in any way to the federal government—we were nonetheless single-minded in our pursuit of truth. Aptly, David Slawson would recall years later, "We were all motivated to find something

Warren Commission photograph of general counsel J. Lee Rankin with assistant counsel and other staff. Front row: Alfred Goldberg; Norman Redlich; J. Lee Rankin; Howard Willens; David Belin; Burt Griffin. Second row: Stuart Pollak; Arlen Specter; Jim Liebeler; David Slawson; Samuel Stern (back); Albert Jenner; John Hart Ely. Missing are assistant counsel Frank Adams; Joe Ball; Bill Coleman; Leon Hubert; Norman Redlich (Estate of David Belin).

unexpected, such as other gunmen or a hidden conspiracy. *It would have made us heroes.*"[17] Those of us who were young lawyers were keenly aware, moreover, that our future careers depended on doing an objective, highly competent, credible job. If we failed, well might our own careers.

The staff exercised an independence from the Commission members that was similar to the independence of a prosecutor from the judge or jury. Until they received a transcript of a witness's testimony or heard the testimony itself, the commissioners were largely ignorant of the fact-gathering being conducted by the staff. When, on one occasion, Chairman Warren declined to approve a staff member using the Swiss government to obtain documents from the Cuban government, the staff member disobeyed the order and obtained the documents.[18]

Your Only Client Is the Truth

On January 20, 1964, the full professional staff met together for the first time. The Commission's conference room was large enough to accommodate the fifteen of us, but scarcely more. Chief Justice Warren presided. For me—and I suspect the rest—this audience with the nation's highest judicial officer, already an icon, was awe-inspiring. On a par with John Marshall's establishment of judicial review (the Court's ability to declare legislative and executive acts unconstitutional), Chief Justice Warren had changed American society by declaring segregation unconstitutional through *Brown v. Board of Education.*

Warren's words set the tone as well as the enormity of our responsibility: "Your only client is the truth."[19] Less than a year later, in his book *Portrait of the Assassin,* Gerald Ford hailed those words as the standard to which we were all committed.[20] We were acutely aware, also, how keenly our work bore upon our nation's security.[21] The nation feared that the Soviet Union or Cuba had planned the assassination. If there had been such a conspiracy to assassinate the president and we failed to find it, our nation faced the gravest peril. Conspiracy or none, however, only the most credible investigation and evidence might avert political tragedy. The era of Senator Joseph McCarthy was less than a decade behind us. Political assault could be unceasing, and unjustified war might follow.

The Commission took care in its final report to define its role for posterity:

> The Commission has functioned neither as a court presiding over an adversary proceeding nor as a prosecutor determined to prove a case, but as a factfinding agency committed to the ascertainment of the truth.[22]

The distinction between a fact-finding agency and a court or prosecutor is critical. A trial court should be neutral, serving to referee a dispute between contestants. It maintains order within the bounds of law as lawyers on different sides present their evidence. The court does not search for evidence. Judges and juries evaluate what is presented by the contesting lawyers.

Lawyers are not necessarily as dedicated to finding the truth as they are to winning. Indeed, a good lawyer avoids presenting evidence that is harmful to his client. A crafty one tries to keep it from his opponent. In rendering a decision, a court (or even a jury) determines only whether a litigant has met its burden of proof.

But our function as fact-finders was different. Just as scientists, physicians, and engineers, our mission was to draw upon established principles and proven procedures to assemble as much relevant evidence as possible. Then we were bound to question everything and each other until we were confident of our findings and conclusions.

We inhabited a realm of continual cross-examination—of investigators, witnesses, and each other. We undertook a perpetual search for missing pieces. When evidence from initial police or federal investigators was not forthcoming or sufficient, we demanded more. And then we questioned everything presented to us. We accepted nothing as true unless it could be verified and corroborated. We sought independent experts to examine the expert opinions of the original investigators. For example, the Commission retained Joseph D. Nicol, superintendent of the Illinois Bureau of Criminal Investigation to determine whether FBI expert Robert A. Frazier had correctly concluded bullets, fragments, and cartridges had come from Oswald's Mannlicher-Carcano rifle. In addition, two other FBI ballistics experts were asked to make independent examinations. All agreed.[23] Even then, we disputed each other until we were satisfied as to what we could rely upon as accurate and reasonable.[24]

We expected that witnesses would be mistaken or outright lie—just as Oswald clearly had. Lee Oswald told Dallas police that he had never possessed a rifle. But his wife, Marina, when shown a photo of him holding a rifle, said she had taken the photograph. A friend, Jeanne de Mohrenschildt, testified that she saw a rifle in a closet at Oswald's residence. Lee's palmprint was found on the rifle that police recovered from the sixth floor of the School Book Depository.

Yet evidence of Oswald's lying about the Mannlicher-Carcano went beyond his possessing it at some time. Sales and postal records showed that the 6.5-mm Mannlicher-Carcano rifle found on the School Book Depository's sixth floor was delivered from the seller to an A. Hidell at a post-office address listed in Lee Oswald's name. Moreover, the police had found on Oswald's person a forged Selective Service card containing a photo of him with Hidell's name on it. Marina testified to the Commission that Lee had used the name A.J. Hidell on Fair Play for Cuba membership cards that he prepared in the summer of 1963 when they were living in New Orleans.

Not as easy to sort as outright lies were exaggerations and speculations. Prominent among these were those occurring in testimony as to whether Oswald and his murderer, Jack Ruby, knew each other. At least five witnesses suggested they did.[25]

A few hours after Ruby killed Oswald, William D. Crowe, Jr., a master of ceremonies at one of Jack Ruby's nightclubs, told news media reporters that there was a possibility that he had seen Lee Oswald at Ruby's Carousel Club. Crowe's repertoire included a memory act. The news reporters made Crowe's identification sound probable. In his Commission testimony, Crowe said, "[T]hey built up a bit of having seen Oswald there, and I never stated definitively, positively, and they said that I did ... what they said in the paper was hardly even close to what I told them."[26]

After Crowe's statements to the media, four others said they believed they saw a man resembling Oswald at the Carousel Club. One gave a specific date. Other testimony established, however, that Oswald was present that entire day at the home of Ruth Paine with Marina.[27]

The Commission, through its staff, examined every claim that Oswald and Ruby had been together and found none to be credible. No witness had ever seen Oswald prior to claiming to have seen him with Ruby. The Commission wrote, "With regard to all of the persons who claimed to have seen Ruby and Oswald together, it is significant that none had particular reason to pay close attention to either man, that substantial periods of time elapsed before the events they assertedly witnessed became meaningful, and that, unlike the eyewitnesses who claimed to have seen Oswald on November 22, none reported their observations soon after Oswald was arrested."[28]

Politics Two

Prejudice and Truth

5

Truth-Finding and Jack Ruby's Trial

Leon D. Hubert, Jr. and I were assigned by the Warren Commission's general counsel, J. Lee Rankin, to investigate Jack Ruby. Our goal was to determine whether Ruby had been part of a conspiracy to assassinate either President Kennedy or Lee Harvey Oswald or both.

Hubert, fifty-two years old, had been born and spent his professional career in New Orleans. He knew the city where Oswald had lived. A scholarly, experienced criminal lawyer, Hubert had been Phi Beta Kappa at Tulane University and graduated Order of the Coif from its law school. Thereafter he served four years as chief criminal prosecutor in New Orleans, twelve years as an assistant United States attorney, and eighteen as a law professor. He had taken a leave of absence from his New Orleans partnership of Hubert, Baldwin, & Zibilieh to join the Warren Commission. He was bright, dedicated, and practical.

At age thirty-one, I was clearly the junior associate. Yet from the beginning, Hubert and I worked as a team. I, too, had been an assistant U.S. attorney. My primary responsibility had been prosecuting criminal cases.

As we began our investigation, Jack Ruby was awaiting trial in Dallas for the murder of Lee Harvey Oswald. Until the Ruby trial ended, we could not go to Dallas to depose witnesses. Such efforts might undermine the trial. Our tasks, meanwhile, were to digest the hundreds of pages of interviews that had already been conducted concerning Ruby and his acquaintances, plan our investigative strategy, and request further investigation from the FBI and other agencies.

We had no doubt that some witnesses might lie. Ruby's self-interest was obvious. Ruby had been interviewed by the FBI, Secret Service, and Dallas police as soon as he was arrested. Ruby said that he acted alone, without encouragement or help. It was unlikely, of course, that anyone who blatantly committed a murder would admit to being part of a conspiracy without pressure, favor, or self-interest. If we could find a connection between Ruby and someone who was also linked to Oswald or wanted to kill him, or to someone who wanted to kill the president, it might prove a basis for pressure, favor, or self-interest to reveal a conspiracy.

Initially Ruby's employees, friends, family, business associates, and acquaintances were all suspects in any possible conspiracy. Even if innocent, they, too, likely had interests that might not be conducive to truth—such as fear of being linked to Ruby, a desire to protect him, a desire for publicity, concern for their own employment security, or a desire to protect the image of Dallas.

Dallas police were also on our suspects list. Although unlikely to be part of a conspiracy to kill President Kennedy, they had ample reason to detest Oswald. He had murdered one of their brethren. Moreover, many of them knew Ruby. Some had patronized his clubs. One was dating one of his strippers. We couldn't rule out that one or more of them might have recruited or encouraged Ruby.

Evidence and Jack Ruby's Trial

Although Ruby's trial prevented us from taking testimony, we followed the evidence that it produced and its outcome closely. Dallas's chief prosecutor, Henry Wade, had every reason to find a conspiracy if one existed. He could become a national hero—perhaps president—if he could find a conspiracy. As occurred in 1969, when New Orleans District Attorney Jim Garrison unsuccessfully attempted to convict businessman Clay Shaw of conspiring to kill the president,[1] Wade might have tried to find a suspect to link Ruby to Oswald. As he told the Warren Commission, numerous individuals claimed, prior to the Ruby trial, that they had seen Oswald and Ruby together. He checked them out. None were credible.[2]

In March 1964, Ruby was tried alone for murder with malice aforethought of Lee Harvey Oswald. Wade got his conviction.[3] Under Texas law, such a conviction did not require premeditation—only that the killing was a "voluntary homicide committed without justification or excuse."[4] A "deliberate intention of the mind was sufficient," regardless of how quickly that intention was formed.[5]

In returning its guilty verdict, the jury at the same time gave Ruby the death penalty. The defense and trial judge were shocked.[6] Hubert and I were surprised. When Ruby shot Oswald, he undoubtedly expected to receive sympathy, if not acclaim. Before the trial, one informal Dallas poll of two hundred people showed the group seven to one in favor of a light sentence. A Dallas newspaper poll found that fifty percent wanted no punishment at all.[7]

Such feelings were not unique to Dallas. In Iowa, just three months before Ruby's conviction, an Iowa judge had given forty-seven-year-old Michael Bohan probation and a thousand-dollar fine for killing his sixty-eight-year-old stepfather with a knife when the stepfather cursed Kennedy as Bohan was watching a broadcast about funeral arrangements for the president. Bohan had pleaded guilty. After killing his stepfather, Bohan called the police and reported his own actions. The sentencing judge told Bohan, "[T]he entire nation was under stress and strain from the tragedy.... But that is not a reason for a citizen ... to release his emotions to the extent of causing another tragedy."[8]

Jack Ruby's initial lawyer, Tom Howard—an experienced Dallas criminal defense lawyer—had hoped to apply the same strategy. In the twenty-five capital cases Howard had tried, not one of Howard's clients had received the death penalty.[9] Ruby, he believed, should plead guilty to a noncapital offense and ask the court for mercy.

If a trial were necessary, Howard would argue to the jury that Ruby had acted without malice, "under the immediate influence of a sudden passion arising from an adequate cause." To prove that, he would call Ruby's friends and family to testify to Ruby's character as well as his conduct once he learned that the president had been shot. He would put Ruby on the stand to describe his emotions upon seeing Oswald in the police basement. Ruby would apologize.[10]

Neither Howard nor his strategy would prevail. Howard was a criminal defense lawyer with a storefront office and no secretary of his own. Even though he had successfully defended many homicide cases, mostly he represented ordinary criminal defendants—thieves, prostitutes, drunk drivers. Ruby's family wanted a lawyer with "class."[11]

Through a friend, they found Melvin Belli—a personal injury lawyer representing the nation's most prominent plaintiffs. Whereas Howard would have sought to keep the trial low-keyed, Belli wanted to gain maximum attention. Ruby's family could not pay Belli's $75,000 fee. Belli expected to cover it by writing a book. He hired one author to write a story of the trial and another Belli's own biography.[12] Ultimately, Belli wrote his own book with Maurice C. Carroll.[13] Belli's strategy was to seek a not guilty or diminished homicide verdict by proving that Ruby was insane at the time he shot Oswald. He wanted to move the law of insanity to what he believed was the perception of modern psychological science. An acquittal for Ruby would achieve that goal and ensure Belli national acclaim.

As customary with an insanity defense, Ruby did not testify. The chief defense psychiatrist advised against Ruby testifying. Belli feared that Ruby would say he wanted to kill Oswald. Ruby was, himself, ambivalent about testifying. Belli said that Ruby ultimately did not want to testify because "I'll go all to pieces."[14] Belli presented minimal

Jack Ruby (center) at his trial conferring with his lawyers Melvin Belli (right) and Joe Tonahill (left) as unknown men look on (Bill Winfrey Collection / The Sixth Floor Museum at Dealey Plaza).

evidence to show Ruby's evolving state of mind once he learned of the president's death. Psychologists and psychiatrists carried the bulk of the defense.

It was famed psychiatrist Manfred Guttmacher who gave Ruby's account of his thoughts after the president's murder. Ruby, Guttmacher testified, "insisted and does insist, whenever I've seen him, the shooting was due to a sudden, momentary impulse." Dr. Guttmacher's opinion was that a condition known as psychomotor epilepsy was a partial factor in Ruby's actions. It was that partial factor upon which Melvin Belli chose to rest Ruby's insanity defense.[15] Ruby had a momentary blackout and didn't know what he was doing.

The State was fierce in countering that claim. Central to the State's case were Dallas police officers who testified to Ruby's expressing his intent. A key witness was Dallas Police Sergeant Patrick Dean. Dean testified that a few minutes after being arrested, Ruby told him that he thought of killing Oswald when he watched Oswald address the press about midnight on November 22 in the basement assembly room of the police department.

After two weeks of testimony and two hours nineteen minutes of deliberation, the jury returned its verdict. In Texas at that time, the jury determined penalty at the conclusion of the guilt/innocence phase without hearing further evidence or argument about the penalty.[16]

Its verdict: guilty and the death penalty.[17]

Melvin Belli rose and shouted to the jury, "May I thank the jury for a victory for bigotry and injustice." Speaking to the press, he called the proceedings a kangaroo court, adding that the jury had made Dallas "a city of shame forever" and that American justice "had been raped."[18]

Justice may well have failed, but whose fault was that? Many experienced criminal defense lawyers would have employed a strategy different from Belli's, focusing on a reduced sentence rather than an unusual insanity defense and acquittal.[19] As Tom Howard had perceived, the challenge was to persuade the jury that Jack Ruby, a man overwrought by the totality of crushing events on November 22, had reacted as many Dallas residents might have and now felt regret.

Years later, Dallas lawyer Bill Alexander, part of the team that prosecuted Ruby, told Robert Blakey, chief counsel and staff director to the House Select Committee on Assassinations, "Jack Ruby was about as handicapped as you can get in Dallas. First, he was a Yankee. Second, he was a Jew. Third, he was in the night club business."[20]

Belli might not have been wrong, however, about the verdict being a victory for bigotry. There were reasons to believe that anti-Semitism underlay part of the state's strategy. Ruby was indicted as Jack Rubenstein, Alias Jack Ruby, even though he had changed his name legally to Jack Ruby nearly fifteen years earlier.[21] Immediately after Ruby shot Oswald, the headlines of the *Dallas Morning News* identified him as "Rubenstein."[22] At a pretrial hearing, Belli accused prosecutor Alexander of referring to Ruby as "that Jew boy from Chicago." Alexander denied saying it, but Belli repeated the accusation throughout the trial, and trial documents confirm that Alexander used opportunities to show the jury that Ruby was Jewish.[23]

Perhaps as a means of overcoming possible anti-Semitism, Belli presented as a defense witness Ruby's rabbi, Hillel Silverman. Silverman testified that after the assassination Ruby had attended a memorial service for the president.

In listing Ruby's three handicaps, prosecutor Alexander omitted two: the city of Dallas was also on trial, and the jury's own integrity was at stake. Before the trial began,

Jurors in Jack Ruby trial and two bailiffs. Front row (left to right): Luther E. Dickerson; Max E. Causey (foreman); Robert J. Flechtner; J.G. "Glen" Holton, Jr.; James E. Cunningham; and Louise Malone. Second row (left to right): Mildred McCollum; Aileen B. Shields; Gwen English; Douglas Sowell; J. Waymon Rose; and Allen W. McCoy (Bill Winfrey Collection / The Sixth Floor Museum at Dealey Plaza).

local newspapers were filled with expressions by city leaders that the assassination of the president and the murder of the accused assassin brought disgrace upon the city.[24] At the pretrial hearing for change of venue, the defense counsel argued that Ruby could not get a fair trial in Dallas. Prospective jurors could not be unaware of or impartial to these perceptions.

One judge on the Texas Court of Criminal Appeals later expressed the view, one probably held by Ruby, that Ruby's prosecution was an atonement for Dallas's own sins—its failure to protect the president and Oswald.[25] After the trial, Ruby became obsessed with the idea that Jews in Dallas were being murdered for his actions.[26]

Although jurors may not have seen themselves as defending their city's honor, they realized they were a part of history. Max Causey, the first juror to be selected, began a diary as he waited days for the full jury to be selected. Two other jurors—Waymon Rose and Alex McCoy—followed his example.[27] A year after the trial ended, Causey turned his diary into a memoir. The memoir was ultimately edited and published after his death in 1997.[28]

From Causey's memoir and the statements of other jurors, it is clear that the jury was quick to reject Belli's insanity defense and find Ruby guilty of murder with malice. It took them roughly another fifteen minutes to vote unanimously for the death penalty.[29] Foreman Causey, who originally favored life in prison, explained in his memoir his reason for ultimately agreeing to the death penalty:

> I would really prefer that an easier and more humane method of major crime deterrent could be found.... I feel it is a moral and civic responsibility to do so.... The law states that when ... a jury ... finds beyond a reasonable doubt that a man is guilty of committing a crime of unprovoked murder, with full and complete sanity then he is subject to being sentenced to death for his crime.[30]

Even with such a finding, Texas law allowed a jury to select a sentence less than death if it deemed the sentence appropriate. In this case, for many of the jurors a decisive factor was that Ruby had shot a manacled, defenseless man and denied him the right of a trial.[31] It was the argument pressed most strongly by the prosecution in its closing argument: "American justice is on trial.... Oswald was entitled to the protection of the law.... He was entitled to be tried in a court of justice."[32]

Change of Counsel

Belli's inability to place Ruby's interests before his own soon ended their relationship. The day after the jury's verdict, Belli photographed Ruby in jail. He offered the photo to *Life* magazine for sale. When Ruby's family learned of the offer, Belli was quickly fired.[33] Through his failed strategy and self-promotion, Belli had antagonized Ruby, Ruby's family, and the City of Dallas. He left Ruby and Dallas to write *Dallas Justice: The Real Story of Jack Ruby and His Trial*. What, one may wonder, had impelled Belli to go for broke by seeking a full acquittal. According to Vincent Bugliosi, Belli had told his law partner, "... [I]f I can do that, I'll be right up there with Clarence Darrow."[34]

For two years, other defense counsel fought to remain as Ruby's lawyers. Joe Tonahill was the principal contender. He filed an appeal for Ruby and appeared with him before the Warren Commission in June 1964. For the appeal, Ruby secured a sympathetic group of new lawyers—Charles Bellows, of Chicago; Sam Houston Clinton, of the Texas Civil Liberties Union; Sol Dann, of Detroit; Elmer Gertz, of Chicago; and William Kunstler, of New York City.[35]

Tonahill did not take it lying down. In proceedings before multiple lower courts, he argued that Ruby was insane and therefore incompetent to discharge him or retain new counsel.[36] The new lawyers argued he was sane.[37] After many months, a civil jury—empaneled especially for the purpose of determining sanity—found Ruby competent to select his own counsel.[38] The new lawyers were on board, and Ruby's criminal conviction was enroute to appellate review.

Reversal in the Texas Court of Criminal Appeals

On October 5, 1966, the Texas Court of Criminal Appeals reversed the Ruby conviction.[39] It found that Ruby could not have received a fair trial in Dallas and held that a motion for change of venue should have been granted.

One concurring judge elaborated:

> Dallas was being blamed directly and indirectly for President Kennedy's assassination and for allowing the shooting of Oswald by Ruby. The feeling and thought had been generated that Dallas County's deprivation of prosecuting Oswald could find atonement in the prosecution of Ruby ... the citizenry of Dallas consciously and subconsciously felt that Dallas was on trial and the Dallas image was uppermost in their minds to such an extent that Ruby could not be tried there fairly....[40]

A possible reason—not mentioned by the appellate court—that the trial judge, Joe B. Brown, did not grant Ruby's request for a change of venue was that Judge Brown was also planning to write a book about the trial. While still overseeing the case, he received a $5,000 advance from his prospective publisher, Holt, Rinehart, and Winston.[41] If the venue had been changed, Brown might not have retained the case. Regardless, Brown's publishing contract was never fulfilled, but he did leave a memoir about the trial, which eventually was edited by retired psychologist Diane Holloway and published in 2001 as *Dallas and the Jack Ruby Trial: Memoir of Judge Joe B. Brown, Sr.*

In addition to granting a change of venue, the appellate court found that Sergeant Patrick Dean's testimony should not have been considered. Under Texas law, an oral statement from a defendant under arrest could not be admitted unless made spontaneously. The appellate court found Ruby's alleged statement was not spontaneous.[42]

Ruby was never retried. On January 3, 1967—three months after his conviction was reversed by the Texas Court of Criminal Appeals—he died in Dallas of cancer. Until his death, he continued to insist that he was not part of a conspiracy to assassinate either President Kennedy or Lee Harvey Oswald. He died fearful that the Jewish community was suffering for his actions.

6

Truth and Self-Interest

While the Ruby trial was proceeding, Leon Hubert and I gathered evidence. Although we wanted to know Ruby's life history and friends, we particularly wanted to know the details of his activities from the first time anyone could have known that President Kennedy planned to come to Dallas—in September 1963—through his arrest and interrogation for shooting Oswald. Considering every possibility of conspiracy, we sought any connection between Ruby and Oswald as well as any relationship Ruby may have had with any individuals hostile to the president. We wanted to know about Ruby's friendships with Dallas police officers, especially any possibly inclined toward vengeance for the murder of Officer Tippit.

We began by taking testimony on how security had lapsed to allow Ruby into the police department basement. An answer to that might lead us to someone who helped, conspired with, or inspired Ruby.[1] In particular, did any Dallas police officer help Ruby gain access to Oswald?

Sergeant Dean as a Key Witness

A significant witness for us was Sergeant Patrick Dean. Dean's testimony had been important to the prosecution in suggesting that Ruby had premeditated Oswald's murder. The Texas Criminal Court of Appeals reversed Ruby's conviction on the ground that Dean's testimony was inadmissible. This same Patrick Dean was in charge of security for the basement garage where Oswald was shot. Dean and Ruby were acquainted, and the breach in security seemed to lie at Dean's doorstep. Leon Hubert and I wondered if Dean had seen Ruby enter the basement but decided not to stop him. Was it possible, even, that Dean had helped Ruby gain entrance?

Our suspicions were heightened by Dean's behavior after Oswald was shot. Dean did not take charge of securing the basement and/or conducting an investigation of Ruby's entry. His first step was to give a TV interview in which he said that he had not seen Ruby enter the basement.[2] He then went to Chief Curry, who asked him to accompany Secret Service Agent Forest Sorrels to a fifth-floor holding cell where Sorrels would interview Ruby.

The interview lasted from five to seven minutes. Sorrels said that Ruby first inquired as to whether Sorrels was a news reporter—suggesting that Ruby sought publicity. When Sorrels answered that he wasn't, Ruby, after some hesitation, continued to talk.[3] Sorrels secured a cursory personal history and asked Ruby how he came to shoot Oswald.

According to Sorrels, Ruby then recounted how he had been at the *Dallas Morning*

News when Kennedy was shot, became very upset, decided to close his businesses for three days, heard a eulogy for Kennedy at a Jewish synagogue that Friday night, became distressed that Mrs. Kennedy might have to testify at any trial of Oswald, and "had worked himself up into a state of insanity ... and that he guessed he felt that he had 'to show the world that a Jew had guts.'"[4]

Dean's memory of the interview differed from Sorrels.' In his initial report to his superiors on November 26, Dean made no mention of what Ruby said or when Ruby decided to shoot Oswald or what motivated him to shoot Oswald. Dean reported, however, "After Mr. Sorrels interrogated the subject, I questioned Ruby as to how he had entered the basement and the length of time he had been there. Ruby then stated to me in the presence of Sorrels that he had entered the basement through the ramp entering on Main Street. He further stated that he would estimate his total time at about 3 minutes before the detectives brought Oswald into his view, then he immediately shot him (Oswald)."[5]

Sorrels did not recall that Ruby made any statement while Dean was present about how he entered the police basement. He remembered Ruby first admitting to Homicide Captain Will Fritz in a subsequent interview later that day that he had entered via Main Street.[6] Police officers, who remembered Ruby being questioned before being taken to Fritz, failed to mention in their initial reports any statements by Ruby about how he entered the basement.[7]

Fritz's memory of his discussion with Ruby about his entry into the basement was explicit. He told the Warren Commission, "He [Ruby] told me he came down that ramp from the outside.... I said, 'No, you couldn't have come down the ramp because there would be an officer at the top and an officer at the bottom....' He said, 'I am not going to talk to you any more, I am not going to get into trouble' and he never talked to me any more.... I asked him when he first decided to kill Oswald, and he didn't tell me that."[8] When FBI Agent C. Ray Hall asked Ruby sometime that day about how he entered the basement, Ruby said only that he entered via the Main Street side and that no one had helped him. Ruby declined to give any details.[9]

Dean and Patrol Officer Roy Eugene Vaughn, stationed at the top of the Main Street ramp, were now the primary focus in the police department's security breakdown on November 24. Both knew Ruby. Vaughn denied that Ruby had walked past him. He said that it would have been impossible for Ruby to have entered without him seeing Ruby and that if he had seen Ruby on the ramp, he would have stopped him.[10] There was evidence, however, that someone did try to stop Ruby. On December 5, in an FBI interview, Detective Thomas D. McMillon claimed that he heard Ruby say on November 24 that some officer hollered at him as he walked down the Main Street ramp.[11] Was it, Hubert and I had to wonder, Officer Vaughn or Sergeant Dean?

In addition to Ruby emerging to shoot Oswald from the Main Street side of the awaiting crowd, there was other evidence to confirm Ruby's claim that he had walked down the Main Street ramp. Jimmie Turner, an employee of television station WBAP, said that he was standing near a railing close to the Main Street ramp and saw a man he was confident was Ruby walking down the ramp about ten feet from the bottom.[12]

Leon Hubert and I were aware that Ruby could conceivably have gotten onto the ramp to where Turner saw him by climbing over the railing alongside the Main Street ramp. We also knew that there were other entrances to the basement in addition to the Main Street ramp. Thus, we faced a dilemma. Was Captain Fritz correct in questioning

Ruby's claim of entry? Was Officer Vaughn correct in saying that Ruby could not have entered from Main Street without being seen by him? Was Dean truthful in saying that he did not see Ruby enter the basement? Who as a matter of self-interest might be trying to protect his job?

Ultimately, we accepted Ruby's explanation. It made sense. When he fired his shot at Oswald, Ruby had emerged from the Main Street side of the group assembled in the garage. Jimmie Turner had seen him walking from the base of the Main Street ramp for about ten feet to the crowd from which he lunged to shoot. Ruby could have entered onto the Main Street ramp without being seen by Officer Vaughn because Vaughn may have walked to the middle of Main Street to block traffic as a police car driven by Lt. Rio Pierce was exiting the ramp. Ruby claimed he edged by Pierce's car unseen as it passed him. When Pierce's car turned on to Main Street, Vaughn may have seen only Ruby's back. Either Vaughn or Dean might have yelled. If Ruby had walked along Main Street from the Western Union office after he wired the money order, it wasn't improbable that he would have reached the garage ramp just as Pierce's police car was exiting.

Special Doubts About Dean

To Leon Hubert and me, resolving the question of how Ruby entered the basement was relevant to whether Ruby had a co-conspirator. If Ruby had not entered as he claimed, he may have been protecting whoever had aided him.

Hubert and I were particularly suspicious of Dean. He knew Ruby well—might even be considered a friend. We wondered if he had, in fact, questioned Ruby in any respect after Sorrels had. Dallas police officers Don Archer, Barnard Clardy, and Thomas McMillon were present when Dean claims he talked to Ruby. In their initial reports on November 24 and 27, they said that Sorrels and FBI Agent C. Ray Hall questioned Ruby on the 24th. They failed to report that Dean was present at any time.

They also failed in those initial reports to mention any explanation by Ruby as to how he entered the basement.[13] Nor did any of their reports mention Ruby's saying, as Dean testified at the Ruby trial, that he had been thinking about killing Oswald for two days. The most vivid recollection of Detective Clardy was that Ruby said shortly after being arrested, "If I had planned to kill Oswald, my timing could not have been more perfect."[14]

We found Dean's behavior after the shooting of Oswald to be especially surprising—almost a sign of guilt in failing to prevent Ruby's entry. After Ruby allegedly told him in the presence of Secret Service Agent Sorrels that he had entered on the Main Street ramp, Dean did not remain at the police station to interrogate Officer Vaughn or otherwise seek to find witnesses who might have seen Ruby enter the garage. Though he wasn't assigned to do so, Dean went to Parkland Hospital.[15] There, he accompanied Oswald's mother in viewing Oswald's body.[16]

While at Parkland, Dean received a phone call from his superior, Lt. Pierce. Pierce instructed Dean to return to police headquarters. Even though Pierce was trying to learn how Ruby got past security, only after he returned to the station, at approximately 2:30 p.m., did Dean tell Pierce what Ruby allegedly said to him three hours earlier about coming down the Main Street ramp.[17] By then the focus was already on Officer Vaughn.

Dean was not, however, relieved of suspicion that he had aided Ruby. On December 8, 1963, a *Dallas Times-Herald* newspaper article reported falsely that Dean had affirmed in a TV interview on November 24 that he had seen Ruby come down the Main Street ramp.[18] Dean denied both making the statement on TV and affirming it to the *Times-Herald* reporter.[19] Nonetheless, the false news was out. Dean remained under a cloud.

Not until February 18, 1964—two weeks before the start of Ruby's trial—did Dean commit the following to paper: "Ruby stated he had thought about this for two days and decided it was senseless to have a long and lengthy trial and subject Mrs. Kennedy to having to return to Dallas for it."[20] Dean had not included this in his November 26, 1963, report to Dallas police Chief Jesse Curry.[21] He had not mentioned it when interviewed on December 2, 1963, by FBI Agent Paul L. Scott. Scott's report ends with the usual statement, "Dean advised he could furnish no additional pertinent information."[22] Captain Fritz, who was in charge of investigating Oswald's death, had never heard anything about such a statement to Dean.[23] Indeed, when Fritz asked Ruby on November 24, 1963, when he first decided to kill Oswald, Ruby declined to tell him.[24]

How unusual, Hubert and I thought, that a police officer having evidence so important to a murder prosecution would have waited nearly three months to report in writing such a statement about premeditation, and that no one would have told the chief homicide investigator once Dean came forward with Ruby's statement.

Sergeant Dean's Deposition

It now became my task to take Dean's deposition testimony. We began cordially in Dallas at 8 p.m. on March 24, 1964.[25] The deposition lasted nearly three hours.

We covered in detail Dean's actions from the time he began work at 9:00 a.m. on November 24 until his day ended. That occupied eighty percent of the deposition. We spoke very little about his testimony at the Ruby trial. My focus was on basement security and what Dean did on November 24 after Oswald was shot.

Dean told me he saw Lt. Pierce's car go up the Main Street ramp. He did not see Ruby come down. He did not deviate from his earlier accounts that Ruby had told him he had walked down the Main Street ramp.

I was unconvinced.

Challenging Sergeant Dean

After about two hours, I suggested that we take a break. We got soft drinks from a vending machine and talked for about twenty minutes without a stenographic reporter present. In a polite manner, I told Sergeant Dean that I doubted some of his testimony. I said that the important matter was that the Commission get the truth, that what might seem of lesser significance to him might be highly relevant to us. I had in mind, of course, the failure of any other officers to mention Ruby's statements in their initial reports even though they were present when Ruby allegedly made those statements to Dean.

I assured him that if he changed his testimony, the Commission would make every effort to protect him. My desire and tone were to appeal to his sense of patriotism, not to threaten him.[26]

We went back on the record. Dean added nothing regarding my topics of concern. We ended as cordially as we had begun.

Two days later, still in Dallas, I received a call from General Counsel J. Lee Rankin. Dean had gone to Prosecutor Henry Wade. Wade reported to Rankin that Dean said that I had threatened him and accused him of perjury.[27] The allegation was untrue. Although I had expressed doubts, I had sought his patriotic cooperation, not threatened prosecution.

Returning to Washington, I provided Rankin with a memo of my off-the-record conversation with Dean:

> ... I told him that in the two or three hours that he and I had been talking I found him to be a likeable and personable individual, and that I believed he was a capable and honest police officer. I tried to approach him on a basis of respect and friendship.... I then stressed that this investigation ... was of extreme importance to the National Security and that ... if there was some way that he could be induced to come forward with a more forthright statement without injuring himself, the Commission would probably be willing to explore a means to afford him the protection that was necessary.... I pointed out to him that if he had any such inclination to change his story it would probably be best that he not approach us directly but that he secure an attorney so the problems that he faced could be worked out without committing himself to anything on the record.
>
> ... I told him what I was particularly concerned with what Ruby told him about how he got into the basement. I explained that although he might not see the significance of that inquiry, he would have to accept my statement that ... it was extremely important to the national security to learn how Ruby entered the basement.[28]

After Dean's assertions to Henry Wade, I was satisfied that Dean was not to be believed.[29] More than fifty years later, I am satisfied that Ruby entered on the Main Street ramp. It is possible that Ruby told Dean he came down the Main Street ramp. He might have found an advantage in telling Dean how he entered. Dean could then tell him whether he would anger the police by showing Vaughn to be at fault.

To this day, for me, the overpowering facts are that Dean waited nearly three months to report to his supervisors in writing his claims about Ruby's statements concerning premeditation.

The information, provided in a letter to Chief Curry, was apparently not given to Captain Fritz. Why would Fritz not be informed? Did the prosecutor and police chief suspect that Dean was not truthful? Did they not want Fritz to know or interfere with Dean's testimony? Or was Fritz, in fact, told but unwilling to admit such knowledge to the Warren Commission?

Probabilities and Possibilities

The issue of premeditation was only one piece of why Dean's unusual behavior was so troublesome to Hubert and me. Whether Ruby had admitted premeditation to Dean or not, confirmation of how Ruby entered the garage could indicate who, if anyone, might have helped him. That in turn might serve eventually to reveal if any police officer had encouraged Ruby out of revenge or whether anyone else played a part in some completely different conspiracy.

We considered the possibility that Ruby did not use the Main Street ramp—that he entered the garage by walking down an alley just before he reached the police station. There was evidence that a door from the Dallas Municipal Building opened onto the alley and that the door would remain unlocked if someone exited the building and did not lock it from the outside.[30] If that door were unlocked, Ruby could have entered the Municipal Building, walked down a staircase into the police garage, and gone past where Sergeant Dean was standing. Under such a scenario, Dean might have been negligent—at least—and both Dean and Ruby would have been lying.

We rejected that conclusion. Our decision was that Ruby "entered the basement unaided, *probably* [emphasis added] via the Main Street ramp...."[31] Fifteen years later, the House Select Committee on Assassinations reached a different conclusion. They wrote that the most likely way in which Ruby entered the police garage was through the door and stairway from the alley next to the Dallas Municipal Building.[32]

The House Select Committee construed Ruby's initial reluctance to describe how he entered the basement as evidence that his ultimate explanation was false. The Committee reasoned further that his explanation gave him less than fifty-five seconds to walk down the ramp and shoot Oswald and that entering through the alley was a more secretive means of entry—evidence of planning to kill Oswald.[33] Without specifically accusing Ruby and other police officers of colluding to kill Oswald, the Select Committee wrote, "Ruby's close relationship with one or more members of the police force may have been a factor in his entry to the police basement on November 24, 1963."[34]

Leon Hubert and I ultimately accepted Ruby's explanation because it seemed most reasonable that Ruby would have walked directly along Main Street from the Western Union office—not through an alley door, then walking through a building to reach the garage floor. Going down the Main Street ramp was most consistent with where he was standing immediately before shooting Oswald, and at least one witness without a motive to lie (Jimmie Turner) was certain that he had seen someone walking part of the way down the ramp. Although we recognized that other routes were possible and that Ruby and Dean might both be lying, we concluded that the ramp explanation was more probable and that other routes less likely.

In the end, we believed that we had seen a classic example of how one's self-interest—the protection of one's job—could cause false or evasive testimony to prevail over justice, national interest, or the standards of one's profession.

7

Jack Ruby Tells His Story

Jack Ruby at first had wanted to testify at his trial. Now, facing a death penalty, Ruby wanted to testify before the Warren Commission. Joe Tonahill, fighting to remain Ruby's chief attorney at this point, urged against it: it would be better to save his testimony for a new jury, should the court of appeals grant him a new trial.

To accept Ruby's request posed problems for the Warren Commission. Evidence indicated that Ruby was psychotic. Too, he had Fifth Amendment rights, and the Commission risked being accused of coercion. Yet Ruby was insistent. He wanted the Warren Commission to hear his story, and he wanted it verified by a lie-detection test—a polygraph examination or sodium pentothal or both. The Commission acquiesced.

On June 7, 1964, Jack Ruby gave sworn testimony to Chief Justice Earl Warren and Representative Gerald Ford in the Dallas County jail.[1] Ruby's desire to testify was so strong that even before the Chief Justice administered the oath, he began reciting how he came to shoot Lee Oswald. After a few minutes, Warren remembered that Ruby was not under oath. The oath was administered, and Warren asked, "Now will you please tell us whether the things you have told us are true under your oath?"

Ruby answered, "I do state they are the truth," and proceeded to open a dialog with the Chief Justice:

> **Mr. RUBY:** Without a lie detector test on my testimony, my verbal statements to you, how do you know if I am tell[ing] the truth? ... I would like to be able to get a lie detector test or truth serum of what motivated me to do what I did at that particular time.... Now Mr. Warren I don't know if you got any confidence in the lie detector test and the truth serum, and so on.[2]
>
> **CHIEF JUSTICE WARREN:** I can't tell you just how much confidence I have in it, because it depends so much on who is taking it, and so forth. But I will say this to you, that if you and your counsel want any kind of test, I will arrange it for you.....
>
> **Mr. RUBY:** I do want it. Will you agree to that, Joe?
>
> **Mr. TONAHILL:** I sure do, Jack.[3]

Satisfied, Ruby began an interchange with Sheriff William Decker:

> **Mr. RUBY:** ... Bill, will you do that for me that you asked a minute ago? You said you wanted to leave the room.
>
> **Mr. DECKER:** I will have everyone leave the room, including myself, if you want to talk about it. You name it, and out we will go.
>
> **Mr. RUBY:** All right.
>
> **Mr. DECKER:** You want all of us outside?
>
> **Mr. RUBY:** Yes.

Mr. DECKER: I will leave Tonahill and Moore. I am not going to have Joe leave...
Mr. RUBY: Bill, I am not accomplishing anything if they are here and Joe Tonahill is here....
Mr. DECKER: Jack, this is your attorney. That is your lawyer.
Mr. RUBY: He is not my lawyer.[4]

(Sheriff Decker and law enforcement officers left room.)

Mr. RUBY: Gentlemen, if you want to hear any further testimony, you will have to get me to Washington soon, because it has something to do with you, Chief Warren. Do I sound sober enough to tell you this?
CHIEF JUSTICE WARREN: Yes, go right ahead.
MR. RUBY: I want to tell the truth, and I can't tell it here. I can't tell it here. Does that make sense to you?
CHIEF JUSTICE WARREN: Well, let's not talk about sense. But I really can't see why you can't tell this commission.[5]

At that Ruby turned to my colleague Joe Ball and said, "What is your name?" Joe Ball was a lawyer from California. Ruby wanted to know if Ball knew his former chief trial counsel, Melvin Belli, also from California. Ball responded that he knew of Belli only by reputation and that they practiced law in different parts of the state. Ruby did not object to Ball's presence.

About an hour into the interview, a remarkable interchange occurred. Ruby wanted to know if anyone in the room was Jewish. The only one in the small delegation from Washington who was Jewish was Arlen Specter, but Specter was waiting elsewhere in the facility. The Chief Justice summoned Specter.[6]

After a brief introduction, Ruby began questioning Specter in a barely audible voice, asking him: "Are you a Yid?" Specter sat expressionless. Ruby asked again, "Are you a Yid?" Again, Specter did not answer. Ruby then jumped from his chair, took the Chief Justice by the arm, pulled him to a corner, and ordered Specter to follow. As Specter remembered it, Ruby said to Warren, "Chief, you've got to get me to Washington. They're cutting off the arms and legs of Jewish children in Albuquerque and El Paso."[7]

His request to go to Washington was related to his belief that he, his family, and Jews in general were in jeopardy:

> Gentlemen, my life is in danger here.... I may not live tomorrow to give any further testimony ... the only thing I want to get out to the public, and I can't say it here, is with authenticity, with sincerity of the truth of everything and why my act was committed, but it can't be said here.
>
> It can be said, it's got to be said amongst people of the highest authority that would give me the benefit of doubt. And following that, immediately give me the lie detector test after I do make the statement.
>
> Chairman Warren, if you felt that your life was in danger at the moment, how would you feel? Wouldn't you be reluctant to go on speaking, even though you request me to do so?[8]

With sympathy and an expression of understanding, the Chief Justice said, "I want you to feel absolutely free to say that the interview is over."[9] Ruby did not accept the invitation. He proceeded to talk about that Sunday morning, the emotional condition that led him to decide to shoot Oswald, his actions on prior days, and accusations about visits to Cuba and some friends whom he thought others might consider unsavory.[10]

For nearly four hours, Jack Ruby took the initiative. Incongruous one might say—one of the most revered figures in U.S. legal history and the manager of a Dallas strip-tease club were conversing as if they were friends. Periodically, Ruby repeated his desire for a lie detector test, and the Chief Justice reiterated his promise to arrange it. The Chief Justice established a relationship of confidence with Ruby, who then related chronologically his actions from the night of November 21 to when he shot Oswald on November 24. Warren, Congressman Gerald Ford, and General Counsel Rankin asked only a few questions. Their roles were to clarify times, ensure that all topics were covered, and get clear statements as to whether Ruby was engaged in a conspiracy and knew Oswald. To those questions, Ruby answered no.

The following reflects what he wanted most to impress upon the Commission:

> ...that thought [of shooting Oswald] never entered my mind prior to that Sunday morning when I took it upon myself to try to be a martyr or some screwball, you might say.
>
> But I felt very emotional and very carried away for Mrs. Kennedy, that with all the strife she had gone through—I had been following it pretty well—that someone owed it to our beloved President that she shouldn't be expected to come back to face trial of this heinous crime.
>
> And I have never had the chance to tell that, to back it up, to prove it.
>
> Consequently, right at this moment I am being victimized as a part of a plot in the world's worst tragedy and crime at this moment.
>
> .... At this moment Lee Harvey Oswald isn't guilty of committing the crime of assassinating President Kennedy. Jack Ruby is.
>
> How can I fight that, Chief Justice Warren?[11]

The Chief Justice assured Ruby, "As far as this Commission is concerned, there is no implication of that in what we are doing." But Ruby had explained earlier his concerns.

> **MR. RUBY:** There is an organization here, Chief Justice Warren, if it takes my life at this moment to say it, and Bill Decker said be a man and say it, there is a John Birch Society right now in activity, and Edwin Walker is one of the top men of this organization—take it for what it is worth, Chief Justice Warren.
>
> Unfortunately for me, for me giving the people the opportunity to get in power, because of the act I committed, has put a lot of people in jeopardy with their lives.
>
> Don't register with you, does it?[12]
>
> **CHIEF JUSTICE WARREN:** No; I don't understand that.

When the session came to a close, Congressman Ford asked, "Is there anything more you can tell us if you went back to Washington?" Ruby responded:

> I want to tell you this, I am used as a scapegoat, and there is no greater weapon that you can use to create some falsehood about some of the Jewish faith, especially at the terrible heinous crime such as the killing of President Kennedy.
>
> Now maybe something can be saved. It may not be too late, whatever happens, if our President, Lyndon Johnson, knew the truth from me.
>
> But if I am eliminated, there won't be any way of knowing.
>
> Right now, when I leave your presence now, I am the only one that can bring out the truth to our President, who believes in righteousness and justice.
>
> But he has been told, I am certain, that I was a part of a plot to assassinate the President.[13]

Conspiracy theorists have suggested that Ruby wanted to go to Washington to reveal a conspiracy to kill President Kennedy. For them, Ruby's testimony about his motives was a cover story; he was withholding the truth from the Chief Justice. It should be clear from a complete reading of Ruby's testimony that the only conspiracy he wished to reveal was one he believed existed to blame him and the Jewish people for the assassination.

In Chief Justice Warren's handling of Jack Ruby, there is a lesson for those who love movies and books about trials. The Chief Justice was an experienced prosecutor. He had spent more than a decade as the chief prosecutor in Alameda County, California. He knew that one way to secure the truth was to allow a witness to speak freely—without interruption and without caustic cross-examination. That is the respectful extension of courtesy that one can read in the questioning of Jack Ruby by Chief Justice Warren. By encouraging the witness to speak freely, one can more readily discern the personality of the witness than is often possible by accusatory questioning. The gathering of other evidence and the questioning of other witnesses can corroborate or discredit the truthfulness and sincerity of the witness. That was the Chief Justice's method.

Jack Ruby's dialogue with Chief Justice Warren and Congressman Ford lasted only a few minutes more. The discussion returned to the importance—to Ruby—of a lie detector test. Six weeks later, on July 18, 1964, a polygraph examination was conducted in Dallas.

Arlen Specter was the only representative from the Warren Commission or its staff. Neither Hubert nor I attended. Specter was the appropriate person to represent the Commission because Ruby had been concerned previously to have someone from the Commission who was Jewish, and Ruby had met him. Specter served that purpose at that time.

Ruby was asked a series of questions: Was he involved in a conspiracy to assassinate President Kennedy? Did he ever meet Lee Harvey Oswald? Did anyone urge him to shoot Oswald or was he otherwise involved in a conspiracy to kill Oswald? To each of these he answered no. As he told Warren and Ford, the idea of shooting Oswald did not occur to him until Sunday morning. And no one gave him any assistance in entering the basement of the Dallas Police Department at the necessary time.[14]

Was the lie-detector test to be trusted? The polygraph examiner, a seasoned FBI professional, believed that if Ruby were mentally competent, the charts generated in the examination "could be interpreted to indicate that there was no area of deception present."[15] Polygraph charts aside, the examiner believed also from Ruby's frowns, smiles, and gestations during the examination that he was truthful. Arlen Specter, the Commission's assistant counsel who was present during the examination, concurred.

Neither of those opinions would have been admissible in court. Dr. William Beavers, a psychiatrist who interviewed Ruby and was present at the polygraph examination, concluded that Ruby was a psychotic depressive. If that diagnosis were accepted, the polygraph examiner said, "there would be no validity to the polygraph examination."[16] The Warren Commission placed no reliance on the polygraph examination.

Regardless of the polygraph examination's validity, there can be no doubt that Ruby was consistent. While in jail, he maintained a diary. His rabbi, Hillel Silverman, visited him almost weekly. Neither in the diary nor to Rabbi Silverman did Ruby suggest that he was part of any conspiracy, either to assassinate the president or murder Lee Oswald.[17]

Forty years later, Silverman was convinced that Ruby acted alone, out of emotion and without the urging of anyone. Being interviewed by Gabrielle Tenenbaum for the NBC-TV documentary *Beyond Conspiracy,* Rabbi Silverman said, "I feel in my heart that Jack Ruby would never lie to me. I was a symbol to him of authority. And he believed that you tell the truth to a rabbi."[18]

Silverman explained, "[Ruby] was so volatile, he was so impetuous, he was so belligerent, that he couldn't control his temper ... he believed that this man [Oswald] killed his President, and he loved his President, and he was taking justice into his own hands."[19]

Another traditional view of Ruby's truthfulness may be found in Ruby's death bed statements—which would have been admissible in some courts. What better time for a man like Ruby to unburden himself of a terrible secret? Dying of cancer in Parkland Hospital in January 1967, Ruby dictated this letter to his brother Earl: "I want you to know I never knew Oswald; I was never involved in a conspiracy, and I did not plan to shoot him. After it happened, I didn't know what I had done. Oh, Earl, how I wish that this had never happened. I never realized that this could cause such grief to everyone."[20]

Shortly thereafter, in a will prepared at his request but too late for him to sign, he authorized: "This being my Last Will and Testament, I hereby reiterate that I have had no association with any persons in connection with the assassination of the late John F. Kennedy and for the world to know that on my death bed I do make this statement."[21]

Rabbi Hillel Silverman's 2009 recollection is supportive: "Was there a conspiracy? Was he paid to shoot Oswald to silence him? Did he know Oswald? Was he associated with conspirators?"

"I discussed this with Ruby many times. I am convinced he was completely innocent of a conspiracy."[22]

Ruby's family and his lawyers believed Jack was psychotic—not only during his trial but continuing until his death from cancer on January 3, 1967. As it happened, four days before Chief Justice Warren heard Jack Ruby's testimony in Dallas, Leon Hubert and I took the testimony of Earl Ruby, Jack Ruby's brother.[23] For Earl there was no doubt that his brother became psychotic shortly after he shot Oswald, if he was not already psychotic at the time of the shooting. The rest of Jack's family and Jack's lawyers agreed. Earl believed that the dominant factor in Jack's decision to kill Oswald was his fear that Jews would be blamed for the assassination of the president. In support of that belief, Earl submitted a thirty-page memorandum prepared by Sol Dann, a Detroit lawyer who served as co-counsel on Jack's appeal of his criminal conviction.[24]

In the memo, Dann described the man who killed Lee Harvey Oswald as "an insane Jack Rubenstein, the son of pious Jewish parents, who suffered a lifetime of persecution as Jews."[25] Dann concluded that when Ruby shot Oswald, he believed he would be acclaimed a hero. But, months later, by the time he was ready to testify to Chief Justice Warren, Ruby's feelings had changed. He "now believes," Dann wrote, that "he brought disgrace and shame upon all the Jewish people for all time . . . ."[26]

Dann cited a series of details from the trial—shocking to contemporary readers—that support his contention that Ruby had been victimized by anti-Semitism as a Jew in Dallas in the early 1960s. Dann claimed that the prosecutor, at trial, had inflamed the jury by referring to Jack Ruby as a "Jew boy from Chicago," a "money grubber," and a "Jewish Messiah."[27] There is disagreement as to whether Bill Alexander used the expression "Jew boy from Chicago" or, in calling attention to Ruby's childhood, referred to him as a Jewish boy discussing baseball scores with someone from Chicago. In any event, the reference was made at Ruby's bail hearing, not at trial, and was not heard by the jury. Nonetheless Dann's memo confirmed for Ruby his belief that the death penalty was imposed because he was Jewish and that other Jews were being persecuted and executed for his behavior.

In 2015, fifty-one years after Hubert and I took Earl Ruby's testimony and read Sol

Dann's memo, a forensic psychiatrist from Australia, Dr. Robert M. Kaplan, offered his appraisal of what motivated Jack Ruby to kill Lee Oswald. Considering Ruby's personal and family history, his conduct beginning November 22, 1963, and his medical history, Kaplan concluded, "Ruby's behavior was driven by a belief that there was an anti–Jewish conspiracy behind the killing of the President. In addition, his use of amphetamines increased.... Ruby's killing of Oswald reflected aspects of the American Jewish immigrant experience, his dysfunctional personality, abuse of amphetamines, and the probably [sic] effect of a slight brain tumor."[28]

8

Friends, Employees, and Truth-Telling

The evidence was strong that Jack Ruby was mentally ill during his trial and at the time he testified before the Warren Commission. From the beginning of our investigation, however, Leon Hubert and I believed that whatever Jack Ruby said and whatever was his mental state, we must seek information from other sources before accepting his credibility on any issue. Our assignment was to determine whether Ruby was part of a conspiracy to assassinate President Kennedy or Lee Harvey Oswald.

Five witnesses—Ralph Paul, George Senator, Curtis Laverne (Larry) Crafard, Lawrence Meyers, and Alex Gruber—seemed especially important. Paul was Ruby's business partner. Senator was his housemate. Crafard was an employee, and Meyer and Gruber were out-of-town friends. They had been in communication with Ruby on November 21, 22, 23, or 24, 1963.

We recognized that each could be affected by both self-interest and a desire to protect their friend. Their closeness to Jack Ruby raised the possibility that they might have encouraged or conspired with him to kill Lee Oswald. At a minimum, they might have had advance knowledge that he intended to shoot Oswald on Sunday morning, November 24. In either event, they might be reluctant to tell us the whole truth.

Ralph Paul

We had no information that Ruby's business partner, Ralph Paul, had been physically present with him on November 22, 23, or 24, but we knew that Ruby had telephoned Paul multiple times. Telephone records showed that at 1:51 p.m. on November 22, Ruby made a brief call to Paul. Paul testified to us that Ruby informed him that he was closing his night clubs for three days. Ruby, in fact, did that. At about 9:00 p.m. that evening, Ruby asked Paul to accompany him to Friday night religious services. Paul declined. Ruby went alone.[1]

The call that attracted our greatest interest occurred at about 10:44 p.m. on Saturday night, November 23. Wanda Helmick, a nineteen-year-old waitress at a restaurant owned by Paul, told the FBI for the first time in June 1964 that she had overheard Paul's end of a conversation. She heard Paul reacting to Ruby with the word *gun* and asking Ruby, "Are you crazy?" Both Ruby and Paul denied that shooting Oswald was the topic of conversation. Paul suggested that the conversation was about Ruby's competitors who had not closed their night clubs and about difficulties Ruby was having with them.[2] Who was telling the truth, we wondered.

Shortly after 11:00 p.m. Saturday, Ruby was at his Carousel Club. He made five short telephone calls, one to three minutes each, between 11:18 and 11:48 p.m. Four were to Paul, and one was to an entertainer, Breck Wall, who was affiliated with the American Guild of Variety Artists (AGVA), a union that represented Ruby's employees. Paul and Wall said the calls related to a dispute Ruby was having with AGVA concerning favorable treatment to his competitors, who had not closed their clubs after Kennedy's death.[3] We had additional evidence that Ruby was, in fact, having such a dispute.[4]

Leon Hubert and I were satisfied that Ruby's calls to Paul and Wall did not justify a conclusion that either man encouraged or conspired with Ruby to kill Lee Harvey Oswald, but we had an obligation to report fully on the calls and the witnesses to them. The Commission and soon the public (in perpetuity) would both be able to weigh the validity and meaning of everything we were able to gather.

Larry Crafard

We were also suspicious that Ruby's employee Larry Crafard had withheld important information from us. Crafard was a twenty-two-year-old with limited education. He had been employed by Ruby for a short time as a night watchman and general handyman. For those services, Ruby gave him room, board, and money for incidental expenses. Before that, Crafard had roamed the country, picking crops, working in carnivals, and doing odd jobs. He had acquired a wife and two children. Yet by November 1963, Crafard wasn't living with them. Leon Hubert observed to me that if he, Crafard, and I were tossed onto the street of a small western town without jobs, it would be Crafard who'd survive. Hubert and I would starve.

At about 5:00 a.m. on Saturday, November 23, Ruby phoned Crafard from his apartment, telling Crafard to secure a small flash camera from the Carousel Club and wait for him and George Senator to pick him up. They drove to a billboard overlooking a Dallas freeway that proclaimed "Impeach Earl Warren." Ruby wanted to photograph it. He believed the billboard was somehow connected to a full-page ad attacking President Kennedy that had appeared that day in the *Dallas Morning News*. Ruby suspected that the billboard, the ad, and the assassination were connected. Ruby was going to solve the crime.[5]

After photographing the billboard, Ruby's investigation proceeded to the main Dallas Post Office. There Ruby tried, unsuccessfully, to inquire who had the post office box with the number that was on the billboard. Thereafter, the trio stopped for coffee and a brief conversation about the billboard, the advertisement, and the assassination. By about 5:45 a.m., Crafard was back at the Carousel Club. Ruby and Senator were on their way home.[6]

At about 8:30 a.m., Crafard telephoned Ruby. Ruby had asked him to feed the six dogs that lived at the Club. Crafard was calling about the food. Ruby, forgetting that he had told Crafard he was not going to bed, responded with anger. Crafard told the FBI that Ruby's anger caused him to make a decision. He fed the dogs, took five dollars that he believed Ruby owed him, left a note for Ruby, and set off hitchhiking to Michigan.[7]

To Hubert and me, this was strange behavior. The president has been assassinated.

Crafard joins Ruby to take photographs at 5:00 a.m. the next day, and a few hours later Crafard leaves Dallas without telling Ruby. Did Crafard know something that we did not know? Did he suspect that Ruby was about to commit a crime and that he—Larry Crafard—might be implicated? As Hubert had said, Crafard knew how to survive.

We were able to bring Crafard to Washington to testify.[8] He repeated what he had previously told the FBI: Ruby was difficult to work for; Ruby's behavior after the assassination was bizarre [my word, not Crafard's]; Crafard had been thinking about leaving Dallas for about a week; Ruby had mistreated him; and he wanted to be with relatives in Michigan.[9] Ruby had not said anything about killing Oswald. Crafard had no information about a conspiracy.

For many years, I thought that Crafard might be the Rosetta Stone to Jack Ruby and that someday he would tell a story that we had not heard. He died on April 19, 2011, at age seventy without writing a book or telling a different story to other investigators.[10] I suspect that after nearly forty-eight years of silence, he was not withholding anything of importance.

George Senator

Unusual behavior by Jack Ruby's fifty-year-old, unmarried housemate, George Senator, also aroused suspicions in Hubert and me. He described Ruby on Sunday morning as "mumbling, which I didn't understand.... Then after he got dressed, he was pacing the floor from the living room to the bedroom, from the bathroom to the living room, and his lips were going. What he was jabbering I don't know."[11] When Ruby left the apartment a few minutes before 11:00 a.m., Senator did not go with him.[12]

Instead, Senator called his friend, William Downey, and offered to visit and make breakfast for Downey and his wife. Downey declined.[13] Senator then went to the Eatwell Restaurant in downtown Dallas for coffee. A waitress following the news suddenly shouted that Jack Ruby shot Oswald. "My God," Senator gasped.[14] He gulped down his coffee, ran to a telephone, and quickly departed. He went directly to the home of his lawyer, James Martin.[15] That was the move that troubled us.

From Martin's home, the two men drove to the Dallas Police Department, where Senator gave a statement.[16] Was Senator seeking help for himself? Did he fear he would be implicated? Or did he turn to Martin to secure help for Ruby? Martin told investigators that Senator's concern was for Ruby, not for himself.

Two months after we took George Senator's testimony, we learned more. On July 18, 1964, Jack Ruby—at his own request—submitted to a polygraph examination. To the polygraph examiner, he filled in an important detail: Before leaving Senator on that eventful Sunday morning, Ruby expressed a hope that someone would kill Oswald.[17]

When we took Senator's testimony, we judged him to be a worried and reluctant witness. It took Ruby, himself, to tell us what he had said that so alarmed George Senator. We could not verify Senator's activities on November 23 after he had gone with Ruby and Crafard to photograph the billboard. He had not disclosed the billboard incident when initially interviewed by the FBI. In the end, however, we decided that he was not involved in a conspiracy of any sort with Ruby. We concluded that on November 24 he was a frightened man enveloped by two shocking crimes.

Lawrence Meyers

We were also concerned with two of Jack Ruby's friends who had more successful backgrounds than Senator and Crafard. They were Alex Gruber, a childhood friend who lived in Los Angeles, and Lawrence Meyers, a friend from Chicago who had been with Ruby on the evening of November 21. Could Meyers or Gruber be links in a conspiracy to kill either Kennedy or Oswald?

Meyers was the sales manager of an auto accessories manufacturer. His brother and sister-in-law lived in Dallas. Meyers, a married man, had come to Dallas with a girlfriend, Jean Aase, and was staying with her at the Cabana Motel. On Thursday, November 21, the night before the president's assassination, Aase and Meyers met with Ruby for about an hour at the Carousel Club and invited him to join them for dinner. When Ruby explained that he had a dinner appointment with his business partner, Ralph Paul, Meyers suggested that Ruby meet them later at the Bon Vivant Room of the Cabana Motel. At about 11:30 p.m., Ruby joined Meyers, his brother and sister-in-law, and Ms. Aase at the Bon Vivant Room.[18]

Two days later, in the evening of November 23, Ruby telephoned Meyers. Meyers told the Warren Commission that Ruby was very distressed about the assassination and was especially disturbed that his competitors, Abe and Barney Weinstein, had not closed their club. He accused them of being "money hungry Jews." Meyers recalled to the Commission that Ruby said he was "going to do something about it."[19] What did that mean?

Leon Hubert and I assumed that if Meyers were a conduit or confederate to Ruby in a plot to kill Oswald, he would not reveal it. Even if he were only an innocent friend, he might, as a witness, want to avoid harming Ruby. Nothing, however, about Meyers' conduct suggested that he was part of a conspiracy. He was in Dallas with a girlfriend. She was present at all of Ruby's meetings with Meyers. Meyers' brother and sister-in-law were present at one. None of these public meetings seemed to lend themselves to conspiring in murder.

We were more skeptical about Meyers' description of Ruby's emotional distress in their phone conversation on Saturday night. Meyers believed that when Ruby said he had "to do something about it," he was referring to the conduct of his business competitors. Ultimately, we accepted Meyers' interpretation. It was consistent with Ralph Paul's and Breck Wall's descriptions of the calls they had received from Ruby at about the same time. Unless Meyers, Paul, and Wall had orchestrated a grand cover-up for their friend, it seemed true that Ruby was distressed about both the assassination and the conduct of his competitors—which from Ruby's perspective embarrassed the Jewish community.

Though we accepted as true the descriptions that Meyers, Paul, and Wall gave us about Ruby's emotions and worries, Leon Hubert and I made sure to include in endnotes to the Warren Commission Report references to anything that might contradict our conclusions. In the text of the Report, we held back one bit of relevant information about Lawrence Meyer—his relationship with Jean Aase. We did not know what Meyers' wife may have known about Ms. Aase. We were not about to reveal it in a text that was about to be the most permanent of all documents.

Alex Gruber

The last of the possibly conspiratorial conversations that Ruby might have had with friends was a phone call to Alex Gruber in Los Angeles. Gruber and Ruby had been friends since grammar school days in Chicago.[20] In the intervening years, Gruber had developed a successful business in Los Angeles. How Ruby and Gruber had maintained contact over the years was not clear, but Gruber told the FBI that on about November 10, 1963, he visited Ruby in Dallas after a trip to Joplin, Missouri.[21]

Gruber never explained the reason for the visit; however, on Sunday, November 17, at 9:28 p.m., Ruby called Gruber in Los Angeles from Dallas.[22] Robert Blakey, former chief counsel to the House Select Committee on Assassinations, was one who believed Ruby might have been inspired by organized crime to kill Oswald. Blakey has suggested, nonetheless, that Ruby may have been simply seeking help with financial problems.[23]

Whatever the reasons for Ruby's call to Gruber on November 17, at the time the president was assassinated, Ruby felt that his relationship with Gruber was important. At 2:37 p.m. on November 22, Ruby again telephoned Gruber in Los Angeles. Gruber told the Warren Commission that Ruby talked about the possibility of purchasing a carwash business, said he was sending Gruber a dog, and became so emotional about the president's death that he ended the conversation abruptly, having lost emotional control.[24]

That was the only information the Commission had linking Ruby to Gruber from November 17 until Ruby shot Oswald on November 24. Gruber may have been withholding evidence or even lying to us about the true nature of his conversations with Ruby. Ruby may have wanted to borrow money from Gruber. Gruber may have hoped that Ruby had contacts for him in Dallas. For Leon Hubert and me, that evidence and such possibilities were insufficient to justify a reasonable suspicion that Gruber was a link between Ruby and anyone interested in assassinating the president or killing Oswald. We ceased pursing a Gruber connection. No later investigation or conspiracy theorist has produced evidence to the contrary.[25]

In sum, as we examined Jack Ruby's contacts with employees, friends, and acquaintances between November 21 and November 24, we found no evidence of a plan to kill President Kennedy or Lee Oswald. We needed, however, to look at Ruby's conduct in more detail.

9

Jack Ruby

The First Conspiracy Investigator

To understand why Jack Ruby killed Lee Oswald and whether he was part of a conspiracy—either to assassinate President Kennedy or to kill Lee Harvey Oswald—Leon Hubert and I believed it was necessary to detail Ruby's activities from the first time someone might have known of President Kennedy's trip to Dallas until Ruby shot Oswald. We compiled an exhaustive account of Ruby's activities in that period and obtained an extensive record of his earlier history, friends, employees, and associates. We checked the interests and activities of those friends, employees, and associates. We verified their claims of contact or lack thereof through telephone records and other witnesses.[1] Nothing connected any of those people to Ruby entering the Dallas police garage or killing Oswald—or in any way to the president's assassination.[2]

In the end, Leon and I were both satisfied that Jack Ruby was not part of any conspiracy. What became most important to our understanding Ruby's conduct was the precise chronology of those activities and attendant emotions from the time he heard the president had been shot until he was arrested for shooting Oswald.[3] To us, what seemed most significant was Ruby's distress over the president's assassination, his fixation on Bernard Weissman's anti-Kennedy ad, his fear that Jews would be blamed for the president's death, and his effort to solve the crime of the century.

Ruby First Hears of the Assassination

By 11:30 a.m. on November 22, 1963, Jack Ruby was at the advertising office of the *Dallas Morning News* placing ads for his two nightclubs, the Carousel Club and the Vegas Club. Newspaper employees recalled Ruby expressing concern about the financial condition of his businesses. They also recalled his complaining about a black-bordered advertisement attacking President Kennedy that the *Morning News* had run that day. It appeared to be signed by one Bernard Weissman as chairman of something called the American Fact-Finding Committee.[4] As disrespectful as the ad seemed to Ruby, what troubled him more was that Weissman seemed to him a Jewish surname. Yet Ruby couldn't believe that anyone Jewish would be associated with such an ad.

At approximately 12:45 p.m., while still at the *Morning News*, Ruby heard that the president had been shot. One newspaper employee recalled that Ruby appeared obviously shaken and "sat for a while with a dazed expression in his eyes."[5] It is a matter of

WELCOME MR. KENNEDY

TO DALLAS...

... A CITY so disgraced by a recent Liberal smear attempt that its citizens have just elected two more Conservative Americans to public office.

... A CITY that is an economic "boom town," not because of Federal handouts, but through conservative economic and business practices.

... A CITY that will continue to grow and prosper despite efforts by you and your administration to penalize it for its non-conformity to "New Frontierism."

... A CITY that rejected your philosophy and policies in 1960 and will do so again in 1964—even more emphatically than before.

MR. KENNEDY, despite contentions on the part of your administration, the State Department, the Mayor of Dallas, the Dallas City Council, and members of your party, we free-thinking and America-thinking citizens of Dallas still have, through a Constitution largely ignored by you, the right to address our grievances, to question you, to disagree with you, and to criticize you.

In asserting this constitutional right, we wish to ask you publicly the following questions—indeed, questions of paramount importance and interest to all free peoples everywhere—which we trust you will answer ... in public, without sophistry. These questions are:

WHY is Latin America turning either anti-American or Communistic, or both, despite increased U.S. foreign aid, State Department policy, and your own Ivy-Tower pronouncements?

WHY do you say we have built a "wall of freedom" around Cuba when there is no freedom in Cuba today? Because of your policy, thousands of Cubans have been imprisoned, are starving and being persecuted—with thousands already murdered and thousands more awaiting execution and, in addition, the entire population of almost 7,000,000 Cubans are living in slavery.

WHY have you approved the sale of wheat and corn to our enemies when you know the Communist soldiers "travel on their stomachs" just as ours do? Communist soldiers are daily wounding and/or killing American soldiers in South Viet Nam.

WHY did you host, salute and entertain Tito — Moscow's Trojan Horse — just a short time after our sworn enemy, Khrushchev, embraced the Yugoslav dictator as a great hero and leader of Communism?

WHY have you urged greater aid, comfort, recognition, and understanding for Yugoslavia, Poland, Hungary, and other Communist countries, while turning your back on the pleas of Hungarian, East German, Cuban and other anti-Communist freedom fighters?

WHY did Cambodia kick the U.S. out of its country after we poured nearly 400 Million Dollars of aid into its ultra-leftist government?

WHY has Gus Hall, head of the U.S. Communist Party praised almost every one of your policies and announced that the party will endorse and support your re-election in 1964?

WHY have you banned the showing at U.S. military bases of the film "Operation Abolition"—the movie by the House Committee on Un-American Activities exposing Communism in America?

WHY have you ordered or permitted your brother Bobby, the Attorney General, to go soft on Communists, fellow-travelers, and ultra-leftists in America, while permitting him to persecute loyal Americans who criticize you, your administration, and your leadership?

WHY are you in favor of the U.S. continuing to give economic aid to Argentina, in spite of that fact that Argentina has just seized almost 400 Million Dollars of American private property?

WHY has the Foreign Policy of the United States degenerated to the point that the C.I.A. is arranging coups and having staunch Anti-Communist Allies of the U.S. bloodily exterminated.

WHY have you scrapped the Monroe Doctrine in favor of the "Spirit of Moscow"?

MR. KENNEDY, as citizens of these United States of America, we DEMAND answers to these questions, and we want them NOW.

THE AMERICAN FACT-FINDING COMMITTEE

"An unaffiliated and non-partisan group of citizens who wish truth"

BERNARD WEISSMAN,
Chairman

P.O. Box 1792 — Dallas 21, Texas

Jack Ruby's copy of the black-bordered anti–Kennedy ad from the *Dallas Morning News* dated Friday, November 22, 1963, found in his car at the time of his arrest for shooting Lee Harvey Oswald on November 24, 1963 (loaned courtesy the Dallas County District Attorney's Office/The Sixth Floor Museum at Dealey Plaza).

dispute as to whether Ruby then went directly to his Carousel Club or first to Parkland Hospital, where the president had been taken.

Seth Kantor, an Associated Press reporter who knew Jack Ruby, wrote on November 25, 1963, that Ruby had approached him at Parkland Hospital barely a minute before the president's death was announced at 1:33 p.m. With tears in his eyes, according to Kantor, Ruby said, "This is horrible. I think I ought to close my places for three days because of this tragedy. What do you think?"[6]

Yet Ruby denied to the FBI and the Warren Commission that he had gone to Parkland Hospital.[7] The Commission failed to ask Ruby if he had talked to Kantor at Parkland Hospital or anywhere else on the day of the president's death. My partner, Leon Hubert, and I were satisfied that Ruby had spoken to Kantor that day, but we thought that in the excitement of the November 22 weekend, Kantor was probably mistaken about the time and place. We checked possible driving times between Parkland Hospital and Ruby's Carousel Club. We decided that it was more likely the conversation had occurred elsewhere on Friday afternoon or evening.

Five decades later, I am less certain that our skepticism was well placed and that Kantor's memory was wrong. Kantor's memory was fresh when he wrote his Associated Press article. The question exemplifies the problem of two eyewitnesses with contradictory memories and contradictory interests. Although difficult, it was possible for Ruby to drive from the *Dallas Morning News* to Parkland Hospital to his Carousel Club in the time available. Ruby was an excitement hound. It would be characteristic of him to follow the news of the tragedy by driving to the hospital. But why should Ruby have forgotten his trip to the hospital? And why should he later deny having made the trip?

Ruby's handmade "Closed" signs placed outside his nightclub (Bill Beal, photographer, *Dallas Times-Herald* Collection/ The Sixth Floor Museum at Dealey Plaza).

In any event, Ruby arrived at his Carousel Club no later than 1:45 p.m.[8] By then he knew that the president had died. He made numerous calls to friends and family. He told his employees that the club would be closed for the next three nights.

Over a course of about six hours, Ruby shopped for weekend food and made at least ten phone calls to relatives and friends in Chicago, Detroit, Los Angeles, and Irving, Texas. He also called his synagogue twice to determine if Friday services would be held. He prepared signs to announce the temporary closing of his clubs and made arrangements with the Dallas afternoon newspaper, the *Times-Herald*, to place ads about the closings. He was described as grief-stricken by all who came in contact with him.

Friday Night, November 22

From about 5:30 p.m. to 7:30 p.m., Ruby was at his sister Eva Grant's apartment for dinner. From there he went to his own apartment and called his business partner Ralph Paul. Paul declined his request to attend religious services. Arriving late at the services, Ruby spoke to Rabbi Silverman after his sermon lamenting President Kennedy's death. When interviewed by the FBI on November 27, 1963, the rabbi recalled that Ruby was not a regular attender at temple services and that he seemed in tears over the president's death. In later accounts, the rabbi most remembered that the only words Ruby spoke were to thank the rabbi for the attention he had shown to his sister, Eva.[9] To Rabbi Silverman, such silence about President Kennedy was a sign of Ruby's own depression.[10]

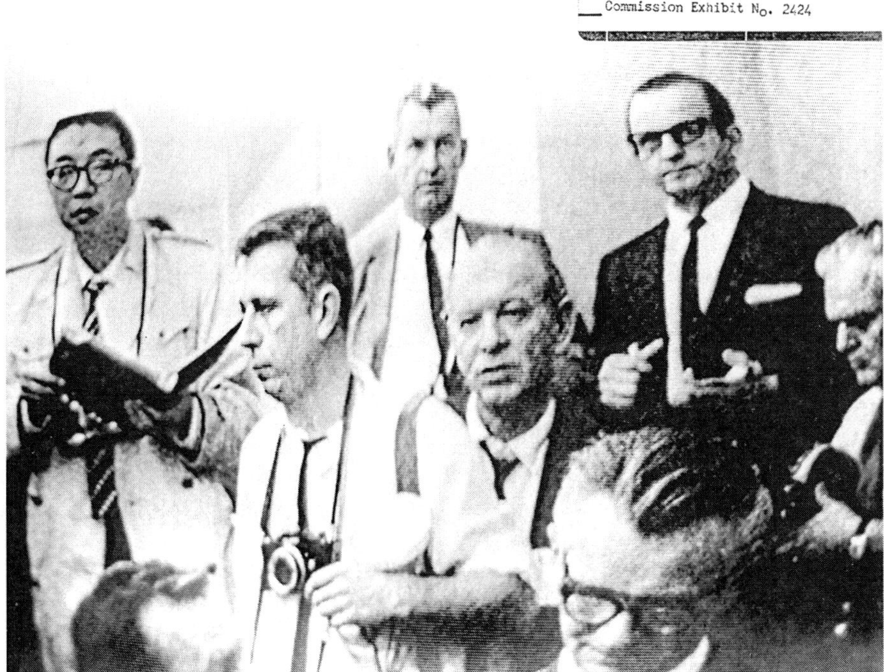

Jack Ruby, last row on right in a dark business suit at Friday's Oswald press conference, with a pen or pencil in right hand and a notebook in left (National Archives. Warren Commission Exhibit CE 2424).

From religious services, Ruby drove past some competitors' night clubs to see if they had closed. They had not. That distressed him. When Ruby heard on the radio that police officers were working late, he stopped at a delicatessen and purchased eight kosher sandwiches and ten bottles of soft drinks. He then called the police department and learned that the officers had already eaten.[11]

Nonetheless, Ruby drove to the police station and ingratiated himself with out-of-state reporters. He told police that he was a translator for the Israeli press. At 11:30 p.m., Prosecutor Wade and Police Chief Curry held a press conference. Oswald was presented to the press. Ruby was there, pencil or pen and a small notebook in hand.[12]

When Wade described Oswald as belonging to the "Free Cuba Committee," Ruby joined a few reporters in shouting to Wade that the committee's proper name was the Fair Play for Cuba Committee (FPCC). It was not surprising that Ruby knew of FPCC. From the time Oswald was arrested, the airwaves had been filled with background on Oswald, and the Committee's correct name was being bandied about by reporters at the police station.[13]

When the press conference ended, Ruby approached Prosecutor Wade, saying, "Hi Henry.... Don't you know me? ... I am Jack Ruby. I run the Vegas Club." Ruby then began distributing cards to the Carousel Club—one to Justice of the Peace David Johnston and another to Ike Pappas, a reporter for New York radio station WNEW. When Pappas had difficulty getting Wade's attention, Ruby directed Wade to Pappas. Thereafter, Ruby brought Wade to a telephone line he'd opened to radio station KLIF and directed KLIF reporter Russ Knight to Wade.[14]

Ruby had succeeded in building his relationships with the press and police and telling them about his night clubs. From the police station, he went to KLIF, arriving at about 1:45 a.m., with his sandwiches and soft drinks. During the 2:00 a.m. newscast, Russ Knight credited Jack Ruby with arranging the interview with Henry Wade.

By then, Ruby's grief was not as pronounced, but his interest in being a sleuth had grown. He suggested to Knight that the assassination had been the consequence of Dallas radicals—meaning the right-wingers who hated Kennedy. From KLIF, Ruby's next stop was the *Dallas Times-Herald*. He needed to look over the ads he had ordered for closing his clubs.[15]

Enroute, he encountered one of his dancers, Kay Helen Coleman, and her fiancé, Dallas Police Officer Harry Olsen. Ruby told the Warren Commission that Officer Olsen was very upset about Oswald. Ruby alleged that in a lengthy conversation, Olsen told him, "They should cut this guy inch by inch into ribbons," and Ms. Coleman added, "In England they would drag him through the streets and would have hung him."[16]

At the *Times-Herald*, employees remembered Ruby as "pretty shaken up" but excited that he had attended Oswald's press conference and was able to arrange interviews for reporters. He also mentioned the Weissman ad, saying that it was an effort to discredit the Jews.

Ever the promoter, Ruby demonstrated a Twist-board that he was selling. This was an exercise and weight-loss device consisting of two pieces of hardened materials joined together by a lazy-susan bearing so that one could twist back and forth while standing on it. Ruby got aboard and did his Twist.[17]

By this time, the Weissman ad and the possibility that Jews would be blamed for the assassination of President Kennedy had become an obsession for Ruby. It was not an unfounded obsession. This was 1963. Anti-Semitism was pervasive in America. It was more evident in Dallas than in many other cities. In January, a Dallas segregationist had burned a cross on the lawn of Jack Oran, a Holocaust survivor. Oran had been speaking out against intolerance. The segregationist was fined ten dollars.[18]

On the night before Easter Sunday 1963, neo-Nazis put stickers reading "We are back" on the homes of Dallas Jews, including that of Dallas department-store owner Stanley Marcus, owner of the Neiman Marcus stores. A few homes were vandalized. The next day swastikas were placed on the windows of retail stores owned by Jewish merchants in Dallas, among them the fashionable Neiman Marcus department store. The next week vandals painted bright red swastikas on Temple Emanu-El, the oldest Jewish temple in Dallas. The vandals left a message claiming a bomb was planted, but police investigation found none.[19]

Some of the vandalized stores were only a few blocks from Ruby's Carousel Club. All of the incidents were the subject of articles in the *Texas Jewish Post*.[20] Ruby must surely have been recalling incidents like these when he talked about the Weissman ad to *Times-Herald* employees in the early morning hours of November 23.

From the *Times-Herald,* Ruby drove to his apartment. Ruby had not slept at all that night. Arriving at about 4:30 a.m., he wakened his housemate, George Senator. Senator testified to the Warren Commission that Ruby began discussing the Weissman ad. Ruby, he said, recalled seeing a billboard on a Dallas roadway urging the impeachment of Earl Warren, and wondered if the same people had sponsored both the billboard and the Weissman ad.[21]

After a few minutes, Ruby made his call to Larry Crafard, telling him to get the Polaroid camera kept at the Club, and wait for him and Senator. The three men drove to the Impeach Earl Warren billboard near Hall Avenue and Central Expressway. Ruby copied the name and post office box number on the sign. They photographed the billboard.

Senator told the Commission, "I [heard] him say, 'This [meaning the sign and the Weissman ad] is the work of the John Birch Society or the Communist Party or maybe a combination of both.'"[22]

The three men drove next to the main post office. There Ruby tried and failed to secure from a postal worker the names of those who had rented the post office boxes for the billboard and the Weissman ad. After that they drove to a coffee shop, where a thirty-minute conversation ensued about the two political advertisements.[23]

After returning to his apartment, Ruby seems to have got some sleep, although wakened by a call from Larry Crafard. Later that morning, he received a telephone call from Marjorie Richey, a Carousel Club waitress. To the Commission, Ms. Richey described Ruby as talking in a shaking voice. She believed it was over the assassination.[24]

Saturday Afternoon, November 23

Ruby recalled to the Commission that sometime between noon and 1:30 p.m. on Saturday, November 23, he drove to inspect wreaths at Dealey Plaza, returned home, went back downtown, and called KLIF announcer Ken Dowe.[25] A police officer at Dealey Plaza remembered Ruby as having been choked, almost in tears.[26] At about 3:00 p.m., Ruby arrived at Sol's Turf Bar.[27] There he talked with Frank Bellochio, a jeweler. Bellochio remembered an impassioned Ruby pointing to a copy of the Weissman ad and showing him the photo he had taken that morning of the Impeach Earl Warren billboard. Linking the billboard and the ad to anti-Semitism in Dallas, Ruby said he regarded the photos as a news scoop.[28]

Without saying goodbye, Ruby left Bellochio abruptly. He then called his civil attorney, Stanley Kaufman, about 4:00 p.m.[29] The Weissman ad was very much on Ruby's mind. By this time Ruby had checked the Dallas phone directory but not found Weissman's name. Kaufman recalled, "Jack was particularly impressed with the [black] border as being a tipoff of some sort—that this man knew the President was going to be assassinated."[30] Ruby told Kaufman he had taken a photo of the Impeach Earl Warren billboard and had gone to the post office to be helpful to the police. At Kaufman's suggestion, Ruby checked a Dallas street directory but couldn't find Weissman's name.[31]

When Ruby arrived at Eva Grant's apartment an hour or two after leaving the Turf Bar, he continued to be obsessed with the Weissman ad. He told Eva that he had not been able to find Weissman's name in the city directory. Both Eva and Jack believed that the inability to find Weissman's name confirmed that the ad, the billboard, and the assassination were connected and were an effort to implicate the Jews. Ruby then called Russ Knight at KLIF and asked who Earl Warren was.[32]

Saturday Evening

At about 8:30 p.m. on Saturday evening, Ruby called his friend former Dallas police officer Tom O'Grady. O'Grady had once worked for Ruby as a bouncer. Ruby mentioned that he had closed his night clubs, criticized his competitors for remaining open, and mentioned the Impeach Earl Warren billboard.[33]

By 9:30 p.m., Ruby was back at his own apartment. He received a phone call from one of his dancers, Karen Carlin, professionally known as Little Lynn. Carlin had come to the Carousel Club expecting to be paid. Because she expected the club to be open, Ruby became angry, but he agreed to give her money.[34]

In an apparently depressed mood, he called his sister Eva, who suggested that he call a friend. Ruby then telephoned Lawrence Meyers, the visiting friend from Chicago, with whom he'd had dinner two nights earlier. Meyers recalled to the Warren Commission that Ruby became highly critical of his competitors Abe and Barney Weinstein for not closing their clubs, and said, "I've got to do something about this." Ruby and Meyers agreed to have dinner together the next evening.[35]

A Flurry of Phone Calls

Ruby returned to his sister's apartment. At 10:44 p.m., he called his business partner Ralph Paul. Paul remembered both Ruby and Eva Grant being in tears as they discussed the assassination. After that call, Ruby went to the Carousel Club, from where over the course of the next hour he made the multiple brief calls to Paul and Breck Wall.

Our Suspicions

Ruby's activities on Saturday aroused suspicions for Hubert and me. Officer Olsen and Kay Coleman had said Oswald should be killed. Why had Ruby called Tom

O'Grady, his ex-bouncer and former policeman? Ruby's conversations with Ralph Paul and Lawrence Meyers also suggested the possibility that Ruby was thinking about killing Oswald.

We asked the FBI to do background and telephone checks on those individuals. No leads were there. Our conclusions were that Ruby had called Breck Wall and Ralph Paul because he was genuinely concerned about the competition he was getting from the Weinsteins, the disrespect that their failing to close their business could bring upon Jews, and AGVA's alleged mistreatment of him. Based on the multiple accounts describing his obsession over the Weisman ad and his photographing the Impeach Earl Warren billboard, we were satisfied that Ruby's distress over the Weissman ad was genuine, as was his belief that the ad, the billboard, and assassination were connected.

Sunday Morning, November 24

Ruby arose sometime between 8:30 and 9:00 a.m. The cleaning lady for his apartment called him at about that time. She found him "terrible strange." He seemed not to comprehend who she was, although it was her custom to clean on Sundays.[36] George Senator, who interacted with Ruby that morning, confirmed Ruby's disorientation.[37]

At 10:19 a.m., Little Lynn telephoned. She still needed money. She asked for twenty-five dollars because her rent was due, and she needed to buy groceries. Ruby said he was going downtown anyway. He would send her a money order from Western Union. A few minutes before 11:00 a.m., he left, taking with him his dog Sheba, a portable radio, a revolver, and $3,000 in cash.[38] It was during that drive, Ruby told the Commission, he first thought about killing Oswald, if he could. His priority for the moment was sending a money order to Little Lynn.[39]

The Western Union office was on Main Street, one block from the police station where Oswald was being held. Normal driving time to Western Union was about fifteen minutes. Ruby parked his car in a lot across from Western Union. He left his billfold and car keys in the trunk, and locked the trunk. He left Sheba in the unlocked car, and placed the trunk key in the glove compartment. He took with him $2,000 in cash, leaving $1,000 in the car. He walked across the street to Western Union.

At Western Union, Ruby waited for another patron to complete a transaction. At 11:17 a.m. he finished sending a money order to Little Lynn. From there, he walked to the basement garage of the Dallas police station. At 11:21 a.m. C.S.T., surrounded by police officers, news reporters, and TV cameras and in full view of a television audience of millions, Jack Ruby shot Lee Harvey Oswald.

Dallas police detective Thomas McMillon, who was standing nearby, would remember Ruby saying, "You rat son of a bitch. You shot the President."[40] A few minutes later, while guarding Ruby on the police department's fifth floor, Detective Barnard Clardy would hear Ruby say, "If I had planned to kill Oswald, my timing could not have been more perfect," and "Somebody had to do it. You all couldn't do it."[41] Ruby denied any such statements. Secret Service Agent Sorrels did not report them. The words recalled by McMillon and Clardy may not have been accurate. The tone and meaning probably were.

Ruby and Organized Crime

To Leon Hubert and me, a brazen shooting amid dozens of police officers and media personnel did not have the earmarks of a planned conspiracy. What rational conspiracy would plan a killing where the gunman—especially one who liked to talk—would be immediately captured? We were well aware, however, that many in the public suspected that Ruby had been a part of a plot by organized crime to kill the president and to kill Oswald. Our task was to seek evidence that might verify such a possibility.

Although the FBI had systematically wiretapped members of organized crime in the northeastern part of the United States, they had not tapped crime figures in Dallas, New Orleans, or other areas where Ruby was known to have friends.[42] Nor did the agency suggest to us that they might tap such people as part of our investigation.

Our investigation depended, therefore, upon circumstantial evidence. We looked at Ruby's past history and the associations he made. As a young man growing up in Chicago, Ruby had known people associated with organized crime. He had been arrested, himself, for ticket scalping. We could find no indication that as a ticket scalper, he was anything but a freelance entrepreneur. Between 1937 and 1940, Ruby was employed through the help of an attorney friend by Local 20467 of the Scrap Iron and Junk Handlers Union. In 1939, his friend was murdered in a union power struggle. Employers who negotiated with the union said they had no indication that the union was connected with organized crime during that period.[43]

After moving to Dallas in 1947, Ruby developed friendships with numerous figures associated with criminal activities. The FBI was unable to link any of those friends to the shooting of President Kennedy or to Ruby's actions on November 24, 1963. What was most important to us in 1964 was whether friends or friends of friends had contacted Ruby after President Kennedy was shot.

In 1977, the House Select Committee on Assassinations expanded on the Warren Commission's investigation of organized crime by identifying numerous suspected members and leaders of organized crime who might have wanted to influence Jack Ruby before and after President Kennedy was shot. It found that, on the night of November 21, Ruby and his business partner, Ralph Paul, had dinner in Dallas at the Egyptian Lounge (owned by reputed organized crime leader Joseph Campisi). A week or so after being arrested, Ruby placed Campisi's name on a list of people that he asked Sheriff Bill Decker to call and request a visit. After that request, made by Decker by phone, Campisi visited Ruby in jail while a deputy sheriff was present. Later, Campisi attended part of a day of Ruby's trial.[44]

The Select Committee produced no evidence that those visits were other than social. After an extended investigation of Ruby's friendships with participants in organized crime, the Committee failed to make a finding that Ruby was involved in a conspiracy either to assassinate the president or to kill Lee Oswald.[45]

The best assessments of Ruby's association with organized crime may come from law enforcement officials in Dallas who knew Ruby. One was given to the House Select Committee on Assassinations in 1978 by Dallas Police Lt. Jack Revill. In 1963 and 1964, Revill was in charge of keeping a watch on organized crime in Dallas. He told the Select Committee, "If Jack Ruby was a member of organized crime, then the personnel director of organized crime should be replaced."[46] Bill Alexander, the chief assistant prosecutor in the trial of Jack Ruby, had a personal view of how Ruby came to murder Oswald.

Through his prosecution of Ruby, Alexander had come to know Ruby well. Thirty years after securing Ruby's conviction, Alexander told author Gerald Posner, "People that didn't know Jack Ruby will never understand this, but Ruby would never have taken that dog with him and left it in the car if he knew he was going to shoot Oswald and end up in jail. He would have made sure that dog was at home with Senator and well taken care of."[47] Ruby's own testimony to the Warren Commission seems to support Alexander's contention of a sudden decision:

> ... Sunday morning ... [I] saw a letter to Caroline [the President's daughter] ... The most heartbreaking letter ... alongside that letter ... it was stated that, Mrs. Kennedy may have to come back for the trial of Lee Harvey Oswald.... I don't know what bug got ahold of me.... I am taking a pill called Preludin.... I use it for dieting. ... I think that was a stimulus to give me an emotional feeling that suddenly I felt, which was so stupid, that I wanted to show my love for our faith, being of the Jewish faith ... suddenly the feeling, the emotional feeling came within me that someone owed this debt to our beloved President to save her the ordeal of coming back. I don't know why that came through my mind.[48]

That was the explanation Jack Ruby would have given if he had testified at his trial. It was the defense his first lawyer, Tom Howard, preferred.[49] It was a human, emotional defense. Ruby told one of his subsequent lawyers, Joe Tonahill, "Joe, you should know this. Tom Howard told me to say that I shot Oswald so that Caroline and Mrs. Kennedy would not have to come to Dallas."[50] It was not a false defense, however, for Ruby had mentioned his concern for Mrs. Kennedy even before talking to Howard.[51]

Ruby's conduct after he left his apartment on Sunday morning seems to support Prosecutor Alexander's assessment. Besides Sheba, Ruby had also taken his portable radio with him downtown. From that he could learn whether Oswald had been moved to the county jail. When he got to Western Union and left Sheba in the car, he had a pistol and $2,000 cash in his pocket. Along with his car keys, he had locked an additional $1,000 in cash in the trunk.[52]

If he should shoot Oswald, Sheba could be rescued. At the same time, Ruby's car could not be moved without a tow truck. If he succeeded, the $2,000 in his pocket might be enough for bond and release from jail. If he needed more, he could direct his lawyer to the additional cash in his trunk. Most important, he would be a hero.

But Ruby might not gain access to Oswald. Killing Oswald at the police station was problematic. No one except the law enforcement officers who were interviewing Oswald knew when Oswald would be moved. As Alexander observed, Ruby's first obligation would have been to Sheba. His next obligation was clearly to send a money order to Little Lynn. Shooting Oswald seemed to come third.

In any event, were those the actions of a grand conspirator—especially one recruited by organized crime? Indeed, was Ruby planning to shoot Oswald ever since Friday night, as Sergeant Dean had testified at the Ruby trial? Was it a last-minute decision based on an unplanned opportunity, as Prosecutor Alexander implies? Was it a thought that arose only when Oswald came into sight—a psychotic episode, as Melvin Belli argued? Or was it the result of emotions that built up over two days and, as Ruby himself told the Warren Commission, a decision that was made Sunday morning in order to spare Mrs. Kennedy the emotional trauma of returning to Dallas—and to show the world that a Jew had guts, as he said when first arrested?[53]

None of us can be certain. I have never believed that concern about Mrs. Kennedy was the driving force for Ruby. With the passage of time, the gathering of more information, and further reflection, I have become satisfied that fear of anti-Semitism, anger at Oswald for killing the president, and the desire for acclaim were Ruby's primary motivators. Concern for Mrs. Kennedy may well have been a factor, but not the most important. Every friend and stranger we interviewed gave remarkably similar descriptions of Ruby in those hours between his learning the president had been shot and his killing Oswald. Consistently they described a general state of agitation and growing obsession with the Weissman ad; a belief that the ad was connected to the shocking murder of the president; fear that Jews would be blamed for the assassination; and a belief, as Ruby said, that if the world saw that "a Jew had guts," Jews would be absolved of blame for President Kennedy's death.

POLITICS THREE

Determining Credibility

10

National Interest, Self-Interest, and Truth

The Commission's staff were acutely aware that some of the investigative agencies or employees upon which they depended might conceal from the Commission information that could damage the agency or its employee.[1] Confirmation of that possibility came early.

The FBI Conceals

Within a month of joining the staff, Norman Redlich, special assistant to the Commission's general counsel, J. Lee Rankin, discovered that a typed copy of Oswald's address book provided by the FBI differed from the actual address book. One entry of Oswald's address book, in his handwriting, was AGENT JAMES HASTY at the FBI's Dallas office address, and included what appeared to be a license plate number, and the date November 1, 1963.[2] Redlich noticed that the reference to HASTY (obviously a misspelling of Hosty) had been omitted from the corresponding page that had been typed by someone at the FBI.

Was the omission deliberate, an attempt to conceal, and if so, by whom within the agency? Other FBI documents provided to the Commission and describing the address book had mentioned the "HASTY" entry. The omission of Hosty's name, as explained by Robert Gemberling, the FBI agent coordinating the Oswald investigation in Dallas, resulted from Gemberling's request for a list of names in Oswald's notebook that were to be checked for investigation. As Hosty was an agent, there was no need to include him on that list.[3]

Yet for those of us on the Commission's staff, the omission seemed to be evidence that the FBI could not necessarily be trusted, particularly if there was evidence that might damage one of them or their agency. Most worrisome, this supported a suspicion that Oswald might have been an FBI informant who had gone astray. Both the Commission and the House Select Committee pursued that inquiry. Both concluded that Oswald had no cooperative relationship with the FBI.[4] Supporting that conclusion was Oswald's outrage toward Hosty on November 22 during the interrogation led by Captain Will Fritz.

A Concealment that Hindered Finding the Truth

Even if Norman Redlich had not discovered the HASTY entry in Oswald's address book, its omission from the FBI's transcript of the book would not have hindered our investigation. From numerous other sources, the Commission knew that Agent Hosty had visited Marina Oswald on November 1, 1963, looking for Oswald, that Oswald wanted Hosty's name and address, and that he wanted to contact Hosty to tell him not to bother Marina.

What the Commission did not learn from the FBI was that at some time near November 8, 1963—approximately two weeks before killing President Kennedy—Oswald had gone to the Dallas FBI office to confront Hosty. As Hosty wasn't there, Oswald left an angry (perhaps threatening) note.[5] For the Commission, that information would have been important in assessing when, why, and with whom Oswald began thinking seriously about killing the president.

If Oswald left a threatening note to an FBI agent shortly before shooting the president, one would have to question whether, at that time, he could already have been planning to kill the president. After all, he should well have expected that he would be quickly questioned, if not arrested, by the FBI for leaving the note.[6] Moreover, for investigators attempting to understand Oswald's state of mind, the note to Hosty would have supported the seeming significance of a change of address card that Oswald sent to the Socialist Workers Party publication, *The Militant,* close to the same time. The card said that he had changed his post office box number on November 10, 1963, and advised the paper that he had moved from New Orleans to Dallas.[7] Oswald's desire to ensure proper delivery of *The Militant* caused us to question whether he could have been planning, at that time, such drastic action as might produce his arrest, flight from Dallas, or death.

To Hosty and his supervisor, Gordon Shanklin, however, the note had relevance beyond the state of Oswald's mind. As Hosty wrote in his 1996 book, Shanklin upbraided him: "This note was written by Oswald, the probable assassin of the president, and Oswald brought this note into *this* office just ten days ago. What do you think Hoover's going to do if he finds out about this note? … If people learn that Oswald gave you guff a week before the assassination, they'll say you should have known he'd kill the president. If Hoover finds out about this, he's going to lose it."[8] Then, on Shanklin's instructions, Hosty claimed, he destroyed the note.[9] Neither Hosty nor Shanklin told the Commission anything about this.

What was the *guff* in the note? Hosty says it was essentially, "If you want to talk to me, you should talk to me. Stop harassing my wife and stop trying to ask her about me. You have no right to harass her."[10]

The note's content is greatly disputed. Oswald had handed the note in an envelope to an FBI receptionist, Fannie Lee Fenner (aka Nancy Lee Fenner). Ms. Fenner told the House Select Committee on Assassinations that the note contained a threat to blow up the FBI headquarters and the Dallas police station. Hosty denied the claim and provided numerous reasons why Ms. Fenner might be unreliable.[11]

The note might well have said little more than what Hosty claims.[12] It might be true that, before the assassination, the note seemed simply to be a mild but angry outburst and that after Oswald's death, Hosty could not see the note's relevance to when Oswald decided to kill the president.

But that decision was not Hosty's or his supervisor's to make. The Commission wanted every bit of evidence about Oswald. Had the Commission's staff seen the note, an intensive investigation would have been launched into who else saw the note, Oswald's demeanor and tone of voice in leaving the note, whether it was written before he arrived at the FBI office or in frustration just before he left, the significance of the precise language of the note, and why the FBI had not promptly pursued the matter.

The Commission might well have reached two conclusions. First, that Oswald was unlikely to have been planning to kill the president when he left the note for Hosty and sent the change of address card to *The Militant*; and second, that the FBI had tragically neglected its duties in not promptly contacting Oswald after receiving his note and in failing to notify the Dallas police and Secret Service that he posed a danger. Thus, at the very least, the interest of Gordon Shanklin and James Hosty in self-protection prevented the public and the Warren Commission from gaining greater insight into Lee Harvey Oswald. At worst, they failed to avert the president's assassination.

Concealment to Protect the Agency's Image

Hosty's and Shanklin's fear of J. Edgar Hoover proved to be warranted. Before the Warren Commission had hired its own staff, Hoover disciplined seventeen FBI agents for failure to engage in proper "preventive intelligence work."

When various agents testified to the Commission, none mentioned the discipline.[13] Instead, on April 6, 1964, Hoover wrote to Warren Commission General Counsel J. Lee Rankin: "The facts available to the FBI concerning Lee Harvey Oswald prior to the assassination did not indicate in any way that he was, or would be a threat to President Kennedy; nor were they such to suggest that the FBI should inform the Secret Service of his presence in Dallas or his employment at the Texas School Book Depository."[14]

On May 5, 1964, Agent Hosty testified to the Commission. He explained that when he interviewed Ruth Paine six months earlier, he decided there was no urgency in speaking to Oswald since he was not employed in a "sensitive industry." Hosty's plan, he asserted, was to wait until he had conducted a thorough interview of Marina before approaching Oswald.[15] Though he never mentioned the note, Hosty did testify that when Oswald reacted to him in anger during the interview by Captain Fritz, Oswald said, "I'm going to fix you FBI ... Don't bother my wife. Come and see me."[16]

To J. Lee Rankin, that a federal agency would withhold from the Commission important information about Oswald's conduct or disciplined FBI agents in relation to Oswald was unthinkable. Fourteen years later, Rankin told the House Select Committee on Assassinations:

> [T]he thought never crossed my mind that they would deliberately withhold something as important as information about what had happened in connection with the assassination, which I thought was of major importance to the country.... I never thought that they would deliberately conceal or withhold anything.... I thought there might be some time when I would have to pull it out of them, and I might have to keep after something a good many times that I should have been able to get the first time, but the other never crossed my mind.... I never believed that Mr. Hoover would deliberately lie to the Commission.[17]

For Rankin, a World War II veteran, the work of the Commission was like that in World War II. Information about the assassination was vital to the security of the nation. It would be treason to withhold from an investigative body or a superior officer information vital to the war effort. As Rankin later admitted to the House Select Committee, that assumption was naive. For him, the FBI's withholding of relevant information from the Warren Commission destroyed his belief that responsible government officials could ultimately be trusted to place the national interest above their personal or agency's interest.

National Security and the Truth

The FBI was not the only agency to conceal relevant information from the Warren Commission's staff. On the very day that the president was shot, a CIA agent was meeting in Paris on a plan to assassinate Cuban President Fidel Castro. Strong evidence exists that Commission member Allen Dulles, Attorney General Robert Kennedy, and even President Kennedy knew that the CIA was pursuing a scheme to assassinate Castro.[18] Neither Dulles nor Robert Kennedy revealed anything of those plans to Commission staff.[19] The Commission staff knew only that Castro had accused the United States of attempting to assassinate him. It did not know that the accusation was true.[20] President Johnson and Chief Justice Warren did not learn of the assassination efforts until 1967.[21]

Johnson learned of those efforts in mid-January 1967, not from the CIA but from his friend, journalist Drew Pearson.[22] After discussing Pearson's revelation with Warren, Johnson asked CIA Director Richard Helms to prepare a full report. In May 1967, Helms disclosed to Johnson that under both Presidents Eisenhower and Kennedy, the CIA had been trying to assassinate Castro.[23] Eight years later, Helms told Secretary of State Henry Kissinger that Robert Kennedy "personally managed the operation" on the assassination of Castro.[24]

The CIA did not admit outside the White House its assassination efforts until former Warren Commission staff member David Belin discovered them in 1975. Belin was then executive director of the Commission on CIA Activities Within the United States. Chaired by Vice President Nelson Rockefeller, it was informally known as the Rockefeller Commission. That commission's goal was to uncover—as its title suggests—improper CIA activities within the United States.

Belin was well aware that agencies work diligently to conceal information that may harm them. Years later he explained his approach to securing candor from the CIA:

> I had to convince the agency that it was in its best interest to cooperate with the [Rockefeller] commission.... I had to make sure that it had a respect for the overall abilities of our staff.... I had to toss in a third factor that would keep them off balance and worry them should there not be full cooperation: the possible use against the CIA of one of the CIA's own tools—the polygraph.[25]

Belin had found those considerations important while serving with the Warren Commission. His theory of using the polygraph to "worry them should there not be full cooperation" was one that he had employed with the Commission. He had induced Jack Ruby to submit to a polygraph as a means of encouraging his truthfulness.[26]

When Belin began his work at the Rockefeller Commission in January 1975, he learned that in 1973 the CIA had done its own internal investigation of its own possibly illegal activities. The investigation had been documented in a 693-page report referred to informally as the "family jewels." Belin asked to see it. He reports his discovery in this way:

> As I pored over the first pages of the family jewels, I noticed a section that was blank. I asked Knoche [his liaison from the CIA] why it was blank. He replied, "Those pages are not within your jurisdiction, because the commission's jurisdiction only pertains to CIA activity within the United States."

> I replied that I was not going to let anyone else determine whether the matter fell within our jurisdiction.
>
> Knoche was hesitant about what to do. He explained that the matters were extremely sensitive and he did not want me to have any copies of any documents in my office....
>
> I suggested a compromise. Instead of taking anything out of the CIA offices ..., I would go to the CIA headquarters....
>
> What next happened was one of the greatest shocks of my life: learning that my country had participated in assassination plans against foreign leaders.[27]

The greatest shock, however, was that during the Kennedy years and before, the CIA had developed plans and recruited assassins to kill Fidel Castro. Castro's claim was true.

Belin's discovery was revealed in 1976. His outrage was shared by former Warren Commission staff members. General Counsel J. Lee Rankin testified before the House Select Committee on Assassinations in September 1978:

> **Mr. Rankin:** [T]he CIA ... did not alert us to the situation at all, give us any opportunity to take action that we should have[,] the chance of investigating that type of information.
>
> **Mr. Klein:** As General Counsel of the Warren Commission, you had no knowledge whatsoever of the assassination plots against Fidel Castro.
>
> **Mr. Rankin:** That is true, I did not.... If we had had the information from the CIA, we certainly would have run out those leads and tried to find out whatever we could in that area.[28]

A decade later Belin suggested, "[T]here may have been an indirect connection between the CIA assassination plots directed against Castro and the assassination of Kennedy by Oswald."[29]

Belin saw the connection as being relevant to motivation. Belin speculated: "I believe that when Oswald shot Kennedy, he felt he was acting on behalf of the man he idolized, the man whose first name was adapted by Oswald to form his alias A.J. Hidell—Fidel Castro. I also believe that there is a substantial possibility that Oswald was influenced by the extreme anti-Castro rhetoric of the Kennedys and perhaps by Castro's call for retaliation."[30]

Castro, indeed, made such a call. On September 9, 1963, both the New Orleans *Times-Picayune* and the *States-Item* reported Castro saying, "United States leaders should think that if they are aiding terrorist plans to eliminate Cuban leaders they themselves will not be safe."[31] It can hardly be a stretch to interpret his words to mean that if Americans were attempting to assassinate Premier Castro, the Cubans might assassinate President Kennedy. Yet Castro would tell the House Select Committee that he did not intend to threaten assassination.[32]

In 1964 Rankin and Assistant Counsel Norman Redlich argued strenuously with Assistant Counsel Jim Liebeler over whether to mention both the September 9, 1963, articles and the fact that right-wing groups had distributed anti-Kennedy leaflets in Dallas on November 21 and 22.[33] The Commission had no direct evidence that Oswald either read the New Orleans articles or saw the Dallas literature. Without such evidence, Rankin and Redlich thought the impact of the statement and leaflets on Oswald were too speculative to warrant treatment. The resolution: The Warren Commission Report failed to mention Castro's accusation about U.S. assassination attempts and his threat of possible retaliation, but a copy of the newspaper article was included in a Commission volume of published exhibits.[34]

The reluctance of the Commission and its staff to speculate reflected a prevailing consideration for the Commission: Speculation not supported by compelling evidence would simply feed political pressure groups. The Commission should not speculate.

Yet circumstantial evidence existed that Oswald was probably aware of Castro's threat. Oswald was a news junkie. On September 9, 1963, he was living in New Orleans. He probably read either the *Times-Picayune* or the *States Item* article or both.[35] Oswald could not have been unaware of Castro's repeated accusations that the CIA was causing Cubans to be murdered under authorization of President Kennedy.[36] The September 9 accusation was not new. A similar accusation was, in fact, reported in the *Dallas Morning News* on April 21, 1963, eleven days after Oswald, himself, attempted to kill right-wing former Maj. General Edwin Walker.[37] In March 1963, both *The Worker*[38] and *The Militant,*[39] to which Oswald subscribed, reported on the basis of an unidentified U.S. government source that the United States was seeking Castro's assassination.[40]

Havana Radio also made the accusation of U.S. assassination attempts repeatedly in its English language broadcasts. Oswald could easily have listened to those broadcasts on a shortwave radio he possessed.[41] Transcripts of those broadcasts were in the possession of government agencies, but Warren Commission staff did not see them.[42] Nor had they seen the articles in the *Dallas Morning News,* the *Worker,* and the *Militant.*[43]

What was unique in the September 9 articles was the implicit threat of retaliation, but no outright call for retaliation may have been needed for a Castro supporter who believed that his idol was a target of assassination.

There should be no doubt that staffers Belin, Liebeler, and Slawson would have pushed hard to find a linkage between Oswald and the CIA's assassination plans if they had known of those plans. In his book, *Final Disclosure: The Full Truth About the Assassination of President Kennedy,* Belin has described his effort in 1976, when he was chief of staff for the Rockefeller Commission, to push such an investigation by the Rockefeller Commission and Congress and ultimately to reopen the Warren Commission investigation.[44] He was the same Dave Belin I knew in 1964. Liebeler and Slawson would have been relentless allies.[45]

Relevance of CIA Attempts to Assassinate Castro

If the CIA had revealed its assassination attempts to Warren Commission staff members, we would have needed to explore thoroughly Oswald's awareness of Castro's accusation and threat. More questioning of Marina Oswald would have been necessary. How regularly did Oswald read the New Orleans papers? Which ones did he read? Had he read the September 9 article? How frequently did he listen to Havana Radio while in Dallas and New Orleans? Had Oswald ever mentioned to her or anyone else a belief that the U.S. was trying to assassinate Castro or other foreign leaders or that Castro had threatened retaliation? If so, when and how had he reacted?

Awareness that the CIA was, itself, engaged in plans to assassinate Castro was even more important. Commission staffer Jim Liebeler told the House Select Committee on Assassinations that, had he known the CIA was attempting to kill Castro, he would have pushed the CIA to disclose whom they were using and would have explored the possibility that such individual or individuals had connections to Oswald.[46]

Warren Commission staff members David Slawson and William Coleman were already investigating whether either Cuba or anti–Castro Cubans in the United States were attempting to assassinate Kennedy.[47] Slawson speculated that anti–Castro Cubans might have devised a scheme to use the pro–Castro Oswald to kill Kennedy, thereby inducing the United States to blame Castro and invade Cuba.[48] If Slawson and Coleman had known that Castro's accusation was true, such knowledge would have prompted an inquiry into whether the CIA's attempts at assassination had triggered retaliation.[49] The most intimate details of the CIA's assassination plots would have been needed: Who were the planners? With whom had the CIA made contact to execute the plans? Did any of those contacts link back to Oswald? Was it possible that Castro himself was, in fact, attempting to retaliate—perhaps through Oswald?[50]

Political and Personal Implications

The possibility that Oswald was motivated by the CIA's attempts to assassinate Castro and Castro's threat of retaliation bore immense political implications. If Oswald had been motivated to kill President Kennedy because he believed the U.S. was trying to kill Castro and if the president had been unaware of the CIA's project, then blame for Oswald's actions could have been attributed to the CIA. If President Kennedy was aware of the CIA's project and approved it, he was inadvertently the architect of his own death.

There are strong reasons to believe that the president was aware and approved of the CIA's actions. Kennedy mentioned such a possibility to *New York Times* reporter Tad Szulc on November 9, 1961,[51] and at another time to Florida Senator George Smathers.[52] When Smathers and Szulc responded disapprovingly, Kennedy expressed his own disapproval, but there can be no doubt that others were pushing an assassination strategy to eliminate Castro. Since the president's brother, Attorney General Robert Kennedy, had responsibility for overseeing the CIA's anti–Castro activities, one might reasonably infer that the president was not only kept informed by his brother, but either gave his own approval or allowed his brother to approve what had been a CIA project that preceded the Kennedy administration.

Indeed, CIA agents were seeking potential assassins among Cuban contacts, and President Kennedy knew that any removal of the Castro regime by an exile force or internal coup was likely to require the killing of Castro.[53] A ready rationale was that assassination meant loss of fewer lives—especially those of innocent civilians—than direct warfare.

Both the nation and the Kennedy family preferred, however, that the president be remembered as a martyr. Consequently, the interests of Robert Kennedy, the Kennedy family, and the CIA were linked inextricably to concealing the possibility that the president had known about and approved CIA efforts to assassinate Fidel Castro.

What kind of onus then was such a concealment for Robert Kennedy and Allen Dulles? Robert Kennedy had suggested to President Johnson that he appoint Dulles to the Warren Commission—perhaps with an understanding between Kennedy and Dulles that the CIA's assassination plots would not be revealed unless essential to finding a conspiracy.[54] Neither the Warren Commission nor its staff ever directly asked Dulles or Robert Kennedy if the Castro assassination allegations were true. In the absence of a direct inquiry, was Dulles obligated to volunteer this information to the Commission? Was it conscionable for Dulles to be engaged in an effort to find the truth yet to be obliged to protect the interests of the CIA, the Kennedy family, and, perhaps, the United States?

However great the weight on Dulles was, how much greater must it have been on Robert Kennedy? Was it possible that Robert feared that his own decision not to stop the CIA from trying to kill Castro had resulted—directly or indirectly—in his own brother's death?[55] We know only that for months after the assassination, Robert was deeply depressed and limited in his ability to function as U.S. attorney general.[56]

11

Scientific Evidence, Physical Evidence, and the Quest for Truth

Even though evidence was overwhelming that Oswald shot President Kennedy, and no eyewitness saw a second shooter or confederate, the Warren Commission was obliged to explore all indications that might lead to a conspiracy. A possible indication was the testimony of Texas Governor John Connally.

When the president was shot, Governor Connally was seated in a jump seat in front of the president. Connally heard a loud sound from over his right shoulder. He turned to his right but did not complete the turn. He looked back over his left shoulder and felt a pain in his back. He believed he was hit by a second shot that he had not heard. He was certain that he and President Kennedy had been struck by separate bullets.[1] If true, there was a possible second gunman, for it would have been extremely difficult for a single gunman to have fired two shots so quickly from a single rifle. No physical or eyewitness evidence showed a second gunman, however.

To the Warren Commission, Connally's description of when he first felt pain and the finding of a bullet near his stretcher posed a major mystery. Where was the other bullet or marks from it? No bullet was found in Governor Connally or President Kennedy, though a few bullet fragments were found in the president's skull.[2] A single bullet was found near a stretcher at Parkland Hospital. The hospital employee who found the bullet said he heard it roll off a stretcher as he moved the stretcher against a wall.[3] Through a process of elimination, the Warren Commission concluded it was the stretcher on which Governor Connally had been placed when he reached the hospital.[4]

No bullets were found in the presidential limousine or anywhere else. Small fragments not constituting a complete bullet were found on the front floor of the vehicle.[5] Only a single, small nick was found inside the limousine's windshield. At first glance, it appeared to the autopsy doctors (as the FBI initially reported) that Connally and Kennedy were struck by separate bullets.[6] Consequently another bullet needed to be found or another explanation was necessary in order to explain the injuries to the two men. The task of explanation fell primarily to Commanders James J. Humes and J. Thornton Boswell, anatomic pathologists who led the team doing the autopsy of the president's body at Bethesda Naval Hospital.[7]

Wounds on President Kennedy and Governor Connally

When these Navy pathologists examined the president's body on the night of November 22, it was clear that the final shot was a bullet that struck the president's head, removing a large portion of the right side of his skull and leaving metal fragments there. The pathologists were satisfied that the head wound was caused by a shot from the rear.[8]

Two other wounds were visible in the president's body—one, an obvious entry wound in his back at the base of his neck; the other, a hole in the front of his neck, apparently caused by a tracheotomy that had been performed at Parkland Hospital in an attempt to save the president's life.[9]

But they found no exit wound for the bullet that had entered the base of the president's neck. After tracing the bullet's path through the president's neck to the point at which the tracheotomy had been performed at Parkland Hospital[10] and talking to the doctors at Parkland, the autopsy physicians in Bethesda concluded that the bullet that caused the back wound had exited the president's neck at the place of the later tracheotomy.[11] The Parkland doctors agreed.[12]

The conclusion has been further confirmed by examination of fibers in the president's shirt where holes were found. The shirt fibers around those holes had been moved in a way consistent with entry and exit of a bullet from the president's back through his neck.[13]

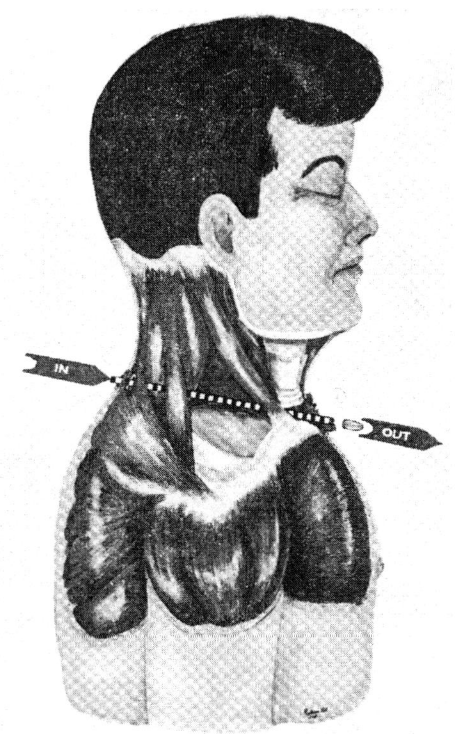

A Single-Bullet Theory Emerges

To lead Navy pathologist James Humes, the possibility of a single bullet striking the president from the rear, exiting his neck, and striking Governor Connally seemed logical.[14] If a bullet went through the president's back at the base of the neck, exited through the front of his neck, left no marks in the limousine, nor was located anywhere in the

***Top:* Diagram showing that the bullet that killed the president made a small entrance wound at the base of his skull and caused a large exit wound on the right side of his skull. It left metal fragments in his head (National Archives. Warren Commission Exhibit CE 388). *Bottom:* Diagram path of the first shot to hit President Kennedy, striking him at the base of his neck and exiting his throat (National Archives. Warren Commission Exhibit CE 385).**

vehicle, where else could it have gone? Unless it was deflected by something, the only place it could have gone was into Governor Connally, who was seated in front of the president.

There was no evidence of any deflection. The bullet that exited the president's throat struck no boney structure in the president. Nothing except air was between the president's throat and the entrance wound in Governor Connally's back. After reviewing films of the shooting and the condition of the presidential limousine, Dr. Humes posited to Warren Commission Assistant Counsel Arlen Specter his suspicion that a single bullet had passed through the president's neck and into Connally's back.[15] Could he be right? Governor Connally had heard no separate shot before he was struck.

Seeking an Answer

The Commission's assistant counsels Joe Ball, Dave Belin, Mel Eisenberg, Norman Redlich, and Arlen Specter debated the question.[16] They worked together to find the answer. They looked at other evidence besides that of Kennedy's and Connally's wounds.

Of particular importance were the bullet found at Parkland Hospital near Governor Connally's stretcher, the rifle found on the sixth floor of the School Book Depository, and motion pictures taken of the motorcade through Dealey Plaza by three amateur photographers—Mary Muchmore, Orville Nix, and Abraham Zapruder.

The Zapruder film was especially valuable. Except for about a second when the president's body was obscured by a freeway sign, the Zapruder film seemed to capture the full shooting sequence, consisting of three shots fired by Oswald. By looking at the movement of the passengers, one could determine the minimum time frame a shooter would have had in order to fire at the president twice and Connally once. By test firing the rifle, one could determine both the minimum amounts of time needed to fire three shots and the accuracy of the rifle. If two shots could not be fired with Oswald's rifle in the minimum time that appeared for the shots from the Zapruder film, there had to be a second shooter unless Humes' single-bullet theory was correct.

Belin Focuses on a Second Shooter

Aware of Humes' theory, after seeing the Zapruder film, Assistant Counsel David Belin set out to determine the probability of a second shooter.[17] He wanted to know whether there was enough time for a single rifleman to have shot Kennedy twice, chamber another bullet, and fire the shot that hit Connally. If there was not sufficient time, there could well have been a second gunman. Further, Belin reasoned, if the bullet found near Connally's stretcher had not come from the rifle found on the sixth floor, there must have been a second gunman.

Consequently, he set forth three challenges: to test-fire the rifle and compare the test bullet to the bullet that went through Connally; to time how quickly the rifle could be fired twice; and finally, to determine from the Zapruder film how much time elapsed between the last moment Kennedy appeared to be unhurt and Connally reacted to being shot. If the bullet found near Connally's stretcher came from Oswald's rifle and a second bullet could be fired in the determined time lapse, Oswald could have shot Connally with a different bullet from the one that went through President Kennedy's neck. But where, then, was the missing bullet?

If the timespan of opportunity revealed by the Zapruder film was not long enough for two shots to have been fired from Oswald's rifle, there could well have been a second shooter, but once again, where was the missing bullet?

The Bullet from Connally's Stretcher

Joseph D. Nicol, chief of ballistics identification for the State of Illinois, and three ballistics experts from the FBI all reached independent determinations that the bullet from Connally's stretcher had been fired from the rifle found at the School Book Depository.[18] So far, the evidence hadn't eliminated Humes' single-bullet theory.

Further Investigation

But the Commission team needed more—much more. They needed to know if a single shot from Oswald's rifle passing through the neck of the president could have caused the wounds on both the president and Governor Connally. The Commission's lawyers turned to U.S. Army wound and firearms experts at the Army's Wound Ballistics Center at Edgewood Arsenal in Maryland. Those experts performed experiments using anaesthetized goats and a model for Governor Connally's body made from the bones of human cadavers, animal skin, and gel.[19]

Reenacting the Shooting of November 22, 1963

Bullets like the one found at Connally's stretcher were shot at the goats and the Connally model with Oswald's rifle from the same distance that the School Book Depository window was from where Kennedy was struck.[20] The tests confirmed for the Army testers that the bullet found on Connally's stretcher could have produced the wounds both Connally and Kennedy sustained.[21]

Those tests were based on assumptions of how Governor Connally and President Kennedy were positioned in the limousine at the time Oswald fired his shot that hit President Kennedy at the base of the back of his neck. To establish those assumptions, the Commission's staff used the Zapruder film of the shooting.

Markings were placed on the backs of two men identical in size to Kennedy and Connally. The two substitutes were seated in the limousine where Kennedy and Connally had been. The markings were at the points where each had been wounded. A man was stationed with Oswald's rifle at the point from which Oswald was believed to have fired. Using the Zapruder film, the limousine was moved frame-by-frame along the motorcade route. When the limousine got to the point where Kennedy could have been shot in the back, the markings on the two substitutes appeared in a virtually straight line to the sights of Oswald's rifle.[22]

The Single-Bullet Analysis Is Confirmed

The reenactment supported the single-bullet analysis. If it hadn't, the Commission's lawyers would have been obliged to look for a possible second shooter on the sixth floor of the Texas School Book Depository. Considering the reenactment, the opinion of the autopsy physicians, the experiments with goats and medical models, and the various ballistics and firearms tests, the Commission's staffers concluded that the president and Governor Connally had been struck in the back by a single bullet fired from a window in the southeast corner of the sixth floor of the Texas School Book Depository. Fourteen years later, the House Select Committee on Assassinations reached the identical conclusion.[23]

The Third Bullet

On November 22, 1963, three empty cartridges were found on the sixth floor of the Texas School Book Depository. One cartridge could have been a previously expended cartridge that had remained in the rifle until Oswald fired his first shot at the president. That seemed unlikely. The Warren Commission concluded that Oswald fired a third bullet which missed the limousine completely. The probabilities suggest that Oswald would not have fired a third shot after hitting the president's head. The Commission drew no conclusion as to which of the shots missed the vehicle.[24]

Author Max Holland has examined circumstantial evidence in detail and has concluded that the first shot was the one that missed.[25] He has captured a range of relevant evidence that neither the Warren Commission nor the House Select Committee on Assassinations fully noted or integrated into their reports. Of fundamental importance to Holland is that the Zapruder film did not begin to depict the motorcade until the presidential limousine was already approximately seventy feet into Dealey Plaza.

The Zapruder film and the recollection of Rosemary Willis confirm Holland's conclusion. The film shows Willis, a twelve-year-old girl running alongside the presidential limousine and suddenly looking up toward the sixth-floor window at least five seconds before the film shows the president reacting to a shot. Willis said that she looked toward that window because she thought she heard a sharp sound coming from that direction.[26]

Max Holland believes the evidence shows that Oswald's first shot was probably deflected by the mast arm of a traffic sign, and that he had more than eleven seconds to fire his second and third shots. For Holland, the only reasonable explanation of the second shot is that it hit both Kennedy and Connally—the only places in the limousine that a well-placed shot could have gone.[27]

The Grassy Knoll and a Puff of Smoke

Both the Warren Commission in 1964 and the House Select Committee on Assassinations between 1977 and 1979 considered the possibility that shots were fired from locations other than the Texas School Book Depository. If there had been such shots, there must have been either a conspiracy or a remarkable coincidence.

For the Warren Commission, circumstantial evidence of a second shooter came from S.M. Holland. Holland was a signal supervisor for the Union Terminal Railroad Co. in Dallas.[28] The company's terminal was a railroad yard adjacent to the Texas School Book Depository. Together with coworkers Frank E. Reilly and Richard Calvin Dodd, Mr. Holland had stationed himself on the railroad overpass crossing Elm Street. There they could get the clearest view of the presidential motorcade. When the president was shot, the three men together with twelve others were watching the motorcade as it proceeded west on Elm Street toward them.

When S.M. Holland heard explosive sounds and realized the president had been shot, he ran with others to a parking lot that was separated by a five-foot-high picket fence from a sloping grassy hill that has come to be known as the grassy knoll. The grassy knoll bordered Elm Street where the motorcade proceeded. A crowd had gathered there to see the motorcade.

Mr. Holland believed he had seen a puff of white smoke beneath some trees on the knoll and that the gunshots had come from behind the picket fence at the top of the knoll. He ran to the spot from which a shot might have come.

At the same time, a motorcycle policeman following the motorcade left the procession, drove his cycle up the knoll, and left it on the hillside when he lost control. Mr. Holland and other civilians joined numerous police in a search for evidence. They looked both behind the fence and in the parking lot for empty cartridges, a rifle, and a possible shooter.[29] None were found.[30]

Any shooter from behind the fence would have had to have been in the parking lot. The lot was reserved for use by sheriffs, police, prosecutors, and courthouse personnel. Access to the lot had been restricted from 10:00 a.m. until after the motorcade. Anyone and any vehicle entering or leaving the parking lot would have been visible both from the overpass on which Holland and the others were standing and from a watch tower occupied by Lee E. Bowers, Jr.[31]

No cartridges, rifles, or other physical evidence of a shooter were found at any location except the sixth floor of the Texas School Book Depository. No one in the watch tower, on the overpass, or watching the motorcade at ground level saw any one with a weapon or otherwise appearing to be a shooter on the grassy knoll or behind the fence. No one saw anyone leaving the parking lot or hiding in or under a motor vehicle.

After leaving the searchers, S.M. Holland promptly contacted Sheriff Bill Decker. That day he provided the Sheriff's Department a sworn affidavit that he heard the sounds of shooting, and he saw a puff of smoke about six or eight feet above the ground in a tree on the grassy knoll. He believed the smoke might be associated with gunfire.[32] Two days later he provided the same information to an FBI agent. The FBI provided the interview report to the Warren Commission.[33]

On April 8, 1964, S.M. Holland gave the following testimony to Assistant Warren Commission Counsel Samuel Stern:

> There was a ... report.... And a puff of smoke came out six or eight feet above the ground right out from under those trees ... from where I was standing you could see that puff of smoke, like someone had thrown a firecracker, ... I have no doubt about seeing that puff of smoke from under those trees....[34]

Holland's description would have placed the puff of smoke on the grassy knoll, approximately eleven feet in front of the picket fence.[35] Most of the overpass witness did not see such smoke. Two saw something which they described variously as "exhaust fumes," "steam," or "smoke."[36] Another person on the overpass, Royce G. Skelton, told the Commission that he saw smoke come up from the cement pavement of Elm Street when he heard a shot. He associated it with a bullet or bullet fragment striking the cement.[37]

What was the Commission to make of this testimony? It had no question that S.M. Holland and the others were truthful witnesses. They were describing what they believed they saw. Even if they saw a puff of smoke, the Commission could not, without more evidence, infer that it was smoke from a firearm. Smokeless gun powder was invented in 1884. No manufacturer of firearms or bullets had used black powder since the early 1900s.[38] If firing some guns did issue "smoke," how visible would it be?

There might well be other explanations for what the witnesses thought was "smoke." There was, in fact, a steam pipe near the fence at the grassy knoll.[39] Some members of the Commission staff believed that any "smoke" could have been an emission from the steam pipe.[40] Mr. Holland, himself, suggested it could have been from a cigarette or other smoker. When he was looking for evidence of a shooter near the fence atop the knoll, Holland observed numerous cigarette butts in the area where a shooter might have been.

Most importantly, the inference that smoke came from a firearm was inconsistent with what did not exist—a witness who saw a shooter or physical evidence of a shooter anywhere in the area that Holland, other civilians, and the police extensively searched.[41] Finally, there is the factor of reason. Unless the assassin desired to be seen or was oblivious to being seen, no reasonable person would choose to shoot from the grassy knoll.

Acoustics Evidence and the Grassy Knoll

No further evidence of a possible shooter at any location except the School Book Depository was reported until September 1977. At that time Mary Ferrell, a Dallas woman researching the assassination, told the House Select Committee on Assassinations that her friend, Gary Mack, had copied an audio tape of communications to the Dallas Police Department's radio dispatcher on November 22, 1963.[42] The tape—made from dictabelts of Dallas Police Department radio Channel 1—covered the period of the assassination. It was believed that the original tapes[43] might contain sounds of gun shots from Dealey Plaza.[44]

In May of 1978 the Select Committee gave the original tapes to an acoustics professional, Dr. James Barger of Cambridge, Massachusetts. The tapes contained no audible sounds that could be identified as gun shots.[45] Dr. Barger cleaned and enhanced impulses on the tapes and charted the impulses on a graph. In July 1978, Dr. Barger notified the Select Committee that he believed the enhanced impulses on the graph showed four gunshots from Dealey Plaza. He thought that the radio transmission to Dallas police Channel 1 had been from an open microphone of a police motorcyclist accompanying the presidential motorcade.[46]

Barger told the Select Committee that the graph and the confirmatory experiments showed a fifty percent chance that a fourth shot had been fired from the grassy knoll.[47] The Committee then conducted experiments to determine whether the lines on the graph corresponded to impulses that might be created by gunshots.[48] Two other acoustics professionals, Mark Weiss and Ernest Aschkenasy, examined the Committee's data, agreed that the impulses were from gunshots, and ultimately testified that there was a ninety-five percent or better probability that the graph showed a gunshot from the grassy knoll.[49]

The Barger, Weiss, and Aschkenasy views evoked quick opposition. On December

13, 1978, Anthony Pellicano, president of Voice Interpretation and Analysis, Ltd, sent the Select Committee a memorandum, saying that the motorcycle microphone upon which the Committee's witnesses relied was not in the motorcade and that what the "impulses detected ... were not shots." He requested that his memo be circulated to Committee members. The Committee's staff did not do so.[50] On January 2, 1979, Dr. Marvin E. Wolfgang, Professor of Sociology and Law at the University of Pennsylvania, wrote to the Committee: "[The] works of Barger and of Weiss and Aschkenasy have been exciting from a scientific perspective.... I think it is premature and inappropriate for a Federal group, like your committee, to make a major policy decision on the basis of their findings."[51]

On January 8, 1979, Dr. Frederick K. Davis, Dean of Science at Drexel University, wrote the Committee: "I certainly think that the 95 percent confidence claim is grossly exaggerated, and it would take considerably more scientific evidence to convince me and most other scientists that their conclusions were valid."[52] The Committee did not seek further experimentation or testimony from other scientists. On March 29, 1979, a majority of the Committee concluded "that the acoustical [sic] scientific evidence established a high probability that two gunmen fired at President John F. Kennedy."[53]

The Committee, nonetheless, recommended that the FBI conduct a further acoustics investigation. Two issues were paramount. Did the impulses on the graph establish that they were caused by gunshots? Were the impulses on the tapes transmitted from a microphone at Dealey Plaza?

Barger, Weiss, and Aschkenasy believed that the tape impulses came from the motorcycle of Officer H.B. McClain. McClain's motorcycle was in the motorcade at Dealey Plaza at the time of the shooting. After McClain had a chance to hear the tapes, he insisted that the transmission had not been from his motorcycle. He based his argument on his belief that the engine sounds on the critical tape were different from his motorcycle's, that a clarion bell heard on the tape could not have come from Dealey Plaza, that there were no crowd noises on the belt, and that the Doppler effect of siren sounds heard on the tape were consistent with a motorcade approaching the microphone instead of leaving the sound of the shooting.[54]

The Select Committee examined each of McClain's objections and rejected them. On March 29, 1979, it accepted the opinion of its acoustics scientists by an eight to four vote.[55] The Committee issued its final report and requested the U.S. Department of Justice to further examine the acoustics evidence. The Justice Department assigned the task to the National Academy of Sciences. The Academy appointed a twelve-member Committee on Ballistics Acoustics. In 1982, the Committee on Ballistics Acoustics decided that the opinions of Barger, Weiss, and Aschkenasy were invalid. The Committee on Ballistic Acoustics found that there was not an acceptable scientific basis for concluding that the impulses were from gunshots, that the analysis itself was incorrect, and that the impulses they were analyzing from the radio recording had occurred approximately one minute after the shots fired by Lee Oswald.[56]

Although the report of the Committee on Ballistics Acoustics was accepted by the FBI, conspiracy advocates continued to challenge it vigorously for more than three decades. In 2013, political science professor Larry J. Sabato hired Sonalysts, Inc., to examine the Dallas Police Department tapes and consider all other evidence. Sonalysts, Inc., concluded that the transmission on the tape did not come from a motorcycle at Dealey Plaza and that the impulses were not necessarily those of gunshots.[57] A sixty-five-page comprehensive chronology and analysis of the controversy may be found in the endnotes of Vincent Bugliosi's *Reclaiming History: The Assassination of President John F. Kennedy.*[58] Another history of the dispute, with strong support for the conclusions of Barger, Weiss, and Aschkenasy, has been provided in *Last Seconds in Dallas* by Josiah Thompson.[59]

Expert Testimony and Establishing Truth

Professionals—referred to as "expert" witnesses—often present conflicting conclusions in court proceedings. As a finder of fact, a juror or judge must decide which expert to believe. What are their credentials and biases? Is their scientific premise widely accepted by their peers? Was their experiment properly conducted? Was the evidence accurately perceived? And how much weight do you give to other evidence that leads to the same or a different conclusion?

In a court proceeding, judge and jury are alerted at the outset to whether an alleged expert may be biased. The litigants have searched for and found witnesses who support their side. The opposing lawyers cross-examine. Cross-examination can reveal biases, disparities in experience or knowledge, failures to consider relevant facts, and faulty analyses. Rules of evidence preclude using theories not accepted in the particular profession.

For the court of public opinion, the demeanor, tones of voice, and possible biases of the scientists relied on by the House Select Committee were not recorded. The Select Committee, itself, did not purport to make a definitive judgment. It said that scientific evidence showed a high probability of a second gunman at Dealey Plaza. It recommended further scientific study.

The analysis of Barger, Weiss, and Aschkenasy did not find support in the acoustics profession. Without widespread professional acceptance of the theory on which their claim is based, their conclusions would not be admissible in most courts of law. In the court of public opinion, however, their claim has been accepted by many. A juror in that court must therefore evaluate the acoustic arguments not only in terms of the validity of the acoustical theory being proposed and the facts on which they relied, but also on the extent to which important physical evidence or lack thereof exists—no witnesses to a gunman at the grassy knoll, no rifle or bullet cartridges near the alleged point of shooting, no one seen fleeing the scene. Ultimately, the test for accepting the opinion of a claimed expert is one of credibility and reasonableness. How strong must the expert's testimony be to overcome the reasonable inferences that are drawn from the non-scientific evidence?

12

Sylvia Odio

A Sincere Witness May Be Wrong

No witness is more perplexing than one who offers potentially significant information, has no apparent motive to lie, has little to gain from the account, yet whose account cannot be corroborated and is inconsistent with other reliable evidence. Such was Sylvia Odio.

Ms. Odio told the Warren Commission that at approximately 9:00 p.m. on either September 26 or 27, 1963, two Cubans and an American had come to her Dallas apartment. She said the American was identified by the Cubans as "Leon Oswald." She had not previously known the Cubans or the American. The Cubans said they were seeking money to finance arms for anti–Castro fighters. They wanted her help in translating into English a fundraising letter they had prepared. Doubting the group's credentials, Ms. Odio turned them down.[1]

The next day, according to Ms. Odio, one of the Cubans telephoned her and described their American companion as an ex-Marine who wanted to go to Cuba to help the anti–Castro insurgents. The Cuban allegedly said that the American had upbraided anti–Castro activists for not assassinating Kennedy when he failed to support them at the Bay of Pigs.

Sylvia Odio's account is vital to many who suspect a conspiracy to assassinate the president.[2] It was vital to the Warren Commission as well. Ms. Odio was the only witness who said that Oswald had a working relationship with Cubans in the United States. Hers was the only claim that, while in the United States, Oswald had said Kennedy should be assassinated.

Ms. Odio's claim had to be pursued. Who were the two Cubans? Was their companion Lee Harvey Oswald? Did they know Oswald, and if so, how? How did they know where Ms. Odio lived? Was Ms. Odio mistaken in her identification of Oswald? Was Ms. Odio telling the truth? The Warren Commission's staff undertook that pursuit. Here is what we found.[3]

In September 1963, Sylvia Odio was a twenty-six-year-old divorcée with four young children. She had been born in Cuba but attended high school for three years at the Eden Hall Convent of the Sacred Heart in Philadelphia. Her father had been a wealthy businessman in Cuba. She had studied law at the University of Villanova in Cuba for nearly three years.

In 1960, after Fidel Castro took power, Ms. Odio and some of her nine siblings fled Cuba. Her father and mother, however, were imprisoned in Cuba as opponents of the Castro regime. By 1963, Ms. Odio had gone from great wealth to near poverty and was emotionally fragile.

In March 1963, Ms. Odio moved to Dallas where she had two sisters. She began to build a new life—becoming popular in Dallas's wealthy community, gaining employment, and even dating. She also established relationships with Cubans who were attempting to form a Dallas chapter of the Cuban Revolutionary Junta (JURE).

The period of March 1963 to September 1963 in Dallas was one of great emotional distress for Ms. Odio. Previously, while living in Miami and Puerto Rico, she had suffered fainting spells and emotional problems. After her divorce, she lost custody of her four children for a short while because of alleged neglect and abandonment. In Dallas, the mental health problems continued.[4] With the help of Lucille Connell, a wealthy Dallas matron, Sylvia began seeing a young psychiatrist, Dr. Burton C. Einspruch, for treatment on a weekly basis.

In the week after being approached by the group she believed included Oswald, Ms. Odio told Dr. Einspruch that a group of two Cubans and an American had approached her. She also sent a letter to her imprisoned father about the group.[5] Her concern was for her own safety and the validity of the group.[6]

Until November 22, 1963, Ms. Odio had no reason to think further about the American who had visited her apartment with the Cuban solicitors in late September. While at work on November 22, she heard that the president had been shot. As she later testified to the Warren Commission, she then began thinking about her September visitors and fainted. She was immediately hospitalized.[7] When she saw Oswald on television, she thought he was the American who had visited her in September.[8]

Sylvia's sister Annie visited her in the hospital later that day. By then, Lee Harvey Oswald had been arrested, and his picture was on television. Sylvia and Annie had seen it separately. Annie had been present with her sister during the visit in September. When Annie entered Sylvia's hospital room on November 22, she said she thought that Lee Harvey Oswald was the American-looking man who had visited Sylvia's apartment. Sylvia agreed.[9]

Within a few hours of Ms. Odio's hospitalization, Dr. Einspruch talked to her by telephone. He saw her personally not long thereafter. In those discussions, Sylvia attributed her fainting to her belief that Lee Harvey Oswald had been the American who came to her apartment in September.

To the Warren Commission staff and later the staff of the House Select Committee on Assassinations, Dr. Einspruch said he regarded Ms. Odio as a person who would not lie.[10] However, he described her as a "histrionic personality" who had "a degree of suggestibility that she would believe something that did not really transpire."[11]

Talking to the Select Committee's staff in 1978, Dr. Einspruch did not recall Ms. Odio's ever telling him what the Cuban who phoned her the next day had said about Leon Oswald—that he thought anti–Castro Cubans should have assassinated Kennedy. Dr. Einspruch believed that if she had, he would have advised her to contact the FBI.

Ms. Odio was first interviewed by the FBI on December 18, 1963, nearly a month after the assassination. The interview resulted from Ms. Odio's reciting her story to her friend, Lillian Connell.[12] Mrs. Connell reported it to the FBI.

Despite Ms. Odio's failure to initiate the contact with the FBI, a number of factors lent credibility to her story. First, it was reasonable that two Cuban men and an American might have visited Ms. Odio in late September 1963 and asked her to help raise funds for anti–Castro rebels.[13] Second, she had shared that general information with Dr. Einspruch in the course of psychiatric treatment before November 22. Perhaps the American's name was Leon—or Oswald or something similar.

But Ms. Odio's description of Leon was not consistent with Lee Harvey Oswald. She estimated that Leon was thirty-four or thirty-five years old. Lee Harvey Oswald was a month shy of twenty-four. She described Leon as having a light trace of hair on his upper lip, being unshaven, and having a greasy appearance. Lee Harvey Oswald had not even a slight mustache, was usually meticulous about being clean shaven, and took pride in appearing neat.

Yet, Ms. Odio mentioned ancillary facts that matched Lee Harvey Oswald. She said she was told that Leon was an ex-Marine who had come to Dallas from New Orleans. Lee Harvey Oswald was an ex-Marine. Prior to September 26, he was living in New Orleans. On September 26, he was known to be enroute from New Orleans to Mexico City. It seemed not impossible for him to go to Mexico City by way of Dallas.

Finally, engaging with anti–Castro Cubans was in keeping with Lee Harvey Oswald's past behavior even though Castro was his idol. In August 1963, Oswald had presented himself to an anti–Castro group in New Orleans, the Student Revolutionary Directorate (DRE), as someone who could help commit sabotage against Castro. Was it not possible that Lee Harvey Oswald would attempt to infiltrate another anti–Castro group, JURE, and come with them to Dallas in late September 1963?

On the other hand, perhaps, as Dr. Einspruch had implied, the story about Leon Oswald was a fantasy that Ms. Odio believed. After her sister Annie independently suggested to Sylvia that Oswald was the man who'd been at Sylvia's apartment with the two Cubans in September, Sylvia had not taken the initiative to contact the FBI. By the time Ms. Odio was interviewed by the FBI, all of the facts about Oswald's past behavior could have been gleaned by her from news media reports or friends.

To determine whether Lee Harvey Oswald could have visited Ms. Odio on September 26 or 27, 1963, as she said, the Warren Commission attempted to establish Oswald's whereabouts on September 25, 26, and 27, and to locate the two Cubans and one American who had come to Ms. Odio's apartment.[14] The Commission was able to establish that between 6:00 a.m. and 2 p.m. on September 26, Lee Harvey Oswald was on Continental Trailways bus 5133 that left Houston, Texas, at 2:35 a.m. on the 26th and crossed the Mexican border at Laredo, Texas, before 2:00 p.m. on that day. It seemed, then, that the only date that Oswald could have been in Dallas at around 9:00 p.m. was September 25—a date not indicated by Ms. Odio. Even so, she might have been mistaken about the date but not the event itself.

Bus company records caused the Warren Commission to conclude that the only time Lee Harvey Oswald might have been at Ms. Odio's apartment was between the morning of September 25, when he was believed to be in New Orleans, and midevening that same day, as at 2:35 a.m. on September 26 he was aboard the bus from Houston to Laredo. It was possible, but difficult, to leave New Orleans on the morning of the 25th, arrive in Dallas by automobile that evening of the 25th, and drive to Houston from Dallas in order to arrive there by 2:35 a.m. on the 26th.

Yet that possibility was contradicted by another witness, Estelle Twiford. Mrs. Twiford, a resident of Houston, told the Commission that Oswald had placed a call to her home in Houston (presumably from Houston) on the evening of the 25th and asked for the possibility of visiting her husband that evening.[15] Moreover, Lee Harvey Oswald had told passengers on the bus from Houston to Laredo that he had come from New Orleans. He did not mention Dallas. The Warren Commission decided that the "evidence was persuasive that Oswald was not in Dallas on September 25 and, therefore, that he was not in that city at the time Mrs. Odio said she saw him."[16]

Among many who later disagreed were Gaeton Fonzi, staff member of the House Select Committee on Assassinations, and authors Jean Davison and Vincent Bugliosi. Fonzi wrote, "There is a strong probability that one of the men [who visited Ms. Odio] was or appeared to be Lee Harvey Oswald."[17] Putting it in lawyers' language, Bugliosi concluded there was "a slight preponderance of evidence" that Lee Harvey Oswald was at Ms. Odio's apartment as she said.[18] The Select Committee was more explicit:

> [T]hree men did visit her apartment as part of an anti-Castro organization and one of them at least looked like Lee Harvey Oswald and was introduced to Mrs. Odio as Leon Oswald,[19]

The Select Committee ultimately concluded, however, that even if Oswald had visited Ms. Odio in September 1963, it was "unable to reach firm conclusions as to the meaning or significance of the Odio visit incident to the President's assassination."[20] Davison conjectured that Oswald was infiltrating JURE in hopes of gaining evidence about them for Castro. Bugliosi attempted no explanation of Oswald's purpose. He was content to show the weaknesses of arguments by conspiracy theorists.

For Davison and Bugliosi, a witness was either truthful or not truthful. Neither recited the possibility, as suggested by Dr. Einspruch, that Ms. Odio might be accurate in describing men who came to her apartment but was fantasizing, based on news accounts she heard nearly two months later, that one of the men was Lee Oswald. She honestly but inaccurately could believe that the non-Hispanic man was named Leon Oswald and was an ex-Marine who thought Kennedy should be assassinated.

13

Mark Lane

A Misleading Advocate

Sylvia Odio may have been wrong, but she did not intentionally mislead the Warren Commission. Lawyer Mark Lane, who testified before the Warren Commission, was different. Thirty-six years old, Lane was a New York criminal defense attorney and political activist who undertook to show that Lee Harvey Oswald was not guilty of murdering either Officer J.D. Tippit or President Kennedy. Under the veil of legal advocacy, he misstated, omitted, and withheld information while making his claims to the Commission.

On December 19, 1963, less than a month after Oswald's death and before the Warren Commission had even assembled a staff, Lane published in the *National Guardian* an article entitled "Oswald Innocent?—A Lawyer's Brief: A Report to the Warren Commission."[1] Lane based his brief on statements to the media by Dallas County Prosecutor Henry Wade, Dallas police officers, and FBI agents. Many of the statements or media reports were inaccurate.

Lane's brief made six assertions: (1) pre-trial publicity would have deprived Oswald of a fair trial; (2) the physical evidence was defective; (3) the eyewitnesses were unreliable; (4) investigative agencies had falsified evidence; (5) character witnesses would have shown Oswald to be a truthful person who admired President Kennedy; and (6) the evidence was insufficient to overcome the presumption of innocence that is required in a criminal trial.

All of these claims were, in fact, among those addressed by the Warren Commission and the House Select Committee on Assassinations. After gathering evidence, both were satisfied that Oswald had fired shots from the sixth floor of the Texas School Book Depository that killed President Kennedy and that he had murdered Dallas police officer J.D. Tippit.

Lane, however, did not wait for the Warren Commission to consider his arguments and criticisms. He was more interested in presenting his defense of Oswald to the court of public opinion. Within weeks of his December 19 article, Lane began speaking on college campuses and on radio and television. On January 27, 1967, Lane claimed in a debate with assistant Commission counsel Wesley J. Liebeler at the University of California, Los Angeles, that he had spoken at eighty-five colleges and universities.[2] Arguing that the Warren Commission had judged Oswald even before it completed its work, he published his own book in 1966, ironically titled *Rush to Judgment.* In 1973, Lane co-wrote the story for the screenplay of the first conspiracy movie, *Executive Action,* a fictional account of Kennedy's assassination. The movie alleged that the president was killed by a right-wing conspiracy of powerful business and government interests. Lane went on to publish three books about the assassination.[3]

On March 4, 1964, Lane made his first appearance before the Warren Commission. At his request, the press was present. He had requested to appear as counsel for Lee Harvey Oswald, maintaining that he had been hired for that purpose by Oswald's mother, Marguerite. Since Oswald's wife Marina believed her husband guilty, Lane argued that his authorization from Marguerite denied Marina the right to designate her husband's defender.[4]

The Commission rejected Lane's request to be recognized as Oswald's official counsel. The Commission designated American Bar Association president Walter E. Craig to perform that function.[5] Nonetheless, the Commission did permit Lane to make his arguments and present his evidence. When asked if he had any witnesses to present, Lane said, "I do not know that I would be able to do that."[6] Lane's presentation, which mimicked a defense attorney's closing argument in a trial in which the client had not testified, rested mainly upon media reporting of evidence before the Commission was formed. Sometimes Lane recited newspaper accounts favorable to his client or opinions he claimed to have received from forensic experts. When asked to provide the name of a purported witness, he often did not have the name available.[7]

Two of Lane's claims were of extreme importance to the Warren Commission. One was that Helen Markham, a witness who said she had seen Oswald shoot Officer Tippit, had given Lane a different description of the man she said was the shooter than she had given to the Commission. Lane said that he had tape recorded his interview with Mrs. Markham.[8]

The second important claim was Lane's assertion that an informant existed who said that Officer Tippit had met with Jack Ruby and Bernard Weissman at Ruby's Carousel Club on November 14, 1963. If true, the evidence suggested a possible conspiracy by Tippit, Ruby, and Weissman to assassinate the president. It was evidence that would have been vital to Dallas County Prosecutor Henry Wade in his prosecution of Jack Ruby. Yet Lane had not shared that evidence with Wade.

The Commission asked Lane to produce the Markham tape and the name of the informant. Lane said they were confidential. On March 4, 1964, in testimony before the Commission, he failed to produce the tape or the name of the informant.[9]

Over the next four months, the Commission attempted unsuccessfully to persuade Lane to produce the Markham tape and the name of the informant. Meanwhile, Lane carried his message about Oswald's innocence to audiences at approximately forty American college campuses and in Europe.[10] Finally, upon a promise from the Commission to pay for his return from Europe, Lane agreed to testify again about the tape and the informant. The Commission expected that he would agree to produce both.

On July 2, 1964, Lane testified again before the Commission. The following dialog ensued:

Mr. Rankin: And you are not willing to have the Commission have the [Markham] recording to check the accuracy of your report about what the testimony or statement was, is that right?

Mr. Lane: I am not in a position to give you that document.... I don't understand why it is not possible to call Mrs. Markham and to call me and to have us confront each other.[11]

****

> **The Chairman**: Mr. Lane.... According to you. Mrs. Markham made a statement that would bear upon the probability of his guilt or innocence in connection with the assassination. Mrs. Markham has definitely contradicted what you have said, and you do not believe that it is in your own interest and in the interests of this country for you to give whatever corroboration you have to this Commission so that we may determine whether you or she is telling the truth.
>
> ****
>
> You did not tell us that you have a recording of what Mrs. Markham said to you. Now, we ask you for verification of that conversation, because she has contradicted you. You say that you have a recording, but you refuse to give it to this Commission.[12]
>
> ****
>
> [H]opefully you would be able to tell us who this informant of yours was in Dallas concerning the so-called meeting between Jack Ruby and others in his nightclub. And we have been pursuing you ever since with letters and entreaties to give us that information so that we might verify what you have said, if it is a fact, or disproving it if it is not a fact. Here we pay your expenses from Europe, bring you over here, and without telling us at all that you won't answer that question, you come before the Commission and refuse to testify. Do you consider that cooperation?[13]

Vincent Bugliosi reports the aftermath of this encounter between Mark Lane and the Warren Commission:

> Lane finally gave up the tape after being given a promise of immunity from prosecution.... The reason for Lane's reluctance to release the tape of the conversation was now obvious. The tape had revealed his blatant attempt to improperly influence, almost *force* an uneducated and unsophisticated witness to say what he wanted her to say.[14]

Lane denied that he produced the tape in response to an assurance that the Commission would not seek to prosecute him. Commission staff member Howard Willens states that such assurance was given him at his request.[15]

Although Lane relinquished the Markham tape, he never revealed the name of the claimed informant with respect to a Tippit, Weissman, and Ruby meeting. Both Ruby and Weissman denied such a meeting vehemently.[16]

Later Lane wrote that the unnamed informant had disclosed the information to Thayer Waldo, a reporter for the *Fort Worth Star Telegram*. When Waldo testified before the Warren Commission, he failed to mention either the informant or a Ruby, Tippit, and Weissman meeting. Waldo was later discharged from the *Star Telegram* for "sensational journalism."[17]

The Commission, satisfied that Lane was not credible, did not pursue the matter further. After fifty-five years, there have been no death-bed declarations to support Lane's allegation that a meeting occurred between Officer Tippit, Jack Ruby, and Bernard Weissman. Both the Warren Commission and the House Select Committee on Assassinations agreed that Mrs. Markham's identification of Lee Harvey Oswald as the shooter of Officer Tippit was accurate.

Commission staffers like myself believed that anyone reading the transcript of Mark Lane's testimony would agree with the Chief Justice that Lane was not a credible person. Lane, while testifying before the Commission, had shown no hesitancy to avoid, invent, or misstate evidence to achieve his purpose. It was our belief that those who honestly sought the facts would reject Mark Lane.

To some extent that has happened. Many serious private researchers of the assassination ultimately shunned Lane after having an opportunity to work with him.[18]

More significantly, however, Lane succeeded in insinuating himself into not only print, radio, television, and movie media—and even the academic world—but also into the unsuccessful prosecution from 1967 to 1969 of Clay Shaw by New Orleans District Attorney Jim Garrison and the creation of the House Select Committee on Assassinations in 1976.[19]

Politics Four

Ambition, Failure, and Assassination

14

Leaving Why to Others

Despite more than 20,000 interviews and testimony from 552 witnesses, the Warren Commission declined to speculate on a motive for killing the president. Chief Justice Warren, himself, decided not to seek Commission agreement on a motive. Neither the staff nor Commission members could have reached agreement.[1] The Commission told the public:

> ...to determine the motives for the assassination of President Kennedy, one must look to the assassin himself. Clues to Oswald's motives can be found in his family history, his education or lack of it, his acts, his writings, and the recollections of those who had close contacts with him throughout his life.... [O]thers may study Lee Oswald's life and arrive at their own conclusions as to his possible motives.[2]

In conclusion, the Commission stated Oswald's purpose in personal, psychological terms: "He sought for himself a place in history—a role as the 'great man' who would be recognized as having been in advance of his time. His commitment to Marxism and communism appears to have been another important factor in his motivation. He also had demonstrated a capacity to act decisively and without regard to the consequences when such action would further his aims of the moment."[3]

But what were his aims in the moment when he fired the fatal shots? The Warren Commission was deliberate in avoiding the possible impact that the political environment might have had on those aims of the moment. Without a statement of aim by Oswald himself, any discussion of Oswald's political motives could be only speculative. Speculation was not the function of a fact-finding commission. There was, nonetheless, a substantial body of evidence for reasoned speculation about Oswald's motive in the Warren Commission's report and in its twenty-six volumes of evidence. Only a few subsequent researchers have gathered more.

Journalist Albert H. Newman was the first to try.[4] He tracked Oswald's activities, so far as possible, on a daily basis from the time he returned to the United States from the Soviet Union in 1962 until he was murdered by Jack Ruby. Newman, being a newspaper man, tried to link the media's coverage of world and national events to an understanding of how Oswald's access to that coverage might have influenced his decision to kill President Kennedy.

Of special importance to Newman were English language broadcasts from Radio Havana. Oswald possessed a shortwave radio. He could listen to those nightly broadcasts in Dallas and New Orleans. The Warren Commission had failed to recognize the significance of Oswald's shortwave radio or to assemble transcripts of the Radio Havana broadcasts. Newman did.

In 1970, Newman published his analysis: *The Assassination of John F. Kennedy: The Reasons Why.* He believed that Oswald killed Kennedy because he hoped to eliminate a threat to the Cuban revolution and to blame Dallas right-wingers and their leader, former Major General Edwin Walker, for the assassination. Newman also believed that when Oswald was stopped by Officer Tippit, he was actually on his way to the home of General Walker. There he would kill Walker, "tamely" give himself up, and use his trial to denounce American imperialism.[5]

Newman concluded, "[Oswald] did not murder Mr. Kennedy as a hated human being but, rather, delivered a most vehement political protest, registering dissent from the administration's policy toward the Marxist Cuba he traitorously supported."[6]

Priscilla Johnson McMillan, a Russian-studies scholar and a news correspondent, was the next to provide new insights and information on Oswald. While a North American News Alliance reporter, McMillan had met Lee Oswald in Moscow in 1959 when he sought Soviet citizenship. In the summer of 1964, when the Warren Commission was gathering information, McMillan signed a contract to become the biographer for Oswald's wife and established a residence near Marina in Richardson, Texas. From mid-July until Christmas 1964, they were together on a daily basis.[7]

McMillan would typically arrive before noon and help with the children until serious discussions would begin about 5:00 p.m. Their discussion would continue late into the evening. For one period of nearly two weeks, Marina and Priscilla were alone together at the home of a generous friend in Sonoma, Arizona. For another two-week period, they lived together at the vacation home of McMillan's cousin in Santa Fe, New Mexico. On November 22, 1964—the first anniversary of the assassination—Marina suffered an emotional collapse and was hospitalized for two or three days. Priscilla was her support system. Through it all, Priscilla had become Marina's friend, confidante, surrogate mother, and psychotherapist. Ultimately, Marina gave McMillan written permission to write Marina's biography as McMillan saw best.[8]

The result, in 1977, was *Marina and Lee*, a book about the lives of the couple, both alone and together. With the help of Marina, Priscilla came to understand Oswald intimately as a person.

Unlike Newman, however, McMillan did not articulate in *Marina and Lee* a specific political objective for Oswald. McMillan was steeped in the psychoanalytic perspective of the 1950s and '60s. And she admired John Kennedy deeply. Her concluding paragraphs were psychoanalytic:

> Lee Oswald's life had been rich in disappointments. He had been disappointed in the mother who, he felt, let him down so egregiously while he was growing up that he came to feel deeply wronged by her. And he had been disappointed by the father who let him down by dying before he was born. It was not President Kennedy's fault, it was his danger, that he stood in a position to magnetize the emotions of a Lee Oswald, who had very little love in his life and whose feelings toward both his parents were so richly compounded of hate.
>
> President Kennedy died, then, because of his plentitude. To some, and Oswald apparently was one of them, the memories and associations that this president stirred were too deep, too charged emotionally, altogether too much to bear. President Kennedy died because he had, as man and symbol, become so many things to so many men.[9]

Jean Davison followed McMillan. She drew upon McMillan's work and added her own original research. In 1983 Davison published *Oswald's Game*, an insightful attempt to understand Oswald as a psychologically disturbed individual acting out his disturbance on the world stage of East-West politics. At the end, she too failed to give a specific political explanation. Her explanation was in terms of a character disorder. She wrote:

> In large part, the assassination was the tragic result of a steady accumulation of chance happenings, the elimination of any one of which might have spared Kennedy's life.
>
> The chain of circumstances began in Oswald's childhood when someone innocently handed him a political pamphlet that gave his anger and resentment a direction. Six years later, he failed in an attempt to sign away his citizenship which meant that he would be able to go back to the United States in 1962. Less than a year after he returned, a bullet intended for General Walker missed. Then in 1963, when he was trying to build a record to impress the Cubans, Castro's warning appeared and gave him a new target. Finally, after his trip to Cuba was blocked, a neighbor of a friend suggested a job at the school book warehouse.
>
> Ultimately, these coincidences came to have a horrible significance, but only because they happened to a particular dangerous individual. The root cause of the assassination wasn't blind fate, but Oswald's sociopathic nature.[10]

Over the next ten years, Gerald Posner studied the evidence that then existed and re-interviewed those who knew Oswald best: his wife Marina, his Dallas acquaintances Michael and Ruth Paine, coworkers in Texas, his friend Ernst Titovets in Minsk,[11] Russian and Cuban embassy employees who had talked with Oswald in Mexico City, and many who had claimed to see him in the United States and Mexico only briefly. Posner wanted a complete picture of Oswald and an ability to assess the credibility of the crucial witnesses before undertaking to determine whether Oswald acted alone or in concert with others.[12]

In 1993, Posner published *Case Closed.* Concerned with whether Oswald was Kennedy's assassin and whether he acted alone, Posner's priority was to determine the truthfulness, accuracy, and completeness of the Warren Commission report and those who disputed it. He refrained from reaching a conclusion on Oswald's motive. Posner added substance, however, to Oswald's behavior during the period most relevant to determining a motive—from Oswald's defecting to the Soviet Union in 1959 until his killing of Kennedy four years later.[13]

Author Norman Mailer was the next researcher to provide new information about Lee Harvey Oswald. After the fall of the Soviet Union, Mailer interviewed Oswald's associates there and gained access to KGB files. Drawing heavily on those Russian sources, his own interviews of those who knew Oswald in the United States, and the work of Davison, McMillan, and the Warren Commission, Mailer in 1995 produced a 791-page biography of Oswald: *Oswald's Tale: An American Mystery.* As the title indicates, Oswald's motive is a mystery to Mailer. Although certain in his own mind that Oswald shot Kennedy, Mailer allowed the reader to have doubts.

In the end, Mailer saw Oswald as the lone killer and his motive in these terms:

> His personal attitude toward Kennedy had little to do ... with his act. In war, one may execute a man for whom one feels respect or even personal affection; Oswald saw it as an execution. One mighty leader was going to be dispatched by another high and mighty personage—of the future. The future would preempt the present.
>
> If he failed to escape, well, he could tell his story. He could becloud the issue and possibly be acquitted, and if it came to twenty years of prison, he would be able to forge his political agenda—even as Hitler, Stalin, and Lenin had done. Should he face capital punishment, then, at the least, he would be immortal. He would take care of that at his trial. He would expound his ideals.[14]

Mailer suggests why Oswald could kill a man that he respected. It was an act of war. But what Oswald expected to accomplish by the act of war—other than personal aggrandizement if he escaped or a chance to tell his story if caught—Mailer does not say.[15] For Mailer, any specific political motive remains a mystery.

The researchers who focused on Oswald as a person added significantly to the argument that no reasonable person interested in assassinating the president would have engaged Oswald as an ally or a foil.[16] In fact, consideration of Oswald's personality, as presented by these biographers, leads one to doubt that he would conspire with anyone—even to dupe them into an act of violence for which he would escape blame.

In 1998, Gus Russo used a wealth of newly discovered evidence about American efforts to assassinate Fidel Castro in the 1960s as a foundation for arguing, in *Live by the Sword: The Secret War Against Castro and the Death of JFK*, that President Kennedy ironically brought about his own death. Russo was a political science graduate of the University of Maryland. In his twenty-year pursuit of assassination evidence, Russo worked as an investigative reporter for the TV series *Frontline* in its documentary *Who Was Lee Harvey Oswald*; as a researcher for ABC's documentary *Dangerous World: The Kennedy Years*; and as a research associate and consultant for the books *The Dark Side of Camelot*, by Seymour Hersch (1997), *Case Closed: Lee Harvey Oswald and the Assassination of JFK*, by Gerald Posner (1993), and *Conspiracy*, by Anthony Summers (1993). In discharge of those tasks and on his own, Russo interviewed witnesses who testified previously to the Warren Commission and the House Select Committee on Assassinations. He was also able to find new witnesses.

Russo began his years of inquiry as a skeptic that Oswald had killed Kennedy. Ultimately, he became satisfied that Oswald was Kennedy's lone assassin. His research led him to conclude that it was the conflict between Cuba and the United States from 1959 to 1963 that inspired Oswald and prevented the Warren Commission from gaining the information needed to reach conclusions as to Oswald's motive and whether he was part of any conspiracy.

Taking into consideration that on September 9, 1963, the New Orleans *Times-Picayune* had published a warning from Castro that American leaders would become victims if their efforts to kill Cuban leaders did not cease, Russo argued that Kennedy's own efforts to kill Fidel Castro had strongly influenced Oswald. Russo wrote, "Oswald acted at least in part for political reasons, and ... in murdering John F. Kennedy, Lee Harvey Oswald clearly thought he was acting in Cuba's behalf."[17] Ten years later Russo wrote more firmly, "He carried out [the] assassination in order to prevent another one, that of Fidel Castro...."[18]

Whose assessment is correct? Was it a psychological need, only coincidentally connected to the politics of the day, as both Priscilla McMillan and Jean Davison seem to suggest? Or was Oswald's motive at least partly if not overwhelming political, as Alfred Newman and Gus Russo maintain? Or, as Norman Mailer seems to believe, is it a mystery that can never be solved?

The answer is important. The Warren Commission's failure to find a motive for either Lee Harvey Oswald or Jack Ruby translated into much of the public (sometimes as high as eighty percent) believing that a grand conspiracy assassinated President Kennedy. Those conspiratorial beliefs reinforced public distrust of government.

Continuing distrust of public findings about that historic event makes examining the evidence of Lee Harvey Oswald's life and the world as he perceived it of continuing importance. Only through mining Oswald's personality, politic actions, ambitions, personal relationships, frustrations, and view of the larger political world can we grasp why he murdered President Kennedy and Police Officer Tippit and attempted to murder Major General Edwin Walker.

15

Becoming a Marxist

Lee Harvey Oswald was born in New Orleans, Louisiana, on October 18, 1939, two months after the death of his father, Robert E. Lee Oswald. Lee was the third son and last child of thirty-two-year-old Marguerite Claverie Oswald.

Lee's eldest brother, John Pic, had been born in January 1932 to Marguerite and her first husband, Edward John Pic, Jr. The middle brother, Robert Oswald, was born in April 1934.

In 1939 the Great Depression had not ended. For the widowed Marguerite, who had only a ninth-grade education, economic survival was a persistent challenge.[1] Marriage and motherhood were not her strong suits.

She was, however, as her son Robert remembered, "remarkably pretty." Husbands came easily but did not last long. Her first marriage lasted only eighteen months. Her first child, John, was born after Marguerite and John's father were separated.[2] Marguerite and Robert Oswald had been married only five years when he died. Their son Robert would scarcely remember him. Edwin A. Eckdahl, her third husband, received a verdict of divorce in 1948 after three years. A jury determined that Marguerite was guilty of "excess, cruel treatment, or outrage."[3] Her middle son might well have concurred; Robert would attribute his brother becoming an assassin to Marguerite's inadequate mothering and personality characteristics.[4]

As a single mother in the midst of the Depression, Marguerite found it difficult to maintain employment and keep her children at home. She admitted to the Warren Commission that she had held more than a dozen jobs by 1964 and been fired from half of them.[5]

Marguerite returned to work two months after Lee was born. In Lee's early months, Marguerite's sister Lillian provided a home. Soon, however, Marguerite secured her own residence and hired a couple to move in with her to provide childcare for fifteen dollars per month and free rent.

After a few months, when the arrangement proved unsatisfactory, Marguerite quit her job to accept full time responsibility for Lee. She soon secured another full-time job, however, and hired another couple to provide childcare. That situation was worse. Lee cried frequently when placed in a highchair. The couple responded by physically abusing him. Marguerite discharged them.[6]

By Marguerite's own admission, Lee was not easy to manage. When he was two-and-a-half, Lee got angry, threw a toy gun at his babysitter, and broke a bedroom chandelier. The babysitter quit after fourteen days.[7]

In January 1942, Marguerite placed Lee's older brothers—John, almost 10, and Robert, age 7—in the Bethlehem Children's Home in New Orleans. She attempted to place

Lee at the Home at the same time, but the Home would not accept him. He was too young—less than three months over two years old. The day after Christmas, 1942, when Lee was slightly more than three, the Children's Home admitted him. Lee remained at the Children's Home with his brothers for thirteen months until he was nearly four and a half.[8] Robert described the Home as having a "cheerful atmosphere" and Lee as being "a happy boy" who didn't talk "about missing his mother."[9]

Marguerite did not plan on a home for three children. While Lee remained with Marguerite until he was seventeen, his older brothers were placed in a boarding school or military academy much of the time. Each left home and school to work when they reached seventeen.

When his brothers were not home, Lee remained with Marguerite, virtually an only child. Sometimes, Marguerite had only a single bedroom. Lee slept with Marguerite in her bed until he was nearly eleven.[10] He was eleven or twelve before she stopped bathing him.[11]

During all of those years, Lee never had a stable residence or a steady school. Before age ten, he lived in thirteen different homes.[12] From his birth until he joined the Marines at age seventeen, Lee and Marguerite lived at twenty-two different locations. Lee attended eleven different schools—three years being the longest he attended any one school.[13] The opportunity to make lasting friends—even if he had wanted—was slim.

In his early years, Lee was a commendable student. Of higher than average intelligence, he tested 103 and 118 on IQ scales.[14] In his elementary school years, he earned As and Bs in first, second, and third grades; Bs, Cs, and an occasional D in fourth, fifth, and sixth.

Rebellion

In August 1952, when both brothers had left home and Lee was nearly thirteen, Marguerite moved with Lee to New York City. It was the beginning of seventh grade and the start of adolescence.[15] For a few weeks, Marguerite and Lee lived with Lee's half-brother John Pic, John's eighteen-year-old wife, and their young baby. Fear of violence by Lee and incompatibility with Marguerite caused John's wife to insist they leave.[16]

Marguerite then rented a one-room, basement apartment. Adolescence, cramped quarters, Marguerite's temperament and neglect, and the consequence of bringing a Southern accent to the Bronx fomented a rebellion in Lee not previously evidenced. He soon stopped attending school, spending his time, instead, at the Bronx Zoo, the library, on the streets, or at home reading and watching television.[17]

Truancy brought Lee to court in January 1953. The charges were that he was excessively truant and "beyond the control of his mother." On April 16, 1953, the court remanded him to Youth House for residence, school, and psychiatric evaluation.[18]

Psychiatrist Dr. Renatus Hartogs described Lee as a thirteen-year-old boy with superior mental resources and "an emotionally quite disturbed youngster who suffers under the impact of really existing emotional isolation and deprivation, lack of affection, absence of family life, and rejection by a self-involved and conflicted mother."[19]

Social worker Evelyn Strickman Siegel's assessment confirmed Dr. Hartogs.' She described Lee in her 1953 evaluation as an "emotionally starved, affectionless youngster

... that has detached himself from the world around him because no one in it ever met his needs for love."[20] He "withdrew into a completely solitary and detached existence where he did as he wanted and he didn't live by any rules or come into contact with people." She observed that Lee "felt that his mother never gave a damn for him. He always felt like a burden she simply had to tolerate." More ominously, as the Warren Commission Report added from Ms. Seigel's report, "He admitted to fantasies about being powerful and sometimes hurting and killing people, but refused to elaborate on them."[21]

In May 1953, the New York court returned Lee to his mother. When not in school, he continued to spend all of his time alone, often on the streets. The streets of New York provided a forum for politics. Outside a subway stop, one woman, paid by the Communist Party, handed Lee a pamphlet urging that Julius and Ethel Rosenberg be saved. The Rosenbergs, one-time members of the Young Communist League, USA, had been convicted in New York by a federal court for conveying atomic secrets to the Soviets. They were to be executed on June 19, 1953. Lee would tell acquaintances in the Soviet Union that the Rosenberg pamphlet and their fate awakened him to Marxism.[22]

At school in the fall of 1953, Lee's rebellion became partly political. He refused to salute the American flag. He also failed to do schoolwork and became disruptive in class. His probation officer and school officials wanted Lee to secure counseling, but Marguerite would not cooperate. When Lee's case was set for a further court hearing in January 1954, Marguerite and Lee did not appear. They had departed for New Orleans.[23]

New Orleans—Reaching for Independence

In January 1954, Lee entered the eighth grade at Beauregard Junior High School in New Orleans. His attendance was satisfactory, but relationships were difficult. He was teased for his newly acquired Yankee accent. Fights occurred, and Lee was not to be intimidated

On May 17, 1954, the Supreme Court under the leadership of Chief Justice Earl Warren decided *Brown v. Board of Education*. Integration was on its way. At some point, Lee sat in the rear section of a bus—clearly reserved for Blacks. Perhaps his sixteen months in New York City caused him to forget what the South was like. More likely he was protesting. A group of white boys beat him for the indiscretion.[24]

Although school did not interest him, Marxism did. At age fifteen, Lee read *Das Kapital* and the *Communist Manifesto*.[25] One must wonder whether Senator Joseph McCarthy had unintentionally piqued Lee's interest. Before Lee entered the ninth grade, McCarthy's claims of communists in the U.S. government had reached their nadir and were making almost daily headlines. The term *McCarthyism*—indiscriminate accusations by members of Congress against citizens suspected of communist leanings—had entered the public lexicon.

By the time he was sixteen, Lee was proclaiming his identity as a Marxist. He told a fellow employee at a shoe store where he worked part-time that they should join the Communist Party—for "their social functions."[26] A fellow high school student, William Wulf, recalled to the Warren Commission that one day, while visiting Wulf's home, Lee:

> started expounding the Communist doctrine ... and then came out with a statement that he was looking for a Communist cell in town to join but he couldn't find any.... [M]y father came in the room, heard what we were arguing on communism, and that this boy was

> loud-mouthed, boisterous, and my father asked him to leave the house and politely put him out of the house, and that is the last I have seen or spoken with Oswald.[27]

In Marguerite Oswald's household, sixteen was nearing the age to leave school. Shortly after that birthday, Lee submitted to the Marine Corps a false affidavit, signed by Marguerite, stating that he was seventeen. His brother Robert had joined the Marines three years before without finishing high school. His half-brother John Pic had also left high school without graduating. Pic did not believe Lee wanted a military career; rather it was "to get from out and under ... the yoke of oppression from my mother."[28]

The Marine Corps was not to be fooled, and Lee was rejected. But Lee did not return to high school. For the next year, he held unskilled jobs as a messenger and office boy and spent countless hours studying a copy of the Marine Corps manual that Robert had given him. Knowing that Lee was waiting for another opportunity to join the Marines, Marguerite moved with Lee in July 1956 to Fort Worth.[29]

Although joining the Marines was his goal, political theory was ever present in his mind. On October 3, 1956, three weeks before entering the Marine Corps and with an application pending, Lee wrote to the Socialist Party of America:

> I am sixteen years of age and would like more information about your youth League. I would like to know if there is a branch in my area, how to join, ect, [sic] I am a Marxist, and have been studying socialist principles for well over fifteen months. I am very interested in your Y.P.S.L.[30]

This was the Socialist Party that ran Norman Thomas for president on five occasions. In 1956 it fielded its last candidate for president.[31] It was definitely not a communist group and definitely anti-Soviet. Oswald's message was on a coupon that he apparently clipped from the Socialist Party's newspaper *The Socialist Call*.[32] The Party responded with literature. One wonders whether the young Marxist, about to enter the Marines, understood the many differences among groups that identified themselves as socialist or Marxist.

The Marxist Marine

On October 26, 1956, having just turned seventeen, Lee Harvey Oswald reported to the Marine Corps' Second Recruit Training Battalion in San Diego, California. For many adolescents, the Marines are a pathway to independence and manhood. For Lee, that pathway was not easy. To fellow recruits, the 5-foot, 8-inch, 135-pound teenager was "Mrs. Oswald," "shit bird," and "Ozzie Rabbit." Deriding him, they threw Lee in the shower fully dressed.[33]

When free time came, he did not join the others to play cards or work out in the gym. On weekend leaves when other recruits were finding entertainment in Tijuana's brothels, Lee immediately separated from them to go alone—to places unknown.[34] Three years later, Lee explained to United Press reporter Aline Mosby, "For two years I've had it on my mind, don't form any attachments, because I knew I was going away. I was planning to divest myself of everything to do with the United States."[35]

The estrangement from his fellow Marines was, of course, more complicated. Lee Harvey Oswald was not your typical Marine. He was not your typical high-school dropout, either. He preferred books, classical music, and political ideas to sports, sex, or popular music. One of the few Marine recruits who got to know Lee while a trainee was Daniel Patrick Powers. Powers recalled to the Warren Commission that, in September 1957, while aboard ship headed to their overseas assignment in Japan, he and Lee spent long hours together playing chess. When not playing chess, Powers remembers Oswald reading Walt Whitman's *Leaves of Grass*.[36] Another recalled Gibbon's classic *The Decline and Fall of the Roman Empire* among his readings.[37]

The Serious Marine

In those early months, Oswald was a serious Marine. He attained a sharpshooter's score with the M-1 rifle and was graded 4.4 out of a possible 5.0 for conduct and proficiency in basic training. By May 1957, he earned 4.5 for proficiency and 4.7 for conduct while in advanced training at the Naval Air Station near Jacksonville, Florida.[38] There he was promoted to private first class.[39]

On September 12, 1957, Oswald arrived in Japan for his first regular assignment—a radar operator with the First Marine Aircraft Wing in Atsugi, Japan, about twenty miles from Tokyo.[40] After nearly a year as a Marine, it was in Japan that he decided that he would remain in neither the Marines nor the United States. One can speculate on the reasons.

Failure and Punishment

Certainly, mishaps as a Marine were not insignificant factors. Perhaps fearful of his fellow Marines, Lee—in violation of Marine Corps rules—kept a loaded derringer pistol in his foot locker. On October 27, 1957, six weeks after arriving in Japan, a bullet from the derringer pierced his left elbow. Some say he deliberately injured himself in order to avoided going with his unit to the Philippines. Oswald explained that when he opened his locker, the derringer fell accidentally to the floor and discharged.[41]

A fellow Marine, Paul Edward Murphy, heard the shot and rushed to Oswald's cubicle. Murphy remembered Oswald sitting on his locker and unemotionally saying, "I believe I shot myself." Lee was taken to the naval hospital where he remained until November 15. Five days later, he left with his unit for the Philippines.[42]

Possession of a privately owned, unregistered firearm was a court-martial offense. A hearing on the incident did not occur, however, until April 1958, when Oswald's unit returned from the Philippines. He was found guilty of that charge. The judge advocate general concluded that Oswald had negligently stored the weapon but that the injury, itself, had not resulted from his "own misconduct." A twenty-day sentence of confinement was suspended pending good behavior for six months. He was, nonetheless, fined twenty-five dollars and reduced in rank to private.[43]

To Oswald's disadvantage, good behavior did not follow. After eighteen months in the Marines, alcohol had become part of his recreational life. On June 20, 1958, Lee was with other Marines at the Blue Bird Café in Yamato, Japan. A sergeant who had assigned Oswald to mess duty was at the café. Their relationship had not been pleasant. Lee spilled a drink on the sergeant, and the sergeant pushed him away. Oswald responded by inviting the sergeant outside to fight. When the sergeant declined, Oswald called him yellow.[44] This was another court-martial offense.

Perhaps because he had already experienced a court-martial proceeding, Oswald, in this second case, declined counsel and chose to represent himself. He cross-examined his accuser. He testified in his own behalf.[45] The court accepted part of his defense but not all. He was found guilty. This time the sentence was twenty-eight days of confinement plus imposition of the previously suspended twenty days. He went to the brig for his sentence.[46]

One must wonder how much stubbornness and defiance played into the lengthiness of his sentence. Acting as one's own defense lawyer often makes it difficult for one to show penitence and to gain leniency. In civilian life, the incident of cursing a supervisor might have resulted in loss of employment.

Confinement in the brig—a facility where inmates were not permitted to talk to one another and were required to stand at attention except when sleeping, eating, or at work—was not easy. He served seventeen of those days at hard labor. A Marine who had been in the brig with Oswald described it as a horror: "far worse than anything in civilian prisons."[47]

Fellow Marine Joseph E. Macedo remembered Oswald to be a changed person when returning to his unit. Before that, Oswald had mixed with others. Macedo now found him to be cold, withdrawn, and bitter. "I've enough of democratic society here," Oswald reportedly said. "When I get out, I'm going to try something else."[48]

We do not know exactly when thoughts about the Soviet Union turned from intellectual interest to active planning. We know that by mid–1958, the eighteen-year-old Oswald was in earnest about an extended visit to the USSR. By then, he had begun the self-study of Russian using an English-Russian dictionary and Russian language publications he purchased while in Japan. His fellow Marines were calling him Oswaldovich.[49]

Russian is hardly an easy foreign language for an English speaker to learn, even with a tutor. The alphabet is Cyrillic, not Roman. And the grammar is like classical Latin, with different endings for nouns, verbs, and adjectives depending on their function in the sentence and their gender. By February 25, 1959, Oswald felt sufficiently confident to take a Marine Corps proficiency test in the Russian language. Testing poorly for native Russian speakers and for students at the military's language schools, Oswald's score of 2 was not bad for one who was self-taught.[50]

On September 14, 1958, Oswald's study of Russian was interrupted. He and his unit set sail for Taiwan. Conflict was brewing between the United States and China over possession of Quemoy in the Matsu Islands. In Taiwan, Oswald helped build artillery embankments to resist a possible Chinese invasion. He viewed building those defenses a form of American imperialism.[51]

In November 1958, Lee's tour in the Far East ended, and he returned to California. His Marine obligation was scheduled to end in a year. With the study of Russian being his principal avocation, the Soviet Union was his goal.[52]

Why Not Cuba?

On New Year's Day, 1959, Fidel Castro drove Fulgencio Batista from power in Cuba. At first, many Americans were filled with admiration for Castro. In short order, Oswald became one of the admirers. When the American media began to turn against Castro, Oswald believed the anti–Castro information was false and that the change of attitude toward Castro was because Castro had driven out American business interests.[53]

Inspired by Castro's victory, Oswald, while in California, began learning Spanish in addition to Russian. His Spanish tutor was Nelson Delgado, a fellow Marine. Similar backgrounds and interests plus living together for ten months in the same Quonset hut facilitated their friendship. Delgado and Oswald were the same age. Each was essentially a loner. Each had come from a disrupted family.[54] Each had dropped out of high school to join the Marines, but both had college-level IQs.[55] Both nineteen-year-olds were dreamers.

The two fantasized about joining the Cuban revolution, becoming officers in Castro's army, and freeing other Caribbean islands. It was not a unique dream. William Morgan, another ex-American soldier, had succeeded in joining the Castro forces.[56] Oswald and Delgado would help "do away with Trujillo," the dictator of the Dominican Republic. Delgado advised Oswald that the best way to be trusted in the Cuban revolution was to learn Spanish.[57]

Oswald threw himself into the task with gusto. He used every opportunity to speak with Delgado in Spanish.[58] Quickly, Delgado recalled, Oswald was able to carry on a social conversation in Spanish, obtain directions, and talk to the Tijuana prostitutes.[59]

At Delgado's suggestion, Oswald contacted the Cuban Consulate in Los Angeles. He received materials from the Cubans, and on one occasion a contact visited him at their Marine base.[60] For Oswald, in early 1959, going to Cuba might also serve a second purpose—reaching the Soviet Union. He'd heard that two Americans had already defected to the USSR by going first to Mexico and then to Cuba.[61]

Testifying before the Warren Commission, Delgado remembered Oswald as an intellectual, "mostly a thinker, a reader."[62] He characterized Oswald as a person who "wanted to become somebody."[63] A George Orwell book—*Animal Farm*—fascinated Oswald. He explained to Delgado that the book involved a group of pigs who took control of a farm. When a copy of Adolf Hitler's *Mein Kampf*, a book he had started while a sixteen-year-old in New Orleans, circulated among Marines in the Quonset hut, Oswald was among those who read it.[64]

Oswald's First Biographer

In early 1959, Lee met Kerry Wendell Thornley. They served together in the same Marine unit for three months. Thornley may have been the Marine who best understood the Oswald of 1959.

Fashioning himself to be an author, Kerry Thornley was intrigued with Oswald. When he heard that Oswald had defected to the Soviet Union in October 1959, Thornley began writing a novel, *The Idle Warriors,* in which Oswald served as the model for its central character.[65]

The Idle Warriors reflected Oswald's and Thornley's shared view of life overseas among the Marines. Thornley claims Oswald said about his experience in Japan, "My fellow Marines equaled any Nazi storm troopers for brutality, given the opportunity to get away with it."[66] Upon assignment to duty in Japan himself, Thornley came to understand what Oswald meant. In a later essay on Oswald, Thornley noted that some

Marines, when they were off base, treated the Japanese with contempt; some Marines regarded all foreigners as subhuman; and sometimes there was brutality. Thornley saw such Marine behavior as juvenile. Oswald saw it as an example of American imperialism.[67]

Thornley concluded that even as a Marine, the future assassin was dreaming of a place in history. Reflecting on his brief acquaintanceship with Oswald, Thornley wrote in 1965:

> [He] looked upon history as God. He looked upon the eyes of future people as some kind of tribunal, and he wanted to be on the winning side so that ten thousand years from now people would look in the history books and say, "Well, this man was ahead of his time."[68]

Another Marine, Mack Osborne, remembered Oswald telling him that "one day he would do something which would make him famous."[69]

Thornley and Oswald first met when Oswald was discussing religion with fellow Marines. Thornley recalled Oswald saying, partly in jest, "the best religion is communism."[70] In a lengthy essay that Thornley began writing shortly after President Kennedy was assassinated, Thornley said of Oswald: "I have never personally known an individual more motivated by what appeared to be a genuine concern for the human race...." Thornley quoted Oswald as having remarked in their discussion of religion, "I'm not a Communist. I think they have the best system ... because they have a purpose.... The Communist way of life is more scientific than ours. You don't have to believe a bunch of fairytales."[71]

George Orwell Defines the World for Oswald

Thornley remembered also that Oswald was intrigued by George Orwell's *1984*. Oswald urged Thornley to read it. First published in 1949, *1984* conjured a brutal, totalitarian London society dominated by an all-powerful dictator, Big Brother. Technology in Orwell's imagined 1984 enabled Big Brother to observe every move of any citizen.

It was a society where the meaning of words was inverted so that "War is Peace. Freedom is Slavery. Ignorance is Strength." It was a society in which the greatest crime was to dispute the dogmas of Big Brother. The most feared agency of government in *1984* was the Thought Police.

In 1959 Oswald likened life in the Marines to life in Orwell's *1984*. He saw Marine commanders as Big Brother. He thought that the Marines exerted a form of thought control similar to Big Brother's, and that the forces of history were moving western capitalism toward the world Orwell depicted in *1984*. Reflecting on Oswald's fascination with George Orwell, Thornley described this perspective of Marine Private Lee Harvey Oswald:

> Oswald ... saw the future of mankind as a dark one filled with the poverty and oppression of 1984, controlled by an all powerful state ... he wanted to believe that somewhere there was freedom.... [He wanted] to work for the creation of an anarchist society.[72]

Of course, an anarchist society was the theoretical vision of Marxism, a society in which the state would wither away. Incomprehensibly to most, Oswald—a U.S. Marine—hoped that the beginnings of such a society might be found in communist Russia.

Yet was such so incomprehensible? In an Afterword to the 1961 edition of *1984*, Erich Fromm parses Orwell's message in this way:

> Books like Orwell's are powerful warnings, and it would be most unfortunate if the reader smugly interpreted 1984 as another description of Stalinist barbarism, and if he did not see that means us, too.

In 1959, Oswald might well have concurred with Fromm. Was Oswald not living in the very era that Orwell said had spawned the oppressive life in *1984?* Indeed, in Orwell's book, the 1950s and '60s were the decades whose political battles brought power to Big Brother.

If Oswald thought that Orwell was forecasting the direction in which all societies were moving, then it was possible for him to imagine that the Soviet Union was not fundamentally different from the United States. If he believed that the Soviet Union had a Marxist—an anarchist—purpose and that it was more scientific than the United States, he might also have conjured that the Soviet Union was building a society that ultimately offered maximum individual freedom.

Albert Schweitzer College—Another Route to Moscow

Despite his preoccupation with Marx and Orwell, by late winter of 1958–59, Oswald had not settled on a route to Moscow. Europe was certainly on the way. On March 19, 1959, he applied for admission to the 1960 spring term at the Albert Schweitzer College in Churwalden, Switzerland.

How Oswald heard of the college, one can only imagine. To call Albert Schweitzer College obscure might be an understatement. The college might better be called a religious study group. In 1964, it had twenty-five to thirty students. Founded in 1900 by the International Council of Unitarian and Other Religious Thinkers and Workers, its mission was to bring together people from all religions—Buddhists, Christians, Hindus, Jews, Muslims, and many others.[73]

Perhaps Oswald heard about Albert Schweitzer College from Kerry Thornley. Thornley was, himself, a free thinker. On March 23, 1959—four days after submitting the Schweitzer College application—Oswald took and passed the high-school graduation equivalency test.[74] Albert Schweitzer College approved his application; on June 19, 1959, Lee mailed the college a twenty-five-dollar registration fee.[75]

Whether the Schweitzer College application was simply a ruse to avoid a Marine reserve obligation and to secure a visa, as some have suggested, or whether it reflected a genuine interest in pursuing a European education, one can debate.[76] Nelson Delgado, with whom Oswald had discussed the application, believed Lee was serious about gaining further education. Another course beside Cuban adventurism—a college education—seemed to Delgado to be genuinely on Oswald's mind.[77]

When, in June 1959, Oswald sent his registration fee to the college, he had expected to be released from the Marines on December 8, 1959.[78] Enrollment for the spring semester would not be that far off. Moreover, Oswald could not be sure that he would be admitted to the Soviet Union. College enrollment in Europe might be a reasonable fallback.

In the period leading up to the Albert Schweitzer application, Delgado had observed the same deterioration in Oswald's military life that Thornley and Macedo noted. Although promoted for the second time to Private First Class,[79] Oswald was frequently "gigged" [given a bad mark] for having an unclean rifle and seldom passed an inspection.[80] He often had political arguments with superior officers, thought they were ignorant, and believed that any discipline he received was for political reasons.[81]

Dos Svidaniya, Marines

On June 6, 1959, Lee wrote his brother Robert: "[P]retty soon I'll be getting out of the corp and I know what I want to be and how I'm going to do it, which I guess is the most important thing in life."[82] By December 8, he would be twenty years old.

By midsummer 1959, however, a means of earlier release arose. His mother, Marguerite, with whom he had almost no communication, had suffered a slight injury at work. She had not returned to her job and was not receiving state compensation. On August 17, 1959, Oswald applied for an early discharge from the Marine Corps, claiming a need to support his disabled mother.[83] On approval of that application, Marguerite received $131.30, and on September 11, 1959, Lee got an early discharge.[84]

Thirty-five days after Lee Harvey Oswald left his Marine unit in Santa Ana, California, to help his mother in Fort Worth, he would be in Moscow. He disclosed his plans to no one. He went to Fort Worth, then arrived in New Orleans by September 17. There he posted a letter to his mother just before he left by boat for Europe:

> Well, I have booked passage on a ship to Europe. I would of had to sooner or later[,] and I think it's best I go now. Just remember above all else that my values are very different from Robert's or yours. It is difficult to tell you how I feel. Just remember this is what I must do. I did not tell you about my plans because you could harly [sic] be expected to understand.[85]

In New Orleans, he booked passage on the *SS Marion Lykes,* a freighter with only four passengers. The *Marion Lykes* left New Orleans in the early morning hours of September 20 and reached Le Havre on October 8. On October 9, Lee was in London. On October 10, he was in Helsinki, Finland, where he received a six-day visa to enter the Soviet Union on October 14. He reached Moscow by train on October 16—two days before his twentieth birthday.[86]

16

To Russia for Love

Going to the Soviet Union—for Lee Harvey Oswald—was a search for a new identity in a new culture. As hard as he'd studied his brother's manual, Oswald the young Marine had mostly met failure, disgrace, and punishment. It was not his failure, he thought. It was because the Marine Corps leaders were incompetent and the American political system immoral. The Soviet Union, he was sure, would welcome an American with the insight to reject his homeland and commitment to building a new society.

Seeking Soviet Citizenship

His visa allowed him four days to effect that transition. Rimma Shirokova, an attractive young woman and guide from Intourist, became his vehicle. She met him at the Hotel Berlin, where he was lodged. Rimma planned sightseeing for the next day's schedule. After a tour of Moscow, including a visit to Red Square and lunch, Lee did not want to sightsee any further. He wanted to tell Rimma about himself. At the end of a biographic discourse, he told her that he wanted Soviet citizenship.[1]

As Oswald wrote later, she was "flabbergasted."[2] Upon instructions from her superiors, Rimma helped Lee write a letter to the Supreme Soviet requesting citizenship.[3] Her role changed from sightseeing guide to sympathetic hand-holder. The next day, October 18—Lee's twentieth birthday—Rimma gave him a copy of Dostoevsky's *The Idiot*. As an inscription she wrote: "Dear Lee, Great congratulations! Let all your dreams come true!"[4]

But his dreams did not come true. Three days passed. He was interviewed by Radio Moscow and a representative of the Passport and Visa Office. His visa expired on October 20. That day Rimma was instructed to tell Oswald he must leave the country. She waited until the next morning, October 21.[5] Years later, author Norman Mailer reported Rimma's account of Oswald's reaction in this way:

> He was shocked. Very depressed, very tense. She tried to calm him, but now it was as if he were dead. He spent a whole morning with her....
>
> After taking her big meal at lunchtime, she waited for him downstairs; usually he was punctual.... So, by two-thirty she was so worried that she went upstairs to his room without permission.
>
> The floor lady at the elevator landing said, "He's still in his room, because I don't have his key."
>
> ... They began knocking. Nobody answered.... [A] locksmith ... joined them.... [T]he locksmith had difficulty opening the door ... and finally pushed it open.[6]

The locksmith and another man found Oswald in the bathroom, unconscious with a slit across his wrist. Oswald later gave this account in his Historic Diary [misspellings preserved]:

> My fondes [sic] dreams are shattered because of a petty offial; because of bad planning I planned too much! 7:00 P.M. I decide to end it. Soak rist in cold water to numb the pain. Then slash my left wrist. Then plaug wrist into bathtub of hot water.... I think to myself "how easy to die" and "a sweet death," (to violins)[7]

His explanation nearly four years later was slightly different, however. To a group of students at Spring Hill College in Mobile, Alabama, according to one in attendance, he said that his apparent suicide was a deception. He planned to be saved. He waited until he heard Rimma's knock on the door before cutting his wrist. He believed that attempting suicide would satisfy the Russians that his desire to remain in Russia was genuine.[8] Had he realized that the Soviets could fear that they might be accused of attempted murder?[9]

Rimma and others summoned medical help. Oswald was taken to a hospital, revived, and placed in a ward for the mentally ill. One may wonder whether Oswald made a genuine attempt at suicide. Physicians who examined his wound called it slight. A vein was not cut; yet the cut was deep, and one physician told Warren Commission staffer David Slawson that such a cut was consistent with other suicides he had studied.[10]

After a few days, Oswald was transferred to a regular medical ward. Rimma visited daily while the Soviets reconsidered his desire to stay in the Soviet Union. On October 28, he was released from the hospital and transferred to the Metropole Hotel. The Soviets were, indeed, reconsidering.

On October 31, uncertain that he would be allowed to remain in the Soviet Union, Oswald went to the United States Embassy and tried to revoke his citizenship. It was Oswald's way of demonstrating to the Soviets that he was sincere in his desire to be a Soviet citizen.[11] The U.S. consul told him that he must return another day and personally complete appropriate papers. On November 3, the Embassy received a letter from Oswald requesting revocation of his citizenship. On November 9, the Embassy wrote him, saying that his request for revocation must be in person. Oswald never returned.

Relinquishment of citizenship is not granted easily. The person seeking to relinquish his citizenship might be mentally ill, emotionally disturbed, temporarily angry, or immature. If Oswald did not gain Soviet citizenship but had revoked his U.S. citizenship, he would become a stateless person—unable to secure protection from any government. Moreover, it was common that when American citizens sought to revoke that citizenship in the Soviet Union, they eventually became disenchanted with life in that country.[12]

Still a U.S. citizen, Lee remained at the Metropole Hotel for two months, awaiting a decision from the Soviet government on his request for its citizenship. He worked intensively on his Russian. At first, he resisted interviews by American journalists.

Then on November 14, he talked for two hours to United Press reporter Aline Mosby. Mosby wrote that Oswald talked like a "type of semi-educated person of little experience who clutches what he regards as some sort of unique truth.... A zealot, he is not remotely touched by what anyone else says."[13]

November 16 was an important day for Oswald and Priscilla Johnson (later to be Priscilla Johnson McMillan). Ms. Johnson was a reporter for the North American

Newspaper Alliance. On November 16, an entry in Oswald's Historic Diary said, "A Russian official ... notifies me I can remain in USSR till some solution [is] found with what to do with me, it is comforting news to me."[14] That evening Ms. Johnson spent five or six hours interviewing him.[15]

She wrote that Oswald "seemed lonely ... very, very young ... lost in a situation that was beyond him ... he's bitter." He was different from other defectors she had interviewed. "He was ... the only ideological defector I met in Moscow." The others "appeared to be fleeing some obvious personal difficulty, such as an unhappy marriage back home." But Oswald was a "little lost boy" who insisted that "my decision is not an emotional one." It was, he claimed, based on an intellectual commitment to Marxism. Johnson saw in him "the desire to stand out from other men," a belief that he was "extraordinary." She felt pity. She regretted that she had failed in an effort to help. "I had reached out, and my fingers had not touched anyone."[16]

Seven more weeks elapsed before Oswald learned the fate of his application for Soviet citizenship. On January 4, 1960, he was told he would be allowed to remain in the Soviet Union for a year under Identity Document for Stateless Persons Number 311479. His requests for permanent residency and Soviet citizenship would be resolved later. He would be sent to Minsk in Belorussia. Although he had hoped to remain in Moscow or go to Leningrad, he told Rimma he was happy.[17]

A New Home: Minsk

In January 1960, Minsk was a large industrial city, still rebuilding from World War II. By Oswald's arrival on January 7, it had a population approximating 510,000, with one cinema, four restaurants, an opera house, and a university. But it also had an outdoors that could be enjoyed—parks, a lake, a river, and woods for hunting.[18]

As a defecting American, Lee was a minor celebrity. On his second day in Minsk, he was greeted by the mayor. Five days later, on January 13, he began his job making parts on a lathe at a large radio factory, Belorussian Radio and Television, known to its workers as Horizon. He was a lowly "checker."[19]

Our most detailed knowledge of Oswald's first year in Minsk comes from his Historic Diary, from Norman Mailer's access to KGB documents reporting their almost daily surveillance of him, from Mailer's interviews of Oswald's acquaintances in Minsk, and from the accounts in *Oswald: Russian Episode* by his Russian friend, Ernst Titovets. Ironically, the KGB's reports may be the most reliable as the intelligence agency had a self-interest in accuracy, and its reports were contemporaneous. Many entries in the Historic Diary were written weeks or months after the recorded events. Interviews and writings of Oswald's Minsk friends may afford valid impressions of him, but such recollections three decades or more later may, in fact, be dimmed and distorted memories.

In Minsk, the newly arrived celebrity received supplemental pay from the Soviet "Red Cross." His total income was equal to that of a factory director. The city gave him an almost rent-free apartment (one room and a kitchen), larger than other single men were allotted. His new Intourist guide, Roza Kuznetsova, became his friend and attended his twenty-first birthday party. Fellow factory workers wanted to master English and, in so doing, helped him learn Russian.

Women interviewed by Norman Mailer remembered Oswald as trim, neat, clean, and even handsome. The greatest attractions, however, were his apartment and that he was an American. Oswald entered in the Historic Diary, "At night I take Rosa to the theater, movie, or operor [sic] almost every day[.] I'm living big and am very satisfied."[20] Perhaps not historic, but in the diary Oswald also notes two conquests—Inna Tachina and Nell Korobka.[21]

More significant was Ella German, a dark-haired, attractive twenty-three-year-old of Jewish heritage. Ella had never been married and never succumbed to his advances. She, too, worked at Horizon. They met in May 1960. Often sitting together at the same table for lunch, their lunches became walks, and walks led to movies, the theater, and the opera hall.

Ella liked Lee. She saw the relationship as an opportunity to learn English and felt sorry for him because he seemed lonely.[22] Following a New Year's Eve party, Oswald wrote, "I think I'm in love with her." On January 2, 1961, he asked her to marry him.[23] It was two days before his one-year Soviet passport expired and had to be renewed.[24]

His diary entries reveal:

> Jan 1. New Years I spend at home of Ella Germain. I think I'm in love with her. She has refused my more dishonourable advanis, we drink and eat in the presenec of her family in a very hospitable atmosfere. Later I go home drunk and happy. Passing the river homeward, I decide to propose to Ella.
>
> Jan 2. After a pleasant handin-hand walk to the local cinima we come home, standing on the doorstep I propose's. She hesitates than refuses, my love is real but she has none for me. Her reasons beside lack of love; I am american and someday might be arrested simply because of that example[.] Polish Intervention in the 20's, led to arrest of all people in the Soviet Union of polish oregen "you understand the world situation there is too much against you and you don't even know it" I am stunned and she snickers at my awkarness in turning to go (I am too stunned too think!) I realize she was never serious with me but only exploited my being an american, in order to get the envy of the other girls who considered me different from the Russian Boys. I am misarable!
>
> Jan 3. I am misarable about Ella. I love her but what can I do? It is the state of fear which was always in the Soviet Union.
>
> Jan 4. On year after I recived the residency document I am called in to the passport office and asked if I want citizenship (Russian) I say no simply extend my residential passport....
>
> Jan 4–31 I am stating to reconsider my disire about staying[.] The work is drab the money I get has nowhere to be spent. No nightclubs or bowling allys no places of recreation acept the trade union dances I have had enough.
>
> Feb. 1st Make my first request to American Embassy, Moscow for reconsidering my position, I stated "I would like to go back to U.S."[25]

Ella's rejection may have triggered an undated request that the U.S. Embassy received from Lee Harvey Oswald on February 13, 1961,[26] but thoughts about leaving the USSR were not generated solely by Ella. That he'd made a mistake in defecting from the U.S. may have been seeded in Oswald's mind nine months earlier, at a May Day party at the apartment of Lee's factory supervisor, Alexander Ziger.

Born in Poland, Ziger had fled to Argentina when the danger of Nazi pogroms became evident but returned to Russia after the war. In the Historic Diary for May 1, 1960, Oswald wrote:

> Zeber advises me to go back to the U.S.A. its the first voice of oppossition I have heard. I respect Zeger. He has seen the world. He says many things, and relats many things I do not know about the U.S.S.R. I begin to feel uneasy inside, its true!-[27]

The Historic Diary for February 28, 1961, records a favorable response from the U.S. Embassy to Oswald's inquiry about returning to the United States: "Richard E. Sneyder [U.S. embassy official] stated, 'I could come in for an interview...."[28]

Another event, however, caused Lee to delay. For March 17, he records in the diary that, at a trade union dance, he has met a "girl with a French hair-do and red-dress with white slipper[.] I dance with her. [T]han ask to show her home. I do, along with 5 other admirers. Her name is Marina. We like each other right away."[29]

Barely a month later, Lee Harvey Oswald proposes marriage to Marina Prusakova, and Marina accepts. On April 30, 1961, they are married.[30] The Historic Diary records:

> May Day 1961. Found us thinking about our future. Inspite of fact I married Marina to hurt Ella I found myself in love with Marina.
>
> May—The trasistion of changing full love from Ella to Marina was very painfull esp. as I saw Ella almost every day at the factory but as the days and weeks went by I adjusted more and more my wife mentaly. I still haden't told my wife of my desire to return to US. She is maddly in love with me from the very start, boat rides on Lake Minsk walks throught the parks evening at home or at Aunt Valia's place mark May[.]
>
> June—A continuence of May. except that; we draw closer and closer, and I think very little now of Ella. in the last days of this month I revele my louging to return to America. My wife is slightly startled. But than ... encourages me to do what I wish to do.[31]

The adolescent Marine had become a married man. Marina Prusakova had given him an adult identity.

Marina Prusakova

Who was Marina Prusakova; why did she marry Lee Harvey Oswald; and why did she agree to go to America? We cannot understand Oswald without understanding Marina and their relationship to each other. In her book *Marina and Lee,* Priscilla Johnson McMillan provides a remarkable entrée.[32]

Marina was a talented, rootless girl. Like Lee, she had not known her father. Born in Russia in 1941 during the darkest days of World War II, her infancy was spent in her grandmother Tatyana's home in Archangel. At fourteen months, Marina gained a stepfather, Alexander Medvedev, who then was away at the war. She met him for the first time when she was almost four. He claimed to be her father. Although Marina did not know it until much later, she had in fact been born out of wedlock. Her stepfather Alexander remained in Archangel for barely a month, then left with her mother for Murmansk.

After a few months Marina joined them. By December 1945, however, Marina was living again with her grandmother Tatyana. Marina was Tatyana's favorite, a "genius" and "marvel of intelligence" in Tatyana's eyes. Shielding her from the influence of the Soviet system, which Tatyana rejected, the grandmother kept Marina from the Soviet schools until she was almost seven.[33]

By that time Marina's mother and stepfather had established a home in Moldavia. Marina joined them there. The household soon consisted of five—Marina, her stepfather, her mother, a brother, and a sister from that marriage. Still believing that her stepfather was her real father, Marina found herself the least loved of the three, treated in some respects like Cinderella.[34]

Two traumas befell her when she was fifteen. First, she learned that she had been born out of wedlock. She yearned, without success, to know whether she was the child of genuine love or merely the product of infatuation. The second trauma precluded an answer. On April 8, 1957, her mother died—at only age thirty-nine.[35]

For practical purposes, at age fifteen, Marina was an orphan. She soon became separated, both physically and emotionally, from the members of her stepfather's household in Leningrad, living sometimes with them, at other times with her maternal grandmother, who had by then moved to Minsk, and frequently with friends in Leningrad.[36]

The next two years for Marina were a rollercoaster. She attended pharmacy school for a while but was told to leave when emotional depression made her performance unsatisfactory. She worked thereafter at a cafeteria and pharmacy in Leningrad before being readmitted to the pharmacy school.[37]

Metaphorically, "rollercoaster" characterized not only her living situation, employment, and schooling but also her social relations and self-image. Before her mother died, Marina seemed prim and proper. But under Soviet law, the discovery of her true birth occasioned her the embarrassment and stigma of changing her last name from Medvedeva (the patronym of her stepfather) to Prusakova (her mother's family name).[38]

A sequence of love affairs, late hours, and an attraction to foreigners caused family and friends to question Marina's morality. She insisted they were wrong. But her friendships did not reassure others. Her crowd defied Soviet rules. She listened with them to the Voice of America, and she came to regard "Lullaby of Broadway" and the songs of Louis Armstrong, Nat "King" Cole, and Eartha Kitt as the theme songs of her youth.[39]

By July 1959, Marina had earned her pharmacy degree, but she did not have a home. Her stepfather Alexander gave her a choice: live in a Leningrad hostel or return to her mother's relatives in Minsk.[40] In early August, Marina, barely eighteen, chose Minsk. By this time her grandmother had died, but her mother's sister and brother were there. This was only five months before Lee Oswald arrived.

Not all of Marina's Minsk relatives received her eagerly. Under Soviet law, a single girl who married had the right to bring her husband into the residence where she lived. The bright, attractive Marina could ultimately be a burden.[41]

Marina found a home with her uncle Ilya Prusakov and his wife Valya. For Marina, it was an ideal setting. Ilya and Valya were childless. Valya regarded Marina as the child she never had. Ilya, an official and engineer with the Belorussian Ministry of Internal Affairs, was a high-ranking official in the local branch of the Communist Party. Attendant privileges enabled him to live as a part of the Soviet upper class. Marina had suddenly gone from being Cinderella to becoming a princess.

Viewed as a snob by some at the pharmacy where she was employed, the attractive and vivacious Marina was nonetheless an object of attention for budding physicians, architects, and sons of aristocratic foreign families. In Minsk, as in Leningrad, her friends composed a small counterculture reading *Dr. Zhivago, All Quiet on the Western Front,* and the novels of Ernest Hemingway and Theodore Dreiser.[42]

It was against that background that Marina Prusakova met Lee Harvey Oswald on March 17, 1961, at a trade union dance. As his own references in the Historic Diary recount and as Marina confirms, after dancing together, Lee accompanied her home with a group of four or five admirers. The next week they met at another dance. This time he walked her home alone.

A few days later, Lee called Marina from a hospital. He was about to undergo adenoid surgery the next day. Marina brought a jar of apricots. She visited him every day in the hospital thereafter.[43]

On April 18, thirty-two days after their first meeting and a week after his release from the hospital, Lee proposed marriage and Marina accepted. Marina was attracted by Lee's good looks, his polite manners, his interest in music, his ability to dance, and his kisses. Thirty-three years later she elaborated, "I was interested in him because he was different, he would broaden my horizons, and all other men I wanted had been taken or didn't want me."[44]

Pragmatic as she felt she needed to be, Marina would seek a second, third, and even fourth opinion regarding her choice of Lee. Before Lee's proposal, Marina took her friend Lyala to Lee's apartment to meet him. When Lyala and Marina left, Lyala said:

> Good God! That boy is really great! He's so neat and polite and good looking, and he keeps his apartment so clean! I'd throw everybody over for a chance at a man like that! You're too choosy, Marina.[45]

Aunt Valya's appraisal was no different. She had not seen Lee's apartment, but he dined with Valya and Ilya at theirs. His politeness set him apart from others Valya had seen.[46] On that superficiality, Valya supported Marina's interest in marriage.

Another factor secured Uncle Ilya's approval. As Lee had his own apartment, Soviet law would not force Ilya and Valya to let Lee and Marina live with them. Ilya missed his and Valya's privacy, and Marina's marriage would recover that.

Marina herself has admitted that Lee's apartment was an inducement for her, as well.[47] In an apartment of her own, she could secure the independence that teenagers seek. But for Marina, the apartment and marriage offered more than independence. It was the first residence since her mother's death that she could claim as a matter of right.

Marina gave Priscilla Johnson McMillan this assessment of why she married Lee:

> I married Alik [Lee's Russian nickname] because he was an American.... I married him because I liked him. He was neat and clean and better looking than Anatoly [another suitor at the time]. I was more in love with him than anybody else at the time.[48]

McMillan's own appraisal is more psychoanalytic:

> There was ... a kinship they shared. He, too, obviously felt "outside" and alone in Minsk, but it went further back. Marina believed that he was an orphan, and that made her enormously sympathetic toward him, as if they were brother and sister.... Both rejected their past so completely that they did not tell each other anything about it—ever.... They would support and take care of each other. Alik was exotic—yet somehow familiar.
>
> There is one other way in which Marina was nearly fated to marry Alik. He brought her the attention she craved. They had only to walk down the street hand in hand for heads to swivel and eyes to pop.... For at a deeper level, Alik's choice of her and the attention it brought, confirmed the feeling she always had that she was different and special. The mere fact of being married to him would mean that for the rest of her life she was going to be singled out as someone special.[49]

McMillan provides her perspective also on why Lee married Marina:

> Marina teased him sexually, exactly as an American girl her age might have done. She led him on, made him desire her, then refused herself unless they were married. Alik could have searched the length and breadth of Russia and not found a girl as American in her sexual behavior as Marina. He, too, may have felt that she was exotic—yet somehow familiar.
>
> But there were other, deeper reasons that enabled Alik, for the first time in his life, to think

> about marriage at all. Emotionally, he was freer than he had ever been before; free, that is, of his mother and the inner conflicts she incited in him....
>
> While Alik's distance from his mother may have been the principal key to his emotional wholeness at this time, it was not the only one. He was, in Russia, receiving tremendous support from his environment; a job from which he could not be fired, an apartment, his "Red Cross" [actually from the Soviet government] subsidy. And ... he was on the receiving end of a great deal of generosity from the men and women he met....
>
> Marina says that Alik was happy in her country, happier than he had ever been before and was ever to be again.... But ... it was not enough, for his dependence was bottomless. He disliked his job as a manual laborer, he disliked the dull provincial city of Minsk. He wanted to continue his education, but thus far Soviet authorities had taken no action on his request to attend the Patrice Lumumba University of Friendship of Peoples in Moscow to study as a full-time student—not technical subjects, but economics, philosophy, and his real forte, so he believed, politics.[50]

Before their marriage, Marina obviously knew little about the real Lee. He presented both a good front and a false one. He told Marina that he was twenty-four when, in fact, he was not yet twenty-two. He said that he was an orphan, like her, when, in fact, his mother was very much alive. He said that he had no intention of returning to the United States. In truth, he had applied to the U.S. Embassy for return of his passport nearly four months earlier. Nonetheless, neither Lee's Historic Diary nor McMillan's biography of Marina suggest that Lee's intense sociopolitical interests invaded their six-week romance. Hormones were in control.

Lee first revealed to Marina his desire to return to the United States in late June 1961, approximately two months after their wedding.[51] In the interim, he had received a letter of rejection from Patrice Lumumba University[52] and had written a second letter to the U.S. Embassy requesting return of his passport, neither of which he had disclosed to Marina. Without telling her about his correspondence with the Embassy, he asked her one night if she would be willing to go to America with him.[53]

Marina's initial answer was no. For three days Lee persisted. Finally, she agreed to write a letter to the U.S. Embassy requesting a visa.[54] Marina has not publicly disclosed why she ultimately decided to leave Russia with Lee. Her reasons may best be explained in the words of advice that she received from two elderly Russian women: "Where your husband goes, you go.... Fish go where water's deeper, man goes where life is better.... Your husband has seen both. He can compare. He knows which is better."[55]

In July 1961, impatient and on his own initiative, Lee flew to Moscow to press the U.S. Embassy for action. When Embassy officials were receptive, Marina joined him a few days later.[56] Eight months elapsed, however, before both Marina and Lee gained permission to emigrate to America. In the meantime, on February 14, 1962, their first child, June, was born. Perhaps named after the month of conception, their daughter, they must have agreed, had to have an American name.

Writing It Up

While in Minsk, probably after he decided to return to the United States, Lee began drafting an account of living conditions in the Soviet Union.[57] The finished product would reach fifty-one pages. It took its title from the words of the first sentence: "The Lives of Russian Workers."[58] When Marina first noticed Lee writing the essay on a yellow pad and saw that he had a diagram and photographs of the radio factory where he worked in Minsk, she thought he might be a spy. She asked what he was writing, but he declined to answer. Finally, he told her, "I'm writing my impressions of Russia.... Maybe there are people in America who will want to read them. Maybe I'll publish them, and maybe I'll keep them for myself."[59]

What he intended with it ultimately, we will never know, but a partially typed version of "The Lives of Russian Workers" was found among Oswald's effects after he shot President Kennedy. There was also a handwritten foreword and brief biography. About himself, Lee wrote:

> Lee Harvey Oswald was born in October, 1939 ... the son of a[sic] Insurance Salesman whose early death left a mean streak of indepence [sic] brought on by neglect.[60]

He was not a man to be led by others. We can only speculate on what he meant by "mean."

17

The *Maasdam* Manifesto

On May 10, 1962, the U.S. Embassy in Moscow notified Oswald that his papers were in order. He could return to the United States.[1] On May 22 or 23, 1962, Lee, Marina, and June left Minsk by train for Moscow. Thanks to a $418 loan from the U.S. Department of State, on June 4 they boarded the Holland-American Line's passenger ship *Maasdam* in Rotterdam. Its destination—Hoboken, New Jersey.[2]

Aboard the *Maasdam*, Oswald held himself in virtual isolation, in large part even from his wife. Unable to speak any language except Russian, Marina had little to occupy her beyond mothering three-month-old June, as Lee walked the decks alone, observing other passengers and the open sea, or continuing to immerse himself in writing. On seventeen pages of *Maasdam* stationery, he drafted a political manifesto:

> I, have lived under both systems. I have sought the answers and although it would be very easy to dupe myself into beliveing one system is better than the other, I know they are not.
>
> I despise the represenatives of both systems weather they be socialist or cristan democrates, weath they be labor or conserative they are all products of the two systems....[3]

Oswald's misspellings cannot be taken simply as betraying ignorance or the price of truancy and recalcitrance. Howard P. Rome, a psychiatrist who once treated Ernest Hemingway, provided a psychological autopsy of Oswald to the Warren Commission. He attributed Oswald's misspellings to dyslexia. He suggested that "for a bright person to be handicapped in the use of language is an especially galling experience ... in Oswald's instance this frustration gave an added impetus to his need to prove to the world that he was an unrecognized 'great man.'"[4]

Even in this version, with the author's errors preserved, it seems clear that in writing his *Maasdam* monograph, Lee Harvey Oswald believed he had a message for the world:

> I have offen wondered why it is that the communist, capitalist and even the fasist and anarchist elements in America, allways profess patrotistism toward the land and the people, if not the government; although their movements must surly lead to the bitter destruction of all and everything.
>
> I am quite sure these people must hate not only the government but the culture, heritage and very people itself, and yet they stand up and piously pronounce themselfs patriots, displaying their war medles, that they gained in conflicts between themselfs.
>
> I wonder what would happen if somebody was to stand up and say he was utterly opposed not only to the governments, but to the people, too the entire land and complete foundations of his socically.
>
> I have heard and read of the resugent Americanism in the U.S., not the ultra-right type, but rather the polite, seemingly pointless Americanism expressed by such as the "American

fore group" and the freedom foundation.[5]

Time Magazine, *The Worker*, and publications of the Communist Party USA were the probable sources of his information about activities in the United States. In Minsk Oswald was able to get English language copies of *The Worker*.[6] Once his mother, Marguerite, knew that he was planning to return to the United States, she began sending him copies of *Time*. From both *Time* and *The Worker*, he could learn about the efforts of anti-Communist groups in the United States.

With that information and his own experiences, Lee grappled for an alternative to two unacceptable sociopolitical systems:

Marina and Lee Oswald on a train leaving Minsk for the United States in 1962 (National Archives).

> To where can I turn? [T]o factional mutants of both systems, to odd-ball Hegelian idealists out of touch with reality[,] religious groups, to revisinists, or too abserd anarchism. No!
>
> [T]oo a person knowing both systems and their factional accesories, their can be no mediation between the systems as they exist to-day and that person.
>
> He must be opposed to their basic foundations and represenatives and yet it is imature to take the sort of attitude which says "a curse on both your houses!"[7]

He embarked on his own analysis of the clash between Soviet Communism and western democratic capitalism and where he saw the solution:

> [A]ny practical attempt at one alternative must have as its nuclus the triditionall idealogical basis of both systems, and yet be utterly opposed to both systems.
>
> [F]or not system can be entirely new, that is where most revolutions[,] industrial or political, go astray. [A]nd yet the new system must be opposed unequipily too the old....
>
> *****
>
> The biggest and key fault development of our eara is of course the fight for markets between the imperalist powers themselfs, which lead to the wars, crises and oppressive friction ... [I]t is this prominent factor of the capitalist system which will undoutly evenually lead to the common destruction of all the imperalistic powers .
>
> *****
>
> [B]ut what is important to remember is that the old system capitalism even within itself is revising and what is most evident, forming imperilist economic coilations, such as the common market.[8]

Having recognized western capitalism was undergoing constant change, the young philosopher addressed the evolution of Soviet communism and noted its fallacies: the failure of "the withering away of the state" and its inability to establish social democracy at the local level:

> [A]s history has shown time again the state remains and grows whereas true democracy can be practiced only at the local level, while centralized state, administrative, political, or supervisual remains their can be no real democracy....[9]

Rejecting the statism of Marx and Engels, Oswald saw a vehicle for averting their errors. It was decentralization of power:

> [I]n equal division, with safe guards against coilation of communties there can be democracy, not in the centralized state delagating authority but in numeross equal, practicing communities practicing and developing democracy at the local level. [T]here have allready been few organizations who have declosed that they shall become effective only after conflict between the two world systems leaves the country....
>
> These armed groups will represent the remaining hard core of feninatical american capitalist supporters....
>
> [T]here will also be many decided religious segments putting forward their own allturnitives and through larger memberships than the minute men etc. [T]here will allso be anarchist pacifist and quit probably fasist splinter groups however all these[,] unlike the minute men and communite partesin groups, will be unarmed.[10]

He expected the armed conflict to end in atomic warfare. When the atomic dust settled, he expected tradition to direct the course of restructuring:

> The mass of survivors however will, not beblong too any of these groups, they will not be fanatical enough to join extremest, and be too disallusioned too support either the communits or capitalist parties in their respective countries[. A]fter the atomic catorahf they shall seek a alturnative to those systems which have brought them misery. But their thinking and education will be steeped in the traiditions of those systems....[11]
>
> But what political structure would tradition produce?

Lee Oswald would offer the solution. He would be its intellectual, perhaps indeed, its political leader:

> I intend to forward just such an allturnative.
>
> In making such a declaration I must say that in order to make this allturnative effective[,] supporters must prepare now ... for pratical application of this allturnative[.]
>
> [I]n this way the minute men and their narrow support of capitalism have been most far-sighted, however they present only a suicide force whereas what is needed is a constructive and practical group of persons desiring peace but stead fastly opposed to the revival of forces who have led millions of people to death and destruction in a dozen wars and have now at this moment led the world into unsurpassed danger.[12]

As he offered his leadership, he shouldered a burden of guilt:

> Whene I first went to Russia in the winter of 1959 my funds were very limited, so after a certain time, after the Russians had assured themselfs that I was really the naivé american who beliyved in communism, they arranged for me to recive a certain amount of money every month[.] ... I told myself it was simply because I was broke and everybody knew it. I accepted the money because I was hungry and there was several inches of snow on the ground in Moscow at that time but what it really was was payment for my denuciation of the U.S. in Moscow ... and a clear promise that for so long as I lived in the USSR life would be very good[.] ... As soon as I became completely disgusted with the Sovit Union and started negotitions with the American Embassy in Moscow for my return to the U.S. my "Red Cross" allotment was cut off....

I have never mentioned the fact of these monthly payment to anyone. I do so in order to state that I shall never sell myself intentionly, or unintentionly to anyone again.[13]

Beyond the Manifesto

Continuing to write without publication after he reached America, he retreated for long hours into his own world. In those hours, he simplified and clarified the political philosophy that he expressed in his *Maasdam* monograph.

We cannot be sure when any of his other theoretical writings were composed. We can only believe that he wanted them read at some time by someone. He preserved and guarded them carefully. All were found among his belongings when he died, including "The Lives of Russian Workers," which he had begun to compose while in Minsk[14]; a short essay entitled "The New Era"[15]; his Historic Diary; and even a memo about his love life while in the Soviet Union. He saw himself as a man of destiny.

He had little respect for the Communist Party of the United States. Sometime after finishing his *Maasdam* manifesto, Oswald wrote:

> The Communist Party of the United States has betrayed itself!
>
> [I]t has turned itself into the tradional lever of a foreign power to overthrow the Goverment of the United States, not in the name of freedom or high ideals, but in servile conformity to the wishes of the Soviet Union and in anticipation of Soviet Russia's complete domination of the American continent....
>
> There can be no sympathy for those who have turned the idea of communism into a vill curse to western man.[16]

But he had a solution—changing the American Communist Party.[17] Overthrow of the American government was not his goal. It would fall through other forces:

> We have no interest in violently opposeing the U.S. Government, why should we manifest opposition when there are far greater forces at work to bring-about the fall of the United States Government, then we could ever Possibly muster.[18]

Nor would his revised Communist Party take power when the existing government fell:

> We do not have any interest in directly assuming the head of Government in the event of such an all-finising crisis.... The emplacement of a separate, democratic, pure communist sociaty is our goal, but one with union-communes, democratic socializing of production and without regard to twisting apart of marxist communism by other powers.
>
> The right of private personal property, religious tolerance[,] and freedom of travel (which have all been violated under Russian "Communist" rule) must be strictly observed.
>
> Resoufullniss and patient working towards the aforesaid goal's are prefered rather than loud and useless manifestation's of protest. Silent observance of our priciples is of primary importance.
>
> But these prefered tactics now, may prove to be too limited in the near future, they should not be confused with slowness, indesision or fear, only the intellectualy fearless could even be remotly attracted too our doctrine, and yet this doctrine requirers the utmost restraint, a state of being in itself majustic in power.
>
> This is stoicism, and yet stoicism has not been effected for many years, and never for such a purpose.[19]

Having identified stoicism as a guiding principle, Oswald reflects (as he had in his *Maasdam* manifesto) on those who would use violence to oppose both his ideas and the

American government: armed groups like the newly emergent Minute Men, communists, anarchists, and even religious groups.[20]

Having relegated the opposition to failure, Oswald turned his attention toward successfully implementing his own ideas:

> There can be no substitute for organization and procurement work. Towards the aforestated ideals and goals. [W]ork is the key to the future door, but failure to apply that key because of possible armed opposition in our hypothetical, but very probable crisis, is as useless as trying to use force now to knock down the door.[21]

While stoicism may be essential to producing Oswald's Marxist democracy, arms would be necessary to protect the reforms:

> Armed Defenses of our ideals must be an accepted doctrine after the crisis, just as refrainting from any demonstrations of force must be our doctrine in the mean time....
>
> Membership in this organization implies adherence to the principle of simple distribution of information about this movement to others and acceptance of the idea of stoical readiness in regards to practical measures once instituted in the crisis.[22]

But what system was to be established? What was the "separate, democratic, pure communist society" that he envisioned? He entitled it "A system opposed to the communists" and began with basic principles:

A. Any person may own private propertty of any sort.

B. Small business or speculation on the part of a single indinviduals be gauranteed.

C. That any person may exchange personal skill or knowledge in the completion of some service, for remuneration.

D. That any person may hire or otherwise remunerate any other single person for services rendered, so long as: that service does not create surplus value.

E. No individual may own the means of production, distribution, or creation of goods or any other process wherein workers are employed for wages, or otherwise employed, to create profit or surplus profit or value in use or exchange.[23]

It was to be a free enterprise system based on cooperatives. As Oswald often emphasized, he was a Marxist, not a communist. Even as a Marxist, he was a free-thinking one.

The Atheian System

At some other time after he returned to the United States, Oswald began to elaborate. He called it the *Atheian* (possibly a misspelling of *Athenian,* but more likely Oswald's adaptation of *atheist*)[24] system, "A system opposed to communism, Socialism, and capitalism."[25] It had sixteen components[26]:

A. That the right of free enterprize and collective enterprize be gauranteed.

B. That Fasism be abolished.

C. That nationilizism be excluded from every-day life

D. That racial segregation or discrimanation be abolished by law.

E. [T]he right of the free uninhibated action of religious insistutions of any type or denomination to freely function.

F. Univeral Sufferage for all persons over 18 years of age.
G. Freedom of desimanation of opions through press or declaration or speech.
H. [T]hat the desemanation of war propaganda be forbidden as well as the manufactor of weapons of mass destruction.
I. [T]hat Free compulsory education be univeral till 18.
J. [N]ationalization or communizing of private enterprize or collective enterprize be forbidden.
K. [T]hat monopoly practices be considered as capitalistic.
L. That combining of separate collective or private enterprizes into single collective units be considered as communistic.
M. That no taxes be levied against indivuals.
N. That heavy grauated taxes of from 30 percent to 90 percent be leveled against surplus profit gains.
O. [T]hat taxes be collected by a single ministry subordanite to individual communities.
P. That taxes be used soley for the building or improvement of public projects.[27]

In his Atheian system, there was a specialized form of gun control. No pistols should be sold; private ownership of rifles could be allowed with police permission; and anyone could have a shotgun.[28] It was the Texan after life in the Marines and Minsk.

As Oswald theorized in his *Maasdam* manifesto, this Atheian system would in many respects be built on "trations"—the traditions that he believed Americans cherished. Free enterprise, prohibition of monopolies, free exercise of religion, universal suffrage, free speech, and freedom of the press—these were the foundation stones of the Atheian system. That system would incorporate the Bill of Rights and the Thirteenth, Fourteenth, Fifteenth, and Twenty-First Amendments of the United States Constitution. Indeed, the Atheian system reflected the deep humanitarian values that Kerry Wendell Thornley saw in Oswald.

Whether the Atheian system was a finished product in Oswald's mind or only the beginning, we cannot know. As outlined by him, it had no courts, police, or jails; no provisions for the ill, the aged, or the mentally disabled; no military force to defend against outsiders; and no structure of governmental decision making or administration other than a single ministry subordinate to individual communities for the collection of taxes. The Atheian system was probably a work in progress.

The Significance of His Writings

In understanding Lee Harvey Oswald, it is probably not so important to know when he wrote his disdain for the Communist Party USA or his proposed Atheian system.[29] What is significant about those writings is that they reveal what preoccupied his thoughts, how he spent much of his spare time, what his political values were, and what political role he envisioned for himself. Of equal importance, they set forth a goal upon which he saw himself embarked as he began a new life in the United States with a new wife and a new child.

From his writings, we discern that Oswald considered himself an innovator, a pioneer, yet not inclined to join any organization. If he did join an organization, he hoped to change it or use the group for his own purposes. He was not a follower. As he'd admitted about himself, he had a mean streak of independence. Yet he saw himself also—at least at one point—as a nonviolent stoic, acknowledging that history would follow its inexorable course as he did his utmost to guide it.

One must wonder then what changed the nonviolent, passive, contemplative stoic, Lee Oswald, into an assassin.

18

Independence and the Changed Man

Before the *Maasdam* docked in Hoboken on June 13, 1962, Oswald had written, for an expected press conference, alternative drafts of possible questions and answers about why he had gone to the Soviet Union. In one draft he wrote:

> I went as a citizen of the U.S. (as a tourist) residing in a foreing country which I have a perfect right to do. I went there to see the land, the people[,] and how their system works.[1]

In another he said:

> I went as a mark of discuss and protest against American political policies in forenign countrys, my personal sign of discontent and horror at the misguided line of reasoning of the U.S. Government.[2]

There was, however, no awaiting press. Only a representative of the Traveler's Aid Society was at the Hoboken dock. Neither FBI agents nor his mother—or even one of his two brothers—appeared. The Traveler's Aid Society referred the three Oswalds to the New York City Welfare Department. The Welfare Department found them a room near Times Square.[3]

With the help of $200 wired by Lee's brother Robert, the Oswalds flew the next day, June 14, to Dallas. For the next month Lee, Marina, and June lived in nearby Fort Worth with Robert's family. Marina's foremost needs were a place to live and a means to pay for it. Lee's foremost thoughts were elsewhere.[4]

The Unfinished Book

On Monday, June 18, even before seeking employment, Lee hired a public stenographer—Pauline Bates—to begin typing "The Lives of the Russian Workers."[5] On June 20, the third day of her typing, he paid Ms. Bates $10 and left with ten pages of what she estimated would be a thirty-page document.[6] He never used the typist again. Nor would he, in the few remaining months of his life, seek any manner of publication for the manuscript. Yet "The Lives of the Russian Workers," a work in progress though it may have been, would become more widely read than perhaps even Oswald could have imagined.

Starting with Lee's employment in the Minsk radio factory where he had worked, the manuscript provided details on how plant leadership was selected and exercised, how political meetings were part of the daily factory schedule, and how promotions occurred. Vignettes on the lives of coworkers added flavor.

As the paper progressed, it transitioned to a geographic and social description of life in Minsk; then to discussions of collective farms, Russian marriage and the family, and the availability of books, movies, theater, and television; and finally, to exposing how political indoctrination and participation dominated everyday life and how so many avoided it.

Oswald was presenting firsthand an unadmiring view of Soviet culture. Coming from one who had rejected America to join an idealized society, "The Lives of the Russian Workers" was a story that, in 1962, might have had a market.

Seeking Employment

For his first week in Fort Worth, "The Lives of the Russian Workers" came first. Lee's sister-in-law, Vada, recalled that Lee spent "hours at a stretch going over his notes and adding to them." She questioned how diligently he was looking for work.

In fact, he harbored a hope. Perhaps, his two-and-a-half years in Russia could be of value. On June 19, he called Peter Gregory, a Russian immigrant who volunteered at the Dallas Library. Lee sought a letter of reference to be a translator of Russian. Satisfied with Oswald's language skills but unaware of his dyslexia, Gregory wrote the letter.[7]

The meeting with Gregory, however, benefited Marina, not Lee. A week later, Gregory visited the Oswalds with his son Paul, a college student, and hired Marina to give Paul Russian lessons.

It was not until June 26 that Lee made his first job application, for a laboring job, not for work as a translator.[8] Three weeks later, in July, he became a sheet metal worker at $1.25 an hour with the Leslie Welding Company in Fort Worth.[9]

Independent Living

Unable to afford their own residence, Lee, Marina, and June remained with Robert and his family until mid-July. They moved then to a Fort Worth apartment that Lee's mother, Marguerite, had found for herself. Marguerite had quit her job in Crowell, Texas, to come to Fort Worth to help with Lee and his family.[10] She planned that they would all live together.

Lee had not, however, and told her so.[11] From the beginning, the arrangement was filled with conflict. Lee's dislike of Marguerite was strong. Marina remembered that there were times in the apartment when Lee would not talk to his mother.[12]

Living together lasted barely a month. On August 10, without notice to Marguerite but with Robert's help, Lee, Marina, and June moved to their own one-bedroom apartment.[13] Lee's first pay check made it possible.[14] Neither Robert nor Lee disclosed the location to Marguerite, who found them nonetheless. Three days after the move, she arrived with clothes for Marina, kitchenware for the apartment, and a highchair for June. Lee was incensed. Although he had solicited Marguerite's help in returning to Texas, now he wanted neither her aid nor her presence. He told Marina not to open the door for Marguerite again.[15]

The move brought independence and convenience. The apartment, near a Montgomery Ward department store in a poorer section of Fort Worth, was within walking distance of Lee's job. Marina indulged her wonderment at American life by strolling with the infant June almost daily through Montgomery Ward.[16] But her penchant for America's consumer economy soon became a source of friction in their marriage.

The friction extended to other issues and was not simply verbal. The friction involved physical fights, as often as twice a week. On one occasion Lee assaulted Marina because, against his wishes, Marina had admitted Marguerite to their new quarters. Other attacks arose during arguments over Marina's housekeeping, her childrearing habits, her smoking, and her drinking at parties.[17] Marina, herself, was not passive or submissive. She could be taunting and caustic, and she struck back physically.[18]

Lee and Marina often quickly made up. Marina's biographer, Priscilla McMillan, reported the relationship this way:

> He, after an hour or two, would repent and beg Marina to forgive him. And the next day he would buy her caviar or a trinket for the baby.
>
> At the smallest sign that he valued her and the baby, Marina forgave him.... Their sexual relationship also began to deteriorate.... Lee did not want sex more than once a week or so, and Marina, dispirited at the turn things were taking, did not want sex much, either.[19]

Although Lee prized his own independence, he did not value it for Marina. Marina's ability to be independent was linked to her ability to speak English. Without being able to speak English, she was inextricably dependent on her husband. Lee made no effort to help her bridge the language barrier. In fact, he discouraged her from learning English and insisted on always speaking Russian together. He claimed that if she learned English, his own ability to speak Russian would diminish.[20]

Friends and Acquaintances

Except for a few months in 1956, Fort Worth had not been home for Lee. He had neither friends nor acquaintances there. Peter Gregory, to whose son Marina was teaching Russian, opened a door to the small community of local Russian expatriates. In mid–August, Peter invited a few of his fellow Russians to meet Marina and Lee at a small dinner party.

Marina was the attraction. Lee was an appendage. She was young, pretty, intelligent, well-spoken in Russian, and had been reared in the society the émigrés had fled. They were eager to learn about current life there. They wanted also to be helpful. The Oswald's furnished apartment was shabby. They did not own a car, and Lee could not drive. How was this twenty-year-old mother of a six-month-old child to function without money, transportation, and English fluency?

George Bouhe, Anna Meller, Elena Hall, Gali Clark, Katya Ford, and George and Jean de Mohrenschildt formed a rescue party. They found June a pediatrician and Marina a dentist. They brought clothes, a crib, a baby carriage, and toys for June. Soon Marina had, perhaps, one hundred dresses. The women became Marina's chauffeurs, taught her English, and even arranged a baptism for June.[21]

The new friends meant freedom for Marina. For Lee, they meant distress. The Russians' gifts and attention affronted his sense of manhood and implied his inability to provide for his wife and child. More importantly, it undermined his determination to control Marina.[22] Their generosity conflicted, also, with the vow Lee had written on the *Maasdam* that he would "never sell [himself] intentionally, or unintentionally to anyone again."

Many of the Russian men came to dislike Lee. Although they shared his rejection of the Soviet Union, they did not embrace his Marxism or his criticisms of the United States. Soon, they became aware of Lee's physical abuse of Marina and wanted to protect her.

A Changed Man?

Marina believed that when Lee returned to the United States, he changed. She told the Warren Commission:

> I would say that immediately after coming to the United States Lee changed. I did not know him as such a man in Russia.... He helped me as before but he became a little more of a recluse. He did not like my Russian friends and he tried to forbid me to have anything to do with them.... He thought [the Russian friends] were fools for having left Russia.... He said that they all only liked money and everything is measured by money.[23]

The reclusiveness that Marina noted was to retreat from her and most others. It was not a retreat from the political world. Marina described Lee as returning often from the public library with an armload of books about political figures, political theory, and spy novels. Through books and his own writing, he was seeking an identity.

Lee's first paycheck permitted him not only to separate from Marguerite but also to establish contact with American Marxists. On August 4, he mailed a subscription to New York for *The Worker*, the weekly published by the Communist Party USA.[24] On August 12, two days after moving from Marguerite's apartment, he wrote to the Socialist Workers Party in New York City for information about its program.[25]

On August 26, after receiving their pamphlet "The Socialist Workers Party—What It Is, What It Stands For," Lee sent the party's publishing house an order for "The Teachings of Leon Trotsky." Was he seeking an alternative to the Communist Party USA, which he had condemned so strongly in his writings aboard the *Maasdam?* Could the Socialist Workers Party (SWP) be the organization in which supporters for the Atheian system could be found?

Organized in 1928 by Communist Party USA members who'd been expelled for their opposition to Stalinist control of the Soviet Union, the SWP now had a more than thirty-year history of opposition to those communists whom Oswald had rejected. Early SWP members were supporters of the Marxist Russian dissident Leon Trotsky. By 1962, the party viewed countries such as Hungary, Poland, Yugoslavia, and China as extensions of Stalinism. More significantly for Oswald, the SWP regarded Fidel Castro's Cuba as qualitatively different. Castro topped Oswald's list of admired Marxists.

In Texas, Lee Oswald observed America's domestic and international activities through a variety of prisms. He had purchased a shortwave radio in Russia. On it he could receive English language broadcasts from Radio Havana. The range of views that came to Oswald from print media was unusually broad. He got American perspectives by subscribing to *Time* magazine and by reading the *Dallas Morning News*, the *Dallas Times-Herald*, and the *Fort Worth Star-Telegram*. He secured Marxist perspectives by subscribing to *The Worker*, *The Militant* (a publication of the Socialist Workers Party), *Soviet Belorussia*, and *Krokodil*, a humor magazine from the Soviet Union containing political satire.[26]

The Militant was critical of the Soviet Union. Its principal topics when Oswald was a subscriber were racial discrimination in the United States, U.S.-sponsored violence or potential violence against Cuba, labor movement struggles in the United States, and third-world resistance to western powers. Completely supportive of Fidel Castro's Cuban government, the eight-page weekly newspaper featured, almost without fail, a front-page article that defended Cuba in its conflict with the United States. Entire speeches of Fidel Castro were reprinted in English.

Nearly every week, *The Militant* challenged the foreign policies of President Kennedy and his failure to provide adequate support for the civil rights movement. *The Worker*, though sharing *The Militant*'s Marxist perspective on domestic issues, often favorably discussed President Kennedy's international policies and never criticized the Soviet Union.

In contrast to *The Militant* and *The Worker*, the Dallas and Fort Worth newspapers were relentlessly hostile to Fidel Castro's Cuba. Destruction of the Castro regime was a top priority. If economic isolation, sabotage, and subversion could not bring it down, armed invasion was justified. Their criticism of President Kennedy was that he was too cautious in dealing with the menace that they believed Castro represented.

The strident but starkly different perspectives of *The Militant, The Worker, The Dallas Morning News, The Dallas Times-Herald, The Fort Worth Star-Telegram,* and even *Time* magazine could only confirm to Oswald the concept about clashing cultures that he had expressed in his writings aboard the *Maasdam* and read in George Orwell.

Texas was not, however, a place to find fellow Marxists. To the contrary, Texas was a center for extreme American conservatives. Among the most extreme was Dallas resident and resigned U.S. Army Major General Edwin Walker. On two occasions, *The Worker* compared Walker to Adolf Hitler. Oswald had read portions of Hitler's autobiography, *Mein Kampf,* and agreed. Walker's political actions in the fall of 1962 and early 1963 would make Walker Oswald's first assassination target. As much as anything, Oswald's increasing obsession with and actions against Walker described a Lee Harvey Oswald that Marina had not known in Russia. To understand Oswald's transformative fixation, one must understand Walker.

19

Edwin Walker

A Target for Murder

When Lee Harvey Oswald arrived in Texas on June 14, 1962, Edwin Walker had become one of America's most vehement, outspoken, and well-known advocates for military action against communist regimes. While still in the Soviet Union, Oswald had learned of Walker from articles in *The Worker*.[1] One *Worker* article on November 12, 1961, carried a headline "Gen. Walker Bids for Fuhrer Role."[2]

Walker commanded the Twenty-Fourth United States Army Infantry Division in Germany. In April 1961, President Kennedy relieved Walker of that command. The initial provocation was Walker distributing John Birch Society literature to troops of the Twenty-Fourth Division. Walker ultimately became an icon for the Society.

By the time Oswald returned to America, the John Birch Society was a rapidly growing movement. In 1962, it claimed more than sixty thousand members, had twenty-eight central staff workers, and boasted more than one hundred chapters.[3] The Society was especially visible in Texas. The Impeach Earl Warren billboard that Jack Ruby photographed on November 23, 1963, was one of its works. The John Birch Society fit the definition of one of the "fasist ... elements ... [that] allways [sic] profess patriotism toward the land and the people if not the government" that Oswald had characterized in his *Maasdam* manifesto.

From the time Walker lost his command of the Twenty-Fourth Division in Germany in April 1961 until Oswald attempted to assassinate him in April 1963, Walker stayed in the media spotlight. He responded to his relief from duty by accusing the Kennedy administration of pro-communist political thought control. Some members of Congress came to Walker's defense. They alleged that Walker had been disciplined because he was too zealously anti-communist.[4]

The Department of Defense investigated Walker's conduct. In September 1961, it issued a report exonerating Walker in some respects, calling him "a sincere, deeply religious, patriotic soldier" but also labeling him an eccentric.[5]

Two months later, on November 2, 1961, Walker announced his resignation from the military. U.S. senators partial to Walker subpoenaed him to testify at hearings covering his being disciplined. The subpoena became a justification for his resigning from the service and freeing himself to speak loudly and often. Through the office of South Carolina Senator Strom Thurmond, Walker released a public explanation: "[N]ow, as a civilian, [I can] attempt to do what I have found it no longer possible to do in uniform."[6]

Walker lost no time in doing just that. He publicly urged military action against international communism, especially against the Castro government in Cuba. He lamented that, in October 1957, he had commanded the U.S. Army troops who facilitated racial integration at Central High School in Little Rock, Arkansas.[7] When he testified in December 1961 at the Senate hearing to which he had been subpoenaed, Walker was asked whether he endorsed the extremist views of the John Birch Society, the American Nazi Party, or the Minutemen. He answered, "I see extremists in all areas basically being inspired by something that will bring us out of the world situation today."[8]

On February 2, 1962, Walker filed in the Democratic primary for governor of Texas.[9] He explained his decision: "[There is] the need to defend the United States under God in a struggle for survival against international communism."[10]

Walker's words were so strident that more established conservative political leaders and political groups began to separate themselves from him. On February 12, 1962, the conservative group Young Americans for Freedom, under pressure from Republican Senator Barry Goldwater of Arizona and Democratic Senator John Tower of Texas, withdrew an invitation for Walker to address a March rally in New York City.[11]

When Walker spoke later that February at a rally in Chicago, *The Worker* noted that Walker appeared in full dress military uniform and concluded his remarks by saying, "Your order is to attack on all fronts." *The Worker* headlined its article: "General Walker: The Man on Horseback."[12]

In April 1962, Walker testified again at a U.S. Senate hearing. This time, he accused President Kennedy, former President Dwight Eisenhower, Eleanor Roosevelt, news reporters Edward R. Murrow and Walter Cronkite, and various other popular reporters and editors of fostering an "unwritten policy of collaboration and collusion with the international Communist conspiracy" that was resulting in a no-win policy. He told the Senate committee that President Kennedy, Secretary of State Dean Rusk, and Secretary of Defense Robert McNamara were "even worse than traitors."[13] They were not prepared to wage preventive war against countries with communist leaders such as Cuba, Congo, and Vietnam. Coming to the hearing to show support for Walker were the American Nazi Party's leader George Lincoln Rockwell and two party members. Each wore a lapel swastika.[14]

On leaving the April 1962 hearing, Walker himself punched a *Washington Daily News* reporter in the eye. The reporter had tried to question him about his views on Rockwell.[15] *The Worker,* continuing to link Walker with Nazism, commented, "Reminiscent of the tough bullying methods of the Hitlerites before they seized power was Walker's striking a reporter with his fist because the reporter had dared to ask him a question."[16]

On May 5, 1962, Walker failed in his quest for the governorship of Texas. In the Democratic primary election, he finished sixth in a field of six.[17] Nonetheless, Walker had a following. In finishing sixth, he garnered 138,387 votes—10.46 percent of the Democratic primary's vote.[18] Thereafter, Walker continued to maintain an office with a stenographer in his Dallas home. He was sought frequently by conservative groups as a featured speaker and had financial backers.

In the draft of a speech that Oswald hoped to give, he philosophized on Walker's danger:

> Americans are apt to scoff at the idea, that a military coup in the US., as so often happens in Latin american countries, could ever replace our government, but that is an idea that has grounds for consideration. Which military organization has the potenitialities of executing such action? Is it the army? with its many constripes, its unwieldy size its scores of bases

scattered across the world? The case of Gen. Walker shows that the army, at least, is not fertail enough for a far right regime to go a very long way. for the same reasons of size and desposition the Navy and air force is also to be more or less disregarded. Which service than, can qwalify to launch a coup in the USA? Small size, a permanent hard core of officers and few baseis is necscary. Only one outfit fits that description and the U.S.M.C is a right wing infiltrated organization of dire potential consequence's to the freedoms of the U.S. I agree with former President Truman when he said that "The Marine Corps should be abolished."[19]

While Walker may not have been able to use the Army to gain governmental control, Oswald's tour in the Marines left him not so sure of the impotence of the Marines. Perhaps Walker, as a civilian, could mobilize a civilian force through groups like the John Birch Society or even the Minutemen. It was, indeed, among those groups that Walker found his strongest supporters.

Civil Rights and Segregation in Summer '62

For Walker, Texas, and all of the South, racial segregation was a central issue by the time the Oswalds returned to America. Pressures to end segregation were widespread. Emotions were high. Violence was frequent. Those who did not live through the era may have difficulty grasping the intensity of emotions or the persistence of violence. Lee Harvey Oswald was watching, almost with detachment, writing:

[The] undemocratic, country wide insitution known as segregation. It, is, I think the action of the active segregationist minority and the great body of indiffent people in the South who do the United States more harm in the eyes of the world's people, than the whole world communist movement.[20]

It becomes clear he envisions delivering this as a speech when he adds:

[A]s I look at this audience there is a sea of white facts before me where are the negro's amongst you (are they hiding under the table) surly if we are a democracy, let our fellow negro citizen's into this hall. Make no mistake, segregationist tendencies can be unlearned. I was born in New Orleans, and I know.[21]

We cannot be sure when Oswald wrote those paragraphs. Authors Vincent Bugliosi and Gary O'Brien believe it was while Oswald was aboard the *Maasdam*, returning to the United States.[22] It is also possible that the words were drafted before leaving the Soviet Union or in August of 1963, when Oswald was in New Orleans, planning to address a Jesuit group at Spring Hill College in Mobile, Alabama. In any event, it evidences a reflective, instead of reactive or aggressive, Oswald.

However detached Lee Harvey Oswald could remain in the battle over segregation and civil rights in 1962, three unrelenting political figures—President John F. Kennedy, Dr. Martin Luther King, Jr., and former Major General Edwin Walker—could not. They were on a collision course that set the stage for Oswald and November 22, 1963.

The conflict was building momentum when the Oswalds reached Texas in 1962. One of the most widely publicized challenges to segregation was occurring in Albany, Georgia. Its leader was Martin Luther King, Jr. Protests had been taking place in Albany since December 1961.[23] A full-court press against segregation had begun there—at lunch counters, at a Holiday Inn dining room, at a bowling alley, at theaters and churches, and at public parks.[24] Every media outlet was reporting it nationwide.

White city leaders in Albany, Georgia, were responding by closing the parks and libraries,[25] by threatening to boycott employment of Black domestic workers,[26] by arresting demonstrators, and by refusing to negotiate unless demonstrations and other confrontations ceased.[27]

White mobs were throwing rocks and bottles at the protesters.[28] More than a thousand white and Black protesters had been arrested since the demonstrations began.[29] By August 1, 1962, Dr. King was in an Albany jail for leading, on the steps of Albany City Hall, a prayer protest against segregation. Though the Dallas-Fort Worth media covered those events softly,[30] *The Worker* and *Time* magazine blazoned what was happening in Albany. The network news programs reported it nightly. The organizations that Walker hoped to mobilize were intimately involved in resisting integration efforts.

As summer light dwindled in August, school desegregation became an issue for Texans. Many Texas school districts were resisting court orders for school integration. Fort Worth was appealing such an order.[31] In neighboring Louisiana, when a Catholic diocese in Buras attempted to integrate its schools, a mob of whites led by local political leader Leander Perez stopped the action temporarily by threatening violence. No Black student thereafter attended that year. A week later, in New Orleans, resistance and threats escalated into shots fired at a public high school, as the *Dallas Morning News* would report on September 8, 1962.[32]

The Dallas-Fort Worth approach to school desegregation was quiet and deliberate, but not speedy. An inside page of the *Dallas Morning News* reported on August 30, 1962, that fifty Black elementary school children would be allowed to attend sixteen previously all white Dallas schools in the coming school semester.[33] That was double the number the previous year. If General Walker disagreed with the Dallas approach, the Dallas news media did not report the disagreement.

The General Leads a Charge

By late September 1962, however, Edwin Walker's views on desegregation were more than visible. Twenty-seven-year-old James Meredith was attempting to become the first African American to attend the University of Mississippi. Walker was determined to stop him. Whatever Lee Harvey Oswald may have theorized about political violence in America and whatever he may have feared concerning the former Major General were confirmed by events unfolding in Oxford, Mississippi.

From September 25 through October 7, Walker, Meredith, President Kennedy, and Mississippi Governor Ross Barnett were in continuing confrontation over integrating the University of Mississippi. In Fort Worth, Oswald could monitor the struggle daily through the *Star-Telegram, Dallas Morning News, Times-Herald,* and local radio.

The pictures from Oxford, Mississippi, were vivid. The words of Barnett and Walker were strident. The University of Mississippi, despite federal court orders requiring Meredith's admission, had twice turned Meredith away. At the state office building on September 25, a crowd of fifteen hundred jeered Meredith and cheered Governor Barnett as he rejected Meredith's application during a personal appearance by the would-be student. At the Ole Miss campus, "groups of students greeted news of the governor's actions with cheers."[34]

The front page of the September 26 *Fort Worth Star-Telegram* reported that

Mississippi's lieutenant governor had scuffled with U.S. Marshals at Oxford as they tried to assist Meredith in gaining admission to the university. The marshals' goal had been to escort Meredith safely to the registrar's office at the university's Lyceum Building. The registrar, notwithstanding Barnett's opposition, had agreed to register Meredith.[35] State troopers, however, intended to encircle the marshals and ask what they planned to do. If the answer was register Meredith, the troopers would arrest Meredith or block his entry to the Lyceum.[36]

On September 28, the *Star-Telegram*'s front-page article had a banner headline: "Walker Stumps for Volunteers."[37] The previous day, General Walker had held a press conference at his home in Dallas calling for "Americans 10,000 strong from every state in the Union" to rally behind Mississippi Governor Barnett. He said he had received a pledge from Louisiana that "10,000 men and women will be there."[38]

Walker declaimed to the press:

> The [Kennedy]Administration has indicated it will do whatever is necessary to enforce this unconstitutional action [to compel Meredith's admission to the University of Mississippi]. I have stated that whatever is necessary to oppose that enforcement and stand behind Governor Barnett (of Mississippi) should be done.
>
> ... The decision for force will be made in Washington.... When and if it is.... [w]e will move with the punches....
>
> It is time to move. We have talked, listened and been pushed around far too much by the anti-Christ Supreme Court....
>
> Rally to the cause of freedom.[39]
>
> ****
>
> It is now or never! Bring your flag, your tent and your skillet.[40]

The *Dallas Morning News* reported, "Ex-General Edwin A. Walker's pronouncements are being received [in Mississippi] with a mixture of admiration and dismay. A taxi driver said, 'Walker'd make a good president.'"[41]

On Friday, September 28, the situation in Oxford grew even grimmer. Access for Meredith to the Ole Miss campus that day was so hazardous that a caravan of escorting U.S. Marshals had stopped twenty miles away.[42] On this same day, the U.S. District Court found Governor Barnett in contempt for disobeying its order to admit Meredith. The court set a daily ten thousand dollar fine for future disobedience and authorized Barnett's arrest if he continued to obstruct the order.[43]

As the governor proclaimed his refusal to obey the federal court, U.S. Attorney General Robert Kennedy announced that he was sending seven hundred U.S. Marshals to Mississippi to escort and protect Meredith. A battalion of U.S. Army Engineers was also being dispatched. Barnett indicated he might stop the marshals with state police, but a Mississippi officer said, "If they bring military troops in here, we will not fight."[44]

The president and the governor had been testing who would blink first. It was Governor Barnett. By the end of the day, the *Fort Worth Star-Telegram* was able to report, "Mississippi Withdraws Forces from Ole Miss."[45] Nonetheless, the *Star-Telegram* editorialized that Mississippi should have the right to make its own rules with respect to who is admitted to its universities.[46]

Claiming that Mississippi law superseded federal law, Barnett suggested that he might close the university rather than acquiesce in Meredith's admission. Closing the university plumbed the depth of public resistance to segregation. Closing Ole Miss would suspend educational opportunities for whites. It would also end the university's football season. Both Mississippi's lieutenant governor and its legislature wanted the university kept open.[47] Football won.

Meanwhile a "peace officer army" of resistance was assembling at Ole Miss, and the Mississippi legislature sent a message to President Kennedy not to use force.[48] At the same time, on Saturday the 29th, Walker continued to make news in Fort Worth, Dallas, and the nation. This time he disavowed any plan to go to Oxford—unless U.S. troops were there: "I would hope that no physical force ever would be used. I am advocating no violence at all." Meeting newsmen at his home, Walker suggested that he was calling only for a demonstration of public opinion that would dissuade the president.[49]

Yet the next day, Sunday, September 30, Walker arrived in Oxford. Federal troops were on their way. Walker announced, "Thousands, possibly tens of thousands of people from Florida to California" were also on their way to Mississippi to support Governor Barnett "in the position he has taken on states' rights."[50]

In a statement read to NBC television, Walker castigated the effort to integrate the University of Mississippi as a "conspiracy of the crucifixion by the anti-Christ conspirators of the Supreme Court in denial of prayer and their betrayal of the nation."[51] He urged "violent vocal protest" against the use of federal troops in Mississippi.[52]

Couched in terms of free speech and states' rights, Walker's words were, in fact, a shrill call to action. Walker's rhetoric linked the cause of freedom to resisting racial desegregation and America's apprehension of the Soviet Union and Castro's Cuba. In Oxford Walker told NBC:

> Now is the time to be heard: 10,000 strong from every state in the Union. Rally to the cause of freedom. The battle cry of the republic: Barnett yes! Castro no!
>
> It's now or never. The time is when and if the President of the United States commits or uses any troops—federal or state—in Mississippi.
>
> The last time in such a situation—I was on the wrong side.... This time I am on the right side and I will be there.[53]

This was the language of the Minutemen that Oswald had mentioned in his *Maasdam* manifesto. Yet, in a carefully nuanced answer to a question about violent action, Walker said, "[A]ny violence or bloodshed in Mississippi, from what I see here ... would only be initiated by the Federal Government, and any bloodshed would be on their heads."[54]

Others were joining in Walker's call. White Citizens Councils in Louisiana offered to bring ten thousand members to Mississippi to support Barnett. A rally of several thousand was held in Shreveport, Louisiana. A Louisiana State Representative planned to lead a caravan of cars to Mississippi's state capital, Jackson. A Citizens Council leader in Florida pledged fifteen hundred armed supporters. The Ku Klux Klan planned a rally in Georgia.[55]

While Walker was issuing statements to NBC and other Southerners were offering support, Governor Barnett was in Oxford on Saturday the 29th of September—attending an Ole Miss-Kentucky football game. He was applauded by adoring supporters. He was also on the phone with President Kennedy. Kennedy was seeking a way for Barnett to retreat manfully.[56]

Before Saturday night ended, Kennedy realized that Barnett was intent on forcing him to impose the ultimate insult on Mississippi—federal troops—the symbol of post–Civil War occupation. Like Mississippi's Jefferson Davis, nearly a hundred years before, Barnett might be conquered or arrested, but he would not surrender.

Unable to persuade Barnett to retreat, Kennedy reached for network help. The next evening, Sunday, September 30, he addressed the nation in a radio and television speech. He called upon Mississippians to obey the federal court order requiring Meredith's admission to the University of Mississippi. He announced that he was sending a battalion of seven hundred military police to Memphis, Tennessee, for use, if necessary, at Oxford. And he federalized the Mississippi National Guard to help maintain peace in Oxford. There would be federal troops, but they would be Mississippi residents.[57]

Anticipating Meredith's arrival with federal protection, students and hundreds of local residents flocked that night to the Oxford airport before Kennedy spoke. Four plane loads of marshals set down. When a seven-truck convoy led by a U.S. Army sedan left the airport, the crowd abated.[58]

The expected confrontation occurred, instead, on the University of Mississippi campus. The president's speech was ill-timed. It was scheduled for 9:00 p.m., Eastern Daylight Time. Meredith arrived at Ole Miss before then. A melee began shortly after Meredith arrived.[59]

Edwin Walker was in the midst of it. He had come to Oxford Saturday night. On Sunday, he was on campus. Lee Oswald could read about it in a front-page *Star-Telegram* article headlined, "Walker Stirs Up Frenzied Mob on Ole Miss Campus" and noting that "his only troops were a band of students and other persons whom he led in a charge on the positions of the federal marshals."[60] A youthful-looking journalist who mingled in the crowd like a student and was six feet from Walker much of the time gave this more detailed account in the *Star-Telegram*:

> Walker first appeared in the riot area at 8:45 p.m. Sunday ... about 300 yards from the Ole Miss administration building.
>
> He was nattily dressed in a black suit, tie and shoes, and wore a light tan hat.....
>
> [A man said] "General, will you lead us to the steps?"....
>
> Walker ... nodded "yes" without speaking....
>
> Walker assumed command of the crowd....
>
> Two men took Walker by the arms, and they headed for the Lyceum and the federal marshals....
>
> We were met with a heavy barrage of tear gas.... [M]any of the rioters hurled their weapons—the bricks, the bottles, rocks and wooden stakes—toward the clustered marshals....
>
> The crowd racing back.... Shortly thereafter, Walker climbed halfway up the Confederate monument and addressed the crowd.[61]

The *New York Times* reported Walker's behavior slightly differently:

> One of the mob's charges on the Lyceum, ... followed a harangue by former Maj. Gen. Edwin A. Walker from the pedestal of a Confederate monument across the mall from the Greek-revival structure of white columns and brick masonry.
>
> "Protest! Protest! Keep it up." Mr. Walker shouted.
>
> He did not advocate violence. But he told the students that help was coming from out of the state. He accused Mississippi officials of a "sellout"....
>
> The Rev. Duncan M. Gray, rector of St. Peter's Protestant Episcopal Church, stepped up on the pedestal and called on the students to end the violence. Some grabbed him and roughed him up....
>
> Mr. Walker then told the students he would give them his "moral support." He turned and strode up a walkway toward the Lyceum with 100 students following behind him.
>
> "Sic 'em, John Birch," a student shouted from across the street.[62]

In any event, students and some adults, many from out of state, fought hand-to-hand with the marshals. A contingent of three hundred U.S. Marshals, wearing steel helmets and aided by Mississippi national guardsmen, responded with tear gas and three-foot sticks. The battle ended only when U.S. Army military police arrived at about 1:00 a.m. from Memphis. More than twenty-five hundred infantrymen and military police were ultimately required to maintain peace.[63]

When the troops were in place, some students responded by cheering, "Go to Cuba, nigger lovers, go to Cuba"—meaning, of course, that rather than occupying one of the fifty states, the Army should be invading Cuba and toppling the Castro government.

The toll of dead and wounded that night was serious. Three died—one a French newsman. At least fifty people were treated at the university infirmary for injuries. Six U.S. Marshals were shot, one wounded critically.[64] Before their duty at Oxford was ended, 160 marshals were wounded—twenty-eight by gunfire.[65]

As bad as it was, the dead and injured could have been greater. Early Sunday morning, a Walker supporter, Ashland F. Burchwell, was arrested in Dallas after his car was searched and found to contain rifles, shot-guns, pistols, and three thousand rounds of ammunition together with a document by Walker about a "call to duty." According to the *Dallas Morning News,* Dallas authorities believed Burchwell was headed to Oxford. Burchwell said he was simply moving to a new residence.[66] Oswald could read about it also in the *Fort Worth Star-Telegram* and *The Worker.*[67]

After his unsuccessful speech on Sunday evening, it was a sleepless night for President Kennedy. At 8:46 a.m. the next day, he began a telephone conversation with Governor Barnett. Barnett agreed to supply state police to maintain order during the daytime even though a U.S. military force, including paratroopers, would remain.[68]

About a half-hour later, the president called Solicitor General Archibald Cox. Kennedy wanted to know what authority he had to arrest General Walker.[69] Before the day was out, Walker was taken into federal custody by a U.S. infantry commander and charged criminally on four counts, including inciting an insurrection and conspiring to overthrow the U.S. government. Unable to post a $100,000 bond, he was committed to the United States Medical Center in Springfield, Missouri, for psychiatric evaluation.[70]

The Rev. Duncan Gray, who had urged Walker to tell the college crowd to disperse, said of Walker, "I didn't feel like I was talking to a rational man.... There was a wild, dazed look in his eyes."[71]

Walker's supporters and lawyers said the prosecution was political. They asked for an investigation by the U.S. Senate Judiciary Committee, headed (conveniently for Walker) by Mississippi Senator James Eastland.[72] Dallas Congressman Bruce Alger accused the U.S. Department of Justice of denying Walker his civil rights.[73]

There were some grounds for such claims. No hearing had been held to determine whether he was competent to stand trial—whether he understood the charges against him, whether he could understand his rights, and whether he could communicate with and cooperate with counsel. Neither he nor his counsel had claimed that his mental health provided a basis for a claim of insanity. A claim of insanity could be made only by Walker, not by the prosecution; thus, the criminal law might not afford the government a basis for obtaining a psychiatric evaluation when Walker was ordered to the federal mental health facility in Springfield, Missouri.

On October 6, the *Dallas Morning News* ran an editorial stating that Walker had not led the assault against federal authorities at Ole Miss, he had warned against violence, he had been unconstitutionally held without counsel, without a hearing, and under an improper order for psychiatric evaluation.[74] At the federal mental hospital in Springfield, Missouri, pickets both protested his hospitalization and extolled him.[75] Their signs read "Walker for President," "Walker was Framed; Are You Next?," and "Interracial Marriages Will Ruin the White Race."[76] The American Civil Liberties Union came to Walker's defense also, agreeing that his being held for a psychiatric determination of competency violated his constitutional right to due process of law.[77]

On October 6, Walker agreed to a psychiatric examination by a team of two doctors, one from Southwestern Medical Center in Dallas and the other selected by the U.S. Department of Justice.[78] He was released on a fifty thousand dollar bond.[79] Returning to Dallas the next day—Sunday, October 7—he was approvingly greeted by a crowd of about two hundred.[80] Their signs read "Walker for President in 1964," "Win with Walker," "Hail to the Returning Hero," and "We're for Walker."[81]

While the showdown at Oxford had been a victory for James Meredith, for the cause of racial integration, for the assertion of federal power, and for John Kennedy, it was also a victory for Edwin Walker. His name was more widely spread. He had become a martyr to his supporters. Three and a half months later, Walker was found competent to stand trial, and all charges were dismissed by the U.S. Justice Department.[82]

After Oxford, it was not difficult for Oswald to fear Walker. One of Oswald's favorite news sources, *The Worker,* expressed that fear. In its October 7, 1962, edition, *The Worker* reprinted an editorial from eleven months earlier, the one headlined "Gen. Walker Bids for Fuhrer Role." The reprinted editorial read in part:

> The general, thus, became the first open candidate for leadership of the mass movement which the military-monopolistic pro-fascist plotters are now hoping to organize throughout the nation.... Unfortunately the swiftness with which the Army proceeded to accept the would-be-dictator's resignation now makes it difficult to punish him and thereby warn the subversive anti-American elements who are boring from within the Armed Services to destroy their tradition and legal foundation.[83]

Was it possible that, just as Hitler's march to power was spurred by his arrest in 1923 for an attempted Nazi putsch in Munich, Walker's arrest in Oxford might be the first step in a march by him to the presidency of the United States?[84] *The Worker* believed so, and so, it seems, did Lee Harvey Oswald.

20

Alone in Dallas

A Chance for Political Reflection

On Sunday, October 7, 1962—the day of Edwin Walker's triumphal return to Dallas—Lee and Marina decided to move from Fort Worth to Dallas. The events may be only coincidental, though Vincent Bugliosi is more certain, suggesting, "The news about General Walker, who lived in Dallas, may have had something to do with it." That the front page of the Sunday edition of the *Fort Worth Star-Telegram* blazoned "Walker Goes Free on $50,000 Bond" does make it likely that Oswald was or became aware of that when friends visited that afternoon.[1] What can be certain is that the move set Lee Harvey Oswald and Edwin Walker on a collision course. Six months later, Oswald would attempt to assassinate Walker.

For Lee and Marina, that day of October 7 commenced with uncertainty. Lee's mother, Marguerite, made an unwelcome appearance at their Fort Worth flat. Her arrival was followed in the late afternoon by visitors from the community of Russian emigres: George Bouhe, Anna Meller, Elena and John Hall, George and Jeanne de Mohrenschildt, George de Mohrenschildt's nineteen-year-old daughter Alexandra, and her young husband Gary Taylor.

Lee lied to the émigrés, saying that he had lost his job at Leslie Welding. He said that the work was seasonal, his rent was overdue, and he urgently needed employment. In truth, the job was not seasonal, and he had not been released from Leslie Welding. In fact, his supervisor viewed him as a good worker.[2]

The falsehoods may have been a ruse to gain sympathy for rent money, secure more satisfying work, or escape from Marguerite. There is no dispute that Oswald did not like the welding work; the pay was clearly meager,[3] and rent may have been overdue. The Russian émigrés were there to assist, not to socialize or to question.

Of the émigrés, only George de Mohrenschildt became Lee's friend. The others were befriending Marina and enduring Lee. After three months, the group came to regard Lee as abusive and neglectful of Marina, insufferably opinionated, and ungrateful.

Their primary purpose in visiting that Sunday was to help the impoverished young mother. Able to speak only the most limited English, Marina was completely dependent on Lee and their friends. To the émigrés, their support of Marina and the baby seemed essential.

Lee's ruse worked.

The visitors fashioned a plan. Gary Taylor told the Warren Commission that his father-in-law, George de Mohrenschildt, probably suggested that Lee look for a job in Dallas. It was a larger city where jobs were likely to be more plentiful.[4] De Mohrenschildt offered to call his Dallas friend Samuel Ballen. John Hall would call his father who worked at the Murray Gin Company in Dallas. Anna Meller's husband, Teofil, would ask his friend at the Texas Employment Commission to give special attention to Lee's plight.

Lee and Marina could move almost immediately. Marina and the baby would stay for a few nights in Dallas with the Taylors. The Taylors had a baby about the same age as June Oswald. Alexandra Taylor's stepmother, Jeanne de Mohrenschildt, and Anna Meller had already arranged for Marina to get desperately needed dental care at the Baylor University Dental Clinic in Dallas. George Bouhe would pay for it. After securing the dental care, Marina and June could return to Fort Worth, living at the home of Elena Hall, where they could stay for the time being without paying rent.

The next evening, October 8, Robert Oswald came to his brother's residence to help pack Marina and Lee's few bulky belongings. John Hall supplied a truck, and they stored the belongings in Elena Hall's garage in Fort Worth. That night Lee took a bus to Dallas. Teofil Meller's connection at the Texas Employment Commission proved its worth. Helen Cunningham, Meller's friend at the Commission, paid special attention to Lee, recognizing his need for immediate income. She was impressed by his neatness, verbal ability, and higher-than-average intelligence, as well as his Marine Corps service.[5]

By Friday, October 12, he had a job as a photoprint trainee earning $1.35 per hour at Jaggars-Chiles-Stovall. His hire was on a trial basis, but it could become permanent.[6] That weekend, as he would every weekend until he could find an apartment for them in Dallas, Lee returned to Fort Worth to be with Marina and June.

A Residential Mystery

No one can be absolutely certain where Lee stayed in Dallas before the fifteenth and after the twenty-first of October. YMCA records reflected that he paid $2.25 per night there from Monday, October 15, until Friday, October 19. The Warren Commission was unable to find records of any other Dallas residence for Oswald prior to October 15 or between the 19th and November 4, 1962. Lee told Marina that he had found a rooming house after staying at the YMCA.[7] The cost of a rooming house would have been half of that charged by the YMCA, but neither Marina nor acquaintances could recount specific, provable locations for Oswald's residence during the unaccounted-for October and early November dates.[8]

The inability to verify a Dallas residence on any of the missing dates has been a source of suspicion for conspiracy advocates. Some have suggested that Oswald had a secret safe house provided by the CIA or that he was "underground," yet no evidence of that exists.[9] Marina and her friends—aware of Lee's lack of money—joked that he was sleeping on a park bench.[10] The greater probabilities are that he stayed at the YMCA or in an undocumented rooming house, as he claimed.[11]

Marital Conflict

Living apart during the week benefited both Lee and Marina. For Marina, the separation reduced conflict and opportunities for Lee's violence—matters that were worrisome both to her and to her Russian friends.[12] Recalling to the Warren Commission one visit with Marina in Fort Worth, George Bouhe said, "[S]he had a black eye. And not thinking about anything unfortunate, I said: 'Well, did you run into a bathroom door?' Marina said, 'Oh, no, he hit me.'"[13]

By early October, the marriage had become shaky. Marina, in Lee's presence, belittled his sexual performance to their Russian friends. When Warren Commission Counsel Wesley J. Liebeler asked Elena Hall if she ever heard Marina making fun of Lee generally or about his sexuality, Ms. Hall recounted, "Oh yes; she would do it.... She was always complaining about him. He was not a man. He is afraid. I don't know, not complete, I guess, or something like that. Not complete man."[14]

Marina was more candid in telling the de Mohrenschildts that Lee's incompleteness extended to his sexual performance. To their shock, Marina said, "He sleeps with me just once a month, and I never get any satisfaction out of it."[15]

The separation from Lee drew Marina even closer to her Russian friends. Through them she not only gained housing, food, and health care, but they also aided her in pursuits that would likely incur Lee's disapproval. On October 16, two days before Lee's twenty-third birthday, Marina took June to an Eastern Orthodox church in Dallas for baptism.[16] Émigré Elena Hall was the facilitator and godmother. The Russian community was becoming Marina's family in an America Marina was embracing for herself and her daughter.

Dallas as a Center for Political Action

For Lee, moving to Dallas accomplished more than employment and more than removal from the frequent irritations of Marina or the intrusions of Marguerite. It also brought Lee closer to the center of Texan political action. In Dallas, Oswald could see and hear Walker and his followers firsthand. He could read about Walker almost daily. On sixteen of the first nineteen days of October, the *Dallas Morning News* carried a story about Walker—often headlining his name on the front page.[17] No Texas politician got fuller coverage.

Walker's efforts were not merely regional. He was laying a foundation for nationwide influence. On September 29, the *New York Times* reported that together with a group from McAllen, Texas, known as the Legion for the Survival of Freedom, Inc., he had purchased the New York–based quarterly *American Mercury.* A highly respected magazine of the 1920s that had developed a reputation by 1960 for anti–Semitism, Walker would be the *American Mercury's* military analyst.[18]

In Dallas, Oswald was not alone in believing that Walker posed political danger. George de Mohrenschildt, who also saw Walker as a national threat, fed Lee's ruminations. It is likely that books from de Mohrenschildt on Hitler and the rise of the Nazis supplied additional fodder.[19]

Lee's Only Friend

Over the next six months, the fifty-one-year-old de Mohrenschildt[20] was the only man in Dallas to genuinely befriend the twenty-three-year-old renegade. De Mohrenschildt told the Warren Commission, "He was clinging to me. He would call me. He would try to be next to me—because, let's face it, I am a promoter and a salesman. So I know how to talk with people."[21]

De Mohrenschildt was intrigued by Oswald's independence and iconoclasm. Their conversations were intense and sympathetic. After Oswald's death, de Mohrenschildt expressed two different views of Oswald, both of which may be valid.

In 1964, to the Warren Commission, de Mohrenschildt said:

> He was a semieducated hillbilly.... All his opinions were crude.... But I thought at the time he was rather sincere.... His mind was of a man with exceedingly poor background, who read rather advanced books and did not understand even the words in them. He read complicated economical treatises and just picked up difficult words out of what he has read, and loved to display them.... But there was always an element of pity I had ... he was sort of a forlorn individual, groping for something.[22]
>
> ****
>
> What was the main thing that I really liked about Oswald.... He was ferociously, maybe too much, for integration.... He said it was hurting him that the colored people did not have the same rights as the white ones, and this is my opinion also, you see. I was very strongly opposed to segregation, and I am sometimes very violent on the subject, because it hurts me that I live in Texas you know and I do not have colored friends. It annoys me. It hurts me. I am ashamed of myself.

In 1977, in an unpublished manuscript, de Mohrenschildt wrote in a different vein about his first meeting with Oswald:

> Only someone who had never met Lee could have called him insignificant. "There is something outstanding about this man," I told myself. One could detect immediately a very sincere and forward man. Although he was average-looking, ... he showed in his conversation all the elements of concentration, thought and toughness. This man had the courage of his convictions and did not hesitate to discuss the[m]. I was glad to meet such a person and was carried away back to my youth in Europe, where as students, we discussed world affairs and our own ideas over many beers and without caring about time.[23]

Marina Oswald did not believe her husband was outstanding. Instead, she thought he had unwarranted fantasies. She described Lee to the Warren Commission in these words:

> [H]is fantasy, which was quite unfounded, as to the fact that he was an outstanding man... [H]e was very much interested, exceedingly so, in autobiographical works of outstanding statesmen of the United States and others.... I think he compared himself to these people whose biographies he read ... [W]hen I would make fun of him ... he said that I didn't understand him....[24]

A realist, Marina was not the ego-building wife that a frustrated but wildly ambitious young husband might crave.

Oswald and Mein Kampf

With de Mohrenschildt's endorsement, Hitler's *Mein Kampf* and William Shirer's *Rise and Fall of the Third Reich* were on Oswald's list of important books. Gary Taylor, de Mohrenschildt's son-in-law, recalled Lee's commenting on *Mein Kampf* while visiting the Taylors in October 1962. From the *Rise and Fall of the Third Reich,* Oswald could see similarities between Edwin Walker of the 1960s and Adolf Hitler of the 1920s. He could liken the world of 1962 to that in George Orwell's *1984.*

Priscilla Johnson McMillan, in her seminal biography, *Marina and Lee*, raises the likelihood that by October 1962, Lee considered Edwin Walker's activities in the United States to resemble those of the emergent Adolf Hitler and his Nazi party thirty-five years earlier.[25] Author Norman Mailer, in *Oswald's Tale: An American Mystery*, has carried the speculation further. Mailer conjectures that Oswald—while detesting Hitler—also identified with him. Mailer found passages from *Mein Kampf* where Hitler described himself in ways that could have resonated deeply with Oswald. In Hitler's words:

> The uncertainty of earning my daily bread soon seemed to me one of the darkest sides of my new life.... I studied more or less all of the books I was able to obtain ... and for the rest immersed myself in my own thoughts. I believe that those who knew me in those days took me for an eccentric.... I had but one pleasure ... my books.... All of the free time my work left me was employed in my studies. In this way I forged in a few years' time the foundations for a knowledge from which I still draw nourishment today.... In this period there took shape within me a world picture and a philosophy which became the granite foundation of all my acts.[26]

Perhaps Norman Mailer, George de Mohrenschildt, Priscilla Johnson McMillan, and Marina Oswald each painted accurate portions of the young man who, in October 1962, was struggling to support a wife and infant, groping for purchase in a world he felt destined to shape, and hanging on the clash of major players in a dangerously political world.

Watching a Titanic Struggle

Larger forces than Oswald and Walker were shaping the world in October 1962. A vanguard of change that was closest and most philosophically appealing to Oswald was taking place in Cuba. When Oswald's room in Dallas was searched after the death of President Kennedy, the room was found to contain 173 "Hands Off Cuba!" hand bills, 26 Fair Play for Cuba Committee pamphlets detailing the Kennedy Administration's "crime against Cuba," four Socialist Worker's Party pamphlets, three speeches of Fidel Castro, two Ian Fleming novels, and one brochure from the New York School of Marxist Studies—a clear picture of Oswald's focus on Cuba in November of 1963.[27] Castro was the vanguard's leader. In October 1962, Cuba came front and center in the struggle that was unfolding for Castro and Cuba's survival as a Marxist country.

At 7:00 p.m., Eastern Standard Time, October 22—not two weeks after Oswald arrived in Dallas—President Kennedy announced to the nation that the Soviet Union had implanted medium range missiles in Cuba. The missiles were capable of striking the United States with nuclear warheads. Lee Oswald watched, listened, and read.

The message from Kennedy was clear:

> This action also contradicts the repeated assurances of Soviet spokesmen both publicly and privately delivered that the arms build-up in Cuba would retain its original defensive character and that the Soviet Union had no need or desire to station strategic missiles in the territory of any other nation.
>
> ***
>
> Neither the United States of America nor the world community of nations can tolerate deliberate deception and offensive threats on the part of any nation, large or small.
>
> ***

> Our unswerving objective, therefore, must be to prevent the use of these missiles against this or any other country; and to secure their withdrawal or elimination from the Western Hemisphere.
>
> ***
>
> Acting, therefore, in the defense of our own security and of the entire Western Hemisphere and ... as endorsed by the resolution of the Congress, I have directed that the following initial steps be taken immediately:
>
> First, ... a strict quarantine on all offensive military equipment under shipment to Cuba is being initiated....
>
> Second, I have directed the continued and increased close surveillance of Cuba and its military build-up.
>
> ***
>
> Third, it shall be the policy of this nation to regard any nuclear missile launched from Cuba against any nation in the Western Hemisphere as an attack by the Soviet Union on the United States requiring a full retaliatory response upon the Soviet Union.
>
> Fourth, as a necessary military precaution, I have reinforced our base at Guantanamo, evacuated today the dependents of our personnel there, and ordered additional military units to be on a stand-by alert basis.[28]

The president outlined three other steps: calls for a meeting of the Organization of American States, a meeting of the United Nations Security Council, and a rescission by USSR Chairman Nikita Khrushchev of the military steps that the Soviet Union had taken in Cuba. The president cautioned, "Any hostile move anywhere in the world against the safety and freedom of peoples to whom we are committed including in particular the brave people of West Berlin will be met by whatever action is needed."[29]

Finally, Kennedy addressed the people of Cuba:

> [Y]our leaders are no longer Cuban leaders inspired by Cuban ideals. They are puppets and agents of an international conspiracy which has turned Cuba against your friends and neighbors in the Americas and turned it into the first Latin-American country to become a target for nuclear war.... Many times in the past the Cuban people have risen to throw out tyrants who destroyed their liberty.[30]

The president proceeded to call for a second revolution to produce the fall of Fidel Castro.

For both Lee Oswald and Castro, this was not only a challenge to Nikita Khrushchev but an implicit suggestion that the United States might invade Cuba. From his own words, spoken in New Orleans ten months later, we know that Oswald was listening and watching closely.[31]

Unequivocally, the president had told Fidel Castro that the United States would not abandon its intent to remove him. Fearing an American invasion, Castro began mobilizing Cuban military forces and placed his country on air alert. Anticipating war casualties, Cuban hospitals began admitting only emergency cases. Sandbags were placed around the entrances to buildings in Havana.[32]

To many in Dallas and Fort Worth, war seemed likely. Dallas gun-store operators reported that the sale of small firearms and ammunition rose dramatically, as much as doubling or tripling.[33] Oswald himself noted that, in anticipation, Texans were hoarding food.[34]

Soviet Premier Nikita Khrushchev called the blockade an act of war and challenged the right of the United States to take such action. He canceled all military leaves in the Soviet Union. Czechoslovakia, East Germany, Hungary, and Rumania—Soviet Bloc countries—acted similarly. Khrushchev said that the world was on the brink of thermonuclear war. He called for a meeting of the United Nations Security Council.[35]

On the evening of Tuesday, October 23, Americans saw continuous live TV coverage of Ambassador Adlai Stevenson confronting the Soviet Ambassador at the U.N. Security Council. Stevenson had photographic proof that the Soviet Union had installed offensive missiles in Cuba. Oswald could well have watched it at the YMCA.

Gary Taylor would recall to author Priscilla McMillan that on the evening of Friday, October 26, he picked Oswald up at the YMCA and drove him to Fort Worth to be with Marina. The topic of conversation was the Cuban missile crisis. Lee and Marina believed that the Soviets would not take further steps to provoke armed conflict. They said they knew the Soviet government and the Russian people. They would not risk war.[36]

Others on the political fringes were not so sure. By the end of the week, two thousand people staged a rally outside the U.N. opposing the belligerence that was underway. Fifteen hundred of them were organized by the Fair Play for Cuba Committee—an organization supporting Fidel Castro. Nine months later, that organization was to become prominent in Lee Oswald's life.[37]

At first, Khrushchev proposed that his country would remove all offensive missiles from Cuba under U.N. supervision if the United States ended the blockade, promised not to invade Cuba, and withdrew its own missiles from Turkey. Kennedy stated publicly that the missiles in Turkey were nonnegotiable.

The larger truth was that the United States already considered the missiles in Turkey to be obsolete,[38] and President Kennedy had already ordered them removed before the Cuban missile crisis occurred. While letters were being exchanged between the United States and the Soviet Union and public statements were being made, Robert Kennedy privately assured Soviet Ambassador Anatoly Dobrynin that U.S. missiles would be withdrawn from Turkey shortly after the Cuban crisis ended.[39] (Indeed the United States would announce withdrawal of the missiles in January 1963, and removal was completed by the end of April 1963.[40])

By Sunday, October 28, an agreement was reached. The United States would promise the Soviets not to invade Cuba and would end the naval blockade. The Soviet Union would withdraw all offensive missiles from Cuba under U.N. supervision.[41]

Though the Soviet Union and the United States believed an agreement had been reached, Cuba did not. Castro wanted more: The promise not to invade should be made directly and formally to Cuba. The United States should leave Guantanamo Bay. It should stop all exile raids. And it should cease aerial inspection. There should also be no U.N. verification.[42]

Khrushchev sent a top diplomat, Anastas Mikoyan, to meet with Castro.[43] After a few days, Castro relented. The United States did not make a no-invasion promise directly to Cuba. Guantanamo was not relinquished. Aerial inspections did not cease. But exile raids abated somewhat, and no final U.N. inspection occurred.[44]

Edwin Walker did not agree that the settlement with Khrushchev represented a victory for America. The Sunday, October 28 *Dallas Times-Herald* carried this headline on page three: "General Walker Studies Crisis." The article said that he opposed appeasement and negotiations, and quoted him as saying that "an equally forceful action to that in Mississippi would have solved the Cuban problem two years ago."

A Stimulus to Action

For Oswald, the Cuban missile crisis was a stimulus to action. Until Kennedy and Khrushchev reached an accord, Oswald had been largely an explorer of communities and ideas. On October 29—the day that Kennedy announced his agreement with Khrushchev—Lee mailed a membership application to the Socialist Workers Party in New York City.[45] In August, he had received from the party its booklet "The Socialist Workers Party—What It Is, What It Stands For," and quickly asked for a copy of "The Teachings of Leon Trotsky."[46] The Party had obviously been on his mind as he followed General Walker's words and observed the actions of Kennedy, Khrushchev, and Castro in the escalating crisis. Now he was asking to join a movement.

But acceptance was not easy. Was he a true believer or a federal agent? On November 5, 1962, the Socialist Workers Party rejected Oswald's application for membership. Farrell Dobbs, the party Secretary, wrote that the party's "constitution requires that there must be a minimum of five members before a branch of the Socialist Workers Party can be formed and it is not our practice to take in individual members where no branch yet exists."[47] Dobbs added, however, "We suggest that you concentrate on seeking subscribers to the Militant and promoting the sale of socialist literature obtainable through Pioneer Publishers ... Let us hope it will be possible before too long to welcome a Dallas, Texas, branch into the party."[48]

Was this a put-off or a come-on? Recruiting readers for *The Militant* or potential party members were obviously not things that Oswald could do easily. He was a stranger to Dallas. Co-workers were unlikely prospects. His only friend was George de Mohrenschildt. But George was not a joiner. He was an entrepreneur. Lee needed another way to build Marxist relationships.

21

Searching for Identity

Rejection by the Socialist Workers Party was not the only roadblock Lee encountered that first week of November. An apartment for Marina and their daughter began another.

On Sunday, November 4, with the help of Gary Taylor, Lee moved Marina and June from Fort Worth to Elsbeth Street in Dallas. The new quarters were cramped and unclean. When Marina saw the apartment, she grew angry, calling the apartment a pigsty.[1]

Lee had rented the unit only the day before and had scarcely touched it. Marina set herself to scrubbing and cleaning. It was 5:00 a.m. the next morning before she went to bed. After helping briefly, Lee left. He claimed he still had a night's rent available at the YMCA and would sleep there.[2] He had a job to report to that morning.

Separation and Reunion

Matters worsened between Lee and Marina. Their very marriage was at issue. Author Priscilla Johnson McMillan, who discussed the events nearly two years later with Marina, described the disintegration:

> Within a day or two, they were fighting again. Lee told Marina that she had been spoiled by the Russians. He said that George Bouhe was trying to "buy" her. "I understand he doesn't want you as a woman. But he wants to have you in his power." He went on to accuse Marina of "whoring" after the Russians because they gave her money and possessions—"If you like them so much, go live with them!"....
>
> Lee had used the Russian *blyad*, a very strong word for "whore," which was simply so insulting and profane that it seemed to give her no choice. Trembling, she ran out the door.[3]

Nine-month-old June was left behind. Marina found a gas station. Despite limited English, she made herself understood. Pay phones cost a dime, and the station attendant gave her one. Marina called Anna Meller. Meller told her to summon a cab; the Mellers would pay for it. As Priscilla McMillan recounted, "Marina went back to the apartment, grabbed the baby and a couple of diapers, and went out again."[4] By 11:00 p.m. she was at the Mellers'—emotionally devastated and determined not to return to Lee.

Again, the Russian community converged to help. For George Bouhe, the separation was a last straw. To Marina he said, "I don't want to advise or interfere.... But if you want my opinion, I don't like Lee. I don't think you can have a good life with him.... If you leave him, of course we'll help. But if you say one thing now and then go back, next time no one will help."[5] To herself Marina said, "I'll never go back to that hell."[6]

But the separation lasted less than two weeks. Marina was receiving conflicting advice. Katherine Ford told her to return to Lee.[7] At first, Marina refused even to take Lee's phone calls. Undeterred, Lee phoned persistently. On Sunday, November 11, face-to-face communication was opened. George de Mohrenschildt had arranged for Marina and Lee to meet at the de Mohrenschildts. The meeting ended in failure—with Marina asking for a divorce.

The de Mohrenschildts then helped Marina transfer all of her belongings to the Mellers.[8]

The stay at the Mellers' modest quarters lasted just a few days. Next Marina and June moved for a week to the larger home of Katherine and Declan Ford.

Meanwhile, Lee's phone calls continued. His determination was buttressed in part by an invitation he had received for Thanksgiving dinner from his brother Robert.[9] Lee felt embarrassed that Marina had left him. He wanted Marina and June present at the Thanksgiving dinner as evidence that he had not failed.

After six days with the Fords, Marina and June moved a third time, this time to the home of Frank and Valentina Ray.[10] Like Anna Meller and Katherine Ford, Mrs. Ray was of Russian origin. She saw Marina's living with her as an opportunity for Marina to learn English and create a foundation for independence.[11]

Marina and June spent only one night at the Rays' home, however. Although Valentina Ray offered her a home for as long as Marina believed necessary, Marina was beginning to miss Lee. The next day, Sunday, November 18, Frank Ray drove Lee to the Ray residence for another attempt at reconciliation.[12]

On this occasion, Marina relented, perhaps because she realized that a long-term stable residence with her Russian acquaintances was unlikely, and perhaps because the ability to be self-supporting seemed too distant in the offing. But Marina explained her decision differently. Priscilla McMillan renders Marina's account of the November 18 meeting in these words:

> Marina realized that Lee needed her. He had no friends, no one to count on but her. Harsh as his treatment was, she knew he loved her. But she brushed him away when he tried to kiss her. He went down on his knees and kissed her ankles and feet. His eyes were filled with tears, and he begged her forgiveness again. He would try to change, he said. He had a "terrible character," and he could not change overnight. But change he would, bit by bit. He could not go on living without her. And the baby needed a father.
>
> "Why are you playing Romeo?" Marina said, embarrassed at his being at her feet. "Get up or someone will come in the door." Her voice was severe, but she felt herself melting inside.
>
> He got up, protesting as he did so that he refused to get up until she forgave him. Both of them were in tears.
>
> "My little fool," she said.
>
> "You're my fool, too," he said.
>
> Suddenly Lee was all smiles. He covered the baby with kisses and said to her: "We're all three going to live together again. Mama's not going to take Junie away from Papa anymore."[13]

In a handwritten narrative for the Warren Commission, Marina offered a more contemplative explanation of her decision on November 18 to return to Lee. Translated from the Russian, it read:

> [I] felt that this man is very unhappy, and that he can not love in any other way. All of this, including the quarrels, mean love in his language. I saw that if I did not go back to him, things would be very hard for him. Lee was not particularly open with me about his feelings, and he

> always wore a mask. Then I felt for the first time that this person was not born to live among people, that among them he was alone. I was sorry for him and frightened. I was afraid that if I did not go back to him something might happen. I didn't have anything concrete in mind, but my intuition told me that I couldn't do this. Not because I am anything special, but I knew that he needed me. I went back to Lee.[14]

Marina was right. Lee needed her. But she had not begun to fathom the hold that another world had upon him.

George Bouhe's prediction about Dallas's Russian émigrés proved correct. Marina's return to Lee ended the supportive relationship of most in that community.[15] With the exception of the de Mohrenschildt and Anna Meller, none who had reached out sought to be helpful after November 18, 1962.[16]

On November 22, four days after they reunited, Marina and Lee were at Robert Oswald's house in Fort Worth for Thanksgiving dinner. Present were the three brothers—Lee, Robert, and John Pic—with their wives and children. Their mother, Marguerite, had not been invited.[17] Marina described the gathering as a gay occasion, a "good American holiday."[18]

No one learned of Marina and Lee's separation; however, Thanksgiving, 1962, was the last time any family member would see or hear from Lee, Marina, or June until a year later. Lee was then in the Dallas county jail, charged with the murders of Dallas Police Officer J.D. Tippit and President Kennedy.

The Husband, Father, and Provider

In some respects, Lee was a dutiful husband, rarely refusing a household chore. It was Lee who did the vacuuming, washed the dishes, turned down the bed, and bathed baby June. At times, Marina even found sexual excitement with him. When Marina feared she might be pregnant from having unprotected sex, Lee became joyous at the thought of another child, perhaps a son.[19] The frequent slaps or punches from meaningless affronts did not end, however. They were behavior that Marina endured as a norm of their marriage.

Work as a photography trainee at Jaggars-Chiles-Stovall was at first gratifying to Lee. He was regarded as an earnest worker—faithful in attendance, never late for work, eager to work overtime and on Saturdays. More important for Lee, the training in photographic printing was leading to a skill that might be politically useful.

Looking for a Political Role

On November 10, having been rejected by both Marina and the Socialist Workers Party, Lee had written to the Socialist Labor Party to inquire about its program.[20] November 11 to November 24 brought only a two-week hiatus from politics as the Thanksgiving holiday intervened, and Lee and Marina grappled with preserving their marriage.

After Marina and June had returned to him, Lee reached out again, on November 25, for a role in politics. This time it was to the Communist Party, USA. He sent to the Hall-Davis Defense Committee sample photos that he had devised for posters that he hoped might generate financial support for the Committee.[21] Gus Hall and Benjamin Davis were leaders of the Communist Party USA. They were being criminally prosecuted for violating registration provisions of the McCarran Act. By then Lee had been employed slightly more than a month as a technician in Dallas at the graphic arts printing firm Jaggar-Chiles-Stovall, Co. but he had learned some fundamentals.

In early December, Lee also wrote the Socialist Workers Party, this time offering to do photographic reproductions and offset printing. On December 9, a New York volunteer worker for the party politely declined Oswald's offer of help but suggested that they maintain contact.[22] On December 17, 1962, Lee sent a one-dollar check to *The Militant*, the party's weekly newspaper, for a four-month subscription.[23] He was grasping for a political home.

In fact, Lee wanted more than an unpaid, supportive political home. As Alexandra Taylor aptly observed:

> [H]e wanted to be a very important person without putting anything into it at all.... He expected to be the highest paid immediately, the best liked, the highest skilled.... My husband told him you can't be something for nothing ... you can't expect to get high pay and receive a good position with no education and no ambition, no particular goal, no anything ... he just expected a lot for nothing.... I don't think he knew what he wanted, and I don't think he was too interested in working toward anything.[24]

Lee did know what he wanted. He knew what he wanted to work toward. Being a husband, a father, and a worker in a photographic print shop were not his priorities. As his Marine friend, Kerry Wendell Thornley observed, Lee wanted to be on the right side of history, and he wanted to effect it.[25] He wanted to be a player in important events.

Questions of Fidelity

Whereas finding a political home was important for Lee, creating a home for herself, June, and even Lee was Marina's priority in December. Yet that month brought Marina's hopes crashing once more.

The precipitating event was a holiday party on December 28 at the home of Declan and Katerina Ford. Marina annoyed Lee by greeting George Bouhe with an affectionate kiss on the cheek and by spending the evening talking with her Russian friends. Lee separated from Marina and the Russians, devoting much of the evening to an attractive young Japanese woman. He reminisced about Japan, and she spoke to him in Russian.[26]

A few days later, Marina found in Lee's pocket the Japanese woman's address. "What a bastard. He is having an affair with her," Marina told George de Mohrenschildt. "That Japanese bitch. We had a fight over her—and look at the result." Marina had new black eyes.[27]

New Year's Eve was not a happy one for Marina, either. On that most celebratory night of the year for Russians, Lee and Marina were alone. At about 10:30 p.m., Lee went to bed without Marina. Marina, quite awake, began thinking of happier times in Russia and about Anatoly, a Russian medical student whose marriage offer she had rejected. She sat down to write a letter.

As she remembered the letter to her biographer, Priscilla Johnson McMillan, she wrote to Anatoly:

> ... I am writing ... because I feel very much alone. My husband does not love me and our relationship here in America is not what it was in Russia. I am sad that there is an ocean between us and that I have no way back....
>
> Alik [Lee's name to the Russians] does not treat me as I should like, and I fear that I shall never be happy with him. It is all my fault, I think.... How I wish that you and I could be together again.
>
> I regret that I did not appreciate the happy times we had together and your goodness to me. Why did you hold yourself back that time? You did it for me, I know, and now I regret that, too.[28]

The next day, January 1, 1963, when Marina was still brooding over Lee's possible Japanese lover—and most Americans his age were watching football—Lee was thinking about politics. In addition to asking Pioneer Publishing to send him the English words to the anthem of the Fourth International, he ordered three political pamphlets by James B. Cannon, one of Leon Trotsky's most ardent supporters and a former National Secretary of the Socialist Workers Party.[29] The Cannon pamphlets were "The Coming American Revolution," "The End of the Comintern," and the "1948 Manifesto of the Fourth International."[30]

Marina had put the letter to Anatoly aside, then mailed it four or five days later, with a twenty-five-cent stamp. When the letter was returned for insufficient postage, Lee retrieved and read it in disbelief. He slapped her twice.

McMillan rendered the rest of Marina's account in this way:

> "Is that true what you wrote?" Lee asked....
>
> "Yes," she said....
>
> "Not a word of it is true," he said. "You did it on purpose. You knew they changed the postage and that the letter would come back to me. You were trying to make me jealous. I know your woman's tricks. I won't give you any more stamps. And I'm going to read all your letters. I'll send them myself from now on. I'll never, ever trust you again."[31]

Walker Becomes a Target

One cannot be certain what caused Lee Harvey Oswald to change from political philosopher to political assassin. We know that the change began when his marriage was failing and his overtures to American Marxists had not borne fruit. We know also that beginning Monday, January 21, 1963, a series of outside events channeled his life in a new direction.

On that day, the U.S. Attorney in Oxford, Mississippi, dismissed all criminal charges against Edwin Walker. A federal grand jury in Mississippi had failed to return an indictment on criminal charges of insurrection, seditious conspiracy, and assaulting, resisting, and impeding federal officers.[32] Not a surprise, perhaps. The same day, national media were reporting that James Meredith might be leaving Ole Miss. He had failed to take a final examination, and two weeks earlier he had said he would not register for the next semester "unless very definite, positive changes are made to make my situation more conducive to learning."[33] To Oswald, the combination of events must have seemed a clear victory for Walker.

With the dismissal of all charges, Walker became even more exalted to many. Supporters came to his home to congratulate him. He told reporters, including those of the *Dallas Morning News,* "Today my hopes returned to the Cubans and millions of others who long to return to their homes having escaped from jails and boundaries of police states."[34] There could be little doubt that Lee would see it.

Walker's Liberation

In Oswald's eyes, dismissal of insurrection charges against Walker could have given Walker the aura to his followers that Hitler gained when released from prison after the Munich beer-hall putsch. Walker was now the wrongly arrested spokesman for the military overthrow of Fidel Castro—if not more. Walker could resume full speed his efforts to build a political movement.

The January 1963 issue of the *American Mercury* magazine demonstrated Walker's influence. Walker's name appeared on the masthead as Military Editor. The January table of contents listed two articles by Walker.

Also featured were an article praising Mississippi Governor Ross Barnett's resistance to the integration of "Old Miss," a lengthy partial reprint of a book favoring state sovereignty, and an article criticizing President Kennedy for failing to await Supreme Court review of the federal appellate court's order that James Meredith should be admitted to the university. At the end of the issue was a letter to the editor criticizing Walker's October arrest at Oxford, Mississippi. From cover to cover, the agenda was Walker's.

To reach the religious right, *American Mercury* made T. Robert Ingram, rector of St. Thomas Episcopal Church in Houston, Religious Editor. By late January, Walker had also formed an alliance with a fundamentalist Oklahoma minister, the Rev. Billy James Hargis.

Hargis was a budding powerhouse. His ministry, the Christian Crusade, was broadcast on more than 500 radio stations and 250 television stations. Its monthly newspaper with a claimed circulation of 55,000 copies[35] exceeded the *American Mercury's.*[36] Both its staff (seventy-eight) and income (nearly $700,000) were considerably larger.[37]

A Speaking Tour for Walker

Together, Hargis and Walker were planning a speaking tour called "Operation Midnight Ride." The tour was to begin in Miami on February 27, 1963, and end in Los Angeles on April 3.[38]

On the tour, Hargis was the main attraction. Walker's role was to rally retired army officers to Hargis's crusade and to discredit the United Nations and the U.S. Department of Defense as tools of communist conspiracy. As Walker was ready to say, "God's Spirit goes before us.... Let there be no doubt that this satanic hatred which we see aimed at the anti–Communist conservative ranks is directed in reality against the Church of Jesus Christ." And Hargis buttressed that before their crowds with an image of Christ superimposed on a map of the United States.[39]

Laying a Foundation for Murder

On Friday, January 25, four days after criminal charges against Walker were dismissed, Lee Harvey Oswald sent $106 to the United States Department of State in final payment of the loan that had financed his return to the United States. That left no obligations that would preclude his regaining an American passport. Two days after that, on January 27, Lee sent $10 in cash to Seaport Traders, Inc., in Los Angeles. It was down payment for a snub-nosed Smith and Wesson .38 caliber revolver, ordered in the fictitious name of A.J. Hidell.[40] The age for the purported purchaser—twenty-eight years old—was also different from Oswald's.

The inference may be obvious: Oswald's purpose was to kill Edwin Walker. Biographer Priscilla McMillan, after conversations with Marina and Dallas acquaintances of George de Mohrenschildt, suggested that the idea may well have been reinforced by de Mohrenschildt, a man who could easily have said, "Anybody who bumps that bastard off will be doing this country a favor."[41]

Yet, killing someone with a snub-nosed pistol was nearly suicidal. Such a pistol could be accurate only at close range. The likelihood of capture would be great. Whatever plan existed on January 27 was not the best.

Coincidence gained Oswald time for more rational planning. Eight weeks would pass before the weapon arrived. Oswald would have no opportunity before Walker returned from the "Operation Midnight Ride" tour in early April. He would, however, have more time to consider his mode of assault.

22

Waiting for Walker

Love and murder were starkly intertwined as Lee edged closer to a plan to kill Walker. In the early morning of the day Lee would order the pistol, Marina felt a passionate need for Lee. McMillan tells us:

> [About three the following] morning Marina woke him, feeling sexual desire.
> "What do you want?" he mumbled.
> "I want a son," she said.
> "But only last time you were crying. I thought you didn't want a baby."
> "I want you to have a son."
> "I want a son very much."
> ... It was a "wonderful night" for Marina. She felt closer to Lee and closer to being satisfied by him sexually than ever before. But the next day she regretted what she had done. Nor did Lee show any happiness over the night before, or elation over the possibility of another child. He had his mind elsewhere.[1]

"Elsewhere" translated to ordering the pistol from Seaport Traders, Inc., and all that it portended. Neither the choice of weapon nor the seller was a likely spur of the moment decision. He must have been researching his options.

Marina believed that any thoughts Lee had of killing Walker may have been bolstered by conversations Lee had on February 13 with Volkmar Schmidt and George de Mohrenschildt at a party at the de Mohrenschildt home. Schmidt, a researcher for the Socony Mobil Oil Company, spent more than three hours talking with Lee.

Although Schmidt did not testify before the Warren Commission, he was interviewed by the FBI. Years later, he would recall that evening to McMillan, Gus Russo, and Edward Jay Epstein in separate interviews.[2] To Russo, Schmidt described Oswald as emotionally detached from Marina, "obsessed with his own political agenda." He was struck by Oswald's "seeming determination to give meaning to his life by doing something political." He seemed so intent on finding political fulfillment that Schmidt feared he would explode into violence, not political violence but violence against Marina.[3]

Contrary to what others recalled about Oswald, Schmidt remembered Oswald's being extremely critical of President Kennedy.[4] According to Schmidt:

> He ... very much idealized the socialist government of Cuba, and he was just obsessed with what America did to support the invasion.... He really felt very angry about the support which the Kennedy Administration gave to the Bay of Pigs. I noticed that he was really, really obsessed with this idea and with animosity towards Kennedy, just obsessed with anger towards Kennedy.[5]

Schmidt recalled that his own response was to turn the conversation away from Kennedy. He raised General Walker as the truly bad man in political life. Schmidt told

Oswald how obnoxious both he and de Mohrenschildt thought Walker was. When Schmidt later learned that Oswald had tried to assassinate Walker, he feared that his observations about Walker had supplied Oswald's motivation.[6]

The de Mohrenschildt party on February 13, 1963, was, for Marina, only a brief respite from Lee's aggression. McMillan reports that the month of February was "...the worst in all her married life... [T]here was a dramatic change in the style and ferocity with which he did it [hit Marina]. No longer did he strike her once across the face with the flat of his hand. Now he hit her five or six times—and with his fists."[7] His work performance and relationships at Jaggars-Chiles-Stovall were deteriorating noticeably; as they did, the quarrels with Marina and beatings increased in frequency and intensity.[8]

The day after the de Mohrenschildt party, February 14, the *Dallas Morning News* announced "Operation Midnight Ride" in a front-page article. The Hargis-Walker tour was likened to one of the famous evangelist Billy Graham. Three days later, on February 17, the *Morning News* carried another article about the "Midnight Ride." This one emphasized the anti-Castro purpose of the speaking tour. With such power and purpose being assembled by Walker, the importance to Oswald of his own mission must have loomed larger.

Yet two days earlier, Lee had learned of a complication: Marina told him she was pregnant with their second child.[9] If Lee were dead or in jail, how would she survive? She had no money and no job. Her English was minimal. All of their Russian friends except the de Mohrenschildts had deserted her. She would be pregnant with a fourteen-month-old child to care for alone. His own children might be abandoned to an orphanage as his own mother had done with him. Not a happy thought for Lee. He came up with a plan.

That same day, Lee forced Marina to write to the Soviet embassy asking for help in returning to the USSR. She wrote to Nikolai Reznichenko, the Soviet consul: "I beg your assistance to help me return to the Homeland in the USSR where I will again feel myself a full-fledged citizen.... I am requesting you to extend to me possible material aid for the trip. My husband remains here, since he is an American by nationality."[10]

Marina told the Warren Commission that she did not want to leave the United States, did not want to write the letter, and was unaware of Lee's plan to kill Walker. "What could I do if my husband did not want to live with me," she said. "At least that's what I thought."[11]

Meeting Ruth Paine

Although Marina had lost most of her Russian friends, the de Mohrenschildts remained supportive. Through that friendship, Lee and Marina were invited on Friday evening, February 22, to a small gathering at the home of Everett Glover.[12] Glover believed the Oswalds would be an interesting couple for his friends to meet, especially those who were interested in speaking Russian or learning about life in Russia.[13]

For nearly four hours, Lee was the center of attention. The guests were interested in Oswald's views on life in Russia and in his disagreements with both Soviet communism and American capitalism. Glover felt that Lee enjoyed the attention, despite being put largely on the defensive.[14]

Glover remembered Ruth Paine, Jeanne de Mohrenschildt, and Marina as the only women at the party.[15] At the outset, Marina tended to baby June in one of the bedrooms.[16] When Junie was settled, Marina joined the larger group.

Ultimately, Ruth Paine and Marina began to talk separately A beginning teacher of Russian, Ruth did her best to carry on a conversation.[17] She was a recently separated mother of two who sang with Glover in a madrigal choir. Over three or four hours, Ruth and Marina became acquainted. Marina invited Ruth to visit her. That visit led to a dinner invitation from Ruth for Marina, Lee, and June.[18] It was a growing friendship that seven months later sheltered Marina from Lee and inadvertently may have enabled the assassination of a president.

Attempted Suicide

After what might have been an enjoyable time at the home of Everett Glover, Saturday, February 23 became a nightmare for Marina. It was the day she attempted suicide. She was reluctant to discuss that day with the Warren Commission. Later, in the privacy of her own home, Marina gave an account to Priscilla Johnson McMillan. McMillan reported it in these words:

> … Lee had asked Marina to fix him something special for dinner, a Southern dish called red beans and rice. Marina had never heard of it. But Hungarian dishes have a good deal of rice, so she took her Hungarian cookbook off the shelf and pored over it. She found nothing helpful there and she fell back as usual on Mother Russia. She put everything in a skillet and cooked it with onions.
>
> Lee started scolding her the second he got home. He told her that she ought to fix the rice separately and then pour the beans over it.
>
> "What on earth difference does it make?" she asked. "You mix the whole thing into a mess on your plate anyway."
>
> "I work," Lee complained. "I come home and I find that you can't even do a simple thing like this for me."
>
> "And of course I sit home all day with nothing to do but spit on the ceiling." Marina threw down her cooking spoon, told Lee to fix it himself, and stomped out of the kitchen.
>
> Lee came after her and ordered her to fix his dinner.
>
> "I won't."
>
> "You will."
>
> "I won't."
>
> "I'll force you to."
>
> Marina stomped back into the kitchen and threw the whole dinner out.
>
> The next thing she knew she was in the bedroom and he was about to hit her. "You have no right," she said. "If you lay a finger on me, I'll throw this at you." She was holding a pretty wooden box, a present from a friend in Minsk. It was heavy with jewelry: Lee's cufflinks and watch and all Marina's beads and pins.
>
> He hit her hard across the face, then whirled and started to leave the room. Marina hurled the box as hard as she could, and it grazed Lee's shoulder. He spun around and came at her white with rage. His lips were pressed together and he had an inhuman look of hate on his face. He hurled her onto the bed and grabbed her throat. "I won't let you out of this alive."
>
> Just at that second the baby cried.
>
> Lee suddenly came to his to his senses. "Go get her," he ordered.
>
> "Go get her yourself." Another second, Marina thinks, and he would have strangled her. She had never seen him in such fury.
>
> Lee went to the baby and sat alone with her in the next room for a long time while Marina

lay on the bed and sobbed. She was shocked and ashamed. Why go on living if Lee would not spare her even while she was carrying their child? ... Lee did not treat her like a human being. For five minutes he was kind to her—then cruel. Why on earth had he brought her to America if only he meant to send her back? A hundred thoughts went through her head, and then turned to apathy. The baby cried and she scarcely heard. She went to the bathroom, glanced into the mirror, and saw bruises all over her face.

"Who on earth needs me?" she wondered. "The one person I came to America for doesn't need me, so why go on living?"

She picked up the rope she used for hanging the baby's diapers, tied it around her neck, and climbed onto the toilet seat.

Lee came in from the living room. A glance at Marina and his face became horribly twisted. Even at that moment he could not control his rage. He hit her across the face.

"Don't ever do that again," he said. "Only the most terrible fools try *that*."

"I can't go on this way, Alka. I don't want to go on living."

Lee lifted her off the toilet seat and carried her gently to bed. He went back to the baby in the living room, with the door open so he could watch Marina. Then he sat beside her on the bed and suddenly stroked her hair.

"Forgive me," he said. "I didn't mean to do what I did. It's your fault. You saw what a mood I was in. Why did you make me so mad?"

"I only tried to do to myself what *you* tried to do to me. I'm sick of it, Alka. Every day we fight, and for no reason. We fight over things so tiny, normal people wouldn't speak of them at all."

Lee lay down and took her in his arms. "I never thought you'd take it so hard. Pay no attention to me now. You know I can't hold myself back."

They both began to cry like babies. "Try to understand," he begged. "You're wrong sometimes, too. Try to be quiet when you can." He started kissing her as though he were in a frenzy. "For God's sake, forgive me. I'll never, ever do it again. I'll try and change if you'll only help me."

"But why, Alka, why do you do it?"

"Because I love you. I can't stand it when you make me mad."

They made love the whole night long, and Lee told Marina again and again that she was "the best woman" for him, sexually and in every other way. For Marina, it was one of the best nights sexually. And for the next few days, Lee seemed calmer, as if his attempt to strangle Marina was a substitute for killing Walker.[19]

Although Oswald had left home that Saturday morning dressed for work, he hadn't gone there. Nor did he tell Marina he was going elsewhere. He may have been hoping the pistol would come before Walker left for Miami.[20] In all probability, Lee was checking the post office for the pistol he was expecting. McMillan speculates that when he returned home at dinner time, Lee felt frustrated that the pistol had not arrived and took out his frustration on Marina.[21]

A Request to Move

As happened so often, the calm that followed the storm on February 23 was short-lived. The arguments and beatings resumed in a few days. The violence was so persistent that the neighbors had been complaining for weeks to the building manager. A window in the Oswald's unit was broken when Lee, in anger after an argument with Marina, forced his way back in. One tenant told the building manager that she feared for Marina's life.[22]

Finally, the building's owner told Lee that the fighting must stop, or they must move.

Without informing Marina about the ultimatum, Lee decided to move. He was truthful in telling her that the cost of another unit he had found was $8 cheaper per month and that she would like it better.[23] On Saturday, March 2, using baby June's stroller to carry their few belongings, the Oswalds moved to a furnished, second floor apartment, less than two blocks away at 214 West Neely Street.[24] It had a balcony, reminding Marina of Minsk, and for Lee there was a tiny room[25] that, by making bookshelves, he converted into a study. Lee told Marina she was not to enter the room or disturb any of his papers.[26]

The cramped study became Lee's closed-door planning room. Therein he assembled schedules for bus routes serving the Walker residence, photographs of the house and nearby areas, the location of windows, estimates of distances to those windows, and a description of his escape route.[27] The data-gathering required multiple trips to the Walker house. An initial trip to reconnoiter and other trips to observe more closely and to photograph were probably necessary. He needed information about Walker's habits, and perhaps even a rehearsal for traveling to the residence, secreting himself, and escaping.

One trip was made on Sunday, March 10, no more than a week after the move to Neely Street. On that trip, Oswald photographed the rear of Walker's house and a railroad right-of-way. Since Oswald possessed a set of small binoculars, his view could be enhanced without approaching too closely.[28]

By then the Walker plan was changing, not only because Walker had left Dallas on February 28. The pistol Lee had ordered on January 27 had not arrived. Lee began searching catalogs and magazines for information about rifles. Firing a rifle from a concealed location could greatly reduce the chance of being detected, apprehended, or killed. On March 12, using the fictitious name A. Hidell once again, Oswald ordered from Klein's Sporting Goods in Chicago a 6.5-mm Mannlicher-Carcano rifle with a telescopic sight. Accompanying the order was a $21.45 postal money order that he obtained that day in the name of A.J. Hidell.[29] The plan now was not to be caught.

But how does one convey a rifle across town if one cannot, as in Oswald's case, drive an automobile? Marina told her biographer that, after the rifle arrived, Lee would practice with it at a secluded spot by carrying it under his raincoat, regardless of the weather and traveling by bus.[30]

Reading, Writing, Revising, and Reflecting

Nearly a month was to elapse from the time Lee ordered the rifle on March 12 until Walker would be back in Dallas and the plan could be executed. What else was on Lee's mind? Marina recalls that after the move to Neely Street, Lee read *All Quiet on the Western Front* and some materials of Leon Trotsky.[31]

Finding privacy in the tiny Neely Street room that Marina called his "little closet," a new calm came over Lee. The hitting stopped. He found joy in baby June, although little in Marina. There were even picnics in the park and ice cream. He could concentrate serenely on what was to come.[32]

Walker was not to return to Dallas until April 8. It might be weeks after that before the opportune moment arrived. By coincidence, the pistol and the rifle were both shipped to Oswald on March 20, 1963—one to his postal box and the other to a depot of REA Express.[33] Lee probably retrieved them by March 25.[34]

In the interim that followed, as Marina recalled, Oswald spent many hours cleaning the rifle and practicing with it. On one occasion, he wrapped the rifle in a raincoat, and she accompanied him with June to a bus stop where he boarded a bus marked Love Field.[35] He had told her there was a field at which to practice near the airport.[36]

Maintaining relations with the Socialist Workers Party also remained important to Oswald. On March 24, he again wrote the party—this time enclosing a newspaper clipping that he deemed important.[37] We do not know what the clipping was. It may well have been an extensive interview with Fidel Castro that the *Dallas Times-Herald* reprinted on March 22 from the Paris newspaper *Le Monde*. The article quoted Castro as saying:

> What support did we get during the blockade last October when we were on the edge of a major conflict? Where were the mass demonstrations in our favor? ... Only the Venezuelans reacted then. But the big parties that call themselves Revolutionary did not budge. They are not Revolutionaries but bureaucrats.... I can not approve Khrushchev's promising Kennedy to withdraw his missiles without the slightest reference to the indispensable agreement of the Cuban government. It is true that it was a matter of Soviet missiles which were beyond our direct control. But they were on Cuban soil and nothing should have been decided without consulting us.[38]

Perhaps Oswald thought it was something that the Socialist Workers Party may not have seen.

The *Dallas Times-Herald* was an important resource for Oswald. It gave almost daily coverage both to Walker and the Cuban conflict. On Tuesday, March 26, for example, the *Times-Herald* reported that Walker had faced pickets in Wichita, Kansas. On March 27, the paper's front page headlined, "Russians Protest Cuba Raid." On March 29, the paper reported a Walker speech in Amarillo, Texas, saying that American media were blacking out his speeches. A March 30 story showed him in Albuquerque, New Mexico, claiming communist subversion in the United States. The article also noted that Walker's Midnight Ride would soon end.

Marina remembers Lee reading a biography of Leon Trotsky in the weeks before Walker returned from his Midnight Ride.[39] Trotsky had been a prolific writer. We do not know which of Trotsky's writings Oswald read. Books about him and his writings were available in many public libraries in 1962 and 1963. The latest of Isaac Deutscher's three-volume biography of Trotsky was published in 1963. In the same year, Random House published *The Basic Writings of Trotsky*, a compilation of Trotsky's writings already available from other sources.

At the top of Trotsky's list of enemies were fascists. To Oswald, Walker was an American fascist. For Trotsky, one of the historic failings of European communists had been their failure to recognize the danger of fascism and stop Hitler before he gained power in Germany.[40] In 1932 Trotsky warned, "If we allow the Fascists to seize power ... [a]ll revolutionary plans ... will prove to be only wretched and disgraceful twaddle...."[41]

In the 1930s Trotsky had given inspiration to the Fourth International. The purpose of the Fourth International was to counter the Soviet Comintern and to invigorate and democratize Marxism worldwide. In the Transitional Program for the Fourth International, Trotsky had suggested:

> [I]t is imperative to propagate the necessity of creating workers' groups for self-defense.... It is imperative wherever possible, beginning with youth groups, to organize groups for self-defense, to drill and acquaint them with the use of arms....
>
> Only with the help of such systematic, persistent, indefatigable, courageous, agitational and organizational work ... is it possible ... to train detachments of heroic fighters capable of setting an example to all toilers; to inflict a series of tactical defeats upon the armed thugs of counterrevolution; to raise the self-confidence of the exploited and oppressed; to compromise Fascism in the eyes of the petty bourgeoisie and pave the road for the conquest of power by the proletariat.
>
> When the proletariat wills it, it will find the road and the means to arming.[42]

In truth, Trotsky might not have approved of assassinating Walker. In 1911, Trotsky had opposed assassination as a political instrument. Anarchists of the nineteenth and early twentieth centuries had promoted killings as a form of "propaganda by deed." Trotsky, on the other hand, regarded assassination as a self-defeating political tool. He wrote:

> The anarchist prophets ... can argue all they want about the elevating and stimulating influence of terrorist acts on the masses.... But [when] the smoke from the explosion clears away ... the successor of the murdered minister makes his appearance, life again settles into the old ... [and] the state is much richer in the means of physical destruction and mechanical repression than are the terrorist groups.
>
> *****
>
> Social Democracy rejects all methods and means that have as their goal to artificially force the development of society and to substitute chemical preparations for the insufficient revolutionary strength of the proletariat.[43]

Trotsky was even more explicit in 1939 after Herschel Grinszpan had assassinated a Nazi official in the German Embassy in Paris:

> We Marxists consider the tactic of individual terror inexpedient in the tasks of the liberating struggle of the proletariat.... A single isolated hero can not replace the masses.
>
> *****
>
> In the moral sense, although not for his mode of action, Grinszpan may serve as an example for every young revolutionist. Our open moral solidarity with Grinszpan gives us an added right to say to all other would-be Grinszpans, to all those capable of self-sacrifice in the struggle against despotism and bestiality: Seek another road![44]

Yet, Walker did not hold public office. He was no longer a part of the government. He did not yet have "the means of physical destruction and mechanical repression" of government to suppress the masses. Perhaps, assassinating Walker did not violate Trotsky's admonition.

We cannot be sure how Oswald would have perceived Trotsky if he had read Trotsky's works extensively. Yet we can be confident that if Oswald had found support in Trotsky, he would have embraced the supportive interpretation. If he had not found support, he would have followed his own conscience and concepts.

Preparing for Fame

On Friday, March 29, a shock befell Oswald. His supervisor told him that, effective April 6, he was fired. The official reason was inadequate production. But there were other factors: an increasingly slovenly appearance, poor relationships with fellow employees, and reading the Russian humor magazine *Krokodil* on the job site. Perhaps realizing that after April 6 he would be free full time to pursue Walker, Lee's reaction to his supervisor and colleagues was one of outward equanimity.

For more than a week, Lee did not tell Marina what had happened with his job. On Saturday afternoon, March 30, perhaps hoping to be seen by his former employer and fellow workers, he placed himself on a street corner a few minutes' walk from Jaggars-Chiles-Stovall with a Viva Cuba placard around his neck and handed out Fair Play for Cuba Committee literature.[45] The next day, he wrote to the Committee reporting what he'd done for the cause and requesting more literature.[46]

On that same day, Sunday, March 31, a most remarkable event occurred, one that spoke to Oswald's pride in trying to kill Walker. In the late afternoon, while Marina was in the back yard hanging diapers, Lee appeared on their balcony dressed in black trousers and a black shirt. He held in his hands his rifle, one copy each of *The Militant* and *The Worker*, and a camera. Strapped to his belt was the pistol he had received a week before. He came down the stairs to the yard.[47]

Priscilla McMillan describes in this way what happened:

> On his face was an expression of sublime contentment. Marina's eyes grew large and round. The diapers fell from her hand. She broke into peals of laughter.
>
> "Why are you rigged out like that?"....
>
> "Take my picture," Lee said. He was serious.
>
> Marina stopped laughing. "Are you crazy? I've never taken a picture in my life. I am busy, and I don't know how. Take it yourself."
>
> He showed her how to do it.... She snapped the shutter, he reset it, and she snapped it again. It was over in a minute....
>
> [Before] going back inside, she asked him why he had the picture taken with guns, of all stupid things? He explained that he was going to send the picture to the *Militant* to show that he was "ready for anything."[48]

Photograph taken by Marina Oswald on March 31, 1963, of Lee with a pistol on his belt and holding a rifle along with a copy of *The Militant* and *The Worker* (National Archives).

McMillan believes that the decision to be photographed may have been prompted by a letter that the

Militant had published on March 11 headed "Dallas, Texas" and signed with the initials "L.H." Among other things, the lengthy, six-paragraph letter criticized *The Militant* for "neglecting any serious discussion of the 'Reform' movement within the Democratic Party." McMillan believed that the letter was written by Oswald.[49] She went on to observe:

> Marina did not know it, of course, but Lee had a special reason for sending his picture to the *Militant*. In the photograph he was holding two newspapers, the *Worker* of March 24, the one that had most recently arrived, and, thrust forward a little more prominently, the *Militant* of March 11, the issue containing the letter from Dallas that was signed "L.H." Hoping to go down in history, Lee wanted the *Militant* to know exactly whom it had the honor of publishing, and that the author had meant every word when he said that he "questioned" the system. He was, indeed, "ready for anything."
>
> "What a weird one you are!" Marina exclaimed. "Who on earth needs a photograph like that?"
>
> Lee probably developed the photographs at work the following day, April 1. He handed one of them to Marina and told her to keep it for the baby. On it he had written: "For Junie from Papa."
>
> "Good God!" Marina was appalled. "Why would Junie want a picture with guns?"
>
> "To remember Papa by sometime."[50]

There were at least three different photos, striking three slightly different poses. On April 5, he sent one to George de Mohrenschildt.[51] On it he wrote "For my friend George from Lee Oswald."[52] At the risk of incriminating himself, Lee was saying to his friend that his own passionate words about Marxism and against the capitalist system were not just idle parlor talk. As for incriminating himself in the forthcoming assault on Walker, perhaps he was preparing the "Who would be so dumb as to do that?" defense.

Lee also sent one of the photos to *The Militant*.[53] His primary purpose, Marina said Lee told her, was to inform the newspaper that he was "ready to do anything."[54] He was seeking approval of the Socialist Workers Party, *The Militant's* parent organization. The Socialist Workers Party, which he had pursued so assiduously, had long embraced Trotsky's views. Lee was the "heroic fighter" whom Trotsky deemed essential.

Not surprisingly, compliments were not forthcoming from either the Party or *The Militant*. Instead, the reaction at *The Militant* was one of bewilderment and fear. Sylvia Weinstein, a handler of subscriptions for *The Militant*, remembered that, when the photo from Oswald arrived, she thought the man in the photo must be "kookie." Nearly thirty years later, she told Gus Russo that she believed Oswald must be "really dumb and totally naive."[55]

When Farrell Dobbs, General Secretary of the Socialist Workers Party, became aware of the photo, he thought Oswald must be a weirdo, acting out a fantasy, or a provocateur.[56] He told Weinstein to bring him any similar materials from Oswald. Dobbs ultimately gave the materials to the party's attorney, William Kunstler, after Oswald was arrested briefly in New Orleans during the summer of 1963.[57]

23

Action and Exit

Once the backyard photographs were developed and mailed, Lee's tensions mounted. At least a week must pass from March 31 when the photos were taken before Oswald could have access to Walker. Marina remembered Lee's talking frequently in his sleep in English, something that had not occurred since mid–February.[1]

Though Lee had yet to tell Marina he had lost his job, his coworkers knew that Saturday, April 6, would be his last day. When coworker Dennis Ofstein asked him what he would do, Lee mentioned "he could always go back to the Soviet Union, and sort of laughed about it."[2]

On the afternoon of Monday, April 1, Lee came home from work as usual. He had been enrolled in a typing class since January 14, a week before the federal criminal charges were dismissed against Walker. Typing classes were from 6:15 to 7:15 p.m. on Mondays, Tuesdays, and Thursdays. He had stopped attending on March 28 but did not tell Marina.[3]

Lee's attendance had, in fact, been sporadic, but the course had given him an excuse to leave home three nights a week. That excuse facilitated his surveillance of Walker's residence and the area around it. It is likely the same occurred on April 1.

The next night, April 2, at Ruth Paine's invitation, Marina, Lee, and June had dinner at the Paine residence with Ruth and her husband, Michael.[4] The relationship between Ruth Paine and Marina was to be crucial in the events leading up to November 22. It was in Ruth Paine's garage that Lee ultimately stored the rifle with which he killed the president.

In early 1963, Ruth and Marina had something else in common besides their desire to bolster each other's new languages and young children: deteriorating marriages. Ruth Paine's own marriage had already withered. She and her husband had separated, although they maintained a social relationship. Ruth wanted a companion. Marina needed support in her relationship with Lee, and the Russian community had forsaken her.

April 2 was the first time that Ruth, Ruth's husband Michael, Marina, and Lee were together. For Michael Paine, that first meeting with Lee was surprising, perhaps shocking. Michael's father had numerous friends who were communists. As Michael recalled in 1993 to author Gus Russo, his father's friends were "mostly intellectually interesting people." But Lee was different. He wanted Michael to know that he was a revolutionary.[5]

Michael wouldn't "put ... together" the dinner table discussion that evening about General Walker—whom the Paines did not like—and the shooting at General Walker eight days later. What both Ruth and Michael did see, however, was that Lee treated Marina with total disrespect. Although Michael could not understand the words that Lee spoke in Russian to Marina, he could understand the tone of voice.[6]

After that April 2 dinner, Ruth felt even closer to Marina. At age thirty, Ruth was nearly a decade older than Marina. Their conversations had become candid enough for Ruth to know that Marina and Lee's marriage was collapsing. Marina had told Ruth that Lee wanted to send her back to Russia without him. Marina regarded that as a de facto divorce. She told Ruth that she wanted to remain in the United States.[7]

On April 7, Ruth drafted a letter to Marina in Russian. In it, Ruth said, "I want to invite you to move here and live with me both now and later when the baby is born. I don't know how things are for you at home with your husband.... It is, of course, your affair, and you have to decide what is better.... But I want to say that you have a choice. When you wish, for days, weeks, months, you could move here."[8] The letter was never sent, but the sentiment persisted. In late September, Ruth Paine was to become Marina's safe haven from Lee's focus on political action and physical abuse, and for the delivery of their second child.

Lee's mind, of course, was elsewhere. Although Edwin Walker's last speech on the Midnight Ride was to be Wednesday, April 3, in Los Angeles, Lee could not be certain when the general would return to Dallas. Nor can we be sure what Lee did—besides work—from April 3 through April 6. Records of Jaggars-Chiles-Stovall do show that he worked a full day on each date and received a clean-up paycheck.

Marina remembers Sunday, April 7, with some particularity. She recalls that Lee left their apartment with his rifle.[9] He would not tell her until after his attempt to assassinate Walker that he had taken the rifle to a secluded wooded area about a half mile from Walker's house and hidden it there. The area for secreting the rifle was probably the area near some railroad tracks that he had photographed a month earlier. The photographs served to preserve his memory of where the favored hiding place lay. The strategy and the photographs bespeak careful planning and numerous trips after work or on weekends to Walker's neighborhood.

On Monday, April 8, Lee dressed again as if going to work. He had yet to tell Marina he'd lost his job. He visited the Texas Employment Commission, came home for supper, left immediately afterward, but came home sooner than if he had gone to a typing class. Walker was due home that evening, and Lee may well have gone to the Turtle Creek area to check Walker's house. Walker remembered his own arrival as having been "in the late afternoon or break of evening."[10]

On that Monday, tucked away in a lengthy article about politically conservative organizations in Dallas, the *Morning News* carried this paragraph about the general's house:

> Walker headquarters on Turtle Creek Boulevard [his home] is still a going thing.... Three women volunteers work there nearly every day.... Also squadron a of men and women will respond for hurry calls to help on mailing and letter writing.[11]

The article reported that Walker received one hundred letters per day and that a group called Friends of General Walker raised money to publish his speeches. Also operating from Walker's home was the American Eagle Publishing Company, a small enterprise with a subscription list of about eight hundred people.

Even though Walker had been away for five weeks, his home was still a beehive of activity. It would be difficult to shoot the general there during the day without being identified and caught. The plan, then, must be to wait for nightfall.

On Tuesday, April 9, Lee told Marina that the day was a holiday, but he was going to work to secure his paycheck.[12] Since Walker had returned to Dallas and Lee was away from home for the entire day, one could speculate again that Oswald was surveilling the Walker house.

Shooting the Fascist

Wednesday, April 10, was the day for action. Marina remembered Lee as pensive and sad when he awoke. With tears, he told her that he had lost his job. "I liked that work so much," he said. "But probably the FBI came and asked about me, and the boss just didn't want to keep someone the FBI was interested in."[13]

A while later he left in his gray suit. The weather that day was blistering hot. The previous day had set a record of 97 degrees for that date. At 3:00 p.m. on Wednesday, the temperature was 94. At 8:00 p.m. it was 82 degrees.[14] All day Oswald must have been waiting, watching, and sweltering. But the suit served a purpose. With his suit jacket off, once he recovered the rifle from its hiding place, he could cover the rifle with the jacket and carry it unnoticed to Walker's house.

Behind and to the southeast of the Walker house was a Mormon church. An alley ran north and south, directly behind the house. The alley led into a church parking lot between the church and the house.[15] A lattice fence about 120 feet directly behind Walker's house separated Walker's property from the alley.[16]

That evening of April 10, a meeting was in progress at the Mormon church. Neatly dressed, Oswald could mix inconspicuously with the congregants as they approached the church or entered the parking lot. From the alley or parking lot, he could see Walker's house and study.[17]

At 9:00 p.m. on April 10, Walker was alone in the study at the rear of his home. The lights were on, windows closed, and air conditioner operating. Walker described the next moments in this way:

> I was sitting behind a desk facing out from a corner, with my head over a pencil and paper working on my income tax return when I heard a blast and a crack right over my head.... I thought that possibly somebody had thrown a firecracker, that it exploded right over my head through the window right behind me. Since there is a church back there, often there are children playing back there. Then I looked around and saw that the screen was not out ... and this couldn't possibly happen, so I got up and walked around the desk and looked back where I was sitting and I saw a hole in the wall.... I went upstairs and got a pistol and came back down and went out the back door, taking a look to see what might have happened.[18]

Walker could see nothing that he could relate to the attack, although, as he was walking downstairs with his pistol, he could see a car "at the bottom of the church alley just making a turn onto Turtle Creek." He believed that it had come from the church parking lot.[19] As he returned to his house, he noticed that a window in his study was shattered and that his right forearm was bleeding. He called the police.

When the police arrived, Walker helped them identify a location in the lattice fence from which the shot could have been fired. According to Vincent Bugliosi, examining the broken window, they noticed that the bullet had probably "struck the 'upper portion' of the 'window frame near the center locking device' as it smashed through both the screen and the window, thus deflecting the bullet just enough to save the general's life."[20] Inside the house, police found the remnants of a damaged bullet. They told newspaper reporters that it was a 30–06.[21] It was an easy shot in which chance had intervened to save Walker and cause police to misidentify the assault weapon.

Flight

Oswald had fled. He had not remained to see whether Walker had been hit. People leaving the church made it expedient to leave quickly.[22] There were a variety of routes Oswald could take: east into the church parking lot and then onto an unmarked alley that intersected near where he had been shooting and led to Turtle Creek Boulevard; east or west onto Avondale; or south from his firing spot and along an alley that led to Irving Street.[23] Oswald must have considered them all as he planned his shooting. If, as Walker saw, a car was leaving the church parking lot to enter Turtle Creek Boulevard, a wiser course was to go in the opposite direction either onto Avondale or down the alley that led to Irvington.[24]

Marina told the Warren Commission that she learned from Lee that "he ran several kilometers and then took the bus."[25] As we are dealing with an interpreter's English translation of her Russian, not to mention a somewhat distant memory, we can be confident only that Lee moved quickly until he reached a bus.[26]

Lee later told Marina that by the time he heard the wail of a police car, he was far away.[27] From various interviews with Marina, it appears that he carried the rifle onto a bus, got off the bus, hid the rifle in a different place from where he had put it on Sunday, and took another bus home. His suit coat must have done its job of concealing the rifle.[28]

A Goodbye Note

When Lee was not home at his usual time after his typing class, Marina became concerned. Priscilla Johnson McMillan reports her concern in this way:

> For months he had been tense, preoccupied, ready, like his rifle, "to go off." … Now it turned out that he had been fired. Marina sensed … that this element on top of the rest made up a recipe for danger….
>
> *****
>
> She paced anxiously from room to room…. On an impulse, about ten o'clock, she opened the door to her husband's study. There on the desk she saw a key with a sheet of paper lying under it. At the sight of the key, Marina felt a thud inside: Lee was never coming back.[29]

The key and the piece of paper were ominous. On the paper, written in Russian, were a set of instructions:

> 1. Here is the key to the post office box which is located in the main post office, downtown on Ervay Street…. There you will find our mailbox. I paid for the mailbox last month so you needn't worry about it.
> 2. Send information about what happened to me to the Embassy [the Soviet Embassy in Washington] and also send newspaper clippings (if there's anything about me in the papers). I think the Embassy will come quickly to your aid once they know everything.
> 3. I paid our rent on the second so don't worry about it.
>
> *****
>
> 6. You can either throw out my clothing or give it away. *Do not keep it.* As for my personal papers (both military papers and papers from the factory), I prefer that you keep them.

7. Certain of my papers are in the small blue suitcase.
*****
10. I left you as much money as I could, $60 on the second of the month, and you and Junie can live for two months on $10 a week.
11. If I am alive and taken prisoner, the city jail is at the end of the bridge we always used to cross when we went to town.[30]

The letter and the money Oswald left for Marina speak clearly to his expectations before the shooting. Author Albert H. Newman has calculated that Marina would have had ninety-four dollars when she added a yet due paycheck to the sixty dollars Lee left on April 2. He had paid the month's rent and purchased groceries for a week.[31] Lee expected her to survive on that and friends until she could return to the Soviet Union with the help of the Soviet Embassy. As Lee saw it, the backyard photo and his papers would be what Junie, the new baby, and history could remember him by.

Newman calculated also that Lee would have had approximately two hundred dollars if needed for escape.[32] When he wrote the note, Lee accepted the possibility that he would be either killed or captured. The money he retained would serve little purpose in jail—not likely to be enough to purchase a bond or pay for a lawyer in a homicide case. If he escaped, the money he retained for himself was enough to take him to Mexico and to Cuba.

Returning to Safety

Lee did escape. Instead of leaving Marina, he came home. Marina had been right when she reunited with him in November. He needed her.

It was 11:30 p.m. when he made his appearance. McMillan's description continues:

> … Lee walked in, white, covered with sweat, his eyes glittering.
> "What happened?" Marina asked.
> "I shot Walker." He was out of breath and could barely get out the words.
> "Did you kill him?"
> "I don't know."
> "My God. The police will be here any minute. What did you do with the rifle?"
> "Buried it."
> *****
> "Don't ask any questions." Lee switched on the radio. There was no news. "And for God's sake don't bother me." He peeled off his clothing and hurled himself on the bed. There he lay, spreadeagled, on his stomach….

Marina could not sleep. She expected the police. McMillan's interpretation of Marina's account proceeds:

> She glanced over at Lee … and she felt sorry for him. She felt a pity almost physical in its closeness and fear of what the police would do to him. "There will be time" she thought, "to scold him and punish him later. But not now. Not while he is in danger."
> An idea flickered across her mind. She would go to the police and tell them, in sign language or some other way, what her husband had done. She put the thought aside.
> *****
> She had grown up in a world where police spies are everywhere and it is your duty by law to inform on anyone, even the person closest to you, if you know he has committed a crime…. In

> such an environment the only honor, the only way of keeping faith, is never, ever, to inform. The law says you must; Marina's private morality says you must not.
>
> *****
>
> So Marina did not go to the police, or consider it for more than a moment or two.... [H]er personal morality stressed loyalty to her husband above everything. And this loyalty was to expose her to a crushing sense of guilt when many people told her that if only she had gone to the police "after Walker," a later, lethal event would not have happened.[33]

For Marina, Lee's shooting at General Walker was frightening. For Lee, it was a confidence builder. He had shot and not been caught. The first news that his bullet had missed came over the radio the next morning.[34] In Thursday morning's *Dallas Morning News,* a front-page headline read, "Close Call: Rifleman Takes Shot at Walker." But the police had not a clue as to who did it. The police had misidentified the ammunition and therefore the weapon.

Reading the article, Lee said to Marina, "They say I had a .30 caliber bullet when I didn't at all. They've got the bullet and the rifle all wrong."[35]

He laughed at the speculation that the gunman had come and left by car. "Americans are so spoiled!" Marina recalls him saying. "It never occurs to them that you might use your own two legs. They always think you have a *car*.... And here *I* am sitting *here!*"[36]

The *Morning News* article suggested also that men in an unlicensed car might have staked out the Walker residence on Monday night. The article reported that a teenage witness, Kirk Coleman, said he saw two cars leave the scene shortly after the shooting.[37]

Oswald's trajectory from defector to activist to assassin would eventually be chartable. But for now, fate had saved Walker. Oswald's careful planning had not succeeded, but his escape had been total.

Despite his elation over the misidentified bullet, Lee could not believe his shot didn't find its mark. Marina told McMillan that over and over again, Lee said, "It was such an easy shot. How on earth did I miss?" He decided that Walker had moved unexpectedly at the last second.[38] The truth was it took no more than a minuscule error to permit the window frame to intervene.

Marina was both frightened and mystified. Why did he do it? she asked. Walker was a fascist, Lee responded. Marina said that made no difference. That did not justify murder. Walker had a family. Lee said, "He lives alone. If someone had killed Hitler in time, many lives would have been saved."[39]

Marina thought that Lee, although scornful of the police, was also fearful. The night of the shooting, Marina remembered, Lee "suffered anxiety attacks in his sleep. He shook all over from head to toe four times at intervals of a half hour or so, but without waking up." The anxiety attacks continued into Friday night's sleep.[40]

What is the significance of the attempt on Walker? The Warren Commission believed it showed a capacity to kill.[41] But it evidenced much more. It showed a capacity to kill for a political purpose. It showed also a willingness to abandon everything for a political goal—marriage, obligations as a father, and, if necessary, his own life. And what could be gained? If Walker were killed, his leadership of a growing political faction would be terminated. If Lee were not caught, self-satisfaction would be won. If apprehended and charged or killed, there might be fame, martyrdom, perhaps a place on the big stage of history.

Yet owing to the manner in which the attempt failed, it was not attributed to Oswald until he himself, was dead. Given that, Priscilla McMillan's assessment may be best: "[B]y far the greatest legacy Lee carried out of the Walker attempt was the conviction that he was invulnerable."[42] If not a sense of invincibility, Oswald did enjoy the freedom of knowing there was nothing to link him to the Walker attempt. And therefore, nothing to prevent from further pursuing his place in history.

Fear and Exodus

Marina worried that Lee's anxiety would not translate to abandoning another attempt to kill Walker. She pressed him to promise not to try again. "I promise," he said. But Marina did not believe him.[43]

Her worry would only grow. On Saturday, Lee went to where he had hidden the rifle, and returned with it concealed in a raincoat. About an hour after returning with the rifle, Marina saw Lee thumbing through the notes he had made to plan the killing and the photographs he had taken of Walker's house. "I had it so well figured out," he exclaimed.[44]

Marina was terrified; Lee had not given up. And the police might come and find the papers, the photos. They were evidence. She told him to destroy them. A few minutes later she saw Lee standing near the toilet, crumpling papers, and lighting them with matches. But he did not destroy them all. His philosophical writings remained, as did a few photographs of the back of Walker's house and the area where he had originally hidden the rifle.[45] Nor did he dispose of the pistol and rifle. As Marina feared, he had not forsaken his goal.

Concerned for her own safety and not trusting Lee, Marina persisted. She appealed to reason. She pointed out how shooting Walker because of his beliefs had contradicted Lee's own belief in freedom of speech. He had praised it so highly when they were in Russia.

She threatened him. She said she would keep the note he had left for her and she had concealed. She would take it to the police if he tried again.[46] Then she tried concern for family: "Even if you didn't think of me, you ought to have thought of Junie."

"I did," he said coldly. "I left you money.... The Russians here like you. They'd have helped."[47]

The Russians who were most attentive were George and Jeanne de Mohrenschildt. That Saturday evening—the day before Easter and three days after the shooting—the de Mohrenschildts arrived with an Easter bunny for Junie. As they came up the stairway, George blurted out in Russian, "Hey Lee, how come you missed?"[48]

It was his provocative—perhaps intoxicated—way of probing. Neither Marina nor Lee was certain that one of them had not let their secret slip. Had Lee revealed to George that he *wanted* to kill Walker? Could George be thinking of the backyard photo Lee had sent him on April 5.[49]

With their backs to the stairwell as the de Mohrenschildts made their way up, Marina and Lee looked at each other in horror. "Shh," Lee said to George. "Junie's sleeping." But George wanted to talk about Walker. After a few more words about the incident, the conversation shifted to other matters.[50]

This was the last time the de Mohrenschildts were to have contact with the Oswalds. On April 19, George and Jeanne went to New York and Washington in preparation for leaving Dallas on May 1. George was to begin a business venture in Haiti. Lee and Marina were losing their most reliable support in Dallas. No one in Dallas was like the de Mohrenschildts.

Out of work, Lee had time on his hands. Marina feared he would try again for Walker. To Marina's plea that he should sell the rifle because "We need the money for food," Lee replied, "Money evaporates like water. I'll keep it."[51]

On Sunday morning, April 21, dressed in his gray suit with pistol at his waist, Lee started toward their apartment door. "Nixon is coming," Marina remembered Lee saying. "I want to go and have a look.... I am going to go out and find out if there will be an appropriate opportunity and if there is I will use the pistol."[52]

Former Vice President Richard Nixon was not coming to Dallas that day. Indeed, he had no plan to do so. Oswald could have read that morning in the *Dallas Morning News* that the previous day Nixon had given a speech in which he had called for armed action against Castro by Cuban exiles.[53] Historian Richard Reiman has speculated that Oswald may not have noticed the Washington dateline on the article and believed Nixon had spoken in Dallas.[54] In any event, that front page article may well have brought Nixon to mind.

But another article might have been even more provocative. On page twelve of the *Morning News*, a headline screamed, "U.S. Decides on Slayings, Says Castro." The article went on to report a Castro speech on April 20, the second anniversary of defeating Cuban exiles at the Bay of Pigs. "The U.S. has abandoned plans for a second invasion of Cuba in favor of a plot to assassinate Cuban leaders," Castro said. If killing Cuban leaders was a substitute for war, why not make another try at Walker, or even Nixon, if he were there? Wasn't it fair game?

Whatever Lee's intent on April 21, Marina was frightened. She lured Lee into the bathroom. She claims she kept him there with threats, tears, argument, and her own body force until he relented. She even took the pistol away from him.[55]

Reflecting on the incident nearly a year later, Marina told the Warren Commission that Lee was probably trying to test her or was engaging in a sadistic joke.[56] Is it possible, however, that Lee's statement about Nixon was a subterfuge—that what he really had in mind was tracking down Walker, killing him with a pistol, and risking his own capture or being killed?

For Marina, there could be no question after the Nixon comment that they must leave Dallas. Lee must be removed to a place where he could not easily gain access to Walker and where the chance of Lee's being arrested seemed lessened.

The place was New Orleans: Lee's birthplace, a place where he had gone to school and where relatives still lived. Marina urged the move to New Orleans. Finally, Lee agreed.[57] He would precede Marina to New Orleans. Once he had found work and a place to live, she would follow with June.

By Wednesday morning, April 24, Lee had packed a duffle bag and suitcases and was ready to leave for New Orleans. What he valued most—his writings, his shortwave radio, his pistol, and his rifle—were with him.[58]

Four days earlier, Ruth Paine had arranged with Marina that they would spend part of April 24 together. When Ruth arrived that day at the Oswald apartment, she was amazed to see that Lee had three packed bags. Marina had given no indication that she and Lee might be leaving Dallas.

Lee and Marina explained that he was going to New Orleans to look for work. He said that he had lost his job, he had family in New Orleans, where he had been born, and

Marina and June would follow once he found work. He asked Ruth to drive him to the bus station.[59]

At the station Lee bought two tickets—one for himself and one for Marina to use once he had found a job and a place for them to live. At that point, it occurred to Ruth that she could be even more helpful. Marina could live with her until Lee sent for them. Since the Neely Street apartment lacked a phone, Lee could more easily reach Marina at Ruth's. As further help, Ruth would later drive Marina, Junie, and their belongings to New Orleans—a far easier trip for a pregnant woman than going by bus.

With that agreed upon, Lee returned Marina's ticket for a refund and gave some money to Marina. He checked his baggage at the bus station. All then returned to Neely Street where Lee loaded Marina and June's clothes, a crib, playpen, stroller, and some dishes into Ruth's car. At about 4 p.m., Ruth drove with Marina and June to Ruth's home in Irving, Texas. There Marina remained as Ruth's friend and companion for 15 days.

Lee's bus did not depart until the evening. He waited at Neely Street until it was time to go to the station.

24

The Big Easy

It was the morning of April 25, 1963, when Lee's bus pulled into the station in New Orleans.[1] New Orleans had once been home. This time he saw it as a way station. Edwin Walker was in Dallas, and America did not offer a promising future for a Marxist defector to the Soviet Union. He needed an accepting country in which to forge his place in history.

In Lee's eyes, Fidel Castro was building for Cuba a model society. Thousands of Soviet troops and advisers were there to assure Castro's control. Lee's knowledge of Russian might make him a valued communicator with the Soviets. His Marine experience might even make him a trainer or a guerrilla with Che Guevera.

The Big Easy would not prove as easy a way station to Cuba as it had been to Russia four years earlier. When Lee sought defection in 1959, he had stayed only three days in New Orleans before embarking unencumbered on the journey that would take him to Moscow.

Now he had a wife, a fourteen-month-old daughter, and another child due in October. Marina's request to return to the Soviet Union had not been granted. With a wife and child in tow, he could not arrive in Cuba on a six-day visa—even if such were attainable—slash his wrists, and plead for mercy as he had in the Soviet Union.

Moreover, he needed credibility. He would need to prove to Cuban officials that he wasn't a spy, potential saboteur, or possible assassin. How, then, could he assemble the needed credentials? And he needed money. Unemployment compensation from Texas could fill the gap for a while in New Orleans. But without a job, he would soon be without funds either to support his family or travel to Cuba. Working in New Orleans for a few months was inescapable.

Temporary Quarters

From the New Orleans bus station, Lee called his aunt, Lillian Murret. He had not told her he was coming. The last she knew, Lee was in the Soviet Union.[2] To Lee's surprise, Aunt Lillian responded with warmth and invited him to stay at her home until he could find work and an apartment.

Lillian Murret had a fondness for Lee. It stemmed from his childhood. She had kept him intermittently during his toddler years while his mother Marguerite worked and before Marguerite placed him in the Bethlehem Children's Home.[3] Aunt Lillian had been at times like a second mother to Lee. To the Warren Commission, Lillian recalled him as a cute, friendly, and intelligent preschooler, an early teenager who absorbed himself in books, and a young adult who believed that formal education had nothing to offer.[4]

The Murrets were lifelong New Orleanians. They were a typical post–World War II, middle-class, American Catholic family. They had reared five children during the Depression and war. One was now a housewife. Two were teachers. One son was a dentist; another son was studying to be a Jesuit teacher. The Murrets did not share Lee's political views, but in their company, he found friendship, support, and respect.[5]

Searching for Roots

For Lee, New Orleans was also a link to a wider and unknown family past. On Sunday, April 28, three days after arriving, he asked Aunt Lillian about the Oswald family history. He wanted to know about his father and possible aunts, uncles, and cousins who might be in New Orleans. But Lillian, an aunt in Oswald's maternal line, knew almost nothing about the Oswalds.

Lee began his own search. On his first Sunday in New Orleans, he rode the Lakeview streetcar to a cemetery at the very end of the line. With the help of a cemetery worker, he found his father's grave. Returning to the Murrets' house and with phone book in hand, he called every listed Oswald until he located a relative—an aunt—Hazel Oswald.[6]

Reboarding the streetcar, Lee visited Aunt Hazel. From Aunt Hazel, he learned about Hazel's son and a grandson living in New Orleans. He learned, also, about his deceased grandfather, Harvey Oswald.[7] It was for Harvey that Lee had been given his middle name.[8]

Hazel Oswald also gave Lee a photograph of his father. Although she invited Lee to keep in touch, Lee never called again. Nor did he contact other Oswald relatives.[9] Lee never showed his father's photograph to Marina, and it was never located after Lee's death.[10]

The quest for Oswald family history filled an empty page in a book to which Lee did not want to return. He had not been seeking to build relationships. He simply sought information. Oswald was determined to be his own person and chart his own direction.

Doing so required, as soon as possible, a job and a place of his own in which to live. The rest of Lee's first two weeks in New Orleans were spent mostly pursuing employment and apartment ads in the New Orleans newspapers.

25

Revolution in America

Preceding the ads was the news. The front-page news in the New Orleans *Times-Picayune* during late April and early May 1963, was about revolution—the civil rights revolution. The site was Birmingham, Alabama. The leader was the Reverend Dr. Martin Luther King, Jr. Dr. King said, "If we can crack Birmingham, I am sure we can crack the South. Birmingham is a symbol of segregation for the entire South."[1] The sights and sounds from Birmingham in April and May set the stage for Dallas on November 22.

The opening event was on April 12, 1963, two days after Lee shot at General Walker. Dr. King together with other African American ministers commenced demonstrations to end racial segregation in Birmingham. The demonstrations lasted for nearly a month.

The sounds and scenery in Birmingham were of praying protestors, marching children, police dogs, fire hoses, and massive arrests. The police dogs and fire hoses separated the Black ministers and the Black children from worried, fearful, and angry whites.

Expecting violence, a state court in Birmingham issued an injunction against marching by African American protestors. Robert Kennedy urged restraint by Dr. King. Eight white ministers urged Dr. King to confine protests to the courts.

But Dr. King's course was fixed. On April 11, when Lee Oswald was gloating about the inability of Dallas police to identify Edwin Walker's assailant, Martin Luther King, Jr. told news reporters in Birmingham, "I am prepared to go to jail and stay as long as necessary."[2] On April 16, his fourth day in the Birmingham jail, Dr. King sent a letter to the eight white ministers who had urged restraint.

Dr. King's "Letter from the Birmingham Jail" set forth the basis for selecting Birmingham to highlight the revolution: "There can be no gainsaying of the fact that racial injustice engulfs this community.... There have been more unsolved bombings of Negro homes and churches in Birmingham than in any other city in the nation."

The number, in fact, was staggering: fifty since World War II; seventeen from December 1956 to March 1963; and six between January 1962 and March 1963. Three in 1962 had been at Black churches pastored by civil rights leaders, and three others had been at the homes or businesses of lay advocates.[3]

Dr. King explained why restraint was to be abandoned:

> On the basis of these conditions, Negro leaders sought to negotiate with the city's fathers. But the latter consistently refused to engage in good faith negotiations.... We had no alternative except that of preparing for direct action.... We started having workshops on nonviolence, and we repeatedly asked ourselves the questions, "Are you able to accept blows

without retaliating? Are you able to endure the ordeal of jail?" We decided to schedule our direct-action program for the Easter season, realizing that except for Christmas, this is the main shopping period of the year.[4]

"Letter from Birmingham Jail" set forth a strategy for nonviolent action that had not been articulated by Leon Trotsky or contemplated by Lee Oswald:

> Nonviolent direct action seeks to create a crisis and foster such a tension that a community which constantly refused to negotiate is forced to confront the issue. It seeks to dramatize the issue that it can no longer be ignored.
>
> ****
>
> The purpose of our direct-action program is to create a situation so crisis-packed that it will inevitably open the door to negotiation. Too long has our beloved Southland been bogged down in a tragic effort to live in monologue rather than dialogue.[5]

Dr. King did not reject, however, all premises of a Marxist view of political change:

> History is the long and tragic story of the fact that privileged groups seldom give up their privileges voluntarily.... We know through painful experience that freedom is never voluntarily given by the oppressor; it must be demanded by the oppressed.[6]

Yet Dr. King had an abiding belief that dialogue and nonviolent protests could produce change in America: "I have no despair about the future. I have no fear about the outcome of our struggle in Birmingham, even if our motives are at present misunderstood. We will reach the goal of freedom in Birmingham and all over the nation, because the goal of America is freedom."[7]

In terms of the role of violence in political change, Oswald's and Dr. King's views were polar opposites. King believed that peaceful protest would produce violence by the political opponent. Such violence by the oppressors in a democratic society would produce the political change that the protestors sought.

Violence against civil rights advocates extended beyond Birmingham. On April 24, as Lee was readying to leave Dallas, a white Baltimore postman, William A. Moore, was killed while walking solitarily through Alabama. He was marching to Mississippi carrying a sign of protest against racial segregation and intending to deliver a letter to Mississippi Governor Ross Barnett, a letter urging equal rights for Blacks.[8] On May 1, a group of nine white and Black supporters picked up the cause. The New Orleans *Times-Picayune* reported that the marchers intended to follow Moore's route and complete his journey.

On May 3, Birmingham was again front-page news in New Orleans. A headline of the *Times-Picayune* said, "Estimated 700 Negroes Jailed." Martin Luther King and other Black ministers had organized a march of children, ages six to sixteen, toward the Birmingham city hall. The news report estimated that from three hundred to four hundred children were arrested and taken to the Juvenile Detention Center. One was said to be a six-year-old girl.

The next day, the Birmingham conflict reached historic proportions. Police dogs were used to bite the marchers. Water from fire hoses drove the marchers back and splayed many along the pavement and sidewalks. Two police officers were injured in retaliation. Two hundred demonstrators were jailed.[9]

On May 5, the Sunday *Times-Picayune* carried another front-page headline: "Pleas by Negro Leaders Halt Mixing March." But the headline did not tell the whole story.

Saturday's demonstrations had involved an estimated one thousand participants. Another thousand cheering bystanders lined the streets. Approximately two hundred arrests were made, including 111 of children. Groups of between ten and fifty had emanated in serial fashion from the Sixteenth Street Baptist Church. One group reached the steps of City Hall and knelt to pray. They were arrested. Ultimately, police sealed the Sixteenth Street Baptist Church, forestalling other marchers.[10] Four months later, white vigilantes sealed the church in a different way—planting a bomb and killing four young girls.

Demonstrations in Birmingham continued until May 8.[11] Approximately twenty-four hundred people had been arrested, and about one thousand were still in jail when a settlement was reached on May 9. The settlement provided for elimination of segregation at department and variety stores in ninety days, promotion of "qualified Negroes" in public and private employment, prompt release of picketers still in jail, recommendation that criminal charges be dropped against all who had been arrested for picketing, and formation of a biracial committee to continue to attempt to resolve grievances and improve relations.[12]

Martin Luther King had won. He had demonstrated the power of nonviolence. But Lee Harvey Oswald, as strongly as he favored desegregation, would not follow Dr. King's lead.

26

Looking at a Different Revolution

In New Orleans, May 9 was a day of significance for Lee Harvey Oswald as well: he found both work and an apartment. He hired on as a general laborer for William B. Reily and Company—a dirty job, oiling and cleaning machines that ground, canned, and bagged coffee. The apartment Lee found was at 4907 Magazine Street, an easy trip to the coffee company. Lee thought Marina would like it. With a fenced-in backyard, Junie—only fifteen months old—might have a place to play.[1]

Lee quickly called Marina at Ruth Paine's home. Two days later, May 11, Marina, Junie, and their limited belongings arrived with Ruth and her own two children. The apartment that so pleased Lee and that Aunt Lillian thought satisfactory was, for Marina, "...dark, none too clean, and shabby. And there was little ventilation but many evident cockroaches...."[2] The aura of New Orleans was a different story, however. Lee walked Marina, Ruth, and their children through the French Quarter to the women's great delight.

Ruth and Marina enjoyed each other's company, but Marina and Lee quarreled frequently. So unpleasant was their conflict that on Tuesday, May 14, Ruth left with her children for Dallas a day earlier than she had planned.[3] Lee spent that day at work learning to grease and clean coffee machines, but his mind was on politics. By day's end, he'd sent a change-of-address card to the Fair Play for Cuba Committee in New York City.

Lee's eyes were locked on social revolution, but as Marina told the Warren Commission, a grander one, worldwide—and beginning, for him, in Cuba.[4] In Dr. King's revolution, Lee could only be a small appendage. In the worldwide revolution, he fantasized he might be a leader.

Feeding the Fantasy

The fantasy was kept alive by thirty-four books, in sum topping ten thousand pages, that Oswald borrowed from the New Orleans Public Library between May 22 and September 19.[5] To secure them required at least nineteen trips to the library. Whether he read them all we cannot know, but we can be sure what piqued his interest.

The first, borrowed on May 22, was Robert Payne's *Portrait of a Revolutionary: Mao Tse-Tung*.[6] The reading was timely. A rift had occurred in the worldwide Communist movement. Mao was challenging Nikita Khrushchev for leadership. Mao believed that Khrushchev, in withdrawing Soviet missiles from Cuba, seeking a nuclear test ban treaty, and pursuing détente with the United States, was abandoning both the worldwide revolution and China.

On May 16, while visiting North Vietnam, Chinese Communist Party leader Liu Shao-chi had spoken out against the Soviet Union. Liu suggested that such Soviet behavior raised the question of "whether the people of the world should carry out the revolutions or not and whether proletarian parties should lead the world's people in revolution or not."[7] To the Chinese, the answer was yes. For the Soviets, the Chinese thought the answer might be no. To resolve their differences top Chinese and Soviet officials had agreed to meet in Moscow on July 5.[8]

Reading about Mao could crystalize for Lee competing ideas about how Marxism should be extended to the non–Marxist world. The book was timely not only in terms of the contemporary struggle for leadership of the communist world, but also for Lee's struggle with his personal future and his own identity.

In *Portrait of a Revolutionary,* Marxists could find a prototypical man they could canonize. As Robert Payne described Mao, he was "a new kind of man, one who single handedly constructs whole civilizations."[9] For Oswald, Mao's biography could either reinforce or discourage his search for an identity and for his fantasy that China might be a place where he could find a role in the Marxist movement. As Lee expressed to Marina, if he did not go to Cuba, perhaps he would go to China.[10]

Mao was presented in *Portrait of a Revolutionary* as a man of patience and perseverance. Like Oswald, Mao took a long, philosophic view of history. He did not expect quick results. He thought deeply about the forces of history. Mao was a man to be emulated. But in many respects, Mao's career was not one with which Lee, even in a moment of high fantasy, might readily identify. Mao had skills, experiences, and a supportive environment which Lee did not enjoy. Mao was native-born and had spent a decade in China's university world before becoming a fulltime revolutionary. Lee was a self-educated, dyslexic, high-school dropout who denied the need for more formal education, and was hoping to be a leader in a country whose language he did not speak.

Mao's impressive literary skills made him a leading revolutionary publicist. Lee struggled to craft a private diary, a private political manifesto, and an unpublished monograph on life in Russia. Mao was easy to admire but difficult to match.

Mao also possessed a supportive family. His first wife shared his revolutionary zeal. She was murdered by Mao's enemy, the Kuomintang. A later wife, while pregnant, accompanied Mao and his troops on their six-thousand-mile march to hide from the Kuomintang. Marina was not such a wife. Even going to Cuba—a country she admired from movies she had seen and books she had read—was not a plan she endorsed.[11] She mocked Lee's ambitions. Equally disheartening, she was beginning to embrace the capitalist materialism that he rejected.

If Lee went to China, he would not be a leader. Perhaps the Chinese communists could use a follower who was fluent in Russian. But going to China would probably end Lee's relationship with Marina and his children. Without friends or family, he would be a small cog in a mighty machine, learning to speak an even more difficult language than Russian. Reading *Portrait of a Revolutionary* was not likely to have conjured for Lee a life that he could pursue optimistically.

Returning the biography of Mao, Lee obtained on June 1 two more books: the newly published *The Huey Long Murder Case* by Hermann Deutsch and Deanne and David Heller's *The Berlin Wall.*[12] It is tempting to speculate that Oswald, obsessed with political murder, searched for a book about assassination. Both books were relatively new publications, however. It is just as likely that the *Huey Long Murder Case* was being showcased by the New Orleans Library among other new titles, and it attracted Oswald's attention coincidentally.[13]

Nonetheless *The Huey Long Murder Case* must have reinforced Lee's thinking on assassination. A message was implicit but clear: nearly three decades after Huey Long was killed, even the obscure assassin Carl Weiss remained a subject of public interest. Through assassination, even someone who was no one could gain a permanent place in history.

27

Beyond Birmingham and Dallas

While Lee Oswald was finding refuge in reading, the challenge that Dr. King had issued in Birmingham was kindling fires elsewhere. And, as often occurs in cultural conflicts, successes and failures inspire greater action on both sides.

Oswald's failed attempt at assassination made Edwin Walker a martyr. It inspired Walker to renew his message. His colleague the Rev. Billy James Hargis told reporters that immediately after Walker had been shot at, "before the news ever reached the public, General Walker called me and said, 'Billy let's make another tour immediately.'" The tour was to be for two weeks and cover nine cities. Beginning May 15 in Salt Lake City, it would end in New Orleans.[1]

On May 27, the day before reaching New Orleans, Walker drew a hero's welcome in Louisiana's capital, Baton Rouge. He strode down the center aisle of the Louisiana state senate to resounding applause. Later, he told a crowd estimated at a thousand that there was no difference between "Kennedyism and Communism" and that former President Dwight Eisenhower and aspiring Republican presidential candidate Nelson Rockefeller were no better.[2] The next day, he gave a similar message to a crowd of similar size in New Orleans. The *Times-Picayune* reported that General Walker and the Reverend Hargis announced that they would be starting another speaking tour soon. Lee Harvey Oswald had not stopped the Walker train. He had fueled it.

Governor Wallace in the Doorway

Events of greater significance were mounting in Tuscaloosa, Alabama—events that would eclipse any Walker-Hargis tour and would launch the newly elected Governor George Wallace as the dominant Southerner opposing Dr. King's revolution.

On June 11, in Tuscaloosa, two Blacks—Vivian Malone and James Hood—were to be admitted for the first time as students at the University of Alabama. A poll of University of Alabama students showed that a majority believed that racial integration was inevitable and that resistance should not be undertaken. But Governor Wallace announced he would use his power to prevent integration.

For ten days, Lee Harvey Oswald could follow that clash on the front pages of the *Times-Picayune*. On June 1, Wallace said that he would not appear for a contempt hearing in federal court.[3] Four days later, the United States District Court enjoined him from interfering with the admission of Malone and Hood.[4] On June 8, Wallace said he would mobilize five hundred national guardsmen to enforce Alabama law and preserve order at the university.[5]

The next day President Kennedy spoke out, not simply to the scene about to unfold in Tuscaloosa but to the broader range of confrontations occurring in the South. He articulated a five-point program for peaceful resolution of the controversies that were enveloping the segregated South.[6]

The president's proposals did not address the issues at the University of Alabama, and Wallace ignored the president's plea. He said he would stand in the doorway at the University's admissions office to prevent violence and to uphold Alabama law.[7]

Oswald could read a step-by-step account in the *Times-Picayune*. First, as he had done in Mississippi, Kennedy federalized Alabama's national guard. He also withdrew federal troops from Oxford, Mississippi.[8]

At 10:47 a.m. on June 11, a three-car motorcade with U.S. Marshals, Deputy U.S. Attorney General Nicholas Katzenbach, and Malone and Hood arrived on the Tuscaloosa campus in the ninety-five-degree heat. There was no jeering crowd. Edwin Walker was absent. Perhaps his arrest at Ole Miss had deterred him.

As he said he would, Governor George Wallace stood at the doorway to the University of Alabama's admissions building. "A solid wall of men stood behind Wallace, some of them heavily armed."[9] Katzenbach approached and said, "I am asking you for an unequivocal assurance that you will not bar entry to these students, Vivian Malone and James Hood."

Walker responded with a statement expressing state's rights.

Katzenbach continued, "I take it from that statement that you are going to stand in the door and that you are not going to carry out the orders of this court."

Wallace replied simply that he stood on his statement of principles.

Katzenbach again requested an affirmative statement admitting the students: "Governor, I'm not interested in a show.... I would ask you once again to responsibly step aside."[10]

Wallace did not respond. Katzenbach left and took Malone to her dormitory room. Kennedy had won.

Yet this was still a personal victory for Wallace. Unlike Governor Barnett in Mississippi, Wallace had kept the rabble rousers and General Walker away. No violence had occurred. George Wallace had become the more attractive symbol around whom Southern whites could rally.

President Kennedy's call on June 11 for local dialogue, resolution of grievances, and civil rights legislation was not embraced by Southern leaders. On June 12, Georgia's Senator Richard Russell, a future member of the Warren Commission, gathered seventeen Southern senators to give a Southern response. The message: they would resist any further extension of federal power over property rights. On June 20, the American Baptist Association said that racial integration was morally wrong.[11] Senator Russell predicted an increase in racial disturbances if Kennedy used "threats of mass violence" to push civil rights legislation.[12] The threats were not from President Kennedy; he feared that if civil rights legislation was not passed, demonstrations would continue, and retaliatory violence would follow.

Both Russell and Kennedy were tragically right. On the same day that Russell convened his Southern colleagues for a statement of resistance and three days after Kennedy's call for dialog, white vigilantes murdered Black civil rights leader Medgar Evers outside his home in Jackson, Mississippi. Evers had been leading a drive to register Black voters. For the next five months—until the climactic event of November 22—it would be Southern violence in response to the civil rights movement that would define the foremost struggle in America.

28

Building a Dossier

In Oswald's eyes, leaders such as Martin Luther King, Medgar Evers, Vivian Malone, James Hood, Nicholas Katzenbach, and John Kennedy were champions of only incidental change. To Oswald, Fidel Castro was a champion of change who could transform the world. Castro's changes were all-encompassing. Equal civil rights were only one piece of the puzzle. Castro's Cuba was a model for the world.

The *Times-Picayune* covered both Castro's revolution and Dr. King's. On May 1—a week after Oswald arrived in New Orleans—page one carried a claim by Cuban refugees that Fidel Castro's militia had used flamethrowers against rebel insurgents. The next day the *Times-Picayune* reported that Castro was observing May Day celebrations in Moscow with Nikita Khrushchev. Castro was seeking Soviet help.

Perhaps Lee Harvey Oswald could assist Castro as well. A starting point might be the Fair Play for Cuba Committee. On May 14 Lee sent a change of address letter to the Committee. The Committee responded by asking that he renew his subscription to their mailings. To that simple subscription request, Oswald answered with a grand plan. He wrote to the Fair Play for Cuba Committee:

> I am requesting formal membership in your Organization.... Now that I live in New Orleans I have been thinking of renting a small office at my own expense for the purpose of forming a F.P.C.C. branch here in New Orleans. Could you give me a charter?
>
> Also I would like information on buying pamphlets, etc. in large lots, as well as FPCC applications.
>
> Offices down here rent for $30 a month and if I had a steady flow of literature I would be glad to take the expense. Of course I work and could not supervise the office at all times but I'm sure I could get volunteers to do it....
>
> Could you add some advice or recommendations? I am not saying this project would be a roaring success, but I am willing to try. An office, literature, and getting people to know you are the fundamentles [sic]of the F.P.C.C. as far as I can see so here's hoping to hear from you.
>
> Yours respectfully,
> Lee H. Oswald[1]

He heard promptly, by letter of May 29 from national director V.T. Lee. The letter was cordial and detailed but less than encouraging:

> It would be hard to conceive of a chapter with as few members as seem to exist in the New Orleans area....
>
> We certainly are not at all adverse to a very small Chapter but certainly would expect that there would be at least twice the amount needed to conduct a legal executive board for the Chapter....
>
> You must realize that you will come under tremendous pressures with any attempt to do

> FPCC work in that area.... Even most of our big city Chapters have been forced to abandon the idea of operating an office in public. The national office here in New York is the only one in the country today and the New York City Chapter uses our office too so it is the only Chapter with an office.... We do have a serious and often violent opposition.... I definitely would not recommend an office, at least not one that will be easily identifyable [sic] to the lunatic fringe in your community....
>
> Naturally, I would like to communicate with you a great deal more concerning yourself so that we can get to know you and possibly be of some assistance to you as we get more information.
>
> We hope to hear from you very soon in this regard and are looking forward to a good working relationship for the future. Please feel free to discuss this matter quite thoroughly with me.
>
> Fraternally,
> V. T. Lee,
> National Director[2]

Oswald did not call Mr. Lee or write for advice. If other supporters of the national Fair Play for Cuba Committee existed in New Orleans, V.T. Lee did not identify them. One needn't be a skeptic to read Mr. Lee's response as an effort to secure information about Oswald without alienating him. For all V.T. Lee might know, Lee Harvey Oswald was an agent of the FBI. Priscilla McMillan has interpreted the letter from V.T. Lee differently. She thought it offered Oswald a "real chance to work with a political group" and that he was "elated by it." Gerald Posner interpreted the initial paragraph—" ... we are certainly not averse to a very small Chapter"—as welcoming.[3] The elation that Marina reported was undoubtedly true. It was characteristic of Lee to grasp at the slightest signs of encouragement from Marxist leaders.

Oswald hadn't waited for V.T. Lee's reply, however, to act on his intentions. On May 29, the day after Edwin Walker's rally in New Orleans and the day that V.T. Lee wrote his cautionary letter, Lee Harvey Oswald, using the fictitious name Lee Osborne, paid $4.00 to the Jones Printing Company in New Orleans to order a thousand copies of a promotional handbill of his own creation:

> HANDS OFF CUBA
> Join the Fair Play for Cuba Committee
> New Orleans Chapter
> Free Literature, Lectures,
> LOCATION[4]:

The location was left blank. To be filled in later.[5] Oswald ultimately sent a copy of this handbill to the Fair Play for Cuba Committee in New York.[6]

On Monday, June 3, when Kennedy and Wallace were moving toward a face-off in Tuscaloosa, Oswald, using a fictitious address, opened another post office box. That same day, again using the fictitious name of Lee Osborne, he ordered from a different New Orleans printing company—Mailers Service Company—five hundred copies of membership application forms for his not-yet-existing Fair Play for Cuba Committee chapter. The cost was $9.34.[7]

One wonders why Oswald used fictitious names and chose different printing companies for the handbill and the membership application forms. Did the fictitious names show fear or were they an attempt to suggest that there were other members of the nonexistent New Orleans committee? Would one company not have the ability to print both orders? Perhaps there was a cost differential. In any event, it took some shopping and indicates that no one else was supporting Lee's effort.

The membership application form gave no address for the Fair Play for Cuba Committee and bore no return address. The form provided for the name and address of the applicant and a designation of the amount of money to be contributed. Unless the applicant handed the form to the committee's recruiter or was given the address orally, the form was useless as a device to build membership.

On June 4, Oswald took delivery of the promotional handbills. The next day, Wednesday, June 5, he returned to Mailers Service Company, not far from Reily Coffee on Magazine Street, to retrieve the membership application forms. On a subsequent undetermined date, he ordered three hundred membership cards to be printed by Mailers. That price was $3.50. Altogether, printing for the New Orleans Chapter of the Fair Play for Cuba Committee cost Lee $26.93—not an inconsiderable amount in 1963 for a low-wage worker and certainly large enough that the costs needed to be spread across several pay checks. The modest quantities (1000 handbills, 500 membership application forms, and 300 membership cards)—given pre–Internet options for outreach—might serve to attract respectable enough attention for a fledgling chapter that might not want, as V.T. Lee hinted, to risk too wide or undesirable attention.

When the membership cards were in hand, Lee signed his own card and had Marina add the signature of the chapter's president, A.J. Hidell, the same name he had used in Dallas to order a pistol and rifle.[8] When Marina mocked him for selecting a name that sounded like Fidel, he explained that, with a name other than his own as president, it would appear that the chapter had more than one member.[9]

Marina believed that Lee's efforts for a Fair Play for Cuba Committee chapter in New Orleans were more personal than political. She told the Warren Commission, "His basic desire was to get to Cuba by any means and ... all of the rest of it was window dressing for that purpose."[10] In creating the framework for a Fair Play for Cuba Committee chapter, she thought, Lee was simply building a dossier. Gaining a few members might win an endorsement from New York when it came time to apply for admission to Cuba.

A serious political organizer would have planned a long-term presence in New Orleans and looked for like-minded people in like-minded organizations. College campuses and college professors would have been a logical starting point. A peace movement in which university people showed interest existed in New Orleans. The Warren Commission found no evidence that Oswald reached out in any personal way to such individuals.[11]

Marina's biographer, Priscilla McMillan, believed that, initially, there was more to Lee's engagement with the Fair Play for Cuba Committee than trying to gain admission to Cuba. Certainly, other Americans had gained entry there without affiliating with the Committee. McMillan saw Lee's objectives as "...two-pronged, both an attempt to change American policy toward Cuba by peaceful political action at the grassroots level and an attempt to win the trust of the Castro government."[12]

Marina's insight may have been sounder than McMillan's.[13] On June 10, Lee took another stab at the credentialing he needed to gain acceptance in Cuba. He wrote the Communist Party paper, *The Worker:*

> I have formed a Fair Play for Cuba Committee here in New Orleans. I think it is best to attract the broad mass of people to a popular struggle.... I ask that you give me as much literature as you judge possible since I think it would be nice to have your literature among the "Fair Play" leaflets (like the one enclosed) and pamphlets in my office.[14]

He included honorary committee membership cards for Benjamin Davis and Gus Hall—Communist Party leaders then under indictment for failure to register under the Internal Security Act and whose defense committee had not accepted Lee's December offer to do printing.

Of course, the claim was false. He had not formed a committee. Oswald did not have an office for the committee. He was the committee's only member, and the suggestion was naive that Communist Party literature would be "nice to have ... among the 'Fair Play' leaflets." Communist literature in a Fair Play for Cuba Committee office would undermine the political organizing he was claiming to do.

Oswald never avoided lying if lying might promote a goal. He knew that his actions would not be favored by the national office of the Fair Play for Cuba Committee, but the letter to *The Worker* might make friends and even gain a squib in the party's newspaper.

Oswald would not receive the requested literature any time soon. A letter to Oswald from the Communist Party USA dated July 31, 1963, indicates, however, that party literature was sent to him then.[15] *The Worker* never publicized him. And Oswald never overtly linked the Fair Play for Cuba Committee to the Communist Party USA.

On June 11, the day after writing to *The Worker* and the evening President Kennedy gave his nationwide speech urging civil rights legislation, Lee was fully absorbed in his own political agenda. That day he added Marina and A.J. Hidell as individuals authorized to receive mail at his post office box. For a number of evenings, he was engrossed in stamping membership cards for his local chapter with his post office box and the name of A.J. Hidell as president.[16]

Political Action

Oswald's haste in preparing "Hands Off Cuba" literature and stamping membership cards may have been because of the presence of the *USS Wasp* in New Orleans from June 13 to June 20. On June 6, the New Orleans *Times-Picayune* had carried an article that the *Wasp* and four accompanying ships would be in New Orleans for public viewing.[17] The *Wasp*—an aircraft carrier—had participated in the embargo of Cuba and Cuba's quarantine during the Cuban missile crisis. While the *Wasp* was in New Orleans, civilians were welcomed aboard.[18] What an opportunity. Distributing pro-Castro literature at the dock of the *Wasp* wasn't likely to garner prospective members or even sympathizers. Many visitors were family of the four-thousand-person crew on the five ships or members of civilian and veterans' organizations supporting the Navy.[19] Even so, what Oswald was doing would likely attract attention—and might even be newsworthy. It could also risk his job at Reily Coffee.

In the mid-afternoon of Sunday, June 16, at the Dumaine Street Wharf where the *Wasp* was docked, Oswald seized the opportunity. Without an assistant and without Marina's knowledge, he began distributing the "Hands Off Cuba" handbills. Also in hand were leaflets from the national office of the Fair Play for Cuba Committee.

The leaflets, "*The Truth about Cuba is in Cuba*," protested the ban on travel to Cuba, urged Americans to seek permission for such travel, and recommended books to read. That leaflet bore the address of the Fair Play for Cuba Committee in New York City. The handbills that Lee had printed still showed no address.[20] The only place a prospective joiner could contact was New York. New York could then refer prospective New Orleans members to Oswald.

What a plan this must have seemed to Oswald. By attracting members for a local chapter, he was proving himself to the national organization. He may not have been Mao in the making, but he was indeed building a resume for Cuba.

Alas, after no more than a few minutes of passing out handbills and leaflets, the activities were reported to port security by the *Wasp*'s deck officer. A local harbor security officer, Girod Ray, was dispatched to instruct Oswald to cease distributing the literature. Officer Ray said he needed a permit to do so.

Oswald questioned why a permit was necessary. He argued that he had a constitutional right to distribute the leaflets and handbills. Ray responded that he'd arrest Oswald if he did not stop. Lee left without further incident.[21]

In his maiden attempt at political organizing, he had failed. No members were recruited, and no publicity ensued. It was August, more than six weeks later, before Oswald communicated that defeat or anything else to the Fair Play for Cuba Committee in New York.[22]

Reacting to Failure

The failure at Dumaine Street Wharf was unnerving. Marina recalled to Priscilla McMillan that the days that followed were ones of intense anxiety for Lee. McMillan recorded, "One night [in late June] he cried, yet when he woke up he could not remember what his dream had been about ... [another night] toward the very end of June he had four anxiety attacks during which he shook from head to toe at intervals of a half an hour and never once woke up."[23]

For a while after the wharf incident, Lee spent his time at home mostly in silence. He read extensively. Some days, even at meals, he did not talk to Marina. On June 24, he took a crucial step toward dissociating himself completely from what was happening in America. Without telling Marina, he applied for a new passport. He told the passport office he would be going to England, France, Germany, Holland, Italy, Finland, Poland, and the Soviet Union sometime between October and December. He said that he might be gone from three months to a year.[24] If the plan was true, it was an inconvenient time to go. Marina was approaching her third trimester; the baby would be born in October.

For weeks, Lee had been pushing Marina to resume contact with the Soviet Embassy and return to Russia—without him. Marina resisted. Then, on either June 29 or 30, something happened. McMillan reported it this way:

> Marina, too, was sleeping badly because of her fear about being sent back to Russia. She looked tired and unhappy all the time. "What's wrong with you?" Lee would ask. "Don't you like it here? Your face is making me nervous."
>
> ****
>
> But one night Marina was sitting in her rocker holding back her tears when she noticed that Lee looked unhappy, too. He stole a glance in her direction, and she saw a look of sadness in his eyes. He put his book down and went into the kitchen by himself. Marina waited a few minutes. Then she put the baby down and followed him. Lee was sitting in the dark with his arms folded and legs wrapped around the back of a chair and his head resting on top. He was

> staring down at the floor. Marina put her arms around him, stroked his head, and could feel him shaking with sobs.
>
> "Why are you crying?" she asked. Then, "Cry away. It'll be better that way." Finally, she said: "Everything is going to be all right. I understand."
>
> Marina held him for about a quarter of an hour, and he told her between sobs that he was lost. He didn't know what he ought to do. At last he stood up and returned to the living room.
>
> She followed him, and he was quiet at first. Then he said suddenly, "Would you like me to come to Russia too?"
>
> "You're kidding."
>
> "No," he said.
>
> "You mean it? You're not just joking?"
>
> "I do."
>
> Marina danced around the room for joy and then curled up in his lap.
>
> "I'll go with my girls," he said. "We'll be together, you and me and Junie and the baby. There is nothing to hold me here. I'd rather have less, but not have to worry about the future. Besides, how would I manage without my girls?"[25]

Of course, Oswald did not say exactly that. This was Marina—with McMillan's help—reconstructing an event years later. Whatever we know of Lee during this period of his life, we know from Marina. One must always be skeptical of a witness's memory, especially one whose interest is in protecting the subject or herself. But why would the incident itself be false?

The essence is probably true. The details may well have been distorted by Marina and dramatized by McMillan, yet the essence is simple. Like many twenty-three-year-olds, Lee was struggling with his identity and his future. He wanted to be a significant player in the Marxist revolutions that were shaking the world—not the revolution that was shaking America. He had been disappointed by Russia. The only role he'd found for himself in the United States—trying to assassinate a potential Hitler—had failed, and might well have been suicidal.

Could he ever really join the revolution in Cuba? So far, he was failing in that effort. Neither the Socialist Workers Party nor the Communist Party was ready to certify his credentials. His wife was not supportive. And Cuba might not accept an American defector with a pregnant wife and very young child. Moreover, his first effort to build a public resume had been futile.

For a moment he was comforted by the arms of Marina. Perhaps, he truly felt he should return to the Soviet Union. They could all be together. Or was this all merely a calculated ruse?

In any event, Marina wrote to the Soviet embassy begging that the embassy expedite visas for both herself and Lee.[26] By the time he mailed the letter for her, however, Lee had other plans for himself.

Unbeknownst to Marina, on July 1, Lee added a note of his own: "As for my entrance visa please consider it *separtably*."[27] As had occurred before, in his moment of emotional need, Marina had come to Lee's rescue. For a few hours, their interests seemed one. Yet, Marina had succumbed, and Lee had returned to his fantasies. She had agreed to return to Russia, but he was going elsewhere. He could now do as he'd told her he would last May: "I'll go to Cuba, then China and you will wait for me in Russia."[28]

29

Fantasies After Failure

July 1, a Monday, was a workday. When Lee returned from work, Marina and June accompanied him to the New Orleans Public Library. Without money for a television set or movies, Lee continued to indulge his fantasies and assuage his anxieties by reading. In June and July, he borrowed more than a dozen books from the public library. Many were about powerful public figures or raised issues of political power. Their subject matter ranged from accounts of the ancient world and a mythical hero, *Ben Hur*, to problems in contemporary Russia and Aldous Huxley's fantasy about the emerging future, *Brave New World*. One withdrawal on this July 1 trip to the library was William Manchester's personality sketch of John Kennedy, *Portrait of a President: John F. Kennedy in Profile*.[1]

One might speculate that reading William Manchester's *Portrait of a President* was a forerunner to assassination—that it inspired the idea or that Oswald was already considering it. Marina did not think so. Yet Priscilla McMillan notes Manchester's speculation: "[Kennedy] has a weaker grip on the nation's heartstrings" [than Lincoln] "and the reason isn't that he hasn't been shot." McMillan comments: "How might Lee Oswald read a passage like that?"[2]

She believed Lee respected John Kennedy, although he may have been jealous of the president's good looks. Those looks captivated Marina.[3] She kept a photo of Kennedy in their apartment and scoured magazines for photos of him. Lee would then read her the accompanying articles.[4] Marina remembered also that they listened together on their radio to at least three of Kennedy's national broadcasts.

Like *The Day Huey Long Was Shot,* William Manchester's book about Kennedy may have been among the new books displayed in the New Orleans library. When Oswald borrowed *Portrait of a President,* Kennedy had made his national broadcast only three weeks earlier on the eve of integrating the University of Alabama. It was one of many books that Lee read that summer about powerful people who had achieved the heights he thought he deserved. Marina recalled to Priscilla McMillan that, while reading *Portrait of a President,* Lee began to fantasize about becoming president.[5]

In fact, there was very little in Manchester's book with which Oswald could identify. *Portrait of a President* was a book about personality, not policy. From the perspective of John Kennedy and his political entourage, the book was a flattering campaign piece, useful for the forthcoming reelection campaign. It gave little insight into how Kennedy gained the pinnacle of power. It showed how the president stroked people, jested, reacted to conflict, and endured physical pain. It showed his athleticism and his heroism on P.T. 109. If Oswald were looking to learn how the president intended to combat communism or overthrow Castro, he would not find it in *Portrait of a President*.

Nonetheless, Manchester's biography of John Kennedy ignited something in

Oswald. Nine days after returning *Portrait of a President* to the New Orleans Library, Oswald checked out John Kennedy's own *Profiles in Courage.*[6] *Profiles in Courage* could have captivated Oswald. It was crammed with vignettes of Americans whom Oswald, even from a Marxist perspective, might respect—men who had risked their political futures by unwavering adherence to their political values.

He kept the book only five days.[7] If he read any of the vignettes in *Profiles in Courage*, the one about Texas's own Sam Houston may have struck closest to home. Houston was a figure of monumental proportions—one about whom it is easy to romanticize. In Sam Houston, Lee Oswald could have seen parallels and dreams for his own life.

Houston, as a teenager, had, on his own, left his boyhood home in Tennessee. He was adopted by a Cherokee family. Living with the Cherokees, Houston learned their language and married a Cherokee woman. How familiar that might well have seemed to Oswald.

Despite youthful impediments, Houston became a towering success. He was able to build political and business bridges between the Cherokee nation and those whose native language was English. After being wounded in the War of 1812, Houston became a protégé of Andrew Jackson. At age thirty-five, Houston became governor of Tennessee.

Politically dissatisfied with Tennessee, Houston went to Texas where his military heroism helped win Texas independence from Mexico. Twice Houston was elected president of the independent Texas nation. After Texas joined the Union, Houston became a U.S. senator and twice was elected governor of Texas. In the battle over secession, he supported remaining in the Union. He left politics rather than join the Confederacy.

As John Kennedy wrote of Sam Houston in *Profiles in Courage:* "He was fiercely ambitious, yet at the end he sacrificed for principle all he had ever won or wanted.... Sam Houston's contradictions actually confirm his one basic quality: indomitable individualism, sometimes spectacular, sometimes crude, sometimes mysterious, but always courageous."[8] Was that not what Oswald wanted to be? Could not an intelligent, courageous man of principle who lacked formal education become a moving force in an emerging revolution? But where was that emerging revolution? For Lee Harvey Oswald it was in Cuba, China, and the countries throwing off Western domination.

The Doors Are Closing

July 8 or 9 might have been a day that lifted Lee from the depression that had engulfed him in June. About that time, he received a letter from his cousin, Eugene Murret. Eugene was a student at the Jesuit House of Study at Spring Hill College in Mobile, Alabama. On behalf of the Jesuits, he was inviting Lee to speak to the Jesuits about "contemporary Russia and communist practices there."[9] The prospect of an audience may have engendered hope.

A few days later another event—notice that he was being discharged from Reily Coffee—would dash hope once again.[10] At Reily, Lee had been neither sociable nor efficient. He performed the simple task of greasing machines poorly. He spoke to almost no one. His supervisor, Charles Le Blanc, estimated that in two and one-half months, Oswald had said a hundred words to him.[11] At lunch, Oswald separated himself from other employees, often spending his break times reading rifle and hunting magazines at a nearby auto garage and returning to work late from his lunch and even midmorning or afternoon breaks.[12]

When he was at work, his behavior was peculiar. Approaching another employee, he would sometimes point his finger in the nature of a pistol, move his thumb as if firing the pistol, and without smiling, utter simply "Pow." To Lee, it may have been a friendly acknowledgment. To fellow workers, it was off-putting.[13]

There was another way in which Lee did not fit in. Marina told Priscilla McMillan that Lee claimed that occasionally he had gone drinking with a Black coworker at Reily Coffee. What didn't ring true about the story to Marina was the drinking—at home Lee's favorite drinks were Coca Cola, Dr. Pepper, and iced tea.[14] As a teenager in New Orleans, he had ostensibly challenged segregation by taking on a bus a seat in the section reserved for Blacks. In Dallas he had expressed to George de Mohrenschildt strong disapproval of the way the South treated African Americans. But no witness has come forward indicating that Oswald had a friendship with any African American at any workplace.

We also do not know how much politics affected Oswald's attention to his job or to other employees. While at work, Lee's mind was more on politics than on Reily's business. One day, he asked his supervisor, Charles LeBlanc, "Do you like it here?" LeBlanc responded, "Well, sure I like it here. I have been here a long time about 8½ years or so." "Oh, Hell, I don't mean this place," Lee said, "This damn country."[15]

We do not know the date of that conversation, and we cannot know what caused Lee Oswald to ask that question. We can know, however, that political matters were attracting his attention.

Among Marxists, the most disputed political matter related to strategies for the world communist movement. The controversy was front page news in the New Orleans *Times-Picayune*.[16] The Soviet Union and the Peoples Republic of China were vying for leadership of that movement. For three weeks prior to Oswald's release from Reily Coffee on July 19, Soviet and Chinese leaders had been meeting in Moscow to reconcile their differences.[17] A primary dispute was over the proper strategy for worldwide Communist expansion. Foremost were whether war with the capitalist countries should be avoided and whether nuclear war should be risked.

On Monday, July 15, the lead story in the *Times-Picayune* was headlined "Communist Giants on Verge of Split." The article reported that the Chinese favored pushing the use of nuclear weapons to the limit. If nuclear war occurred, the Chinese leaders believed, "Communism can build a thousand times higher civilization on the corpses of hundreds of millions of persons." The dispute sounded like Oswald's reflections in his manifesto written on the *Maasdam*.

The Chinese argued that nuclear war should be risked if it would free developing countries from capitalist control. They believed that the West, desiring peaceful co-existence, was unwilling to take the nuclear risk. The Chinese argued that the West—the United States in particular—would relent in the face of communist military power.

With that philosophy, the Chinese accused the Soviets of deserting Cuba in October 1962 by removing their missiles under U.S. naval threat. The Soviets countered that in 1962, they had information that the United States was planning to invade Cuba. By building missile bases, they had prevented an American invasion; and, by agreeing to remove the bases, they had obtained a U.S. promise not to invade. Castro's Cuba had been saved.

Even if the October missile crisis had reduced the immediate likelihood that the United States would invade Cuba, it did not reduce, in Oswald's mind, Castro's need for him. Another imminent danger—invasion by exiles—loomed still. The Soviets and

Cubans saw it. The *Times-Picayune* reported that according to Cuban exiles, the Soviet Union, although removing its missile sites, had increased the number of its own troops in Cuba, added other bases, and was providing more military equipment.[18] Castro could certainly use an American who spoke Russian fluently, had been trained as a Marine, and could speak on Havana Radio to the American people.

If the need for Oswald was growing, the ease in reaching Cuba was diminishing. On July 6 the *Times-Picayune* reported that the United States was determined to isolate Cuba economically and that the ban on travel to Cuba was tightening. On July 9 the headline on page one of the *Times-Picayune* was "Cuban Assets Seized by U.S." Cuba responded by seizing the U.S. Embassy.[19] When Oswald had defected to Russia, there was at least a U.S. Embassy in Moscow. The door to Cuba was closing. Perhaps that was weighing on Lee when he asked LeBlanc whether he liked it here.

It was likely that Oswald's question to LeBlanc pertained as well to the ongoing struggle over civil rights. Conflict was growing. For weeks, news of civil rights violence filled the New Orleans media.[20] By July 1963, the battles had expanded northward. On July 4, a riot erupted in Maryland as an attempt was made to integrate an all-white amusement park.[21] On July 5, protesters staged a sit-in at the Brooklyn, New York, Board of Education.[22] The next day white teenagers threw rocks, eggs, and tomatoes at civil rights demonstrators from the Congress of Racial Equality who picketed a White Castle drive-in restaurant in New York City.[23]

In the South, on July 7, ninety-nine people, including three rabbis and nine other clergy, were arrested for continued integration efforts at the Maryland amusement park.[24] On July 10, in Savannah, Georgia, police used tear gas to quell a two-thousand-person march.[25] In Cambridge, Maryland, on July 11, two National Guardsmen were fired upon as they drove through a Black neighborhood. Elsewhere in Cambridge, both Blacks and whites shot at each other from automobiles.[26] Martial law was imposed the next day.[27]

President Kennedy had decided that the way to quell the storm was to enact legislation that would give African Americans the rights they were seeking through civil protest. He proposed a bill to end segregation in public accommodations. The bill was under consideration before the Senate Commerce Committee. Hearings brought forth inflammatory accusations. Mississippi Governor Ross Barnett testified that Robert and John Kennedy were aiding a "world communist conspiracy to divide and conquer" the United States by encouraging sit-ins, picketing, and violence against local leaders and by sowing the seeds of hate and violence.[28] Alabama Governor George Wallace testified that "the Air Force is encouraging its personnel to engage in street demonstrations with rioting mobs...."[29]

Depression and Further Fantasy

Of all the weighty events of late July 1963, probably the most concerning for Oswald was his termination from Reily Coffee. Unless he could find another job, the family would have to live on unemployment compensation that would be fifty dollars less per month than he had been earning. For a family, at 1963 levels, such a reduction would be crushing. Beyond paying for food, rent, and Marina's prenatal care, Lee needed to fund the prospective Cuba journey.[30]

It is likely that Lee received notice as early as July 12, and carried the burden silently for almost a week. July 17 was Lee's last day at Reily.[31] It was also Marina's birthday. When Marina appeared morose at dinner that evening, Lee asked why. She answered, "Today was my birthday"—her twenty-second. He had not remembered. After a few minutes, Lee responded, "Come on. Let's go out." He took her to a nearby drugstore, where he bought her face powder and a Coca-Cola.[32] He wouldn't tell her he'd lost his job until the next day.[33]

He never told her that he was discharged for poor performance. She attributed his dismissal to current widespread unemployment in the United States. To Lee she said, "Don't worry. You'll have a little vacation, and then you'll find a job."[34]

Priscilla McMillan believed that Lee used this break to immerse himself deeper into his political fantasies. Marina hoped that Lee would get a college education. She recognized that without a college education, Lee had no future—even in the political world. McMillan reported Marina's thoughts in this way:

> She was ashamed of Lee because he lacked a college education, and in five years or so, when the children were in school, it was her intention to go to work and support him so that he could study philosophy and economics. Those were his choices, and she approved of them, because she thought they might straighten out his thinking and help him see his mistakes.[35]

Whether it was his need for action or fear of failure (possibly exacerbated by his dyslexia), Lee rejected the idea of further education. Instead, he persisted with his dreams. After reading Manchester's *Portrait of a President*, he told Marina that in twenty years their next child—surely to be a boy—would be president or prime minister. "Okay," she laughed. "Papa will be prime minister. Son will be president. And what will I be—chief janitor in the White House?"[36]

On Monday, July 22, Lee applied for unemployment compensation. To receive it, Louisiana required him to show that he was seeking work. Each week, Oswald dutifully listed four or five employers that he had allegedly contacted. The evidence that he actually did is scant.[37] The state itself required no corroboration; nor could the Warren Commission find any. Moreover, when Louisiana's Department of Labor learned on August 22 that he had become involved in provocative political activities, it ceased making job referrals.[38] Nothing shows that Lee Oswald was employed in any capacity anywhere in New Orleans after July 19.

Late July brought another setback. Lee had been seeking a reversal of his undesirable discharge from the Marines that resulted from his seeking to renounce his citizenship while in the Soviet Union and living there for two and one-half years. On July 25, the U.S. Navy issued notice that his undesirable discharge had been upheld.[39]

For a while, Lee became lost in his thoughts and his books. Marina recalled that Lee, melting in the summer heat, would sit silently in a chair for hours at a time.[40] Formerly meticulous about his appearance, he stopped shaving on weekends even while still employed. He ceased washing his face in the morning, stopped using soap when taking a bath, and reduced his fastidious teeth brushing from three times to once a day.[41] One cannot be sure whether it was because of depression or an effort to cut costs until he found a new job or amassed enough to go to Cuba. Remarkably, though unemployed for twelve days, he saved forty-nine dollars in July.[42]

Anger and depression were surely affecting him. As his job became less satisfying and discharge finally came, his discontent showed in his treatment of Marina and in his self-care. McMillan reported: "…Marina used to beg him to brush his teeth, especially if he was going to kiss her. 'You're my wife. You're supposed to love me any way I am,' and he would come at her, his mouth open, breathing as hard as he could. He would try to kiss her, yet his eyes were so full of hate she thought he was going to kill her instead."[43] Marina did not see this as hostility toward her. She believed he had lost all desire to care for himself.

30

Another Try at the Dossier

Even though July brought anger, depression, and financial crisis, the last week in July and first weeks of August rekindled Oswald's fantasies of greatness. On Saturday, July 27, Lee, Marina, June, Lee's aunt and uncle, his cousin Joyce, and her two children left New Orleans in a station wagon to visit Lee's cousin Eugene Murret at Spring Hill College in Mobile, Alabama.[1] Gene, having obtained undergraduate and law degrees at Loyola University, was at age thirty-one a Jesuit scholastic at Spring Hill, planning to be a Jesuit scholar. He had invited Lee to address the Jesuits about his experiences in the Soviet Union.[2]

Joseph Reardon, a Jesuit scholastic in attendance, remembers Lee pulling a few crumpled papers from his pocket and beginning his presentation with an assault on capitalism.[3] The prepared remarks continued with a discourse on day-to-day life in Russia. Lee noted particularly that political propaganda was inescapable: radio programming that intruded upon public places and private lives and could not be changed, factory floors with constant political messages, the workday ending with a political meeting, and workplace votes where no one voted no.

Reardon recalled that Oswald's monologue was interrupted by questions, some of which became personal. Why had he returned to the United States? What was the role of religion in the Soviet Union and Lee's view of it? Without his saying so, his listeners concluded that he was an atheist. He was more explicit in saying that he believed neither communism, socialism, nor capitalism were good systems; that capitalism was a form of gambling; and that the best system would be one that combined the better parts of each. His presentation was so well delivered that many of his listeners inferred he was a college graduate.[4]

It is possible that his talk with the Jesuits inspired Lee to write the one page, sixteen-point outline, "The Atheian System," found among his belongings after his arrest on November 22, 1963.[5] Consistent with Oswald's statements to the Jesuits that the good qualities of communism, socialism, and capitalism should be combined in a new system, the outline for "The Atheian System" included the elements of those systems that he approved. His discussion with the Jesuits about atheism might well have induced him to label his system Athean.

In any event, after speaking to the Jesuits, Oswald's mind, as usual, was on politics not employment. On August 1, he wrote a remarkable letter to V.T. Lee at the Fair Play for Cuba Committee in New York City:

> Through the efforts of some Cuban-exile "gusanos," a street demonstration was attacked and we were officially cautioned by the police. The incident robbed me of what support I had, leaving me alone.

> Nevertheless, thousands of circulars were distributed and many, many pamphlets which your office supplied.
>
> We also managed to picket the fleet when it came in and I was surprised in the number of officers who were interested in our literature.[6]

Except for that letter, no record exists of a street demonstration and an attack by Cuban exiles before or on the date of the letter; yet four days later the basis for such an attack began to evolve. Authors Priscilla McMillan, Norman Mailer, and Vincent Bugliosi agree that Oswald's claims of assault, distributing thousands of circulars, and interested naval officers were false.[7] They may be wrong. A confrontation with Cuban exiles could have occurred at the Dumaine Street wharf on or prior to August 1 without warranting a police report. What is significant is that the letter to V.T. Lee reveals that by then, Oswald was aware that distributing pro–Castro literature in New Orleans could produce threatening behavior from Cuban exiles.

When Oswald mailed the letter three days later, on August 4, he was feeling a restored sense of power. The Jesuits had showed him respect. He had probably also just received a polite three sentence letter from Arnold Johnson, director of the Information and Lecture Bureau of the Communist Party, USA, dated July 31.[8] Marina remembered Lee's treating the letter as recognition of his own importance from a man he respected.[9] Johnson had merely acknowledged an earlier letter from Oswald, commended him for founding a chapter of the Fair Play for Cuba Committee in New Orleans, and said he was sending Communist Party literature under separate cover.

August 5 was the beginning of more grandiose and impulsive efforts. On that day, Oswald made his first known contact with Cuban exiles. By gathering information on Castro's foes, perhaps he might establish credentials for joining the revolution in Cuba. The idea may have been generated by front-page articles about anti–Castro activities that appeared in the New Orleans *Times-Picayune* on August 1 and 2. The articles reported that on July 31, the FBI had seized explosives from a cottage on Lake Pontchartrain. The cottage was linked to anti–Castro Cuban exiles and their American supporters.[10]

Whether in response to those articles or otherwise, Oswald called a New Orleans newspaper to secure information about local Cuban exiles' groups and placed three addresses in his address book.[11] One address was that of the Cuban Student Directorate. Its New Orleans leader was Carlos Bringuier. Oswald could have learned from a Fair Play for Cuba Committee pamphlet—"Cuban Counter Revolutionaries in the United States"—that the Cuban Student Directorate was suspected of planning, with CIA support, a reinvasion of Cuba.[12]

Bringuier owned Casa Roca, a clothing store at 107 Decatur Street. The store's window contained an anti–Castro sign: a drawing of the Statue of Liberty with a hand, labeled USSR, putting a knife in the statue's back, and bearing the warning "Danger. Only 90 Miles from the United States Cuba Lies in Chains."[13]

When Oswald entered Casa Roca, Bringuier was present with his brother-in-law Rolando Pelaez, and two teenagers, Philip Geraci and Vance Blalock. Overhearing Bringuier talking with them about anti–Castro activities, Oswald joined in, saying that he was against Castro and communism. He asked where the headquarters of CSD (known by its Spanish initials DRE) was located and how it was organized.[14]

Bringuier was suspicious. He did not know Oswald and feared being infiltrated by the FBI or a Castro agent. He responded to Oswald with caution. When Oswald asked if this was the Cuban exile headquarters, Bringuier said it was not.[15] The headquarters was in Miami. When Oswald said he was an ex-Marine and offered to train anti-Castro fighters and join the fight in Cuba, Bringuier said his group's activities involved only propaganda and public information. When Oswald reached in his pocket to make a small financial contribution to CSD, Bringuier declined.[16]

The teenagers and Pelaez were more receptive listeners. Oswald intrigued them with advice on blowing up the Huey Long Bridge, derailing a railroad train without using explosives, and making gunpowder and zip guns. He said he had received guerrilla training while a Marine. Perhaps remembering how important as a teenager his own brother's Marine manual had been to him, he offered to bring the teenagers a copy of the manual he had saved.[17]

The next day, Oswald returned to Casa Roca and dropped off the manual. It had the name "L.H. Oswald" on the top of the first page. Bringuier, not there at the time, would read it with interest and retain it.[18] Author Albert Newman speculated that Oswald had actually hoped to become part of an exile group intending to invade Cuba. He would either sabotage the group or expose it either to Castro or the FBI.[19] The manual might have been a door opener.

Whatever had been Oswald's goal, the effort at infiltration failed. Bringuier did not contact Oswald after he left the manual and would not hear of Oswald again until three days later on August 9.

For the nation and the Oswalds, August 9 began with deep sadness. Early that morning, news reached Marina and Lee by radio that Patrick Kennedy, the two-day-old son of Jacqueline and John Kennedy, had died. Marina was in tears. She loved the Kennedys.

She also had personal fears. To that day, Marina had received no medical attention for her own pregnancy. She had a premonition that she would lose the child she was carrying. If the Kennedys could lose their baby, the same might happen to her. Lee should end his vacation and look for employment. How, she asked, could they pay for the birth of their child?[20]

Marina remembered Lee's answer this way:

> "No, no, you're not to worry.... You'll be taken care of. Once you're in the hospital, the doctors don't care whose baby it is. They do the same for everyone. I'll borrow money. I promise you, you'll never be thrown out of the hospital....
>
> *****
>
> We haven't any money and maybe we can't get good doctors. But you're strong. We've got a baby already. Ours will be healthy. Everything will be all right."[21]

In fact, neither Patrick Kennedy's death, Marina's pregnancy, nor the Oswalds' lack of money were first on Lee's mind. Political action was paramount. At about 2:00 p.m. on that same day, an anxious Celso Hernandez entered Casa Roca and told Carlos Bringuier that a young man with a Viva Fidel sign was distributing literature on Canal Street. Bringuier, Hernandez, and a teenage visitor, Miguel Cruz, quickly grabbed Casa Roca's Statute of Liberty sign and left to confront the demonstrator with a counter demonstration.[22]

After searching more than an hour, they found him in the 700 block of Canal Street. A sign on his chest said Viva Fidel, Hands Off Cuba.[23] Bringuier was shocked and angered. The demonstrator was Lee Harvey Oswald. Oswald offered his hand and smiled. When Bringuier threatened to punch Oswald, Lee crossed his arms and responded, "O.K. Carlos if you want to hit me, hit me." Carlos withheld. But people in the crowd began shouting, "Traitor! Communist! Go to Cuba! Kill him!"[24]

Meanwhile, a police officer—alone at the scene—called for support. Two police cars arrived, and Oswald, Bringuier, Hernandez, and Cruz were arrested for "disturbing the peace by creating a scene."[25] It was a Friday, and a court hearing would not occur until Monday.

The Cubans quickly made bond, but Oswald, at first, could not. Ultimately, through a friend of his uncle "Dutz" Murret, contact was made with a New Orleans jury commissioner who arranged for Lee's release Saturday evening on a low bail.[26]

Making Himself Known

When Lee arrived home that Saturday night, Marina remembers him as tired and dirty but with an air of prideful good spirits.[27] His conversations with New Orleans Police Lieutenant Francis L. Martello, and FBI Agent John Lester Quigley had been gratifying. Lt. Martello, he said, was like a "kindly uncle [who had] ... listened to my ideas and let me out."[28]

Martello interviewed Oswald on Saturday morning. Before the questioning, Martello had examined Oswald's wallet and found two membership cards for the Fair Play for Cuba Committee: one from the New York office of FPCC and the other, a local card, signed by A.J. Hidell.[29] He was interested in the local chapter. Oswald would not provide details, but was eager to discuss Marxism and the differences between Russia and the United States. When asked about Russian communism, Oswald said it "stunk." He spoke favorably of President Kennedy.

Martello found Oswald to be "a very cool speaker ... no aggressiveness or emotional outbursts in any way, shape, or form." The coolness, Martello believed, came through most clearly in his handling of the confrontation with Bringuier: "[H]e never reacted to the action that was being directed against him [by Bringuier] ... He seemed to have set them up ... to make an incident...." No one was more surprised than Martello when he learned on November 22 that Oswald had shot the president.[30]

Oswald's coolness continued on Saturday afternoon with FBI Agent John Quigley. Oswald requested the interview. His reason for doing so is unclear. Author Priscilla McMillan could conceive of five different reasons.[31] Quigley told the Warren Commission that it was not unusual for people arrested by local police to ask to talk to the FBI.[32] Better to get your story to the FBI before they have a chance to investigate you. Moreover, becoming a target of the FBI might be helpful to one needing credentials for the Cuban government. Perhaps it might reach the press and build the dossier. Why not, then, tell the FBI that you were a dedicated Marxist in support of Fidel Castro?

When Lieutenant Martello notified the FBI of Oswald's desire to be interviewed, he did not give the name of the prisoner who wanted to talk, so Special Agent Quigley was unaware that his office already had a file on Oswald. Oswald falsely identified himself to Quigley. He gave his name properly, but he said that he had an honorable discharge from the Marines, had met and married Marina in Fort Worth, and that he had come to New Orleans from Fort Worth four months earlier. He avoided placing himself in Dallas at the time he shot at Walker. He made, of course, no mention of his two and a half years in the Soviet Union.[33]

Lieutenant Martello had given Quigley papers that the police had retrieved at the arrest scene on August 9—some "Hands Off Cuba" flyers, a thirty-nine-page article by Corliss Lamont entitled "The Crime Against Cuba," and Fair Play for Cuba Committee membership application forms. Quigley also saw Oswald's own membership card, signed by A.J. Hidell. From that Quigley began to ask questions about the Committee and Hidell.

Quigley knew of the Fair Play for Cuba Committee at the national level but was unaware of a New Orleans chapter. Quigley wanted to know about it. Having put number *33* on his own membership card, Oswald said the chapter had about thirty-five members. He did not know the names of the other members except the chapter's president, A.J. Hidell. He said he had never met Hidell but had attended two or three monthly meetings with about five persons present. He would not give the locations, although he claimed one meeting was at his own residence.

Oswald said that Hidell had sent him a note on August 7 urging him to conduct the August 9 leafleting. Although he and Hidell had never met, Oswald said they had talked by telephone—apparently forgetting that such a call would have been difficult since the Oswalds did not have a telephone. Conveniently, Oswald did not remember Hidell's phone number and said that it had been disconnected.[34] For Oswald, his interviews with Martello and Quigley on August 10 were a success.

Media Coverage

Monday, August 12 was court day for Lee Harvey Oswald, Carlos Bringuier, and the other Cubans. Oswald arrived last. He quietly took a seat in the section designated COLORED.[35] It was his public statement. He pled guilty, was fined $10, and said nothing more.

Bringuier, having been trained as a lawyer in Cuba, spoke for the refugees. He pled not guilty, showed the judge the Marine Corps manual that Oswald had left him, explained how provocative Oswald had been, and was found not guilty.[36]

Johann Rush, a television cameraman, was in the second-floor courtroom. Rush began filming Oswald as he was walking down the stairs. He told Oswald a report of the hearing and his photo would be on station WDSU-TV that evening. Rush gave Oswald his card and suggested that Oswald call him if he planned another demonstration.[37]

Almost as soon as he returned home, Lee began stamping leaflets. Marina tried to dissuade him. Biographer Priscilla McMillan described Marina's account this way:

> He and Marina sat many nights after that, she sewing and he pausing now and then to listen as she tried to talk him out of it. Sometimes he stole the leaflets from the closet when she was not looking and tried to stamp them on the sly. She told him to do it openly. "Up to your old games again, are you, big boy?"
>
> "For God's sake shut up," he said. "Why did God send me a wife with such a long tongue?"....
>
> Marina was trying to drag him back to reality and make him see himself as others saw him....
>
> "Be content to be an ordinary mortal, as you are....You're nobody special. Cuba has lived without you, and it can continue to get along without you now...."
>
> "Look at our neighbors," she said, "the people living all around us.... They are peace-loving people, busy with their families. They don't want a revolution. No one does, here. If it's a revolution you're waiting for, I tell you, this country isn't ready for it yet."

> "You're right," Lee sighed. "I ought to have been born in some other era, much sooner or much later than I was...."
>
> Marina did not mention the obvious—that he ought to be out looking for work.... But she did say, "Poor great man sits here all by himself. He's part of a great cause, and yet he has nothing to eat. Nobody sees that he is a genius."
>
> "You laugh now," Lee said to her. "But in twenty years, when I am prime minister, we'll see how you laugh then."[38]

Of course, this was Marina remembering more than a decade later events that she must have recalled many times. The dialogue could not have been precise. The reader must decide how much has been reported in self-interest and how much is true. But even if the details are embellished, McMillan may nonetheless have painted a valid picture of how the man who murdered the president was evolving and what was affecting him.

On Tuesday August 13, the day after Oswald's sentencing, the *Times-Picayune* carried a short article about the skirmish on Friday and the sentencing on Monday. The headline read, "Pamphlet Case Given Sentence." That same day, Oswald mailed Communist Party Secretary Arnold Johnson a short note with a copy of the article.[39]

Another Chance for Publicity

The newspaper article and Rush's request to be notified encouraged Oswald. Friday, August 16, was the next event. The International Trade Mart near Canal Street was the site. The time, noon. Oswald notified Rush, other television stations, and newspapers. Only Rush and WWL's cameraman Mike O'Connor appeared. Oswald and two

Oswald distributing pro–Cuba literature in New Orleans (National Archives).

others began distributing leaflets. Dressed in a white shirt and tie and carrying a briefcase, Lee had gone to the local unemployment office on Canal Street and paid two of the men waiting there each two dollars to hand out leaflets for twenty minutes.

He told one of the men, twenty-year-old Charles Hall Steele, Jr., that the leafleting was being done by a group affiliated with Tulane University. It turned out that Steele's father was a local deputy sheriff and a state Democratic Party committeeman. When Steele became concerned that the Fair Play for Cuba Committee might have a communist affiliation, he stopped passing out literature and later attempted to have his identity removed from any television broadcast.[40]

With three men passing out literature, Oswald could more easily claim to the media that his Committee was an organization with supporters. That evening the Trade Mart leafleting made the television news. Carlos Bringuier got word of the leafleting but didn't get to the Trade Mart until it was over. He did succeed, however, in securing Oswald's address from one of the leaflets, and a counter-espionage effort took shape. Before the evening was out, Bringuier's associate, Carlos Quiroga, went to Oswald's home posing as a Castro supporter. When little June spoke to her father in Russian, Quiroga became suspicious and reported to Bringuier that Oswald might be connected to the Soviet Union.[41]

A Radio Interview

Oswald was on a roll, however. Local media had found him. At 8:00 a.m. Saturday, August 17, William Stuckey, a radio show host from station WDSU was at Oswald's door. Stuckey was surprised. Oswald was not the long-haired hippie he had expected. Instead, he had neatly trimmed hair, was clean shaven, and was wearing Marine fatigue pants. He was articulate and intelligent. Oswald told Stuckey that he'd been a Marine, had lived in Texas before coming to New Orleans, and was employed as an assistant to a commercial photographer.[42]

Their conversation ended with Oswald's giving Stuckey a copy of Jean-Paul Sartre's *Ideology and Revolution* and Corliss Lamont's *Crime Against Cuba*. Oswald agreed to meet Stuckey at the WDSU studios at 5:00 that evening to record an interview to be aired two and one-half hours later.[43]

Lee's adrenalin was flowing. Before even reaching the station, Lee wrote and mailed another letter to V.T. Lee:

> … I was invited by Bill Stucke[y] to appear on his T.V. show called "Latin american Focus" at 7:30 P.M. Saturdays on WDSU—Channel 6. After this 15 minute interview which was filed on magnetic tape…. I was flooded with callers and invitations to debate's ect, as well as people interested in joining the F.P.C.C., New Orleans branch….
>
> You can I think be happy with the developing situation here in New Orleans.[44]

How many falsehoods could there be in three sentences? The program had not occurred. The invitation was to a radio show, not television. The broadcasted interview was only four and a half minutes. Of course, there were no callers, no interest expressed in joining FPCC, and no invitations to debate. To Oswald's letter, Vincent Lee did not respond. He was leery of Oswald.

Stuckey's radio program was *Latin Listening Post*. He had been on the lookout for members of the Fair Play for Cuba Committee but had heard of none in New Orleans until Oswald was arrested. Oswald arrived at WDSU as promised at 5:00 p.m. He was dressed in white shirt and tie and carried a loose-leaf notebook. It was Oswald's opportunity to influence the American media. He handed Stuckey a 1961 article by a Brandeis University professor distributed by the national office of the Fair Play for Cuba Committee. The article criticized the American press, especially the *New York Times*, for withholding full information about the CIA's support of the invasion of Cuba at the Bay of Pigs and failing to report that the United States had rejected a request by Castro for economic help when he first gained power.[45] *Latin Listening Post* was Oswald's chance to plead his case.

Although his broadcast segment was only four and one-half minutes, the taped interview lasted thirty-seven minutes.[46] Stuckey began by sharply questioning Oswald about his New Orleans chapter, how long it had existed, its membership, its leadership, whether the Fair Play for Cuba Committee was an arm of the Communist Party, and whether Oswald believed that Cuba was a satellite of the Soviet Union. He answered, "[A]s secretary [of the New Orleans chapter of the FPCC] I am responsible for the keeping of the records and the protection of the members' names ... [O]ur organization has a president, a secretary and a treasurer."[47]

Perhaps he had forgot that he had told FBI Agent Quigley that he did not know the names of his chapter's members or their addresses. He went on:

> In regards to ... whether I myself am a Communist, as I said I do not belong to any other organization....
>
> This organization is not occupied at all with the problem of the Soviet Union or the problem of international communism. Hands Off Cuba is the main slogan of this committee. It means it follows our first principle, which has to do with non-intervention, in other words keeping your hands off a foreign state which is supported by the constitution.... As I say we are not occupied at all with the problem of the Soviet Union.[48]

Remembering that Fidel Castro's failure to cooperate in the settlement Kennedy and Khrushchev had been reached nearly ten months earlier, Oswald said of Castro:

> He is an independent person. An independent leader in his country and I believe that was pointed out very well during the October crisis when Castro very definitely said that although Premier Khrushchev had urged him to have on-site inspection at his rocket bases in Cuba, that Fidel Castro refused.[49]

When asked if Cuba was a Communist regime, Oswald responded:

> [W]ell, they have said that they are a Marxist country. On the other hand so is Ghana, so is several other countries in Africa. Every country which emerges from a sort of feudal state as Cuba did, experiments, usually in socialism, in Marxism. For that matter, Great Britain has socialized medicine. You cannot say that Castro is a Communist at this time because he has not developed his country, his system thus far.[50]

Here was an informed, articulate, and elusive—when he wanted to be—speaker. At times, however, Oswald's facts were demonstrably wrong.[51] When the taping was over, Stuckey was so interested in Oswald that he asked Oswald to call him Monday just in case they might be able to air a longer broadcast with him.[52] Lee's adrenalin was being stoked again.

A Public Unmasking

When Oswald called on Monday, August 19, Stuckey said that his program director did not want a longer interview. He wanted a debate between Oswald and two anti-Castro activists—Carlos Bringuier and Edward S. Butler—on one of WDSU's daily programs, *Conversations Carte Blanche.* Butler was executive director for the Information Council of the Americas. One of the Council's speakers was Castro's anti-Communist sister, Juanita. The proposed date was Wednesday, August 21. Although Oswald asked Stuckey, "How many of you am I going to have to fight?" he agreed to the time, place, and participants.[53]

Stuckey, Bringuier, and Butler came fully prepared. On Monday, Stuckey had learned from the FBI that Oswald had defected to the Soviet Union and had married Marina there. Butler had obtained newspaper clippings on Oswald from the files of the House Un-American Activities Committee. Together with Bringuier, they planned a trap.[54]

Dressed in a heavy Russian-made suit and carrying his usual notebook, Oswald was the first to arrive at the station on Wednesday. Butler came next with stack of literature. Bringuier came last. As at the Canal Street confrontation, Oswald extended his hand. This time Bringuier was cordial. He hoped to make friends and dislodge Oswald from his support of Castro—perhaps enlist him in the exiles' cause. He believed that a former Communist who became an anti-Castro advocate could be especially influential.[55]

Stuckey opened the radio program with an explanation of the national Fair Play for Cuba Committee, the confrontation between Oswald and Bringuier on August 9, and their subsequent arrest. Stuckey ended with:

> Mr. Oswald had attempted to renounce his American citizenship in 1959 and become a Soviet citizen. ... Mr. Oswald had returned from the Soviet Union with his wife and child after having lived there three years. Mr. Oswald, are these correct?[56]

The surprised Oswald answered with "That is correct. Correct, yea."

From there, nearly twenty minutes of the twenty-five-minute program focused on whether the Fair Play for Cuba Committee was a communist-front organization and whether Cuba was controlled by the Soviet Union. It was a good night for Edward Butler and Carlos Bringuier. Not so good for Lee Harvey Oswald.[57]

When the program ended, Stuckey invited Oswald to join him alone at Comeaux's Bar, a half-block from WDSU. Stuckey recalled to the Warren Commission, "Oswald looked a little dejected." But for the first time, he seemed to Stuckey to relax. It was as if the revelation of his past on the WDSU program had relieved him of a burden, and he began to speak freely to Stuckey over the course of an hour. As Stuckey testified to the Warren Commission:

> [H]e told me that he was reading at that time about Indonesian communism, and that he was reading everything he could get his hands on. He offered an opinion about Sukarno [President of Indonesia], that he was not really a Communist, that he was merely an opportunist who was using the Communists.... He told me that he had begun to read Marx at the age of 15, but he said the conclusive thing that made him decide that Marxism was the answer was his service in Japan. He said living conditions over there convinced him something was wrong with the system, and that possibly Marxism was the answer. He said it was in Japan that he made up his mind to go to Russia and see for himself how a revolutionary society operates, a Marxist society ... he wasn't very pleased apparently with some of the aspects of Russian political life. Particularly in the factories he said that a lot of the attitudes and this sort of thing was the same sort of attitude that you would find in an American factory. There was a lot of deadheading, as we say in Louisiana.[58]

Oswald's candor may, in fact, have been a way of reclaiming face. Stuckey remembered him as one who "regarded himself as living in a world of intellectual inferiors. ...[T]his was a man who was intelligent, who was aware that he was intelligent, and would like to have an opportunity to express his intelligence."[59] Sharing with Stuckey his knowledge of Indonesia, his experiences in Japan and Russia, and his study of Marx may have enabled the twenty-three-year-old high-school dropout to regain a sense of superiority in dealing with the college-educated Stuckey.

The relief that Stuckey's chat provided was short-lived. McMillan later reported Oswald's feelings when he got home:

> "Damn it," he said to Marina... "I didn't realize they knew I'd been to Russia. You ought to have heard what they asked me! I wasn't prepared and I didn't know what to say."[60]

The encounter had been taped for later broadcast. McMillan tells us further, "Long before the program was to go on the air, Lee switched on the radio and sat in the kitchen waiting. 'Come quickly,' he called out to Marina, 'I'm about to speak now.... Maybe the debate will help and others will join.' 'Twenty minutes!' he said when the program was over. 'And I spoke longer than any of them. Every minute costs a lot on radio. And I talked by far the most.'"[61]

A Dream Damaged

Despite his spin on the broadcast to Marina, reality would soon set in. Lee Harvey Oswald may have gained materials for a dossier, but his career as a spokesman or organizer for the Fair Play for Cuba Committee had ended. What was next?

A week after the debacle at WDSU, Oswald did something unusual. He confessed error and sought advice. On August 28, he wrote to the Central Committee of the Communist Party USA:

> Comrades:
>
> Please advise me upon a problem of personal tactics. I have lived in the Soviet Union from Oct. 1955 [sic] to July 1962. I had, in 1959, in Moscow, tried to legally dissolve my United States Citizenship, however I did not complete the legal formalities for this.
>
> Having come back to the U.S. in 1962 and thrown myself into the struggle for progress and freedom in the United States, I would like to know weather, in your opinions, I can continue to fight, handicapped as it were, by my past record, can I still, under these circumstances, compete with anti-progressive forces, above ground or weather in your opinion I should always remain in the background, i.e., underground.
>
> ****
>
> Here in New Orleans, I am secretary of the local branch of the "Fair Play for Cuba Committee," a position which, frankly, I have used to foster communist ideals. On a local radio show, I was attacked by Cuban exile organization representatives for my residence, etc., in the Soviet Union. I feel I may have compromised the F.P.C.C., so you see I need the advice of trusted, long time fighters for progress. Please advise.
>
> With Fraternal Greeting
Sincerely
Lee H. Oswald[62]

Three days later, on August 31, Lee wrote to the managing editor of the Communist Party's newspaper, *The Worker,* in New York City, seeking employment:

I am sure you realize that [as] a program person with a knowledge of photography and printing, the greatest desire imaginable is to work directly with the "Worker."

However, I understand that there might be many loyal comrades who want the same thing, i.e., to work for the "Worker." So if you say there is no openings I shall continue to hope for the chance of employment directly under the "Worker."

My family and I shall, in a few weeks, be relocating into your area.

In any event, I'm sure you shall give my application full consideration. Thank you.

Sincerely
Lee H. Oswald[63]

That same day, he wrote two other letters.[64] One was to the Communist Party in New York City:

Dear Sirs,

Please advise me as to how I can contact the Party in the Baltimore-Washington area, to which I shall locate in October.

Fraternally,
Lee H. Oswald[65]

The other letter was to the Socialist Workers Party in New York City. A few days before, he had received from the Socialist Workers Party literature and a description of the party's philosophy that he had requested on August 12. This new letter said:

Dear Sirs:

Please advise me as to how I can get into direct contact with S.W.P. representatives in the Washington D.C.-Baltimore area.

I and my family are moving to that area in October.

As you know, there is no S.W.P. branch in the New Orleans area where I have been living.

I am a long time subscriber to the Militant and other party literature of which, I am sure, you have a record.

Thank you,
Lee H. Oswald[66]

October would hardly be the best time to relocate the Oswald family to the Baltimore-Washington area. Marina expected their second child to be born about October 8, although a nine-month pregnancy could bring the delivery date to October 22.[67] As the Oswalds lacked sufficient residency in Louisiana, Marina could not get free obstetrical care at a state hospital.[68] Dallas was, however, still an option. Ruth Paine had written Marina on August 24 that she was coming to New Orleans on September 20 to visit them.[69] Ruth's purpose, if Marina and Lee agreed, was to take Marina and Junie back to Dallas.[70] There Marina could have the baby and remain under Ruth's care.

Actually, Ruth had been proposing that plan to Marina for three months. The proposal seemed, at first, almost incredible: Ruth would not only relieve Marina of household responsibilities in the early weeks after delivery, but Ruth and her estranged husband, Michael, would pay Marina's medical and living expenses and give her $10 per week for clothing and incidentals for up to a year—perhaps longer.[71] Lee would be free to pursue his dreams.

The generous proposition arose from the Paines' need to restructure their own lives and from Ruth's affection and empathy for Marina. Michael and Ruth Paine had been separated since September 1962. In the fifteen days that Marina had lived with Ruth during late April and early May, the two women had become close. Ruth saw Marina's living with her as a way to help Marina achieve her goal of remaining in the United

States and a way for Ruth not only to learn Russian fluently but also to relieve her own loneliness.[72]

When Lee suggested to the Communist Party and Socialist Workers Party on August 31 that he might come to Baltimore or Washington, D.C., in October, the arrangement for Marina to be in Dallas had not been finalized, but Lee was aware that it could be. His own goal was not employment as he'd written. That was only a fallback in the event he could not reach Cuba.

But what a challenge it was proving to get to Cuba. The United States had imposed tight restrictions on travel to Cuba. If he made the journey without State Department permission, he faced indictment when he returned.[73] Such was the fate of V.T. Lee, national director of the Fair Play for Cuba Committee.[74] Securing permission from the State Department would be well-nigh impossible for one who had defected to the Soviet Union.

The Solution: Marina to Dallas, Lee to Cuba

As one by one Oswald's roles as pamphleteer, infiltrator, and radio spokesman for Castro's cause met failure, his emotional isolation from Marina grew. Marina remembered her husband spending many August days and evenings reading on the screened-in porch of their apartment, bringing a lamp onto the porch as the daylight hours dwindled.[75] She described him sitting silently on the darkening porch, staring out at the street for extended periods.[76] His conversations with her were mostly about Cuba.[77]

One day, in late August, he announced to Marina his solution. He and Marina would hijack a passenger plane at gunpoint and order the pilot to fly them to Havana. Between May 1, 1961, and October 26, 1961 (while Oswald was still in Minsk), six U.S. airline planes were hijacked from the U.S. to Cuba. The hijackings succeeded because there was no airport security system, and airline policy held that pilots should comply with hijackers' demands once threat of force was clear. No hijacking had occurred since.[78] The prospect of publicity for a hijacking appealed to Lee.[79]

The FBI reported Marina's account of the hijacking plan in this way:

> He told MARINA that he, OSWALD, would sit in the front of the airplane with the pistol which he owned and MARINA would be at the back of the plane with a pistol which he would buy for her. They would have their daughter, JUNE, with them. They would force the crew to fly the plane to Cuba. OSWALD told MARINA that she was to stand at the back of the airplane at the appointed time and yell out "Hands up" in English. She told OSWALD she could not say that in English. He replied for her to say it in Russian and stick the gun out and everyone would know what she meant.[80]

The scheme was almost humorous—but true. Marina would repeat the account with varying degrees of detail in testimony to the Warren Commission,[81] in interviews with authors Norman Mailer[82] and Priscilla McMillan,[83] and to her friend Katherine Ford.[84]

Lee's planning the hijacking may have lasted as long as two weeks. He measured distances on a map, secured airline schedules from New Orleans, figured the routes planes took, and considered the prospect of changing planes before committing the hijacking. He and Marina discussed the basic idea on at least four occasions. Marina claimed that each time she tried to dissuade him. Not only did it seem a generally bad idea, but the idea of a woman eight months pregnant holding a gun seemed laughable to her.[85]

When it was clear that Marina would not join him, he considered finding a Cuban to help him. He told Marina that he rejected that possibility because "Your accomplice is your enemy for life."[86] He meant, of course, that an accomplice can be a witness against you. Every conspiracy theorist might well consider Oswald's own stance on partnering in assessing whether Oswald had or was an accomplice in either the attempt on Edwin Walker or the assassination of President Kennedy.

Committed to reaching Cuba, Lee began studying Spanish in late August. He used Marina as his tester, relying especially on her to develop a more satisfactory pronunciation of the letter "r."[87]

To the amusement of Marina and Junie, in August he began exercises to strengthen himself for both the hijacking and service in Fidel Castro's army. To qualify himself further, he spent many evenings sitting on their apartment's screened-in porch dry-firing his rifle.[88] And for those in the Cuban government who would determine his loyalty and merit, he drafted a resumé outlining his adherence to Marxism, his residence in the Soviet Union, his language skills, his experience as a photographic technician, his training as a Marine, and his activities as a pamphleteer and public speaker on the radio and at Spring Hill College.[89]

His most surprising conduct was that which only a psychoanalyst could interpret. It was early September. Priscilla McMillan rendered Marina's description in these words:

> It was fearfully sultry and hot, and their only air-conditioning was an old kitchen fan. Lee went naked around the apartment a good deal of the time and sometimes spent the whole day lying on the sofa on his stomach, without a stitch on, reading a book....
>
> He played with Junie continually, took baths with her, and spent a good hour and a half putting her to bed every night. These were boisterous sessions, with Lee getting so much into the spirit that he sometimes leaped into Junie's bed himself, as if the two of them were babies going to sleep together....
>
> He was at his most babyish when he and Junie emerged from the tub. "Wipe my back first," he would say to Marina in baby talk.[90]

Late September came before Lee received any response related to his August 31 letters about moving to the Baltimore-Washington area. There were no offers of employment. Only Arnold Johnson answered for the Communist Party:

> Since I received your letter of September 1st indicating that you are moving to Baltimore, I suggest that when you do move that you get in touch with us here and we will find some way of getting in touch with you in that city.
>
> While the point you make about your residence in the Soviet Union may be utilized by some people, I think you have to recognize that as an American citizen who is now in this country, you have a right to participate in such organizations as you want, but at the same time there are a number of organizations, including possibly Fair Play, which are of a very broad character, and often it is advisable for some people to remain in the background, not underground. I assume that this is pretty much of an academic question now, and we can discuss it later.[91]

It was yet another letter that was cordial and advisory but not inviting. The message was clearly "Contact us when you move to Baltimore, and we can talk to you then."

By then, however, Lee was implementing his plan. He was confident that Ruth Paine would fulfill her offer to care for Marina, the new baby, and June in Dallas. In early September, Lee kept asking Marina, "When is Ruth coming?"[92]

Until Ruth arrived, he remained a steady patron of the New Orleans Public Library. On September 5, he returned *From Russia with Love, The Sixth Galaxy Reader,* and *Portals of Tomorrow.* On September 9, he withdrew *Goldfinger, Moonraker, Brave New World,* and *Ape and Essence.* His final returns were on September 23, the day Ruth and Marina left for Dallas: *Ben Hur, Bridge Over the River Kwai,* and *The Big Book of Science Fiction.*[93] Unless Oswald merely skimmed these books, one must wonder how he had time for anything else.

An article in the September 9 New Orleans *Times-Picayune* may indeed have diverted him. On that day the *Times-Picayune* reported that Castro had accused the United States of attempting to assassinate him and other Cuban leaders. Headlined "CASTRO BLASTS RAIDS ON CUBA, Says U.S. Leaders Imperiled by Aid to Rebels," the article quoted Castro as saying, "We are prepared to fight them and answer in kind. United States leaders should think that if they are aiding terrorists' plans to eliminate Cuban leaders, they themselves will not be safe." A similar story appeared in the *New Orleans States Item.*[94] A fuller Castro quotation added, "Let Kennedy and his brother Robert take care of themselves since they too can be victims of an attempt which will cause their death."[95]

The likelihood is slim that Oswald was too buried in his books to be aware of all this. He could well have read either or both articles in the public library, heard Castro's warning from Radio Havana over his shortwave set, or followed the coverage by the *Militant.* By mid–September he could have had little doubt that as an ally of Castro's government, he would be welcomed in the Cuban Embassy at Mexico City.

On September 17, he visited the Mexican consulate in New Orleans and obtained a fifteen-day tourist card[96] as a transit tourist.[97] With this tourist card, he could remain in Mexico City long enough to go to the Cuban Embassy, seek admission to Cuba, and secure transportation there. Marina and June would go with Ruth to Dallas to await the new baby. If the Cubans granted him admission, it might be months before Lee could see Marina and his children again, if ever.

True to her promise, on September 20, Ruth Paine arrived in New Orleans. After a conversation about plans for Marina, it was agreed that Marina, June, and Ruth's two children would leave for Dallas on September 23. The baby would be delivered in Dallas. Ruth would provide support as long as needed.

They never told Ruth of Lee's plan to go to Mexico City and Cuba. Marina was to keep it a secret, and Marina did not trust Ruth.[98] Lee told Ruth that he would be looking for work in Houston, where he said he had a friend, and perhaps also in Philadelphia.[99]

For Ruth's help, Lee was grateful and supportive.[100] While Ruth and Marina toured the French Quarter, Lee washed dishes and did the packing for Marina. One packed item was his rifle—disassembled and placed in a large duffle bag.[101] His pistol he retained for travel to Mexico City and Cuba.

Ruth gave this description of Lee on that weekend:

> He appeared to me to be happy, called cheerily to Marina and June as he came in the house with a bag full of groceries.... And particularly in parting on the morning of September 23 I felt he was really sorry to see them go. He kissed them both at the house as we first took off and then again when we left from the gas station where I had bought a tire.[102]

Priscilla McMillan's account of the first goodbye is more intimate: "When he kissed Marina goodbye, his lips were trembling, and it was all he could do to keep from crying.... Marina remembers that he looked at her 'as a dog looks at its master.' And in that pathetic look she thought she could see that he loved her."[103]

The second parting resulted when Ruth noticed a tire going flat as she pulled away from the house. With Lee following on foot, she drove to a nearby gas station. There he and Marina kissed goodbye again, and in a motherly fashion, Marina told him to be careful and eat properly. "Stop," he said. "I can't stand it. Do you want me to cry in front of Ruth?"[104]

He had to have known the risk he was taking. If he managed to get to Cuba from Mexico, it would be without permission from the State Department. He would not be able to return to the United States without being criminally prosecuted.[105]

The Oswalds had not paid their September rent. When their landlord, Jesse Garner, had noticed Lee packing Ruth's car on Sunday, September 22, he asked Lee if they were moving out. Lee said that Marina was going to Texas to have their baby, but he was staying. At about 7:00 or 7:30 p.m. the next evening, the Garners heard noises in the Oswald apartment. Either that evening or the next, another tenant, Eric Rogers, saw Oswald run to catch a bus, suitcases in hand.[106] A bus driver, who did not know Oswald, remembered picking up a man with suitcases at that bus stop. The man asked for directions to a bus station, and the bus driver dropped him off on Canal Street where he could board a streetcar that could take him to another bus that would go to a Continental Trailways bus station.[107]

Whether Oswald took his suitcases to the Continental Trailways bus station on the evening of September 23 or 24[108] and returned to his apartment to sleep or slept at the bus station those nights cannot be determined. The FBI checked with owners of forty-one inexpensive hotels near the bus station. It could find no evidence that Oswald stayed at a hotel on either night.[109]

What is known with certainty is that on the morning of Wednesday, September 25, Oswald collected a thirty-three-dollar unemployment compensation check from his New Orleans post office box, cashed it at a Winn-Dixie grocery store six blocks from his apartment, and arrived in Houston in time to take a Continental Trailways bus leaving at 2:35 a.m. on September 26 for Laredo, Texas. There is uncertainty as to what he did from the time he cashed his unemployment check on September 25 in New Orleans until records and witnesses place him clearly on a bus from Houston to Laredo in the early hours of September 26.

That uncertainty has been fodder for conspiracy theorists who maintain that Oswald had a secret, undiscovered conspiratorial life in New Orleans. Relying on the testimony of those who knew Oswald, his personality, and his patterns of behavior, the Warren Commission was unable to find any relationships, conspiratorial or otherwise, that existed at any time while he lived in New Orleans.[110]

In the days that I was a Warren Commission lawyer, I too worried that Oswald had an undiscovered secret life. I realized that individuals who might have conspired with Oswald to kill the president would not admit that they had an acquaintanceship with him. Finding such relationships was our task and that of the FBI. The FBI and others interviewed more than twenty thousand possible witnesses. I am satisfied that all investigators tried earnestly to find possible relationships of Oswald with individuals and foreign governments who might have had an interest in killing the president.

After nearly sixty years, no credible witness has come forward to establish that Lee Harvey Oswald had a secret life in New Orleans with potential conspirators. Those who knew Oswald best—Marina in particular—were correct in saying that Lee Harvey Oswald had no unknown relationships while in New Orleans.[111] He was not a man that others would have wanted as an associate in a well-planned criminal activity. Nor was he one to seek out others unless they served his political purpose—to build a dossier for admission to Cuba. Otherwise, his time was spent at home—stamping pro-Castro pamphlets, reading one of the thirty-four books he withdrew from the New Orleans public library, planning to hijack an airplane, dry-firing his rifle, exercising to improve his fitness as a revolutionary, or tending to his daughter June. In the summer of 1963, his focus was on reaching Cuba. America's politics were important only in achieving that goal.

Onward to Mexico City

The Warren Commission concluded that regardless of where he slept on the nights of September 23 and 24, spending nothing for overnight accommodations would have left Lee with approximately two hundred dollars when he left New Orleans. We concluded also that he probably departed at 12:20 p.m., September 25, on Continental Trailways trip number 5121, and that he arrived in Houston at approximately 10:50 p.m. on September 25.[112]

Oswald had approximately four hours in Houston before a bus left at 2:35 a.m. for Laredo, Texas. The wife of Horace Elroy Twiford told the Warren Commission that at about 10:00 p.m. on the evening of the 25th, a man identifying himself as Lee Oswald called their home in Houston. Mr. Twiford, a member of the Socialist Labor Party, had sent party literature to Oswald. A merchant seaman, Twiford was at sea when his wife received the call. Mrs. Twiford remembered that the caller spoke about his membership in the Fair Play for Cuba Committee, wanted to meet Mr. Twiford, was curious as to how Twiford had secured his name, and said that he had only a short time in Houston before flying that night to Mexico. The Warren Commission concluded that Oswald made the call probably from Beaumont or some other stop on the route to Houston or that Mrs. Twiford was mistaken about the time she received the call.[113]

The reader may speculate as to why Oswald called Twiford. If he was hoping to go from Mexico City to Cuba, why would he want to build a relationship with a Marxist in Houston? Perhaps, he wanted a Marxist name to add to his dossier when he arrived in Cuba. Perhaps, as he had done with Arnold Johnson of the Communist Party in New York, he was still reaching out for possible ideological colleagues in the United States, ones who might help him secure employment. Perhaps he realized that he might not quickly make it to Cuba.

In any event, we know from bus passengers, tickets, and other documents that on September 26, Oswald did indeed board the 2:35 a.m. Continental Trailways bus to Laredo and arrived in Laredo at approximately 1:20 p.m. on that date. He crossed the border into Mexico between 1:30 and 2:00 p.m., took Flecha Roja Bus Line trip No. 516 from Nuevo Laredo at about 2:15 p.m., and arrived in Mexico City at 9:45 a.m. on Friday, September 27.

Possibly, this many hours into his journey, it was a growing sense of optimism that caused normally incommunicative Oswald to overcome all secrecy and reticence. Sometime between 6:00 a.m. Thursday, September 26, and his arrival in Mexico City the next day, Oswald spoke with two British tourists—Dr. John McFarland and his wife Meryl

McFarland—who were also aboard both buses from Houston to Mexico City. They said Oswald told them he was on his way to Cuba, he had been the secretary of the Fair Play for Cuba Committee in New Orleans, and he hoped to see Fidel Castro in Cuba.[114]

Cuba was clearly his urgent mission. Within an hour of arriving in Mexico City, he registered at the Hotel del Commercio and then proceeded to the Cuban Embassy. In his address book were the telephone number and address for a Cuban airline that he obtained at the hotel. He could not be a tourist or rest until Monday. Friday must be put to good use.[115]

31

Mexico City

Secrecy, Bureaucracy, Credibility, and the Cold War

The Cold War—a war of words, feints, and negotiations—was at its height in 1963. On Friday, September 27, Mexico City was the springboard from which Oswald hoped to join the Cuban revolution. Seven months later, it was where the Warren Commission sought to ascertain whether Cubans had encouraged or conspired with Oswald to assassinate President Kennedy. Nearly all of the witnesses had a national or personal interest in being less than truthful.

The CIA in 1963 was secretly taping phone conversations of the Soviet and Cuban embassies and attempting to photograph all who entered or left the Soviet Embassy. When the CIA learned on November 22 that Lee Harvey Oswald was the prime suspect in President Kennedy's death, agents remembered Oswald as the subject of taped phone calls between the Soviet and Cuban embassies in Mexico City on September 27.[1] On that date, Silvia Duran of the Cuban Embassy had phoned the Soviet Embassy. She told the Soviets that Oswald had just come to the Cuban Embassy. As part of a projected trip to Russia, he said he was seeking a transit visa to Cuba and intended to go there on Monday, September 30.[2] His goal, he said, was to remain for two weeks or longer and then proceed to Russia.[3] Duran wanted to know from the Soviets if they had agreed to issue Oswald a visa to Russia. They told her no.[4]

On November 22, talking to Senora Duran was of great importance to the CIA. Silvia Duran—a Mexican citizen—was a married, twenty-five-year-old mother of one child.[5] She was employed by the Cuban government to help process visa applications at the Cuban Embassy. From the taped telephone conversation, the CIA concluded that Duran had obviously spoken with Oswald. Diplomatic considerations, among others, made it inadvisable for the CIA to make direct contact with Duran. For any American investigator, without permission from the Mexican government, to interview a Mexican citizen on Mexican soil brought both political and legal obstacles.[6]

The CIA had another option. It could ask Mexican security officials to interview Duran.[7] Mexican security promptly complied. By midday November 23, Silvia Duran was in Mexican custody—under arrest—along with four members of her family and a friend. By 6:00 p.m. on that day, she signed a two-page typed statement of her contact with Oswald at the Cuban Embassy.[8] Until the summer of 1978, that statement was the only eyewitness account that the United States had of Oswald's activities at the Cuban Embassy.

For the Warren Commission, the FBI summarized the Mexican authorities' two interviews with Duran as follows:

> [I]in the last days of September ... [Oswald] appeared at the Cuban consulate and applied for a visa to Cuba in transit to Russia. ... [He presented] his passport in which it was recorded that he had been living in the latter country for a period of three years, his work permit for that same country in the Russian language, ... as well as proof of his being married to a woman of Russian nationality and being the apparent Director in the city of New Orleans of the organization called 'Fair Play for Cuba.'... [He said he had] the desire that he should be accepted as a "friend" of the Cuban Revolution,.... [As] a result of which [Senora Duran] ... received all of his data and filled out the appropriate application, and he left to return in the afternoon, this time with his photographs ... and [Sra. Duran] called the Russian Consulate by telephone because of her interest in facilitating the handling of the Russian visa for Lee Harvey Oswald ...[T]hey answered her that the operation would require approximately four months, which annoyed the applicant, since as he affirmed he was in a great hurry to obtain the visas ... [Upon returning to the Cuban Embassy] insisting that he was entitled to them because of his background and his partisanship and personal activities in favor of the Cuban movement... [H]e became highly agitated and angry, as a result of which [Duran] called Consul [Azque], who ... came out ... and began to argue in English with Oswald in a very angry manner and [Azque] concluded by saying to him that, "As far as he was concerned, he would not give him a visa" and that "A person like him, in place of aiding the Cuban Revolution, was doing it harm."[9]

Duran told Mexican security that when she learned that Oswald had been arrested in connection with President Kennedy's murder, she had recognized Oswald from a newspaper photo as the man whose activities she described to them. In order for Oswald to contact her about progress on securing a visa to Cuba, she said she had written her name and telephone number on a piece of paper, which she gave to Oswald.[10] Two weeks later the Cuban government approved Oswald's request for a visa, conditional upon his receiving a transit visa to the Soviet Union.[11] Oswald did not contact her to check on his visa application.[12]

Finding the Truth and Silvia Duran

But was Silvia Duran truthful? The Warren Commission's staff was not satisfied with a signed affidavit from Senora Duran and an FBI summary of two interviews by Mexican authorities with her.[13] In April 1964, Commission staff members William Coleman, David Slawson, and Howard Willens went to Mexico City to see the scene first-hand, meet with all of the local investigators, and interview Senora Duran. They wanted her sworn testimony.[14]

The political and diplomatic difficulties that had caused both the CIA and FBI to rely on Mexican authorities had not abated, however. A meeting with Mexico's acting minister of the interior, Luis Echevarria, found him resistant to having American investigators interview Mexican witnesses. He wanted only informal discussions over coffee or lunch. No oaths. No stenographic transcripts. No other trappings of a formal investigation. Coleman, Slawson, and Willens returned to the United States without interviewing any Mexican witnesses.[15]

In the United States they considered another strategy. The Commission might invite Silvia Duran by letter to come voluntarily at Commission expense to Washington to testify under oath before the Commission. That strategy, however, had its own difficulties, and it required the permission of Chief Justice Warren. A concern was that one could not be certain how Senora Duran would react to a formal letter of invitation. Her husband was extremely distressed by the way Mexican authorities had treated them. She had been held in custody for eight hours before her signed statement was obtained. She was terrified.[16] Slawson suspected that her statement might have been the result of torture.[17] The Durans were, after all, supporters of the Castro regime. Even a polite invitation might be used adversely for propaganda purposes.

Willens, Coleman, and Slawson believed, nonetheless, that Duran was basically truthful. Her statement was consistent with what the secret telephone recordings had revealed and what Marina said her husband had told her of his disappointment with the Mexico City trip. Back in Washington, they were about to dismiss the idea of inviting Duran when the Chief Justice happened to enter the room and concurred. In that era of the Cold War, he believed no communist could be trusted.[18]

But that did not end the possibility of putting Silvia Duran under oath in Washington. A month or so later, Willens and Slawson learned from the CIA that Senora Duran was willing to come to Washington to testify. They notified the chief justice. He again decided that Senora Duran's testimony was not necessary.

In the end, the Commission incorporated in its Report excerpts from the translated text of the Mexican interrogators' account of Duran's statement to them.[19] The Commission added:

> The Commission has reliable evidence from a confidential source that Senora Duran as well as other personnel at the Cuban Embassy were genuinely upset upon receiving news of President Kennedy's death.... By far the most important confirmation of Senora Doran's testimony, however, has been supplied by confidential sources of extremely high reliability available to the United States in Mexico. The information from these sources establishes that her testimony was truthful and accurate in all material respects. The identities of these sources cannot be disclosed without destroying their usefulness to the United States.[20]

The confidential sources were the telephone tapes.

As time elapsed, of course, reliance on confidential sources undermined rather than enhanced the acceptability of the Warren Commission's conclusions. On June 6, 1978, Senora Duran finally provided sworn testimony in a deposition to staff of the House Select Committee on Assassinations.[21] She confirmed her earlier statement to the Mexican security officials and gave details that Slawson, Coleman, and Willens had hoped to obtain in 1964. Oswald had visited the Cuban consulate three times, not twice, all on Friday September 27. On his third visit, he lied by stating that the Soviet Embassy had approved a visa for him.

It was at that point that Senora Duran called the Soviet Embassy and reported to Oswald that the Soviets had not approved his visa application—that it would be three or four months before the visa could be approved.[22] Oswald, according to Duran, then got so angry that "he was almost crying." His anger caused her to seek help from Consul Eusebio Azque.[23]

Duran was troubled not only by her inability to quell Oswald but also by the questionable nature of the documents he had used to prove his acceptability for admission to Cuba. He had told her that he was a member of the Communist Party in the United States, but he did not have an introduction or recommendation from the Party. The Cubans feared that Americans seeking entry to Cuba might be either spies or saboteurs. The surest way to have forestalled such fears and gained quick admission to Cuba would have been to make arrangements through the Communist Party.[24]

After a brief discussion of the problem with Duran, Azque came out from his office, and explained to Oswald that any visa must be approved in Havana, that approval might take two weeks, and that a transit visa from the Soviet Union would be necessary. With that Oswald's anger escalated. He accused Azque of bureaucratic intransigence. According to Duran, Azque then told Oswald that "if he didn't go away at that moment he was going to kick him out or something like that." Duran said Azque went to the door, opened it, and told Oswald to leave. She told the Select Committee's investigators, "I was feeling pity for him because he looked so desperate."[25]

Russians Speak

The House Select Committee was not the last to fill in the gaps on Oswald's visits to the Soviet and Cuban embassies in Mexico City. In 1993, two years after the Soviet Union collapsed, it was time for the Russians to contribute. Russia had become a separate state. Freedom to speak and to make money in the private market became possible for former Soviet officials. Colonel Oleg Maximovich Nechiporenko was one who seized the opportunity. Having retired from the KGB in May 1991, he set out to render his recollection of Oswald at the Soviet Embassy in Mexico City.[26] There was, of course, a possibility that Nechiporenko hoped to quell any suspicion that Oswald had killed Kennedy as an agent of the Soviet Union. Yet on the basis of its phone recordings of the Soviet Embassy in Mexico City, the CIA concluded that Oswald's visit to the embassy was "nothing more than a grim coincidence" and not related to assassinating President Kennedy.[27]

In September 1963, when Oswald applied for a transit visa, Nechiporenko had been a KGB agent assigned to the Soviet Embassy in Mexico City. He talked with Oswald at that time. Thirty years later with the help of KGB colleagues, friends, and the Russian Intelligence Service, the Russia Ministry of Security, and the Belarus KGB, he published his book on the Oswald encounter.[28]

As Nechiporenko recalled, Oswald came to the Soviet Embassy at about 12:30 p.m. on Friday, September 27, 1963. The Soviet and Cuban embassies were about a block apart. Oswald already had been informed at the Cuban Embassy that he needed a Soviet visa in order to secure a Cuban visa for a stopover in Cuba.

Valery Kostikov, the KGB officer with particular responsibility for Soviet spying activities in the Western hemisphere,[29] was the first to speak with him. Oswald quickly gave his history of having lived in the Soviet Union, being married to a Russian woman, and returning to the United States. He said that he wanted to return to the Soviet Union because he was under constant surveillance by the FBI.[30]

On his way to another appointment, Kostikov turned Oswald over to Nechiporenko. As Nechiporenko recalled Oswald was at first aloof, but over the course of their conversation:

> [his] mood changed from discomfort to a state of great agitation, creating the impression of a high-strung, neurotic individual.... When I asked him to provide specific information about the FBI's following him, he replied that it all began after his return from the USSR ... His wife was still being questioned in his absence, and he claimed that the FBI had even been in contact with his friends. When I then asked him the reason for his return to the United States, Oswald fidgeted, changed the subject, and avoided answering the question.... From my first impressions of him it was clear that he was not suitable agent material."[31]

As the conversation proceeded, Nechiporenko explained that visas must be issued by the embassy in the country where the applicant is living and that it would take three or four months for the Washington, D.C. Embassy to act. At that, writes Nechiporenko, Oswald shouted "This won't do for me! This is not my case! For me it's all going to end in tragedy!"[32]

Nechiporenko stood up, ending the interview, and extended his hand to Oswald. Nechiporenko estimated that the meeting lasted an hour. He writes, "He departed, obviously dissatisfied with the results of our talk. He appeared to be extremely agitated."[33]

Kostikov said, "As soon as I came back from lunch.... I got a call from the Cubans. It was Silvia Duran.... It turns out that our 'friend' had been to see them after us and supposedly told them that we had promised him a visa, so she decided to call and double-check.... I told her we hadn't promised him anything and that ... it would take at least four months.... Is our man schizoid?"[34]

Nechiporenko answered, "I don't think so, judging by our conversation. But there is no doubt he's neurotic."[35]

If Nechiporenko and Kostikov are to be believed, we can feel the frustration that Oswald had a few minutes later at the Cuban Embassy when he attempted to pressure Azque for a visa, lost his temper, and was forced to leave. By the end of Friday afternoon, Oswald's only recourse was one more attempt to persuade Soviet officials to expedite his approval for a visa.

Returning to the Soviet Embassy

Saturday, September 28, was not a workday for KGB officers. They were meeting at the office for their regularly scheduled volleyball game against other embassy officials. It was to begin shortly after 10:00 a.m. Pavel Yatskov, chief of the consular office, was first to arrive. Waiting for him was Lee Harvey Oswald. Yatskov remembered Oswald this way:

> He was carelessly dressed, in a gray suit. His pale features and the extremely agitated look on his face were especially noticeable.... The visitor, without waiting for any questions, spoke to me in English. My limited knowledge of English nonetheless allowed me to understand that my guest was an American, a Communist, pro-Cuban, and that he was asking for a visa to Cuba and the USSR. I was also able to discern that someone was persecuting him and that he feared for his life.... While relating his story, the foreigner fidgeted in his chair, and his hands trembled, as though he didn't know what to do with them.... Then the door opened, and Valery [Kostikov]... stood smiling in the doorway.[36]

Nechiporenko lets Kostikov continue the story:

> [A]t the attached desk to the right ... was the American who visited us the previous day. He was disheveled, rumpled, and unshaven. He had the look of someone who was hounded and he was much more anxious than the day before.... I explained to Pavel [Yatskov] that the visitor had been here the previous day.... I turned him over to Oleg, who spent time explaining everything to him.[37]
>
> At this point Oswald, on his own initiative, turned to me and quickly began to retell his story.... Throughout his story, Oswald was extremely agitated and clearly nervous, especially whenever he mentioned the FBI, but he suddenly became hysterical, began to sob, and through his tears cried, "I am afraid ... they'll kill me. Let me in!" Repeating over and over

that he was being persecuted and that he was being followed even here in Mexico, he stuck his right hand into the left pocket of his jacket and pulled out a revolver, saying "See? This is what I must now carry to protect my life," and placed the revolver on the desk where we were sitting opposite one another.

I was dumbfounded and looked at Pavel who had turned slightly pale but then quickly said to me, "Here, give me that piece." I took the revolver from the table and handed it to Pavel... [he] grabbed the revolver, opened the chamber, shook the bullets into his hand, and put them in a desk drawer.[38]

Yatskov resumes the narrative:

Oswald began to droop. Most likely the peak of his tension had passed, but his eyes were wet with tears, and his hands shook. I poured him a glass of water and offered it to him. Oswald ... took a few swallows and placed it down in front of him. I began to console him ... we explained our rules once again, but in view of his condition, I offered him the necessary forms to be filled out. If he thought this was acceptable, we would send them on to Moscow, but it was absolutely out of the question that we would issue a visa to him at that very moment.

In response to his persistent requests that we recommend that the Cubans give him a visa, as an alternative to obtaining our visa, we told him that Cuba was a sovereign nation and decided visa questions for itself. Oswald had explained his desire to travel to Cuba earlier in the conversation saying he wanted to help the Cubans "build a new life."

Oswald gradually calmed down, evidently after having understood and reconciled himself to the fact that he was not about to get a quick visa. He did not take the forms we offered him. His state of extreme agitation had now been replaced by depression. He looked disappointed and extremely frustrated.[39]

As Yatskov relates the events, Oswald then arose from his chair, took back the revolver, and placed it under his jacket. Yatskov returned the bullets to Oswald. Oswald then left. The KGB officers never got to play volleyball. Immediately they sent a cable to their Moscow office describing the sessions with Oswald.[40] Presumably the cable was a basis for the book Nechiporenko wrote in 1993.

The account seems too bizarre to believe, yet also too bizarre to have been fabricated. After thirty years, it is unlikely, of course, that anyone recalled the dialog precisely or that the story hadn't improved, as recollections are wont, with each retelling.[41] But the described emotions and reactions ring true. That Nechiporenko and his colleagues would immediately cable Moscow seems to reflect the level of concern such an encounter would evoke. The refusals of both the Soviets and Cubans to issue Oswald a visa are consistent with political realities of the day and with what we know.[42] The erratic behavior attributed to Oswald is consistent with the extreme steps he took when he was at first denied Russian residency in 1959. It is consistent also with Marina's account of his plan to hijack a plane when he could see no other way to reach Cuba.

A Threat to Kill President Kennedy

An allegation that Oswald, while at the Cuban Embassy, either threatened or offered to kill President Kennedy is one to scrutinize with care.[43] The allegation stems from a letter dated June 17, 1964, from J. Edgar Hoover to Warren Commission general counsel J. Lee Rankin. The letter states that a reliable confidential informant had told the

FBI that after being rejected at the Cuban Embassy, Oswald said, "I'm going to kill Kennedy for this."[44]

The letter does not provide the source of that statement. Hoover's letter was unsupported by evidence of who actually heard the alleged statement. The Commission's staff regarded it simply as a rumor.[45] Although the letter bore a 1964 date, it was not discovered by private researchers until 1975. No copy of the letter is in the Warren Commission files. Copies were found in files of the FBI and CIA.[46]

Silvia Duran and Consul Azque say that no such statement was ever made in their presence.[47] Staff of the House Select Committee on Assassinations attempted to talk to everyone employed by the Cuban Embassy when Oswald was there. None heard such a statement made or mentioned by anyone.[48] The Select Committee said that it "did not believe that Oswald voiced [such] a threat to Cuban officials."[49]

The statement, itself, seems inconsistent with Oswald's having been rebuffed at the Cuban Embassy. Logically, any anger should have been directed at embassy personnel—as Duran said it was—not Kennedy. On the weekend of November 9, 1963, when Oswald drafted a letter to the Soviet Embassy in Washington describing his failure in Mexico City, he blamed Consul Azque.[50] The House Select Committee on Assassinations investigated the Hoover letter and concluded that the informant's claims should not be credited.[51]

Filling in the Gaps

What has not been clarified since 1964 is what Oswald did in the three and a half days from the time he left the Soviet Embassy on Saturday, September 28, 1963, until he departed Mexico City on Wednesday morning, October 2. His priority certainly must have been to persuade the Soviet or Cuban embassies to allow him to go to Cuba.

Marina testified to the Warren Commission that Lee told her that, in that intervening time, he went to a bullfight, visited museums, and shopped for a gift for her.[52] She later found papers and a map on which he had marked places to visit. The Commission believed that he may have seen several movies, either in English or with English language subtitles.[53] Oswald never mentioned encounters with anyone except at the two embassies.

People who had not previously known Oswald claimed, nonetheless, that they saw him at various locations other than the Cuban and Soviet embassies in the period from Saturday, September 28 to October 2. Although some of these alleged sightings are possible, none has been verified.[54]

The most exotic claim was that of Elena Garro de Paz, a Mexican novelist who was related to Senora Duran by marriage and vehemently opposed Duran's support for Castro. Garro told a CIA informant that she had seen Oswald with two beatnik Americans at a twist party for pro-Castro colleagues of Silvia Duran and that Duran had an affair with him.[55] Senora Duran emphatically denied that she ever saw Oswald after he left the Cuban Embassy on September 27.[56] In December 1964, an FBI agent interviewed Senora Garro. He decided her allegation was a case of mistaken identity.[57] Garro, herself, had not spoken with the man she believed was Oswald and did not become aware of Oswald until he assassinated the president. Her description of the man's clothing and other aspects of his appearance did not correspond with what was known of Oswald.[58] Oswald was not known to have American acquaintances in Mexico or friends of any sort who could be described as beatniks.

The allegation was one, however, that would not die. In 1978, the House Select Committee on Assassinations attempted to verify Garro's allegations. Both Elena Garro and the reputed CIA informant failed to accept invitations to talk to the Committee or its staff.[59] Ruben Duran told the Committee's staff that he had hosted a twist party in 1963 but that no Americans had attended.[60] Garro's family members claimed, however, that they saw Oswald at the twist party. The Select Committee attempted to find confirmation of Garro's claim from other guests who had attended the party. It could find no one who remembered Oswald.[61] The Select Committee decided that it was "unable to obtain corroboration for the Elena Garro allegation."[62]

Nonetheless the story of Oswald attending a party of Castro supporters and having an affair with Duran continued to have legs. It was marketable. In 2006, the German TV documentary, *Rendezvous mit dem Tod*, featured an interview with Garro's daughter, Elenita. She said that, as a teenager, she had been at the now legendary twist party with her mother. According to Elenita, she asked the man she remembered as Oswald to dance with her. He declined. The next day, she claimed, she saw the same man with his American companions as she sat at a Mexico City restaurant.[63]

Seven years later, in 2013, author Philip Shenon made Garro's claim a signal feature of his book *A Cruel and Shocking Act: The Secret History of the Kennedy Assassination*. Shenon located a Mexican artist who Shenon believed had first brought the Garro claim to the CIA's attention and claimed that Duran had told him she had an affair with Oswald. The artist acknowledged that he knew Duran but denied to Shenon that he was a CIA informant or that Duran had said she'd had a sexual relationship with Oswald.[64] Undeterred, Shenon located Duran in Mexico City in April 2013.[65] Again she denied seeing Oswald anywhere except at the Cuban Embassy.[66]

For over fifty years, relentless efforts by government and private researchers to account for Oswald's last three days in Mexico City have been unavailing. No reliable witness has been found that Oswald did anything more than what he told Marina—tried unsuccessfully to secure a visa to Cuba, attended museums and a bull fight, purchased jewelry for her, and returned to the United States angry at Cuban bureaucrats.

But let us assume that claims like those of Elena Garro and others are true. In the end, one must ask what relevance they have for determining Lee Oswald's motive in killing President Kennedy or whether he had conspirators. The missing days in Mexico City took place in late September when neither Oswald nor anyone else in Mexico knew that the president was going to Dallas on November 22, 1963, or that Oswald would be there himself. Oswald's indisputable goal had been to join the Castro revolution in Cuba. When he arrived in Mexico City, he had no intention of returning to the United States. He had not purchased a return ticket.

What we best know about his activities after leaving the Soviet Embassy on Saturday, September 28, is established by documents. On Monday, September 30, he purchased a return bus ticket for the United States. On Tuesday morning, October 1, he telephoned the Soviet Embassy, this time to determine the status of his visa application.[67] He also prepaid his hotel bill to remain that night.[68] On Wednesday morning, October 2, he was aboard a bus to the United States that was scheduled to leave Mexico City at 8:30 a.m. At 1:35 a.m. on Thursday, October 3, the bus crossed the International

Bridge from Nuevo Laredo into Texas; at 2:20 p.m. that day it arrived in Dallas.[69] On October 4, he was seeking employment in Dallas.

His effort to join the Castro revolution had failed, and he knew it. Returning to America and to Dallas had become the only option for the jobless, friendless, young revolutionary. In three weeks, he would have a second child. That he knew was imminent. What he did not know was that in seven weeks he would murder the president of the United States.

32

Setting the Stage for Assassination

When Lee Harvey Oswald returned to Dallas on October 3, 1963, America offered little promise for his political ambitions. In New Orleans, he had been exposed as a defector to the Soviet Union. In Mexico City, he had been rebuffed as a potential soldier for Fidel Castro. And Marxist leaders in New York City had been polite but not encouraging.

In America, he could not or would not join the two powerful political dramas that were unfolding—the civil rights movement and the 1964 presidential election. The civil rights movement commanded his sympathy, but it could not welcome his involvement. He had been a defector to the Soviet Union. He could not successfully be a visible player on the American political stage. Indeed, partisan politics was not his interest. His desire, as was stated so clearly in his *Maasdam* manifesto, was to be an agent of fundamental change on the world stage.

Yet he was confined to America for the moment. He was confined also to Dallas. Marina was expecting their second child in two weeks. For that there was a reason to stay, Yet, Dallas was a center for organizations on the extreme political right—the John Birch Society, the Committee for the Retention of the Poll Tax, the Committee for the Monroe Doctrine, the National Indignation Convention, the Dallas Committee to Impeach Earl Warren, and the Dallas Committee for American Freedom Rallies—to name a few.[1]

The spotlight in the unfolding political drama was on its star actors: Martin Luther King, Jr., and President Kennedy. On August 28, millions had watched Dr. King on Washington's mall as he shared his American dream. King was mobilizing the nation to bring pressure on Washington. Civil rights were at the forefront of the president's reelection campaign, already taking shape. Also at the forefront of that campaign was Cuba, where Fidel Castro was fending off assaults by exiles and pushing his own agenda for revolution in Latin America.

Those were the highly volatile issues that dominated American political theater. Vietnam was in the wings, only beginning to enter that stage.

Violence and Civil Rights

When Oswald left for Mexico City, violence had reached a tragic climax in the civil rights movement. On Sunday morning, September 15, in Birmingham, Alabama, four members of the Ku Klux Klan, using sticks of dynamite, bombed the Sixteenth Street Baptist Church.[2] The church had been a primary gathering spot for civil rights marchers. The dynamite killed an eleven-year-old and three fourteen-year-old girls. Twenty other adults and children were injured. The bombing followed the opening of integrated schools in Birmingham on September 4. In New Orleans, the bombing brought headlines that Lee Oswald could read. For the nation, the Sixteenth Street Church bombing came to symbolize the awfulness of white violence in the struggle for civil rights.

Violence in the Cold War

A different form of violence—assassination of third world leaders—had entered the Cold War. It had garnered only faint attention from American news media, but it was real. For more than two years the CIA, with President Kennedy's knowledge and oversight by Attorney General Robert Kennedy, had been sponsoring plans to assassinate Fidel Castro.[3] It was one part of President Kennedy's two-part strategy to remove Castro.[4] In his 1988 *Remembering America: A Voice from the Sixties,* presidential assistant Richard Goodwin recalls Defense Secretary Robert McNamara indicating in August 1962 that the only way to get rid of Castro was by "Executive Action"—assassination.[5]

By the summer of 1963, a Kennedy family friend, Desmond FitzGerald, was overseeing a CIA assassination attempt to be carried out by a Castro military officer, Rolando Cubela Secades. It was to be in connection with a proposed reinvasion of Cuba in July of 1964. The overall plan was that Cuban exiles would stage another invasion; Cubela, in league with others in the Cuban military, would assassinate Castro once the invasion was underway; the United States would provide needed military support; and the United States would recognize the new Cuban government.[6]

A companion strategy for dealing with Castro involved secret negotiations to render Castro a more contained threat, akin to Josip Broz Tito in Yugoslavia. Yugoslavia was a Marxist state that was not trying to export its revolution through armed force. By 1963 openings to possible discussions with Castro had been secured by two news reporters—Jean Daniel, a French journalist who edited the Socialist news weekly *Le Nouvel Observateur* and Lisa Howard, an American Broadcasting Company television news broadcaster. Both were friendly with Castro.[7]

Kennedy was willing to explore, through Daniel and Howard, the possibility of rapprochement with Castro.[8] The message that the president hoped to convey privately to Castro was simple. If Castro stopped trying to export communism to other nations and became the Tito of the Caribbean, then, like Yugoslavia, Cuba could receive U.S. recognition and aid.[9]

Planning for Reelection

While Dr. King was pushing for civil rights legislation and various strategies were underway to neutralize Cuba, President Kennedy was preparing in 1963 for his 1964 reelection campaign. He had won Texas in 1960 by only 46,233 votes.[10] After the Cuban missile crisis in October 1962, the president's national approval rating reached a high of 82 percent.[11] However, by October 1963, a Gallup poll showed the president's national rating had fallen 25 points to 57 percent. Another Gallup poll released on October 12 showed the president with an approval rating in southern states of only 35 percent. A Harris poll appearing in the *Washington Post* on October 15 predicted that he would lose more than half the southern states. Other polls showed Senator Barry Goldwater beating President Kennedy 59 percent to 41 percent in 13 southern states.[12]

By September 1963, polls gave the president an approval rating of only 50 percent in Texas.[13] Many Southern Democrats were unsympathetic to the president's support for civil rights reform and his apparent hesitancy to use military force against Cuba.[14] The structure of a political campaign in Texas was a major worry for Kennedy. Its liberal and conservative Democratic Party factions were in conflict. A healing process was necessary before a successful reelection campaign could be launched.

On Friday, October 4, 1963—when Lee Harvey Oswald was interviewing in Dallas for employment—Texas Governor John Connally and President Kennedy were meeting in Washington to plan a major political effort in Texas. It was to be a whirlwind, two-day visit to five Texas cities: San Antonio, Houston, Fort Worth, Dallas, and Austin in that order. Jacqueline Kennedy would be a star attraction.[15] Stops in Dallas, Fort Worth, Houston, and San Antonio would be used to build grass-roots support and resolve intra-party conflicts.[16]

The Texas visit would begin on November 21 with a 1:30 p.m. motorcade in San Antonio leading to a speech at the Aerospace Medical Center. The trip would continue that day with a flight to Houston for a testimonial dinner honoring Congressman Albert Thomas. After dinner the presidential party would proceed to Fort Worth. There the president would speak the next morning, November 22, at a breakfast meeting. From Fort Worth, the president would fly to Dallas for a motorcade from the airport to a luncheon speech at a place yet to be determined.

A reason for flying between Fort Worth and Dallas rather than making the short drive between the two cities was to have a motorcade from Dallas's Love Field to wherever the president would speak. The specific route of the motorcade was to be decided later by the Secret Service. After the Dallas luncheon, the presidential party would fly to Austin for the only fundraiser.[17] Thereafter, the president would spend the weekend with Vice President and Mrs. Johnson at the Johnsons' LBJ Ranch.

Motorcades were a routine part of presidential campaigning in post–World War II America. What was unusual was that First Lady Jacqueline Kennedy would co-star on the trip. In the past she had held herself at a distance.[18] Most recently, she had been emotionally crushed by the death in August of their newborn son, Patrick Bouvier Kennedy. At her husband's urging, she had gone to the Mediterranean for an extended period of rest.

But the attractive Mrs. Kennedy could be a genuine asset in winning the support of Texans. When asked to be a central figure in the Texas tour, she responded enthusiastically. Whatever one might think of President Kennedy's policies, it was difficult for political leaders and Texas voters not to adore Mrs. Kennedy. Indeed, when the decision to include her was announced, it made front-page news in Dallas. The visit to Dallas, itself, had been announced on September 13 in the *Dallas Morning News* and *Dallas Times-Herald*.[19]

Dallas in 1963

Dallas was not expected to be a welcoming place. In addition to anti–Kennedy activists such as Edwin Walker, the president had another strident opponent in

Dallas—Ted Dealey, the owner, editor, and publisher of the *Dallas Morning News.* Two years before, in October 1961, Dealey and eighteen other Texas publishers had met with Kennedy in the White House. Armed with a nine-page, five-hundred-word statement, Dealey had launched an outspoken assault upon the president in the Red Room of the White House:

> The general opinion of the grass roots thinking in this country is that you and your administration are weak sisters.... We need a man on horseback to lead this nation—and many people in Texas and the Southwest think you are riding Caroline's tricycle.... We should lead from strength not from weakness....We can annihilate Russia and should make that clear to the Soviet government. This means undoubtedly that they can destroy us. But it is better to die than to submit to communism and slavery.... We are not morons to be led around the nose by an invested bureaucracy. .[20]

Kennedy had Texan supporters, however. Some of the publishers rose to their feet and said "No." One publisher said, "Ted, you're leading the worst fascist movement in the Southwest, and you don't realize that nobody else is with you."[21] Finally, Dealey responded: "My remarks were not meant to be personal in nature. They are a reflection of public opinion as I understand it."[22]

Lee Harvey Oswald, in Russia at that time, may not have known what Dealey said to Kennedy in 1961. But in October 1963, when Dealey's paper reflected, as he claimed, the atmosphere in Dallas, Oswald knew it.

Oswald was not alone in that perception. There were those in Dallas who hoped to change the political atmosphere. A leader among them was Dallas department store mogul Stanley Marcus. No store in the nation was more prestigious than Neiman-Marcus. Stanley Marcus was hoping to foster a counter-front to the *Morning News,* a newspaper in which he was a major advertiser. By early October 1963, Marcus and his friends were planning for United Nations Ambassador Adlai E. Stevenson to address a Dallas crowd on United Nations Day, October 24. Stevenson's message, of course, would be the importance of bringing peace through international cooperation.

Larrie Schmidt and the Walker Movement

Edwin Walker was not expected to be part of the welcoming party for Stevenson's October message of peace. Indeed, he might be part of an un-welcoming party for Kennedy in November. One Walker supporter in Dallas was Larrie Schmidt, a U.S. Army veteran, who became a Walker supporter while serving in Munich, Germany.[23] Unwittingly Schmidt would play a significant role in the tragic Dallas events of November 22 and November 24.

In his tour of duty overseas, Schmidt had formulated a grandiose plan to infiltrate and become a leader in the American conservative movement. On September 30, 1962, Schmidt, Bernard Weissman, and three other noncommissioned soldiers swore allegiance to each other to bring true conservatism to the United States. The project was to commence when their periods of military service ended in the ensuing twelve months.

Their plan was to build political influence through a business partnership and a not-for-profit political foundation. The concept, they thought, was akin to the Ford Motor Company's relationship to the Ford Foundation. A common purpose of their business partnership and the proposed foundation was to further "conservative political thought in the U.S.A." The business arm was called American Business, Inc. or AMBUS. It began with no financial assets—only the efforts of the five partners. The political foundation was called CUSA—Conservatism U.S.A. Businesses of AMBUS would provide jobs to the five partners and fund CUSA. CUSA's strategy was to influence existing conservative organizations by gaining control of them.[24]

Under their agreement signed in Germany, Larrie Schmidt was the president and acknowledged leader of both AMBUS and CUSA.[25] Little could any of the five have known that the culmination of their efforts—a full page, black-bordered ad appearing in the *Dallas Morning News* November 22, 1963—would appear to Jack Ruby as an attempt to frame Jews for the assassination of President Kennedy.

Dallas was to be the starting point and headquarters for AMBUS and CUSA because Dallas was a center for conservative political groups like the National Indignation Convention and the John Birch Society., Schmidt believed if one could control those and similar organizations in Dallas, one could control conservatism throughout the nation. AMBUS and CUSA unwittingly became stagehands for the political drama in which Lee Harvey Oswald became a central player.

In late 1962, after his release from the Army, the newly married Schmidt moved with his wife to Dallas. He quickly developed friendships with leaders of the National Indignation Convention and the John Birch Society. One new friend was Robert Morris, legal counsel for Edwin Walker.[26]

By September 1963, Larrie Schmidt's brother, Bob, had become Walker's chauffeur and a confidante. Through his contact with Robert Morris, Larrie Schmidt became an organizer of a newly formed Dallas chapter of Young Americans for Freedom, a national voice for conservative young Americans.[27]

While Lee Harvey Oswald was thinking of joining Fidel Castro in Cuba, Schmidt and his newfound Texas friends learned that opportunities might soon arise in Dallas for a face-to-face confrontation with liberals over policies they most detested in the Kennedy administration. Not only was President Kennedy being scheduled to visit Texas in November, but Adlai Stevenson, the U.S. ambassador to the United Nations, would be the featured speaker in Dallas on October 24 at the United Nations Day event being planned by Stanley Marcus. What an opportunity for Schmidt and CUSA. Governor Connally had been persuaded to establish October 23 as United States Day—a day to stand in competition to United Nations Day.[28]

Together with his new conservative friends, Schmidt began preparing for a countervailing rally on United States Day. The rally would be highlighted by General Walker appealing for anti-Communist patriotism. Walker's words would contrast with Stevenson's speech the following night and might stimulate citizen action. Larrie Schmidt hoped to enlist Young Americans for Freedom and other youth in that effort.[29]

Calling Bernard Weissman

Bernard Weissman, the ultimate signatory on the advertisement that attracted Jack Ruby's attention on November 22, was not in Dallas in late September 1963 when Schmidt and his colleagues began planning for the Walker rally and their opposition to Stevenson. Weissman had been released from the Army only the month before. In October, he was still in his hometown, Mt. Vernon, New York, readjusting to civilian life.

Feeling abandoned by his CUSA partners, Schmidt urged Weissman to come to Dallas. Weissman did not arrive, however, until November 4.[30]

As Weissman received Schmidt's letters from Dallas, he was, in fact, having second thoughts about the relationships Schmidt was forging. The individuals with whom Schmidt was making alliances were not the pure conservatives that Weissman envisioned. Their brand of conservatism was infused in many ways with an element of bigotry.

The bigotry extended beyond the racial prejudice that was so widespread in the South. Religious prejudice was also visible. Some supporters of General Walker may have attributed Oswald's April attempt on Walker's life to Jews. On April 15, five days after Oswald fired at Walker, black swastika stickers were plastered on the home of Stanley Marcus, on his Neiman-Marcus department store, and on the stores of other downtown Jewish merchants. Under the stickers on Marcus's home were scribbled the words "We Are Back!"[31]

Evidence of Dallas bigotry came early to Weissman. In November 1962, shortly after arriving in Dallas, Schmidt had written Bill Burley, another partner in CUSA, about the attitudes of some Dallas conservatives:

> One bad thing though. Frank [McGee of the National Indignation Convention] gives me the impression of being rather anti-Semitic. He's Catholic. Suggest "Bernie" [Weissman] convert to Christianity—and I mean it. We must all return to church. These people here are religious bugs.
>
> ....
>
> [D]own here a negro is 'nigger.' No one—and I mean no one—is ever to say one kind word about niggers. Only liberals do that. Liberals are our enemies. Never forget that! Set Bernie straight on that.... Don't say anything good about niggers—but don't talk about harming them either. The Conservative isn't against the niggers, he just wants to keep him in his place for his own good.[32]

Schmidt's letter was passed on to Weissman. Weissman was offended by Schmidt's suggestion that he should submit to anti-Semitism—especially by becoming a Christian. Weissman did not believe that conservatism should be allied with bigotry. For Weissman, Arizona's Senator Barry Goldwater was the model for true conservatism. Goldwater was Mr. Conservative. An objective of CUSA should be to secure Goldwater's election as president in 1964.[33]

Yet this was the Dallas stage on which a sweeping political drama was unfolding when Lee Harvey Oswald returned from Mexico on October 3, 1963. Oswald was not on the playbill; Jack Ruby was not even an extra. Neither could even have imagined how the weekend of November 22 would catapult them into principal roles.

33

Looking for a New Life

On returning to Dallas, Lee Harvey Oswald was looking not only for a job but also a place to live. Marina and June were with Ruth Paine in Irving, but the Paine home was not a place for Lee. Marina told the Warren Commission she, in fact, preferred living with Ruth and without Lee.[1] Her baby was due in the next two weeks, and she felt Ruth could be more helpful than her husband. For a few months, Marina, June, and the new baby could stay without cost with Ruth. After that, the responsibility for Marina and their children had to be Lee's, more so than Lee or Marina actually knew at that time. The Soviet Union had rejected their requests to return. Marina's aunt and uncle did not want her.[2]

Even though Marina's due date was imminent, Lee did not call Marina or the Paine household when he arrived in Dallas shortly after 2:00 p.m. on October 3. He went first to the Texas employment office, where he renewed his application for unemployment compensation and registered for employment opportunities.[3] The Warren Commission estimated that on October 2, he had slightly less than $130 cash.[4] That cash together with $33 in weekly unemployment compensation might sustain him for a few weeks.[5]

He went next to the YMCA. As a former Marine, he could stay without joining. The next day, Friday, October 4, after seeing a newspaper ad, he interviewed for work at the Padgett Printing Corporation.[6] At first, being "well dressed and neat," Oswald made a favorable impression at Padgett. Afterwards, Frank Gangl, Padgett's plant superintendent, telephoned an acquaintance at Jaggars-Chiles-Stovall, Oswald's prior employer in Dallas. From that conversation, Gangl learned that employees at Jaggars-Chiles-Stovall "did not like him because he was propagandizing and had been seen reading a foreign newspaper." The acquaintance thought Oswald was a Communist.[7] Gangl did not offer Oswald employment.

After the Padgett interview, Lee called Marina. Ruth Paine was unable to meet him in Dallas, so Lee hitchhiked to the Paine residence in Irving. Priscilla McMillan gives this account of the reunion:

> He kissed her and asked if she had missed him? Then he started right in: "Ah, they're such terrible bureaucrats that nothing came of it after all.... The same kind of bureaucrats as in Russia. No point in going *there.*" ... Indeed, Lee's disenchantment with Castro and Cuba was complete. He never again talked about "Uncle Fidel" ... nor used the alias "Hidell."
>
> In spite of his disappointment, Marina thought he seemed happy, his spirits vastly improved over what they had been before he went to Mexico. He followed her like a puppy dog around the house, kissed her again and again, and kept saying, "I've missed you so."[8]

Lee spent the weekend at the Paines. On Monday, October 7, Ruth drove him to the Irving bus station, where he took a bus to Dallas.[9] Advertisements for room rentals were in Ruth's *Dallas Morning News*. Lee found a vacancy at 621 North Marsalis, in the Oak Cliff section of Dallas. The weekly rental was $7.00, prepaid.[10]

Mary Bledsoe was the landlady. As she told the Warren Commission, she remembered Lee Oswald well. He was not forgettable; after only five days, she had asked him to leave. Later, on November 22, she had recognized him on a bus, shortly after the president was shot.[11]

When Mrs. Bledsoe rented to Lee Oswald on October 7, she viewed him positively at first—a polite, recently released Marine with a wife and young child. She became annoyed, however, when he insisted on storing a bottle of milk in her refrigerator and taking food to his room. But those incidents were minor. His rent was more important, and she wanted to assist the young ex-Marine in finding work.

On Tuesday morning, October 8, she helped Lee make telephone calls for jobs. She again became annoyed when he returned that day at about 1:30 p.m., disturbing her regular afternoon nap. The same annoyance recurred on Wednesday and Thursday as he failed to find employment. Even more distressing was his presence all day on Friday. She had, after all, expected her tenants to be fulltime workers who would not disturb her daytime hours.

Oswald's bedroom was, in fact, immediately next to hers. She could easily see and hear his activities. Particularly distressing were some personal phone calls he made on the home's only telephone. He spoke to Marina two or three times a day; the calls were in Russian and often angry in tone. Although she could not understand the language, the fact that the calls were in a foreign language bothered her.

Mrs. Bledsoe was a widow who was confined largely to her own home because of health problems. She was able to observe Lee's daily life more closely than anyone other than Marina. Except for the few hours when he was away job hunting, she was regularly in a position to see or hear him. Mrs. Bledsoe told the Warren Commission that in his five days as a roomer at her home, Oswald had no visitors and talked to no one except the businesses he telephoned about employment and the person to whom he spoke in a foreign language.

On Saturday morning, October 12, Mrs. Bledsoe saw Lee leaving with a duffel bag. She asked if he was leaving for good. Lee responded that he was going only for the weekend. At that, she said he should not return—that she was terminating the rental. Without argument, he asked her to remit two dollars rent. She declined.[12]

He was, of course, going to spend the weekend with Marina. After a week, he still had neither a job nor a place to live. As always, limiting both where he might live and the jobs he might perform was his lack of a driver's license. He had never learned to drive, not even in the Marines.[13] Ruth Paine offered to give him some lessons. Although he did not have a learner's permit, she allowed Lee to practice with her in an empty parking lot in Irving that weekend of October 11 to 13.[14]

Reflecting on that weekend, Ruth recalled Lee as a good houseguest and husband. At her request, he planed down a door. He played with her own son, Chris, and watched television with him. There were only good words between Marina and Lee.[15]

To Marina the weekend was idyllic. They held hands, she sat on his lap, and he "spoke sweet nothings into her ear."[16] She thought that Lee, after his disappointment in Mexico City, might be shifting his focus from politics to family life.

Whether the assessment was right or wrong, Lee returned to Dallas on Monday, October 14, without a job, a place to live, or the expectation of long-term unemployment compensation. Fortunately, a twenty-two-unit rooming house at 1026 North Beckley

Street had a vacancy. When he had visited it on October 7, there were no vacancies, but the landlady, Mrs. A.C. Johnson, had encouraged him to keep an eye out for vacancy signs. The available unit rented for $8 per week, one dollar more but also slightly nicer than Mrs. Bledsoe's. This time he registered not as Lee Oswald but as O.H. Lee.[17]

More good fortune occurred on October 14. Concerned for Lee, Ruth Paine discussed with a neighbor, Linnie Mae Randle, Lee's inability to find employment. Linnie Mae believed that a job might be available at the Texas School Book Depository. Her brother, Buell Wesley Frazier, worked there. Ruth called the School Book Depository, and Roy Truly, the superintendent, invited her to refer Lee for an interview.

The next day, Tuesday October 15, Lee went to see Truly. As he had often done before, Lee implied to Truly that he had been recently released from the Marines and told him that he had an honorable discharge. He addressed Truly as "Sir." Truly offered Oswald a seasonal job filling schoolbook orders. Truly needed extra help because a few of the permanent employees were busy installing new flooring on the Depository's sixth floor. In a few weeks, when the fall demand for schoolbooks abated and the flooring work was completed, Lee's job would end. The hours were 8:00 a.m. to 4:15 p.m., Monday through Friday. Lee accepted and began the next day.[18]

Oswald's political interests had neither closed the door to a job nor did they interfere with his relationships when at work. The job was simple and solitary. He would obtain a list of orders to be filled, go to the floor where the books were kept, retrieve them, place them on a freight elevator, and take them to the shipping department. Most of the orders he filled were for books published by Scott Foresman and stored on the sixth floor.[19]

The workday was steady, with little opportunity for conversation about anything besides the orders to be filled. Roy Truly remembered Oswald as competent, efficient, and reliable. He also recalled Oswald reading a book or a newspaper on breaks but not talking to others.[20]

Buell Wesley Frazier recalled that he was Oswald's only friend at the School Book Depository. In the few conversations with coworkers that Frazier heard, Oswald used big words, for which others made fun of him.[21]

What began as a bad week ended as one of Lee's best. He had a new job, a place to live, and a coworker who could drive him to Irving to visit Marina on weekends. When Friday arrived, life got even better.

Friday, October 18, was Lee's twenty-fourth birthday. Marina and Ruth surprised him with a small birthday party, replete with table decorations, wine, cake, and the singing of "Happy Birthday." Lee was so touched that he cried and could not blow out the candles even though there were fewer than twenty-four.[22]

The present that Lee wanted most was that their expected baby be born on his birthday. He said to the group, "I'd like the baby to be born today, my birthday. I don't like late birthday presents. I don't accept them."[23] He did everything he could to bring it about. He rubbed and kissed Marina's ankles and legs. The next night, Saturday, October 19, they made love.[24]

During the day, Lee's mind remained on Marina and the expected baby. Aware that with two children, Marina would need a washing machine, Lee scoured the *Dallas Morning News* for ads for used washing machines. He also looked in the paper for secondhand cars, but his priority was a washing machine. He told Marina he could always go to work by bus.[25]

Some of their conversation was about naming the baby. If it was a boy, the name would be David Lee. Fidel had been abandoned. If a girl, Marina wanted Audrey Rachel. For Marina, their children should be American. The name Audrey was for Audrey Hepburn. Lee's preference, if the baby were a girl, was to name her Marina.[26]

On Saturday night, with Marina dozing off in his arms, they watched two movies.[27] Ironically, they were about assassinations: *Suddenly,* starring Frank Sinatra in the role of a psychotic serviceman who is hired to kill the president of the United States; and *We Were Strangers,* a 1949 remake in which James Garfield portrays an American who tries to murder the dictator of Cuba in 1933.[28]

Sunday, October 20, was another day of waiting. Lee arose early and scanned newspaper ads for automobiles and washing machines.[29] Politics was not first on his mind that day. For dinner Ruth cooked Chinese food. The sight made Marina ill. "I'll get ready to go," she said. Soon labor pains began, and Ruth went to the car. Lee remained with Junie and the two Paine children while Ruth drove Marina to Parkland Hospital.[30]

At about 9:00 p.m., Ruth left as Marina was taken to the delivery room. Returning home, Ruth sensed that Lee was asleep. The door to Marina's room was closed and the light out. Lee made no inquiry as to his wife or the baby. At about 11:00 p.m., Ruth called the hospital and learned that Audrey Marina Rachel Oswald had been born. Lee did not learn of his new daughter, always to be called Rachel, until he was leaving for work the next morning.[31]

Lee at first feared on Monday morning that, if he visited Marina and Rachel at Parkland Hospital, he would be obliged to pay for the delivery and other maternity expenses. Ruth assured him that the hospital already knew he was now employed and that it would make no difference.[32]

He went to Parkland after work that day. Marina wrote this account of Lee's visit:

> Monday evening Lee visited me in the hospital. He was very happy at the birth of another daughter and even wept a little. He said that two daughters were better for each other—two sisters. He stayed with me about two hours. In his happiness he said a lot of silly things and was very tender with me, and I was very happy to see that Lee had improved a little, i.e., that he was thinking more about his family.[33]

Indeed, he was, at least a bit. Lee's twice daily telephoning continued—at his noon lunch breaks and when he got back to his rooming house. But his focus was still on politics.

A Return to Politics

On Wednesday, October 23, the *Dallas Morning News* reported that Edwin Walker would speak at 8:00 p.m. that night at the Memorial Auditorium, the same theater at which Adlai Stevenson was to speak the following night. The October 23 event featuring Walker was the United States Day rally organized, in part, by Larrie Schmidt. Its purpose was to contrast with Stevenson's United Nations Day talk that Stanley Marcus had helped organize. On the evening of October 23, Oswald was in Walker's Memorial Auditorium audience, not at Parkland Hospital with Marina and Rachel.

Priscilla McMillan explained Lee's behavior this way:

> What Marina, like everyone else, failed to observe was that far from being better after his trip to Mexico, Lee was worse.... More than ever he inhabited a world of delusions.... Living alone five days a week with no one to talk to, he was not exposed to the scrutiny of those who knew

> him, and the strain was off him of keeping his inner world out of sight. And on weekends, in a world of women who were exhausted by the rituals of child rearing, he escaped for hours on end in front of the television set.... Thus, all through October it was as if the little household in Irving was perfectly geared, indeed, existed for no other purpose but to help Lee keep his inner world whole.[34]

Living most of the week alone was only part of what enabled Lee, in October, to keep his inner world intact. His room at 1026 North Beckley was, itself, a special container. For fourteen hours a day, it separated him and his delusionary world from ordinary people.

Vincent Bugliosi described the room on North Beckley as "little more than a large closet."[35] Fifty years later, tourists could visit the room, for a fee of twenty dollars apiece to the granddaughter of Oswald's landlady.[36] Scarcely more than seven feet wide and twelve feet long, it was indeed a place that could lend itself to inner sanctum and harboring dreams. When it was his, the room contained a single bed fitted snugly into one corner, and, by landlady Gladys Johnson's accounting, also had an "old fashioned clothes closet to hang your clothes and drawer space for your underwear, your socks and everything, a cabinet space anyone could have stored food . . and then ... a heater, and a little refrigerator."[37] In the room, Lee kept his shortwave radio, books, papers, and a holstered pistol.

Mrs. Johnson told the Warren Commission that Lee spent ninety-five percent of his time in the room and never had visitors.[38] The housekeeper, Earlene Roberts, said that Lee "was always in his room at night. He never went out." He left for work each morning between 6:30 and 7:00 and returned each afternoon at about 5:00 p.m.[39]

Three decades later, tenant Leon Lee recalled to Gus Russo that other tenants went out for dinner together, but not Oswald, who "just stayed in his room all night while the rest of us would be in the living room watching television.... He only came out to watch 'the Fugitive,' which he loved."[40]

Sadly, a crucial enabler in Lee's re-immersion into political fantasy was Ruth Paine's generosity. Providing room, board, and personal support to Marina, June, and Rachel was in effect relieving Lee of day-to-day responsibility as husband and father. In the isolation of his tiny cell at 1026 North Beckley, Lee could let imagination hold sway. And tragically, what imagination set in motion would, indeed, change the world.

Photograph of the author taken October 2013 in the room rented by Oswald at 1026 North Beckley in Dallas during November 1963 (author's photograph).

34

Resuming Political Pursuit

We can only speculate as to why Lee Oswald attended Edwin Walker's speech and the rally of his followers on Wednesday, October 23—United States Day. Was Oswald merely monitoring Walker and the right-wing movement? Was he planning another assassination attempt? Whatever the reason, watching Walker was more important to him than being with Marina and Rachel.

Edwin Walker's movement was not the only political force on Lee's mind. Saving Cuba was still a priority. A.C. Greene, former editorial page editor for the *Dallas Times-Herald* believed that a few weeks before November 22, 1963, Oswald, wrote to the *Times-Herald* under the name O.H. Lee expressing views of the Fair Play for Cuba Committee.[1] Lee had listed the FPCC as a recipient when he secured a post office box on November 1. In an oral history, Greene told John Weeks of Dallas's Sixth Floor Museum that after receiving the letter, he called the phone number on the letter and reached O.H. Lee, who asked, "You aren't going to publish it, are you?" Oswald may have worried that fellow roomers would read the letter and recognize his name. Perhaps in providing Greene a phone number, Oswald hoped only to influence the politically moderate *Times-Herald*—to persuade Green to appreciate and publish FPCC's point of view.

Oswald would well have expected that Cuba would be a target of Walker's speech on October 23. Political tensions over Cuba were running high. On Sunday, October 13, a headline on page 7 of the *Dallas Morning News* read, "Fighters See Return to Cuba in Six Months."[2] Perhaps he hoped to hear what Walker and his followers had to say about that.

It was equally likely that on the evening of October 14, he heard Radio Havana air statements by two American defectors. How that must have exacerbated the sting of having been rejected at the Cuban Embassy in Mexico City. Those men had succeeded where Lee Oswald had failed.

One defector accused the American Red Cross of being a branch of the U.S. government that was "sworn to destroy the Cuban Revolution." The other said, "It's a well-known fact that … the American government has been trying to smash the Cuban Revolution in every way that it can." A Canadian commentator added, "Stop trying to overthrow our government."[3] Those men were living what Oswald had dreamed.[4]

In mid-October, Cuba was in a crisis mode. Hurricane Flora had just ravaged the island, and the Cuban government was accusing the United States of hypocritically maintaining an embargo on Cuba while offering token amounts of aid through the Red Cross. On October 21, Fidel Castro claimed that the U.S. had deliberately withheld hurricane-hunter planes from Flora. He said, "The US imperialists are four times worse for Cuba and the world than Hurricane Flora."[5]

Walker Speaks

On October 23, however, General Walker's primary target was not Cuba. It was the United Nations and Adlai Stevenson's speech in Dallas the next day. The United States Day rally was designed to mobilize conservatives to disrupt Stevenson's speech on October 24.[6] On stage for Walker's speech were local politicians, including members of the Texas state legislature. That body had passed a bill to make it a crime to fly the United Nations flag. A welcoming telegram was read from Dallas Congressman Bruce Alger. He had offered federal legislation to withdraw the United States from the United Nations.[7]

Walker's opening words made the issue clear: "... The main battleground in the world is right here in America, and it involves the United States vs. the United Nations.... Tonight we stand on a battleground, identified on this stage as U.S. Day—the symbol of our sovereignty. Tomorrow night there will stand here a symbol of the communist conspiracy and its United Nations.... Adlai's going to sell his hogwash, and here's who is sponsoring him in Dallas."[8]

Walker then named the enemies—the Boy Scouts of America, the YMCA, the League of Women Voters, Kiwanis clubs, Optimists clubs, Rotary clubs, and more—sixty-one Dallas organizations, including the conservative Southern Methodist University.[9] Next came national names: Kennedy, Eisenhower, Roosevelt, Truman, the CIA, Nixon, and the State Department. Local federal officials—U.S. Attorney Harold Barefoot Sanders and U.S. District Judge Sarah Hughes—were also included.[10] Each listing drew a round of boos. Walker continued, "I'll tell you who started the UN. It was the Communists."[11]

Condemnations from other speakers went further. Oswald remembered anti-Semitic and anti-Catholic statements.[12] They reflected the sentiments of members of the John Birch Society and other ultra-right-wing attendees, sentiments echoing those Larrie Schmidt had reported to his CUSA colleagues a month before.

Finally, General Walker issued his marching orders. He told the crowd to go to the Stevenson speech tomorrow night: "Buy all the tickets you can afford. Bring noisemakers ... and handbills." Handbills were available to Walker's audience. Some bore a photo of President Kennedy and the words "Wanted for Treason."[13] Bumper stickers reading "U.S. Day or United Nations Day: There Must Be a Change" and "U.S. Out of U.N." were also available.[14]

There was to be more than placards, handbills, and bumper stickers, however. When Walker ended the rally, he remained behind to oversee the creation of a surprise. One may surmise that Larrie Schmidt participated. A large sign had been created bearing the words WELCOME ADLAI. Concealed behind it was a less welcoming message. Walker supervised the sign's attachment to hang from the auditorium's ceiling, just behind the speaker's platform. When Stevenson was speaking, a Walker supporter was to go behind stage where a rope could be pulled, releasing the second message.[15]

The Stevenson Affair

Oswald did not attend the Stevenson speech. Neither did the Young Americans for Freedom, whom Larrie Schmidt helped organize,[16] but hundreds of others from the Walker rally did. Schmidt succeeded in recruiting eleven students from the University of Dallas.[17] The students arrived early at the auditorium on October 24, forming a picket line in the lobby and taking strategic positions in the auditorium. So successful had been Walker's rally that according to estimates, nearly half of Stevenson's almost two-thousand-person audience were Walker supporters.[18]

As people entered, they faced signs held by Walker supporters: "Adlai, Who Elected You?" and "Get the U.S. Out of the U.N." Other supporters waved Confederate flags or rattled Halloween noisemakers. A well-known segregationist dressed in an Uncle Sam suit waved an American flag and shouted that the U.N. was for "communist race mixers."[19]

The most ingenious attention-grabbing stunt was staged by Schmidt. The dress code for his college student picketers was sport coats and ties. He arranged for another Walker supporter, posing as a Stevenson advocate and not so nicely dressed, to begin yelling at the student picketers, calling them Nazis and grabbing at their signs, hoping to provoke a fight. The idea was that U.N. supporters were to be seen as the ones opposed to free speech, out of control, and initiating violence.[20] Schmidt later told the *New York Times,* "I wanted to show people the difference between conservative pickets and leftist beatniks."[21]

As the auditorium filled, Stanley Marcus became restive. He realized that Stevenson would face hostility. Walking to the stage to introduce Stevenson, Marcus was met by a shower of boos and catcalls. Visibly shaken by jeers, he moved awkwardly through his introduction. Stevenson, a professional, was better. He welcomed the cheers and ignored the hisses.[22]

A few lines into Stevenson's remarks, Frank McGhee—an ally of Schmidt and founder of the National Indignation Convention—rose from the audience. "Why was Stevenson negotiating with communists?" he asked. Stevenson's responded, "I'll be delighted to give you equal time after I have finished." A physical struggle then ensued between McGhee and a man next to him. The police arrived, and McGhee was ejected.[23]

Yet the disruptions—initiated by Schmidt and others—continued. More scuffles occurred, but Stevenson was not deterred. Calling for polite and respectful behavior, he said, "Surely my dear friend, I don't have to come here from Illinois to show Texas manners, do I? … For my part, I believe in the forgiveness of sin and the redemption of ignorance."[24]

But the discourtesies abated only partially. Midway through Stevenson's speech, the Walker supporter assigned to convey the surprise package did his job. He pulled the rope on the WELCOME ADLAI sign. Unfurled beneath it was another sign: "Get the U.S. Out of the U.N. and U.N. Out of the U.S."[25]

The Aftermath

When Stevenson finished, his supporters gave him a three-minute standing ovation. Others apologized as he walked off stage.[26] Even though the speech was over, all was not peace and quiet. A policeman informed Marcus and Stevenson that a group of nearly one hundred were waiting outside, surrounding his automobile and chanting anti–U.N. slogans. Larry Schmidt's followers were there. A driver moved Stevenson's limousine; the crowd pursued it. Dallas police then established a rope line to protect Stevenson and Marcus as they walked to the vehicle.[27]

Hoping to mollify the angry crowd, Stevenson chatted and shook hands with supporters while walking to the waiting car. Suddenly a middle-aged woman—a Walker supporter who had been at the United States Day rally—lunged forward. She was wielding an "Adlai, Who Elected You?" sign fastened to a length of wood. Her sign dropped onto Stevenson's forehead, not causing serious injury but engendering nationwide publicity.[28] She, of course, denied responsibility. "I was pushed from behind by a Negro," she later explained. Photos showed no Blacks near her.[29]

For Larrie Schmidt, the Walker rally, disruption of the Stevenson rally, and Stevenson's strike on the forehead made his efforts a smashing success. CUSA had brought nationwide publicity to the conservative cause in Dallas. For Stanley Marcus and other Dallas leaders, the city had been disgraced. For those planning President Kennedy's visit to Dallas in November, the Stevenson incident brought worry. What would Walker's supporters plan for the president?

Summoning Weissman

Larry Schmidt had an answer. On October 24, immediately after the Stevenson incidents, he telephoned Bernard Weissman in Mount Vernon, New York. To the Warren Commission, Weissman recalled Schmidt saying, "I have made it. I have done it for us.... And he said, 'You better hurry down here and take advantage of the publicity, and at least become known among these various right-wingers, because this is the chance we have been looking for to infiltrate some of these organizations and become known.'"[30]

For weeks, Schmidt had been pushing Weissman to join him in Dallas. After phoning Weissman on October 1, Schmidt followed up with a two-page typed letter predicting huge demonstrations when Stevenson and Kennedy came to Dallas. In the letter, Schmidt admonished Weissman for not being there yet. Said Schmidt, "I think it is often overlooked that CUSA was founded for patriotic reasons.... We ... took an oath: Not for the purpose of becoming wealthy, but for 'duty, honor, and country.'"[31] For Schmidt, building a conservative movement was a mission. Opposing Stevenson and Kennedy were milestones in the mission.

Waiting for Weissman, Schmidt wrote again on October 29:

> To[sic] much has happened in the past few days. I don't know where to begin. First of all, what appeared at first to have been a great blunder of ours has rapidly turned into a great victory. I refer to [the] STEVENSON incident....
>
> I personally had nothing to do with the sign-hitting and spitting incidents ... the press reports were so outrageously exaggerated it is unbelievable.... [T]he fact our mayor and City Council have issued an official apology on behalf of Dallas, has aroused the scorn and anger of all Dallasites, the overwhelming majority of whom are right wingers.
>
> The ultra liberals of Dallas, led by STANLEY MARCUS, ... went to [sic] far in pressuring for denunciation of "extremists" and "Fascists" in Dallas. As a result, a bomb has exploded everywhere here against them. This town is a battleground.... Never before have Dallas conservatives from the GOP to the John Birch Society ever been so strongly united.
>
> ....
>
> I am the only organizer of the demonstration to have publicly identified himself. I have been interviewed by UPI, AP, the two local daily newspapers, TV stations, CBS, and local radio. I am a hero to the right—a storm trooper to the left.
>
> ....
>
> [D]ue to this international incident, I have become overnight a "fearless spokesman" and

"leader" of the right wing in Dallas. What I worked so hard for in one year—and nearly failed—finally came through one incident, in one night.

Politically, CUSA is set.... What you achieve is up to you. All I can do is pave the way.[32]

Dallas's Apology

The "official apology" to which Schmidt referred was a telegram sent by Mayor Earle Cabell to Stevenson on October 25: "The city of Dallas is outraged and abjectly ashamed of the disgraceful discourtesies you suffered at the hands of a small group of extremists here last night.... [The attackers] do not represent the heart or the mind of this great city."[33]

That same day the *Dallas Times-Herald* printed its own front-page apology: "Dallas has been disgraced. There is no other way to view the storm trooper actions of last night's frightening attack on Adlai Stevenson.... [T]his misguided brand of 'patriotism' is dragging the name of Dallas through the slime of national dishonor."[34] The *Dallas Morning News* chastened, "This city should examine itself."[35]

On October 27, Mayor Cabell issued another public statement: "Let us look these so-called patriots in the face.... These are not conservatives, they are radicals.... We have an opportunity to redeem ourselves when the President pays us a visit next month.... But good behavior is not enough. This cancer on the body politic must be removed."[36]

General Walker felt differently. For days after Mayor Cabell's statements, he flew the American flags outside his home upside down—a naval sign of distress.[37] Other Dallasites canceled their Neiman Marcus credit accounts.[38] As Larrie Schmidt told Weissman, Dallas was, in fact, a "battleground."

Democrats Worry

The further Adlai Stevenson distanced himself from Dallas, the more his own worries grew. Initially, he described the incidents as "the violent behavior of a few." He asked that the woman whose sign struck him not be prosecuted: "I don't want to send them to jail. I want to send them to school."[39] Once in Washington, however, he began to hear heightened concerns from Stanley Marcus and others.[40] The next day he told historian Arthur Schlesinger, at that time a special aide to President Kennedy, "They wondered whether the President should go to Dallas. And so do I."[41]

Ultimately, Stanley Marcus called Vice President Johnson and urged him to persuade the president not to include Dallas on his Texas itinerary.[42] Johnson knew the president well. He was not going to be intimidated by General Walker. Johnson replied to Marcus, "I don't care what you think, nor does it make any difference what I think about the President's coming down to Dallas. He is coming to Dallas so go out and raise the money."[43]

As the days wore on, Johnson downplayed the Dallas incident as the disruptions of "a minute handful ... a few zealots." Many in Dallas saw it differently. Bob Walker, news director of Dallas's WFAA-TV, wrote to Stevenson that the right wing was "winning their fight in Dallas." What happened to Stevenson on October 24 was front-page news in Dallas for four days.

Kennedy, himself, interpreted the Stevenson incidents merely as forms of disruptive political protest, which of course they were. Larrie Schmidt and others on the political right were political activists, not assassins. They might place hostile words on signs and banners. They might even hurl vegetables or something more disagreeable, but they were not assassins. Their goal was to gain power by winning elections.

Dallas Prepares

Dallas city officials also viewed any likely disruptions as unruly rather than dangerous. Their concern was for civic embarrassment. Nonetheless, the city council passed an ordinance outlawing interference with lawful assembly. Police Chief Curry said he would enforce anti-littering laws if demonstrators left leaflets or other matter on the ground. Yet police were concerned that anything unduly restrictive would leave them accused of preventing free speech.

Despite the disruptions, nothing that had transpired during Stevenson's visit had caused local or federal officials to worry that there might be a rifleman in a building overlooking the proposed presidential motorcade. The Warren Commission concluded no police or federal official had concern for a potential assassin.

There is, however, some evidence to the contrary. On November 22, 1963, after the president had been shot, Dallas Police Officer Jack Revill wrote a letter to a departmental supervisor saying that FBI Agent James Hosty had told him that afternoon that the FBI knew that Oswald "was capable of committing the assassination of President Kennedy." The statement was made apparently in relation to a suggestion that Oswald was a "member of the Communist party." Revill and Hosty were friends. Revill told the Warren Commission he had assumed Hosty would reveal the information himself, but Hosty, in his own testimony, denied making the statement to Revill.[44] There is no evidence, moreover, that on November 22, 1963, anyone but Marina knew that Lee Oswald had attempted to kill General Edwin Walker.

Oswald Looks Ahead

On Wednesday, October 23, not even Lee Oswald could expect that within a month he might murder the president of the United States. As Oswald's subsequent behavior suggests, until a few days before November 22, he may not have imagined that assassination was even a possibility.

Adlai Stevenson's speech on October 24 was apparently not of overriding interest to Oswald. There is no evidence that he attended. He may well have been listening to Havana Radio. That night its broadcaster said, "The CIA acts under the direct orders of the president, in this case Mr. Kennedy, and is responsible solely for their activities and adventures. When they launch a pirate attack against the Cuban coast line, and murder a militiaman or a teacher … they are acting under the direct orders of the United States president."[45] We can be sure that Oswald knew of the turmoil and concerns in Dallas that followed the Stevenson event. A week later he mentioned them in a letter to Arnold Johnson, secretary to the Communist Party USA.[46]

On Friday afternoon, October 25, Lee rode again to Irving with Buell Wesley Frazier for a weekend with Marina, his daughters, and Ruth Paine. As often occurred on

Fridays, Ruth's husband, Michael, came for dinner. Rachel was then five days old. But politics preempted a family evening. Michael invited Lee to join him after dinner for a meeting of the American Civil Liberties Union. Lee accepted.

Learning About the ACLU

As Michael drove to the meeting at Southern Methodist University, he was surprised to learn that Lee had not heard of the ACLU. Michael hoped the organization might become a constructive interest for him.[47] At the meeting, Lee became outspoken, rising to his feet at one point to say that he had been at the Walker rally two nights before and that speakers from the John Birch Society were both anti-Semitic and anti-Catholic. When the ACLU meeting ended, Oswald engaged with at least two members—one of whom he thought might be a Communist. Lee explained to Michael that the man expressed sympathy for Cuba.[48]

Michael recalled his conversation with Lee in the thirty-five-minute drive back to Irving:

> I was describing to him the purpose of the ACLU, and he said specifically ... that he couldn't join an organization like that, it wasn't political and he said something or responded in some manner, which indicated surprise that I could be concerned about joining an organization simply to defend, whose purpose it is, shall we say, to defend free speech, free speech, per se, your freedom as well as mine....And I think it took him by surprise that a person could be concerned about a value like that rather than political objective of some sort....
>
> I am sure I told him that it came to the defense of all people who didn't seem to be receiving adequate help when it seemed to be an issue involving the Bill of Rights.[49]

Yet, Lee had taken a membership application from the meeting. A week later, on Friday, November 1, he mailed the application with two dollars in payment to the ACLU's New York office. This was the same day he rented post office box number 6225 at the Terminal Annex Post Office, two blocks from the Texas School Book Depository, paying three dollars for two months' rental. Listed as authorized recipients were the American Civil Liberties Union and the Fair Play for Cuba Committee.[50]

What could he be planning? A post office box for the ACLU and FPCC are not necessary to assassinate the president. Taking a post office box for two months on November 1 would indicate he was not planning to leave Dallas in November. On that same Friday, November 1, he mailed a letter to Arnold Johnson, secretary of the Communist Party USA with whom he had previously corresponded. To Johnson he wrote:

> [M]y personal plans have changed and I have settled in Dallas, Texas, for the time.
>
> Through a friend, I have been introduced into the American Civil Liberties Union Local chapter, which holds monthly meeting[s] on the campus of Southern Methodist University. The first meeting I attended was October 25th, a film was shown and afterwards a very critical discussion of the ultra-right in Dallas. On October 23rd, I had attended a ultra-right meeting headed by General Edwin A. Walker, who lives in Dallas. This meeting preceded by one day the attack on A.E. Stevenson at the United Nations Day meeting at which he spoke.
>
> As you can see, political friction between the "left" and "right" is very great here. Could you advise me as to the general view we have on the American Civil Liberties Union? And to what degree, if any, I should attempt to heighten its progressive tendencies? The Dallas branch of the A.C.L.U. is firmly in the hands of "liberal" professional people, (a minister and two

Law professors conducted the October 25th meeting) however, some of those present showed marked class-awareness and insight.[51]

Mailed on November 1, a full week after the Friday ACLU meeting, the letter seems to have been carefully drafted and cannot be separated from his membership application to the ACLU or his listing both the ACLU and FPCC on his post office box rental. It reflects fundamental decisions: to remain in Dallas at least for the time being and to explore how the ACLU might fit into furthering his goals.

Oswald's inner world still focused on how Marxism could expand and be protected in Latin America. On November 6, Oswald borrowed *The Shark and the Sardines* from the Dallas Public Library, a 1961 book by the former president of Guatemala, Dr. Juan Jose Arevalo.[52] Arevalo had a doctorate from the University of La Plata, had been elected president of Guatemala from 1945 to 1951, and had been prevented in 1963 by the Guatemalan military from seeking election again—a timely book for one hoping to spread revolution to Latin America.[53] Writing especially for American readers, Arevalo described his book as "a book that speaks out against your State Department's dealings with the peoples of Latin America during the Twentieth Century."[54]

As one might glean from its title, *The Shark and the Sardines* was written in graphic terms. The shark was the United States and its military and economic leaders. The sardines were the smaller countries of Latin America. The sea was Latin America where the shark was consuming the smaller countries. For Oswald, the book could be inspirational reading.[55]

The Shark and the Sardines reinforced what Lee was hearing in the isolation of his Beckley Street room from Radio Havana and reading in *The Militant*. The November 4 edition carried an editorial titled "Lift the Blockade," referring of course to President Kennedy's blockade of Cuba.[56] Could a new revolutionary path be opening for Lee Oswald right there in Dallas? Perhaps he could indeed "heighten … progressive tendencies" and forge allies within the ACLU; he could support revolution in Latin America, and stymie the efforts of Walker's supporters. So many possibilities lay before him. Yet Oswald would never have any further contact with the ACLU.

35

Agent Hosty Disrupts the Inner World

As Lee Oswald was exploring a new course for political action, Special Agent James Hosty of the FBI's Dallas office was in search of him. Hosty had inherited his agency's Oswald file from a retired FBI agent in October 1962. From September 1, 1962, to January 1963, the Oswalds had lived at three different addresses. Hosty had been unable to locate them before they moved in May to New Orleans. When Oswald became visible in New Orleans, responsibility transferred to an agent there. The New Orleans FBI office found Oswald only when he made newspaper headlines, was arrested, and then asked for an FBI interview.

But by October 1, 1963, the Oswalds were lost to the FBI again. On that date, the FBI's New Orleans office notified Dallas that Marina had been seen moving from their residence with another woman in a car bearing Texas license plates, and their apartment was vacant.[1] The Oswald file landed, therefore, back in Hosty's hands.

Hosty was obligated to be concerned with Marina as well as Lee. In recent special training on security and counterespionage cases, Hosty had learned that the Soviets were "recruiting and training young, highly educated Soviets" to be intelligence agents in the United States.[2] Could Marina be one of these? The FBI had also learned from the CIA's telephone intercept that Lee had visited the Soviet Embassy in Mexico City on September 27.[3] Had he been receiving instructions from the Soviets?

Both Lee and Marina were, thus, important subjects to be located, watched, and ultimately interviewed. Marina, as a foreign resident, was required to file a record of her address annually with the United States Immigration and Naturalization Service. From INS records, Hosty learned that Marina was living at 2515 West Fifth Street in Irving, Texas—the home of Ruth Paine.

Hosty determined that background on Ruth was important before he proceeded too far with Marina. He wondered, at first, if Ruth was a Communist.[4] By the end of October, he was satisfied that she was a well-meaning Quaker whose interest in the Oswalds was probably no more than humanitarian.[5] His ultimate goals were to locate Lee and Marina, "to conduct an in-depth interview of Marina to determine whether she posed any national security risk," and to make a similar determination for Lee.[6]

On October 29, Hosty drove to Ruth Paine's street in Irving. No other agent was with him. In the Paines' driveway, he saw a station wagon with Texas plates. Through a neighbor, Dorothy Roberts, Hosty confirmed that a Russian woman who spoke no English and had a small child was living with Ruth. Special Agent Hosty was sure he had located Marina.[7]

In the afternoon of Friday, November 1, Hosty was back in Irving, this time at Ruth Paine's house. Once again, no other agent was with him. His conversation began alone with Ruth. It was a visit that did not surprise Ruth. As might be expected, Dorothy Roberts had told her that an FBI agent had been inquiring about her and Marina.

From Ruth, Hosty learned that Lee was living in Dallas—at an unknown address—and that he worked at the Texas School Book Depository. After a few minutes, Marina appeared. When she learned that Hosty was from the FBI, her initial reaction was one of fright.[8] She was especially concerned that the FBI's interest would cause Lee to lose his job. Hosty, having a demeanor and style that tended to put people at ease, succeeded after a while in reassuring Marina.[9]

As their discussion came to a close, Ruth asked Hosty to stay until Lee came home. It was Friday, and Lee was expected at 5:30. Hosty declined. He did not say so, but he was not ready to proceed with a serious interview. He wanted to gather more background information, and he wanted another agent with him. He excused himself, wrote his name and phone number on a piece of paper for them,[10] and said he'd like to return for a further discussion. Marina and Ruth were agreeable.[11]

Lee arrived at the accustomed time, also in an agreeable mood. Only a few hours before, he had rented the post office box to support his new political strategy and posted his letter to the Communist Party. Things were going well. But when Marina told him about Hosty's visit, "his face darkened."[12] As Priscilla McMillan reported: "He wanted to know everything—what had Ruth said, how long the man stayed, and what he had said. Marina explained that she had not understood much, and Lee scolded her. Marina was astonished at how nervous he had suddenly become, and at the effort he was making to conceal it."[13]

At dinner, Ruth too told Lee about the Hosty visit. Her goal was to be reassuring. Her brother had been a conscientious objector during World War II, and the FBI had been fair-minded and protective of his rights. She urged Lee to seize the initiative, meet Hosty at the FBI office, and tell him whatever he wanted to know.[14] According to McMillan, Marina watched Lee's reactions closely:

> To her eye he was a changed man. He was sad and subdued throughout the supper, and he scarcely spoke a word all evening long. For the first time since his return from Mexico, there was no sex at all between them that weekend, not even the limited sex that had been possible since Rachel's birth. The next day he again asked Ruth about the visit. Marina could tell that he was straining to catch every word, yet at the same time trying not to betray his nervousness.[15]

On Sunday, November 3, Lee had another driving lesson with Ruth.[16] He returned proud and elated, but the elation was short-lived, according to McMillan:

> [F]or the rest of the weekend Lee was withdrawn, taken up with thoughts of his own. Marina tried to leave him in peace, but by now she, too, was annoyed at the FBI. Not at Mr. Hosty—she knew he was only doing his job—but at the astonishing change his visit had wrought in Lee and in their relationship. Everything between them had been wonderful, or nearly wonderful, for a month. Now he would hardly speak to her.[17]

Had Hosty's intrusions torpedoed new political hopes and intentions? The answer would appear to be "Yes", for Lee never returned to an ACLU meeting, and never undertook again to act in behalf of Fair Play for Cuba. Instead, he focused his energies on Agent Hosty. In every phone call to Marina that week, Lee asked if the FBI had returned.

Each time Marina answered *nyet*, even though Hosty had, in fact, visited again on Tuesday, November 5. Despite Marina's denials, on some lunch hour during the ensuing week, probably on November 6, 7, or 8, Oswald went to the Dallas FBI office to confront Hosty.[18] Learning that Hosty was out, he left the note in which he told the FBI to cease contacting Marina and that Hosty later destroyed.

On Friday afternoon of November 8, at about 5:30 p.m., Lee arrived at the Paine residence for a three-day weekend. Veterans Day was Monday, November 11. Marina remembered that his first question was, "Have they been here again?" She answered yes.

With that, Lee erupted in anger, "Why didn't you tell me before?"

Evasively, she responded, "I had a lot on my mind. I forgot. Besides, it wasn't that important to me.... He's such a nice man," Marina continued. "All he did was explain my rights and promise to protect them."[19]

Utterly naive—or worse—Lee thought. "You fool.... You frivolous, simple-minded fool. I trust you didn't give your consent to having him defend your rights."[20] Then he asked if she had written down Hosty's license plate number. She had.[21]

Lee wanted to know what had been discussed, but Marina could not tell him. She had been present only briefly, and the conversation was in English. Ruth later recalled that the FBI agent had asked if Lee was mentally ill. Ruth said that she thought he was illogical and a self-proclaimed Trotskyite.[22]

Hosty's visit had been brief. Hosty and Ruth Paine both told the Warren Commission that their conversation began on the Paine doorstep. Ruth remembered Hosty coming inside but standing the entire time while Marina probably checked his car. It was remarkable that Marina had been able to walk outside, view the car, and obtain its license plate without being seen.[23]

This second intrusion by Hosty on November 5 shaped Lee's entire holiday weekend. For the remainder of Friday evening, he was withdrawn and consumed by worry. Early the next morning, he asked to use Ruth's typewriter.[24] At some time, probably immediately after he left his note for Hosty, Lee had prepared a handwritten draft to the Soviet Embassy in Washington, D.C. The draft began: "This is to inform you of events since interviews with comrade Kostine in the Embassy of the Soviet Union, Mexico City, Mexico."

The handwritten version continued:

> I was unable to remain in Mexico City indefinitey[sic] because of my Mexican visa which was for 15 days only. I could not apply for an extension unless I used my real name so I returned to the U.S. I and Marina Nicholayeva are now living in Dallas, Texas. The FBI is now not interested in my activities in the progressive organization FPCC of which I was secretary in New Orleans, Louisiana, since I no longer live in that state. The FBI has visited us here in Texas on Nov. 1st, An agent of the FBI James P. Hosty warned us that if I attempted to engage in FPCC activities in Texas the FBI will again take an 'interest' in me. The agent also 'suggested' that my wife could remain in the U.S. under FBI protection, that is she could defect from the Soviet Union. Of course, my wife and I strongly protested the tactics by the notorious FBI.[25]

The draft ended by relieving the Soviet representatives in Mexico City of any responsibility for frustrating his goals in Mexico City:

> I had not planned to contact the Mexican City Embassy at all so of course they were unprepared for me. Had I been able to reach Havana as planned the Soviet Embassy there would have had time to assist me, but of course the stupid Cuban consul was at fault here. I'm glad he has since been replaced by another.

The draft seemed to be building a case for return to the Soviet Union, its subtext fairly shouting, *It will be better for everyone if we are in Russia.* It is difficult to be certain when and where the handwritten draft was initially composed. Ruth saw it Saturday when Lee was using her typewriter. The draft had numerous changes. It was written on two sides of a single sheet of paper with words crossed out, modified, or added.[26]

When Ruth noticed the draft as it lay partially exposed near the typewriter, she was so troubled by references to the FBI's interest in him and the interview at the Soviet Embassy in Mexico City that she made a copy when Lee put his typing aside. She thought of perhaps revealing it to the FBI.[27]

The letter writing stopped to enable Ruth to take Lee, Marina, and the children on a trip to Dallas—an unsuccessful trip for Lee to the closed drivers' license bureau but a successful one of dime store shopping for the children. Returning to Ruth's home, Lee spent the afternoon watching football on television and shepherding the Paine children on a walk to buy popsicles.[28]

Leaving America had not left Lee's mind, however. He raised it, perhaps in a playful way, while in bed that night with Marina. Priscilla McMillan provides this account:

> Half teasing, half thinking out loud, he said: "We'll go to Russia.... I'll work, you'll work, the children will go to kindergarten. We'll see Erich and Pavel."
> "I don't want to go to Minsk. Let's go to Leningrad."
> "I don't want Leningrad. Let's go to Moscow," he said.
> "Alik, if you want Moscow, I won't go. Come on, Alka, let's not go to Moscow at all."
> "Okay," he said.
> "Hooray," Marina nearly shouted, pouncing around the bed like a kitten. "Do you swear?"
> "I swear."
> "Word of honor?"
> "How you need my word of honor?"
> "Because sometimes you promise one thing and do another."
> "I won't betray you this time."[29]

Was it a promise to stay in the United States or an offer to go to Russia if they could live together in Leningrad? Lee's final version of the letter, which he finished that weekend, made an even stronger case for readmitting him, Marina, or both to Russia.[30] It read:

> From: Lee H. Oswald, P.O. Box 6225, Dallas, Texas
> Marina Nichilayeva Oswald, Soviet Citizen
> To: Consular Division
> Embassy, U.S.S.R.
> Washington, D.C.
> Nov. 9, 1963
>
> Dear sirs:
> This is to inform you of recent events sincem [sic] my meeting with comrade Kostin in the Embassy of the Soviet Union, Mexico City, Mexico
> I was unable to remain in Mexico indefinily [sic] because of my mexican visa restrictions which was for 15 days only. I could not take a chance on requesting a new visa unless I used my real name, so I returned to the United States.
> I had not planned to contact the Soviet embassy in Mexico so they were unprepared, had I been able to reach the Soviet Embassy in Havana as planned, the embassy there would have had time to complete our business.
> Of corse [sic] the Soviet embassy was not at fault, they were, as I say unprepared, the Cuban consulate was guilty of a gross breach of regulations, I am glad he has since been replced. [sic][31]

> The Federal Bureu [sic] of Investigation is not now interested in my activities in the progressive organization "Fair Play for Cuba Committee," of which I was secretary in New Orleans (state Louisiana) since I no longer reside in that state. However, the F.B.I. has visited us here in Dallas, Texas, on November 1st. Agent James P. Hasty warned me that if I engaged in F.P.C.C. activities in Texas the F.B.I. will again take an "interest" in me.
>
> This agent also "suggested" to Marina Nichilayeva that she could remain in the United States under F.B.I. "protection," that is, she could defect from the Soviet Uion., of couse, [sic] I and my wife strongly protested these tactics by the notorious F.B.I.
>
> Please inform us of the arrival of our entrance visa's [sic] as soon as they come.
>
> Also, this is to inform you of the birth, on October 20, 1963, of a daughter, Audrey Marina Oswald in DALLAS, TEXAS, to my wife.
>
> Respectfully,
> s/Lee H. Oswald[32]

The changes from the draft were few but, for Lee, significant. In the final letter, Lee specifically requested to be notified when his and Marina's visas were issued. He seemingly had hopes of leaving the United States legally and was unaware that the visa applications had already been denied. He tried to strengthen his case for granting the applications by mentioning the birth of his new daughter.

Finally, he restructured the letter so that employees at the Soviet Embassy in Mexico City were more clearly relieved of responsibility for aborting his mission to Cuba. He also softened his anger with Consul Azcue. Instead of calling him stupid, he accuses Azcue of grossly breaching regulations. The various drafts reflected long, careful, and anguished thought.

Although dated November 9, we know that the letter was not mailed until November 12.[33] Ruth Paine, who had worried so about the letter, said that she definitely did not mail it for Oswald but could not be sure that Oswald hadn't put it in her mailbox himself.[34]

Distress over Hosty's persistent interest in him was clear during that November 8 weekend but thinking about the president's visit to Dallas seemed far from Oswald's mind. Ruth, Michael, and Marina were with him throughout the weekend. He was in communication with no one else.[35]

Ruth and Marina recalled to the Warren Commission that when not voicing his anger at Hosty, typing a letter to the Soviet Embassy, or immersed in silence, his focus was domestic and personal. On Saturday, November 9, Ruth took him to the Texas Drivers' License Examining Station to secure a learner's permit, but the station was closed because it was an election day.[36] In the afternoon, he played with the children and watched television. Michael Paine thought it hypocritical that such an ardent Marxist should spend so much time spread out on the living room floor watching football.[37]

Can we fathom what Oswald's immediate intentions were once the November 8 weekend was over? It is doubtful that Lee himself knew. On top of Hosty's persistence, his temporary job at the Book Depository would end before long. Perhaps even before, he might hear back from the Russian Embassy, most likely before he and Marina could obtain visas. In any case, he was likely to be dependent on unemployment compensation once again. His employment prospects were not encouraging. He had no favorable references. With his undesirable discharge, it was risky for him to traffic on being an ex-Marine. Next time, someone might check. His future in Texas—or anywhere in the United States—was precarious at best.

36

Fathoming the Unknown

Except for his working hours, we know little explicitly about what Lee Oswald did from the time he left Ruth Paine's house on Tuesday morning, November 12, until he reappeared unexpectedly at the Paine residence about 5:30 p.m. on Thursday, November 21. We know he was still employed at the School Book Depository, and that he never missed a day of work. We know that he continued to live at his North Beckley Street rooming house. Residents remembered him there every day and night.

On Tuesday, November 12, Wednesday, November 13, and Thursday, November 14, Lee made his usual noon and dinnertime calls to Marina. In the Thursday evening call, Marina suggested that it would be best if he not visit Irving in the coming weekend of November 15 through 17. He had spent three and a half days in Irving the prior weekend, and on Saturday, November 16, Ruth would be hosting a birthday party for her four-year-old daughter, Lynn. Lee understood that it was to be a family weekend for the Paines. "Fine," he told Marina, "I'll read, and I'll watch T.V."[1]

Alone in Dallas for Friday, November 15, Saturday, November 16, and Sunday, November 17, Lee almost certainly spent part of his time reading newspapers and listening to Havana radio and perhaps also reading *The Shark and the Sardines* and watching televised football on Saturday and Sunday. His landlady recalled his taking his laundry on Saturday morning to a laundromat across the street from the rooming house.[2]

When he called Marina on Saturday afternoon, he told her he had arrived too late at the driver's licensing station to take the driver's test but had obtained a license application form.[3] In his evening call, he said that he had taken her advice and sat in a park, then found a restaurant where he could get steak, French fries, a salad, and dessert for $1.25.[4]

Buying a Car?

An intriguing possibility is that Lee spent part of Saturday looking for a car.[5] He knew that without a driver's license and automobile, his employment opportunities were limited. Ruth Paine had been teaching him to drive, and he felt proud of his driving skills. Lee knew that Ruth's husband, Michael, had recently purchased a used car for two hundred dollars.[6] Lee had also discussed the possibility of purchasing a used car with Buell Wesley Frazier as well.[7] Such a purchase was within Lee's reach.

The possibility that Oswald had been looking for an automobile arose after the president was killed. On November 22, around 5:00 p.m., Albert Bogard, an auto salesman, was watching television with fellow employees at Downtown Lincoln Mercury when he heard that Oswald was in custody for allegedly shooting the president. The business was a short walk from the Texas School Book Depository.[8] Bogard told his coworkers that he had helped Oswald look for a car and that he had written "Lee Oswald" on a business card. With that statement, Bogard tore up the "business card and threw it into a wastebasket, saying 'He won't be a prospect any longer because he is going to jail.'"[9]

A coworker, Jack Lawrence, urged Bogard to tell the FBI. When Bogard was reluctant to do so, Lawrence called the FBI himself.[10] On November 23, the FBI arrived at the auto dealership, and Bogard repeated his story. Before the FBI arrived, Bogard's supervisor, Frank Pizzo, with the assistance of other employees, searched the dumpster in which the business card and other confirming documents would have been found. Nothing was located. Later that day, the dumpster and other parts of the auto agency were searched a second time in the presence of FBI agents. Once again nothing was found.[11]

On February 24, 1964, Bogard was subjected to a polygraph examination.[12] There were no indications of deception.[13] On April 8, 1964, Bogard gave similar testimony to the Warren Commission. He was emphatic that his sales encounter with Oswald occurred on November 9, 1963, a day when Ruth Paine and Marina said that Lee was with them all day in Irving, Texas. Bogard stated that Oswald was inquiring about a car that would cost three thousand dollars and required a down payment of two or three hundred dollars; that Oswald test drove the vehicle on Stemmons Freeway in a speedy and reckless manner; and that he said he would be coming into money in about three weeks to make a down payment for the vehicle.[14]

After interviewing and taking testimony from other employees of the Downtown Lincoln Mercury dealership, the Commission decided that Bogard's testimony was not reliable. Neither the business card bearing the name Lee Oswald nor any sort of document confirming that Oswald had been at the dealership were ever found.[15] Bogard had not taken the initiative to notify the FBI and told his story to investigators only after a coworker had notified the agency. Bogard's recollection that Oswald's alleged inquiry occurred on November 9 was inconsistent with the statements of Marina and the Paines that Lee was with them at all times on that day.

It is true that Oswald had searched newspaper ads for an automobile, but the search was for a used car—hopefully for one as low as two-hundred dollars, the amount that Michael Paine had paid for his. The Commission concluded that although other employees of the auto agency had confirmed parts of Bogard's account, it was at the very best a case of mistaken identification.[16] At the time of its investigation, the Commission did not have character or psychiatric evidence concerning Bogard. The Commission never knew that on September 17, 1964, Bogard was held in the Dallas County jail on charges of "passing bad checks and theft by conversion." Seventeen months later he committed suicide.[17]

Ruth Paine—A Crucial Witness

In deciding whether to accept the testimony of Albert Bogard and other witnesses who lacked prior knowledge of Lee Oswald, the most important testimony to the Warren Commission was often that of Ruth Paine. She knew Lee well. In the period from May through November 1963, he had stayed at her home in Irving, Texas, for fourteen full days, and she stayed at the Oswald flat in New Orleans for four days. Only Marina knew Lee better.

Ruth Paine could account for Lee's activities on the days that they had been together. She could confirm or refute the accuracy of Marina's testimony about those days. Ruth could also assess Lee's personality and his likely activities when they were not together.

In reviewing Ruth Paine's testimony, one should be aware that Ruth and Marina had virtually no communication with each other from the time that Marina was taken from the Paine house on November 23, 1963, until after she and Marina had testified to the Warren Commission. Lee's brother Robert and his mother Marguerite had never previously met Ruth. For reasons that the reader must conjecture, they did not trust Ruth and wanted Marina to have no contact with her.[18] The result was that collusion between Marina and Ruth in what each told investigating officers and the Commission was virtually impossible.[19] For nearly every instance in which Marina and Ruth had been together, their accounts coincided.

If Ruth Paine's memory was good, her integrity high, and her testimony accurate, she would be a check on every other witness for the time period in which Oswald was with her. An extensive FBI investigation found nothing but positive information about her. Ruth had attended Antioch College and, while there in 1950, had embraced the religion of the Society of Friends, the Quakers. Two principles became paramount for her: truthfulness and a life of service to others. Her desire for a life of service was one of her reasons for offering her home and help to Marina and continuing as a teacher and school psychologist throughout her working life.[20] Truthfulness was a value that she carried with her when questioned by the Warren Commission. Thirty-five years later, she told her biographer Thomas Mallon, "I wanted to lay out what I did know that could be in any way useful; and to consider then that I had done what I needed to do for history. So I wanted it to be as complete as I could make it and as accurate."[21] Mallon has observed she was "determined to supply every morsel she actually had."[22]

To Mallon, she related a portion of her Warren Commission testimony that almost humorously communicates her concern for accuracy, completeness, and honesty. At one point, she announced to the Commissioners that she previously had withheld information. She wanted to correct the record: When she had been giving driving lessons to Lee, she had not only allowed him to practice in a parking lot (which was legal), but she had also allowed him to drive from her home to the lot (which was illegal).[23]

Her concern for accuracy and objectivity was constant. Shortly after the Commission issued its report on September 24, 1964, she wrote Commission counsel Wesley J. Liebeler expressing doubt about whether the atmosphere of a Commission hearing was conducive to a witness's adequately expressing the "truth about a person's character and personal feelings.... The search [for the truth] requires opportunity to stumble over half-formed thoughts, vaguely recalled impressions, and one's own personal biases and feelings."[24] She was thinking about the speculations she had offered about Lee's personality and motivations.

A draft version of the letter contained a paragraph not included in the letter she mailed:

> I've been seeing a psychiatrist in Dallas for the purpose of.... [dealing with] a wish to distinguish accurately between what I think and what the facts warrant thinking.... My mother has said we can only be as honest as our insight permits us. It's true, but I still pursue honesty as an end in itself.[25]

Ruth Paine may be the only witness in history who sought help from a psychiatrist to gain self-assurance that she was being totally truthful. Without the benefit of Ruth's self-examination, the Warren Commission accepted her assurance that Lee did not visit Downtown Lincoln Mercury on November 9 as Albert Bogard had insisted. Her testimony supported the Commission's doubt that Lee shopped for a car—new or used—at that dealership on any date.[26]

Ruth Paine's testimony was also vital in evaluating the accuracy of other witnesses who did not know Lee but insisted that they had seen him on occasions when Ruth and often Marina were with them. Ruth and Marina said such incidents did not occur.[27] Some believed that they had encountered Oswald looking for a job. Two believed they had been his barber. One thought he had sold Oswald groceries. More than a dozen thought they had seen him at a rifle range. In some instances, Oswald had an associate. If true, that associate might be a conspirator in assassinating the president. Ruth and Marina testified, of course, that they had never seen Lee with an associate in either Irving or Dallas after he returned from Mexico City.

On February 22, 2016, this author interviewed Ruth Paine at the Friends Home, a Society of Friends retirement community in Santa Rosa, California. Her commitment to the Society had been a continuing part of her life. Even though she had been divorced from her husband Michael for more than forty years, she continued to care for him while he occupied a separate portion of the retirement home. When a senior at Antioch College she wrote in a paper about her goals and values: "I seek to fulfill the needs of those whom I meet, to give the fullest of my ability to all who ask of me.... Too often we have not the time, or the inclination, to reach out to those who need help, to concern ourselves with their sorrows, to care how the world is treating them."[28]

The Barber and the Grocer

Clifton Shasteen and Leonard Hutchison were small businessmen in Irving who believed that Oswald had patronized them in October and November 1963. Shasteen was a barber. Hutchison ran a small market. Certainly, Oswald might have needed a haircut; but, while in Irving, he did not buy food. Ruth Paine provided all he needed. She said that he never went shopping with her for food; that she never patronized Hutch's Market; and that Lee never got a haircut while he was staying at her home.[29]

Shasteen's account of cutting Oswald's hair contradicted what we knew about Oswald. Shasteen said that Oswald was in his shop five or six times in October and November. That would have been on every occasion that he stayed at the Paine residence. Even for a fastidious man, five or six haircuts in seven weeks would have been excessive. Oswald spent little money even for necessities. Shasteen said Oswald came by car,[30] but Oswald did not own one, and Ruth Paine never took him to a barber shop. The Warren Commission concluded that Hutchison was mistaken.[31] Shasteen was so obviously in error that he is not mentioned in the Commission's report.[32]

The Parking Lot Manager

A more perplexing identification came from Hubert Morrow. Morrow was a manager of Allright Parking at the Southland Building on Commerce Street in downtown Dallas.

He believed he had encountered Oswald but was not immediately forthcoming other than to tell acquaintances. He was first interviewed on January 24, 1964, by Dallas police after they learned from others that Morrow had been claiming that Oswald applied for a job at Allright. The next day he was interviewed by two FBI agents. When Morrow first talked to the police, he said the encounter with Oswald had been six or seven days before the assassination. That would have been Friday, November 15, or Saturday, November 16, the weekend when he was in Dallas rather than Irving. To the FBI, Morrow said it was about two weeks before the assassination—a time Ruth Paine and Marina said he was in Irving.

Morrow said that Oswald had come to Allright seeking employment, had asked how tall the Southland building was, and inquired whether it had a good view of Dallas. Morrow said he last saw Oswald talking to Morrow's boss, Garrett Claud Hallmark. Hallmark had no recollection of Oswald's seeking employment at Allright and could find no record of an application. He told the FBI that Morrow's story was a fabrication.[33] The Warren Commission did not take Morrow's sworn testimony or ask the FBI to follow up on his story with other Allright employees. Morrow's initial reluctance to come forward, his change of dates when the incident occurred, and the lack of corroboration from company records or his boss indicated that, at best, Morrow was guilty of mistaken identification. The Commission included his statements in its published exhibits but did not discuss his claims in its report.

Yet in 1993, in a Public Broadcasting Service *Frontline* documentary, Morrow would elaborate on his 1964 account:

> It was about ten o'clock [at night] when he came into the garage and he asked if he could see Main Street from the top of the roof. I said "You probably can but you're not allowed up on the roof...." He asked me about the motorcade—would the motorcade be going down Elm Street or Main Street?.... He was carrying a long item that appeared to be about as long as a rifle. But it was wrapped up in a brown paper or canvas sack.[34]

Frontline followed up Morrow's statement with an interview of Viola Sapp. Ms. Sapp had been a cashier at Allright Parking in 1963. She recalled to *Frontline* that Oswald had come in looking for a job, was told that no job was available, had asked to go up on the roof, but rejected a suggestion that Allright had job vacancies at other Dallas locations. Mr. Hallmark told *Frontline* that Ms. Sapp had told him on the day of the assassination, "That crazy Oswald was in here looking for a job." Hallmark rated her as levelheaded and said it was quite possible that he told her not to report the incident to the FBI.[35]

Morrow's account years later to *Frontline* is an example of how memories can become distorted. When he spoke to the FBI in 1964, Morrow recalled that Oswald had come to the parking facility in the early morning, stayed for forty-five minutes or an hour, and left at about 7:00 or 7:30 a.m. To *Frontline*, his recollection was that Oswald came at about 10:00 p.m. To the FBI, Morrow said nothing about Oswald's mentioning the motorcade. If the applicant was responding to Allright's employment ad—which was published between October 28 and November 8—the motorcade had not yet been announced. Moreover, Morrow's statement to the FBI mentioned nothing of Oswald's carrying an item as long as a rifle.[36]

Practice at the Shooting Range

More compelling was information from at least a dozen individuals who reported to the Warren Commission that they had seen Oswald—sometimes alone, sometimes with another person—practicing with a rifle. In every instance, the Commission concluded that the man was not Oswald.[37] The most pertinent testimony came from four witnesses: Malcolm Price, Garland Slack, Sterling Wood, and Dr. Homer Wood. All were certain they had seen Oswald test firing a rifle at the Sports Drome Rifle Range in Dallas.

Price believed he had adjusted the scope for Oswald's rifle on September 28—a date when Oswald was known to have been in Mexico City. Slack described the man he believed was Oswald as having blonde hair, wearing a "Bulldogger Texas style" hat, and chewing either bubble gum or tobacco. None was an Oswald characteristic reported by Ruth Paine or Marina Oswald.

Homer Wood was certain that he and his thirteen-year-old son, Sterling, had seen Oswald at the Sports Drome. It was in the afternoon of Saturday, November 16, a day that Oswald could have been there. Wood and his son had recognized the man separately as Oswald when they observed him on television. They each also identified him to the Warren Commission from a photo display.[38]

The most specific information came from the teenaged Sterling. A gun fan, he said the man had a rifle similar to Oswald's but with a different sight. His father said the rifle belched fire when it was shot. Sterling recalled that the man remained at the rifle range about thirty minutes and left with a companion in a new model car.[39] Commission counsel Wesley J. Liebeler asked Sterling and his father if they had any other information to offer. They didn't.[40]

If the identifications of Homer and Sterling Wood were accurate, they had special significance, for the Oswald they saw had a companion—a potential conspirator—at the rifle range. The Commission decided that the Woods' identifications could not be relied upon. Three reasons were paramount. The firearm described was different from that owned by Oswald. Marina Oswald's testimony showed that Oswald's own rifle remained in Ruth Paine's garage until the morning of November 22.[41] And, third, there would be no reason for him to target shoot with a rifle that was different from the one with which he shot the president.

The identifications by Albert Bogard, Leonard Hutchison, Hubert Morrow, Clifton Shasteen, and the Shooting Drome witnesses are typical of others in Louisiana, Mexico, and Texas who did not know Lee Oswald but said, often in complete good faith but sometimes less scrupulously, that they had seen him.[42] Morrow and the Woods are examples of unreliable witnesses to whom respected members of the media afforded uncritical attention.

Watching the Outside World

The probabilities are greatest that on the weekend of November 15 to 17, Lee Oswald was in his private, contemplative world. He told Marina that he intended to "read and watch T.V." The Warren Commission found no credible evidence that he had contact with anyone that weekend except those who might have been at the laundromat where he did his laundry on Saturday morning, at the licensing station where he obtained an application later that day, in the park where he told Marina he sat for a while in the afternoon, at the restaurant where he got a full dinner for $1.25 on Saturday evening, and in the rooming house where, on Saturday and Sunday, he may have watched hours of televised football.

In his tiny room, however, he was never removed from the political world. There Radio Havana, the daily Dallas newspapers, *The Militant*, and *The Worker* held sway. That weekend he may also have still been reading *The Shark and the Sardine*. In the nine days that he was alone in Dallas from November 12 to 21, all these shaped his grasp of the infinitely complex dance that still held the would-be revolutionary in thrall.

Perhaps most important was Radio Havana, the English language voice for Castro to spread the revolution. In fall 1963, Venezuela was a focal point. Both Radio Havana and the Dallas papers covered conflict there. On November 5, the *Morning News* had reported that Venezuelans had voted in democracy. It was not, however, the democracy that Castro wanted. The rebel group Fuerzas Armadas de Liberación Nacional (FALN) was employing revolutionary violence to oppose the elected government, and Radio Havana said the United States was planning to send troops to stop FALN.[43] Encouragement for FALN was explicit on Radio Havana. On November 14, its nightly broadcast reported jubilantly that rebels had placed eight black coffins with exploding bombs in the streets of Caracas. When the bombs exploded, they released anti-government literature. On Friday night, November 15, Radio Havana urged support for the rebels. On Saturday, November 16, the station began its "Week of Solidarity of the Venezuelan People." It repeated its fear that U.S. armed forces would intervene to stop FALN.[44]

Cuba received special attention from the Socialist Worker's Party's *The Militant*. Its November 11 issue, one that Lee would have been reading while alone in Dallas, contained an article headlined "Cubans Nab CIA Agents in Sabotage"—another confirmation for Castro that the Kennedy administration was trying to overthrow him. And it was all the more reprehensible, Castro asserted, because the sabotage was intended to exacerbate suffering imposed on Cuba by a recent hurricane and by America's blockade.

Of more importance to Dallas residents, however, President and Mrs. Kennedy would be arriving in a week. On Wednesday, November 13, page one of section four in the *Morning News* was headlined "Try to Be Fair." Worried leaders were hoping to forestall any repetition of what happened to Adlai Stevenson at the United Nations Day event. Friday's *Morning News* headline, "JFK Motorcade Seems Unlikely," seemed, however, to diminish possibility of further damage to Dallas's reputation.[45]

Yet, by noon that Friday, the news of a motorcade was released. The afternoon edition of the *Times-Herald* on November 15 reported a motorcade would proceed from the Dallas airport, Love Field, to downtown and then north and west along Main Street and the Stemmons Freeway to the Dallas Trade Mart. The next morning, Saturday, November 16, the *Morning News* announced the motorcade in a frontpage headline. Both Dallas papers gave a detailed map of the motorcade route. Lee Oswald could have readily determined that the motorcade would proceed close to and in a direct line of unobstructed sight from the Texas School Book Depository.

Was it likely or possible that Lee Harvey Oswald could have planned to shoot the president before he read those articles and saw their accompanying maps? On Wednesday, November 13 and Friday, November 15, publicity had indicated there would be no motorcade at all. On Saturday morning, Lee seemed intent on obtaining a driver's license. Would that have been the priority of one planning to kill the president the next Friday, or would he have gone to Irving, at least by Sunday, to secure his rifle?

Biographer Priscilla McMillan believes that another event that made the November 16 Dallas dailies may have been important to Lee in deciding his future. The event was the Soviets' release from jail of Yale political science professor Frederick C. Barghoorn.

Barghoorn had been arrested on November 12 while visiting the USSR. He was charged with being a spy. After negotiations that included breaking off cultural relations by the United States, Barghoorn was released on November 16—in time to make the Dallas papers.[46]

Lee mentioned the newspaper articles to Marina in one of his calls to her on Saturday, the 16th. She remembered him saying, "Poor professor. He's the victim of a Russian provocation. It isn't the first time and it won't be the last."[47]

McMillan believed that Lee could easily have identified with Barghoorn's plight. If Lee were to return to the Soviet Union, he might be similarly victimized; yet the United States government might not protect the ex-defector with the same concern it had shown for a Yale professor. Having not heard from the Soviets on his request for a transit visa and unable to gain entry to Cuba, Lee could now feel utterly trapped in a country that offered him no future.

Whatever may have been Lee's despondency about life in Dallas on November 16, Dallas residents had other fears—that Kennedy opponents would disrupt President Kennedy's visit as they had that of Ambassador Stevenson in October. On Sunday, November 17, the *Dallas Morning News* carried a headline: "Incident-Free Day Urged for JFK Visit."[48] On Tuesday, November 19, the former Republican county chairman, Maurice Carlson, gained a *Morning News* headline, "Carlson Calls for Civilized Reception,"[49] and the next day the *Dallas Times-Herald* announced, "Dallas Security Net Spread for Kennedy."[50] Local news did not have left-wing zealots in mind.

37

Distractions from Dallas Dangers

While Lee Oswald was leaving an angry note for Agent Hosty, writing to the Soviet Embassy, taking driving lessons from Ruth Paine, and contemplating his personal and political future in the solitude of his North Beckley room, President Kennedy and his staff were attending to the business of government and planning for his visit to Dallas. On Tuesday evening, November 12, Secret Service Agent Winston Lawson flew from Washington to Dallas. His mission was to coordinate security with Special Agent in Charge Forrest Sorrels of the Dallas Secret Service office. Their primary concern was "extremist ... rightwing groups."[1]

Dallas police had given the Secret Service a list of persons of interest. Included in the list was Ashland Burchwell, the Walker follower who had been arrested in Dallas with a carload of weapons and ammunition on the 1962 weekend when Walker had been arrested at Ole Miss. Also on the list was Robert Hatfield, another Walker supporter. On October 24, Hatfield had spat upon Ambassador Adlai Stevenson after Stevenson's Day UN speech. Not surprisingly, Walker himself was a "person of interest."[2] Walker was so concerned he might be blamed or arrested for incidents connected with the president's visit to Dallas that he arranged to be in Mississippi on November 18 and in Louisiana on November 20, 21, and 22.[3] Nowhere on any list for Secret Service attention was Lee Harvey Oswald.

The person contributing most extensively to the list was Dallas Police Lt. Jack Revill. Revill headed the Intelligence Section of the Dallas Police Department. Believing that conservative political activists might be planning to disrupt President Kennedy's visit, Revill assigned his men to infiltrate groups that were prime suspects: the Indignant White Citizens Council, the National States Rights Party, the John Birch Society, the local White Citizens Council, and General Walker's group.[4]

That focus led Revill's unit to a cadre of students from North Texas State University. The students had been visiting Walker's home. One had allegedly made a threat against Kennedy: "We will drag his dick in the dirt." The Secret Service was notified. Over the next few days, one-on-one conversations with those students brought to a halt any plot they might be considering to disrupt the Kennedy visit.[5]

Walker's Followers Prepare

Revill's list of Walker supporters did not include Larrie Schmidt. Schmidt was bursting with pride over the publicity he had received after organizing the disruption of

Adlai Stevenson's U.N. Day speech in October. November 22 was to be the day that would cement Schmidt and CUSA's influence among conservative activists in Dallas. Bernard Weissman and Bill Burley, CUSA members from the East Coast, were to be central players. Motivated by Schmidt's exuberant October 29 letter to Weissman, the two arrived in Dallas on November 4.[6] Weissman, Burley, and Schmidt set to work on Schmidt's plan.

The plan was to assault Kennedy with words, without being violent or inciting violence.[7] Schmidt had been a journalism major in college. He believed he had media skills. His plan was to publish a full-page advertisement in the *Dallas Morning News* on November 21 and 22 denouncing President Kennedy on a policy basis. On about November 12, Schmidt, Weissman, and Burley began drafting the ad.[8] The cost was $1,462. To finance it, Schmidt had developed a relationship with a young Dallas oil man, Joseph Grinnan. Grinnan, a member of the John Birch Society, raised the total in increments of $400 or less from oilman Nelson Bunker Hunt, H.R. "Bunt" Bright (later an owner of the Dallas Cowboys), and others in the Society.[9]

Borrowing from John Birch Society literature, Weissman and Schmidt became the primary crafters of the ad. One of Grinnan's contributors insisted on an accusation that caught the tenor of the times: "Why has the foreign policy of the United States degenerated to the point that the CIA is arranging coups and having staunch anti-communist allies of the U.S. bloodily exterminated?"[10] It reflected the fact that on November 1, South Vietnamese military leaders with American concurrence had overthrown South Vietnam's chief of state, Ngo Dinh Diem. Within a few hours, the military leaders murdered Diem and his brother-in-law, Ngo Dinh Nhu.[11]

The ad's final version began cordially in large, heavy black letters:

WELCOME MR. KENNEDY
TO DALLAS....

In starkly political terms, Dallas was then described as:

> ... A CITY so disgraced by a recent Liberal smear attempt that its citizens have just elected two more Conservative Americans to public office.
> ... A CITY that is an economic "boom town" not because of Federal handouts but through conservative economic and business practices.
> ... A CITY that will continue to grow and prosper despite efforts by by you and your administration to penalize it for its non-conformity to "New Frontierism."
> ... A CITY that rejected your philosophy and policies in 1960 and will do so again in 1964—even more emphatically than before.

Weissman, Schmidt, and Burley, with Joe Grinnan's help, then launched their attack:

> ****
> WHY is Latin America turning either anti-American or Communistic or both, despite increased U.S. foreign aid, State Department policy, and your own Ivy-Tower pronouncements?
> WHY do you say we have built a "wall of freedom" around Cuba when there is no freedom in Cuba today?....
> ****
> WHY did you host, salute and entertain Tito—Moscow's Trojan Horse—just a short time

> after our sworn enemy, Khrushchev, embraced the Yugoslav dictator as a great hero and leader of Communism?
>
> WHY have you urged greater aid, comfort, recognition, and understanding for Yugoslavia, Poland, Hungary, and other Communist countries, while turning your back on the pleas of Hungarians, East German, Cuban and other anti-Communist freedom fighters?
>
> ***
>
> WHY has Gus Hall, head of the U.S. Communist Party[,] praised almost every one of your policies and announced that the party will endorse and support your re-election in 1964?
>
> ***
>
> WHY have you ordered or permitted your brother Bobby, the Attorney General, to go soft on Communists, fellow travelers, and ultra-leftists in America, while permitting him to prosecute loyal Americans who criticize you, your administration, and your leadership?
>
> ***
>
> WHY has the Foreign Policy of the United States degenerated to the point that the C.I.A. is arranging coups and having staunch Anti-Communist Allies of the U.S. bloodily exterminated?
>
> WHY have you scrapped the Monroe Doctrine in favor of the "Spirit of Moscow"?[12]

The ad bore a somber black border and was signed "THE AMERICAN FACT-FINDING COMMITTEE ... Bernard Weissman, chairman." Except for Weissman, Schmidt, Burley, Grinnan, and those who had helped finance the ad, the committee was non-existent. The committee's name concealed its financial supporters—members of the John Birch Society.

Weissman suggested the black border as a way of attracting attention. Schmidt declined to place his own name on the ad because his life had been threatened after the Stevenson incident. Instead, Weissman was listed as chairman of the committee in order to show that conservative organizations were not anti-Semitic.[13]

From a far-right, conservative perspective, the ad captured the Cold War issues of the day: giving foreign aid and selling food to communist or socialist regimes; failing to dislodge Castro; and being soft on, sympathizing with, or accepting support from domestic communists. Those were, in fact, issues that Kennedy was coming to Dallas to confront.

Being President—Campaigning and Policy Making

By the fall of 1963, the president's 1964 re-election campaign had already begun. The last week in September, when Lee Oswald was in Mexico City seeking admission to Cuba, Kennedy was in Wisconsin, Montana, Wyoming, Utah, and California giving speeches and making ceremonial appearances. Returning to the White House on October 1, he left two days later to dedicate a dam in Arkansas. On that trip, Arkansas's Democratic Senator J. William Fulbright made clear his view that Kennedy's going to Dallas would be a mistake.[14] Said Fulbright, "Dallas is a very dangerous place. I wouldn't go there. Don't *you* go."[15] But the president would not heed the warning. One day later, on October 4, Kennedy met with Texas Governor John Connally at the White House to finalize the proposed Texas trip.[16] Dallas remained on the itinerary.

Greater dangers than those in Dallas were on the president's mind. A civil war, with American involvement, was raging in South Vietnam. Buddhists were in rebellion, and communist forces were attacking from North Vietnam. President Ngo Dinh Diem was an unreliable leader of the South Vietnamese government. Diem had responded to the Buddhists by allowing special forces—trained by United States advisers—to invade the Buddhist pagodas, damage their shrines, and arrest and beat more than a thousand priests and nuns.[17] To unite South Vietnam, a faction of military leaders was suggesting to U.S. Ambassador Henry Cabot Lodge that they would stage a coup.

On Saturday, October 5, President Kennedy met with Defense Secretary Robert McNamara, Chairman of the Joint Chiefs of Staff General Maxwell Taylor, and National Security Adviser McGeorge Bundy to consider options. One possibility was to support a coup.[18] This was, of course, the very strategy that Bernard Weissman's black bordered ad opposed.

President Kennedy ended his Saturday meeting by instructing Bundy to cable Ambassador Lodge that an "urgent covert effort ... to identify and build contacts with alternative leadership" was needed. Also agreed upon was a plan "to withdraw 1000 U.S. military personnel by the end of 1963."[19] The plan did not depend upon Diem's remaining in or losing power.

The next two weeks for Kennedy were a volatile mixture of domestic and international politics. On Thursday, October 10, the president met with Soviet Foreign Minister Andrei Gromyko.[20] Cuba was a topic of conversation.

On weekends, relaxation, if it deserved that name, was mixed with politics. On Saturday morning, October 19, Kennedy was in Orono, Maine, delivering a speech at the University of Maine. In the afternoon, he was hailed by a crowd in Cambridge, Massachusetts, at his alma mater Harvard's annual football game with Columbia.[21]

On Wednesday, October 23, matters grew grim, however. Word came to Kennedy that the suspected coup in South Vietnam was about to occur.[22] Kennedy dispatched his college roommate, Torbert "Torby" Macdonald, to Saigon to warn Diem that his life was in danger and recommend that he take shelter in the U.S. Embassy.[23] It was advice that Diem either did not heed or did not hear.

Meanwhile, on Thursday, October 24, Kennedy's attention returned to Cuba. At Kennedy's request, journalist Jean Daniel was in the Oval Office to discuss Daniel's forthcoming November trip to Havana. There Daniel hoped to meet with Castro.[24]

A recording of Daniel's thirty-minute conversation with Kennedy does not exist, but Daniel took what purport to be detailed notes of Kennedy's words. As if talking to Castro, Kennedy told Daniel:

> I believe there is no country in the world ... where economic colonization, humiliation, and exploitation were worse than in Cuba, in part owing to my country's policies during the Batista regime.... In the matter of the Batista regime, I am in agreement with the first Cuban revolutionaries.
>
> ....
>
> But it is also clear that the problem has ceased to be a human one and has become international, that it is has become a Soviet problem. I am the President of the United States and not a socialist. I am the President of a free nation which has certain responsibilities in the Free World. I know that Castro has betrayed the promises he made in Sierra Maestra, and that he has agreed to be a Soviet agent in Latin America. I know that through his fault ... the world was on the verge of nuclear war in October 1962.[25]

Turning his thoughts directly to Daniel, Kennedy continued, "I must say I don't even know if he realizes this or even cares about it. You can tell me whether he does when you come back."[26]

In addition to sympathy for the Cuban people, there was a carrot for Daniel to take to Castro: "The United States has the possibility of doing as much good in Latin America as it has done wrong in the past. I would say we alone have this power—on the essential condition that communism does not take over there."[27]

To that Daniel asked a question: Would Kennedy end the Cuban blockade? Kennedy's answer: Yes, if Castro would stop subverting other Latin American nations. Stated more specifically, Castro must stop sending military aid to rebels in places like Venezuela. If he did so, the United States could recognize Castro's government and provide economic aid, as with Yugoslavia.

It was a policy that might not satisfy Lee Oswald and definitely not assuage the indignation of Edwin Walker or Bernard Weissman. Oswald saw Castro as the vanguard for Marxism in the Americas. To Oswald, the movement must continue. To Walker and Weissman, nothing short of removal of Castro would suffice.

When their conversation ended, Kennedy said to Daniel, "Castro's reactions interest me."[28]

On Friday, October 25, Kennedy heard from both Saigon and Dallas. Ambassador Lodge cabled that a coup was imminent. At the same time, the news media, nationwide, were reporting that Dallas had been deluged with ant-Kennedy handbills saying "Wanted for Treason" and that Ambassador Stevenson had been struck and spat upon as he left Dallas's Memorial Auditorium the previous evening.[29]

To his aide, Arthur Schlesinger, Kennedy requested that Stevenson be congratulated for his restrained handling of the Dallas incidents.[30] By the time Schlesinger reached him, Stevenson had heard that Stanley Marcus had worries about Kennedy's coming to Dallas in November. Stevenson told Schlesinger he, too, was concerned. He doubted that Kennedy should include Dallas on his Texas itinerary. It was not only liberal Democrats who feared the trip to Dallas. The Rev. Billy Graham, America's most prominent evangelist, tried to warn Kennedy through their mutual friend, Sen. Ralph Flanders of Florida, that the Dallas stop should be canceled.[31]

One probable reason that Schlesinger never shared Stevenson's warning with the president is that Stevenson called Schlesinger back the next day and withdrew his opposition to a stop in Dallas.[32] Too, Schlesinger was keenly aware of more pressing priorities in South Vietnam and Cuba. Schlesinger could have been reluctant to divert the president by discussing Dallas. To cancel Dallas altogether would have required conferences with Governor Connally, Vice President Johnson, and the Kennedy political team. Cancelation would have constituted capitulation to Walker. By October 25, it was not a viable option.

The next day was Saturday. More pleasant politics were on the Kennedy schedule. This time it was a college speech in Amherst, Massachusetts. Robert Frost had spoken at the Kennedy inaugural in 1961, and Kennedy was in Amherst to dedicate the groundbreaking for the Robert Frost Memorial Library at Amherst College. Schlesinger, who was on the flight to Amherst helping draft the speech, mentioned neither Stevenson's nor Marcus's concerns about Dallas. The Frost speech took priority.

For the students at Amherst, Kennedy left an important message: "There is inherited wealth in this country and also inherited poverty.... [U]nless the graduates of this college and others like it who are given a running start in life ... are willing to put back into our society ... to put back into the service of the Great Republic, then the presuppositions upon which our democracy is based are bound to be fallible."[33] One may wish it was a message Lee Oswald could have heard.

Monday, October 28, Oswald was back to the business of filling book orders at the Texas School Book Depository. Kennedy was back to governing. He reached agreement with Democratic members of the House Judiciary Committee on amendments to the proposed civil rights bill that might attract Republican votes. They included provisions for a Fair Employment Practices Commission, one that might appeal to northern liberal Republicans but would be anathema to conservative Southern Democrats.[34]

On Tuesday, October 29, South Vietnam again dominated the president's time. The coup was beginning. Equal numbers of pro- and anti-Diem forces, about 9,800 on each side, were facing each other around Saigon. National Security Advisor McGeorge Bundy, Secretary of Defense McNamara, CIA officials, and Attorney General Robert Kennedy were with the president in the Cabinet Room. Cables were exchanged between Washington and Ambassador Lodge. On Friday, November 1, the coup succeeded. Diem and his brother were seized. One cable from Kennedy urged that the victors afford safe passage out of South Vietnam for Diem and his family. The next day, Saturday, the President learned that Diem and his brother-in-law had been murdered.[35]

General Maxwell Taylor remembered that Kennedy took the news with "a look of shock and dismay on his face which I had never seen before." Schlesinger said the president looked "somber and shaken." Deputy National Security Adviser Michael Forrestal thought the killings "shook him personally" and were taken by him "as a moral and religious matter."[36]

The assassinations in Saigon, nearly nine thousand miles from Dallas, were just one horrendous image in a tapestry of domestic and international political violence that, in the fall of 1963, filled news channels in Dallas and the rest of America. In Dallas, the Saigon assassinations caused those who financed Bernard Weissman's black-bordered advertisement to blame Kennedy for deserting Diem. Edwin Walker and his colleague Robert Surrey felt similarly as they prepared "Wanted for Treason" leaflets for November 22.[37]

Whether Dallas Democratic National Committeeman Byron Skelton connected the events in Saigon to the coming Kennedy trip to Dallas, we do not know. We do know that Skelton feared trouble for President Kennedy in Dallas. On Monday, November 4, Skelton sent Attorney General Kennedy a copy of a *Dallas Morning News* article describing General Walker's most recent protest—flying the American flag upside down outside his home. Walker was protesting because civic leaders and political officials in Dallas had apologized for mistreatment of Ambassador Stevenson on October 24. In an accompanying note, Skelton wrote to Attorney General Kennedy, "I would feel better if the President's itinerary did not include Dallas."[38]

In addition to the assault on Stevenson ten days earlier, Skelton was probably remembering what happened in the last days of the 1960 presidential campaign, when Lyndon and Lady Bird Johnson had campaigned in Dallas. Just as the Johnsons were about to enter a Dallas hotel, an unruly Dallasite spat upon Mrs. Johnson, tore off her white gloves, and threw them in a gutter. The opposition—organized by Republican Congressman Bruce Alger—was so disruptive that it took the Johnson party thirty minutes to get through the hotel's lobby.[39] Skelton wanted nothing similar for the president. Whether he feared something worse, we can only speculate. In any event, the president's close advisor Kenneth O'Donnell, Lyndon Johnson's right hand man Walter Jenkins, and Democratic National Committee member Jerry Bruno all felt that Skelton's fears were unwarranted. They knew, also, that the president would reject Skelton's plea.[40]

On Tuesday, November 5, Cuba, Vietnam, and civil rights legislation—not Dallas—continued to command the president's attention. Not only was journalist Jean Daniel expected to meet in two weeks with Premier Castro, but Associated Press reporter Lisa Howard—Castro's friend—was also making progress. Howard had put William Attwood, an aide to Ambassador Stevenson, in touch with Cuba's United Nation's Delegate, Carlos Lechuga. Lechuga had contacted a Castro confidant, Dr. Rene Vallejo. After talking to Castro, Vallejo called Howard and indicated that Castro was interested in flying Attwood from Mexico City to a secret location where Castro could talk privately about how relations between the United States and Cuba might be explored.[41] It seemed that an inroad might be evolving through Lisa Howard's efforts and that Jean Daniel might be producing insight into Castro's attitude toward rapprochement.

On November 5, National Security Adviser McGeorge Bundy reported the possibilities to President Kennedy. Kennedy was cautious. He believed that before Attwood went to Cuba, he should be temporarily removed from a U.S. payroll, a maneuver, apparently, to forestall any claim that Attwood was acting in an official capacity. Kennedy also wanted to know what the agenda would be before he approved a meeting on Cuban soil.[42]

Lisa Howard continued as the intermediary. At 2:00 a.m. on November 19, Attwood talked with Vallejo in Cuba from Howard's New York apartment. Attwood remembered that when Kennedy heard about his phone conversation with Vallejo, Kennedy said he wanted to discuss any proposed agenda with Attwood at the White House. The president would "decide what to say and whether to go [to Cuba] or what we should do next."[43]

What neither Attwood, Howard, nor Daniel knew was that Kennedy's companion strategy of unseating Castro by force was being actively pursued. On Tuesday, November 12, the president had met with CIA officials. Hearing that the strategy was failing, Kennedy authorized several sabotage operations for the coming November 16 weekend.[44] The claims from Castro that Lee Oswald was hearing over Radio Havana about Kennedy were true.

Moreover, as an even more aggressive part of the strategy of violence, Desmond FitzGerald, the CIA's chief of Cuban operations, was scheduled to leave for Paris where a CIA case agent would meet with Rolando Cubela on November 22. Cubela was the member of Castro's military who said that he would assassinate Castro if the United States undertook its plan to support an invasion of Cuba by exiles in July 1964.[45]

The weekend of November 16 and 17 were mixed days of campaigning and relaxation in Florida for President Kennedy. They were not worry-free, however. The president would be speaking in Tampa and Miami on Monday, November 18, after motorcades in those cities. The Secret Service had learned from an informant that on November 9 a right-wing believer, Joseph Milteer, had commented to the informant in Miami that the best way to kill President Kennedy would be "from an office building with a high-powered rifle." The transcript of that conversation suggested that Milteer was engaged in hypothetical speculation; to be safe, the Secret Service placed Milteer under surveillance in Georgia where he lived.[46]

When Secret Service Agent Floyd Boring learned about Milteer, he spoke with the president and suggested that Secret Service agents be stationed on the rear steps of the president's motorcade vehicle. To that the president responded, "Floyd, this is a political trip. If I don't mingle with the people, I couldn't get elected dog catcher."[47] Boring apparently disregarded Kennedy's statement, and when the president noticed in Tampa that agents were riding on his car's running boards, he said to Boring, "Ralph, have the Ivy League charlatans drop back to the follow-up car."[48] Apparently Boring gave in, for that was where Secret Service agents were positioned in the Dallas motorcade.

In Miami on November 18, Kennedy's speech was well received. Crafted in part by Arthur Schlesinger, the speech was intended to offer a chance for rapprochement:

> It is important to restate what now divides Cuba from my country and from other countries of this hemisphere. It is the fact that a small band of conspirators has stripped the Cuban people of their freedom and handed over the independence and sovereignty of the Cuban nation to forces beyond the hemisphere. They have made Cuba a victim of foreign imperialism ... a weapon in an effort dictated by external powers to subvert other American republics. This and this alone divides us. As long as this is true, nothing is possible. Without it, everything is possible. Once this barrier is removed, we will be ready and anxious to work with the Cuban people in pursuit of those progressive goals which a few short years ago stirred their hopes and the sympathy of many people throughout the hemisphere.[49]

News of the Miami speech reached Dallas. On Tuesday, November 19, the *Dallas Times-Herald*'s headline on page 1A said, "Kennedy Virtually Invites Cuban Coup." The first paragraph read, "President Kennedy all but invited the Cuban people today to overthrow Fidel Castro's communist regime and promised prompt U.S. aid if they do."[50] One can imagine what news junkie Lee Oswald's gut reaction would have been when he read those words.

What Oswald wouldn't read about, unfortunately, is what the president learned on November 19. Lisa Howard and Bill Attwood had talked with Rene Vallejo and shared that Fidel Castro was open to conversation about U.S.-Cuban relations.[51]

On Wednesday, November 20, Jean Daniel had his first conversation with Castro. Castro had not interpreted the speech as had the headline writer of the *Times-Herald.* Forty years later Daniel remembered Castro saying, "Maybe he has changed. Maybe things are possible with this man ... [who] may at last understand that there can be coexistence between capitalists and socialists, even in the Americas."[52] In 1963, after Kennedy's death, Daniel recalled Castro saying, "I know.... Kennedy is a man you can talk with.... Other leaders have assured me that to obtain this goal [coexistence] we must first await his reelection.... If you see him again, you can tell him that I'm willing to declare Goldwater my friend if that will guarantee [his] reelection."[53]

Waiting for the President

November 20 was a hopeful day for Fidel Castro and Jean Daniel. For John Kennedy, Edwin Walker, and Lee Oswald, the day was different. After removing himself to New Orleans on the 20th, Edwin Walker met with segregationist leader Judge Leander Perez. None was more bigoted than Perez. Perez once said that the civil rights movement was the work "of all those Jews who were supposed to be cremated in Buchenwald and Dachau but weren't."[54] Walker had no intention of returning to Dallas until after the president left.

In the White House, November 20 began with the president's weekly Wednesday meeting with Democratic Congressional leaders. The forthcoming trip to Texas and, more specifically, to Dallas was on the minds of many. Remembering the episode with Stevenson a month earlier, some expressed concern. Congressman Hale Boggs of

Louisiana told Kennedy he was going into "quite a hornet's nest," to which Kennedy responded, "That always creates interesting crowds."[55]

The day ended with a small cocktail reception upstairs at the White House for Supreme Court justices and their wives. Robert Kennedy and his wife Ethel were downstairs at a larger reception being held for federal judges and Justice Department officials. After the president joined the larger reception, Ethel Kennedy would notice him appearing somewhat withdrawn as he sat in a rocking chair.[56] Others would remember the conversation turning to Dallas. At one point Chief Justice Warren called jocularly to the president that Texas would be rough.[57] It was probably not violence that the Chief Justice anticipated but the political climate in Texas, one that Warren knew well from his own days as a politician.

November 20 was also Robert Kennedy's thirty-eighth birthday. Ethel and Robert went home with a smaller group of friends to celebrate. Present at both the judicial reception and the more intimate birthday party was Jack Ruby's childhood friend, former middle-weight boxing champion Barney Ross, whose friendship Ruby recounted with pride. President and Mrs. Kennedy did not go to Hickory Hill for the birthday party. They were to leave the next morning for Texas and a challenging four days.

38

Waiting for the President

On Wednesday, November 20, the president's motorcade may well have loomed large for Oswald. The previous three days had seen a bitter breakdown in his and Marina's relationship.

Though Lee had called twice on Saturday the 16th, on Sunday the 17th he hadn't called by his usual time. When Marina saw June playing with the telephone, she said, "Let's call Papa." As Marina spoke only limited English, Ruth Paine called the number she had for Lee's North Beckley Street rooming house.[1]

In her testimony to the Warren Commission, Ruth recalled:

> I said, "Is Lee Oswald there?" [The person who answered] said, "There is no Lee Oswald living here." As best I can recall. This is the substance of what he said. I said, "Is this a rooming house?" [The answerer] said "Yes." I said, "Is this WH-3-8993?" He said "Yes." I thanked him and hung up.[2]

The Commission's counsel then asked Mrs. Paine, "What happened next?" Ruth remembered that Marina looked surprised. Neither was aware that Lee had registered as O.H. Lee.

The next day, Monday, Lee made his usual noontime call to the Paine residence. Ruth answered and handed the phone to Marina. Ruth and Marina gave to the Commission only brief descriptions of that call.[3] Based on more extensive conversations with Marina, Priscilla McMillan has provided the following account:

> The next day, Monday, November 18, Lee called as usual at lunch time. "We phoned you last evening," Marina said. "Where were you?"
>
> "I was at home watching TV. Nobody called me to the phone. What name did she ask for me by?" Marina told him. There was a long silence at the other end. "Oh damn. I don't live there under my real name."
>
> Why not? Marina asked.
>
> Lee said he did not want his landlady to know he had lived in Russia.
>
> "It's none of her business," Marina retorted.
>
> "You don't understand a thing," Lee said. "I don't want the FBI to know where I live, either." He ordered her not to tell Ruth. "You and your long tongue," he said; "they always get us into trouble."
>
> Marina was frightened and shocked. "Starting your old foolishness again," she scolded. "All these comedies. First one, then another. And now this fictitious name. When will it all end?"[4]

Marina ended the conversation abruptly. Ruth remembered Marina turning to her and saying, "This isn't the first time I felt twenty-two fires," a Russian expression indicating being caught between two loyalties—one to her husband and the other to her recognition that what he was doing was wrong.[5]

That evening, Lee made his usual after work call to Irving, Texas. Marina took the phone reluctantly. This time the conversation contained even stronger criticism. McMillan reports the conversation this way:

> Lee started right off by addressing her as *devushka* or "wench," a word that in Russian has such an insulting ring that a man might use it to a servant, perhaps, but not to his wife. When spoken by a husband to a wife, it suggests that everything is over between them. It is a word designed to annihilate intimacy.
>
> "Hey, wench," he said, "you're to take Ruth's address book and cross my name and telephone number out of there."
>
> "I can't," Marina said. "It's not my book and I have no right to touch it."
>
> "Listen here." Lee was angry. "I order you to cross it out. Do you hear?"
>
> "I won't do it."
>
> Lee started to scold Marina in as ferocious a voice as she had ever heard. She hung up the telephone.[6]

That Monday evening call was Lee's last call to Marina.[7] They did not speak again until the late afternoon of November 21—the night before Lee assassinated the president. Twice a day phone calls had been his routine. Why had he not called Marina on Sunday after calling her twice Saturday? Had something in Saturday's calls already strained their relationship? Or had the extra weekend hours of isolation in his tiny North Beckley room plunged him too deeply into his inner world? Thanks to *The Shark and the Sardines,* was he dwelling too much on the shared vulnerability he felt with Professor Barghoorn? Or how trapped he felt under FBI scrutiny, and how impossible the FBI might make things for him once his Book Depository employment ended after the Thanksgiving or Christmas holidays?

In the midst of those thoughts, was he also thinking about the arrival of President Kennedy? Sunday's *Morning News* had carried a front-page headline, "Incident-Free Day Urged for JFK Visit." The article recited the fears of Dallas leaders that Walker's supporters would reprise the tactics they unleashed against Adlai Stevenson.[8] Could Oswald have been thinking that such widespread attention on Walker's followers would focus suspicion on them if he shot Kennedy but wasn't caught? And, if he were caught, wouldn't they at minimum prove grounds for claiming he was a patsy? If Oswald's attempt on Walker's life shows us anything, it is how obsessively detailed a planner Oswald was. Were thoughts about Walker in Oswald's planning for November 22?

On Monday, November 18, while Kennedy was giving his speech in Miami, Oswald put in a full day's work at the Texas School Book Depository. That day, the president's motorcade route was approved and a late edition of the *Dallas Morning News* reported that the motorcade would pass through Dealey Plaza as it headed to the Stemmons Freeway.[9] The article did not mention that the motorcade would turn right onto Houston Street and then left onto Elm Street, a car's length from the Depository, before entering the freeway, but any employee of the Depository would have known that the turns would be necessary. The motorcade and its route would have been subjects for discussion among the Depository's employees on Monday. By Monday, November 18, no employee would have been ignorant of the route.

We don't know how closely Oswald was monitoring the activities of the far right in Dallas that Monday. We know that on October 23, he had attended a Walker rally and that on October 25, he had talked about the rally at an ACLU meeting. There is every reason to believe Oswald was continuing to monitor Walker and his allies in that week of November 18.

We know with certainty that after Marina abruptly terminated Lee's call on November 18, Governor George Wallace of Alabama spoke to a group of about two hundred at Dallas's Baker Hotel. He had picked that night, that audience, and that location to announce he was running against John Kennedy for the Democratic nomination for president in 1964.

General Walker was present and received Wallace's praise. When a television cameraman attempted to film Walker, he suddenly rose to his feet, knocked the camera from the newsman's grasp, and shoved him against a table.[10] Could there be any better way to secure media attention? Could there be any more effective reinforcement of the fear of Dallas's civic leaders that the president's visit might not be trouble-free? Could there be any more vivid reminder for Lee Oswald that Dallas was a place of violent political conservatism?

Authors Vincent Bugliosi and Gerald Posner believe that Tuesday, November 19, was the day that Oswald began thinking seriously about assassinating President Kennedy. As the *Times-Herald* headlined Kennedy's Miami speech that day, Radio Havana, Oswald's favorite station, may well have been criticizing the president for organizing attacks on Cuba.[11]

Posner most succinctly makes the argument that Tuesday, November 19, was the crucial day for Oswald's decision making. Referring to Oswald's learning of the precise motorcade route on either Monday evening or Tuesday, Posner says:

> [I]t is hard to overestimate the impact of that discovery. Oswald, who thought his contribution to his revolutionary cause would be the death of Walker, was suddenly faced with the possibility of having a much greater impact on history and the machinery of government. Failed in his attempts to find happiness in Russia or the U.S., rejected by Cubans, barely able to make a living in America, frustrated in his marriage, and hounded, in his view, by the FBI, he was desperate to break out of his downward spiral. He had endured long enough the humiliations of his fellow Marines, the Russian and Cuban bureaucrats, the employers that fired him, the radio ambush in New Orleans, the refusal of V.T. Lee and other Communist leaders to acknowledge his efforts and letters. Lee Oswald always thought he was smarter and better than other people, and was angered that others failed to recognize the stature he thought he deserved. Now, by chance, he had an opportunity that he knew would only happen once in a lifetime.[12]

Bugliosi summed up the same factors by saying:

> [W]as it possible he was thinking that if he killed Fidel Castro's most powerful enemy, he might avert the assassination of Castro, forestall the invasion of Cuba, and bring him at last to the status he craved as a hero of the Cuban Revolution? And that if he died in the attempt, Castro would see what Cuba had lost when its petty bureaucrats frustrated his ardent desire to serve the cause?[13]

The argument seems strong that Tuesday, November 19, was important in Oswald's thought process. It was the day that Dallas newspapers both first publicized the exact route of the president's motorcade and led with Kennedy's call in Miami for the removal of Castro. Oswald's frustrations were high, but his ambitions had not abated. The opportunity presenting itself could not be ignored. And surrounding events were amplifying his reasons and need to become an actor in a great moment of history.

Wednesday, November 20, supplied possible reinforcement to Oswald's dream. That day the *Dallas Morning News* carried a front-page headline reading, "Terrorism Leaves 17 Dead in Caracas."[14] If not in the United States, the revolution was blossoming in Latin America. Saving Castro could save the revolution.

Also on November 20, a random event at the Texas School Book Depository may have buttressed Lee's developing plan. At about 1:00 p.m., Warren Caster brought two rifles to the School Book Depository. Caster was a tenant in the building, not an employee. He had purchased the rifles on his lunch hour and proudly displayed them to Depository superintendent Roy Truly and others.[15] Oswald was present and saw Caster with the rifles.[16]

Priscilla McMillan believed the incident with Caster's rifles was seminal.[17] Speculated McMillan, "If anyone should accuse him later of keeping a rifle there, he had a pretext. There were two rifles in the building already, so why should he be under suspicion?"[18] Moreover, Oswald's Mannlicher-Carcano had been purchased in the name of A. Hidell. Who was to say that any rifle found on the Depository's sixth floor was Oswald's? Lots of Texans owned rifles. Anyone could have purchased the rifle from Hidell.

If he could shoot the president without being identified, others might be blamed. He had not been caught or identified when he fired at Walker in April. Suspicions had focused on known enemies of Walker. Perhaps the same thing would happen if Oswald was not caught or identified in shooting Kennedy. A possible Walker supporter—A.J. Hidell, who had purchased the rifle—would be sought. Such thinking was consistent with Oswald's repeated assertions to Captain Fritz that he was innocent and his claim to news reporters that he was a patsy.

Late Wednesday evening, November 20, Oswald was not in his room. He took his laundry to a washateria a half block from his rooming house. He remained there past its closing at midnight, reading magazines. A night watchman had to pressure him to leave.[19] Why did he need to do laundry Wednesday night? He told Marina on Saturday that he had done laundry that day. Was he anxious as he contemplated the next two days? Had he not made a firm decision about Friday?

McMillan believed he had not. He did not take his pistol with him when he left for work Thursday morning. He knew he had to retrieve his rifle from Ruth Paine's garage. He hoped to spend Thursday night there, and return with the rifle to work on Friday with his usual ride from Buell Wesley Frazier. He might need the pistol on Friday if he were able to leave the Book Depository after the shooting. He should not leave it at his rooming house. In McMillan's view, his decision to attempt an assassination was still evolving when he left for work Thursday morning and talked to Marina that evening.[20]

McMillan's assessment is reasonable but not necessary. Few murderers plan the perfect crime. It is just as likely that Oswald did not plan or expect to leave the building after the shooting, that he realized he might be searched at the Book Depository, and that there would be no easy way to conceal the pistol when he was at Ruth Paine's house.

Thursday morning for Lee was an unusual indulgence. He arose early enough to walk two blocks to the Dobbs House diner for a breakfast of two eggs, cooked over light,[21] not the usual coffee in his Beckley Street room. At about 9:30 a.m., before the mid-morning break, he asked Wesley Frazier if he could ride with him to Irving after work.[22] Frazier answered sure and asked Lee why he was going to Irving on Thursday night rather than on the usual Friday.[23]

"I'm going to get some curtain rods," Lee responded. "You know, put them in my apartment."[24] Yet his room already had curtain rods and curtains.[25] When Frazier asked Lee if he would be going out to Irving on Friday night as well, Lee responded that he wouldn't.[26] By 5:30 Thursday evening, he was at the Paine residence.

39

Semifinal Acts

On Thursday, November 21, the CUSA activists—Bernard Weissman, Larry Schmidt, and Bill Burley—were making the final payment and reading the final copy for their full-page, black-bordered advertisement attacking President Kennedy.[1] General Walker's follower and publishing partner, Robert Surrey, was ensuring that a "Wanted for Treason" leaflet bearing President Kennedy's photograph was being distributed on the streets of Dallas.[2]

For the president, the day was absorbed by the Texas trip. He used the early morning in Washington to review and revise his Texas speeches.[3] One was the speech never given in Dallas. It would have issued a challenge to those who did not share his views:

> Ignorance and misinformation can handicap the progress of a city or a company, but they can, if allowed to prevail in foreign policy, handicap the country's security. In a world of complex and continuing problems, in a world full of frustrations and irritations, America's leadership must be guided by the lights of learning and reason—or else those who confuse rhetoric with reality and the plausible with the possible will gain popular ascendancy with their seemingly swift and simple solutions to every world problem.
>
> ***
>
> We cannot expect that everyone, to use the phrase of a decade ago, will "talk sense to the American people." But we can hope that fewer people will listen to nonsense. And the notion that this Nation is headed for defeat through deficit, or that strength is but a matter of slogans, is nothing but just plain nonsense.[4]

The words about deficits and slogans were aimed squarely at his Republican opponents. A Texas newspaperman read the draft and called it a "withering blast at his right-wing critics."[5] "Talking sense to the American people" harkened back to Adlai Stevenson's campaign for president in 1952.

At 10:45 a.m., about the time Lee Oswald was arranging a ride to Irving, the president was boarding a helicopter for Andrews Air Force Base.[6] At 11:05 he and the First Lady were aboard Air Force One for their three and one-half hour flight to San Antonio.[7] Over the next two days, they would spend nearly as much time traveling as politicking—two and one-half hours in San Antonio including a motorcade and a speech, a forty-five-minute flight to Houston, another motorcade and a testimonial dinner for Congressman Albert Thomas, followed by a flight to Fort Worth that landed at 11:07 p.m. in order to accommodate a breakfast speech on Friday before the presidential party went by plane to Dallas for another motorcade that would precede the president's luncheon speech.[8]

Much of the travel time was occupied by Kennedy, his friends, and staff struggling with a cordial protocol to placate Governor Connally and Texas Democratic

Senator Ralph Yarborough. The liberal Yarborough and the conservative Connally detested each other. Who would sit where at the head tables; who would ride in which car; and who would introduce whom? Caught in the middle was Vice President Johnson. When Yarborough declined to ride in a vehicle with Johnson, Kennedy ordered him to do so.[9]

Between 4:45 and 5:00 p.m. on Thursday, when the president was shaking hands in Houston, Lee Oswald was about to arrive unexpectedly at Ruth Paine's home in Irving. Ruth had not returned from her afternoon grocery shopping. Marina was in the bedroom with the baby, Rachel. When she saw Lee leave Wesley Frazier's car and walk to the front door, Marina did not leave the bedroom.[10]

Priscilla McMillan describes their meeting best:

> She did not go to greet him. She looked sullen as he entered the bedroom. Inwardly she was pleased that he had come.
>
> "You didn't think I was coming?"
>
> "Of course not. How come you came out today?"
>
> "Because I got lonesome for my girls." He took her by the shoulders to give her a kiss.
>
> Marina turned her face away and pointed at a pile of clothes. "There are your clean shirt and socks and pants. Go in and wash up."
>
> Lee did as he was told. "I'm clean now," he said, as he emerged from the bathroom. "Are you angry at me still?"
>
> "Of course," she said, turning away another kiss.
>
> Marina tried to leave the bedroom, but he blocked the door and would not let her go until she allowed him to kiss her. With utter indifference, like a rag doll, she acceded.
>
> "Enough," Lee said, angry that she was not glad to see him. "You get too much spoiling here. I'm going to find an apartment tomorrow and take all three of you with me."
>
> "I won't go," Marina said.
>
> "If you don't want to come, then I'll take Junie and Rachel. They love their papa, and you don't love me."
>
> "That's fine," said Marina. "Just you try nursing Rachel. You know what that's like. It will be less work for me."
>
> Lee then spoke of the FBI. "I went to see them," he said. "I told them not to bother you anymore."[11]

Of course, those were not the exact words but the result of McMillan helping Marina reconstruct what they said to each other. Even so, the result is reasonably consistent with the tone of their exchange and their personalities, and had Marina's approval. McMillan continues:

> Marina left the bedroom and went outside to bring the children's clothes in off the line. Lee went to the garage for a few minutes, then the two of them came inside and sat on the sofa in the living room folding diapers. "Why won't you come with me?" Lee begged. "I'm tired of living all alone. I'm in there the whole week long, and my girls are here. I don't like having to come all the way out here each time I want to see you."
>
> "Alka," Marina said. "I think it's better if I stay here. I'll stay till Christmas, and you'll go on living alone. We'll save money that way. I can talk to Ruth, and she's a help to me. I'm lonesome by myself with no one to talk to all day."
>
> "Don't worry about the money," Lee said. "We have a little saved up. I'll take an apartment, and we'll buy you a washing machine."
>
> "I don't want a washing machine. It'll be better if you buy a car."
>
> "I don't need a car," he said. "I can go on the bus. If you buy a used car, you have to spend money to get it fixed. It's not worth it. I don't want my girl to have to do all the laundry in the

bathtub. Two babies are a lot of work." Lee pointed to the pile of clothing. "See what a lot of work it is? With two babies you just can't do it all alone."

"We'll see," Marina said.[12]

Just then Ruth arrived with a load of groceries. Marina and Lee went outside to help. As Lee returned to the house with groceries, Marina lingered to apologize to Ruth for Lee's unannounced presence. Both women guessed that Lee had come to apologize. It is likely, however, that when Marina went outside to gather laundry and Lee went to the garage, he did so to wrap his rifle in the paper bag he may have made while at the School Book Depository.[13]

Although Lee was to take the most momentous step of his life the next day, he made every effort to conceal it that Thursday evening. When Marina and Lee were sitting on the couch folding laundry, Marina said, "Lee, Kennedy is coming tomorrow. I'd like to see him in person. Do you know where and when I could go?" "No," he said blankly.[14]

When Ruth, upon entering the house, said to Lee, "Our President is coming to town," Lee responded indifferently with a characteristic, "Ah, yes."[15]

Again, Priscilla McMillan, based upon her interviews with Marina, best recounts Lee's behavior after the groceries were unloaded:

> Lee went out on the front lawn and played with the children until dark—the Paine children, the neighbors' children, and June. He hoisted June to his shoulders, and the two of them reached out to catch a butterfly in the air. Then Lee tried to catch falling oak wings for June.
>
> Marina stood nearby as Lee and June sat on a red kiddie cart together. Lee spoke with all the children in English, and then turned to Marina and said in Russian, "Good, our Junie will speak both Russian and English. But I still don't like the name Rachel. Let's call her Marina instead."....
>
> It was while they were outside, Marina thinks, that Lee asked her for the third and last time to move in to Dallas with him. His voice was now very kind, quite different from what it had been in the bedroom. Once again he said that he was tired of living alone and seeing his babies only once a week. "I'll get us an apartment, and we'll all live peacefully at home."
>
> Marina, for a third time, refused. "I was like a stubborn little mule," she recalls. "I was maintaining my inaccessibility, trying to show Lee that I wasn't that easy to persuade. If he had come again the next day and asked, of course, I would have agreed. I just wanted to hold out one day at least."[16]

One must wonder, as I and my Warren Commission colleagues did, whether this plea for Marina to resume living with him was Lee Oswald, the frequent liar, covering up a firmly committed plan to kill the president, or whether it was Lee, the lonely, uncertain man, who wanted fervently to restore his life with Marina and had not made a firm decision as to Friday.

The dinner hour was quiet at Ruth Paine's house on Thursday evening. Lee was mostly uncommunicative, and the conversation was so unexceptional that neither Ruth nor Marina remembered it well.[17] President Kennedy's visit to Dallas did not provoke a response, and when Marina asked about the expected motorcade route, Lee said he didn't know anything about it.[18] Marina recalled that at some point during the evening when Lee claimed that he had gone to the FBI office and left a stern note for Agent Hosty, she did not believe him, thinking that he was "a brave rabbit" exhibiting some bravado.[19]

After dinner, Marina stacked dishes, put away the children's toys, and nursed Rachel. While Marina fed the baby, Lee put June to bed and then returned to watch television with Rachel on his lap until she fell asleep. At about 9:00 p.m., Lee came into the kitchen to say goodnight, earlier than his usual bedtime. Marina thought he looked sad. He said, "I probably won't be out this weekend…. It's too often. I was here today."[20]

After Lee had gone to bed, Ruth had occasion to go into the garage. She was painting blocks for the children. Noticing that the garage light was on, she thought that Lee might have been there looking for winter clothes. She was certain it was not Marina, for Marina was careful about turning off lights.[21]

Marina, as usual, was the last to go to bed. It was at least an hour, perhaps two, since Lee had retired. Lee was lying on his stomach with his eyes closed. At about 3:00 a.m., Marina put her foot on Lee's leg. Once more, McMillan best reports what happened:

> Lee was not asleep and suddenly, with a sort of wordless vehemence, he lifted her leg, shoved her foot hard, then pulled his leg away.
>
> "My, he's in a mean mood," Marina thought. She realized that he was sleepless, tense, and she believed that he was so angry at her for refusing to move to Dallas right away that it was no use trying to talk to him. She thinks that he fell asleep about five o'clock in the morning.[22]

40

Friday, November 22

Let us continue with McMillan's recitation of Marina's recollection:

> On the morning of Friday, November 22, the alarm rang, and he [Lee] did not wake up.
> Marina was awake and after about ten minutes she said, "Time to get up, Alka."
> "Okay."
> He rose, washed, and got dressed. Then he came over to the bed. "Have you bought those shoes you were going to get?"
> "No, I haven't had time."
> "You must get those shoes, Mama. And, Mama, don't get up. I'll get breakfast myself."
> Lee kissed the children, who were sleeping. But he did not kiss Marina, as he always did before he left in the morning. He got as far as the bedroom door, then came back and said, "I've left some money on the bureau. Take it and buy everything you and Junie and Rachel need. Bye-bye." Then Lee went out the door....
> Then she fell back to sleep.[1]

He left more than money. In a cup on the dresser, he left his wedding ring, which he had never done before. The total money for Marina was $170.[2] He took with him about $15—enough for bus fare from Dallas to the Mexico border.[3]

At about 7:15 a.m., Linnie Mae Randle, the sister of Wesley Frazier, was looking out her kitchen window and saw Lee walking toward their house carrying a long brown package. He opened the rear passenger door of her brother's car and placed the package inside.[4]

When Frazier became aware that Oswald was there, he left the house and walked to the car. As Frazier opened the driver's door, he noticed the package on the back seat. "What's the package, Lee?" he asked. "Curtain rods," Lee responded.[5] Unlike other days when Lee had ridden with Frazier, he didn't bring his lunch.[6]

The morning was misty, cloudy, and raining as Frazier and Oswald rode to the School Book Depository—not a good day for a motorcade unless the clouds lifted.[7] Not a good day for spectators. The weather forecast indicated, however, that cold air from the west might clear the skies.[8]

Lee and Frazier arrived at the Book Depository before 8:00 a.m. in ample time to begin work. Lee left the car first, got his package from the back seat, and walked quickly ahead to the Depository without waiting for Frazier. Lee entered, perhaps fifty feet ahead.[9]

In Fort Worth that morning, a welcoming crowd in raincoats and umbrellas had gathered beneath the president's hotel room.[10] Scheduled for a 9:00 a.m. breakfast speech, Kennedy awoke to bad news. A front-page headline of the *Dallas Morning News* blazoned, "Storm of Political Controversy Swirls Around Kennedy on Visit."

Senator Yarborough's feud with Governor Connally was the subject. Two other articles picked up the theme. The president put the paper aside angrily, failing to reach page 14, which bore the full-page, black-bordered advertisement bearing the name of Bernard Weissman.[11]

The Weissman ad reached Kennedy after his breakfast speech. Press Secretary Malcolm Kilduff had seen it as the president was giving the speech. Joining Kennedy in the room of aide Ken O'Donnell, he showed the ad to the president. With a grim face, Kennedy read every word and handed it to Mrs. Kennedy. As she scanned it, the president shook his head and turned to O'Donnell: "Ken, can you imagine a paper doing a thing like that?" Turning back to Jackie, he said, "We're heading into nut country."[12]

O'Donnell reread the ad as Kennedy, in the words of William Manchester, "prowled the floor."[13] The president paused in front of Jackie: "You know, last night would have been a hell of a night to assassinate a President." He said it casually, in a murmur, and knowing his humor, Jackie took it lightly. "I mean it," he added.[14]

As the presidential entourage left for their plane at Carswell Air Force Base in Fort Worth, the skies were clearing. The winds were blowing the clouds east and away from Dallas. The limousine waiting at Dallas could have its top down. The president issued his order, enroute to Carswell Field, that Senator Yarborough must ride in the same vehicle with Vice President Johnson. The next issue of the *Morning News* would be deprived of another article on Democratic disunity.

At 11:23, President and Mrs. Kennedy were aboard Air Force One for the fifteen-minute flight to Dallas.[15] Waiting to greet him were a cross-section of the powerful in Dallas. The official welcoming party had been carefully selected by Governor Connally—nine Republicans, two Dixiecrats,[16] and not a single labor leader.[17] In the overwhelmingly warm crowd of a thousand or more were a welter of hostile placards—"Help Kennedy Stamp Out Democracy," "In 1964 Goldwater and Freedom," "Yankee Go Home and Take Your Equals with You," "Mr. President, Because of Your Socialist Tendencies and Because of Your Surrender to Communism, I Hold You in Complete Contempt,"—plus a Confederate flag bearer and a large group of hissing teenagers from a public high school.[18]

Yet even among the most hostile, no one fathomed what was about to unfold.

41

Answering Why?

When a full history of Lee Oswald was in hand, the Warren Commission wanted to know what motivated him and whether a more welcoming response from Marina on November 21 might have averted the outcome on November 22. On July 9, 1964, Commissioners Dulles and McCloy and six staff members—Rankin, Willens, Redlich, Jenner, Liebeler, and Slawson—held a seven-hour conference with three psychiatrists, Drs. Dale C. Cameron, Howard P. Rome, and David A. Rothstein, from whom they hoped to gain insight. The conference covered a range of issues: Oswald's relationship with his mother, the effect of his childhood upon him, his interest in Marxism, his being demeaned by fellow Marines, his defection to the Soviet Union, his apparent rejection by the Soviets, his marriage to Marina and her various rejections and emasculations of him, his shooting at General Edwin Walker, his retention of records related to the Walker shooting, the possibility that his shooting at both Walker and Kennedy were suicidal, his failed attempt to gain entrance to Cuba, and his consideration of hijacking an airplane. No one suggested he was psychotic. The *why* and *whether* that had prompted the conference turned out to be questions that the psychiatrists could not and did not answer.[1]

Commission staffer Jim Liebeler made a last-minute try. In July 1964 he telephoned Robert Oswald for his views on his brother's motive. Robert was reluctant to answer.[2] Four years later, Robert published his thoughts in *Lee: A Portrait of Lee Harvey Oswald by His Brother.* After detailing the pitfalls in Lee's life, Robert concluded, "... the whole pattern of failure throughout most of his twenty three years led to an outburst of violence in April and the final tragedy in November 1963.... The violent end of his life was determined, I believe, by the time he was thirteen. The only question was what form the end would take...."[3]

The Warren Commission did not answer why. They left that mission to others. The Commission was satisfied beyond any doubt that the totality of evidence showed that Lee Harvey Oswald fired the shots that killed the president. It was satisfied that no evidence of a conspiracy had been uncovered. While there might be suspicions of a conspiracy, no evidence showed any probability of a conspiracy or pointed to any possible conspirator.

A wealth of evidence—both actions and words—do permit us to reach reasonable conclusions about Lee Oswald's thinking and motives. His actions speak more clearly than his words.

Parsing the Language of Actions

Oswald's actions show clearly that he hoped not to be caught. He shot the president from a hiding spot on the sixth floor of the Texas School Book Depository. He fled quickly to a second-floor lunchroom. After Officer Baker confronted him, he paused to purchase a soft drink before swiftly exiting the Depository, walking hurriedly seven blocks to a passing bus, and knocking on its door to gain admission. It was not a bus that would take him to his rooming house. Had he waited only a few minutes, he could have taken one that would have stopped near his doorstep.[4]

When the bus, four blocks later, was delayed by heavy traffic, Oswald got off, obtaining a transfer ticket as he left. *Why a transfer ticket?* you might ask. Oswald never used the transfer. He walked two blocks to a Greyhound bus station and secured a just-arriving taxi.

My Commission colleague, David Belin, spent weeks struggling with the mystery of the unused bus transfer ticket. As he recounted nine years later, "On Memorial Day weekend [1964] the idea germinated.... One possible answer was that he took a transfer because he expected to use a bus again and wanted to save a bus fare ... [I]f he was trying to get another Dallas bus ... where would that bus take him.... To me, the most obvious destination was Mexico and then Cuba."[5]

Belin discussed the idea with me, our colleagues Jim Liebeler and Dave Slawson, and the Secret Service. Liebeler mentioned that Oswald's Marine friend Nelson Delgado had said that Oswald once told him that if he were trying to escape from the United States he would go to Mexico, and from there to Russia via Cuba. Slawson said that the Secret Service had secured bus schedules from Dallas to Mexico and had marked maps to show their stops. Belin found one Greyhound bus that made a flag stop Oswald could have reached had he boarded a Dallas bus at a stop a few blocks in the direction he'd been headed when he shot Officer Tippit.[6]

The transfer ticket had to be used within a time limit. Belin checked further. The transfer was valid when the needed Dallas bus arrived at Marsalis and Jefferson streets at about 1:30 p.m. Oswald shot Tippit at about 1:15 p.m. He could have caught the Dallas bus to the Greyhound bus flag stop if Tippit had not stopped him.

As Belin remembered, "By Monday, June 15, I had the answers."[7] It was likely that Oswald was headed to Mexico.

To me, Belin's hypothesis has always made the most sense. As I have had time to reflect, three other facts support Belin's conclusion. First, when Oswald left $170 for Marina on the morning of November 22, 1963, he was careful to keep approximately $15 for himself—sufficient to get him by bus to the Mexican border and perhaps further. Second, he retained a photo identification card in the name of Alek Hidell. Showing it at the border would indicate that Hidell, the man who had purchased the murder weapon, had fled to Mexico. At either the Soviet or Cuban Embassy in Mexico City, he could claim that he had fled Dallas to avoid prosecution for a crime committed by another man.[8]

The third supporting fact was that he secured his pistol after fleeing the School Book Depository. The pistol could enable Oswald to commit a theft or intimidate someone for help once he crossed the border into Mexico. As he had allegedly done in September 1963 at the Soviet Embassy in Mexico City, he could show the pistol to confirm his fear of wrongful prosecution by American authorities.

In Mexico, Cuba, or the Soviet Union, he could proclaim his innocence as he did in Dallas. He was an innocent man who was being accused because he was a Marxist. Others were more likely suspects.

Others Would Be Blamed

Oswald was politically well-informed. He knew Dallas politics. The most logical suspects in Dallas were those whose animosity for the president had been most open and vocal. They included the most avid supporters of Edwin Walker. Those supporters had assaulted Adlai Stevenson a month before. Jack Ruby, among the least of the politically aware, died believing that Walker's followers were part of a conspiracy to assassinate the president and were blaming Jews for the crime.

Walker, himself, feared he would be blamed for any misconduct against Kennedy. To avoid it, he was aboard a plane from New Orleans to Shreveport, Louisiana, when he heard the president had been shot. So fearful was Walker of being blamed that he swiftly sought out flight attendants and secured their names as proof that he was not in Dallas when the president was shot.[9]

Warren Leslie, a Neiman Marcus executive and former *Dallas Morning News* reporter, remembered, "The first thought in the mind of scores of people I've seen since the assassination was that it must have been done by a member of the rightwing. Many of the local rightists themselves thought so. I watched the color go completely from a man's face at the Imperial Club [a favorite Dallas spot for the wealthy] when the murder was announced. Politically he stands well to the right of Goldwater. At that moment he was convinced that one of his colleagues had committed the murder."[10]

Is it not reasonable to conclude that Lee Harvey Oswald believed that supporters of Edwin Walker—probably Walker himself—could and would be blamed for assassinating President Kennedy?

A Purpose in Blaming Walker

Walker topped Oswald's list of the politically dangerous. He had attempted to assassinate Walker to keep him from gaining power. There is no evidence that Oswald expected American foreign policy to change after Kennedy's death. After being charged with killing President Kennedy, Oswald told Secret Service Inspector Thomas J. Kelley that he did not expect U.S. policy to change in the area most important to him—Cuba. If that statement is to be believed, Oswald's political goal was not to secure an immediate change of political policy or to secure a new chief of state. Was it not more likely that on November 22, 1963, Edwin Walker remined an important part of Oswald's focus as it was on October 23? Was it not likely that the same suspicions that caused local law enforcement and others in Dallas to fear disruptive conduct by Walker's followers would cause Oswald to believe that President Kennedy's death could readily be blamed on Walker? If that were Oswald's belief, then killing Kennedy could destroy the Walker movement. The goal that Oswald had sought in April could be achieved on November 22, 1963.

Why Kill a Man You Do Not Hate?

Oswald had never expressed personal dislike for the president and, indeed, respected many of Kennedy's policies. But, in all likelihood, it was not Kennedy, the person, whom Oswald was shooting. A study of attempts at presidential assassination in the United States completed for the Secret Service in 1997 found that potential or actual presidential assassins rarely had personal animosity toward the president. Presidents were targeted because of the power of their office and its symbolism.[11] Oswald was shooting the leader of the capitalist world in a clash of civilizations. His was a political action in keeping with the vision expressed in his *Maasdam* writings. He was affecting the course of history, not settling a personal score.

He was also following the rules of the game. This was the Cold War. Assassinating a chief of state was within those rules. It was easy for Oswald to believe that President Kennedy himself was playing by those rules. In attempting to assassinate Fidel Castro and supporting assassination of other Marxist leaders, America had deprived Kennedy of moral superiority and provided to Oswald a justification, if he wanted it, for murder under contemporary rules of war.

Meeting a Personal Need

To say the assassin's objective was political but not personal is not to deny that killing Kennedy fulfilled for Oswald some personal need. In 1963 Lee Oswald was still fashioning his adult identity. As Marina told the Warren Commission, he wanted to "...get into history."[12] Being accused of killing the president could get one there.

In his classic work *Identity: Youth and Crisis*,[13] the eminent psychoanalyst Erik Erikson discussed the issue of identity in early adulthood. In the transition from adolescence to adulthood, most people are engaged in identity formation—to be a doctor, lawyer, nurse, mother, teacher, artist, athlete, carpenter, politician—whatever that identity may be. As Oswald's writings confirmed, his grandiose dream was to be remembered as a great political figure. He feasted on the biographies of political leaders: Mao Tse Tung, John Kennedy, Sam Houston, and others. His account of his defection to the Soviet Union was labeled "Historic Diary."

What grandiose dream, what identity was to be fulfilled, however, by assassinating or being accused of assassinating John Kennedy? The destruction of Walker's movement might be sufficient, but Oswald's need for grandiosity might be fulfilled on another scale—a personal one. Perhaps for Lee Oswald, it was sufficient that partisans remember him—like Julius and Ethel Rosenberg—as the wrongly accused assassin of President Kennedy.

Life Without a Future

It is likely that by November 22, 1963, Lee Oswald's search for an identity had reached a crisis point. Had John Kennedy come to Dallas on October 22 instead of November 22, Oswald's life and our nation's history might have been different. Yes, Lee Oswald would have been employed at the Texas School Book Depository. Yes, his Mannlicher-Carcano would have been available. Yes, he would have been dwelling too much in his inner world on North Beckley, but Lee Oswald might not have shot the president.

His life changed significantly between October 22 and November 22.

The newborn child, the return to Marina, and the new job he had on October 22 might have been signs of hope and importance rather than the sources of despair they presented on November 16, when the opportunity to perform an historic political event became apparent. Soon after October 22, Lee Oswald's personal life began to collapse. On November 1 and 5, Agent Hosty appeared at Marina's residence. The resumption of FBI surveillance posed threats to future employment, to his relationship with Marina, and to any political future in the United States.

By mid–November, he was beginning to see that the political possibilities he had fancied in the United States had faded. Efforts to become a Marxist leader had already failed. He could not become a member of the Trotskyite Socialist Workers Party while living in Dallas. One must first form a local chapter with five members. Lee had not sought to find even one other. The Socialist Workers Party had not accepted his minimal offer to do printing. The Communist Party USA had not invited him to join, accepted his offer of help, nor responded to his latest letter.

There was no other country in which he could have political success. Cuba's consul in Mexico City had rejected him. The Soviets had not responded to his visa request. He did not, in fact, want to live in Russia. He wanted another country—which he could not find. He must have thought intensely about his plight in the lonely nights between November 12 and November 21.

Until the afternoon of November 15, it is unlikely that Oswald could have conceived the possibility of assassinating President Kennedy by firing from the Texas School Book Depository. On that morning, the *Dallas Morning News* reported that a motorcade was unlikely, but that afternoon news came that a motorcade was planned.

On Saturday, November 16, Oswald could infer from the Dallas newspapers that President Kennedy's motorcade might pass within rifle-shot of the Texas School Book Depository. On Monday, November 18, Kennedy spoke in Florida urging the overthrow of Castro.

That same day, Marina became upset upon learning that Lee was living in Dallas under a fictitious name. The next day when he called, she hung up in anger. On Tuesday, they did not talk, and both Dallas papers showed the motorcade route passing the School Book Depository. On Wednesday, a tenant at the School Book Depository displayed two rifles to admiring employees, with Lee watching. By Wednesday, November 20, he saw an opportunity, had reasons, and found a possible cover for killing the President of the United States. On Thursday morning, he asked Buell Wesley Frazier if he could ride to Irving after work.

Sadly, but understandably, the significance of Marina's rejection is a question that Marina may never be able to put aside. Norman Mailer may be the last author who secured a conversation with her about her feelings. He assessed Thursday night in this way:

> She will never forget that last night in Irving, he had kept making advances to her until he went to bed, and she had refused. She had said to herself, "No, if I don't teach him this lesson right now, this lying will continue. O.H. Lee will continue. Don't butter up to me." She tried to discipline him.
>
> Afterward, she had to think, What if he really wanted to be close to me? What if I put him in a bad mood? It torments her. What if they had made love that last night? But she is the wrong person to talk to about this, she would say, because she is not a sexual person. Sensuous but not sexual.[14]

It is tempting to think that if Marina had not rejected Lee on November 21, he might not have shot the president. But we know that intimacy had not deterred Lee from ordering the .38 caliber pistol on January 27, 1963, the same morning, as Marina recalls it, that she and Lee had hoped passionately they were making a son. A reconciliation might only have strengthened his resolve.

We do know that Lee Harvey Oswald died insisting he was wrongly accused. He died without knowing what effect the assassination had on Edwin Walker's quest for power or on the future of Marxism. Being accused of killing the president gave him a place in history. For a rejected, ambitious young man, that may have been success. What other effects were yet to be seen.

POLITICS FIVE

Coping with Truth in Assassinations

42

Marina and America

It was 12:30 p.m., Central Standard Time, in Irving, Texas, on November 22, 1963. Ruth Paine was preparing lunch. Marina was in her bedroom tending to Rachel and June. Marina had spent part of the morning watching a Dallas television channel, thrilled by the scenes of President and Mrs. Kennedy.[1]

In the kitchen, Ruth could hear the broadcast. Suddenly the announcement came. The president had been shot. Ruth summoned her children, and they prayed together. Marina retreated to her bedroom and cried. After a few minutes, Marina went outside to hang up laundry.[2]

Ruth remained inside listening to the coverage. Soon, Ruth called to Marina that the shots had come from the Texas School Book Depository. Marina's heart sank.[3] Quickly, she went to the garage where she knew Lee kept his rifle. Viewing the still folded blanket that had contained the weapon, her anxiety was eased.[4] But the ease was short lived.

In about an hour, Dallas deputy sheriffs and city police were at the door. Ruth gave permission for them to enter. Some commenced an immediate search while others asked questions. Did Lee Oswald own a rifle? Yes, Marina answered. It was in the garage. With the sheriffs, Marina went to the garage. She pointed to the blanket that had held the rifle. A sheriff lifted the blanket. It fell limp. No rifle was there.[5]

Marina Oswald—the Crucial Witness

At that moment, Marina Oswald's life changed forever. She became the most important witness in investigating the assassination of President Kennedy. She and Ruth were taken immediately to Dallas police headquarters for questioning. When Marina returned to the Paine residence that night, her fears that Lee was the shooter were further confirmed.

Although the Dallas investigators had taken everything they believed might be relevant to a crime involving the Oswalds and the Paines, they had not taken a demitasse cup that had belonged to Marina's grandmother. A family keepsake, obviously. On returning to the Paine residence that Friday evening, Marina looked in the demitasse cup. There she found Lee's wedding ring. He had never removed the ring before. It was a message she could not forget,[6] a message also that might have affected her ultimate decision to be a cooperative witness.

At first Marina was a resistant witness—destroying, in particular, copies of the photos she had taken in March 1963 of Lee holding a pistol and rifle.[7] By February 1964, she began to be a cooperative one. To the FBI and Secret Service, she explained their life together from the time they returned to the United States in June 1962, until Lee left their bedroom early on November 22, 1963. It was information she could not have been compelled to give if there had been a trial of Lee Harvey Oswald. The doctrines of spousal immunity and spousal privilege would have precluded her testifying against her husband. The prosecution would not have learned that he admitted to her that he tried to murder Edwin Walker. It would not have learned about the repeated troubles in their married life. It would not have learned the details of the various political ambitions and fantasies that led to three shootings. Without Marina's testimony, it would have been far more difficult for the Warren Commission and others to understand why he killed the president.[8]

Marina remained at Ruth Paine's house for only twenty-four hours after the assassination. By Saturday afternoon, Marina and her two children were at the Hotel Adolphus in Dallas under Secret Service protection.[9] James Hosty was the first FBI agent to interview her on November 27. Their relationship was not good. She had initially declined to be interviewed, and he did not trust her. She denied that she had ever seen Lee with a gun although five days earlier she had led deputy sheriffs to Ruth Paine's garage where she believed he had hidden his rifle.[10]

At the outset, the Warren Commission's staff would also view her statements with skepticism. She did not readily disclose that Lee had admitted trying to kill Walker. She provided that information only after a note written in Russian was discovered in a cookbook entitled "Book of Useful Advice," which she had kept while living at Ruth Paine's home.[11] The staff doubted that she had held Lee in a bathroom when a few days after shooting at Walker, he had a pistol with him and said he was going to observe an appearance of Richard Nixon in Dallas.[12]

In the end, however, the Commission and its staff came to believe her.[13] Ballistics and other circumstantial evidence were consistent with her account of the Walker shooting.[14] She spoke freely about aspects of her life that never needed to be revealed. She had reasons to be thorough and truthful. First, she wanted to remain in the United States, as she stated the day of her first interview. FBI agent Hosty believed that assurances from the Immigration and Naturalization Service on that date impaired his ability to secure truthful statements from her.[15] Yet Marina knew that everything she said would be checked, wherever possible, and that, if she was found to have lied to the Warren Commission, her chances of remaining freely in the United States would be diminished.

She knew also that other witnesses could verify or refute much of what she said. Ruth Paine could testify to Marina's life and much of Lee's conduct after October 4, 1963. The de Mohrenschildts and others in the Russian community could be witnesses about Lee's behavior in 1962.

Over the period of Marina's interrogation by law enforcement agencies and the Warren Commission, her views of the interrogators changed. She became less apprehensive about the FBI. She quickly came to like and trust the Secret Service. She found also that the American public sympathized with her as an attractive young mother abandoned without money or family by a despicable husband. Donations flowed to her within days.[16] It was in Marina's self-interest to be truthful, trusting, and complete.

We do know that her greatest trust was in Chief Justice Warren. She told Priscilla McMillan that the silver-haired Chief Justice reminded her of her grandfather. She loved her grandfather and would never lie to him. Marina told McMillan she would never lie to Chief Justice Warren.[17]

The Chief Justice may, himself, deserve special credit for Marina's candor with the Commission. Over the objections of staff members, her questioning occurred, at first, without the presence of any staff member except General Counsel J. Lee Rankin. As a result of staff protest, Assistant Counsel Norman Redlich, the Commission's most knowledgeable staff member, was permitted to attend after the first day of questioning in order to assure a thorough interrogation of Marina.[18] The setting was a small conference room. No one else besides Commission members, Marina's lawyer, Marina's interpreter, and a stenographer were there. Warren understood the discomfort that testimony on the central issues could cause this twenty-two-year-old mother of two who could barely speak English and had only recently come to this country. He opened the hearing with these words:

> [W]e propose to ask her questions for about 1 hour, and then take a short recess for her refreshment.... At 12:30 we will recess until 2 o'clock and then we may take her to her hotel where she can see her baby and have a little rest.... If at any time otherwise you should feel tired or feel that you need a rest, you may feel free to say so and we will take care of it.[19]

It was Grandfather Warren speaking. After four consecutive days of testimony, Marina's lawyer spoke on her behalf:

> To begin with, she wanted me to express to you, Mr. Chairman, and members of your Commission, her extreme gratitude to you for the consideration and kindness that has been shown to her in these proceedings. She feels you have certainly gone out of your way to make her comfortable, and she has been comfortable, in spite of the sad and tragic events we have been discussing.[20]

As time has passed, her account did not vary significantly from the testimony she gave to the Warren Commission. To Priscilla McMillan, to Norman Mailer, and to the House Select Committee on Assassinations—those to whom she has spoken most extensively for publication since her Commission testimony—she gave essentially the same accounts.

This consistency across the years is particularly noteworthy in contrast to her changing views on her husband's guilt. Testifying to the Warren Commission, she believed that Lee had shot the President and was the lone assassin. Twenty-five years later she no longer believed that he had acted alone.[21] By 2017, she doubted that he was even the killer.[22] Others, she thought, were probably responsible for President Kennedy's death.

In between, she may have explained her feelings best to Norman Mailer for his 1995 book *Oswald's Tale*:

> If we go through Lee's character, I myself would like to find out: Who is he? Was he really that mean of a person?—which I think he was—but it's hard for me to take because I do not want to understand him. I have to tell you in advance that, as far as Lee is concerned—I don't like him. I'm mad at him. Very mad at him, yes. When a person dies, people have such anger. They loved their husband or wife for a long time so they say, "How dare you die on me?" Okay, but that's not my reason. For me, it's "How dare you abandon me? In circumstances like that? I mean, *you* die but I'm still here licking my wounds."
>
> All the same, I'm definitely sure he didn't do it, even if I'm still mad at him. Because he shouldn't involve a wife and family if he was playing those kinds of games. Yes, I do believe

he was on a mission, may be even when he went to Russia, but first I have to figure out what he was doing here. It wasn't just happening here all of a sudden in America. It was a continuation. In my mind, I'm not trying to convince you or the American public—I have to resolve it for myself. But I think he was sent over to Russia, maybe. I think so. I have no proof. I have nothing. I do think he was more human than has been portrayed.[23]

In the years that followed, Marina has remained in the United States. After the assassination, Americans embraced her. Within six months of Lee's death, she received $57,000 in donations. She gained financial security. She sold Lee's diary to *Life* magazine for $20,000. *Parade* magazine paid her $1,000.[24] The photo that she took of Lee holding a rifle and bearing a pistol brought $5,000. By the end of 1964, she owned an air-conditioned house in the Dallas area.[25] In 1965 she owned a home in Richardson, Texas, and married a Texan, Kenneth Jess Porter. Though Porter never adopted them legally, the girls would use Porter's last name when they were growing up.[26] Marina and Porter divorced in 1974 but returned to each other as soon as the divorce was final six months later and have been together since.[27] With skill and determination, she spent years shielding her children from the tragedy she can never escape. Though Marina spoke with Norman Mailer in 1993 for his book *Oswald's Tale: An American Mystery,* she declined to facilitate interviews with her daughters who were then thirty-one and twenty-nine. Yet June would be interviewed that same year by NBC, and in 1995, an interview with Rachel appeared in *Texas Monthly.* Both daughters praised Marina for the protection she provided.[28]

Perhaps to protect herself as much as her children, she cut herself off from those who had known her best during the time of the tragedy and those first years thereafter: Ruth Paine, who had been her mainstay for nearly three months before Lee's death, and Priscilla McMillan, who was with her nearly five months in 1964 gathering information for her biography. For over three decades after 1985, Marina declined to speak with either Ruth or Priscilla.[29]

Ruth Paine would explain Marina's breaking off all contact and coming to believe in Lee's innocence as the only way Marina could deal with "the worst thing that has happened to each of us."[30] To have maintained a relationship with Ruth or Priscilla McMillan would have been too painful and too constant a reminder of the week that ended with Lee's death and the possibility that had she dealt differently with Lee, he might not have assassinated the president. Better to deny that Lee was the killer and not communicate with those who differed.[31]

43

The Assassination's Long Arm

Just as life changed for Marina Oswald, so life changed for others close to the assassination—power seekers, power wielders, and innocent bystanders.

Bernard Weissman

At 12:30 p.m. on November 22, 1963, Bernard Weissman was in the automobile of his CUSA colleague Bill Burley. Headed to the Ducharme Club in Dallas, they were to meet with Larrie Schmidt and their fundraiser, Joe Grinnan. They were to have lunch and discuss next steps. Weissman and Burley believed the black-bordered advertisement they had created would make their point against the president without inciting the kind of disturbance that had accompanied and followed the speech of Ambassador Stevenson on October 24.[1]

Suddenly on the car's radio, a broadcaster was announcing rumors that the president had been shot. Nearing downtown, Weissman and Burley could see police officers pulling people off the street. They decided a roundabout route to the Ducharme Club would be best.[2]

When they arrived at the club, it was closed. Larrie Schmidt was waiting outside, but Joe Grinnan was absent. Grinnan and Schmidt had also heard the news while driving to the club.[3] Preferring not to be seen in a public place, Grinnan had left Schmidt to wait for Weissman and Burley.[4]

The three CUSA members found another bar where they could watch the television. The immediate speculation was, as Lee Oswald could well have expected, that a member of the ultra-right—perhaps a racist—had shot the president. Within a few hours, however, it became known that the primary suspect was a Marxist defector to the Soviet Union. The CUSA organizers felt relieved. When the Ducharme Club opened, they took refuge there, not leaving for their apartments until the dark of evening.[5]

For five days, the sponsors of the black-bordered advertisement remained out of sight as best they could. Initially, they feared that—with Weissman's name on a newspaper ad and Schmidt having gained publicity after the Stevenson incident—a mob might try to find them. On early Sunday morning, Weissman, Burley, and another CUSA supporter went to the post office to obtain letters that had been accumulating from their black-bordered ad. Letters with the earliest postmarks contained praise. Letters mailed after the president died were angry, some containing threats.

Weissman believed that a bystander at the post office was watching him and tried to follow him.[6] He later told Schmidt, "If there are the kind of 'nuts' on the other side who don't hesitate to attack and kill the President of the United States, there are some who wouldn't hesitate to do the same to me."[7]

Once Oswald was killed, Weissman considered going to the FBI and fully describing how and why the ad had been created. In a phone conversation, Grinnan persuaded him, "If they want you, they will find you."[8] Weissman left Dallas on Wednesday, November 27, and remained out of contact with Schmidt. The FBI did find Weissman and interviewed him in Mt. Vernon, New York, on December 5, 1963. He became a helpful witness for the Commission.[9]

Schmidt left Dallas after being interviewed by the FBI on December 3, 1963.[10] During the work of the Warren Commission, he was never able to be located to give testimony, and CUSA never functioned again.[11] Weissman, himself, never returned to politics. Years later, he made Detroit his home. Irony of ironies, his dry cleaner was Jack Ruby's brother Earl. Weissman never told Earl Ruby about his relationship to the events of November 22, 1963.[12]

Edwin Walker

The fears that engulfed the CUSA activists beset Edwin Walker as well. His fear that he might be blamed for the assassination was not unfounded. While Walker was still in Shreveport, one of his supporters told the FBI that an irate man drove his car to the Walker home, removed an American flag that flew outside the house, and threw it to the ground in a symbolic gesture against the general.[13] On December 5, the Washington, D.C. offices of the conservative TV and radio program *Life Line* received an anonymous letter threatening the lives of Walker and officials of the program. Walker himself notified Dallas police that he had received a threatening phone call from someone in Louisiana accusing him of paying Oswald to shoot Kennedy. The flurry of threats caused him to cancel a speech scheduled for the Garden City Hotel in New Jersey on December 9.[14]

Walker was not to be silenced, however. On December 2, he held a press conference at the Baker Hotel in Dallas, claiming the president had been killed by a communist conspiracy that confirmed the warnings he had long been giving.[15] The message was echoed by Walker's allies throughout 1964. When he testified before the Warren Commission on July 23, 1964, he was more defensive, but his goal was clear: "I am tired of them blaming the right wing, and I am tired of this, and it is about time that the Commission cleared the city of Dallas."[16]

In 1965 Walker himself made the FBI's list of people dangerous to the president as it warned the Secret Service six times that Walker's activities merited watching.[17] Although Walker continued for years to be a featured speaker at ultra-right political gatherings, he was never again an independent political force.

Governor George Wallace of Alabama became the standard-bearer for political conservatives. He was the American Independent Party's candidate for president in 1968, gaining 13.5 percent of the popular vote and 46 electoral votes.[18] In 1977, Walker ceased to have political power. He was arrested for soliciting a sexual favor from a park ranger in a public men's restroom.[19]

Howard Brennan—An Unseen Victim

On November 22, 1963, Howard Brennan was an unknown pipefitter. He did not realize that his life would be deeply changed because he reported seeing a man shoot President Kennedy from the sixth floor of the Texas School Book Depository. After becoming a vital witness in the Kennedy assassination, Brennan suffered continual intrusions and anxiety. He experienced sharply increased blood pressure, sleeplessness, and repeated nightmares about what he had observed that day.[20]

Like so many, he feared that Kennedy was the victim of a conspiracy. He suspected that a conspirator might have been in a car he saw parked near the Book Depository just before the shooting.[21] He feared that conspirators might try to eliminate him if he was publicly named as a crucial witness. Jack Ruby killing Lee Oswald did not eliminate that fear.

Nor did the FBI's efforts to provide security. Within hours of learning that Brennan was a witness, the FBI assigned a detail to protect him, providing a car to maintain 24-hour watch outside his house, and following him wherever he went.[22] Brennan himself was determined that he should not be publicly identified as a witness until he gave testimony at trial—or as later became the alternative—to the Warren Commission.

Brennan also did not trust some in the Dallas Police Department to protect his identity. In his book, *Eyewitness to History,* Brennan said that he refrained from stating with certainty in a police line-up that Oswald was the man he saw shooting because he didn't trust a particular Dallas detective who was present at the line-up to protect his identity.[23]

After the line-up, Brennan's fears were aggravated by the multiplicity of daily phone calls he received from people he had never met. A group of calls came from a woman who ultimately identified herself as Marguerite Oswald. That caller threatened Brennan for claiming the shooter was Lee Oswald.

Brennan's greatest resentment was towards the news media; many he believed were arrogant and insensitive. He argued that the media had undermined justice by publishing Oswald's photograph before he and others had seen Oswald in a line-up. In so doing, he thought the media had impaired both the credibility and accuracy of any trial identification.[24] He also believed that the media attempt to interview him in Dealey Plaza minutes after the shooting probably prevented him from identifying Oswald as he left the Texas School Book Depository.[25]

Fidel Castro

On November 22, 1963, Jean Daniel, a French journalist, was in Cuba with Fidel Castro, trying to lay a foundation for rapprochement between Cuba and the United States. When word reached Castro of Kennedy's death, Danie claims Castro exclaimed, "This is terrible. They are going to say we did it . .. This is the end of your mission of peace."[26]

The next night, in a two-hour radio address, Castro mixed fear with sorrow: "The death of a man, although that man is an enemy, should not cause jubilation."[27] But fear dominated the talk. With the death of Lee Oswald, Castro began to articulate a conspiracy theory not dissimilar from some American writers: Oswald was a well-trained instrument of rightists.[28] He might even be innocent. Oswald could not have fired two accurate shots from his rifle because, as Castro knew, the telescopic sight would cause the rifle to go substantially off target after the first shot and chambering a second bullet. Moreover, Ruby had killed Oswald to prevent Oswald from revealing the true assassins.[29]

Castro's fears were not without foundation. In Paris, at almost the same time that Kennedy was shot and before news of the president's death reached that city, Nestor Sanchez was meeting with Rolando Cubela to consider weapons for Castro's assassination. Sanchez was the CIA case officer responsible for Cubela. Cubela was a Cuban military officer trusted by Castro who may have been a double agent—pretending to be willing to work for the CIA but, in fact, still loyal to Castro. The weapon offered by Sanchez was a Paper Mate pen to be filled by Cubela with a deadly substance called Black Leaf 40. The pen allegedly had a microfilm-thin needle that could imperceptibly pierce Castro's skin, inject the poison, and cause his death.[30]

Fifteen years later, in statements to the House Select Committee on Assassinations, Cubela said it was his intention to kill Castro but that he found Sanchez's method unacceptable. He wanted a rifle. Sanchez said he would supply one with a telescopic sight and a silencer plus money for doing the job.[31] The pen was not accepted. The promised rifle and silencer were supplied in December 1964 through an intermediary.[32]

The Select Committee did what the Warren Commission could not—talk to Castro. In 1978 its chairman, Congressman Louis Stokes, traveled with other Committee members and staff to Havana to interview him. Castro denied that he or his government desired or attempted to assassinate Kennedy. It would be a suicidal effort, he asserted:

> That [the Cuban Government might have been involved in the President's death] was insane.... I am going to tell you here that nobody, nobody ever had the idea of such things.... That would have been the most perfect pretext for the United States to invade our country.... Since the United States is much more powerful than we are, what would we gain from a war with the United States? The United States would lose nothing. The destruction would have been here.... I can tell you that in the period in which Kennedy's assassination took place Kennedy was changing his policy toward Cuba. I was here talking to that man [referring to Jean Daniel] who was bringing a message from him.[33]

Castro denied also that he had told a reporter in September 1963 that Cuba might assassinate Kennedy in retaliation for American efforts to assassinate him or his associates. To the Select Committee, Castro put his conversation with the news reporter this way:

> I said something like those plots start to set a very bad precedent, a very serious one—that could become a boomerang against the authors.... but I did not mean to threaten by that.... I did not mean by that that we were going to take measures—similar measures—like retaliation for that.... For 3 years we had known there were plots against us. So the conversation came about very casually, you know....[34]

On November 25, 2016, Fidel Castro died at age ninety of natural causes. His brother, Raul, had been Cuba's president since February 2008.

The Soviets, the CIA, and Truth

On November 22, 1963, Soviet Premier Nikita Khrushchev was in his Kremlin study, while the remnants of a birthday party for him was still taking place on the Kremlin first floor.[35] He was ready to retire for the evening when his government telephone rang.[36] It was Soviet Foreign Minister Andrei Gromyko. He was calling to say that President Kennedy had been shot. As Khrushchev's son Sergei recalled, his father was greatly disturbed. With his wife and son, he waited for details. When word arrived that Kennedy was dead, Khrushchev decided quickly that a delegation of the highest level, headed by Anastas Mikoyan, should be dispatched to Washington to honor Kennedy.[37]

Sergei Khrushchev believed that his father respected Kennedy. Their meeting in 1961 and negotiations during the Cuban missile crisis left the Soviet premier with a sense that Kennedy could be trusted. He was not sure of Lyndon Johnson. Through future negotiations, Khrushchev hoped that the Soviets and the United States could conduct a joint space flight.[38] Those negotiations never occurred.

On November 22, 1963, Khrushchev did not realize that his own power was in jeopardy. On October 13, 1964, in a vituperative session, the leadership of the Soviet Presidium and the Soviet Communist Party called for his resignation. The next day he capitulated. In the nearly eleven months after Kennedy's death, Khrushchev's rivals had secretly engineered a coup. Aleksei Kosygin and Leonid Brezhnev succeeded him.[39]

There is no evidence that John Kennedy's death caused Khrushchev's loss of power.[40] It is clear that all Soviet leaders in Moscow, upon learning that Kennedy had been shot, shared Fidel Castro's fear of being blamed for Kennedy's assassination. Although Lee Harvey Oswald had lived in the Soviet Union for more than two years beginning in 1959, Soviet leaders in Moscow had little knowledge of the Minsk factory worker who had married a Russian woman and returned to the United States. The primary Soviet file on Oswald and those with responsibility for surveillance were in Minsk. Upon learning that Oswald was Kennedy's accused assassin, Moscow called upon Minsk to fly Oswald's file immediately to Moscow. Yuri Ivanovich Nosenko, a KGB officer in Moscow, told CIA investigators that he was assigned to read it. He became America's first source of what the Soviets knew about Oswald.[41]

Nosenko had been supplying the CIA useful information on other matters since 1962. In January 1964, he arrived in Geneva, Switzerland, as part of a Soviet disarmament delegation. He soon contacted his CIA handlers. Requesting asylum in the United States, he indicated that he feared arrest by his own country and said he had information about Oswald.[42] Nosenko's message was that the KGB had regarded Oswald as mentally unfit and had not used him in any way.[43]

His CIA handlers were dubious. They had never been certain that Nosenko was not a double agent. Was it not now likely that he was a Soviet plant—sent on a mission of disinformation? If, however, he was truthful, the CIA could not abandon him to personal danger in Europe. After a few weeks, they brought Nosenko to the United States to determine the truth.

The CIA pursued truth by attempting to force Nosenko to recant his claim that Oswald had not been in league with the KGB. Nosenko was subjected to four years of extreme psychological and physical intimidation. The details are recited in Richard Posner's *Case Closed: Lee Harvey Oswald and the Assassination of JFK*. Nosenko never recanted.[44]

Meanwhile, FBI agents believed that Nosenko was truthful. Having gathered information in depth about Oswald's behavior in the United States and his personality, they agreed that Oswald was unfit for any government to use. They argued for acceptance of Nosenko's claims.

Through it all, neither the Warren Commission nor its staff saw or questioned

Nosenko. The CIA kept Nosenko in hidden custody. The Commission had only conflicting information on his credibility. Commission staffer Howard Willens recalls that the Commission received a five-page report from the FBI of its single interview with Nosenko. The memo did not assess Nosenko's credibility. The CIA presented nothing in writing. Richard Helms told the Commission that the CIA could not draw a conclusion as to Nosenko's credibility.[45] Unable to establish the credibility of Nosenko, the Commission decided not to mention either Nosenko or his information in its final report.[46]

The first governmental investigative body other than the CIA or FBI to question Nosenko, was the House Select Committee on Assassinations. In its final report, it reflected that it was unable to reach a conclusion as to his credibility: "The fashion in which Nosenko was treated by the [CIA]—his interrogation and confinement—virtually ruined him as a valid source of information on the assassination."[47]

The CIA, it seemed, had rendered it impossible for others to determine with confidence how the KGB had reacted to Oswald's being charged with Kennedy's assassination. Yet when the Soviet Union collapsed in 1991, the KGB disclosed some of its files. Authors Gerald Posner, Norman Mailer, and others gained access. The files confirmed what Nosenko had recounted.

Among the most significant revelations was a memorandum dated November 23, 1963, from KGB chairman Vladimir Semichastny. On that date, as an immediate response to Oswald's arrest, Semichastny recommended publishing in a "progressive paper in one of the Western countries" an article "explaining the attempt by reactionary circles in the USA to remove the responsibility for the murder of Kennedy from the real criminals—the racists and ultra-right elements guilty of the spread and growth of violence in the United States."[48] No Soviet disinformation program has been more successful.

Two months after Semichastny made his recommendation, the British journal *Labour Monthly* alleged that the CIA planned the Kennedy assassination and used Oswald as a "fall guy" to do the killing.[49] In June 1964, Joachim Joesten published similar accusations in his book *Oswald: Assassin or Fall Guy*. Joesten's publisher, Carl Aldo Marzani, an Italian-born American communist, reportedly received KGB subsidies during that period.[50]

Author Mark Lane also drew the KGB's attention. The KGB used an intermediary, probably without Lane's knowledge, to provide a thousand dollars to assist in publishing his first book, *Rush to Judgment,* and five hundred dollars for travel in 1964 to Europe to spread his views.[51]

A part of the KGB's strategy was to link the CIA to President Kennedy's assassination. That strategy passed one rumor after another from the print media to New Orleans prosecutor Jim Garrison and then to movie maker Oliver Stone. The sequence began in March 1967 when the Rome, Italy, newspaper *Pease Sera* repeated the KGB's claim. Three days after Garrison arrested Clay Shaw for an alleged conspiracy to assassinate President Kennedy, Garrison told the news media that he intended to prove that the CIA engineered Kennedy's death. Garrison never did present such evidence at the Shaw trial. Later, however, he made the allegation in his own book, *On the Trail of the Assassins.* Garrison's publisher subsequently passed the book to Oliver Stone, who used the claim in his movie *JFK,* hiring Zachary Sklar, Garrison's editor, to write the screenplay.[52] In *JFK,* Garrison was the unsuccessful but justified prosecutor.[53]

Lyndon Johnson and the Warren Commission

When news of Kennedy's death reached Paris, Moscow, and Havana, Lyndon Johnson was already functioning as the thirty-sixth President of the United States. He had actually become president automatically upon Kennedy's death, but wanting there to be no question, he had been sworn in by United States District Court Judge Sarah Hughes aboard Air Force One before it left Love Field in Dallas.[54]

From the outset, fear of a conspiracy beset the Secret Service agents protecting Johnson.[55] When, within an hour of the president's death, the primary suspect became Lee Oswald, a defector to the Soviet Union and a supporter of Fidel Castro, conspiracy suspicions focused on Cuba and the Soviet Union. Rumors of a coup in the United States and military action in Germany were also afoot. It was necessary to have a president who could act with unquestioned authority.

There was no doubt of Johnson's ability to exercise that authority. There were questions in his own mind of how long the public would accept him. To biographer Doris Kearns Goodwin, he expressed his concerns years later:

> I took the oath. I became President. But for millions of Americans I was still illegitimate, a naked man with no presidential covering, a pretender to the throne, an illegal usurper. And then there was Texas, my home, the home of both the murder and the murder of the murderer. And there were the bigots and the dividers, and the Eastern intellectuals, who were waiting to knock me down, down before I could even begin to stand up. The whole thing was almost unbelievable.[56]

Lyndon Johnson was not a man to be knocked down easily. The only man to do so on that terrible weekend was Secret Service Agent Rufus Youngblood. Youngblood was in the front seat of Johnson's car when the shots rang out on November 22. "Get down. Get down," he yelled as he grabbed Johnson's right shoulder, pulled him to the floor of the car, and shielded him.[57]

The possibility of a conspiracy to wipe out the administration, as accompanied Lincoln's death in 1865, occurred to those with Johnson. Both Governor Connally and the president had been hit by bullets, raising the fear that it must be a conspiracy. Increasing the anxiety, six cabinet officers including the secretary of state and the secretary of the treasury were in flight over the Pacific west of Hawaii heading to a conference in Japan.[58] They were called back immediately.

The anxiety about a conspiracy eased as, within a few hours, there was no evidence of hostile action outside of Dallas, and, within a few days, sounds from the State Department, the CIA, FBI, and Secret Service indicated that no other members of the government were in danger.[59] But the nation was angry and despairing. It desperately needed leadership to restore calm and confidence and to address the civil rights, economic, and international problems that Kennedy himself had been facing.

Johnson's appointment of the Warren Commission on November 29 was one instrument for restoring calm. From the date of its appointment and for at least a year after the issuance of its Report on September 24, 1964, the Warren Commission brought the reassurance that Johnson and the country needed. Freed from the distractions of investigating a crime and conspiracy and using the martyrdom of Kennedy, President Johnson was able to secure enactment of the Civil Rights Act of 1964, the Civil Rights Act of 1965, tax reductions, a budget that would fund Medicare and Medicaid, and the beginnings of a nationwide anti-poverty program. All were programs that Kennedy had wanted but failed to achieve.

As Johnson told Doris Kearns Goodwin, "Everything I have learned in the history books taught me that martyrs have to die for causes. John Kennedy had died. But his cause was not really clear. That was my job. I had to take the dead man's program and turn it into a martyr's cause."[60] Johnson brought Kennedy's program to fruition by mobilizing the country and the Congress behind a cause: a legislative legacy for John Fitzgerald Kennedy.

The Warren Commission played its role by remaining silent until its report was issued. There was no press presence at Commission hearings unless the witness requested a public hearing. Only Mark Lane made that request. No press releases were issued or press conference held with respect to any commission evidence. Transcripts of testimony and some evidentiary documents were marked "Top Secret." In effect, the Commission functioned like a grand jury—making its report to the president for his use.

On September 24, 1964, the Commission delivered its 888-page report to President Johnson. Shortly thereafter, its evidence was published in twenty-six volumes.

The report had an immediate impact. A Gallup poll conducted in November 1963 showed that 52 percent of Americans believed that the president had been the victim of a conspiracy. A Harris poll conducted shortly after the Warren Commission's report was issued found that 55.5 percent of those surveyed believed that Lee Harvey Oswald was the lone assassin. Only 31.6 percent still believed there was a conspiracy.[61] By May 1967, however, the number who believed Oswald was the lone assassin had fallen to 35 percent, while 44 percent believed there was a conspiracy.[62] As years passed, the number who believed there was a conspiracy continued to climb, reaching as high as 81 percent in 1975 and again in 2002.[63] In October 2017, the percentage of conspiracy believers had fallen to 61 percent, with belief among college graduates being the lowest at 52 percent.[64]

The Warren Commission and its staff remained, for the most part, silent in the years that followed issuance of its report.[65] The Chief Justice of the United States had been our leader. Judges issue their rulings and remain silent. Earl Warren's model was not to be a spokesman for the Commission's report. The report, like Supreme Court opinions, was to speak for itself. As staff members, even though we knew and understood the evidence far better than any of the Commission members, nearly all of us believed that we should follow the Chief Justice's example. If we were requested to speak about our work, we did so. But we did not seek audiences.

Until 2013, among our staff members, only David Belin wrote a book—two, in fact—about how we reached our conclusions.[66] In November 2013, Howard Willens, who had been with the Commission since its inception as the General Counsel's first assistant, published *History Will Prove Us Right: Inside the Warren Commission Report on the Assassination of John F. Kennedy*. The title was taken from Chief Justice Warren's answer as to why the Commission's members and its staff had not aggressively defended their work.

Brothers in Grief

No one could have been more devasted by President Kennedy's assassination than the president's two brothers: Attorney General Robert Kennedy and Massachusetts

Senator Edward Kennedy. Senator Kennedy describes their reactions in his 2009 memoir, *True Compass*. For nearly two months after their brother's death, Robert could not return effectively to his duties as attorney general. His powers of concentration were overcome by the tragedy. Senator Kennedy repressed his grief by becoming the family's consoler-in-chief.[67]

When the report was issued in September 1964, Robert Kennedy praised the report but said he would not read it.[68] It was too long and too painful. Robert instead asked Edward to meet with Chief Justice Warren. Edward described a four-hour meeting he had with Chief Justice Warren at the Commission's former offices in this way:

> He told me quite persuasively that he'd felt a responsibility to the nation to get it right. He personally made the case to me, showing me its weaknesses and walking me through the thinking of the Commission members.... I was satisfied that the Commission got it right.... I know how strongly Bobby felt that it was imperative that the inquiry be through and accurate. In my subsequent conversations with him, when all was said and done, I believe that Bobby accepted the Warren Commission's findings too.[69]

Neither Robert nor Edward ever read the report. They relied on the judgment of others. Edward was satisfied with the conclusions of the report and believed that Robert shared that satisfaction.[70]

J. Edgar Hoover

When the FBI relinquished its investigatory authority to the Warren Commission, its leader, J. Edgar Hoover, had a competing goal—to protect the agency's image. From the outset, he had objected to Lyndon Johnson's appointment of a commission to review his agency's work.[71] The Commission, he believed, should find the FBI's evidence correct and give it credit for determining who killed the president.[72] In the end, however, the Warren Commission got primary credit—and blame—for that conclusion.

Of overriding importance for Hoover was protecting himself and his agency from blame. He feared that the Warren Commission would blame the FBI for not warning the Secret Service about Lee Oswald's presence on the motorcade route.[73] On November 23, 1963, just one day after Oswald's arrest, Hoover ordered James Gale, assistant director in charge of the FBI's Inspection Division, to conduct an internal probe of the FBI. Gale concluded that both Marina and Lee should have been interviewed fully before November 22, that Lee should have been placed on the FBI's Security Index, and that the Secret Service should have been informed that he was a security risk.[74]

Most significant to Gale were Oswald's defection to the Soviet Union, his political activities after returning to the United States, his contact with the Soviet Embassy in Mexico City, and his employment in a building along the route of the motorcade.[75] Fourteen years later, Secret Service Agent Forrest Sorrels told the House Select Committee on Assassinations that, if Oswald had been listed on the FBI's Security Index and the Secret Service so informed, "I would have picked him up as part of presidential protection."[76]

Gale's report was all that Hoover needed. On December 10, 1963, before the Warren Commission had hired its own staff, Hoover disciplined seventeen FBI supervisors and agents serving in Dallas, New Orleans, New York City, and in the District of Columbia.[77] They had responsibility for monitoring Oswald or had information about him.[78]

Hoover also changed the criteria for inclusion on the FBI's Security Index—providing that henceforth all defectors to the Soviet Union would automatically be in the index.[79]

Neither the Warren Commission nor the general public were informed of Hoover's disciplinary action. Twelve of those sanctioned got what Assistant Director Cartha DeLoach called slaps on the wrist—letters of censure.[80] The other five were placed on probation. Underlings at the FBI believed that no discipline was appropriate.[81]

Unaware of that discipline, the Warren Commission, nonetheless, criticized the FBI for failing to share information with the Secret Service. It stated:

> [The] FBI took an unduly restrictive view of its responsibilities.... However, there was much material in the hands of the FBI about Oswald ... enough to have induced an alert agency, such as the FBI ... to list Oswald as a potential threat to the safety of the President...[A] more alert and carefully considered treatment of the Oswald case by the Bureau might have brought about such a referral [to the Secret Service] ... Under proper procedures[,] knowledge of the pending Presidential visit might have prompted Hosty to have made more vigorous efforts to locate Oswald's rooming house address in Dallas and to interview him.... FBI instructions to its agents outlining the information to be referred to the Secret Service were too narrow ... the liaison between the FBI and the Secret Service prior to the assassination was not as effective as it should have been.[82]

It was a criticism that Hoover, himself, might have written. Scribbling on an internal FBI report the same day the Commission's report was issued, Hoover commented that the failure of subordinates to place Oswald's name in the Security Index "could not have been more stupid. I intend to take additional administrative action."[83]

To the Commission's report, however, J. Edgar Hoover responded differently. The report, he said publicly, was "a classic example of Monday morning quarter-backing." His deputy, FBI Inspector James Malley, was more vehement. He telephoned the Commission's General Counsel J. Lee Rankin to say that the Commission had "out-McCarthyed McCarthy."[84]

Hoover never told the Commission that he disciplined eight agents on September 28, 1964, four days after the Commission issued its report.[85] Of the eight, five received more than "slaps on the wrist." Ken Howe, Agent Hosty's immediate supervisor in Dallas, was reduced to the rank of agent and transferred to Kansas City. An agent in New Orleans was transferred to Springfield, Illinois, and two supervisors in the District of Columbia were transferred to field positions.[86] Yet Gordon Shanklin—the supervisor who had told Hosty to destroy Oswald's note—received no discipline.

This second round of discipline fell most heavily on Hosty. Hosty was censured, placed on probation again, suspended for thirty days with loss of pay, and transferred to Kansas City.[87] The stated reason for the transfer—that he had experienced conflict with the Dallas police and the matter was receiving attention from the local press.[88] Under any conditions, the sudden uprooting alone would have been difficult on the Hostys, already the parents of eight, including a severely disabled four-year-old, and expecting their ninth child in just four months.

Hosty's friends, both within and outside the Bureau, became his salvation. Fellow agents took up a collection to compensate him for lost wages. Friends and neighbors contributed funds to buy his house so that he and his overwhelmed family could move quickly to Kansas City. Taking sympathy, his new supervisor in Kansas City gave him a manageable assignment.[89]

J. Edgar Hoover died in 1972, never learning, so far as we know, that Hosty had received a threatening note from Oswald before the assassination and, on Gordon Shanklin's order, had destroyed it. Neither Shanklin's supervisors nor the public learned of the note until 1975. Shanklin's supervisors decided that even though Shanklin's actions might have been criminal, too much time had elapsed to warrant prosecution. Shanklin never experienced any discipline or even disgrace. In 2003 the FBI headquarters building in Dallas was named the J. Gordon Shanklin Building.[90]

The Secret Service and Presidential Protection

The Secret Service, the president's primary protector, found its integrity and reputation more threatened by President Kennedy's assassination than any other federal agency. Its job had been to identify potential assassins and to assure the president's safe travel.

The Secret Service's approach to the Commission was resistance. Other than to claim the need for secrecy and to doubt the Commission's authority to investigate presidential protection,[91] the Secret Service responded to the president's death and the Commission's report with silence and passivity. No Secret Service agent was disciplined. Nor did the Secret Service issue any public criticism of the Commission.

In the end, the Warren Commission prevailed. It criticized the Secret Service candidly: "The arrangements relied upon by the Secret Service ... were seriously deficient."[92] The Service had not provided "well-defined instructions" to local law enforcement. Its surveillance of buildings along the motorcade route had been inadequate.[93] Its criteria for identifying potential assassins were seriously deficient.[94]

The Commission specifically recommended, "The Secret Service should develop as quickly as possible more useful and precise criteria defining those potential threats to the President which should be brought to its attention by other agencies."[95]

Developing criteria for identifying potential assassins is no easy task. In 1963, the Secret Service issued criteria for identifying individuals possibly dangerous to the president only to the White House mailroom. They requested information on any communication "that in any way indicates anyone may have possible intention of harming the President."[96] When asked by the Warren Commission if there were more detailed criteria, Robert Bouck, chief of the Protective Research Section (PRS) of the Secret Service, answered, "Our criteria is [sic] broad in general. It consists of desiring any information that would indicate any degree of harm ... to the President, either at the present time or in the future.... We had not had a formal written listing of criteria ... everything that might indicate a possible source of harm to the safety of the President."[97]

On December 26, 1963, the FBI issued its own criteria for individuals it deemed potential threats to the president. The FBI criteria were:

> Subversives, ultra-rightists, racists, and fascists (a) possessing emotional instability or irrational behavior, (b) who have made threats of bodily harm against officials or employees of Federal, state, or local government or officials of a foreign government, (c) who express or have expressed strong or violent anti–U.S. sentiments and who have been involved in bombing or bomb-making or whose past conduct indicates tendencies toward violence, and (d) whose prior acts or statements depict propensity for violence and hatred toward organized government.[98]

In June 1964, before the Warren Commission issued its report, the Secret Service issued to other federal and local law enforcement agencies its own guidelines for identifying potential assassins: "*The Secret Service should be furnished with any information* coming to the attention of an agency *of a threat to physically harm the President, ... or to cause him ... embarrassment....*"[99] [Emphasis added.]

Barely more specific than past guidance, these would not have identified Lee Harvey Oswald. The Commission ultimately said to the Secret Service, "It is apparent that a good deal of further consideration and experimentation will be required before adequate criteria can be framed.... It will require every available resource of our Government to devise a practical system which has any reasonable possibility of revealing [potential assassins]."[100]

In 1964 the practicalities were that the Secret Service and its PRS had neither the skill nor sufficient staff to develop more detailed criteria. In 1963, PRS had consisted of twelve specialists and three clerks. Between November 1961 and November 1963, that staff reviewed 8,709 cases[101]—too many for that small a staff to identify a potential assassin who had not made a clear threat or otherwise demonstrated a physical danger to the president.

For nearly thirty years, PRS struggled with the problems of needed research and necessary staff.[102] It would not be until five years after Squeaky Fromm's 1975 attempt on President Ford's life that the Secret Service, having had no success in developing more sophisticated criteria for identifying potential assassins, would ask the National Academy of Sciences for help. In early March 1981, less than a month before John Hinckley shot President Ronald Reagan, the Academy convened a three-day conference of researchers and clinicians to discuss "Problems in Assessing and Managing Dangerous Behavior."[103] The conferees concluded, "Prediction, judgment, and making decisions are highly fallible and difficult tasks ... and the Secret Service should not expect a panel of experts to be able to help them improve their capability in these areas to a dramatic degree."[104]

Between 1992 and 1997, the PRS undertook its own effort to develop improved criteria. Robert Fein and Bryan Vossekuil examined eighty-three attempted assassinations and near-lethal approaches on prominent public persons from 1949 to 1997.[105] Known as the Secret Service Exceptional Case Study Project (ECSP), Fein and Vossekuil focused on the thoughts and behaviors of the offenders.[106]

Twenty-five incidents were attacks or lethal approaches on the president.[107] "In every case," as Fein and Vossekuil reported, "the attack or near attack was the end result of an understandable and often discernible process of thinking and action."[108] The offenders did not fit any one profile. Some were mentally ill. Some were not. There were both men and women. Ages ranged from sixteen to seventy-three.[109]

None had expressed a verbal or otherwise observable threat to the president.[110] Each had engaged, however, in a planning process—often brief—designed to achieve a specific goal that met a specific rational or unconscious need of the offender.[111]

For many, attempting assassination was the culmination of a downward spiral in the offender's personal life: a loss of significant relationships, a change in financial situation, a change in living arrangement, or a feeling of humiliation.[112] For some, the assassination attempt was an attempt at suicide. Death by police or criminal conviction would end personal pain and bring notoriety or fame.[113]

The offender's personal needs were often accompanied by a goal of producing political change, but few assassinations had a purely political motive.[114] Nonetheless, extreme political ideas were common among would-be political assassins. The offender was, however, rarely more than a fringe member of a political group. In only one case—the attempted assassination of President Harry Truman by Puerto Rican nationalists—was the attempt a group activity.

The potential assassin often had a past history of violence or crime. He or she owned a firearm. Most importantly, the offender's personal life had reached a breaking point.[115]

The ECSP study was conducted to help law enforcement personnel, but it bore a lesson for politicians and the mass media: "Assassinations are stimulated by television and newspaper images, movies, and books.... [and assassins] may transfer their interest from one target to another."[116] Politicians and the media must understand the weaknesses of their audiences and the possible impact of their messages. Their words can provoke actions.

Although the significant factors that Fein and Vossekuil identified in their ECSP study fit Oswald's life, personality, and thought processes almost perfectly, the authors and those who later relied upon them scarcely discussed Oswald in their publications.[117] One may wonder why. Perhaps it was because by 1999, Oswald's role in Kennedy's death had become a matter of persistent public controversy. Highlighting Oswald in the ECSP might have brought a wave of negative attention in the mass media, thereby calling into question the conclusions they conveyed.[118]

Assassination as a United States Policy Option

Assassination of foreign leaders as an unarticulated option for the United States did not formally end with President Kennedy's death. Although Allen Dulles, Robert Kennedy, President Kennedy, and a few others knew of the plan to assassinate Fidel Castro, the planning occurred, apparently, without knowledge of the new president or the CIA's director, John McCone.[119] It remained for consideration by CIA operatives into 1965.[120]

Over a decade elapsed until ending assassination attempts on foreign leaders would be addressed at the presidential level. On February 18, 1976, President Gerald Ford, responding to discoveries of the Rockefeller Commission and Senator Church's committee on foreign intelligence, issued Executive Order 11905. The order provided "No employee of the United States Government shall engage in, or conspire to engage in, political assassination." Two years later, on February 24, 1978, President Jimmy Carter amended Executive Order 11905 by issuing Executive Order 12036: "No person *employed by or acting on behalf* of the United States Government shall engage in, or conspire to engage in, assassination." The word *political* was removed from Executive Order 11905. In neither order was the word *assassination* defined.

Politics in Dallas

No bystanders to the tragedies of November 22–24, 1963, were more devastated than the political and civic leaders of Dallas.[121] When news that the president had been shot reached the luncheon site for President Kennedy's expected speech, one man shouted, "Those damn fanatics. Why do we have to have them in Dallas?"[122]

Others spoke more publicly. A fourth-grade Dallas public school teacher wrote to *Time* magazine saying, "Dallas is as responsible as anyone." A Dallas business leader wrote similarly in *Look* magazine.[123] The superintendent of schools suspended the teacher briefly. The business leader was ostracized by the president of the Chamber of Commerce as "one of the 'gratuitous defectors' and journalistic buzzards that are still circling our town.'" A load of cement was dumped in the "gratuitous defector's" outdoor swimming pool.[124]

In his posthumously published memoir, Dallas Judge Joe B. Brown, Sr., who presided over the trial of Jack Ruby, wrote, "Within hours after President Kennedy died, our city was being blamed for his death and earned the epithet, 'City of Hate.' In our national grief, people wanted to blame somebody, and even some of the citizens of Dallas blamed the city and themselves."[125] Responding to how they thought the world was perceiving Dallas, the Citizens Council—an alliance of elite Dallas business leaders—mobilized to remove Congressman Bruce Alger from power.[126] Alger, the voice in Congress for Dallas's extreme right wingers, was a symbol of political distaste for Kennedy. In November 1960, Alger had orchestrated a confrontation by protestors upon Lady Bird and Lyndon Johnson. Just a month before the president's assassination, Alger sent his praise to the rally for General Walker, which recruited followers to disrupt Ambassador Stevenson's U.N. Day speech on October 24.

President Kennedy's death turned the tables on Alger. Six members of the politically powerful Dallas Citizens' Civic Association met with the organization's president, John Stemmons, to persuade Dallas Mayor Earle Cabell to resign as mayor and run for Congress against Alger. On Monday, February 3, 1964, upon Cabell's resignation, the Dallas City Council elected a new mayor, Eric Johnson, a recent president of the Dallas Citizens' Association's Council. Nine months later Cabell defeated Alger.[127]

Addressing History: a City Heals

President Kennedy's death brought not only political change to Dallas. It brought tourists also. Topping the sight-seeing list was Dealey Plaza. What was Dallas to do about that constant reminder of its disgrace?

Within six weeks of the president's death, a small group of political leaders and private citizens united to form the John F. Kennedy Citizens Memorial Commission. Using funds only from volunteers, the Commission hired architect Philip Johnson to design a prominent memorial. The memorial would take more than six years to complete. Intended to enable Dallas residents to forget the event of November 22 but to both commemorate the president and to distract visitors from Dealey plaza, it was to be located a block away from the plaza.[128]

Meanwhile, in memory of the president, residents and tourists regularly placed wreaths at Dealey Plaza. In November 1966, the Dallas Park Board erected at the plaza two five-hundred-pound bronze plaques acknowledging the assassination but saying no more.[129] Three and one-half years later, on June 24, 1970, Phillip Johnson's Kennedy Memorial—a pillared, thirty-foot high, fifty-foot square monument—was dedicated. Within easy sight of Dealey Plaza, the memorial is a striking tribute to the president.[130]

The shooting site could not, however, escape public interest. No sooner had the president been buried than tourists asked to see the sixth floor of the Texas School Book Depository. In self-protection, the building's management locked the entrance door and posted a sign: "NO ADMITTANCE except on official business."[131]

The steady stream of visitors also attracted commerce to Dealey Plaza. In 1970, a few months after Johnson's Kennedy Memorial was dedicated, two private collectors of Kennedy memorabilia, John and Estelle Sisson, chose to display their collection in retail space at Elm and Houston streets, directly across from the Texas School Book Depository. The Sissons charged viewers two dollars for admission and called their business, a for-profit enterprise, the John F. Kennedy Museum. Several hundred visitors per day were said to visit the museum.[132]

It was the Texas School Book Depository, however, that was the primary site for those who remembered November 22, 1963. In 1969, the Texas School Book Depository ceased to be a warehouse for books. The top three floors were empty. Built in 1901, the building could be torn down or kept as an historic site. In 1970, the owner listed it for public auction.[133] Nearly two decades of political controversy followed.

Aubrey Mayhew was the purchaser for $650,000. Mayhew, a country-music promoter and collector of Kennedy memorabilia, had created a John F. Kennedy Memorial Center in Nashville, Tennessee.[134] Mayhew proposed fashioning the entire School Book Depository as a Kennedy Museum. At the rear would be a PT boat like the one Kennedy piloted in World War II. Inside would be Kennedy automobiles and approximately 200,000 artifacts. For a dollar, visitors could gain admission to the sixth floor from which Oswald fired his shots. The museum's expected cost, eighteen million dollars.[135]

It was a grandiose idea. But, by early 1972, Mayhew was delinquent in payments on his purchase. On August 1, 1972, the building's seller, the only bidder in a foreclosure sale, recovered the property. The building remained unoccupied.[136] For four years, it was the source of controversy: Should it be preserved as an historic site—to remain as a site of infamy, as some argued—or should it be demolished to destroy the shame. The city council voted 9–2 to seek recognition as a national historic site.[137]

In 1976, Dallas County secured an option to buy it. In 1977, the voters approved a bond issue that included funds to exercise the option. Dallas County became owner of the Texas School Book Depository. Most of the building would be used for county offices and a county court. The sixth floor would remain vacant pending future plans.[138]

What then was to happen to the premises from which the president was shot? Securing an answer took ten more years of political dispute, one that engaged nearly every perspective on how the assassination might be remembered—if memory were to be preserved at all.[139]

Three Dallas leaders felt the memory should be preserved. Judson Shook, the public works director for Dallas County, engineered the county's acquisition of the building not simply for county offices but also because of its historical importance.[140] Lindalyn Adams, chairperson of the Dallas County Historical Commission, shared Shook's belief that President Kennedy's death made the building historically important. Shook and Adams enlisted the support of Martin Jurow, a retired Hollywood movie producer who had become an assistant county attorney. When Jurow was taken through the vacant Book Depository he thought, "It must not be destroyed. It must be preserved, and the only way of preserving it is to make sure that it [becomes] a museum."[141]

Those who disagreed were not just Dallas residents. Ted Sorensen, President Kennedy's aide and biographer, feared that a museum would "glorify the crime more than the victim."[142] If the Kennedy family and their friends opposed the museum, the public might see it as "morbid or disgusting or both." Charles Daly, director of the John F. Kennedy Presidential Library in Boston, was one who thought so.[143]

Although not a politician, Lyndalyn Adams understood politics. She turned to her friend Nancy Cheney. Cheney and her daughter had become friends of Senator Edward Kennedy by working in the senator's unsuccessful quest for the presidency in 1980. At Adams's request, Cheney toured the Depository's sixth floor. Impressed with the museum plans, she joined the board of the Dallas County Historical Foundation and agreed to meet with Senator Kennedy in Washington. When the meeting ended, Kennedy said, "Nancy, I have all the confidence in the world in you, and if it's going to be all right, I know it will be."[144]

How could the museum meet Kennedy's expectation? The museum's promoters had enlisted Conover Hunt to develop the museum's concept.[145] Hunt, a museum professional and historian, had recently moved to Dallas. She was intrigued by the challenge of commemorating a national tragedy in a manner that would communicate a positive heritage.[146] Somehow, she thought, the site from which Kennedy was killed could be linked to the times in which Kennedy lived, his vision for a better America, and the Kennedy legacy upon which Lyndon Johnson had built his successes in 1964 and 1965.[147]

The result? The Sixth Floor Museum begins by describing President Kennedy and his times, transitions to evidence about his assassination, and ends with his legacy and public grief over his death. There are digressions to exhibits about Lee Oswald, Jack Ruby, and the dispute over whether Oswald had confederates. One can ignore them if one likes. Whether Conover Hunt met her political challenge, the museum's visitors must decide. Ted Sorensen, Charles Daly, and Senator Kennedy accepted it.

44

The Unending Search for Truth

When Jim Liebeler and I walked from our Commission offices for the last time in September 1964, we had no doubt that Lee Oswald had been the sole shooter on November 22, 1963, that Jack Ruby was not part of any conspiracy to kill Oswald, that Oswald had acted alone, and that we had found no probative evidence that Oswald was part of any conspiracy, foreign or domestic.[1] We understood that the evidence was insufficient, however, to prove the negative to a certainty: that Oswald was not part of a conspiracy. As the Commission's staff was drafting its final report, I expressed serious criticism of its conspiracy investigation. My colleagues had not insisted that all of Oswald's contacts during the prior three years of his life be interrogated for connections and motives to assassinate the president.[2]

My colleagues and I accepted the possibility that there might be evidence yet to be discovered. If new evidence developed or suggestions could be made for better ways to investigate areas of concern, we would support further investigation.

We hoped that the public would view our work as competent and conducted with complete integrity. It was what we tried our best to do. That is why our 888-page report contained seventy-two pages of source notes and why we were about to publish 26 volumes of evidence. Both supportive and contradictory evidence was intentionally included in those volumes. We wanted the public to be able to follow our analysis, read everything that informed our investigation, and judge for itself.

In early 1965, Chief Justice Warren learned that the National Archives, following an established protocol, was not making available to the public the reports and other documents that the Commission staff had read but not published in its 26 supporting volumes. At Warren's request, President Lyndon Johnson required those unpublished documents to be made available. Thus, the only materials not available for public examination at that time—with the exception of the autopsy photographs and x-rays—were documents that the Commission's staff had not seen.[3]

For two years after the Commission issued its report, criticisms came largely from those who had made up their minds before the Commission finished its work.[4] In 1966, five books challenging the Commission began to have an impact.[5] Mark Lane's *Rush to Judgment* sold 150,000 hardcover copies and remained on the *New York Times* bestseller list for six months.[6] Richard Popkin in *The Second Oswald* suggested that another person, either impersonating or mistaken for Oswald, killed the president. Harold Weisberg's *Whitewash* questioned the Commission's integrity.

Those criticisms had limited impact until Edward Jay Epstein, a Ph.D. candidate in

American government at Harvard University, published in 1966, in book form, his Cornell University Master's thesis, *Inquest: The Warren Commission and the Establishment of Truth.*[7] Working from the Warren Commission's volumes of evidence and interviews with five Commissioners and nine staff members,[8] Epstein produced a 156-page analysis of the Commission's work.

Of paramount significance, Epstein believed that a report from FBI agents about the autopsy contradicted the final report of the autopsy doctors and that the Zapruder film showed that the single-bullet theory, first proposed by an autopsy physician, was impossible.[9] He concluded his book by stating, "Evidence arose which showed it was not possible that both men [President Kennedy and Governor Connally] were hit by the same bullet.... There is a strong case that Oswald could not have acted alone."[10]

My colleagues were outraged by Epstein's book.[11] All of the evidentiary matters troubling Epstein had been considered by our staff and found to be unpersuasive. Epstein had never returned to staff members to reveal his use of their statements or to discuss his conclusions and comments.[12] Epstein, they discovered, had taken their statements out of context and misused their candor when they had criticized the thought processes of some of the Commissioners.[13]

Two examples were particularly egregious. In February 1964, Norman Redlich had stated in a staff memorandum his belief that Marina Oswald was lying.[14] In the end, Redlich said, "I find her to be a credible witness." He relied heavily on Marina's testimony in documenting Lee's behavior from May 1961 to November 21, 1963. Epstein reported only Redlich's early memo.[15] William Coleman had a similar experience. Epstein had written that Coleman doubted Marina's credibility because he wanted her to be questioned further. Coleman, in fact, never thought Marina was lying. He believed simply that she should undergo additional questioning. Ultimately, Marina testified before the Commission for six days and was interviewed by staff members and federal agents forty-six times.[16] Coleman believed she was a truthful witness.

Jim Liebeler was a colorful, blunt staff member whose candor Epstein misunderstood. When Liebeler told Epstein that Commission members did "nothing", he meant that it was the staff members who reviewed the work of the investigative agencies, called for more investigation, took the witnesses' testimony, evaluated the evidence, and initially wrote the report.[17] Commission members were, in effect, jurors—five of whom had demanding full time jobs. None sought further investigation.

During the last months of the Commission's work, Liebeler was relentless in calling for changes in the report's language and in seeking further investigation. All of his criticisms were carefully considered by his fellow staff members. His criticisms produced many changes.[18] When the Commission's work had ended, Liebeler said that there was not a single instance in which his request for further investigation was denied.[19]

Nonetheless, Epstein used Liebeler's statement that Commissioners did nothing and his repeated critique of the staff's work in progress to suggest that the Commissioners and their staff had misunderstood or failed to develop essential evidence. Eleven years later, Liebeler told the House Select Committee on Assassinations:

> All of the investigation I wanted to do was conducted. Much of the disagreement was about how the report should be written.... The staff was highly motivated and competent with no inclination or motive not to pursue the issues to the truth.... I have never doubted the conclusions of the report and I do not now.[20]

Notwithstanding the criticisms by Warren Commission staff, Epstein's book *Inquest*—carrying a strong endorsement by a respected journalist, Richard Rovere—was a clear success. Unlike the Warren Commission Report, Epstein's 156-page book was short and readable. Equally important, *Inquest* bore, so it seemed, the cloak of academic respectability. Norman Redlich, himself a law professor at New York University Law School, believed Epstein's work violated academic standards. On June 2, 1966, Redlich wrote Prof. Andrew Hacker, Epstein's academic supervisor, identifying numerous factual errors in *Inquest* and calling it "a wholly specious work."[21]

"Whatever its shortcomings, *Inquest* gave credibility to the conspiracy theorists."[22] With academic credentials and ease of reading, Epstein's work created uncertainty in the minds of two former members of the Kennedy administration, both with Harvard affiliations: Richard Goodwin, a White House assistant to President Kennedy, and Arthur Schlesinger, who had recently published *A Thousand Days,* a history of Kennedy's presidential years. After reading *Inquest,* Goodwin urged in July 1966, that the Warren Commission's report be assessed by a small group of prominent citizens who had no connection to government. They should consider, he suggested, whether the assassination should be reinvestigated.

In November 1966, Arthur Schlesinger went further. He recommended a Congressional investigation.[23] Neither proposal was implemented, but the comments of Goodwin and Schlesinger lent credibility to those who had doubted from the outset that Lee Harvey Oswald was the lone assassin, if he were the assassin at all.

The active skeptics—through letters, telephone calls, exchanges of writings, and annual conferences—began to organize. As authors and speakers at conferences, they called themselves researchers, although, for the most part, their research was done in the volumes of evidence published by the Warren Commission. The overwhelming number were sincere, bright, and tireless. They shared a belief that the evidence of Oswald's guilt was deficient, there was a likelihood of conspiracy, and the Commission's overriding goal had not been to find the truth but to calm the public.

From 1966 to 1976, the Warren Commission's critics pushed to create a new, full-scale governmental investigation of President Kennedy's assassination. They achieved partial success in 1968. Attorney General Ramsey Clark, with the support of former Warren Commission staff, appointed a four-member panel of respected forensic pathologists to reexamine whether President Kennedy and Governor Connally were struck by the same bullet. Their conclusion: the "single bullet theory" was valid.[24]

In 1976, a chain of governmental events resulted in Congressional action to reopen the entire investigation of President Kennedy's death. The chain began in 1975 after former Warren Commission staff member David Belin was appointed by President Gerald Ford to become executive director for the Commission on CIA Activities within the United States. Popularly known as the Rockefeller Commission, it was chaired by Vice President Nelson Rockefeller.

It was through his work on the Rockefeller Commission that Belin learned that the CIA had been attempting—prior to President Kennedy's assassination—to assassinate Fidel Castro. That information had actually become known to President Johnson in 1967 when he asked CIA Director Richard Helms to report to him on a rumor to that effect from newspaper columnist Drew Pearson. Johnson did not disclose Helms's confirmation.[25] By July 1975, it became known that FBI Agent James Hosty had received an angry note from Lee Oswald that had never been disclosed to the Warren Commission.[26] The Warren Commission's trust in two of its primary investigators—the CIA and the FBI—had been misplaced.

When the Rockefeller Commission finished its work, Belin reported his evidence about the CIA to the United States Senate's Select Committee to Study Governmental Operations with Respect to Intelligence Activities. Headed by Senator Frank Church, the Committee took up the subject of CIA attempts to assassinate foreign leaders.[27] Belin's discovery, the Church Committee's verification, and evidence that FBI Agent Hosty had withheld information from the Warren Commission reinforced continuing claims of Warren Commission critics that the Kennedy investigation should be reopened.

The political closer, however, was uncertainty about the assassination of Dr. Martin Luther King, Jr. That death occurred in 1968. After eight years, only James Earl Ray had been prosecuted. Like Lee Oswald, King's assassin had shot, unseen at first, from a nearby building. Suspicions abounded that James Earl Ray was the agent of a conspiracy yet to be discovered.

In 1976, Coretta Scott King—Dr. King's widow—persuaded the Congressional Black Caucus to push for a reinvestigation of the King murder.[28] The result: Warren Commission critics and advocates for the Black community coalesced to secure House Resolution 1540, creating in 1976 the House Select Committee on Assassinations.[29]

On March 29, 1979, the Select Committee concluded that Governor Connally and President Kennedy were struck by the same bullet. The single-bullet theory was validated again. Oswald fired that bullet.[30] The Select Committee endorsed every factual conclusion of the Warren Commission that related to Oswald's activities in shooting the president, fleeing from the scene, killing Officer Tippit, and attempting to kill General Walker.[31]

In searching for a motive, however, the Select Committee did no better than the Warren Commission. It agreed with all of the personal factors that the Commission found beset Oswald, but it could be no more specific than the Commission as to a precise motive. The Select Committee concluded simply, "The best single explanation for the assassination was his conception of political action, rooted in his twisted ideological view of himself and the world around him."[32]

Nonetheless, nine of the twelve members of the House Select Committee believed that evidence showed there probably was a conspiracy. Eight of those members were persuaded by the testimony of acoustics specialists that a shot fired from the grassy knoll missed the president, the limousine, its passengers, and all spectators.[33] Who was in the conspiracy and how they were connected to Oswald, the Select Committee's majority did not know.

If the Committee's acoustics witnesses were correct, either Oswald was part of a conspiracy involving two shooters or coincidentally there was a second shooter acting independently. Not having an answer, Congressman Christopher Dodd, who accepted with reservations the House Select Committee's second-shooter conclusion, recommended, "a general review of the acoustical evidence and all other scientific evidence bearing on [the question of a second gunman] be conducted by the National Science Foundation or some other appropriate body."[34] Such an inquiry might resolve the dilemma that the second shooter theory posed.

On that recommendation, the United States Department of Justice asked the

National Academy of Sciences in 1980 to review the acoustical analysis. In 1982, the Academy reported that experts relied upon by the Select Committee had mistaken sounds occurring one minute after the assassination as being sounds occurring at the time of the assassination. The National Academy concluded that there was no credible evidence of shots from the grassy knoll.[35] The Justice Department accepted the Academy's decision and closed its examination of the case. So far as the government was concerned, Lee Harvey Oswald was the lone assassin.

For a dozen years after the House Select Committee issued its 1979 report, questions of conspiracy and cover-up were in the hands of private-sector advocates. Then, in 1991, movie maker Oliver Stone released the movie *JFK*, a fictionalized account of the prosecution of New Orleans businessman Clay Shaw by New Orleans prosecutor Jim Garrison. In the minds of both Garrison and Stone, Oswald was a patsy, a fall guy for more powerful people.

In 1969, Garrison—with the help of Mark Lane and other conspiracy advocates—had brought Clay Shaw to trial on an allegation that he had conspired with Oswald and others to assassinate President Kennedy.[36] In Garrison's mind and Stone's movie, Oswald was an innocent man who'd been manipulated by Shaw and the CIA.[37]

Yet at trial, Shaw was acquitted by a jury after less than an hour's deliberation. Author Max Holland believes that both Garrison and Stone were duped into pursuing the CIA conspiracy theme by the Russian intelligence (KGB) plant of disinformation in the Rome, Italy, newspaper *Paesa Sera* in 1967. The article brought extensive coverage in the New Orleans *States-Item* when Garrison was preparing his case against Clay Shaw. Prior to trial, Garrison repeatedly called Shaw a CIA agent, but he did not make such accusation at the Shaw trial. In 1988, however, Garrison published his memoir, *On the Trail of the Assassins*. The memoir repeated the claim that Shaw was a CIA agent. Garrison's publisher gave the memoir to Oliver Stone. The memoir became a foundation for Stone's movie, *JFK*. The allegation was central to the movie.[38]

To the credit of conspiracy advocates who came to New Orleans to help Garrison, many became disenchanted after spending only a short time with him.[39] Garrison's disgrace did not deter Oliver Stone, however. *JFK's* closing call was that the government had concealed important evidence—especially CIA files—and that the investigation should be re-opened.

It was a call with which I partially agreed. I wrote an op-ed article for my local newspaper, the *Cleveland Plain Dealer*, calling *JFK* an artful movie but a work of fiction. I agreed that no documents should be kept secret any longer. The Warren Commission had not sealed its documents. Our intent was complete openness for the public.

I soon telephoned my Cleveland friend, Congressman Louis Stokes. Congressman Stokes had been the chairman of the House Select Committee on Assassinations. He had seen the movie with one of his daughters. He, too, was distressed. For him, *JFK* "flagrantly falsified factual material and fictionalized history."[40] He told me that as he had walked from *JFK* with his daughter, she had said to him, "Daddy, you've got to do something about this."

Oliver Stone was right about one thing, I said to Congressman Stokes. There was no reason to keep assassination documents secret. Nearly thirty years had passed. No evidence I had seen in 1964 had warranted secrecy.

Congressman Stokes said that I should telephone his committee's general counsel, Bob Blakey. Blakey had been the one who had dealt with the CIA and FBI about maintaining secrecy. It was necessary to bring Bob on board. I called Bob, then a law professor at Notre Dame University.

After an extended discussion about the need for the CIA and FBI to maintain the confidentiality of some of their sources and procedures, he agreed to call Congressman Stokes and give his approval for opening the files that had been ordered to be kept sealed for fifty years. Next, I called Jim Liebeler in California. Jim agreed that we should attempt to convene all of our former staff members, especially Norm Redlich, Howard Willens, Dave Belin, Al Goldberg, Dave Slawson, Arlen Specter, and Sam Stern.[41]

The meeting occurred, and we agreed that Belin and Redlich would hold a press conference announcing our support for opening the files. All twelve of the living staff members signed a letter to the National Archives asking that all of the archived assassination files be made publicly available.[42] Arlen Specter had by then become a senator from Pennsylvania. He and Congressman Stokes agreed to sponsor appropriate legislation. Howard Willens testified in support of that legislation.[43]

The end result was the Assassination Records Review Board, created by an act of Congress in 1992.[44] Under the leadership of United States District Judge John R. Tunheim, the Board functioned from 1994 to 1998 to collect records. More than four million documents related in any way to the assassination of President Kennedy were delivered to the National Archives.[45] All except those awaiting redaction of names of confidential informants and investigative techniques or tax records required by law to remain private were made immediately available to the public.[46] None revealed a conspiracy.

45

A Conversation about Conspiracy, Truth, and Trust

The absence of direct evidence has not quelled suspicions that a conspiracy underlies the tragedies of November 22 and 24. Many conspiracy advocates have been bright, honest, avid researchers, both well-educated and well-informed. Among the ablest is G. Robert Blakey. Before being chief counsel to the House Select Committee on Assassinations, he had been a principal drafter of the federal Racketeer Influenced and Corrupt Organizations Act (RICO).[1] He retired ultimately as the William and Dorothy O'Neill professor of criminal law at the University of Notre Dame Law School.

Bob and I became friends when he interviewed me at my home for the Select Committee and later called me to testify. When the Committee's work ended, we had differences, but our friendship remained. On February 21, 2017, we met at his home in Phoenix, Arizona, to explore our differences. Our conversation began with Bob's view of the Warren Commission's statement that it could find no evidence of a conspiracy. Bob said:

> You couldn't find any evidence of a conspiracy and you concluded that all the government agencies had fully cooperated with you.
>
> .... Among other things you were not told of the CIA/Mafia plots [to assassinate Fidel Castro].... The other thing is that the FBI had a comprehensive surveillance program on organized crime. Bugs on most of the people in the northeast for sure. And there were discussions on those tapes about whether or not to kill Kennedy or to kill Bobby or whether to kill Hoover [FBI director J. Edgar Hoover].... So the issue was raised ... if we were trying to kill Castro through the Mafia, did Castro retaliate and get Kennedy first?[2]

Those early words set our agenda. When our conversation ended, Blakey said, "What you did was great. You had a great shooter investigation.... you didn't have a good conspiracy investigation; you weren't given the tools or all of the evidence you needed."[3]

On many issues, we agreed. We agreed that Lee Oswald had fired from the sixth floor of the Texas School Book Depository the shots that killed President Kennedy. No one else was there. We agreed that the single-bullet theory was correct.

We disagree on whether there was a second shooter on the grassy knoll. Bob said that acoustics evidence showed a shot that hit no one was fired from that location. We agreed that no eye witness saw that shooter, no one was seen fleeing the area, and no rifle or cartridges were found. Our difference was over whether one should believe the acoustics specialists who testified before the Select Committee or the later specialists who said that acoustics evidence did not prove a shooter at the knoll. If Bob's acoustics witnesses were right, there probably was a conspiracy to kill the president.

On who the conspirators were not, we even had agreement. Neither Castro's government nor the Soviet Union was involved in killing President Kennedy. There was no evidence, and such a conspiracy would have been foolish and too dangerous.

What was the conspiracy that Bob posited? Bob's experience as an organized crime investigator led him to his theory. He said that Carlos Marcello, an organized crime leader in New Orleans, was probably the leader of the conspiracy. Marcello had a motive—to remove Attorney General Robert Kennedy from power.

Marcello was an illegal alien. In April 1961, Robert Kennedy had caused the United States Immigration and Naturalization Service to deport Marcello to Guatemala, although Marcello quickly found a way to gain reentry to the United States through Miami.[4] He wanted to assure his continued U.S. residency.

Bob's belief—that to achieve that goal, Marcello wanted to kill the president—came from a claim by an FBI informant. The informant alleged that Marcello, in September 1962, had said with respect to Robert Kennedy, "Don't worry about that little Bobby son-of-a-bitch. He's going to be taken care of." Marcello allegedly then uttered a Sicilian curse: "Take the stone out of my shoe."[5] Using a metaphor about removing the tail of a dog by cutting off the dog's head, Marcello then analogized the president to the dog's head and Robert Kennedy to its tail. By killing John Kennedy, the dog's tail and the stone in Marcello's shoe—Robert Kennedy—would be rendered harmless.[6] In addition, Bob believed that a cellmate of Marcello was credible in saying subsequently that Marcello had admitted to him that he had arranged for the president to be killed.[7]

The plot to kill the president, Bob believed, was to be consummated by using a patsy to perform the murder. In that way, Marcello and any of his colleagues would not be implicated.[8]

The patsy, of course, was Lee Harvey Oswald. Under Bob's theory, Oswald was recruited by Marcello through anti–Castro Cuban exiles who posed as Castro supporters and wanted Kennedy killed to prevent Kennedy from dislodging Castro. Bob admitted he had no evidence or names of such Cubans. It was a conjecture to use in pursuit of an investigation.

Bob elaborated to me that Oswald, after he was arrested on November 22, realized that his co-conspirators had misrepresented their identity when John Abt, the noted Communist Party lawyer that Oswald sought, did not respond to his request for counsel. Oswald then recognized, Blakey concluded, that he had been duped. He would then testify against his fraudulent co-conspirators.

Bob theorized that the Cubans who had duped Oswald were in league with Marcello. Upon killing Kennedy, Oswald would be murdered by the Marcello-Cuban conspiracy. The murder of Oswald was to be accomplished by a second gunman, probably a Cuban, on the grassy knoll in Dealey Plaza. The killing would take place as Dallas police were transporting Oswald from the Texas School Book Depository to the nearby Dallas police headquarters.

But, as Bob perceived it, that part of the plan misfired. Oswald escaped arrest at the School Book Depository and fled without the grassy knoll gunman being able to kill him. Jack Ruby was, then, recruited to do the job.

That was the conspiracy theory that Bob Blakey suggested to me in our conversation on February 21, 2017. He acknowledged that it was a theory to be used for investigative research, not necessarily a final conclusion. As an investigator, he told me, he was attempting to find the missing pieces in a jigsaw puzzle.

He was certain of the general parameters of the puzzle because of five factors: (1) acoustics evidence showing there was a shooter on the grassy knoll; (2) confirming witnesses who thought they heard sounds or saw smoke at the knoll; (3) Oswald shot and killed the president from the School Book Depository; (4) Ruby killed Oswald; and (5) organized crime leaders wanted President Kennedy killed. From witnesses providing that testimony, he was confident there were two shooters at the president, a third shooter to murder Oswald, and a group of Kennedy opponents capable of planning the murders. What he needed was evidence connecting the principal players: Oswald, the grassy knoll shooter, Jack Ruby, and the members of organized crime, all in a plan to kill the president.

In our conversation, Bob admitted readily that he lacked essential evidence—people, places, or dates—that anyone contacted Lee Harvey Oswald after Oswald returned to Dallas from Mexico City on October 3, 1963. He also agreed that it was unlikely that Oswald joined any plan to kill Kennedy until after he left his threatening note for FBI Agent Hosty. Bob even further agreed that it was reasonable to conclude that neither Oswald nor anyone else devised a final plan until the president's motorcade route was published in Dallas newspapers on November 16 and 17. The elaborate Blakey conspiracy, involving organized crime leaders, anti-Castro Cubans, and the pro-Castro Oswald in New Orleans and Dallas, would be planned and executed in a very few days

An initial plan, Blakey told me later, was probably conceived in New Orleans where Oswald publicly identified himself with Castro's cause. It was an evolving plan. Those who wanted Kennedy dead saw Oswald as a likely patsy when, in August 1963, they learned that he had lived in Texas and later learned, in September 1963, that Kennedy planned a political trip there.

Still, pieces of Bob's jigsaw puzzle were missing. All of us—the Warren Commission, the House Select Committee, Bob, and me—would have liked more evidence of activities by Kennedy's enemies in the weeks after Oswald left New Orleans. Bob suggested we lacked the evidence because the CIA had not told the Warren Commission about its many plans to assassinate Castro; the FBI had not told the Commission about its illegal bugs on members of organized crime[9]; and the Warren Commission had not requested appropriate organizations (as I had suggested in 1964) to freeze all long-distance telephone, hotel and airline manifests, and immigration records for the six-month periods before and after November 22, 1963. If those efforts had been taken, Bob believed a wealth of information might have been available to find the missing pieces of the puzzle.

A beginning question I posed to Bob was how Carlos Marcello or his colleagues would be able to contact Oswald in Dallas after he returned from Mexico City. For Bob, the starting points of an Oswald to Marcello inquiry were David Ferrie and Oswald's uncle, "Dutz" Murret. For three months when Oswald was sixteen years old and living in New Orleans, Ferrie had led a Civil Air Patrol unit to which Oswald had belonged. Ferrie knew Marcello. Bob admitted that no evidence existed that Ferrie had any contact with Oswald after those three months, but their knowledge of each other remained.

Oswald's uncle Dutz Murret, Bob believed, knew Marcello because, as a bookmaker, Murret paid tribute to Marcello. Bob offered no evidence of any other connection between Murret and Marcello. When asked how Marcello might know of Oswald, Bob thought that Marcello could have read about Oswald when he was arrested in August 1963 after his confrontation with Carlos Bringuier and other anti–Castro Cubans.

Bob did not suggest that Dutz Murret was a part of any conspiracy to kill President Kennedy, only that he worked in Marcello's world. From my perspective, Murret did not seem to be the kind of man with whom an organized crime leader would discuss the possibility of murdering the president. Indeed, besides being a bookie, Murret had been a successful father. In November 1963, one son was studying to be a priest; another son was a dentist; one daughter was a teacher; and a second daughter was a housewife. Moreover, Murret could not have known how to contact his nephew in Dallas since Oswald was then living in a rooming house under a fictitious name. Even Marina and Ruth Paine could not contact him by telephone.

How, then, could Marcello or his colleagues contact Oswald in Dallas after early November 1963? Bob suggested that it could be through anti–Castro Cubans who knew Oswald in New Orleans. But how could those Cubans contact Oswald? They would be as ignorant as Dutz Murret, Marina, and Ruth Paine of how to reach him. In our conversation, Bob suggested that Oswald, once he had returned to Dallas, may himself have initiated the contact.

What evidence is there of such a contact, I wondered? No likely phone numbers were in Oswald's address book. Bob said that someone claimed to have heard Oswald speaking in Spanish on the rooming house telephone. I noted to Bob that Oswald was not known to converse in Spanish—only Russian.[10] Bob replied that perhaps he made only an initial greeting and spoke in English thereafter.

Our conversation moved to Jack Ruby. Bob agreed that a primary motive for Ruby might have been "to show the world a Jew had guts." The House Select Committee had not mentioned Ruby's obsession with the idea that Bernard Weissman's ad attacking Kennedy was, in some way, connected to the assassination.[11] It had not called Bernard Weissman as a witness. My impression was that the Select Committee had not given serious consideration to Ruby's two-day effort to find Weissman. In any event, Bob said that wanting to show the world a Jew had guts was not inconsistent with killing Oswald at the request of someone else. I concurred. Leon Hubert and I had pursued the possibility that Ruby had been induced by someone to kill Oswald despite our awareness that Ruby was obsessed with the Weissman ad.

Where were the linkages from Ruby to Marcello, I inquired? Bob acknowledged that Ruby might not be directly connected to Marcello, but they probably had mutual acquaintances. As the proprietor of a striptease club, Ruby obtained his entertainers from a club in New Orleans controlled by Marcello and through a mob-connected labor union. Ruby had telephoned union leader, Breck Wall, on Saturday evening, November 23. Also important to Bob was that Ruby often ate dinner at a Dallas restaurant owned by mob figure Joseph Campisi and that Campisi had visited Ruby once, at Ruby's request, in December 1963 while Ruby was in the Dallas County jail.

For me, an all-important issue, was whether Ruby had told his lawyers that he had been recruited by someone to kill Oswald. Ruby was initially represented by Tom Howard, a streetwise Dallas lawyer. His lawyers at trial were two of the nation's best: Melvin Belli and Joe Tonahill. On appeal, he was represented by four other respected lawyers. It is difficult to believe that at least one of his lawyers would not have asked if anyone urged or persuaded him to kill Lee Oswald.

Ruby was given the death penalty. Providing evidence that someone had persuaded or helped him in killing Oswald could have saved Ruby's life. Evidence of a conspiracy to kill the president would have been even more valuable. There could be no reason for keeping it a secret. A self-interested lawyer could have written a best-selling book with the information. To his death, Ruby asserted he acted on his own, and no one who knew him—lawyer, relative, friend, business associate, or rabbi—has ever said otherwise.

Bob agreed that disclosing that he had been recruited by someone else would have given Ruby a strong bargaining point for a lesser penalty. Bob said he did not think that Ruby had told his lawyers about being recruited by someone to kill Oswald. He said that Ruby did not tell his lawyers because he might have been afraid for his own life. Organized crime figures, said Bob, controlled the sheriff who managed the Dallas County jail where Ruby was being held.

The possibilities had not been discovered, Bob believed, because the FBI had not adequately tapped the offices of organized crime in New Orleans; the Warren Commission had not frozen telephone, hotel, airline, and immigration records; and the CIA had concealed its involvement with anti-Castro Cubans and its efforts to assassinate Fidel Castro.

Of paramount concern to Bob was that the CIA had concealed information from him. In our conversation, Bob put it this way:

> We went to the [CIA] and we entered into a long agreement with the agency. You've got to tell us the truth, and you've got to tell the people we're interviewing that they can't lie to us because [of] some government permission to lie that the agency had. So did the people tell us the truth? … [T]he agency made the presentation to me that why don't you let us get you a facilitator who will listen to what your researchers want, and then go get it for them.

What seemed to be an unvarnished offer of help contained a concealment:

> What we were <u>not</u> told is that the facilitator, a man named Joannides [George Joannides][12] was the agent who had the charge of an anti-Castro Cuban group, a group that Oswald had a contact with, at least. That person … would have been a witness and under oath. He would not have been a facilitator.
>
> As I know now, everything that was given to my researchers went through an editor before it got to my researchers and I wasn't told the whole truth about him.
>
> *I disbelieve everything that the CIA says about the assassination. The only thing that I would believe is if they admitted that they did it, but I would still corroborate it.*[13] [Emphasis added]

For Bob Blakey, withholding information about the CIA's facilitator was tantamount to withholding information about possible conspirators. If a person withholds some information from a confidante (in this case Blakey and his staff), no information that the withholder facilitates should be regarded as complete or truthful without independent confirmation.

Our four-hour conversation on February 21, 2017, ended with an effort to identify what our Warren Commission and House Select Committee experiences had taught us about government witnesses and truth. Bob began:

> …. We can't depend on the agencies because the agencies themselves are engaging in illegal behavior. Because they will do everything in their power to cover it up. I think the FBI did not investigate seriously the organized crime for the Warren Commission because they would have to have revealed to the Warren Commission that they were bugging the Mob … even though in those transcripts there are engrossly [sic] incriminating statements … those tapes were illegal. They weren't going to give them up because that would embarrass them. And the one thing you don't want to do if you work for the FBI under J. Edgar Hoover is embarrass the

> Bureau. That's why the note was grabbed and thrown away… [I]f we had honest investigating agencies, we could conduct those kinds [honest] of investigations.[14]

My question followed:

> How do we bring that about?

Bob answered:

> Well, we got to make certain that the people in the FBI know the rules and stay within them. We got to make sure the people in the CIA stay within the rules, and are candid.[15]

I picked it up from there. I suggested to Bob that there were three levels of concern that caused investigating personnel to be deceitful. First, if their own jobs were at risk. That included FBI Agent James Hosty, his supervisor Gordon Shanklin, and Dallas police officers Patrick Dean and Roy Eugene Vaughn. Second was a leader who wanted to protect the image of the agency. That was J. Edgar Hoover. He not only did not tell the Warren Commission that he had disciplined FBI agents for inadequate supervision of Lee Harvey Oswald, he criticized the Commission for criticizing that very deficiency. Finally, there was concealment of questionable conduct that officials believed was in the interest of national security: the CIA's plan to assassinate Fidel Castro and the FBI bugging communications of organized crime leaders.

How do future investigations foster the full truth from investigating agencies that share the same goals as the independent investigators? Bob and I left that for another day, for the scholars, the teachers, and the rule makers.

I suggested to Bob a final lesson that could be learned from our investigations: "Disturbed individuals can be affected by serious events" in the political environment. "Our own national leaders need to think about the risks they're raising, not only for the country, but for themselves when they stir up passions in this country that can lead disturbed individuals like Ruby and Oswald to violence."

Bob concluded with memorable insight:

> This is a violent country. This country is armed…. I think people in public life have to worry about assassination. Not only as the result of conspiracies, but also disturbed people…. I think we have to lower the tone of the way we behave. There's a reason for civility. And I think we have to return as a public to civility. Or we're going to have more of what you … and I had to investigate.
>
> It's not the kind of thing in a free society we should have to do.[16]

46

Truth and Trust in a Political World

"Truth is your only client." That was Chief Justice Warren's charge to his Commission staff at our first full meeting. Throughout our investigation, they remained the words we lived by. When asked a few years later why so many of the public doubted the Commission's work, the chief justice's answer was concise: "History will prove us right."

If public opinion polls are history's judgment, that time has not arrived. As many as sixty-one percent of Americans still believe a conspiracy remains to be discovered. Some, including Lee Oswald's widow and a daughter, believe that Lee Harvey Oswald was innocent.

If reasonableness is the standard of history, there should be no reasonable doubt that Lee Oswald killed both President Kennedy and police Officer J.D. Tippit. There can be no doubt that Jack Ruby killed Oswald. The Warren Commission and the House Assassinations Committee conducted their investigations fourteen years apart. They agreed that Oswald fired his rifle from the sixth floor of the Texas School Book Depository and killed Kennedy. Neither of those exhaustive investigations, nor any investigation since, has produced probative evidence linking Lee Oswald to a conspiracy to assassinate President Kennedy.

When the Commission had finished assembling the eyewitness testimony of Lee Oswald's conduct on November 22, Earl Warren had no doubt that Oswald had assassinated President Kennedy. He told a Commission staff member that he could have convicted Oswald in three days. His evidence would have been simple. Two witnesses saw Oswald shooting from the sixth-floor window. Oswald's rifle was found on the School Book Depository's sixth floor. There was a photograph of Oswald holding the rifle on an earlier date. He fled the School Book Depository. When stopped by a police officer, he killed the officer. What else was necessary? "Keep it simple" is a prosecutor's maxim. For a decade in the 1930s, the Chief Justice had been a California county prosecutor handling homicide cases.

Historians now have an essential role to play. They are the custodians of truth. Their challenge is to put President Kennedy's assassination in its place in history, to assess why Lee Oswald murdered President Kennedy and Officer Tippit, and to explain why so many are relentless in rejecting the evidence that Oswald and Ruby each acted alone.

One answer may be that everyone loves a mystery. For many, mysteries are more interesting than facts. My own first experiences with assassination mystery writers may be illustrative.

The first influential conspiracy movie, *Executive Action,* appeared in November

1973, the tenth anniversary of JFK's assassination. Burt Lancaster, Robert Ryan, and Will Geer were its stars. Mark Lane wrote the initial screen play.[1] *Executive Action* alleged that the president was killed by a right-wing conspiracy of powerful business and government interests. A friend and high school classmate of mine was a co-producer. He had minimal political interests. He was a businessman.

About a week before *Executive Action* premiered, my friend called to ask if I would attend and say a few words to his investors. He had never asked me to be a consultant for the movie. He did not tell me that Mark Lane had provided the story line. I did not see the movie until I was in attendance with my classmate's investors and other friends.

When, the showing ended, its director preceded me on stage. With passion, he told the audience that the movie presented important evidence of a conspiracy that caused the assassination—that his only mission was to find the truth. He hoped a new investigation would be instigated.

I followed by saying that the movie was fiction—that the audience should be assured that there was no government/business conspiracy to murder President Kennedy. I had no doubt that the marketplace, not politics or truth, was what had attracted my friend and his investors. Politics had been Mark Lane's business, and he knew how to use the marketplace.

Three years later, the political hopes of Mark Lane and the movie's director were fulfilled. The House Select Committee on Assassinations was created.[2] Neither my friend nor *Executive Action* should be fully credited or fully blamed. Other factors were at work.

In late February and early March 1975, the Columbia Broadcasting System, the Associated Press, the *New York Times*, and the *Washington Post* reported that the CIA had been involved in three successful assassinations. They renewed earlier reports that the CIA had not told the Warren Commission about the agency's failed attempt to assassinate Fidel Castro.[3] Six months later, on August 31, 1975, the *Dallas Times-Herald* revealed another government concealment—that the FBI had destroyed Lee Oswald's threatening note to Agent James Hosty.[4] On November 22, 1975, my former Warren Commission colleague David Belin formally requested that Congress reopen the investigation of President Kennedy's death.[5] In September 1976, the House Select Committee on Assassinations was established.[6] *Executive Action*, determined private and public researchers, Dr. Martin Luther King, Jr.'s widow, David Belin, and the news media had combined to generate a second full inquiry into the assassination of President Kennedy.

After two years of investigation, the House Select Committee agreed unanimously that Lee Oswald was President Kennedy's killer. No conspirator was identified. The Committee's members differed, however, on whether acoustics evidence showed a second shooter. The U.S. Justice Department asked the National Academy of Sciences to review the acoustics evidence. In 1982, a special committee of the National Academy concluded that the acoustics specialists used by the House Select Committee were wrong. In 1988, the Justice Department closed its case, satisfied that no evidence existed to warrant its continued investigation.

In 1991, however, another movie—Oliver Stone's *JFK* (based on Jim Garrison's 1988 memoir, *On the Trail of the Assassins*)—reopened the door. A year later, the Assassinations Record Review Board was created and began to collect all records related to the assassination and its investigation. The Board finished its work in 1998. No evidence was found to warrant resuming a criminal investigation.

For more than a half century, obsession with conspiracy theories has distracted us from what is important about the tragic weekend of November 22, 1963—that the murders on that weekend brought a turning point in the Cold War and the civil rights movement; that, acting alone and independently, two insignificant men, driven by very personal considerations of failure, fear, and ambition, had produced monumental political change; and that a violent environment infused by political extremism and bigotry made murder seem reasonable to those perpetrators.

That is the simple story—supported by mountainous evidence. Too much, certainly for a two-hour feature film. Too much for a few days of reading. Yet it is fascinating. A story of men who want to gain or retain the highest levels of power, of men whose fortunes were in a downward spiral, a story of a marriage gone sour, a story of racial and religious bigotry.

Historians have a mission, should they be willing: Replace fiction with fact. Show that truth is stranger and can be more interesting than fiction. Do your best, historians, to teach future generations that the assassination of President Kennedy and his assassin, Lee Harvey Oswald, are not unsolved murder mysteries. Single killers did it alone. Lee Oswald and Jack Ruby were history's change agents. They were not conspirators in an unsolved murder mystery. Most importantly, their lives and actions tell us poignantly about the early 1960s and what followed the tragic weekend.

Chief Justice Warren believed that history would prove us right. Historians, he is waiting.

Postscript

Continuing the Search for Truth

As a student of history, you will be making history's judgment on the assassination of President Kennedy. You must make your own search for the truth. In that search, you will be judging both the witnesses and the authors. Is the author thorough and honest? Is the presentation complete? Are the sources accurate? You must begin with the evidence.

As a serious searcher for evidence about President Kennedy's death, you will want four books at your side:

1. *Report, The President's Commission on the Assassination of President Kennedy.*
2. *Marina and Lee,* by Priscilla McMillan
3. *Case Closed,* by Gerald Posner
4. *Reclaiming History,* by Vincent Bugliosi

They are your best guides to the evidence and the issues.

Since the Warren Commission investigation is the target of all assassination theorists and the source of most evidence, it is the starting point for assessing criticisms and for locating vital testimony and exhibits. You should possess the *Report* of *The President's Commission on the Assassination of President Kennedy.* You can access its 26 volumes of testimony and exhibits online through The Mary Ferrell Foundation and the National Archives.[1]

Priscilla McMillan's *Marina and Lee* (1977 and 1993) is a love story about murder. It is one of the few sources of new evidence. McMillan knew Lee Oswald. She interviewed him in Moscow in November 1959. Beginning in the summer of 1964, she was with Marina Oswald almost daily for over five months, recording Marina's account of her life with Lee. McMillan is honest and factual. She draws heavily on Warren Commission sources and documents them carefully. McMillan took a dozen years to write her book. She has provided the best account of Lee Oswald and his wife for the period most relevant to the assassination.

Gerald Posner's *Case Closed* (1993) addresses in a readable fashion all of the significant conspiracy theories. This is a concise but comprehensive study of all the main factual issues in the assassination. Posner re-interviewed numerous witnesses. Especially helpful, too, is his study of the Soviet defector Yuri Nosenko.

Vincent Bugliosi's *Reclaiming History* (2007) is the most comprehensive reference book available. Bugliosi took over twenty years to write it. The book contains 1,488 pages of relevant text and a compact disc with more than 15,000 source and endnotes. Bugliosi uses 472 pages to analyze the principal conspiracy theories and their authors. Although his analyses are often caustic, Bugliosi is accurate and comprehensive. The most valuable portion of *Reclaiming History* may be its 71-page index. In it one can look for almost any topic, witness, author, or agency that Bugliosi addresses in his text and notes.

Three Warren Commission participants provide firsthand accounts of how the Warren Commission did its work. *Portrait of the Assassin* by Gerald R. Ford and John R. Stiles, published in 1965, gives Commissioner Ford's assessment of the witnesses he believed credible and his judgment of Oswald's possible motive.

David Belin's *November 22, 1963: You Are the Jury* (1973) is the Warren Commission Report he hoped would be written. Belin's responsibility for the Commission had been to trace Oswald's activities from the week before President Kennedy was killed until Jack Ruby killed Oswald. *You Are the Jury* recites testimony at length. Belin asks the reader, as juror, to evaluate the testimony—both supportive and contradictory—relevant to the Commission's conclusions. In that way, Belin explains how he became satisfied that Oswald was Kennedy's lone assassin, why he believes Oswald was headed to Mexico in search of a refuge, and why his theory of Oswald's destination was not included in the text of the Commission's report.

The third book of a Commission participant is Howard Willens's *History Will Prove Us Right*. The title quotes Chief Justice Warren. Published in 2013, it is based on the diary Willens kept while coordinating the work of the Commission's staff. It is a detailed chronology of the Commission's investigation, the issues among the staff, and their controversies in searching for truth.

The documentary film *Truth is the Only Client* provides an opportunity to see and hear some principal participants and investigators of the events of November 1963-Warren Commission witnesses Ruth Paine and Bernard Weissman, private researcher Steve Barber, House Select Committee counsel G. Robert Blakey, authors Vincent Bugliosi and Priscilla McMillan, and members of the Warren Commission's staff. Seeing and hearing an individual is important to judging credibility.

Finally, Dealey Plaza in Dallas and The Sixth Floor Museum at Dealey Plaza are sites that serious students of President Kennedy's assassination should visit. The shooting is most readily understood if one sees where it occurred. From the sixth floor of the Texas School Book Depository, one can have the view that Oswald had of the president's limousine as he fired the fatal shots. You can see the packing boxes that Oswald used as a parapet from which to shoot. You can watch the film of the shooting taken by Abraham Zapruder. An archivist will help you find documents, physical exhibits, and oral histories that may interest you.

Chapter Notes

Abbreviations: HSCA—Report, Select Committee on Assassinations, U.S. House of Representatives, 85th Congress, 2d Session (1979); WCH—Hearings, President's Commission on the Assassination of President Kennedy (1964); WCR—Report, President's Commission on the Assassination of President John F. Kennedy (1964)

Introduction

1. Christopher Andrew and Vasili Mitrokhin, *The Sword and the Shield: The Mitrokhin Archive and the Secret History of the KGB* (1999) at pp. 146–148, 172–175. See also Rudolph Abel, Wikipedia; https://en.m.wikipedia.org/wiki/Rudoph_Abel; James B. Dovovan, *Strangers on a Bridge: The Case of Colonel Abel* (1964).

Chapter 1

1. Newspaper reporter Hugh Aynesworth takes the claim further: "There's never been a homicide investigated to this extent in the history of the world." Sabato, Larry J. *The Kennedy Half-Century: The Presidency, Assassination, and the Lasting Legacy of John F. Kennedy* at p. 160, n.3—from an interview with Aynesworth on March 18, 2011.

2. President's Commission on the Assassination of President Kennedy (popularly known as the Warren Commission) (1963–1964); House Select Committee on Assassinations (often referred to as the HSCA) (1976–79).

3. HSCA Report at p. 67; Vincent Bugliosi, *Reclaiming History: The Assassination of President John F. Kennedy* (2007), Endnote at pp. 156, 158–159.

4. HSCA Report at pp. 95–103.

5. Seven members of the Committee voted to find the probability of conspiracy. Four dissented. One recommended further investigation of the acoustical evidence. Report, Select Committee on Assassinations, U.S. House of Representatives (March 29, 1979) at p. 483.

6. For the conclusion that JFK's death was "probably" the result of a conspiracy, HSCA Report at p. 1. For the acoustic evidence see, HSCA Report at pp. 65–93.

7. Vincent Bugliosi, *Reclaiming History: The Assassination of President John F. Kennedy* (2007), Endnote at p. 198.

8. The committee included six members from academia with scientific specialties and six from industries specializing in acoustical technologies. Vincent Bugliosi, *Reclaiming History: The Assassination of President John F. Kennedy* (2007), Endnote at p. 198.

9. Report, Committee on Ballistic Acoustics, National Academy of Sciences (May 14, 1992) (National Academics Press) at pp. 1, 4–5, 12, 17, 29, 34, and 89.

10. Letter from William F. Weld, Assistant Attorney General, Criminal Division, U.S. Department of Justice to Hon. Peter W. Rodino, Jr., Chairman, Committee on the Judiciary, House of Representatives of Representative, Washington, D.C. enclosed in letter to Mr. Rodino from Thomas M. Boyd, Acting Assistant Attorney General, dated March 28, 1988. A pdf is available at http://jfk.hood.edu/Collection/Weisberg%20Subject%20Index%20Files/J%20Disk/Justice%20Department%20of/Justice%20Department%20of%20JFK-King%20Reinvestigation/Item%2014.pdf.

11. President John F. Kennedy Assassination Records Collection Act of 1992, Public Law 102–526, 106 Stat 3443, 42 USC 2107.

12. John R. Tunnheim, "The Assassination Records Review Board: Unlocking the Government's Secret Files on the Murder of a President," *The Public Lawyer*, Vol 8. No. 1, Winter 2000.

13. Final Report of the Assassination Records Review Board (U.S. Gov. Printing Office, 9/30/98); Federal Register (June 28, 1995); Wikipedia, *President John F. Kennedy Assassination Records Collection Act of 1992.*

14. John R. Tunheim, "The Assassination Records Review Board: Unlocking the Government's Secret Files on the Murder of a President," *The Public Lawyer*, Vol. 8, No. 1, Winter 2000. See also, University of Phoenix *Final Report of the Assassination Records Review Board* at http://fas.org:8080/sgp/advisory/arrb98/part12.html A

few hundred documents that pertain to the conduct of the investigations but do not contain facts as to the assassination itself have been withheld from public examination for national security reasons. National security includes confidentiality of the identity of informants and information about surveillance techniques. Those documents may remain undisclosed until 2063. See Deb Reichmann, Associated Press (April 26, 2018).

Chapter 2

1. 3 WCH at pp. 143–144 (Howard Brennan testimony).
2. 2 WCH at p. 204 (Amos Lee Euins testimony).
3. 3 WCH at p. 158 (Howard Brennan testimony).
4. Bugliosi at p. 52.
5. 3 WCH at p. 144 (Howard Brennan testimony).
6. WCR at pp. 145–146.
7. WCR at pp. 143–145.
8. Howard L. Brennan with J. Edward Cherryholme, *Eyewitness to History: the Kennedy Assassination as Seen by Howard Brennan* (1987), at p. 25. See also id at pp. 18–29.
9. WCR at pp. 64–68. It was 1964 and the first name of Mrs. Cabell is not given, even in her sworn testimony. Shortly after the president was shot, a spectator, 18-year-old Arnold Louis Rowland, reported seeing a man on the sixth floor of the School Book Depository holding a rifle with a telescopic sight about 15 minutes before the presidential motorcade arrived at Dealey Plaza. He believed it was a Secret Service agent and did not claim to be able to make an identification. CE 357. 16 WCH at p. 953; CE 358, 16 WCH at p. 954.
10. 3 WCR at pp. 282–286 (Luke Mooney testimony).
11. 3 WCH at pp. 283–285 (Luke Mooney testimony).
12. 3 WCH at p. 292 (Eugene Boone testimony).
13. WCR at p. 76; 6 WCH at pp. 286–288 (Lee E. Bowers, Jr., testimony). Officer Haygood, contrary to Bowers' testimony, stated that he left his cycle on the street. 6 WCH at pp. 96–301.
14. 3 WCH at pp. 294–295; (Eugene Boone testimony); 17 WCH at pp. 224–226 (CE 515, 516, & 517). A police officer talking to news media first reported the rifle to be a "Mauser." Before being moved, it was photographed and marked with the name of Lt. J.C. Day. That weapon was later properly identified as a 6.55 mm Mannlicher-Carcano. Belin (1988) at p. 9.
15. WCR at p. 9.
16. 3 WCH at pp. 245–250 (M. L. Baker testimony); 3 WCH at pp. 221 (Roy Truly testimony).
17. 3 WCH at pp. 247–251 (Marion L. Baker testimony); Belin (1973) at p. 263; 3 WCH at p. 240 (Roy Truly testimony). Author Alan Adelson walked it in sixty-six seconds without losing his breath from the spot on the sixth floor of the School Book Depository where Oswald's rifle was found to the point in the lunchroom where Oswald was observed. Alan Adelson, *The Ruby Oswald Affair* (1988), pp. 116–117.
18. WCR at p. 151.
19. WCR at pp. 152–153.
20. WCR at pp. 154–155.
21. Bugliosi at pp. 48–49; Gerald Posner, *Case Closed: Lee Harvey Oswald and the Assassination of JFK* (1993) at pp. 245 and 269. The young reporter may have been Robert MacNeil, later to become co-anchor on the Public Broadcasting Service's *MacNeil/Lehrer NewsHour.*
22. WCR at pp. 157–165.
23. WCR at p. 157; Belin (1973) at p. 414.
24. 2 WCH at p. 275 (Cecil J. McWatters testimony).
25. 2 WCH at p. 275 (Cecil J. McWatters testimony).
26. WCR at p. 163.
27. WCR at pp. 157–160.
28. WCR at p. 157.
29. 2 WCH at p. 256 (William Whaley testimony).
30. 2 WCH at pp. 258–262 and 292–294 (William Whaley testimony). In various interviews, Whaley gave inconsistent reports as to how Oswald was dressed and the precise location where Oswald left the cab. However, Oswald, himself, admitted that he took a cab from downtown Dallas to his rooming house. WCR pp. 162–163. Author Norman Mailer, drawing on Whaley's testimony, stated that Oswald walked five blocks from Whaley's cab to 1026 North Beckley. Norman Mailer, *Oswald's Tale: An American Mystery* (1995) at p. 680.
31. WCR at p. 163.
32. WCR at pp. 163–165.
33. A thorough analysis of evidence related to Oswald's actions from the time he left his rooming house until he was arrested may be found in Dale K. Myers, *With Malice: Lee Harvey Oswald and the Murder of Officer J.D. Tippit* (1998).
34. Warren Commission staff member David Belin speculated that Oswald was headed to a bus stop where he could get a local bus connection to another bus to Monterrey, Mexico. See draft, Chapter 6, Warren Commission Report (August 7, 1964). That Oswald had a local bus transfer ticket, enough money for further bus fare to Monterrey, a pistol, 15 rounds of ammunition, and a false identification card bearing his photo and the name Alex Hidell are consistent with such an escape plan. David E. Belin, *November 22, 1963: You Are the Jury* (1973) at pp. 425–428; Seth Kantor, *Who Was Jack Ruby?* (1978) at pp. 204–206; Warren Commission Report, p. 650 (Oswald not headed to Jack Ruby's apartment).
35. 17 WCH at p. 406 (CE 705); 3 WCH 144 (Howard Brennan testimony).
36. Author Dale Myers has speculated that what most attracted Tippit's attention was that Oswald may have changed directions when he was walking west on Tenth Street, saw Tippit's car approaching

him from the west, and turned around to avoid recognition—a most suspicious move. Dale K. Myers, *With Malice—Lee Harvey Oswald and the Murder of Officer J.D. Tippit* (1998) at pp. 64–65.

37. WCR at pp. 165–167.

38. Report, HSCA, U.S. House of Representatives, 95th Congress, 2d Session, pp. 58–59.

39. WCR pp. 166–168; Dale K. Myers, *With Malice: Lee Harvey Oswald and the Murder of Officer J.D. Tippit* at pp. 59–94; Bugliosi, pp. 77–79 see also, Bugliosi, footnote on p. 74. Myers provides a detailed description of the shooting, flight of the gunman, and analysis of testimony together with diagrams and photos of the shooting scene and flight.

40. WCR at pp. 165–171.

41. 7 WCH at p. 4 (Johnny Brewer testimony).

42. 7 WCH at pp. 10–11 (Julia Postal testimony).

43. WCR p. 178; Bugliosi, p. 96.

44. CE 1974, p. 83.

45. WCR at p. 178.

46. 46 WCR at p. 178.

47. WCR at p. 178.

48. WCR at pp. 178–179.

Chapter 3

1. WCR at p. 9.
2. WCR at p. 180.
3. WCR at pp. 180, 199–200.
4. 7 WCH at p. 180 (Testimony of Richard Sims).
5. 7 WCH at p. 135 (Testimony of Elmer Boyd); Elmer Boyd, Oral History Collection, Sixth Floor Museum, Dallas, Texas (February 22, 2007) at p. 9.
6. James P. Hosty, Jr., *Assignment Oswald* (1996) at p. 20.
7. Hosty at pp. 59–60, 181–193.
8. Bugliosi at pp. 841–843.
9. WCR at pp. 163 (bus and cab), 181(had a gun); 4 WCH at pp. 214, 223 (Cap't J.W Fritz testimony).
10. 3 WCH at pp. 308–311 (Helen Markham testimony); 7 WCH at pp. 502–503 (Helen Markham testimony); see also, 3 WCH at p. 322 (William Scoggins testimony).
11. WCR at p. 168; 3 WCH at pp. 343–350 (Barbara Jeanette Davis testimony); 6 WCH at pp. 454–468 (Virginia Davis testimony).
12. Kelley Exhibit A, 20 WCH at p. 443 (Report of Secret Service Agent, Inspector Thomas J. Kelley).
13. WCR at p. 181; 7 WCH at p. 299 (Harry D. Holmes testimony).
14. WCR at pp. 118–119, 181.
15. WCR at pp. 131–137, 740.
16. Bugliosi at pp. 260–261.
17. Bugliosi at pp. 259–260.
18. WCR at p. 201.
19. Wikipedia, "John Abt."
20. 10 WCH at p. 116 (John Abt testimony).
21. Bugliosi at p. 188.
22. Bugliosi at pp. 187–189.
23. Bugliosi at p. 194.
24. Bugliosi at pp. 114–115.
25. Bugliosi at p. 240.
26. Bugliosi at pp. 242–245.
27. Bugliosi at p. 242.
28. WCR at pp. 209–213.
29. WCR at pp. 354–357.
30. Author's conclusion and that of the Warren Commission. The House Select Committee on Assassinations believed Ruby entered through a different route.
31. WCR at p. 216.
32. This was the Commission's conclusion; WCR pp. 221–222. Vaughn acknowledges the police car passing by at this time but denies that Ruby could have gotten by without Vaughn seeing him. 12 WCH 360–361 (Roy Vaughn testimony); Bugliosi at pp. 270–271.
33. WCR at pp. 215–216, 357.
34. Bugliosi, see footnote at p. 275.
35. Bugliosi at p. 290.
36. 24 WCH at pp. 138–139 (CE 2002) (Statement of T.D. McMillon, November 24, 1963).
37. 21 WCH at p. 537 (Sorrels Exhibit No. 1).
38. 20 WCH at p. 507 (Leavelle Exhibit No. 5089) (FBI Interview of Detective James R. Leavelle, December 11, 1963).

Chapter 4

1. Bugliosi at pp. 60–61, 73, 123, 161–162, 237, 339.
2. Willens at pp. 18–19.
3. Robert A. Caro, *The Years of Lyndon Johnson: Passage of Power* (2012) at p. 354.
4. Bugliosi at p. 322; Willens at pp. 22–23.
5. Willens at p. 24.
6. Among the advisors was Abraham Fortas (later appointed by President Johnson to the U.S. Supreme Court) and Assistant U.S. Attorney General Nicholas Katzenbach. Howard Willens, *History Will Prove Us Right: Inside the Warren Commission Report of the Assassination of John F. Kennedy* (2013) at pp. 23–24. The idea of a presidential commission was first recommended to Katzenbach and Johnson by Eugene V. Rostow, former dean of Yale Law School whose brother was Walt W. Rostow, Johnson's national security advisor. Johnson also received confirmatory consultation from *Washington Post* columnist Joseph Alsop and his own mentor, Senator Richard Russell, Democrat of Georgia. Max Holland, *The Kennedy Assassination Tapes* (2004) at pp. 96–103, 108, 149–59, 187–89, 195–206.
7. Willens at p. 26; Bugliosi at pp. 324–325.
8. Willens at p. 26; Gus Russo, *Live by the Sword: Lee Harvey Oswald and the Assassination of JFK* (1998) at p. 34.
9. Holland (2004) at pp. 159–160.
10. Holland (2004) at pp. 159–160.
11. Holland (2004) at pp. 195–206.
12. G. Ed, *Chief Justice, A Biography of Earl Warren* (1997), pp. 60–61.

13. Executive Order No. 11130 (November 29, 1963); WCR at p. 471 (Appendix I).

14. Willens, at pp. 43–49. David W. Belin, *November 22, 1963: You Are the Jury*; New York: Quadrangle/New York Times (1973) pp. 14–15.

15. https//en.m.wikipedia.org/wiki/J.Lee. Rankin.

16. This younger group had outstanding records from highly competitive law schools: University of Chicago, Harvard, Michigan, and Yale. The older group were leaders in their fields. One had been clerk to a Supreme Court justice and later became a cabinet officer. Another was a member of advisory committees to the Supreme Court on federal rules of civil procedure and evidence.

17. Bugliosi, p. xx.

18. HSCA, Attachment E, Testimony of W. David Slawson at pp. 183–184. The documents were visa application forms from the Cuban Embassy in Mexico City that bore Lee Harvey Oswald's signature. For a description of how the evasion of Warren's wishes occurred, see Willens, p. 178.

19. My recollection. Also, that of David Belin; see Belin (1973) p. 9. Other staff members attribute the statement to the Commission's General Counsel, J. Lee Rankin. See Bugliosi, pp. 363–364. Whether Rankin or Warren said it, Warren was present and affirmed the statement.

20. Gerald R. Ford and John R. Stiles, *Portrait of the Assassin* (1965) at p. 538.

21. See memorandum of Warren Commission staff counsel, Howard P. Willens, *The Imaginary Conspiracy: Unmasking JFK's Invisible Shooter on The Grassy Knoll*, p. 23 (February 1, 2019) available in e-mail dated Sat. Feb. 2, 2019, 4:13, at Paul Hoch @mindspring.com. docx, Invisible Shooter, Final 02011).

22. WCR p. xiv.

23. WCR at pp. 84–85.

24. HSCA, Appendix, Vol. 11, pp. 448–449 (Testimony of Howard Willens as to how staff attempted to deal with problem of lack of a court room adversary system.)

25. WCR pp. 359–362.

26. WCR p. 360.

27. WCR p. 361.

28. WCR p. 362.

Chapter 5

1. Patricia Lambert, *False Witness: The Real Story of Jim Garrison's Investigation and Oliver Stone's Film JFK* (1998); Fred Litwin, *On the Trail of Delusion: Jim Garrison: The Great Accuser* (2020); Aleci Long, *Cruising for Conspirators: How a New Orleans DA Prosecuted the Kennedy Assassination* (2021), Posner at pp. 144–148; Bugliosi at pp. 1347–1437; Garrison at pp. 266–297.

2. 5 WCH at pp. 232–234 (Henry Wade testimony).

3. See John Kaplan and Jon R. Waltz, *The Trial of Jack Ruby: A Classic Study of Courtroom Strategies* (1965); Diane Holloway (editor), *Dallas and the Jack Ruby D Trial: Memoir of Judge Joe B. Brown, Sr.* (2001); Dan Abrams and David Fisher, *Kennedy's Avenger: Assassination Conspiracy, and the Forgotten Trial of Jack Ruby* (2021).

4. Kaplan and Waltz at pp. 17 and 43; *Lovelady v. State* (Texas Crim. App., 1947), 198 S.W.2d 570, 573.

5. *Steadham v. State,* 47 Tex. Crim. 475, 43 S.W.2d 944 (Tex. Ct. Crim. App., 1931).

6. Judge Joe B. Brown, Sr., *Dallas and the Jack Ruby Trial: Memoir of Judge Joe B. Brown, Sr.*, edited by Diane Holloway, Ph.D. at p. 133 (2001) at pp. 8, 12, 13. Judge Brown believed that in a properly defended case, Ruby would have received a prison sentence. Holloway at p. 13. He thought Tom Howard would have put Ruby on the witness stand, allowing the jury to have a direct understanding of Ruby's personality and the factors that affected him. Holloway at p. 62. He believed that by presenting insanity defense, Belli gave the jury nothing to fall back on if they rejected the insanity defense. Holloway at pp. 15, 58.

7. Kaplan and Waltz, at p. 20.

8. Kaplan and Waltz, at pp. 372–373.

9. Kaplan and Waltz at p. 20; Abrams and Fisher at p. 29.

10. Kaplan and Waltz at pp. 21–23.

11. Kaplan and Waltz at p. 23; Wills and Demaris at pp. 88–92.

12. Kaplan and Waltz at pp. 32, 57–58, & 63–68; Melvin M. Belli with Maurice Carroll, *Dallas Justice: The Real Story of Jack Ruby and His Trial* (1964) at pp. 8–9.

13. Melvin M. Belli with Maurice C. Carroll, *Dallas Justice: The Real Story of Jack Ruby and His Trial* (1964).

14. Kaplan and Waltz, at pp. 243–45; Bugliosi at p. 1475; Belli and Carroll at pp. 39–40, 53–54.

15. Kaplan and Waltz, pp. 222–233.

16. Kaplan and Waltz at pp. 304–340. Unlike in many states, the Dallas jury did not have a separate hearing for the penalty. It decided without further argument to impose the death penalty. *Rubenstein v. State* (Texas Crim. App. 1966), 407 S.W.2d 793 at 794.

17. Kaplan and Waltz, at pp. 338–339.

18. Belli and Carroll at p. 257; Kaplan and Waltz at p. 340.

19. For an analysis of a preferred defense strategy, see Bugliosi pp. 1479–1483.

20. Blakey and Billings (1992) at p. 353.

21. See *Rubenstein v. State,* 407 S.W.2d 793 (1966). He changed his last name to Ruby on December 30, 1947, shortly after moving to Dallas. WCR pp. 793–794.

22. Bugliosi, p. 1479.

23. Kaplan and Waltz at pp. 59, 70; Belli and Carroll at p. 100; 15 WCH at pp. 524–525 (Stanley M. Kaufman testimony); Adelson, pp. 283–284.

24. Warren Leslie, *Dallas: Public and Private* (1964) at pp. 8–12, 209–218.

25. *Rubenstein v. State* (Texas Crim. App. 1966), 407 S.W.2d 793.

26. 5 WCH 210–211 (Jack Ruby testimony). Ruby calls himself a "scapegoat" and says Jews are being "exterminated."

27. Diaries on file at Sixth Floor Museum, Dallas, Texas.

28. *The Jack Ruby Trial Revisited: The Diary of Jury Foreman Max Causey* edited by John Mark Dempsey (2000).

29. Kaplan and Waltz, at pp. 338–339.

30. Dempsey at p. 34.

31. Kaplan and Waltz, p. 339.

32. Kaplan and Waltz at p. 314.

33. Kaplan and Waltz at p. 341.

34. Bugliosi at p. 1484.

35. Kaplan and Waltz at pp. 356–361; Wills and Demaris at pp. 168–181.

36. Kaplan and Waltz at pp. 343–363.

37. The term "sanity" is used under criminal law to address whether one knew the nature of one's alleged criminal act and the difference between right and wrong when the crime was committed. Sanity can also refer to the ability of one to cooperate with his attorney, understand the nature of the criminal proceeding, and have the ability to testify. A person can be mentally ill, even psychotic, but still legally sane for those purposes. When Ruby subjected himself to a polygraph examination (popularly known as a lie detector test) on July 18, 1963, a psychiatrist who had also examined Ruby said that he was a "psychotic depressive" and that the test was, accordingly, not reliable. WCR p. 815.

38. Adelson at pp. 89–90.

39. *Rubenstein v. State* (Texas Crim. App. 1966), 407 S.W.2d 793.

40. *Rubenstein v. State* (Texas Crim. App. 1966), 407 S.W.2d 793.

41. Adelson, *The Ruby Oswald Affair* (1988) at p. 87.

42. *Rubenstein v. State* (Texas Crim. App. 1966), 407 S.W.2d 795.

Chapter 6

1. WCR at pp. 219–225.

2. 12 WCH at p. 430 (Patrick T. Dean testimony); 19 WCH at pp. 442–444 (Dean Exhibit No 0115).

3. 13 WCH at p. 67 (Testimony of Forest Sorrels); 21 WCH at pp. 536–537 (Sorrels Exhibit No. 1); 19 WCH at pp. 438–439 (Dean Exhibit No. 5009); 19 WCH at pp. 432–437 (Dean Exhibit No. 5008); 19 WCH at p. 440 (Dean Exhibit No. 5010).

4. 21 WCH at p. 537 (Sorrels Exhibit No. 1).

5. 19 WCH at 439 (Dean Exhibit No. 5009).

6. 23 WCH at pp. 66–72 (Forrest Sorrels testimony); Sorrels Exhibit 1, 21 WCH at pp. 536–538; Sorrels Exhibit 2-A, 21 WCH at p. 539. 19 WCH at p. 439 (Dean Exhibit No. 5009).

7. 12 WCH 401–402 (Don Ray Archer testimony); 12 WCH at pp. 412–413 (Barnard S. Clardy testimony); 13 WCH at pp. 49–51 (Thomas Donald McMillon testimony).

8. 4 WCH at p. 244 (Testimony of J.W. Fritz).

9. 15 WCH at pp. 66, 68 (Testimony of C. Ray Hall); 20 WCH at pp. 43–44 (Hall Exhibit No. 2).

10. 12 WCH at p. 362 (Roy Eugene Vaughn testimony).

11. 20 WCH at p. 558 (McMillon Exhibit No. 5017).

12. WCR at p. 221.

13. 20 WCH at pp. 565–570 (McMillon Exhibit No. 5020); 19 WCH at pp. 20–23 (Archer Exhibits Nos. 5092 and 5093); 19 WCH at pp. 331–333 (Clardy Exhibit No. S5061).

14. 19 WCH at p. 337 (Clardy Exhibit 5063).

15. 12 WCH at pp. 433–435 (Patrick T. Dean testimony). 19 WCH at p. 439 (Dean Exhibit No 5009).

16. 12 WCH at p. 434 (Patrick T. Dean testimony).

17. 12 WCH at pp. 434, 436 (Patrick T. Dean testimony).

18. 12 WCH at p. 442 (Patrick T. Dean testimony).

19. 19 WCH at pp. 442–444 (Dean Exhibit No. 5011).

20. 19 WCH at p. 440 (Dean Exhibit No. 5010).

21. 19 WCH at pp. 438–439 (Dean Exhibit No. 5009).

22. 19 WCH at pp. 436–437 (Dean Exhibit No. 5009).

23. 4 WCH at p. 244 (J. W. Fritz testimony).

24. 4 WCH at p. 244 (J. W. Fritz testimony).

25. 12 WCH at p. 415 (Patrick T. Dean testimony).

26. See memorandum, Burt W. Griffin to J. Lee Rankin, March 31, 1964, in author's possession and National Archives.

27. Willens, p. 104.

28. March 31, 1964, memo to J. Lee Rankin from Burt W. Griffin regarding letter of Henry Wade dated March 25, 1964, in possession of author and National Archives.

29. Unknown to Hubert and me, on May 28, 1964 (eleven days before testifying to the Warren Commission), Dean asked Dallas Police Chief Jesse Curry for a polygraph examination. One may wonder if Dean's request reflected his hope that a polygraph would allay my doubts as to his veracity. By his own admission, Dean failed the polygraph test. (See the HSCA Report, p. 139). Dean did not comply with the Select Committee request for an opportunity to depose him. He also failed to answer written interrogatories from the Committee. Unfortunately not even the Select Committee was able to find the polygraph examiner's report or the questions Dean was asked. (HSCA Report at p. 158.) Alan Adelson, who was counsel for probating Ruby's estate, claims he spoke with police officials in Dallas who told him that the polygraph examiner concluded that Dean lied about his claim that Ruby told him he premeditated the shooting of Oswald. (Alan Adelson, *The Ruby Oswald Affair* [1988] at p. 33.) We do not know whether the polygraph examiner questioned Dean about how Ruby entered the police basement.

30. HSCA Appendix to Hearings—Volume IX, pp. 132–148. James Kelleher, *He Was Expendable* (2014) at pp. 163–164.
31. Warren Commission Report, p. 219.
32. HSCA Report, pp. 156–158.
33. HSCA Report, pp. 156–158.
34. HSCA Report, p. 156.

Chapter 7

1. Neither Leon Hubert nor I were present at the Ruby testimony. I provided a memo of questions for the Chief Justice.
2. Ruby's decision to request a lie detector test is a story of its own—one of staff independence. Chief Justice Warren and most staff members opposed use of "lie detector tests." The tests were inadmissible in court proceedings. Commission staffer David Belin had pushed and failed to persuade the Chief Justice and staff members to administer such a test to Marina Oswald. Recognizing that such a proposal would also be rejected for Ruby, Belin pursued another route. He had met Ruby's rabbi, Hillel Silverman, the previous summer as part of a study group to Israel. On his first trip to Dallas, Belin renewed his friendship with Silverman. After the Ruby trial, Belin—without seeking Commission approval—asked Silverman if he would suggest to Ruby that he request a lie detector test from the Warren Commission. Silverman made the proposal to Ruby. Ruby made the request. Belin, *Final Disclosure: The Full Truth About the Assassination of President Kennedy* (1988) at pp. 37–38; Willens at p. 206.
3. 5 WCH at pp. 181–182 (Jack Ruby testimony).
4. 5 WCH at p. 194 (Jack Ruby testimony).
5. 5 WCH at p. 194 (Jack Ruby testimony). When Ruby took a polygraph exam after testifying to the Warren Commission, he also requested that Tonahill leave but allowed prosecutor Bill Alexander to remain and formulate questions. Bugliosi, at p. 1482.
6. Arlen Specter with Charles Robbins, *A Passion for Truth* (2000) at p. 113.
7. Specter at p. 113. The episode involving Specter and Ruby and then Ruby, the Chief Justice, and Specter does not appear in the Warren Commission's transcript of Ruby's testimony. Specter explains that the questioning of Specter was inaudible, and the encounter in a corner of the room occurred when the court reporter ran out of paper and had to replenish her machine. Specter at p. 113.
8. 5 WCH at p. 196 (Jack Ruby testimony).
9. 5 WCH at p. 196 (Jack Ruby testimony).
10. 5 WCH at pp. 197–211 (Jack Ruby testimony).
11. 5 WCH at pp. 197–198 (Jack Ruby testimony). With respect to when he decided to try to kill Oswald, Ruby added, "So my purpose was to go the Western Union—my double purpose—but the thought of doing, committing the act, wasn't until I left my apartment." 5 WCH at p. 199.
12. 5 WCH at p. 198 (Jack Ruby testimony).
13. 5 WCH at p. 211 (Jack Ruby testimony).
14. WCR 809–812.
15. Howard Willens, *History Will Prove Us Right: Inside the Warren Commission Report of the Assassination of John F. Kennedy* (2013) at p. 244. The House Select Committee asked a group of polygraph professionals to review the records of Ruby's examination. Those professionals concluded that the FBI's examination was invalid. Report, Select Committee on Assassinations, U.S. House of Representatives, Ninety-Fifth Congress, Second Session, at p. 159.
16. WCR 813–816.
17. Russo (1998) at pp. 491 and 501.
18. *Peter Jennings Reports, Beyond Conspiracy*, NBC-TV (2003) (Transcript, Job Tracking Number 44146, Spring Media, Inc. WWW.Transcripts.net).
19. *Peter Jennings Reports, Beyond Conspiracy*, NBC-TV (2003) (Transcript, Job Tracking Number 44146, Spring Media, Inc. WWW.Transcripts.net).
20. Adelson at p. 310.
21. Adelson at p. 281.
22. Hillel E. Silverman, *The Time of My Life: Sixty Fulfilling Years as a Congregational Rabbi* (2009) at pp. 60–61.
23. 14 WCH at pp. 364–429 (Earl Ruby testimony).
24. 21 WCH at pp. 321–350 (Earl Ruby, Exhibit No. 1).
25. 21 WCH at p. 325 (Earl Ruby Exhibit No. 1).
26. 21 WCH at p. 331 (Earl Ruby Exhibit No. 1).
27. 21 WCH at p. 339 (Earl Ruby Exhibit No. 1).
28. Robert M. Kaplan, "Jack Ruby's Complex: The Factors Driving the Assassination of Lee Harvey Oswald," *Forensic Research and Criminology International Journal* 1(6): 00032.D01(2015); https://medcraveonline.com/medcrave.org/index.php/FRCIJ/article/view/16394/30739

Chapter 8

1. WCR at pp. 338–340.
2. WCR at p. 350.
3. WCR at p. 350.
4. WCR at pp. 350, 796–797.
5. WCR at p. 345.
6. WCR at p. 345.
7. WCR at p. 345.
8. 13 WCH at pp. 402–506 (Larry Crafard testimony); 14 WCH at pp. 1–95 (Larry Crafard testimony).
9. WCR at pp. 357–358.
10. Peter R. Whitney on-line account of his pursuit and interviews on Crafard in December 2000. http://mcadams.posc.mu.edu/creatingapatsy.htm (2007).
11. 14 WCH at p. 236 (George Senator testimony).
12. WCR at p. 354.
13. WCR at p. 371.
14. 14 WCH at p. 245 (George Senator testimony).
15. WCR at p. 372.
16. WCR at p. 372.
17. WCR at p. 372; 14 WCH 532 (Jack Ruby

testimony to Arlen Specter); WCR at p. 810 (Polygraph testimony of Jack Ruby).

18. Bugliosi, at pp. 1121–22.

19. 15 WCH at pp. 632–635 (Lawrence V. Meyers testimony).

20. Kelleher at p. 144; WCR at p. 337.

21. Blakey and Billings (1992) at p. 329.

22. Blakey and Billings (1992) at p. 335.

23. Blakey and Billings (1992) at p. 330.

24. Blakey and Billings (1992) at 339; WCR at p. 337.

25. Blakey and Billings (1992) discuss Gruber at pages 329, 330, 335, and 339. They question his credibility but do not add facts. James at page 144 in *He Was Expendable* (2014) notes that Gruber had six arrests in his life, one for grand larceny and another for procuring. Warren Commission Document 1144, pp. 5–6. Neither Blakey, Billings, nor Kelleher suggests that Gruber was a member of organized crime or that he had a motive to kill the president or Oswald.

Chapter 9

1. See Narration by G. Robert Blakey to HSCA, Vol. IV HSCA pp. 539–568 (Outline of needed work and investigative requests in memos from Leon Hubert and Burt Griffin, February 24, 1964, to June 1, 1964). Vol. IX HSCA 188–196.

2. WCR at pp. 359–374. Compare Bugliosi (2007) at pp. 1071–1188 and Posner (1993) at pp. 343–403 to Blakey and Billings (1992).

3. WCR, at pp. 333–359.

4. WCR at pp. 334–335.

5. See WCR at p. 335.

6. Kantor, *The Ruby Cover-up* (1978) at pp. 352–353. See also Kantor, *Who Was Jack Ruby?* (1978) at pp. 41, 188–199.

7. WCR at p. 812; 14 WCH at pp. 561–562.

8. WCR at p. 336.

9. CE 1485, 22 WCH at pp. 906–907; WCR at p. 340.

10. Author's interview, July 14, 2020.

11. WCR at p. 340.

12. WCR at p. 342.

13. WCR at p. 342.

14. WCR at p. 342.

15. WCR at 343.

16. WCR at pp. 343–344.

17. WCR at p. 344.

18. Bill Minutaglio and Steven L. Davis, *Dallas 1963* (2013) at pp. 193–194; *Texas Jewish Post*, January 31, 1963, p. 1.

19. Minutaglio and Davis, at pp. 218–219; *Texas Jewish Post*, May 2, 1963, at p. 4.

20. *Texas Jewish Post*, May 2, 1963, at p. 4; email to author from Jessica Schneider, archivist, Dallas Jewish Historical Society, October 7, 2020, stating that Carousel Club was within a few blocks of the vandalized stores.

21. 14 WCH at pp. 218–219 (George Senator testimony).

22. 14 WCH at pp. 222 (George Senator testimony).

23. WCR at p. 345.

24. 15 WCH at p. 196 (Marjorie R. Richey testimony).

25. WCR at p. 346.

26. Bugliosi at p. 248.

27. WCR at p. 347. Author Gerald Posner placed Ruby meeting with Bellochio beginning at about 2:00 p.m. and going to the Dallas police station thereafter, passing out cards to his Carousel Club. Gerald Posner, *Case Closed: Lee Harvey Oswald and the Assassination of JFK* (1993) at pp. 384–385. Author Vincent Bugliosi agreed with Posner about when Ruby spoke to Bellochio. Vincent Bugliosi at pp. 248–249. The timing of activities is always difficult to determine, especially when the specific time of an event may not be important to the witness, and the witness is not being asked to recall the event soon after it occurs. Ruby's own statements confirm the actual events at Dealey Plaza. The Commission differed with Posner and Bugliosi as to when they occurred.

28. WCR at p. 347.

29. Kaufman described the call as ten to fifteen minutes or longer. Kaufman was active in the local Jewish Community Federation and B'nai B'rith. He was a logical person for Ruby to call about members of the Dallas Jewish community. Kaufman characterized Ruby as an impulsive person who would often take action and call later for advice as to whether his actions were proper. 15 WCH at pp. 519, 521–522 (Stanley M. Kaufman testimony).

30. WCR at pp. 347–348.

31. 15 WCH at p. 521 (Stanley M. Kaufman testimony).

32. WCR at p. 348.

33. WCR at p. 348.

34. WCR at p. 348.

35. WCR at p. 349.

36. 13 WCH at p. 231 (Elnora Pitts testimony).

37. 14 WCH at pp. 236, 239 (George Senator testimony).

38. WCR at p. 354. George Senator and all of Ruby's employees were on our suspect list. We asked the FBI to check their backgrounds and their activities from November 22 through November 24. Aside from Little Lynn's telephone call on November 24 and Kay Coleman's statements on November 23, nothing raised suspicions for a possible connection to killing Oswald.

39. 5 WCH at p. 199 (Jack Ruby testimony).

40. 20 WCH at p. 556 (McMillon Exhibit 5017); 8 WCH at pp. 37–55 (Tomas McMillon testimony).

41. 20 WCH at p. 556 (McMillon Exhibit 5017); 19 WCH at pp. 335, 337 (Clardy Exhibits 5062 and 5063); 12 WCH at pp. 403–414 (Bernard Clardy testimony).

42. Email from G. Robert Blakey to author, December 26, 2017.

43. WCR at pp. 787–788.

44. Profile and testimony of Joseph Campisi, HSCA vol IX, at pp. 335–417.

45. HSCA Report at pp. 1–263.

46. HSCA, Vol IV at p. 570. See also, testimony of organized crime expert Ralph Salerno before the Committee that "Jack Ruby cannot be characterized as an organized crime figure in any way ... Jack Ruby would not have been a pimple on the neck of a real organized crime figure." http://mcadams.posc.mu.edu/russ/jfkinfo2/jfk5/saler.htm at p. 23.

47. Posner at p. 394 (footnote). For Alexander's personal relationship with Ruby, see Wills and DeMaris at pp. 60–62.

48. 5 WCH at pp. 198–199 (Jack Ruby testimony).

49. It was also the explanation that he gave the FBI polygraph examiner who, at Ruby's request, administered a so-called lie detector test to Ruby on July 18, 1964. Report, President's Commission on the Assassination of President Kennedy, pp. 807–814, Appendix XVII (1964).

50. HSCA Report at p. 158.

51. John McAdams, *JFK Assassination Logic: How to Think About Claims of Conspiracy* (2011) at pp. 81–83; 13 WCH at pp. 67–68 (Testimony of Forest Sorrels); 20 WCH at pp. 557–558 (Testimony of T.D. McMillon); 12 WCH at p. 413 (Testimony of Barnard Clardy).

52. Stanley Kaufman, attorney for Ruby in civil matters, believed that Ruby's possession of this amount of money and leaving his dog in the car were evidence that Ruby's shooting of Oswald was a spur-of-the-moment decision—that he would not have carried so much money and left his dog in the car if he had been thinking of shooting Oswald when he left his car in the parking lot. 15 WCH at pp. 527–528 (Stanley M. Kaufman testimony).

53. For other views on when Ruby decided to shoot Oswald, see Alan Adelson, *The Ruby Oswald Affair, Reflections by Alan Adelson* (1988); G. Robert Blakey and Richard N. Billings, *The Plot to Kill the President* (1981); Bugliosi at pp. 1071–1144; Mailer at pp. 731–759; Posner at pp. 343–403.

Chapter 10

1. Willens at pp. 66–73. On August 22, 1978, staff counsel Samuel Stern recalled in an interview by Mike Ewing of the HSCA that "at the outset we realized that there was no possible way to penetrate any *official* involvement in a cover-up or conspiracy if there was such complicity." He told Ewings that the staff had discussed that the CIA and FBI could maintain a cover-up that no one could ever penetrate. By 1978, cover-ups relative to CIA and FBI misbehavior had been discovered. Stern did not believe either in 1964 or in 1978 that such cover-ups related to agency involvement in the assassination of President Kennedy. See HSCA memo dated August 22, 1978, by Mike Ewing.

2. CE 18, 16 WCH at p. 64; Shenon at pp. 203–204, 343–345, 377.

3. Hosty at pp. 27, 234; Bugliosi at p. 1337.

4. WCR at pp. 659–660; Report, HSCA at pp. 185–196.

5. Hosty claimed that the note was unsigned and that, when he received it, he could not be certain of the note's author. James P. Hosty, Jr., *Assignment: Oswald* (1996) at p. 21. Hosty's statement is difficult to believe. The source of the note was clear enough to Hosty's supervisor, Kenneth Howe, that he was able, on his own, to find the note in Hosty's "work box" without help from anyone else. *Report*, Select Committee on Assassinations, House of Representatives, 95th Congress, Second Session (1979) pp. 195–196; Deposition of Kenneth Howe, Select Committee on Assassination, House of Representatives, December 12, 1975, pp. 562–629; maryferrell.org/showDoc.html?docld=60937 at pp. 118–193.

6. Conspiracy theorists infer that the incident supports an intent to kill the president: "He might have been trying to get himself into trouble, perhaps to stop him from committing a terrible act; he might have been trying once again to make FBI files show him as a hostile leftist; or he might have been simply cracking under the strain of what he was about to do." David Kaiser, *The Road to Dallas* (2008) at p. 354.

7. 19 WCH 569–570 (Dobbs Exhibit No. 5).

8. Hosty, pp. 29–30.

9. Affidavit of James P. Hosty, Jr., to Federal Bureau of Investigation, July 17, 1975. https://maryferrell.org/showDoc.html?docld=118828/lsearch=kyle_clark++HSCA#relPageld=1&tab=page.

10. Affidavit of James P. Hosty, Jr., to Federal Bureau of Investigation, July 17, 1975. https://maryferrell.org/showDoc.html?docld=118828/lsearch=kyle_clark++HSCA#relPageld=1&tab=page.

11. Affidavit of James P. Hosty, Jr., to Federal Bureau of Investigation, July 17, 1975. https://maryferrell.org/showDoc.html?docld=118828/lsearch=kyle_clark++HSCA#relPageld=1&tab=page. at 194–200.

12. Author Max Holland believed, after interviewing Hosty and many of his colleagues, that, as a father himself, Hosty had not acted on the note because he felt sorry for Oswald, a father of a newborn and one other daughter, and did not want to cause Oswald to lose his job. Email dated October 25, 2019, from Holland to Sam Stern together with responses to questions. The note might have been closer to Fenner's account, however. Dallas police Lt. Jack Revill told news reporter Hugh Aynesworth in April 1964 that Hosty had told him on November 22 or 23, 1963, that the FBI knew that Oswald posed a security threat. Philip Shenon, *A Cruel and Shocking Act: The Secret History of the Kennedy Assassination* (2013) at p. 341; WCR at p. 441. Reville wrote Dallas police captain W.P. Gannaway on November 22, 1963, that Hosty had told him that day that the FBI had prior "information that [Oswald] was capable of committing the assassination of President Kennedy." James P. Hosty, Jr., *Assignment Oswald* (1996) at p. 266 (copy of letter).

13. Years later, Howard Willens, the Commis-

sion's lawyer most closely involved in outlining the scope of the Commission's investigation, said that if the Commission had known that agents were disciplined for faulty surveillance of Oswald, "the Commission could have explored in more detail exactly what the disciplined agents had done... It might have led to the Commission learning about the Oswald note to Hosty." Howard Willens, *History Will Prove Us Right: Inside the Warren Commission Report on the Assassination of John F. Kennedy* (2013) at p. 258.

14. Letter of J. Edgar Hoover to J. Lee Rankin, April 6, 1964; see also, 5 WCH at p. 112 (J. Edgar Hoover testimony).

15. 4 WCH at pp. 450–452 (James Hosty testimony); see also, Willens at pp. 149–151.

16. 4 WCH at pp. 466–467 (James Hosty testimony).

17. HSCA Vol. III, pp. 606–642 (Testimony of J. Lee Rankin, September 21, 1978).

18. Belin (1988) at pp. 104–107, 119–126; Russo (1998) pp. 50–51, 363–66, 433–34; https://washington.blogs.nytimes.com/2007/06/26/a-plot-to-assassinate-castro-was-approved-by-cia-director-allendulles/?mntrref=www.google.com&gwh=58225FB0619911B7C2C681EOA3806BCD&gwt=pay (Dulles). President Kennedy was present at a meeting in the oval office on March 16, 1962, when the possibility of assassinating Castro was discussed, David Corn and Gus Russo, "The Old Man and the CIA: Kennedy Plot to Assassinate Castro," *The Nation* (March 26, 2001). Kennedy acknowledged to Senator George Smathers and *New York Times* reporter Tad Szulc that government officials had suggested to him the assassination of Fidel Castro. Robert Kennedy played an oversight role in anti-Castro policy. Dulles, himself, has reportedly said that "the CIA has never carried out any action of a political nature ... without appropriate approval of a high political level, outside the CIA unless it believed that it had presidential approval." Russo (1998) quoting David Wise and Thomas B. Ross, *The Espionage Establishment* (1967) at pp. 174–75. The inference is that Robert Kennedy, as his brother's surrogate, gave approval to trying to assassinate Castro.

19. General Counsel J. Lee Rankin testified to the House Select Committee on Assassinations that neither he nor Warren knew of the CIA working with others to assassinate Castro. Report, House Select Committee on Assassinations, Vol. III pp. 612–632 (Testimony of J. Lee Rankin, September 21, 1978). See also House Select Committee on Assassinations, Attachment E, Testimony of W. David Slawson at p. 187. CIA Director John McCone admitted that he did not tell the Commission of the attempts to assassinate Castro. David Robarge, "DCI John McCone and the Assassination of President John F. Kennedy," *Studies in Intelligence,* Vol. 57, No. 3, p. 12 (September 2013), an excerpt from Robarge's book, *John McCone as Director of Central Intelligence, 1961–1965*, published in 2003.

20. HSCA vol IX, Attachment E at page 168 (Testimony of W. David Slawson, November 15, 1977; pp 144–209).

21. Max Holland, *The Kennedy Assassination Tapes* (2004) pp. 414–418; Max Holland, *The Atlantic Monthly: The Assassination Tapes* (June 2004), http//www.WashingtonDecoded.com/site/2004/12/the_atlantic_mo.html.

22. Max Holland, *The Kennedy Assassination Tapes* (2004) at p. 392. No witness or document has been found indicating that Johnson was informed prior to the Warren Commission beginning its work that the CIA was supporting efforts to assassinate Castro. In 1975, CIA Director Richard Helms told the Senate Committee headed by Senator Church that he had no information about Johnson being informed of efforts to assassinate Castro until Drew Pearson talked to him. Helms said he assumed that the chair of the AMLASH supervisory committee would have informed President Johnson. For practical purposes, the chairman was Robert Kennedy. https://history.state.gov/historical documents/focus1964–68v32/d315 "Foreign Relations of the United States, 1964–1968, Volume XXXII, Dominican Republic; Cuba; Haiti; Guyana." On January 14, 2020, David Robarge, historian for the CIA, informed the author, "I found no reference that [LBJ] learned about [CIA attempts to assassinate Castro] while McCone was DCI and haven't seen any references to him knowing about them until after Drew Pearson's article appeared on 3 March 1967.

23. Max Holland, *The Atlantic Monthly: The Assassination Tapes* (June 2004), http.//www.WashingtonDecoded.com/site/2004/12/the_atlantic_mo.html.; Willens at p. 303.

24. Holland, *The Kennedy Assassination Tapes* (2004) at p. 419.

25. Belin (1988) at p. 83.

26. Belin states that he approached Rabbi Silverman to encourage Jack Ruby to request a lie detector test. Belin (1973) at pp. 429–434.

27. Belin (1973) at p. 92.

28. HSCA Vol. III, at pp. 614–616 (Testimony of J. Lee Rankin, September 21, 1978).

29. Belin (1988) at p. 212.

30. Belin (1988) at pp. 218–219.

31. Daniel Harker, "Castro Blasts Raids on Cuba," New Orleans *Times-Picayune,* September 9, 1963, at p. 7; https://nola.newsbank.com/doc/image/v2:1223BCE5B718A166@NGPA-NOLA-12D9C6A94C900049@2438282-12D9BE0351B83216@6-12D9BE0351B83216@?search_terms; CE 1348, 22; WCH at p. 578 (*Times-Picayune* article); CE 1349, 22 WCH at p. 579 (States-Item article); See also, Bugliosi at pp. 1284–1285 (doubting both the accuracy of Harker's quotation and the alleged intent of Castro).

32. Report, Select Committee on Assassinations, U.S. House of Representatives, 95th Congress, 2d Session (1979) at p. 127.

33. Memo from "Mr. Liebeler to Mr. Rankin, September 16, 1964," National Archives, Warren Commission files.

34. HSCA, Vol. XI, at pp. 248–249 (Wesley J. Liebeler testimony) and pp. 451–452 (Howard Willens testimony); CE 1347–1350; email of Howard Willens to author, January 28, 2018. The Commission's report also mentioned articles that Oswald might have read in the Dallas *Times Herald*, the *Militant*, and the *Worker* reporting Kennedy's calls for overthrow of the Castro government and his policies which weakened the Cuban economy. WCR at p. 414.

35. Jean Davison, *Oswald's Game* (1983) at pp. 182–184.

36. Albert H. Newman, *The Assassination of John F. Kennedy: The Reason Why* (1970) at pp. 24, 26, 88–90, 208, 331, 310, 406, 409, 481.

37. "U.S. Decides on Slayings, Says Castro," *Dallas Morning News*, April 21, 1963, at p. 12. https://infoweb.newsbank.com/apps/news/document-view?p=AMNEWS&t=pubname%3A0F99DDB671832188%21Dallas%2BMorning%2BNews/year%3A1963%211963/mody%3A0421%21April%2B21&action=browse&year=1963&format=image&docref=image%2Fv2:0F99DDB671832188@EANX-0FF7D15BCECB8589@2438141-0FF7D15C0CF8B6F6@11-0FF7D15F292F012C&origin=image%2Fv2%3A0F99DDB671832188%40EANX-0FF7D15BCECB8589%402438141-0FF7D15BDAB073D8%400.

38. *The Worker*, March 19, 1963, at p. 2.

39. *The Militant*, March 25, 1963, at p. 7.

40. Davison, at pp. 136–137.

41. For an extensive exploration of that hypothesis, see Newman at (1970).

42. Email from Warren Commission staff member W. David Slawson to author.

43. Email, David Slawson to author, February 17, 2021.

44. Belin (1988) at pp. 107–128, 160–186.

45. Although Oswald was not my area of investigation, I would have joined them. Lee Rankin's testimony before the House Select Committee on Assassinations and his willingness to support continued investigation of Sylvia Odio until the Commission's Report was issued satisfies me that the CIA planning to assassinate Castro was so important to the Commission staff and Rankin that the Commission's investigation could not have been closed without a thorough investigation of the Castro assassination effort.

46. HSCA, Vol. XI, at p. 259 (Testimony of Wesley J. Liebeler).

47. HSCA, Vol. XI at p. 148 (Testimony of W. David Slawson).

48. W. David Slawson interview for video documentary *Truth Is the Only Client*, transcript at p. 25.

49. HSCA, Vol XI at p. 171 (Testimony of W. David Slawson).

50. HSCA, Attachment E, Testimony of W. David Slawson at p. 168. William Coleman told author Philip Shenon that he met secretly with Castro on a boat in the Caribbean while working for the Warren Commission. Shenon (2013) at pp. 388–392. The statement is probably false. Coleman was in advanced stages of Alzheimer's disease when he talked to Shenon, denied it in an earlier letter to author Anthony Summers, and did not mention such a meeting in his own autobiography, *Counsel for the Situation: Shaping The Law to Realize America's Promise* (2010) co-authored with his law partner, Donald T. Bliss. Bliss has told this author that Coleman never mentioned such a meeting to him and that he doubts the validity of Coleman's statement to Shenon. No record relevant to such a meeting has been found in any government files. Coleman also did not mention such a meeting to the HSCA when interviewed by the Committee in 1978. Assassination researcher Paul Hoch believes that as Coleman's memory problems evolved, he mistakenly reported past desires as actual events. Email from Paul Hoch to author, January 18, 2018.

51. Don Bohning, *The Castro Obsession: U.S. Covert Operations Against Cuba, 1959–1965* (2005) at p. 78; *Alleged Assassination Plots Involving Foreign Leaders: An Interim Report of the Select Committee to Study Government Operations* (W.W. Norton, 1976) at p. 138; Davison (1983) at p. 91.

52. Davison at pp. 90–91; Russo (1998) at p. 64, citing Anthony Summers and Robbyn Summers, "The Ghost of November," *Vanity Fair*, December 1994 at p. 100.

53. Russo (1998) at pp. 176–184. Although Robert Kennedy never admitted a role in the assassination attempts, none was closer to the president. See, e.g., Arthur M. Schlesinger, Jr., *A Thousand Days: John F. Kennedy in the White House* (1967) at p. 428. Some were certain that Robert was his brother's overseer of the Castro attempt. Alexander M. Haig, Jr., *Inner Circles: How America Changed the World* (1992) at p. 112. Robert's biographer, Arthur M. Schlesinger, Jr., insisted that both Robert and the president were unaware of the CIA efforts. Arthur M. Schlesinger, Jr., *Robert Kennedy and His Times* (1978).

54. Shenon (2013) p. 60.

55. Lester David and Irene David, *Bobby Kennedy—The Making of a Folk Hero* (1986) at pp. 224–230.

56. Robert Kennedy did not return to work until January 1964, and for weeks thereafter had limited ability to concentrate on the tasks at hand. Caro (2012) at p. 572; David and David at pp. 216–217, 219–223. (According to his administrative assistant, "he carried the pain all day." Family and friends feared for his sanity.) Schlesinger (1986) at pp. 640–641 ("refused to involve himself in the problem of who murdered his brother").

Chapter 11

1. WCR at pp. 49–50.

2. WCR at p. 87.

3. 6 WCH 130 (Testimony of Darrell C. Tomlinson).

4. WCR at p. 81.

5. 3 WCH at p. 435 (Testimony of Robert Frazier).

6. WCR at pp. 88–89. When the FBI wrote its initial report on December 9, 1963, it had not been aware of the discussion between Parkland and Bethesda physicians.

7. WCR at pp. 86–87.

8. WCR at pp. 86–87

9. WCR at pp. 87–91.

10. WCR at p. 88. The Parkland physicians had believed initially that the neck wound was an entry wound. They had been unaware of the wound in the president's back. The autopsy doctors initially thought that a possibility existed that the bullet entering the president's back might have been retained in the president's back muscles and had been dislodged at Parkland Hospital by external heart massage. No bullet was found in an operating room at Parkland Hospital. After tracing the path of bruises in the president's body, finding no bullets in the president's body, and talking to the Parkland physicians, the autopsy doctors were certain that the bullet that entered the back had exited from the neck.

11. WCR at p. 89.

12. WCR at p. 89

13. WCR at pp. 91–92.

14. 2 WCH pp. 375–376 (Testimony of James J. Humes).

15. Specter at pp. 80–82; 2 WCH at pp. 375–376, entire testimony at pp. 348–376 (Testimony of James J. Humes).

16. Willens at pp. 85–87.

17. Belin (1988) 50–55; a detailed analysis is at Belin (1973) 302–383.

18. WCR at pp. 84–85.

19. 5 WCH at pp. 76–90 (Dr. Alfred G. Olivier testimony); WCR at 91–92, 109, and 580–585.

20. 5 WCH at pp. 76–80 (Dr. Alfred G. Olivier testimony); WCR, 582–585.

21. WCR at pp. 95, 584–586.

22. WCR at pp. 96–109.

23. HSCA Report at pp. 43–44; and HSCA Vol. VII. Only one forensic pathologist, Cyril Wecht, in the advisory panel to the Committee dissented from the panel's conclusion that the same bullet that went through the president's neck also struck Governor Connally. Wecht agreed that the bullet passed completely through the president but believed a different bullet struck Connally. For a discussion between Wecht and Vincent Bugliosi on the subject, see Bugliosi at pp. 859–864.

24. WCR pp. 111–117.

25. Max Holland, "The Truth Was Out There," *Newsweek* (November 28, 2014) at pp. 26–27; Frank S. DeRonja, MS Engr, and Max Holland, "A Technical Investigation Pertaining to the First Shot Fired in the JFK Assassination," *Association for Crime Scene Reconstruction Journal,* 20: 9–33 (2016). Holland's analysis is strongly disputed by Dale K. Myers and Todd W. Vaughan in *Mr. Holland's Opus: Max Holland and National Geographic Channel's "The Lost Bullet,"* JFKfiles. blogsport.com/search?q=max+holland.

26. Richard A. Reiman, "Six 'Shots' in Dallas: 'Framing' the Perpetrator of the Kennedy Assassination through the Zapruder Film, 1963–2012," *Journal of Perpetrator Research* (2019) at p. 189; Kenneth Scearce, *The Girl in the Red Skirt, a Micro-Study of the Zapruder Film.* 11 December 2013, https://www.washintondecoded.com/site/2013/12/reedskirt:html#more.

27. Max Holland, "The Truth Was Out There," *Newsweek* (November 28, 2014) at pp. 26–27; Frank S. DeRonja, MS Engr, and Max Holland, "A Technical Investigation Pertaining to the First Shot Fired in the JFK Assassination," *Association for Crime Scene Reconstruction Journal,* 20: 9–33 (2016).

28. 6 WCH at p. 239 (S.M. Holland testimony).

29. 6 WCH at pp. 244–247 (S.M. Holland testimony).

30. WCR at p. 72.

31. WCR at p. 72.

32. 20 WCH at p. 163 (Holland Exhibit D).

33. 6 WCH 244 (S.M. Holland testimony).

34. 6 WCH 243–244.

35. Bugliosi, p. 897.

36. WCR at p. 76. Mr. Holland's most immediate companions—Mr. Cobb and Mr. Reilly—did not report seeing anything such as a puff of smoke. See, 6 WCH at pp. 229–231 (Frank E. Reilly testimony); Vincent Bugliosi, *Reclaiming History: The Assassination of President John F. Kennedy* (2007) at Endnote p. 499 (interviews with Cobb and Nolan H. Potter). On November 22, 1963, Austin Miller said that he saw "smoke or steam coming from a group of trees" near the School Book Depository. 24 WCH at p. 217 (CE 2003). On March 17, 1964, James Simmons told the FBI that he believed he saw "exhaust fumes of smoke near the embankment in from of the Texas School Book Depository." 20 WCH at p. 833 (CE 1416). In 1969, at the trial of Clay Shaw, Simmons used the terms "puff of smoke or wisp of smoke" to describe what he saw. Josiah Thompson, *Last Second in Dallas* (2021) at p. 394.

37. 6 WCH 237–238 (Royce G. Skelton testimony).

38. William H. Hallahan, *Misfire: The History of How America's Small Arms Have Failed Our Military* (1994) pp. 230–231.

39. 7 WCH 109 (Seymour Weitzman testimony).

40. Author Gerald Posner had a similar belief. Posner learned that after 1963, the steam pipe had been removed. Posner, at p. 256 and n. 163 to Chapter 11 (Interview with Jim Moore).

41. WCR at p. 76.

42. Blakey and Billings (1992) at pp. 102–103. Bugliosi, Endnotes, pp. 156–157; citing Gary Mack, "Dallas Police Radio Assassination Tape" in *Continuing Inquiry* (August 22, 1977), p. 22.

43. The Select Committee actually received a dictabelt and two tape recordings. Report, House Select Committee on Assassinations (1979) at p. 67. The author will refer to them as "tapes.

44. Blakey and Billings at p. 102. See *Mary Ferrell,* Wikipedia.

45. 45 HSCA Report at p. 67.
46. HSCA Report at pp. 75–70.
47. HSCA Report at p. 72 fn. 7.
48. HSCA Report at pp. 67–75.
49. Blakey and Billings at pp. 102–122. HSCA Report at pp. 65–75.
50. V HSCA at pp. 652–670, "Analysis and Comments, Re: The Dallas Police Tapes, et. al. Submitted by Anthony J. Pellicano, December 13, 1978; Bugliosi, Endnotes at pp. 172–173; Cohen and Goodman, "Contrary Data Withheld from Assassination Panel," *Los Angeles Times* (January 27, 1979).
51. HSCA Report at p. 497.
52. HSCA Report at p. 497.
53. HSCA Report at p. 93.
54. HSCA Report at pp. 75–78.
55. HSCA Report at p. 93.
56. Report of Committee on Ballistics Acoustics, National Academy of Science (1982) at pp. 1, 5; Bugliosi at p. 380; Willens at p. 330. Crucial information came from a private researcher, 24 year-old Steve Barber of Shelby, Ohio, who listened to a cardboard recording of the tape and noticed that the sound that the experts relied upon occurred approximately one minute after the shots that struck the president. www.seanmunger.com/2013/11/22/the-sound-of-history-the-fascinating-story-of-the-audio-reconstruction-of-the-jfk-assassination.
57. Larry J. Sabato, *The Kennedy Half Century: The Presidency, Assassination, and Lasting Legacy of John F. Kennedy* (2013) at pp. 245–246; Sonalysts, Inc. *Analysis of the Dallas Police Department Tapes relating to the Assassination of President John F. Kennedy* at p. 14; Sonalysts, Inc. *Observation on Properties of Impulses Attributed to Gunfire* (June 11, 2013).
58. Bugliosi, Endnotes at pp. 153–218. See also re-analysis of the tapes confirming analysis of Committee on Ballistics Acoustics by Sonalysts, Inc. *Analysis of the Dallas Police Department Tape Recording Relating to the Assassination of President John F. Kennedy* (2013) at p. 14 and *Observations on Properties of Impulses Attributed to Gunfire* (June 11, 2013).
59. Josiah Thompson, *Last Second in Dallas* (2021) at pp. 275–332.

Chapter 12

1. 11 WCH at pp. 369–371 (Sylvia Odio testimony).
2. See, e.g., Anthony Summers, *Not in Your Lifetime: the Defining Book on the J.F.K. Assassination*, New York: Open Road, 1998 (2013 edition) at pp. 355–363. See also Sheno at pp. 212–217. For a strong rebuttal, see Posner at pp. 175–180. Bugliosi leans slightly to the possibility that Odio saw Oswald but rules out "second Oswald" conspiracy theories, Bugliosi at pp. 1299–1315.
3. See Warren Commission Report pages 321–324 for the Commission's analysis of the evidence related to the alleged visit of Oswald to Sylvia Odio.
4. Posner at p. 178.
5. 11 WCH at p. 368 (Testimony of Sylvia Ohio)
6. HSCA, Testimony of Dr. Burton C. Einspruch, July 11, 1978.
7. 11 WCH at p. 381 (Testimony of Sylvia Odio).
8. Bugliosi at p. 1303.
9. Bugliosi at p. 1303.
10. Warren Commission memo from Burt W. Griffin to W. David Slawson, April 16, 1964, concerning interview of Dr. Burton C. Einspruch by Griffin on April 13, 1964.
11. HSCA, Testimony of Dr. Burton C. Einspruch, July 11, 1978.
12. 11 WCH at p. 369 (Sylvia Odio testimony); CE 3108, 26 WCH 738 (FBI interview of Mrs. C.L. Connell on November 29, 1963).
13. HSCA Report at pp. 137–139. Bugliosi at p. 1308.
14. Three individuals who might have been the visitors were ultimately located by the FBI. That information turned out to be false. WCR p. 324; Bugliosi at p. 1306 and Endnotes pp. 746–747. The House Select Committee on Assassinations was also unable to locate the visitors. Bugliosi, Endnotes p. 749.
15. 11 WCH at pp. 179–180 (Estelle Twiford affidavit).
16. WCR at p. 324.
17. HSCA, Hearings, Vol. X, at p. 35.
18. Bugliosi at p. 1309.
19. HSCA Report at p. 139.
20. HSCA Report at p.140.

Chapter 13

1. http://www.ratical.org/ratville/JFK/OI-ALB.html
2. *Lane and Liebeler at UCLA, January 25, 1967,* UCLA Communications Studies Archives, YouTube, https://youtube.com/watch?=faDAGY71jP.
3. Mark Lane, *A Citizen's Dissent* (1968); Mark Lane, *Plausible Denial: Was the CIA Involved with the Assassination of JFK?* (1991); Mark Lane and Robert K. Tannenbaum, *Last Word: My Indictment of the CIA in the Murder of JFK* (2011).
4. 2 WCH at p. 56 (Mark Lane testimony).
5. Willensi at pp. 73–76.
6. 2 WCH at p. 57 (Mark Lane testimony).
7. 2 WCH at pp. 33–55 (Mark Lane testimony).
8. Willens at pp. 227–228.
9. 2 WCH at pp. 32–61 (Mark Lane testimony); 5 WCH at pp. 546–561 (Mark Lane testimony). Willens at p. 227.
10. 5 WCH at p. 560 (Mark Lane testimony).
11. 5 WCH at p. 558 (Mark Lane testimony).
12. 5 WCH at p. 559 (Mark Lane testimony).
13. 5 WCH at p. 559 (Marj Lane testimony).
14. Bugliosi at pp. 1008–1009.
15. Willens at p. 228.
16. WCR at pp. 297, 368. For the denials, see

5 WCH at pp. 203–204 (Jack Ruby testimony); 5 WCH 515–516, 521–524 (Bernard Weissman testimony).

17. Bugliosi, p. 1010, Endnote pp. 557–558; Adelson, pp. 46–48. When asked at the conclusion of his Warren Commission testimony by Warren Commission counsel Leon Hubert whether he had "anything ... to add further," Waldo responded, "No," and then said that he had an unpublished manuscript entitled "The Dallas Murders." Nowhere in his testimony did he mention information about a Ruby, Tippit, Weissman meeting. XV WCH 585–596 (Thayer Waldo testimony).

18. Email to author and 53 others from assassination researcher, Paul Hoch, May 29, 2016.

19. Bugliosi at pp. 372, 1351, and 1402.

Chapter 14

1. Howard Willens and Richard M. Mosk, "The Truth About Dallas," *The American Scholar*, Vol. 85, No. 3 (Summer 2016).
2. WCR at p. 22.
3. WCR at pp. 423–424.
4. Newman (1970).
5. Newman at p. 568.
6. Newman at p. 571.
7. Interview of Priscilla McMillan by author on July 25, 2017.
8. Interview of Priscilla McMillan by author on July 25, 2017.
9. McMillan at p. 582.
10. Davison at p. 293.
11. For Mr. Titovets' experiences with Oswald in Minsk, see Ernst Titovets, *Oswald: Russian Episode* (2010).
12. Posner at pp. xi, 501–504.
13. Posner at pp. 3–223.
14. Mailer at p. 782.
15. Mailer at pp. 782–784.
16. Mailer at pp. 778–779.
17. Russo (1998) at p. 457.
18. Gus Russo and Stephen Molton, *Brothers in Arms: The Kennedys, the Castros, and the Politics of Murder* (2008) at p. 471.

Chapter 15

1. Robert Oswald, *Lee: A Portrait of Lee Harvey Oswald* (1967) p. 43.
2. Oswald at p. 29.
3. Oswald at p. 36.
4. Ultimately Robert had no doubt that his brother had no co-conspirators. See www.pbs.org/wgbh/frontline/article/interview-robert-oswald/ "Interview of Robert Oswald," November 19, 2013; see also, https//www.youtube.com/watch?v=3DVQgFelUiuM. See also, 1 WCH at pp. 254–469 (Robert Oswald testimony); Oswald (1967) at pp. 229–241.
5. Posner at p. 6 (footnote); 1 WCH 126–263, inter alia 254 (Marguerite Oswald testimony).
6. David Abrahamsen, "A Study of Lee Harvey Oswald: Psychological Capability of Murder," Vol. 43, No. 10 *Bulletin of the New York Academy of Medicine* (October 1967) at p. 870.
7. Abrahamsen at p. 870.
8. WCR at p. 671.
9. Oswald at pp. 34–35. In contrast Allen Campbell, a resident of the Home when the Oswalds were there, has called the Home "deplorable." Russo (1998) at p. 90. Campbell told author Gus Russo that a clergyman at the Home had sexual intercourse with girls at the Home when they turned 16 and that he and Lee Oswald saw it occur. *Ibid.* If true, the impact on Oswald could have been substantial; however, other factors raise questions as to credibility. Campbell did not provide that evidence to either the Warren Commission or the House Select Committee on assassinations. Neither Robert Oswald nor John Pic reported such misconduct. One must ask why Campbell first publicly reported the incidents nearly 50 years after he became aware of them.
10. WCR at p. 382; Robert Oswald at p. 40; 11 WCH at p. 29 (John Pic testimony).
11. Mailer at p. 367. Evelyn Strickman Siegel, Exhibits No. 1.493. See all of Siegel Exhibits Nos. 1 and 2, 21 WCH at pp. 484–509.
12. Russo (1998) at p. 89.
13. WCR at pp. 669–681.
14. WCR at pp. 10, 381, 675.
15. WCR at pp. 379, 676.
16. Oswald at pp. 52–53; Bugliosi at p. 528; WCR at pp. 378–379, 676.
17. WCR at pp. 379, 675–676.
18. WCR at pp. 379, 677.
19. WCR at p. 380.
20. 21 WCH at p. 485 (Siegel Exhibit No. 1).
21. WCR at p. 380.
22. WCR at p. 388; Mailer at p. 376; Bugliosi at p. 539; Davison at pp. 54–55.
23. Bugliosi at pp. 538–540.
24. WCR at p. 83.
25. 16 WCH at p. 339 (CE 93).
26. WCR at p. 384; 22 WCH at pp. 711 (CE 1386).
27. WCR at p. 384.
28. WCR p. 384; 11 WCH 3–4 (Edward John Pic testimony).
29. WCR pp. 680–681.
30. WCR p. 681.
31. Gary W. O'Brien, *Oswald's Politics* (2010) at p. 49.
32. HSCA, Administrative Folder G8B, https://www.maryferrell.org/showDoc,html?dodd=99458relPageld=208.
33. The story of Oswald being thrown in the shower is in Epstein (1978) at pp. 68–71. Epstein interviewed 62 of Oswald's Marine colleagues (pp. 337–338).
34. WCR p. 682.
35. Bugliosi, footnote p. 571. CE 1385, 22 WCH 705.
36. WCR at p. 386.
37. Fellow Marine Zack Stout, reported in Epstein (1978) at pp. 69.

38. WCR at pp. 681–682.
39. WCR at p. 682.
40. WCR at p. 683.
41. WCR at p. 683; Bugliosi at p. 554.
42. WCR at p. 683; Mailer at pp. 383–384.
43. WCR at p. 683.
44. WCR at p. 684; Mailer at p. 387; 19 WCH at p. 683 (Folso, Exhibit No. 1, Court-Martial findings).
45. Bugliosi at p. 556.
46. WCR at p. 684; Bugliosi at p. 556.
47. Epstein (1978) at pp. 78–79; Bugliosi at p. 557; Mailer at p. 388.
48. Epstein (1978) at p. 79; Bugliosi at p. 557.
49. Bugliosi at p. 559.
50. Bugliosi at p. 559.
51. Epstein (1978) at p. 80.
52. Bugliosi at pp. 558–560.
53. 8 WCH at pp. 240–241 (Nelson Delgado testimony).
54. 8 WCH at pp. 230–233 (Nelson Delgado testimony).
55. 8 WCH at p. 245 (Nelson Delgado testimony).
56. http://mailstrom.blogspot.com/2006/lee-oswald-why-did-he-do-it.html.
57. 8 WCH at p. 241 (Nelson Delgado testimony).
58. 8 WCH at p. 233 (Nelson Delgado testimony).
59. 8 WCH at pp. 246–247 (Nelson Delgado testimony).
60. WCR p. 687; 8 WCH at pp. 240–242 (Nelson Delgado testimony)
61. 8 WCH at pp. 260 (Nelson Delgado testimony).
62. 8 WCH at p. 237 (Nelson Delgado testimony).
63. 8 WCH at p. 265 (Nelson Delgado testimony).
64. 8 WCH at p. 254 (Nelson Delgado testimony).
65. 11 WCH at pp. 96–97 (Kerry Wendell Thornley testimony); Thornley, *Oswald* (1965) at pp. 45–49. Thornley's novel, *The Idle Warriors,* featuring Lee Oswald as the model for the central figure, was completed in February 1962; https://en.wikipedia.org/wiki/Kerry_Wendell_Thornley.
66. Kerry Thornley, *Oswald* (1965) at p. 37.
67. Kerry Thornley, *Oswald* (1965) at p. 38.
68. 11 WCH at p. 97 (Kerry Wendell Thornley testimony).
69. Bugliosi at p. 565.
70. 11 WCH at p. 87 (Kerry Wendell Thornley testimony).
71. Thornley, *Oswald* (1965) at p. 24.
72. Thornley, *Oswald* (1965) p. 27.
73. Greg Parker, *Oswald and Albert Schweitzer College,* http.CovertHistory.blogspot.com.br/2005/07/Oswald.
74. Bugliosi at p. 566.
75. Bugliosi at p. 566.
76. Compare Epstein (1978) at pp. 89–90, 126; Bugliosi at p. 566.
77. Bugliosi at pp. 564–565; 8 WCH at pp. 242–243 (Nelson Delgado testimony).
78. Bugliosi at p. 566.
79. Parker (2005).
80. 8 WCH at pp. 233–234.
81. Bugliosi at pp. 560–561.
82. Bugliosi at p. 566; 16 WCH at p. 824 (CE 296).
83. WCR at p. 688; Bugliosi at p. 567.
84. WCR at pp. 688–689; Bugliosi at pp. 567–568.
85. WCR at p. 690.
86. WCR at pp. 689–690.

Chapter 16

1. Mailer at pp. 43–45.
2. WCR at p. 691.
3. WCR at p. 691.
4. WCR at p. 691.
5. WCR at pp. 691–692.
6. Mailer at pp. 49–50.
7. 16 WCH at pp. 94–95. CE 24.
8. Author's interview October 9, 2019, with Joseph Reardon who attended on July 27, 1963. Lee Oswald's description of his experiences in the Soviet Union.
9. See Mailer at pp. 50–52; Davison at p. 84.
10. W. David Slawson, interview for documentary film *Truth Is the Only Client,* transcript p. 12.
11. Bugliosi at pp. 579–582. CE 24, 16 WCH 96–97; Mailer at p. 55.
12. W. David Slawson, interview for documentary film *Truth Is the Only Client,* transcript p. 19.
13. Bugliosi at p. 587.
14. 16 WCH at p. 97 (CE 24 at p. 4).
15. Bugliosi at pp. 588–89; see also, Priscilla Johnson McMillan, *Marina and Lee* (1977) at pp. 74–77; 11 WCH at pp. 442–444 (Testimony of Priscilla Mary Post Johnson, later Priscilla Johnson McMillan); 20 WCH at pp. 277–311 (Priscilla Johnson Exhibits 1–6, her writings about Lee Harvey Oswald from 1959–1964).
16. Bugliosi at p. 59; McMillan at pp. 74–77.
17. Bugliosi at p. 593. Author's interview: Spring Hill College student Joseph Reardon recalled on October 9, 2019, that Oswald said at his Spring Hill presentation on July 27, 1963, that he had hoped to stay in Moscow.
18. Bugliosi at pp. 593–595.
19. WCR at p. 697; 16 WCH p. 99; Bugliosi at p. 597.
20. 16 WCH at p. 99 (CE 24).
21. 16 WCH at p. 101 (CE 24); See also Mailer at p. 117–119. An extensive account of Oswald's friendships with female students at the Foreign Language Institute in Minsk has been provided by his friend Ernst Titovets. Titovets at pp. 126–137, 175–181.
22. Mailer at pp. 102–109, 117–119.
23. Bugliosi at p. 604.
24. Mailer at p. 132. See also Mailer at pp. 127–131 for a detailed description of the relationship between Ella and Lee.
25. 16 WCH at pp. 101–102. A third-party account of Oswald's relationship with Ella German is given by his friend Ernst Titovets. Titovets at pp. 63, 78–79, 136, 158–160.
26. WCR at p. 701.
27. 16 WCH at p. 100. Oswald obviously

misspelled Ziger as "Zeber." Oswald's friend Ernst Titovets provides other details about Oswald's relationship with Ziger and his family. Titovets at pp. 49, 91–96, 148, 204, 207, 224.

28. 16 WCH at p. 102. Oswald has misspelled Snyder's last name.

29. 16 WCH at p. 102. Some punctuation and spelling corrected for clarity. Marina recalls that she had arranged to meet two medical students at the dance. Priscilla Johnson McMillan, *Marina and Lee* (1977) at p. 73. Oswald's friend, Ernst Titovets, attended the dance with Oswald and was in the group that accompanied Marina home. He provides a detailed description of the evening. Titovets at pp. 219–260.

30. For details of the period March 17 to April 30, 1961, see Mailer at pp. 165–195; McMillan at pp. 83–112; Titovets at pp. 261, 276.

31. 16 WCH at p. 103.

32. McMillan at pp. 3–53.

33. McMillan, at pp. 8–10.

34. McMillan, 15–20.

35. McMillan at p. 34.

36. McMillan at p. 43.

37. McMillan at pp. 46, 48.

38. McMillan at p. 38.

39. McMillan at pp. 40–48.

40. McMillan at p. 52.

41. McMillan at p. 55.

42. McMillan at pp. 57–60.

43. Since Marina was working in Minsk as a hospital pharmacy assistant, she may have had easy access to him. Priscilla Johnson McMillan, *Marina and Lee* (1977) at pp. 67 and 93–94.

44. Mailer p. 785.

45. McMillan at p. 86.

46. McMillan at pp. 85–86.

47. McMillan at p. 91.

48. McMillan at p. 92.

49. McMillan at pp. 92–93.

50. McMillan at pp. 93–95.

51. 16 WCH at p. 103 (CE 24).

52. 16 WCH at p. 234 (CE 72).

53. McMillan at p. 114.

54. McMillan at p. 115.

55. McMillan at p. 128.

56. McMillan at pp. 116–120.

57. 16 WCH at pp. 285–336 (CE 92).

58. This essay is apparently the same composition that Priscilla Johnson McMillan refers to as "The Collective." See, McMillan at pp. 135–136.

59. McMillan at p. 133.

60. 16 WCH at p. 285 (CE 92).

Chapter 17

1. WCR at p. 712.

2. WCR at p. 773.

3. 16 WCH at p. 120 (CE 25).

4. 4 26 WCH at pp. 812–817 (CE No. 3134).

5. 16 WCH at pp.106–107 (CE 25).

6. 1 WCH at p. 101 (Marina Oswald testimony). Marina referred to the paper as *The Daily Worker.* The U.S. Communist Party published its paper on a weekly basis while Lee was in Minsk; however, the British version of *The Worker* was published daily at that time. https://en.wikipedia.org/wiki/Morning_Star_(British_newspaper)#Postwar).

7. 16 WCH at pp. 107–108 (CE 25).

8. 16 WCH at pp. 108–112 (CE 25).

9. 16 WCH at p. 116 (CE 25).

10. 16 WC at pp. 116–118 (CE 25).

11. 16 WCH at pp. 118–119 (CE 25).

12. 16 WCH at pp. 119–120 (CE 25).

13. 16 WCH at pp. 121–122 (CE 25).

14. 16 WCH at pp. 285–336 (CE 92).

15. 16 WCH at p. 421 (CE 96).

16. 16 WCH at p. 422 (CE 97).

17. 16 WCH at pp. 422–430 (CE 97).

18. 16 WCH at pp. 425–42 (CE 97).

19. 16 WCH at pp. 426–427 (CE 97).

20. 16 WCH at pp. 427–428 (CE 97).

21. 16 WCH at pp. 428–429 (CE 97).

22. 16 WCH at pp. 429–430 (CE 97).

23. 16 WCH at pp. 431–432 (CE 98).

24. 16 WCH at p. 433 (CE 98). As a nonreligious person, Oswald may have deliberately contrasted his system with one that had any religious or other contemporary ideological basis.

25. 16 WCH at p. 433 (CE 98).

26. In providing letters to enumerate his proposals, Oswald omitted the letters P and Q.

27. 16 WCH at p. 433 (CE 98). Letters F, P, and Q were omitted by Oswald from his draft.

28. 16 WCH at p. 434 (CE 98).

29. Author Priscilla McMillan believes Oswald wrote his description of the Atheian system and his philosophy of political action while he was living on West Neely Street in Dallas before attempting to assassinate Edwin Walker. McMillan (1977) at pp. 338–339.

Chapter 18

1. 16 WCH at p. 438 (CE 100).

2. 16 WCH at p. 436 (CE 100).

3. WCR at p. 713.

4. WCR at p. 713.

5. 16 WCH at p. 287 (CE 92). Oswald never gave a title to this document. Those are its opening words.

6. WCR at p. 714.

7. WCR at p. 714.

8. Although Oswald used the Texas Employment Commission for job referrals, the Employment Commission was unable to locate records on Oswald for 1962; 23 WCH at p. 698 (CE 1895).

9. WCR at pp. 714–715.

10. Oswald (1967) at p. 120.

11. McMillan at p. 222.

12. Bugliosi at p. 643.

13. McMillan at p. 225; Bugliosi at p. 643; 16 WCH at p. 866 (CE 2189).

14. WCR at p. 715.

15. Bugliosi at p. 645; McMillan at p. 230.

16. McMillan at pp. 225–226.
17. McMillan at pp. 230–232.
18. 5 WCH at p. 598 (Marina Oswald testimony); 9 WCH at pp. 231–233 (George de Mohrenschildt testimony); 9 WCH at 312–313 (Jeanne de Mojrenschildt testimony); McMillan at pp. 281–282, 289–290, 315–16, 390, 457–459; Titovets at pp. 280–281.
19. McMillan at p. 231.
20. McMillan at p. 235.
21. 9 WCH at p. 230 (George DeMohrenschildt testimony); McMillan at pp. 240–245, 254.
22. McMillan at pp. 244–246, 282–284.
23. 1 WCH at p. 10 (Marina Oswald testimony).
24. 21 WCH at pp. 271–272 (CE 1172).
25. 19 WCH at p. 575 (Farrell Dobbs Exhibit No. 9).
26. Bugliosi at p. 770; Posner at p. 126.

Chapter 19

1. Bugliosi at p. 672, n. 1047 citing Newman at pp. 211–212.
2. Newman at p. 211; *The Worker*, November 12, 1961.
3. PublicEye.org-John Birch Society.
4. Caulfield at pp. 321–323.
5. "Walker Member of Birch Society." *New York Times*, September 8, 1961, page 13. https://timesmachine.nytimes.com/timesmachine/1961/09/08/118924582.html?pageNumber=13.
6. "Excerpts from Walker Statement to Senators on Resignation." *New York Times*, November 3, 1961, page 22. https://timesmachine.nytimes.com/timesmachine/1961/11/03/97256488.html?pageNumber=22.
7. Federal Bureau of Investigation, FOA, file No. 716–16549481 (Edwin Walker interview, September 29, 1962).
8. Milton Bracker. "Walker Declares He'll Work Alone." *New York Times*, December 4, 1961, page 23. https://timesmachine.nytimes.com/timesmachine/1961/12/04/issue.html.
9. "Ex-General Walker Enters Race for Governor." *New York Times*, February 3, 1962, page 1. https://timesmachine.nytimes.com/timesmachine/1962/02/03/issue.html.
10. *New York Times*, February 4, 1962, page 77. https://timesmachine.nytimes.com/timesmachine/1962/02/04/89842952.html?pageNumber=77.
11. "Talk by Walker Is Canceled Here." *New York Times*, February 13, 1962, page 16. https://timesmachine.nytimes.com/timesmachine/1962/02/13/issue.html; Russell Baker. "An Objection by Goldwater Led to Cancellation of Walker Talk." *New York Times*, February 14, 1962, page 20. https://timesmachine.nytimes.com/timesmachine/1962/02/14/issue.html.
12. *The Worker*, February 18, 1962, p. 1.
13. *Ibid.* See also, *The Worker*, April 10, 1962.
14. John W. Finney. "Walker Asserts He Is Scapegoat of 'No-Win' Policy." *New York Times*, April 5, 1962, p. 1, 17. https://timesmachine.nytimes.com/timesmachine/1962/04/05/issue.html.
15. John W. Finney. "Walker Challenges Rusk and Rostow on Loyalty." *New York Times*, April 6, 1962, pp 1, 17. https://timesmachine.nytimes.com/timesmachine/1962/04/06/89854520.html?pageNumber=1; "Walker Charges Jabs." New York Times, April 11, 1962, p. 4. https://timesmachine.nytimes.com/timesmachine/1962/04/11/86702930.html?pageNumber=4.
16. *The Worker*, April 10, 1962, p. 4.
17. Caufield at p. 327.
18. Bugliosi at p. 672.
19. 16 WCH at p. 441 (CE 102).
20. 16 WCH at p. 441 (CE 102).
21. 16 WCH 441 (CE 102).
22. Bugliosi at pp. 636–638; O'Brien (2010) at pp. 65–67.
23. *Time Magazine*, August 10, 1962, at p. 14.
24. "Albany Gets Negro Plea on Issues," *Dallas Morning News*, August 16, 1962, Section 1, p. 2. https://infoweb.newsbank.com/apps/news/document-view?p=AMNEWS&t=pubname%3A0F99DDB671832188%21Dallas%2BMorning%2BNews/year%3A1962%211962/mody%3A0816%21August%2B16&action=browse&year=1962&format=image&docref=image%2Fv2%3A0F99DDB671832188%-40EANX-100110C7E7851106%402437893-100110C7F77A6BC9%401&origin=image%2Fv2%3A0F99DDB671832188%40EANX-100110C7E7851106%402437893-100110C7F2379755%400.
25. "Albany Police Padlock Parks, Library." *Dallas Morning News*, August 12, 1962: 2. *NewsBank: America's News—Historical and Current.* https://infoweb.newsbank.com/apps/news/document-view?p=AMNEWS&docref=image/v2%3A0F99DDB671832188%40EANX-100111F0C75CE177%402437889-100111F0D5D57A50%401-100111F380A781AC.
26. "Whites Plan Reprisals in Albany," *Dallas Morning News*, August 18, 1962, Section 1, p. 7. *NewsBank: America's News—Historical and Current.* https://infoweb.newsbank.com/apps/news/document-view?p=AMNEWS&docref=image/v2%3A0F99DDB671832188%40EANX-100110D5C3D8356E%402437895-100110D5ED131AFA%406-100110D74B86DDD6.
27. Hedrick Smith. "Georgians Balk Albany Movement for Civil Rights." *The New York Times*, August 18, 1962, page 44. https://timesmachine.nytimes.com/timesmachine/1962/08/18/90177401.html?pageNumber=44.
28. *Time Magazine*, August 3, 1962, p. 12.
29. *Time Magazine*, August 10, 1962, p. 14.
30. See, e.g., "Georgia Marchers Defy Court Order." *Fort Worth Star-Telegram*, July 22, 1962, p. 1. https://www.newspapers.com/image/640184457/; Don McKee. "Negros May Suspend Protest After Violence." *Fort Worth Star-Telegram*, July 25, 1962, p. 1. https://www.newspapers.com/image/640227373/.

31. *Fort Worth Star Telegram*, August 18, 1962. Section 1, p. 1.

32. "Shots Fired at Integrated School." *Dallas Morning News*, September 8, 1962: 4. *NewsBank: America's News—Historical and Current*. https://infoweb.newsbank.com/apps/news/document-view?p=AMNEWS&docref=image/v2%3A0F99DDB671832188%40EANX-100111491F873FFD%402437916-10011149316F4278%403-1001114A54C3F436.

33. Carlos Conde. "Integration Expected in 9 More Schools." *Dallas Morning News*, August 30, 1962: 1. *NewsBank: America's News—Historical and Current*. https://infoweb.newsbank.com/apps/news/document-view?p=AMNEWS&docref=image/v2%3A0F99DDB671832188%40EANX-100110BB49EBC052%402437907-100110BBE503F6D7%4040-100110BF170F7AE2.

34. "U.S. Troop Use Looms as Negro Tries Again." *Fort Worth Star-Telegram*, September 26, 1962, Section 1, pp. 1, 8. https://www.newspapers.com/image/640226972.

35. "Negro Again Refused Ole Miss Admittance." *Fort Worth Star-Telegram*, September 28, 1962, Section 1, pp. 1, 4, Morning 3 Edition. https://www.newspapers.com/image/640192284.

36. "U.S. Halts Try to Enroll Negro." *Fort Worth Star Telegram*, September 28, 1962, Morning Edition, Section 1, pp. 1, 4. https://www.newspapers.com/image/640192759.

37. "Walker Stumps for Volunteers." *Fort Worth Star-Telegram*, September 28, 1962, Morning Edition. Section 1, p. 1. https://www.newspapers.com/image/640210746/.

38. "Walker Stumps for Volunteers." *Fort Worth Star Telegram*, September 28, 1962, Morning Edition. Section 1, pp. 1, 4. https://www.newspapers.com/image/640210802.

39. "Walker Asks Drive to Support Barnett If Troops Are Used." *The New York Times*, September 28, 1962, p. 23. https://timesmachine.nytimes.com/timesmachine/1962/09/28/82768120.html?pageNumber=23.

40. John Mashek. "R. Kennedy Considers Using Troops at Oxford." *Dallas Morning News*, September 28, 1962: 1. *NewsBank: America's News—Historical and Current*. https://infoweb.newsbank.com/apps/news/document-view?p=AMNEWS&docref=image/v2%3A0F99DDB671832188%40EANX-1001116B41F0628B%402437936-1001116B4B8F281C%400-1001116C4FC93C93.

41. Richard M. Morehead. "Mississippi Shows Signs of Weakening." *Dallas Morning News*, September 29, 1962: 1. *NewsBank: America's News—Historical and Current*. https://infoweb.newsbank.com/apps/news/document-view?p=AMNEWS&docref=image/v2%3A0F99DDB671832188%40EANX-1001117069337E7A%402437937-100111707496BC9D%400-100111718245E57D.

42. John Mashek. "R. Kennedy Considers Using Troops at Oxford." *Dallas Morning News*, September 28, 1962: 1. *NewsBank: America's News—Historical and Current*. https://infoweb.newsbank.com/apps/news/document-view?p=AMNEWS&docref=image/v2%3A0F99DDB671832188%40EANX-1001116B41F0628B%402437936-1001116B4B8F281C%400-1001116C4FC93C93.

43. "Pass Negro or It's Jail, U.S. Court Tells Barnett." *Fort Worth Star-Telegram*, September 29, 1962, Evening Edition. Section 1, p. 1. https://www.newspapers.com/image/640230029/.

44. "U.S. Puts Squeeze on Barnett." *Dallas Morning News*, September 29, 1962: 1. *NewsBank: America's News—Historical and Current*. https://infoweb.newsbank.com/apps/news/document-view?p=AMNEWS&docref=image/v2%3A0F99DDB671832188%40EANX-1001117069337E7A%402437937-100111707496BC9D%400-1001117185981251.

45. "Mississippi Withdraws Forces from Ole Miss." *Fort Worth Star-Telegram*, September 28, 1962, Evening Edition. Section 1, p. 1. https://www.newspapers.com/image/640229211/.

46. *Fort Worth Star-Telegram*, September 28, 1962.

47. Richard M. Morehead. "Segregation Musters a Last Stand." *Dallas Morning News*, September 30, 1962: 1. *NewsBank: America's News—Historical and Current*. https://infoweb.newsbank.com/apps/news/document-view?p=AMNEWS&docref=image/v2%3A0F99DDB671832188%40EANX-10011176191BA5FA%402437938-10011176246C6A98%400-100111784697311C.

48. "Kennedy Is Urged to Ease Tension." *Fort Worth Star-Telegram*, September 29, 1962, Evening Edition. Section 1, p. 2. https://www.newspapers.com/image/640230042.

49. "Walker Lets Up in Drive for Crusade." *Fort Worth Star Telegram*, September 29, 1962, Evening Edition. Section 1, page 2. https://www.newspapers.com/image/640230042.

50. "Mississippi Guard Put Under Federal Control." *Dallas Morning News*, September 30, 1962: 1. *NewsBank: America's News—Historical and Current*. https://infoweb.newsbank.com/apps/news/document-view?p=AMNEWS&docref=image/v2%3A0F99DDB671832188%40EANX-10011176191BA5FA%402437938-10011176246C6A98%400-1001117840C49544.; "Walker Demands a 'Vocal Protest.'" *The New York Times*, September 30, 1962. P. 69. https://timesmachine.nytimes.com/timesmachine/1962/09/30/121653913.html?pageNumber=69.

51. "Walker Demands a 'Vocal Protest.'" *The New York Times*, September 30, 1962, p. 69. https://timesmachine.nytimes.com/timesmachine/1962/09/30/121653913.html?pageNumber=69.

52. "Walker Demands a 'Vocal Protest.'" *The New York Times*, September 30, 1962. Page 69. https://timesmachine.nytimes.com/timesmachine/1962/09/30/121653913.html?pageNumber=69.

53. "Walker Asks Force to Back Up Barnett."

Fort Worth Star-Telegram, September 28, 1962, Morning Edition. Section 1, page 1. https://www.newspapers.com/image/640192717.

54. "Walker Demands a 'Vocal Protest.'" *The New York Times,* September 30, 1962. Page 69. https://timesmachine.nytimes.com/timesmachine/1962/09/30/121653913.html?pageNumber=69.

55. "Citizens Rally to Support Barnett Stand." *Fort Worth Star-Telegram,* September 30, 1962, Evening Edition, Section 1, page 2. https://www.newspapers.com/image/640195807.

56. Schlesinger (1978) at pp. 320–321; Sorensen at p. 484; Caufield at p. 358.

57. "'My Responsibility Was Inescapable,' Kennedy Says." *Dallas Morning News,* October 1, 1962.

58. Thomas Buckley. "Tear Gas and Sticks Repel Wild Student Charges." *New York Times,* October 1, 1962, page 23. https://timesmachine.nytimes.com/timesmachine/1962/10/01/issue.htmlhttps://timesmachine.nytimes.com/timesmachine/1962/10/01/90192583.html?pageNumber=23.

59. Caufield at p. 361.

60. Relman Morin. "Walker Stirs Up Frenzied Mob on Ole Miss Campus." *Fort Worth Star-Telegram,* October 1, 1962, Evening Chaser Edition. Section 1, page 1. https://www.newspapers.com/image/640185039/.

61. Van Sevell. "Rioter Asked Walker to Lead Crowd; He Did." Fort Worth *Star-Telegram,* October 3, 1962, Chaser Evening Edition. Section 1, page 1. https://www.newspapers.com/image/640185802/.

62. Claude Sitton. "Tear Gas Is Used." *New York Times,* October 1, 1962, pp. 1, 23. https://timesmachine.nytimes.com/timesmachine/1962/10/01/90192375.html?pageNumber=1.

63. Claude Sitton. "Tear Gas Is Used." *New York Times,* October 1, 1962, pp. 1, 23. https://timesmachine.nytimes.com/timesmachine/1962/10/01/90192375.html?pageNumber=1. Some sources claim even higher numbers were necessary. See Daniel Levitas, *The Terrorist Next Door: The Militia Movement and the Radical Right* (2002) at p. 76 asserting figures from 12,000 to 23,000 troops.

64. Claude Sitton. "Tear Gas Is Used." *New York Times,* October 1, 1962, pp. 1, 23. https://timesmachine.nytimes.com/timesmachine/1962/10/01/90192375.html?pageNumber=1.

65. Levitas (2002) at 76.

66. Harry McCormick. "Youth Carrying Arsenal Arrested." *Dallas Morning News,* October 2, 1962: 12. *NewsBank: America's News—Historical and Current.* https://infoweb.newsbank.com/apps/news/document-view?p=AMNEWS&docref=image/v2%3A0F99DDB671832188%40EANX-10011067AB1EF4B6%402437940-10011067D82470A0%4011-100110691D23B751%40Youth%2BCarrying%2BArsenal%2BArrested.; Bugliosi at p. 673 (Note that Bugliosi refers to Burchwell as Burchell).

67. "Mental Exam Possible for Arrested Walker." *Fort Worth Star-Telegram,* October 2, 1962, Evening Chaser Edition, Section 1, page 1. https://www.newspapers.com/image/640185374/; *The Worker,* October 21, 1962, page 2.

68. Tape 4G3, Cassette B, John F. Kennedy Library, President's Office Files, Presidential Recordings Collection.

69. Tape 4G4, Cassette B, John F. Kennedy Library, President's Office Files, Presidential Recordings Collection.

70. "Walker Is Facing 4 Federal Counts." *The New York Times,* October 2, 1962, pp. 1, 27. https://timesmachine.nytimes.com/timesmachine/1962/10/02/90194280.html?pageNumber=1.

71. "Walker Is Facing 4 Federal Counts." *The New York Times,* October 2, 1962, pp. 1, 27. https://timesmachine.nytimes.com/timesmachine/1962/10/02/90194280.html?pageNumber=1.

72. "Walker Aides Want Inquiry." *Dallas Morning News,* October 4, 1962: 1. *NewsBank: America's News—Historical and Current.* https://infoweb.newsbank.com/apps/news/document-view?p=AMNEWS&docref=image/v2%3A0F99DDB671832188%40EANX-10011072188AA616%402437942-1001107223406DA7%400-10011073A581C4AB.; "Inquiry on Senate by Walker Asked." *The New York Times,* October 4, 1962, page 30. https://timesmachine.nytimes.com/timesmachine/1962/10/04/90581772.html?pageNumber=30.

73. Robert E. Baskin. "Alger Says Walker Deprived of Rights." *Dallas Morning News,* October 4, 1962: 10. *NewsBank: America's News—Historical and Current.* https://infoweb.newsbank.com/apps/news/document-view?p=AMNEWS&docref=image/v2%3A0F99DDB671832188%40EANX-10011072188AA616%402437942-10011072 38ED182B%409-10011073F4492086.

74. "General Walker." *Dallas Morning News,* October 6, 1962: 2. *NewsBank: America's News—Historical and Current.* https://infoweb.newsbank.com/apps/news/document-view?p=AMNEWS&docref=image/v2%3A0F99DDB671832188%-40EANX-100110807A1A5DC8%402437944-10011080F4C7A37B%4035-10011083502427AA.

75. "Seven March for Walker." *Dallas Morning News,* October 7, 1962: 8. *NewsBank: America's News—Historical and Current.* https://infoweb.newsbank.com/apps/news/document-view?p=AMNEWS&docref=image/v2%3A0F99DDB671832188%40EANX-10011085F19E5CCA%402437945-10011086116E083F%407-100110884739A5A4%40Seven%2BMarch%2Bfor%2BWalker.

76. "Walker Attorneys May Delay Appeal on Writ." *Fort Worth Star-Telegram,* October 5, 1962, Evening Chaser Edition, Section 1, page 2. https://www.newspapers.com/image/640187363/.

77. "Civil Liberties Union Cautions U.S. on Its Legal Action Against Walker." *The New York Times,* October 5, 1962, page 18. https://timesmachine.nytimes.com/timesmachine/1962/10/05/90595051.html?pageNumber=18.

78. "Walker Goes Free on $50,000 Bond." *Fort*

Worth Star-Telegram, October 7, 1962, Evening Chaser Edition, Section 1, page 1. https://www.newspapers.com/image/640188244/.

79. "Walker Is Freed on $50,000 Bond." *The New York Times,* October 7, 1962, page 1. https://timesmachine.nytimes.com/timesmachine/1962/10/07/121475623.html?pageNumber=1.

80. Jack Castleman. "Crowd Welcomes Ex-Gen. Walker's Return to Dallas." *Dallas Morning News,* October 8, 1962: 1. *NewsBank: America's News—Historical and Current.* https://infoweb.newsbank.com/apps/news/document-view?p=AMNEWS&docref=image/v2%3A0F99DDB671832188%40EANX-10011092324314E9%402437946-1001109240465310%400-1001109316308972. "Walker Greeters Hail Their Hero." *Dallas Morning News,* October 8, 1962: 1. *NewsBank: America's News—Historical and Current.* https://infoweb.newsbank.com/apps/news/document-view?p=AMNEWS&docref=image/v2%3A0F99DDB671832188%40EANX-10011092324314E9%402437946-100110929F3C3F9E%4034-10011094CAC48CC8.; "Walker Returns to Home in Texas." *The New York Times,* October 8, 1962, page 14. https://timesmachine.nytimes.com/timesmachine/1962/10/08/issue.html.

81. "Walker Greeters Hail Their Hero." *Dallas Morning News* (Dallas, Texas), October 8, 1962: 1. *NewsBank: America's News—Historical and Current.* https://infoweb.newsbank.com/apps/news/document-view?p=AMNEWS&docref=image/v2%3A0F99DDB671832188%40EANX-10011092324314E9%402437946-100110929F3C3F9E%4034-10011094CAC48CC8.

82. "Riot Charges Against Walker and 6 Others Dropped by U.S." *The New York Times,* January 22, 1963, Section 1, pp. 1, 5. https://timesmachine.nytimes.com/timesmachine/1963/01/22/89514837.html?pageNumber=1; "Judge Dismisses Walker Charges." *Dallas Morning News,* January 22, 1963: 1. *NewsBank: America's News—Historical and Current.* https://infoweb.newsbank.com/apps/news/document-view?p=AMNEWS&docref=image/v2%3A0F99DDB671832188%40EANX-0FF7D1E8D2385B7E%402438052-0FF7D1E8DE73BB56%400-0FF7D1E9DA66440F.

83. *The Worker,* October 7, 1962, p. 1.

84. *The Worker,* October 21, 1962, p. 2.

Chapter 20

1. Bugliosi at p. 650. "Walker Goes Free on $50,000 Bond" *Fort Worth Star-Telegram,* October 7, 1962, Evening Chaser Edition, Section 1, p. 1. https://www.newspapers.com/image/640188244/

2. 10 WCH at p. 165 (Tommy Bargas testimony); Bugliosi at pp. 650–651; WCR at 717–718.

3. WCR p. 742. The Warren Commission calculated that at the end of September he had only $22.34. Even at 1962 prices, $22.34 was not enough to pay rent and support a frugal wife with an infant child for much more than a week.

4. 9 WCH at p. 96 (HGary Taylor testimony).

5. 10 WCH 125–127, 133 (Helen Cunningham testimony).

6. WCR at pp 403, 719, 724; Gus Russo (1998) at p. 128 (Interview of David Ofstein on June 16, 1993).

7. 1 WCH at pp. 8, 33 (Marina Oswald testimony).

8. See 1WCH 8, 33 (Marina Oswald testimony) (Believed he rented a room at one point but could not give a location); 9 WCH 88–89 (Gary Taylor testimony).

9. See, e.g., Epstein (1978) at p. 190. Epstein relies on a letter that Oswald wrote on August 28, 1963, about 10 months after Oswald's undocumented period in Dallas. The word 'underground" was used by Oswald in a request for advice from the Communist Party U.S.A. in New York as to whether "I should compete in anti-progressive forces above ground, or whether I should always remain in the background, i.e., 'underground.'" Id at p. 316, note 1. There is simply no evidence that Oswald was living "underground" when records could not be found for his residence in Dallas during October 1962.

10. McMillan, at p. 253.

11. Mailer speculated that on the October dates for which no rental records exist, Lee stayed in Dallas with either the de Mohrenschildt or George Bouhe. But neither acquaintance—who were candid when testifying before the Warren Commission—acknowledged that. Indeed, Bouhe spoke critically of his relationship with Lee during this period, saying that Oswald would curtly telephone him to say that he was fine, never saying thank you or offering any other conversation.

For the first few days of Oswald's move to Dallas—October 9 and 10—Marina lived temporarily, until her dental work was done, with Gary and Alexandra Taylor. The Taylors told the Warren Commission that Lee did not stay overnight. The YMCA was within walking distance of their home. Gary Taylor remembered dropping Lee off at the YMCA and picking him up there on various occasions, at least one of which was after October 21. He was also able to reach Lee by telephone there. Alexandra Taylor said that on one occasion, Lee gave them a North Beckley street address that they could not find.

From October 9 through October 11, the Dallas Y might have extended its charity to Lee, a newcomer to Dallas. After Marina returned from the Taylors' to Elena Hall's home in Fort Worth, the weekend of October 13 and 14 was spent with Marina in Fort Worth at no cost. WCR at p. 718; 1 WCH at pp. 8, 33 (Marina Oswald testimony); 11 WCH at p. 137 (Mrs. Donald Gibson testimony). Lee then paid the YMCA for the period October 15 through October 19. The weekend again took him to Fort Worth to be with Marina.

By October 22, Lee had paid the YMCA once. A YMCA attendant might well have seen him checking newspaper ads for work and calling for possible apartment rentals. Perhaps his prior ability to pay, his good conduct, his status as a husband and veteran, and his politeness might have earned him the charity of a sympathetic YMCA employee. If he were a non-paying resident, the Y might not have kept a record, or the record might have been lost.

12. WCR at p. 718.

13. 8 WCH at p. 365 (George A. Bouhe testimony).

14. 8 WCH at p. 397 (Elena A. Hall testimony).

15. Bugliosi, p. 654.

16. WCR at p. 719.

17. Newman at p. 56.

18. "American Mercury Is Sold to Texans" *The New York Times,* Sept. 30, 1962, p. 58. https://timesmachine.nytimes.com/timesmachine/1962/09/30/121653845.html?pageNumber=58; Singleton at p. 241.

19. McMillan (1977) at pp. 257–258; Mailer at pp. 456–460.

20. Born April 17, 1911, in Russia, de Mohrenschildt came from a Czarist-era family of wealth, influence, and education. In 1938, he came to the United States after receiving a doctorate in International Commerce from the University of Liège in Belgium. In 1945, the University of Texas awarded him a master's degree in petroleum engineering. Over the next thirty years, he engaged in a variety of foreign business ventures. Albert H. Newman, *The Assassination of John F. Kennedy: The Reasons Why* (1970) at p. 283. Married four times, he delighted in shocking friends with both his ideas and his behavior. After President Kennedy died, de Mohrenschildt became increasingly depressed as theorists attempted to link him conspiratorially or motivationally to the assassination. To clear both himself and Oswald, he ultimately drafted an eighty-nine-page monograph, "I am a Patsy! I am a Patsy!," about his relationship with Oswald. Shortly after being interviewed by Warren Commission critic Edward Jay Epstein and in anticipation of an interview by Gaeton Fonzi, investigator for the House Select Committee on Assassinations, de Mohrenschildt committed suicide on March 29, 1977. Staff Report of the Select Committee on Assassinations, U.S. House of Representatives, 95th Congress, Second Session, March 1979; http://mcadams.posc.mu.edu/russ/jfkinfo4/jfk12/hscademo.htm.

21. 9 WCH 238 (George de Mohrenschildt testimony).

22. 9 WCH 236–237 (George de Mohrenschildt testimony).

23. George de Mohrenschildt, *I Am a Patsy!* http://mcadams.posc.mu.edu/russ/jfkinfo4;jfk12/hscapatsy.htm at p.3. His wife delivered the monograph to the HSCA on April 1, 1977.

24. 1 WCH at p. 23 (Marina Oswald testimony).

25. McMillan notes that Oswald connects with Walker with fascism already in October 1962 (Macmillan at pp. 298, 320). The Hitler-Walker connection is more explicit in Oswald's conversations of February 1963 (McMillan at pp. 318–321). See also Marina Oswald's testimony to the Warren Commission that Lee didn't like the United States because of its fascist organizations. 1 WCH 22 (Marina Oswald testimony).

26. Condensed from Mailer's citation of Hitler in *Oswald's Tale: An American Mystery* (1995) at p. 457.

27. Newman at p. 17.

28. "Text of Kennedy's Address on Moves to Meet the Soviet Build-Up in Cuba." *New York Times,* October 23, 1962, page 18. https://timesmachine.nytimes.com/timesmachine/1962/10/23/90541679.html?pageNumber=18.

29. "Text of Kennedy's Address on Moves to Meet the Soviet Build-Up in Cuba." *New York Times,* October 23, 1962, p. 18. https://timesmachine.nytimes.com/timesmachine/1962/10/23/90541679.html?pageNumber=18.

30. "Text of Kennedy's Address on Moves to Meet the Soviet Build-Up in Cuba." *New York Times,* October 23, 1962, p. 18. https://timesmachine.nytimes.com/timesmachine/1962/10/23/90541679.html?pageNumber=18.

31. 21 WCH 622–632 (Stuckey Exhibit No. 2).

32. "Cuba Girds for Invasion." *Dallas Morning News,* October 28, 1962: 18. *NewsBank: America's News—Historical and Current.* https://infoweb.newsbank.com/apps/news/document-view?p=AMNEWS&docref=image/v2%3A0F99DDB671832188%40EANX-1001128A444D78BB%402437966-1001128A81F28ECC%4017-1001128D038A3C4D.

33. "Crisis Builds Gun Demand." *Dallas Morning News,* October 28, 1962: 15. *NewsBank: America's News—Historical and Current.* https://infoweb.newsbank.com/apps/news/document-view?p=AMNEWS&docref=image/v2%3A0F99DDB671832188%40EANX-1001128A444D78BB%402437966-1001128A73EABBB7%4014-1001128CE03EBB2C.

34. McMillan at p. 256.

35. "Cuban Crisis: A Step-by-Step Review." *New York Times,* November 3, 1962, pp.1, 6, 7. https://timesmachine.nytimes.com/timesmachine/1962/11/03/90584910.html?pageNumber=6.

36. McMillan at p. 256.

37. "2,000 Here Protest Blockade of Cuba." *New York Times,* October 28, 1962, page 32. https://timesmachine.nytimes.com/timesmachine/1962/10/28/89883811.html?pageNumber=32.

38. Polaris submarines stationed in the Mediterranean and armed with nuclear missiles were considered more formidable, less vulnerable to attack, and exposed Turkey to less danger. Robert Kennedy, *Thirteen Days* (1969) (posthumously) at p. 71.

39. R. Kennedy at pp. 81–83.

40. Thomas Blanton, "Annals of Brinksmanship," *The Wilson Quarterly* (Summer, 1997); Andreas Parsch, "Jupiter, Historical Essay," www.astronautix.com/IVS/Jupiter.htm.

41. Jack Raymond. "Patrols Maintain Blockade Of Cuba." *New York Times,* October 29, 1962,

p. 1. https://timesmachine.nytimes.com/timesmachine/1962/10/29/90567543.html?pageNumber=1.

42. E. W. Kenworthy. "Capitol Hopeful. Plans to End Blockade as Moscow Lives Up to Vow." *New York Times*, November 1, 1962, pp. 1, 16. https://timesmachine.nytimes.com/timesmachine/1962/10/29/90567536.html?pageNumber=1.

43. "Cuban Head Firm." *New York Times*, November 2, 1962, pp. 1, 14. https://timesmachine.nytimes.com/timesmachine/1962/11/02/81797745.html?pageNumber=1.

44. A. Walter Dorn & Robert Pauk, *Unsung Mediator: U Thant and the Cuban Missile Crisis* in Diplomatic History, Vol. 30 (April 2009) pp. 261–292. https://walterdorn.net/pub/144-unsung-mediator-u-thant-cuban-missile-crisis-abstract.

45. Newman at pp. 270–271; 19 WCH at p. 576 (Dobbs Exhibit 9).

46. Bugliosi at p. 645.

47. 19 WCH 578 (Dobbs Exhibit No. 11).

48. 19 WCH 578 (Dobbs Exhibit No. 11).

Chapter 21

1. McMillan at p. 257.
2. McMillan at p. 258
3. McMillan at p. 258.
4. McMillan at p. 258.
5. McMillan at p. 259.
6. McMillan at p. 259.
7. McMillan at p. 284 (1977 edition).
8. Bugliosi at p. 662.
9. The Warren Commission's recitation of events and Marina's recollection differ. The Commission said that Robert Oswald wrote a Thanksgiving invitation to Lee on November 17. WCR at p.721. Marina recalled to Priscilla Johnson McMillan that Lee already had the invitation by the time of the de Mohrenschildts' reconciliation effort. McMillan at p. 281.
10. WCR at p. 721.
11. McMillan at p. 284 (1977 edition).
12. Bugliosi at p. 662.
13. McMillan at p. 281.
14. 18 WCH 623, CE 993 and 994.
15. Newman at pp. 294–295; cf. 1 WCH at pp. 34–35 (Testimony of Marina Oswald).
16. Marina and Lee continued to be curiosities for those who were aware of them, and they were invited to a few social events. However, efforts by the Russian émigré community to be helpful were limited to the de Mohrenschildts and Anna Meller.
17. McMillan at pp. 285–286.
18. 18 WCH 625, CE 993.
19. McMillan at pp. 306–308.
20. 21 WCH 681 (Twiford Exhibit 1). For a discussion of the significance of this inquiry on Oswald's thought process, see Newman at pp. 279–280.
21. Newman (1970) at p. 281; 20 WCH at p. 269 (Johnson Exhibit 5-A).
22. 19 WCH at p. 579 (Dobbs Exhibit No. 12).
23. 19 WCH at p. 565 (Dobbs Exhibit No. 1). When this exhibit was identified for the record by the testimony of Farrell Dobbs, the court reporter mistakenly typed his testimony as stating that the subscription was dated September 17, 1962. The court reporter, moreover, typed other dates that do not correspond to the exhibits which were being identified. See, 10 WCH at pp. 109–110 (Farrell Dobbs testimony).
24. 11 WCH at pp. 128–129 (Alexandra Taylor aka. Mrs. Donald Gibson testimony).
25. 11 WCH at pp. 97–98 (Kerry Wendell Thornley testimony); Bugliosi at p. 939.
26. Bugliosi at p. 667; McMillan at p. 302; 9 WCH at pp. 245–246 (George de Mohrenschildt testimony); 9 WCH at pp. 319–320 (Jeanne de Mohrenschildt testimony).
27. HSCA, Vol. XII, p. 172 (Appendix to unpublished manuscript by George de Mohrenschildt); see also, 9 WCH at pp. 245–246 (George de Mohrenschildt testimony); Mailer at p. 479.
28. McMillan at p. 304.
29. https://en.wikipedia.org/wiki/James_P._Cannon.
30. Bugliosi at pp. 666–667 (footnote). Bugliosi erroneously lists Mr. Cannon as James B. Cannon.
31. McMillan at p. 305.
32. "Riot Charges Against Walker and 6 Others Dropped by U.S." *New York Times*, January 22, 1963, p. 1. https://timesmachine.nytimes.com/timesmachine/1963/01/22/89514837.html?pageNumber=1.
33. "Riot Charges Against Walker and 6 Others Dropped by U.S." *New York Times*, January 22, 1963, pp. 1, 5. https://timesmachine.nytimes.com/timesmachine/1963/01/22/89514837.html?pageNumber=1; and "Civil Rights Gain Seen Even If Meredith Quits," *New York Times*, January 22, 1963, p. 5. https://timesmachine.nytimes.com/timesmachine/1963/01/22/89514868.html?pageNumber=5.
34. "Judge Dismisses Walker Charges." *Dallas Morning News*, January 22, 1963: 1. *NewsBank: America's News—Historical and Current.* https://infoweb.newsbank.com/apps/news/document-view?p=AMNEWS&docref=image/v2%3A0F99DDB671832188%40EANX-0FF7D1E8D2385B7E%402438052-0FF7D1E8DE73BB56%400-0FF7D1E9DA66440F.
35. http://en.wikipedia.org/wiki/Billy_James_Hargis.
36. https://en.wikipedia.org/wiki/The_American_Mercury. The once popular *American Mercury* had declined from a 1959 circulation of over 60,000 copies; Singleton at p. 241.
37. James H. Redekop, *The American Far Right: Billy James Hargis and the Christian Crusade* (1968) at p. 22.
38. McMillan at p. 320.
39. See generally, Caufield at pp. 374–417; Redekop at p. 33.
40. WCR at p. 723. Total cost $19.95 due on delivery. Total expense $31.22. Shipment made

on March 20, 1963. VII WCH at p. 376 (Heinz W. Michaelis testimony); Michaelis Exhibit No. 2, XX; WCH at p. 616. Final payment made in March. WCR p. 743.

41. McMillan at p. 319.

Chapter 22

1. McMillan at p. 311.
2. Russo (1998) at p. 118; McMillan at pp. 318–320; Epstein (1978) at pp. 203–205.
3. Russo (1998) at p. 118.
4. Russo (1998) at p. 119.
5. Russo (1998) at p. 120.
6. Russo (1998) at pp. 124–126.
7. McMillan at p. 315.
8. McMillan at pp. 317–318, 324–327.
9. McMillan at p. 322.
10. 18 WCH at p. 501 (CE 986).
11. 1 WCH at p. 35 (Marina Oswald testimony).
12. WCR at p. 722.
13. 10 WCH at p. 25. (Everett Glover testimony). Present were George and Jeanne de Mohrenschildt, Norman and Elke Fredericksen, Michael and Ruth Paine, Richard Pierce, and Betty McDonald. Epstein (1978) at p. 206.
14. 10 WCH at pp. 25–27. (Everett Glover testimony).
15. 10 WCH at p. 28.
16. Mallon at p. 26.
17. 2 WCH at pp. 434–437 (Ruth Paine testimony); Mallon at pp. 26–27.
18. WCR at p. 723.
19. McMillan (1977) at pp. 325–327.
20. McMillan at p. 325; Allen Duckworth. "Walker Preparing for Crusade." *Dallas Morning News*, February 17, 1963: 16. *NewsBank: America's News—Historical and Current*. https://infoweb.newsbank.com/apps/news/document-view?p=AMNEWS&docref=image/v2%3A0F99DDB671832188%40EANX-0FF7D2888519003C%402438078-0FF7D288C5AA7EF6%4015-0FF7D28B5264A903%40Walker%2BPreparing%2Bfor%2BCrusade.
21. McMillan at p. 325.
22. McMillan at pp. 327–329.
23. Bugliosi at p. 679.
24. Bugliosi at p. 679; McMillan at p. 328 (location of apartment).
25. Vincent Bugliosi viewed and measured the room 40 years later. It was 3'9" by 4'5".
26. McMillan at p. 330.
27. McMillan at p. 336.
28. 16 WCH at p. 485 (CE 114).
29. WCR at p. 119.
30. McMillan at p. 335.
31. McMillan at p. 331.
32. McMillan at p. 337.
33. 7 WCH at p. 365 (William Waldman testimony); 7 WCH at pp. 376–377 (Heinz Michaelis testimony).
34. McMillan at pp. 334–335.
35. 22 WCH at pp. 447–448; CE 1404 (FBI interview of Marina Oswald, February 22, 1964).
36. 1 WCH at p. 15; 5 WCH at pp. 397–398 (Marina Oswald testimony).
37. 19 WCH at p. 580 (Dobbs Exhibit 13); 10 WCH at pp. 114–115 (Farrell Dobbs testimony).
38. Newman at pp. 323–324.
39. McMillan at p. 331.
40. See Leon Trotsky, "For a Workers' United Front Against Fascism" (1932) and "The German Catastrophe" (1933) in Irving Howe, *The Basic Writings of Trotsky* (1963) at pp. 245–266.
41. Quoted in Irving Howe, *The Basic Writings of Trotsky* (1976 edition) at p. 247.
42. "The Picket Line—Defense Guards/Workers' Militia and the Arming of the Proletariat," Leon Trotsky, *Death and Agony of Capitalism and the Task of the Fourth International* (1938) as published online at http://www.marxists.org/archive/trotsky/1938/tp/tp—text.htm.
43. Leon Trotsky, "On Terrorism" (1911) in *Marxism and Terrorism* at pp. 10–11.
44. Leon Trotsky, "For Grinszpan: Against the Fascist Pogrom Gangs and Stalinist Scoundrels," (1939) in *Marxism and Terrorism* at pp. 28 and 30.
45. Newman at pp. 327–328; Bugliosi at p. 684; see CE 1409, 22 WCH at p. 796. Researcher Paul Hoke has checked the location where Oswald was handing out literature and believes it was about a seven minute walk from Jaggars-Chiles-Stoval. Email to author from Hoch, January 19, 2018.
46. The date of the letter is arrived at through a combination of inferences drawn from the text of the letter.
47. McMillan at p. 338.
48. McMillan at pp. 338–339.
49. McMillan is probably correct that *The Militant* published a letter from Oswald, and that this helped motivate the photographs. Parts of the letter may not be from Oswald and may have been re-written by the editors. This issue of *The Militant* is available online at: https://themilitant.com/1963/2710/MIL2710.pdf.
50. McMillan at p. 339. Conspiracy theorists have disputed the photograph's fidelity. Based on Oswald's denial during police interrogation that the photo was genuine, conspiracy theorists have asserted that the shadows in the pictures and the canting of Oswald's head show that his head has been taken from another photograph and transposed on a body in the photo which was not his. But, after the Warren Report was issued, various forensic photographic experts examined the photos available to the Warren Commission, compared them to photos taken at the same time and date in a re-enactment years later, and conducted electronic tests on them. Their conclusions, concurred in by the HSCA in 1979, was that the photographs had not been altered. HSCA Report at pp 54–56; Posner at pp. 107–109. For information concerning possession of the photographs after they were taken, how they came to be found, and how

they were utilized in the police investigation, see Bugliosi at pp. 179, 225, 234–238.

51. 2 HSCA at p. 247 (JFK Exhibit F-383). The photo bears the inscription "5/IV/63," the common way of writing April 5, 1963, in the U.S. military and many parts of the world, including Russia. Author Patricia Johnson McMillan incorrectly believed that the notation should be interpreted as May 4, 1963. McMillan (1977) at p. 360. McMillan concluded from talking with Marina that Jeanne de Mohrenschildt saw the rifle in the Oswald apartment on April 4 or 5. McMillan, at p. 347. Author Norman Mailer believed that Jeanne de Mohrenschildt visited the Oswald apartment on April 5. Mailer at p. 520. If McMillan and Mailer are correct, it is entirely possible that Marina handed Jeanne the photograph that Lee hand inscribed. It is even possible that the writing "Hunter of the Fascists—ha—ha—ha" was Jeanne's, although Marina believed it might be her own. Posner at p. 1 (footnote).

52. Also written in Russian on it in an undetermined handwriting were the words "Hunter for the Fascists—ha-ha-ha!!!" Neither Marina, George de Mohrenschildt, nor Jeanne de Mohrenschildt admits to having made the notation; but it would seem that one of the three must have done so. If one of the de Mohrenschildts did so, it would be understandable that they would deny it since such a notation would contradict their claim that they did not discover the photo until after the Warren Commission concluded its work.

53. McMillan at pp. 339, 361.

54. 23 WCH at p. 408 (CE 1792).

55. Russo (1998) at p. 117 (interview of Sylvia Weinstein by Russo on June 12, 1993).

56. Russo (1998) at p. 117.

57. Russo (1998) at p. 117 fn15; see p.537 fn15. Dobbs denied to the Warren Commission that the Socialist Workers Party had received the photograph. 11 WCH at p. 209 (Farrell Dobbs affidavit, June 4, 1964). We do not know exactly when Dobbs gave the photo and other Oswald records to his lawyer. The thoughtful reader must ask why Weinstein would not have told the Warren Commission in 1964 what she said to Russo thirty years later and why Dobbs might have lied to the Commission about the photo in 1964. Were both fearful in 1964 of the McCarthyism of the era and that Dobbs and others might be unjustly prosecuted? Did Weinstein not want to be a witness in 1964 in a possible case against her political allies but was willing to talk to Russo decades later when times had changed and when Dobbs (7/25/1909–10/31/1983) and other political friends of the 1960s were dead?

Chapter 23

1. McMillan at p. 347.

2. 10 WCH at p. 203 (Dennis Hyman Ofstein testimony).

3. WCR at p. 723; 1 WCH at p. 9 (Marina Oswald testimony); 26 WCH at p. 73 (CE 2699).

4. McMillan at p. 344 (1977 edition).

5. In 1993, Michael also recalled to Gus Russo that when meeting Lee at the Oswald apartment on April 2, 1963, Lee had shown him the photo Marina had taken with him holding a rifle and carrying a pistol. Gus Russo, *Live by the Sword: The Secret War Against Castro and the Death of JFK* (1998) at pp. 116–17. Michael Paine did not testify to the Warren Commission about seeing this remarkable photograph at any time. He also did not tell his wife, Ruth, about it. Author Thomas Mallon has discussed this delayed recollection with both Michael and Ruth. Both Mallon and Ruth believed Michael was truthful despite his delayed recollection. Thomas Mallon, *Mrs. Paine's Garage and the Murder of John F. Kennedy* (2002) at pp. 174–187. Email communication with author from Ruth Paine. November 4, 2019.

6. Mallon (2002) at pp. 28–29.

7. McMillan at pp. 379.

8. 17 WCH 140 (CE 442).

9. 1 WCH 17 (Marina Oswald testimony).

10. McMillan at p. 348 and note no. 18.

11. Allen Duckworth. "Conservatives Organize, Expand, Consolidate." *Dallas Morning News*, April 8, 1963: 12. *NewsBank: America's News—Historical and Current*. https://infoweb.newsbank.com/apps/news/document-view?p=AMNEWS&docref=image/v2%3A0F99DDB671832188%40EANX-0FF7D43C807800D9%402438128-0FF7D43CA474B74A%4011-0FF7D43DE42735DE.

12. McMillan at p. 349.

13. Bugliosi at p. 690; McMillan at p. 349.

14. "Weather Facts and Figures." *Dallas Morning News*, April 11, 1963: 4. *NewsBank: America's News—Historical and Current*. https://infoweb.newsbank.com/apps/news/document-view?p=AMNEWS&docref=image/v2%3A0F99DDB671832188%40EANX-0FF7D3D435E0DAFC%402438131-0FF7D3D4CFD0D884%4045-0FF7D3D9687623B1.

15. 18 WCH at p. 655 (CE 1005) (Sketch of streets and building near Walker house).

16. 18 WCH at p. 658 (CE 1011) (Photo of fence behind Walker property); 11 WCH at p. 409 (Edwin Walker testimony).

17. 18 WCH at p. 655 (CE 1005) (Sketch of streets and building near Walker house).

18. 11 WCH at p. 405 (Edwin Walker testimony).

19. 11 WCH at pp. 405–406 (Edwin Walker testimony).

20. Bugliosi at p. 692.

21. Eddie Hughes. "Rifleman Takes Shot at Walker." *Dallas Morning News*, April 11, 1963: 1. *NewsBank: America's News—Historical and Current*. https://infoweb.newsbank.com/apps/news/document-view?p=AMNEWS&docref=image/v2%3A0F99DDB671832188%40EANX-0FF7D3D435E0DAFC%402438131-0FF7D3D443875FD5%400-0FF7D3D577D77E42.

22. McMillan at p. 348 and chapter note no. 18.

23. Newman at p. 142 (map of shooting location relative to Walker's house, church, streets, and alleys).

24. See 18 WCH at pp. 648–661 (CE 997–1014) (photos and diagrams relative to shooting site, Walker house, and vantage points of witnesses).

25. 1 WCH 17 (Marina Oswald testimony).

26. That is also Vincent Bugliosi's conclusion from her testimony. Bugliosi at p. 693.

27. McMillan at p. 354.

28. Bugliosi at p. 693; McMillan at pp. 354–355; 1 WCH at pp. 16–19 (Marina Oswald testimony); 22 WCH 756 (CE 1401).

29. McMillan at p. 350.

30. Translation is from McMillan at pp. 350–351 which is presumably Marina's translation since it differs slightly from that in the Warren Commission Report. CE 1, XVI WCH 1–2.

31. Newman at pp. 333 and 337.

32. Newman at p. 337.

33. McMillan, at pp. 352–353.

34. 18 WCH at p. 628 (CE 994) (Translation of Marina Oswald's memo to FBI).

35. McMillan at p. 355.

36. 36 McMillan at p. 355.

37. McMillan at p. 355.

38. McMillan at pp. 354–355.

39. McMillan at p. 354. Author Gus Russo said that FBI Agent James Hosty reported that George de Mohrenschildt claimed that he had told Oswald that if someone had killed Hitler in the 1930s, World War II might not have happened. Russo (1998) at p. 124.

40. McMillan at pp. 356–357.

41. WCR at p. 23.

42. McMillan at p. 372.

43. McMillan at p. 357.

44. 11 WCH at p. 293; McMillan at p. 358 (1977 edition). The date that Lee retrieved the rifle is in dispute. Marina told the Warren Commission it was the same day that Lee burned the papers, Saturday, April 13. Thirteen years later, she told Priscilla Johnson McMillan that it was Easter Sunday. McMillan at 363. The earlier testimony seems more reliable.

45. McMillan at 356.

46. 1 WCH at pp. 17–18 (Marina Oswald testimony).

47. McMillan at p. 357.

48. McMillan at 358.

49. McMillan at 358–359; HSCA at p. 56.

50. McMillan at 358.

51. McMillan at 364.

52. 5 WCH at pp. 387–388, 392 (Marina Oswald testimony).

53. "Nixon Calls for Decision to Force Reds Out of Cuba." *Dallas Morning News*, April 21, 1963: 1. *NewsBank: America's News—Historical and Current.* https://infoweb.newsbank.com/apps/news/document-view?p=AMNEWS&docref=image/v2%3A0F99DDB671832188%40EANX-0FF7D15BCECB8589%402438141-0FF7D15BDAB073D8%400-0FF7D15E1C5D75C0. For a detailed discussion of the possible significance of the *Dallas Morning News* article, see Vincent Bugliosi, *Reclaiming History: The Assassination of President John F. Kennedy* (2007) at 697–699.

54. Email, Richard Reiman to author, February 19, 2020.

55. WCR at p. 188.

56. 5 WCH at p. 389.

57. 18 WCH at p. 629 (CE 994); McMillan at pp. 365–366; 2 WCH at p. 458 (Ruth Paine testimony).

58. 2 WCH at p. 463 (Ruth Paine testimony).

59. WCR at p. 725; Bugliosi at p. 699; McMillan at p. 379.

Chapter 24

1. Posner at p. 123.

2. 2 8 WCH at p. 133 (Lillian Murret testimony).

3. 8 WCH.at pp. 106–107 (Lillian Murret testimony).

4. 8 WCH at pp. 106, 122, 136 (Lillian Murret testimony).

5. McMillan at p. 383; Bugliosi at p. 700–701 (referencing Warren Commission testimony).

6. WCR at p. 725.

7. WCR at p. 725; 8 WCH at pp. 135–136 (Lillian Murret testimony); 8 WCH 165–166 (Marilyn Murret testimony); 23 WCH at pp. 717–718 (CE 1919) (Hazal Oswald interview); Bugliosi at p. 701.

8. Bugliosi at p. 701.

9. Numerous other Oswald relatives were in New Orleans. Bugliosi at p. 701 footnote.

10. Bugliosi at p. 701 (referencing Warren Commission testimony).

Chapter 25

1. Foster Hailey. "Truce Bid Pushed at Birmingham. Dr. King Confident." *New York Times*, May 6, 1963, p. 59. https://timesmachine.nytimes.com/timesmachine/1963/05/06/86705834.html?pageNumber=59.

2. Foster Hailey. "Negroes Defying Birmingham Writ." *New York Times*, April 12, 1963, page 1. https://timesmachine.nytimes.com/timesmachine/1963/04/12/90561719.html?pageNumber=1.

3. "Bombing Is 21st at Birmingham." *New York Times*, September 16, 1963, page 26. https://timesmachine.nytimes.com/timesmachine/1963/09/16/461053162.html?pageNumber=26.

4. Martin Luther King, Jr., *Letter from the Birmingham Jail* [Foreword by Bernice R. King] (HarperCollins Publishers 1994) at pp. 4–5.

5. Martin Luther King, Jr., *Letter from the Birmingham Jail* [Foreword by Bernice R. King] (HarperCollins Publishers 1994) at p. 7.

6. Martin Luther King, Jr., *Letter from the Birmingham Jail* [Foreword by Bernice R. King] (HarperCollins Publishers 1994) at p. 8.

7. Martin Luther King, Jr., *Letter from the Birmingham Jail* [Foreword by Bernice R. King] (HarperCollins Publishers 1994) at p. 30.

8. https//www.npr.org/2013/08/14/2117895/a-postmans-1963-walk-for-justice-cut-short-on-an-alabama-road; Mary Stanton, *Freedom Walk: Mississippi or Bust* (2003). A copy of Moore's letter is attached to the internet site. It is signed William L., not William A., Moore. See Wikipedia, William Lewis Moore.

9. Foster Hailey. "Dogs and Hoses Repulse Negroes at Birmingham." *New York Times*, May 4, 1963, pp. 1, 8. https://timesmachine.nytimes.com/timesmachine/1963/05/04/81808290.html?pageNumber=1; Don M'Kee. "5 Negroes, 2 Officers Hurt." *New Orleans Time-Picayune*, May 4, 1963, Section 1, p. 16. https://nola.newsbank.com/doc/image/v2:1223BCE5B718A166@NGPA-NOLA-12D87ABBE672309C@2438154-12D61A4EF5E662DC@15?pdate=1963-05-04.

10. "Pleas by Negro Leaders Halt Mixing March." *New Orleans Times Picayune*, May 5, 1963, pp. 1, 27. https://nola.newsbank.com/doc/image/v2:1223BCE5B718A166@NGPA-NOLA-12D87AD3D63C5E4F@2438155-12D8708FAF62CA18@0?pdate=1963-05-05.

11. Don M'Kee. "Truce Retained in Birmingham." *The Times-Picayune*, May 9, 1963, Section 1, pp. 1, 2. https://nola.newsbank.com/doc/image/v2:1223BCE5B718A166@NGPA-NOLA-12D87AE25014EF49@2438159-12D8737319E4F950@0?pdate=1963-05-09.

12. Claude Sitton. "Birmingham Talks Reach an Accord on Ending Crisis." *New York Times*, May 10, 1963, p. 1. https://timesmachine.nytimes.com/timesmachine/1963/05/10/82066657.html?pageNumber=1.

Chapter 26

1. WCR at p. 726; Bugliosi at p. 702.
2. Bugliosi at p. 703.
3. Posner at p. 126.
4. 1 WCH at p. 44 (Marina Oswald testimony).
5. See Judyth Vary Baker, *Lee Harvey Oswald, the Reader: Oswald's Reading Habits in New Orleans, and Evidence Manipulation*, http://lee-harvey-oswald.com/images/lee_harvey_oswald_and_His_Reading_Habits_in_New_Orleans.pdf.
6. Robert Payne, *Portrait of a Revolutionary: Mao Tse Tung* (1961); Holloway, Diane, *The Mind of Oswald* (2000) at p. 147.
7. Robert Trumbull. "Chinese Red Chief Casts Doubt on Soviet Parley." *New York Times*, May 17, 1963, Section 1. p. 1. https://timesmachine.nytimes.com/timesmachine/1963/05/17/90560130.html?pageNumber=1.
8. Seymour Topping. "Suslov Will Head Russian Team in Ideological Talk with Chinese." *New York Times*, May 16, 1963, Section 1, p. 1. https://timesmachine.nytimes.com/timesmachine/1963/05/16/84796070.html?pageNumber=1.
9. Robert Payne at p. 1.
10. McMillan at p. 400.
11. 18 WCH at pp. 631–632 (CE 994).
12. Holloway (2000) at p. 148.
13. Also in 1963, journalist David Zinman resurrected the Huey Long assassination in a book entitled *The Day Huey Long Was Shot*. Zinman raised questions as to whether the alleged assassin, Dr. Carl Weiss, had done more than punch Long and that Long had actually been killed accidentally by a stray bullet from Long's bodyguards in the act of killing Weiss. Hermann Deutsch's book, *The Huey Long Murder Case*, which Oswald acquired, took the position that Weiss was the assassin. See also "Controversy, mystery still surround the death of Huey P. Long," by Robert Travis Smith, *New Orleans Times-Picayune*; https://www.nola.com/news/politics/article_1f01fd4b-424d-55d6-95cc-b3782e81da79.html.

Chapter 27

1. "Walker, Hargis to Include N.O. *The Times-Picayune*, May 2, 1963, Section 1, p. 11. https://nola.newsbank.com/doc/image/v2:1223BCE5B718A166@NGPA-NOLA-12D87AB502933B89@2438152-12D86CB55584B00F@10?pdate=1963-05-02.
2. "JFK, Ike, Rocke Walker Target." *The Times-Picayune*, May 28, 1963, Section 1, p. 2. https://nola.newsbank.com/doc/image/v2:1223BCE5B718A166@NGPA-NOLA-12D81A0E5698B2A2@2438178-12D61B4D70FDD307@1?pdate=1963-05-28.
3. Don M'Kee. "Ban on Wallace Will Be Fought." *The Times-Picayune*, June 2, 1963, p. 2. https://nola.newsbank.com/doc/image/v2:1223BCE5B718A166@NGPA-NOLA-12D7D73D23A684B8@2438183-12D61C9A5DA0C549@1?pdate=1963-06-02.
4. Relman Marin. "U.S. Court Forbids Wallace to Act." *The Times-Picayune*, June 6, 1963, Section 1, p. 1. https://nola.newsbank.com/doc/image/v2:1223BCE5B718A166@NGPA-NOLA-12D7D73F602CCEE0@2438187-12D7D267C5347381@0?pdate=1963-06-06.
5. Rex Thomas. "500 Guardsmen Will Be Called, Wallace Says." *The Times-Picayune*, June 9, 1963, Section 1. p. 1. https://nola.newsbank.com/doc/image/v2:1223BCE5B718A166@NGPA-NOLA-12D7D740F97D2E9D@2438190-12D7D34B1E05D2C3@0?pdate=1963-06-09.
6. Douglas B. Cornell. "Back Rights Goals, JFK Urges Mayors." *The Times-Picayune*, June 10, 1963, Section 1, pp. 1, 20. https://nola.newsbank.com/doc/image/v2:1223BCE5B718A166@NGPA-NOLA-12D7D74183DA65CF@2438191-12D7D5A28B0A37B5@0?pdate=1963-06-10.
7. Rex Thomas. "Kennedy Message Futile; Wallace Flies to Ala. U." *The Times-Picayune*, June 11, 1963, Section 1. p. 1. https://nola.newsbank.com/doc/image/v2:1223BCE5B718A166@NGPA-NOLA-12D7D741E7F4B221@2438192-12D7D5E05ED1924F@0?pdate=1963-06-11.
8. Rex Thomas. "Alabama Segregation Barrier

Is Overcome." *The Times-Picayune*, June 12, 1963, Section 1, pp. 1, 3, 27. https://nola.newsbank.com/doc/image/v2:1223BCE5B718A166@NGPA-NOLA-12D7D7425AC06C4C@2438193-12D7D60AF816AED2@0?pdate=1963-06-12. Stanley Meisler. "JFK Order Federalizes Guard." *The Times-Picayune*, June 12, 1963, Section 1, p. 4. https://nola.newsbank.com/doc/image/v2:1223BCE5B718A166@NGPA-NOLA-12D7D7425AC06C4C@2438193-12D61C9CC08997AC@3?pdate=1963-06-12.

9. Rex Thomas. "Alabama Segregation Barrier Is Overcome." *The Times-Picayune*, June 12, 1963, Section 1, pp. 1, 3, 27. https://nola.newsbank.com/doc/image/v2:1223BCE5B718A166@NGPA-NOLA-12D7D7425AC06C4C@2438193-12D7D61E0DFEA065@26?pdate=1963-06-12.

10. Claude Sitton. "Governor Leaves." *The New York Times*, June 12, 1963, page 1. https://timesmachine.nytimes.com/timesmachine/1963/06/12/80448099.html?pageNumber=1.

11. "Integration Hit by Church Body." *The Times-Picayune*, June 21, 1963, Section 4, p. 10. https://nola.newsbank.com/doc/image/v2:1223BCE5B718A166@NGPA-NOLA-12D8203057F41E8A@2438202-12D61C9F17E1A0AC@57?pdate=1963-06-21.

12. Stanley Meisler. "Killing Stirs Shock Wave." *The Times-Picayune*, June 13, 1963, Section 1, p. 1. https://nola.newsbank.com/doc/image/v2:1223BCE5B718A166@NGPA-NOLA-12D7D742CF409AAD@2438194-12D7D63BC0A55F16@0?pdate=1963-06-13. Carroll Kilpatrick, "President Calls Others to Talk on Racial Crisis," *The Washington Post-Times Herald*, June 13, 1963, at pp. 1, 9.

Chapter 28

1. 20 WCH at pp. 512–513, Lee (Vincent T.) Exhibit No. 2.

2. 20 WCH at pp. 514–516, Lee (Vincent T.) Exhibit No. 3.

3. McMillan at p. 399; Posner at p. 128.

4. 20 WCH at pp. 522–523 (V.T. Lee Exhibit No. 4); 10 WCH at pp. 89–90 (Testimony of V. T. Lee).

5. Later literature used the address 544 Camp Street, the address of the headquarters of the anti–Castro Cuban Revolutionary Council. Sergio Arachas Smith, Director of the Cuban Revolutionary Council, told author Gus Russo that he believed Oswald used that address in order to embarrass the Council. (Email, April 3, 2019, from Russo to this author.) Inquiries or applications for the Fair Play for Cuba Committee would be received at the Council's office and would demonstrate to anti–Castro organizers that support for Castro existed in New Orleans. 544 Camp Street was a block from Oswald's employment at the Reily Coffee company, close enough for Oswald to become aware of the Council's location. If, in fact, Oswald were to establish a Fair Play for Cuba Committee office at that location, it would have posed a sure opportunity for conflict—a source for publicity in building a resume for Castro.

6. 10 WCH at pp. 89–90 (Testimony of V. T. Lee).

7. 22 WCH at pp. 800–802 (CE 1411).

8. John Heindell, who was in the Marine Corps with Oswald, was nicknamed Hidell by their fellow Marines. Heindell suggested that Oswald may have used the "Hidell" name because of that association. VIII WCH p. 318 (John Rene Heindell affidavit).

9. 5 WCH at p. 401 (Marina Oswald testimony).

10. 1 WCH at p. 47 (Marina Oswald testimony).

11. 10 WCH at p. 55 (Frances L. Martello testimony); 26 WCH at p. 791 (Interview of Dr. Leonard Reissman) (CE 3128).

12. McMillan at p. 406.

13. Oswald's other biographers have agreed that his primary objective in New Orleans was to build a resume to impress Cuban officials. See Epstein, *Legend* (1978) at p. 218; Norman Mailer, *Oswald's Tale: An American Mystery* (1995), p. 554; Vincent Bugliosi, *Reclaiming History: The Assassination of President John F. Kennedy* (2007) p. 709.

14. 20 WCH at pp. 257–258 (Johnson (Arnold) Exhibit No. 1).

15. 20 WCH at p. 260. (Johnson (Arnold) Exhibit No. 2).

16. McMillan at p. 407. McMillan mistakenly states that the informational literature for the Fair Play for Cuba Committee distributed by Oswald in New Orleans contained those names and addresses, but Warren Commission documents do not support that.

17. "5 Navy Ships Will Visit Here." *The Times-Picayune*, June 6, 1963, Section 3, p. 10. https://nola.newsbank.com/doc/image/v2:1223BCE5B718A166@NGPA-NOLA-12D7D73F602CCEE0@2438187-12D61C9B72EC9A5D@67-12D61C9B72EC9A5D@?search_terms

18. "Wasp Gets New Skipper Today." *The Times-Picayune*, June 19, 1963, p. 16. https://nola.newsbank.com/doc/image/v2:1223BCE5B718A166@NGPA-NOLA-12D8202F42B3CB22@2438200-12D61C9EB4C2798A@14?pdate=1963-06-19; "New Command on Board Wasp." *The Times-Picayune*, June 20, 1963, p. 7. https://nola.newsbank.com/doc/image/v2:1223BCE5B718A166@NGPA-NOLA-12D8202FCC5EFE11@2438201-12D81DA9061BD707@6?pdate=1963-06-20.

19. Podine Schoenberger. "Aircraft Carrier Wasp Ties to Dumaine Wharf." *The Times-Picayune*, June 14, 1963, Section 3, p. 15. https://nola.newsbank.com/doc/image/v2:1223BCE5B718A166@NGPA-NOLA-12D7D7435759ACC6@2438195-12D7D6D88FACC76B@48?pdate=1963-06-14.

20. 22 WCH at p. 807 (CE 1412).

21. 22 WCH, 808 (CE 1412).

22. On August 1, 1963, he penned a letter to the Fair Play for Cuba Committee in New York mentioning for the first time the Dumaine Street incident. 20 WCH at pp. 524–525 (V. T. Lee Exhibit No. 5).

23. McMillan at p. 415.
24. 17 WCH at pp. 666–667 (CE 781); McMillan at p. 415; Bugliosi at p. 712.
25. McMillan at pp. 415–416.
26. McMillan at p. 417.
27. 18 WCH 526 (CE 986).
28. McMillan at p. 400.

Chapter 29

1. Others in this diverse group were John F. Kennedy, *Profiles in Courage* (1954); Alexander Werth, *Russia Under Khrushchev* (1962); George B. Cressey, *Soviet Potentials: A Geographic Appraisal* (1962); Alexander Solzhenitsyn, *One Day in the Life of Ivan Denisovitch* (1963); Robert Leckie, *Conflict: The History of the Korean War, 1950–53* (1962); C.S. Forester, *Hornblower and the Hotspur* (1962); Alan Moorehead, *The Blue Nile (1962*); Noel B. Gerson, *The Hittite* (1963); F.R. Cowell, *Everyday Life in Ancient Rome* (1961); Lew Wallace, *Ben-Hur—A Tale of the Christ* (Reprinted, 1961); Pierre Boulle, *The Bridge Over the River Kwai* (1954); Aldous Huxley, *Ape and Essence* (1958); Whit Burnett, ed., *This Is My Philosophy: Twenty of the World's Outstanding Thinkers Reveal the Deepest Meanings They Have Found in Life* (1958).
2. McMillan at p. 425.
3. McMillan at pp. 411.
4. McMillan at pp. 411–412.
5. McMillan at p. 424.
6. Diane Holloway, *The Mind of Oswald* (2000) at p. 154.
7. Holloway (2000) at p. 154.
8. John F. Kennedy, *Profiles in Courage* (1961) (HarperCollins, 2003) at pp. 98–99.
9. 25 WCH at p. 919 (CE 2648) (Invitation for Oswald to speak at Jesuit House).
10. WCR at p. 726. Norman Mailer says that Lee was notified of his discharge on July 17 (Marina's birthday), Mailer at p. 563. If so, it may explain why Lee forgot the birthday when he arrived home on July 17.
11. Posner at p. 130.
12. 10 WCH at pp. 225–226 (Adrian Alba testimony).
13. 10 WCH at p. 216 (Charles Joseph LeBlanc testimony).
14. McMillan at p. 462.
15. 10 WCH at p. 215 (Charles Joseph LeBlanc testimony).
16. George Syvertsen. "Moscow Talks Fail—Red China." *Times-Picayune*, July 13, 1963, Section 1, p. 1. https://nola.newsbank.com/doc/image/v2:1223BCE5B718A166@NGPA-NOLA-12D876FB844AA292@2438224-12D87188A5F75CFA@0?pdate=1963-07-13; Preston Grover. "USSR Blasts China Policy." *The Times-Picayune*, July 14, 1963, Section 1, p. 1. https://nola.newsbank.com/doc/image/v2:1223BCE5B718A166@NGPA-NOLA-12D8771B626E225D@2438225-12D871D0D2946372@0?pdate=1963-07-14; Preston Grover. "Communist Giants on Verge of Split." *The Times-Picayune*, July 15, 1963, Section 1, p. 1. https://nola.newsbank.com/doc/image/v2:1223BCE5B718A166@NGPA-NOLA-12D8771C6253C924@2438226-12D873BBEFC39EF1@0?pdate=1963-07-15.
17. George Syvertsen. "Moscow Talks Fail—Red China." *The Times-Picayune*, July 13, 1963, Section 1, p. 1. https://nola.newsbank.com/doc/image/v2:1223BCE5B718A166@NGPA-NOLA-12D876FB844AA292@2438224-12D87188A5F75CFA@0?pdate=1963-07-13; Preston Grover. "USSR Blasts China Policy." *The Times-Picayune*, July 14, 1963, Section 1, p. 1. https://nola.newsbank.com/doc/image/v2:1223BCE5B718A166@NGPA-NOLA-12D8771B626E225D@2438225-12D871D0D2946372@0?pdate=1963-07-14; Preston Grover. "Communist Giants on Verge of Split." *The Times-Picayune*, July 15, 1963, Section 1, p. 1, See also front-page articles in *The Times-Picayune* on July 16, 17, and 18, 1963.
18. "No Soviet Cuba Pullout, Claim." *The Times-Picayune*, July 1, 1963, Section 1, p. 1. https://nola.newsbank.com/doc/image/v2:1223BCE5B718A166@NGPA-NOLA-12D876766AB6D056@2438212-12D61CA06E3D202D@0?pdate=1963-07-01; "Soviets Rush Cuba Bases on Vast Scale, Is Report." *The Times-Picayune*, July 17, 1963, Section1, p. 1. https://nola.newsbank.com/doc/image/v2:1223BCE5B718A166@NGPA-NOLA-12D885B437542870@2438228-12D87B9F8476DE32@0?pdate=1963-07-17.
19. "Cuba Expropriates the U.S. Embassy." *New York Times*, July 25, 1963, p. 1. https://timesmachine.nytimes.com/timesmachine/1963/07/25/89946832.html?pageNumber=1.
20. See, e.g., "Jackson Police Arrest National Nego Leader." *The Times-Picayune* June 2, 1963, Section 1, p. 1. https://nola.newsbank.com/doc/image/v2:1223BCE5B718A166@NGPA-NOLA-12D7D73D23A684B8@2438183-12D7D114CE616FBD@0?pdate=1963-06-02; Rex Thomas. "Guardsmen Standing by to Keep Down Violence." *The Times-Picayune* June 10, 1963, Section 1, p. 1. https://nola.newsbank.com/doc/image/v2:1223BCE5B718A166@NGPA-NOLA-12D7D74183DA65CF@2438191-12D7D5A28B0A37B5@0?pdate=1963-06-10; Rex Thomas. "Alabama Segregation Barrier Is Overcome." *The Times-Picayune* June 12, 1963, Section 1, p. 1. https://nola.newsbank.com/doc/image/v2:1223BCE5B718A166@NGPA-NOLA-12D7D7425AC06C4C@2438193-12D7D60AF816AED2@0?pdate=1963-06-12; W.F. Minor. "Near Riot Averted After Evers Funeral Services." *The Times-Picayune* June 16, 1963, Section 1, p. 1. https://nola.newsbank.com/doc/image/v2:1223BCE5B718A166@NGPA-NOLA-12D8202DA88F24D5@2438197-12D61C9E1F9429E4@0?pdate 1963-06-16.
21. "Dr. Blake Among 283 Held in Racial Rally in Maryland." *New York Times*, July 5, 1963, p. 1. https://timesmachine.nytimes.com/timesmachine/1963/07/05/89940384.html?pageNumber=1.

22. Leonard Buder. "Racial Sit-In Blocks Main Headquarters of Education Board." *New York Times*, July 6, 1963, p. 1. https://timesmachine.nytimes.com/timesmachine/1963/07/06/82073829.html?pageNumber=1.

23. "Picketing by CORE Stirs Riot in Bronx." *New York Times*, July 7, 1963, p. 1. https://timesmachine.nytimes.com/timesmachine/1963/07/07/107175792.html?pageNumber=1.

24. Ben A. Franklin. "99 Seized in New Demonstration at Segregated Maryland Resort." *New York Times*, July 8, 1963, p. 1. https://timesmachine.nytimes.com/timesmachine/1963/07/08/84988767.html?pageNumber=1.

25. Claude Sitton. "Savannah Police Battle Rioters." *New York Times*, July 11, 1963, p. 1. https://timesmachine.nytimes.com/timesmachine/1963/07/11/89541269.html?pageNumber=1.

26. "Five Whites Shot in Cambridge, Md." *New York Times*, July 12, 1963, p. 1. https://timesmachine.nytimes.com/timesmachine/1963/07/12/82075746.html?pageNumber=1.

27. Hedrick Smith. "Martial Law Is Imposed in Cambridge, Md., Riots." *New York Times*, July 13, 1963, p. 1. https://timesmachine.nytimes.com/timesmachine/1963/07/13/86713064.html?pageNumber=1.

28. E. W. Kenworthy. "Barnett Charges Kennedys Assist Red Racial Plot." *New York Times*, July 13, 1963, p. 1. https://timesmachine.nytimes.com/timesmachine/1963/07/13/86713062.html?pageNumber=1.

29. E. W. Kenworthy. "Wallace Asserts Air Force Offers Aid to Race Riots." *New York Times*, July 16, 1963, p. 1. https://timesmachine.nytimes.com/timesmachine/1963/07/16/82080431.html?pageNumber=1.

30. WCR pp. 726–727, 744–745.

31. Mailer at p. 563.

32. McMillan at p. 422.

33. McMillan at p. 422.

34. McMillan at p. 422.

35. McMillan at p. 423.

36. McMillan at pp. 422–423.

37. Author Priscilla McMillan, based on conversations with Marina, believed that Oswald was "diligent at first" in looking for work. McMillan at p. 426. But he limited his interests to jobs in photography or as a clerk. See 20 WCH at pp. 204–215 (Burcham Exhibit No. 1). He claimed job applications on August 5 and August 9, but we know that on August 5, he attempted to infiltrate the Cuban Student Revolutionary Directorate and on August 9 he was arrested for a confrontation with the local leader of that organization while distributing pro-Castro leaflets.

38. WCR at p. 404.

39. WCR at p. 727; 19 WCH at p. 689 (Folsom Deposition Exhibit No. 1, p. 39).

40. McMillan at p. 449.

41. McMillan at pp. 413–414.

42. WCR at p. 744.

43. 43 McMillan at p. 414.

Chapter 30

1. Chris McFadyen, *Sixties Flashback: Lee Harvey Oswald Visits Spring Hill,* http://mobilebaymag.com/Mobile-Bay/January-2014/Sixties-Flashback-Lee-Harvey-Oswald-Visits-Spring-Hill/.

2. 25 WCH at p. 919 (CE 2648) (Invitation from Eugene Murret to Lee Oswald); 25 WCH at pp. 920–928 (CE 2649) (FBI interviews of Jesuit House attendees at Oswald talk); 8 WCH at pp. 147–148 (Lillian Murret testimony); 8 WCH at pp. 186–187 (Charles Murret testimony).

3. Interview October 9, 2019, by author with Joseph P. Reardon, a fellow student of Murret who met Lee Harvey Oswald at the Spring Hill presentation on July 27, 1963.

4. 25 WCH at pp. 924–928 (CE 2649) (FBI interview with Robert J. Fitzpatrick).

5. 16 WCH p. 433 (CE 9). There is no specific evidence as to when Oswald wrote the document. Author Vincent Bugliosi believed that Oswald wrote "The Atheian System" while planning to shoot General Walker, but it is difficult to see a connection between thinking about shooting Walker and "The Atheian System." Bugliosi at pp. 681–683.

6. 20 WCH at p. 524 (V. T. Lee Exhibit No. 5); 20 WCH at p. 533 (Vincent T. Lee Exhibit No. 9).

7. McMillan at p. 428; Mailer at p. 569; Bugliosi at p. 719.

8. Johnson (Arnold) Exhibit No. 2, XX WCH 260.

9. McMillan at pp. 435–436.

10. Russo (1998) at pp. 70, 183–188.

11. 16 WCH at p. 67 (CE 18) (Oswald's address book containing the names of "N.O City Editor 'cowan' and 'David Crawford reporter'").

12. Russo (1998) at p. 195.

13. 10 WCH at p. 37 (Carlos Bringuier testimony).

14. 10 WCH at p. 83 (Vance Blaylock testimony).

15. 10 WCH at pp. 36–37 (Carlos Bringuier testimony); 10 WCH at p. 77 (Philip Geraci III testimony).

16. 10 WCH at p. 36 (Carlos Bringuier testimony).

17. 10 WCH at p. 85 (Carlos Blaylock testimony).

18. 10 WCH at p. 37 (Carlos Bringuier testimony).

19. Newman at pp. 379–380.

20. McMillan at p. 433.

21. McMillan at p. 434.

22. 10 WCH at p. 37 (Carlos Bringuier testimony).

23. 10 WCH at p. 37 (Carlos Bringuier testimony).

24. 10 WCH at pp. 36–37 (Carlos Bringuier testimony).

25. 22 WCH at p. 820 (CE 1413).

26. Bugliosi at p. 725.

27. McMillan at p. 431.

28. McMillan at p. 432.

29. 10 WCH 53–54 (Vincent Martello testimony).

30. 10 WCH 59–61 (Vincent Martello testimony).

31. McMillan at pp. 430–431. Norman Mailer suggested that Oswald might have believed that if the New Orleans police knew that the FBI was interested in him, he would receive better protection while in the New Orleans jail. Mailer at p. 576.

32. 4 WCH at p. 835 (John Lester Quigley testimony).

33. 4 WCH at pp. 432–440 (John Lester Quigley testimony); 17 WCH at pp. 756–768 (CE No. 826) (Report of Quigley, August 15, 1963).

34. 17 WCH at pp. 759–760 (CE No. 826) (Report of Quigley, August 15, 1963).

35. Bugliosi at p. 725. Mailer at p. 578. 10 WCH at p. 39 (Carlos Bringuier testimony).

36. 10 WCH at p. 39 (Carlos Bringuier testimony).

37. Bugliosi at p. 725, Source notes p. 88, note 1316 (Telephone call and letter between Johann Rush and Vincent Bugliosi).

38. McMillan at pp. 434–435.

39. 20 WCH at p. 261 (Arnold Johnson Exhibit No. 3); 10 WCH at p. 99 (Arnold Johnson testimony).

40. Charles Hall Steele, Jr. was the only leafleteer located by the Warren Commission. Steele did not see Oswald contact the other man but saw Oswald trying to recruit people. 10 WCH pp. 63–71 (Charles Hall Steele, Jr. testimony). See also, 10 WCH 71–73 (Charles Hall Steele, Sr. testimony). Fifty-three years later the identity of the other man became an issue when Republican Party presidential candidate Donald Trump implied that the unidentified leafleteer might have been the father of candidate Ted Cruz. Author Vincent Bugliosi reported that the unidentified leafleteer "seemed embarrassed by the entire affair, grinning a lot, and soon left with his companion..." Vincent Bugliosi, *Reclaiming History: The Assassination of President John F. Kennedy* (2007) p. 727.

41. Bugliosi at pp. 727–728; 10 WCH at p. 41 (Carlos Bringuier testimony). One may question the accuracy of this claim. June Oswald was then 18 months old. How many words could she know, and how could Quiroga determine she was speaking Russian?

42. 11 WCH at p. 172 (William Stuckey testimony).

43. 11 WCH at pp. 160–162 (William Stuckey testimony).

44. 20 WCH at pp. 529–530 (V. T. Lee Exhibit No. 7). Author Vincent Bugliosi makes a strong case for this letter having been written before Stuckey interviewed Oswald, although the letter was postmarked after the interview. See Bugliosi footnote at p. 731. Whether it was written before or after the interview, it was replete with lies.

45. 21 WCH at pp. 606–619 (Stuckey Exhibit No. 1); 11 WCH at p. 161 (William Stuckey testimony).

46. 11 WCH at pp. 163–164 (William Stuckey testimony).

47. 21 WCH at p. 622 (Stuckey Exhibit No. 2).

48. 21 WCH at pp. 622–623 (Stuckey Exhibit No. 2).

49. 21 WCH at pp. 623 (Stuckey Exhibit No. 2).

50. 21 WCH at pp. 623–624 (Stuckey Exhibit No. 2).

51. At various points during the taping, Stuckey, who had been a columnist for the *New Orleans States-Item*, caught Oswald in outright misstatements, such as a claim that the United States had adopted an emergency censorship law during the Korean War and that recent immigrants from Cuba had been mostly supporters of the deposed Cuban dictator, Fulgencio Batista. The claims did not correspond with Stuckey's experience. Stuckey Exhibit No. 2, XXI WCH pp. 625–629. See also, Vincent Bugliosi, *Reclaiming History: The Assassination of President John F. Kennedy* (2007) at pp. 729–730.

52. 11 WCH at p. 166 (William Stuckey testimony).

53. Bugliosi at p. 731.

54. Bugliosi at pp. 731–732.

55. 10 WCH at p. 42 (Carlos Bringuier testimony).

56. 21 WCH at p. 634 (Stuckey Exhibit No. 3).

57. 21 WCH at pp. 633–641 (Stuckey Exhibit No. 3).

58. 11 WCH at pp. 171–173 (William Stuckey testimony).

59. 11 WCH at p. 175 (William Stuckey testimony).

60. McMillan at p. 439.

61. McMillan at pp. 439–440.

62. 20 WCH at pp. 262–264 (Johnson [Arnold]) Exhibit No. 4.

63. 20 WCH at pp. 266–267 (Johnson [Arnold] Exhibit No. 5.

64. These two letters were both dated September 1; however, the letter to the Socialist Workers Party was postmarked August 31 and marked "Received" by the Socialist Workers Party on September 3, the day after Labor Day. 19 WCH at p. 577 (Dobbs Exhibit No. 10). No similar markings were available for the letters to the Communist Party. It would seem most likely that all three letters were written on the same day, although they might have been mailed on different days.

65. 20 WCH at p. 270 (Johnson [Arnold]) Exhibit No. 6).

66. 19 WCH at p. 577 (Dobbs Exhibit No. 10).

67. 17 WCH at p. 115 (CE 415).

68. McMillan at pp. 402–403. Marina did not see an obstetrician until her ninth month of pregnancy, when Ruth took her to see a doctor. McMillan at pp. 402–403, 469.

69. 17 WCH at pp. 137–138 (CE 421).

70. 17 WCH at pp. 148–149 (CE 224).

71. 17 WCH at p. 109 (CE 412).

72. 2 WCH at pp. 449, 493 (Ruth Paine testimony).

73. McMillan at p. 441.

74. Bugliosi at p. 733.

75. New Orleans library records and Oswald's neighbors confirmed his isolation in reading once he lost his employment. In the two-month period

from his discharge from Reily Coffee until he left for Mexico City, Oswald borrowed twenty-two books from the New Orleans Public Library. 25 WCH at pp. 929–930 (CE No. 2630); Bugliosi at pp. 742–743.

76. McMillan at p. 449.

77. 1 WCH at p. 22 (Marina Oswald testimony).

78. The first hijacker—an American—was imprisoned by Castro on suspicion that he was a spy. No hijacking between Cuba and the U.S. occurred in 1962 or 1963. https://en.wikipedia.org/wiki/List_of_Cuba-United_States_aircraft_hijackings; https://listverse.com "Top 10 U.S. Airline hijackings of the 60's."

79. 1 WCH at p. 22 (Marina Oswald testimony).

80. 20 WCH at p. 785 (CE 1404).

81. 1 WCH at p. 23 (Marina Oswald testimony).

82. Mailer at pp. 596–597. This interview was not with Mailer, himself, but with an interviewer working for Mailer.

83. McMillan at pp. 442–443.

84. 2 WCH at p. 317 (Katherine Ford testimony).

85. 20 WCH at p. 785 (CE 1404); McMillan at p. 443.

86. McMillan at p. 444.

87. McMillan at p. 447.

88. 1 WCH at pp. 21–22 (Marina Oswald testimony); McMillan at p. 450; Bugliosi at p. 743.

89. 16 WCH at pp. 337–346 (CE 93).

90. McMillan at pp. 455–456.

91. 20 WCH at p. 265 (Arnold Johnson Exhibit 4-A).

92. McMillan at p. 450.

93. Diane Holloway (2000) at pp. 190–191.

94. Davison (1983) at pp. 182–183.

95. Russo (1998) at p. 249.

96. WCR at p. 730.

97. Bugliosi at p. 745.

98. 22 WCH pp. 196, 198 (CE 1156).

99. 9 WCH 389 (Ruth Paine testimony).

100. 9 WCH 350 (Ruth Paine testimony).

101. Specifically told to author in corrections Ruth Paine made to a draft of this sentence where the author had referred to the packing as "wrapped as if camping equipment." Witnesses later testified that, after the rifle was placed in the Paine garage, it was retained in a "rolled up blanket." WCR at p. 15.

102. 9 WCH 350 (Ruth Paine testimony).

103. McMillan at p. 461.

104. McMillan at p. 461.

105. McMillan at p. 447.

106. 10 WCH at pp. 272–273 (Mrs. Jesse Garner testimony); 10 WCH at p. 276 (Jesse Garner affidavit); 11 WCH at pp. 462–463 (Eric Rogers testimony). The Warren Commission concluded that Eric Rogers testified that he saw Oswald board a bus on the evening of September 24; however, a close reading of Rogers' testimony would seem to be that Rogers was testifying to the evening of September 23. Mr. Garner's affidavit refers to him checking the Oswald apartment the "day after the station wagon left," which he misidentified as September 25. The author believes that these witnesses are testifying that Oswald was seen boarding the bus on September 23 and that the apartment was found empty on September 24. Author Vincent Bugliosi believes that Oswald spent the night of September 23 in the apartment where there was a bed to sleep in, that he took his baggage to the bus station the next night, and that he slept in the bus station the night of September 24. Bugliosi at p. 747. We know that on the morning of September 25, he obtained a check at his post office box and cashed it at a Winn-Dixie store six blocks from his apartment. It is the reader's decision as to what the witnesses are saying and what actually occurred.

107. WCR at p. 730.

108. WCR at pp. 730–732.

109. Bugliosi p. 747.

110. WCR at pp. 321–325, 726–731.

111. For a discussion of claims that Oswald had a secret life in New Orleans, see Mailer at pp. 616–623; Russo (1998) at pp. 196–206; Bugliosi at pp. 1347–1436.

112. WCR at p. 731.

113. WCR at p. 731.

114. 11 WCH at pp. 214–215 (Dr. McFarland); CE 2534.

115. WCR at pp. 733–734; Bugliosi at p. 753, Source notes p. 91, note # 1429.

Chapter 31

1. See April 21, 1964, Warren Commission memorandum by W. David Slawson of his verbatim notes on CIA recording of those phone calls. http://www.maryferrell.org/showDoc.html?docld.=26314#relPageld=1 (CIA record 104-10054-1022, JFK series, File No.88TOB571).

2. As he told Marina, in fact he had no intention of proceeding to the Soviet Union. I WCH 23 (Marina Oswald testimony).

3. WCR at p. 734.

4. WCR at p. 734.

5. 24 WCH at p. 587 (CE 2121 at p. 35).

6. Willens at p. 124.

7. Willens at p. 109.

8. 24 WCH at pp. 589–590 (CE 2121 at pp. 39–40).

9. 24 WCH at pp. 589–590 (CE 2121 at pp. 39–40).

10. 24 WCH at p. 590 (CE 2121 at p. 40).

11. HSCA, Vol. III-6, JFK Exhibit F-440A (Silvia Duran testimony).

12. 24 WCH at p. 590 (CE 2121 at p. 40).

13. W. David Slawson, interview for documentary film *Truth Is the Only Client* (2019), transcript p. 27.

14. Willens at pp. 124–134.

15. Willens at pp. 129–130; W. David Slawson, interview for documentary movie *Truth Is the Only Client* (2019), transcript p. 28.

16. HSCA, Vol. III-6, JFK Exhibit F-440A (Silvia Duran testimony).

17. W. David Slawson, interview for documen-

tary film *Truth Is the Only Client*, transcript pp. 26–27; Shenon, p. 308.

18. Willens at p. 133. Duran denied that she was a communist. She said she was a socialist. Shenon at p. 310.

19. WCR at pp. 301–302; WCR at p. 303 gives CE 2564 with the documents and translation. See also 24 WCH at pp. 567–569 (CE 2120 at pp. 3–7) (Confidential memorandum from Mexican government to U.S. Embassy in Mexico City regarding efforts to secure U.S./Mexico border on November 22, 1963.

20. WCR at pp. 304–305.

21. HSCA, Volume III-6, JFK Exhibit F-440A (Silvia Duran testimony).

22. Former consul Eusebio Azque testified before the House Select Committee that the call back from the Soviet Embassy had been directed to him, and that he had been told that Oswald's visa request could not be approved for three or four months. House Select Committee on Assassinations, Vol. III, at p.127; https://www.maryferrell.org/showDoc.html?docId=954#relPageId=131. W. David Slawson, interview for documentary film *Truth Is the Only Client*, transcript p. 20. Azque also gave a different identification for the man using the name Oswald and did not believe the man was Lee Harvey Oswald. HSCA III pp. 136–139. See also Dan Hardway and Edwin Lopez (1978, revised 2003), "Oswald, the CIA, and Mexico City." Staff Report for House Select Committee on Assassinations. http://www.history-matters.com/archive/jfk/hsca/lopezrpt_2003/contents.htm. Since Oswald's photo was on the visa application received by the Cuban embassy, and Oswald himself later told Marina and wrote to the Soviet Embassy in Washington, D.C., that he had been rejected at the Cuban embassy in Mexico City, one must conclude that Azque was mistaken in saying that the man using the name Oswald was not Lee Harvey Oswald. He may also be mistaken in saying he personally received the call from the Soviet Embassy.

23. The consul's last name has been spelled Azque, Azcue, and Asque by various authors and reporters. The author is using the spelling Azque because that spelling was used by the Warren Commission.

24. HSCA, Volume III-6, JFK Exhibit F-440A (Silvia Duran testimony).

25. HSCA, Volume III-6, JFK Exhibit F-440A (Silvia Duran testimony).

26. Oleg Maximovich Nechiporenko, *Passport to Assassination: The Never Told Story of Lee Harvey Oswald by the KGB Colonel Who Knew Him* (1993) at p. vii.

27. David Robarge, *DCI John McCone and the Assassination of President John F. Kennedy, Studies in Intelligence*, Vol. 57, No. 3, p. 3, fn. 9 (September 2013), an excerpt from Robarge's book, *John McCone as Director of Central Intelligence, 1961–1965*, published in 2003. Robarge accepts as essentially true Nechiporenko's account of Oswald's visit to the Soviet embassy.

28. Nechiporenko at p. viii. Approximately two years later, an interviewer for author Norman Mailer spoke with Nechiporenko. Mailer relied upon Nechiporenko's account. Mailer at pp. 640–641.

29. Kostikov was also in charge of assassination efforts for the region. W. David Slawson, testimony before the House Select Committee on Assassinations, November 15, 1997. The Soviet Union had undertaken assassination efforts in Europe and elsewhere. *Ibid.*

30. 30 Nechiporenko at p. 67.

31. Nechiporenko at pp. 69–70.

32. Nechiporenko at p. 70.

33. Nechiporenko at p. 71.

34. Nechiporenko at p. 74.

35. Nechiporenko at p. 74.

36. Nechiporenko at pp. 75–76.

37. Nechiporenko at p. 76.

38. Nechiporenko at pp. 76–78.

39. Nechiporenko at pp. 78–79.

40. Mailer at p. 640.

41. Nechiporenko has made at least one claim about Oswald that is untrue. He states that a KGB friend told him that the FBI discovered a letter in Oswald's North Beckley Street room from the Soviets rejecting his visa application when the room was searched on the day of Oswald's arrest. Nechiporenko at p. 95. No record of such a letter exists either in U.S. or Soviet files. If such a letter was sent to Oswald, one could be sure that the Soviets would have been waving it to the world as evidence that it was not involved in a conspiracy with Oswald.

42. On October 13, 1963, the Cuban foreign ministry authorized issuance of a visa to Oswald, conditioned on his securing a transit visa from the Soviets. On October 25, 1963, the Soviet embassy in Washington, D.C., rejected Oswald's request. Vincent Bugliosi, *Reclaiming History: The Assassination of President John F. Kennedy* (2007) p. 759. There is no evidence that Oswald was informed of these decisions.

43. Shenon at pp. 381–383.

44. HSCA Report at pp. 122–123. The ultimate source was believed by Vincent Bugliosi to be Gilberto Alvarado Ugarte, whom Bugliosi regards as not reliable. Bugliosi, pp. 1285–1286 and Source notes p. 150 numbers 12–21. For authors who accept Ugarte's account, see Russo (2008) at pp. 375–382 relying, in part, on National Archives and Records Administration #124-10230-1045, FBI, November 28, 1963 and National Archives and Records Administration, CIA document #104-10015-10244 (November 29, 1963).

45. Commission staffer W. David Slawson, who should have received the letter, says he does not remember seeing it. Slawson interview for documentary film *Truth Is Our Only Client*, transcript pp. 30–31. Howard Willens, who oversaw the investigation, believes that he saw the letter and that it probably went to staff member Norman Redlich and was deemed to lack probative value.

Emails from Willens to author, dated March 31, 2015, and March 30, 2019.

46. The essence of the statement was published in 1967 in an article by British journalist Comer Clarke, writing for the October edition of the *National Inquirer.* Clarke claimed that Fidel Castro had told him in an interview that Oswald said at the Cuban Embassy, "Someone ought to shoot that President Kennedy.... Maybe I'll try to do it." When Castro was interviewed by the House Select Committee on Assassinations on April 3, 1978, he denied making the claim, denied ever having been interviewed by Clarke, and denied that Oswald ever made such a statement to people at the Cuban Embassy. Bugliosi at pp. 1285–1286.

47. HSCA, Volume III-6, JFK Exhibit F-440A (Silvia Duran testimony).

48. Bugliosi at p. 1286.

49. HSCA, Report, Part 2 (March 29, 1979) at p. 123.

50. 16 WCH at pp. 443–444 (CE 103).

51. HSCA, Report, Part 2 (March 29, 1979) at p. 123.

52. WCR at pp. 735–736.

53. WCR at p. 735.

54. For a discussion of other possible activities, see, Bugliosi, Endnotes at pp. 607–611; Russo (1998) at pp. 225–226.

55. The claim has been put forth in detail by Philip Shenon in his book *A Cruel and Shocking Act: The Secret History of the Kennedy Assassination* (2013) at pp. 5–9, 496–498, 506–507, 520–521, 527–534.

56. HSCA, Volume III-6, JFK Exhibit F-440A (Silvia Duran testimony). Author Philip Shenon also reports that a sister-in-law of Duran told him in 2013 that Duran admitted that she had lunch with Oswald at a restaurant near the Cuban embassy but does not provide a day. Shenon at p. 553. Another individual who had not previously met Oswald told Shenon that Oswald had encountered him at Mexico City University and asked advice on how to secure a visa to Cuba. Shenon at p. 554. None of this information was provided to the Warren Commission.

57. Shenon at pp. 497–498.

58. Senora Garro said that she observed Oswald wearing a black sweater and that the late evening party occurred on either Monday, September 30; Tuesday, October 1; or Wednesday, October 2. Philip Shenon, *A Cruel and Shocking Act: The Secret History of the Kennedy Assassination* (2013) at p. 497. Oswald is not known to have possessed a black sweater in Mexico City, was dressed in a suit when visiting the Cuban and Soviet embassies, and left Mexico City by bus early on the morning of October 2. Much later, while being interviewed by author Priscilla McMillan, Marina uncovered papers that Lee had saved from Mexico City. They included a map of Mexico City marked in ink for places to visit, a list of possible tourist activities for the period he was there, plus a marked list of English language and English subtitled movies that were playing. Priscilla McMillan in conversation with author, August 2017.

59. Lopez Report, "Oswald, the CIA, and Mexico City," at pp. 228–235, https://www.Maryferrell.org/showDochtml?clucld=799#relPageid=138tab=pag.

60. Lopez Report, "Oswald, the CIA, and Mexico City," at p. 229, https://www.Maryferrell.org/showDochtml?clucld=799#relPageid=138tab=pag.

61. Bugliosi at p. 1288, Endnotes p. 733. Bugliosi does not provide a source for this statement.

62. HSCA Report at p. 124.

63. Russo (2008) at p. 316.

64. Shenon at p. 520, footnote.

65. By then, Duran's accuser, Elena Garro, had died.

66. Shenon at p. 552.

67. WCR at p. 736.

68. WCR at p. 736.

69. WCR at p. 736.

Chapter 32

1. Paul H. Santa Cruz, *Making JFK Matter* (2015) at p. 31.

2. See en.wikipedia.org/wiki/16th_Street_Baptist_Church_bombing. Robert E. Chambliss was arrested a few days after the bombing and charged with illegally possessing sticks of dynamite. He was fined $100. In 1977 he was convicted of murder and sentenced to life in prison for the bombing. Thomas Blanton was convicted of murder for the bombing in 2001 and also received a life sentence. In 2002, Bobby Cherry was similarly convicted and sentenced. A fourth suspect died in 1994 without being charged. See Frank Sikora, *Until Justice Rolls Down: The Birmingham Church Bombing Case* (1991); Elizabeth Cobb, *Long Time Coming: An Insider's Story of the Birmingham Church Bombing That Rocked the World* (1994); Susan Anderson, *The Past on Trial: The Sixteenth Street Baptist Church Bombing, Civil Rights Memory and the Remaking of Birmingham* (2008); Lisa Klobuchard, *The 1963 Birmingham Church Bombing; The Ku Klux Klan's History of Terror* (2009).

3. For a detailed account, see Russo (1998) at pp. 49–84, 155–209, 231–321.

4. Haig (1992) at pp. 106–116. See also Bohning p. 176 (8 assassination plots). Although Robert Kennedy never admitted a role in overseeing assassination attempts, those close to him said that he was the overseer for his brother. See, e.g., Schlesinger (1967) at p. 428; Schlesinger (1978) at p. 700.

5. Richard Goodwin, *Remembering America: A Voice from the Sixties* (1988) at p. 189.

6. Russo (1998) at pp. 63–65, 83, 175–177, 239–240, 250, 427–428, 433.

7. Russo (1998) at pp. 234–235.

8. LeoGrande and Kornluh at pp. 70–78. Bohning at pp. 167–176.

9. T. Clarke at p. 252. For a detailed discussion of overtures toward secret negotiations between

the U.S. and Cuba in 1963, see LeoGrande and Kornbluh at pp. 60–78.

10. Manchester (1967) at p. 3.

11. Russo (1998) at p. 231; Beschloss (1991) at pp. 641–642.

12. For polls in general on Kennedy in 1963, see Caro (2012) at p. 267; for polls on Kennedy and Cuba, see Russo (1998) at pp. 232–233.

13. Caro (2012) at p. 268.

14. Polls and judgments of politicians in Alabama, Mississippi, and North Carolina showed white voters who had supported Kennedy in 1960 unwilling to vote for him in 1963. Theodore C. Sorensen, *Kennedy* (1965) at p. 505.

15. Caro (2012) at pp. 273–274; Manchester (1967) at pp. 8–9; WCR at p. 737.

16. 4 WCH at p. 130 (Gov. John Connally testimony); 7 WCH at pp. 441–442 (Kevin O'Donnell testimony).

17. Manchester at p. 22; Caro (2012) at p. 300.

18. See videoed interview of Malcom Kilduff, assistant presidential press secretary, April 6, 1993, on file at the Sixth Floor Museum, Dallas Texas.

19. WCR at p. 40.

20. Minutaglio and Davis at pp. 108.

21. Minutaglio and Davis at pp. 108–109.

22. Ted Dealey. "'Grass-Roots Sentiment' Told." *Dallas Morning News*, October 28, 1961: 1. *NewsBank: America's News—Historical and Current.* https://infoweb.newsbank.com/apps/news/document-view?p=AMNEWS&docref=image/v2%3A0F99DDB671832188%40EANX-100119BC2081A14F%402437601-100119BC29C36AB3%400-100119BD2B10777F.

23. That was Schmidt's second tour of military service. He dropped out of high school in 1955 at age 17 and enlisted in the U.S. Army, served in Germany, was honorably discharged in 1957, entered Miami University, served a journalism internship at the Miami *Herald*, dropped out of college in 1959, re-enlisted in the Army, and was assigned again to Germany. Http://educationforum.ipb;host.com/index.php?/topic/6397-larrie-schmidt/&page=3 at 13/47.

24. 11 WCH at pp. 430–432 (Bernard Weissman testimony).

25. 18 WCH pp. 841–842 (CE 1034); 5 WCH 489, 494–496; (Bernard Weisman testimony); 11 WCH 430 (Bernard Weissman testimony).

26. 18 WCH at pp. 837–888 (CE 1033, CE 1036, CE 1037, CE 1038, CE 1040, CE 1044, CE 1047, CE 1049) (Communications from Larrie Schmidt to CUSA members); Minutaglio and Davis at pp. 195–200.

27. Minutaglio and Davis at p. 200.

28. Minutaglio and Davis at p. 234; Chris Cravens, "Edwin A. Walker and the Right Wing in Dallas, 1960–1966 (Master's Thesis, Texas State University—San Marcos, 1991).

29. Minutaglio and Davis at p. 237.

30. 18 WCH at pp. 837–840 (CE 1033); 5 WCH at p.489 (Bernard Weissman testimony).

31. "Swastikas Plastered on Stores." *Dallas Morning News*, April 16, 1963: 5. *NewsBank: America's News—Historical and Current.* https://infoweb.newsbank.com/apps/news/document-view?p=AMNEWS&docref=image/v2%3A0F99DDB671832188%40EANX-0FF7D13727EB2A31%402438136-0FF7D13743DE0DF3%404-0FF7D1389234164F.; Minutaglio and. Davis at pp. 218–19.

32. 18 WCH at pp. 848–849 (CE 1036).

33. 11 WCH at pp. 430–431 (Bernard Weissman testimony). "Although raised as an Episcopalian, Goldwater was the first candidate of Jewish descent (through his father) to be nominated for president by a major American party." Wikipedia biography of Barry Goldwater as of 24 June 2021.

Chapter 33

1. 1 WCH at p.28 (Marina Oswald testimony).

2. Nechiporenko at pp. 94–96.

3. Bugliosi at p. 761.

4. WCR at p. 743.

5. 1 WCH at p. 29 (Marina Oswald testimony).

6. Bugliosi at p. 762.

7. 11 WCH at p. 479 (Frank Gangl affidavit), Gangl Exhibit 1.

8. McMillan at p. 469. McMillan may be wrong in stressing that Oswald never again used the name Hidell. We know that, when arrested on November 22, 1963, he had on his person an identification card with the name Hidell and his own photograph.

9. Bugliosi at p. 763.

10. Bugliosi at p. 763.

11. WCR at pp. 159–160, 653.

12. 6 WCH at pp. 405–406 (Mary E. Bledsoe testimony).

13. Growing up in a large city and entering military service at age 17, he had not learned to drive when most teenagers do. He had no opportunity to do so while in Russia and lacked money to purchase a car when he returned to the United States. Michael Paine remembered Oswald as being embarrassed at being unable to drive. 2 WCH at p. 413 (Michael Paine testimony). Inability to drive was now both an economic and psychological disability.

14. Bugliosi at p. 764; Mallon at pp. 105–106.

15. Bugliosi at p. 763.

16. McMillan at p. 471.

17. WCR at p. 737.

18. WCR at p. 738; 3 WCH at p. 237 (Roy Truly testimony).

19. 3 WCH at pp. 215–216 (Roy Truly testimony).

20. 3 WCH at pp. 216–218 (Roy Truly testimony).

21. Russo (1998) at pp. 264–265; Video interview of Buell Wesley Frazier available at *The Sixth Floor Museum at Dealey Plaza*, Dallas, Texas.

22. McMillan at pp. 472–473.

23. McMillan at p. 473.

24. McMillan at pp. 473–474.

25. McMillan at p. 473.

26. McMillan at p. 476.

27. McMillan at pp. 473–474. Vincent Bugliosi concluded that these movies were watched on October 12. Bugliosi at p. 764. His conclusion was based on Marina's testimony to the Warren Commission in which she expressed the belief that they had watched the movies "Several days. Some five days" before Rachel was born. 1 WCH at p. 71. Five days would have been October 15, a date that was impossible since Lee was not in Irving on that day. Marina clarified her recollection in conversations with Priscilla McMillan.

28. McMillan at pp. 473–474. See also, Bugliosi at pp. 764–765. Some have speculated that Lee might have been inspired by one or both movies to assassinate President Kennedy. John Loken, *Oswald's Trigger Films: The Manchurian Candidate, We Were Strangers, and Suddenly* (2000). There is no evidence that, when Oswald saw these films, he was thinking about killing the president.

29. McMillan at p. 473.

30. McMillan at pp. 474–475.

31. McMillan at p. 475.

32. McMillan at p. 475.

33. 18 WCH at p. 636. (CE 994. Translated from Marina's memoir in Russian. CE 993.)

34. McMillan at pp. 471–472.

35. Bugliosi at p. 765.

36. Author's personal experience.

37. 10 WCH at p. 297 (Gladys Johnson testimony).

38. 10 WCH at pp. 296–298. (Gladys Johnson testimony).

39. 6 WCH at p. 442 (Earlene Roberts testimony).

40. Russo (1998) at pp. 256–257.

Chapter 34

1. Oral history of A.C. Green at The Sixth Floor Museum at Dealey Plaza, Dallas, Texas; A.C. Greene, "The Sixth Floor Museum: A Personal View" *Southwestern Historical Quarterly*, Vol. 94 (July 1990–April 1991) at p. 174; "Old Times" [November 1987], *Texas Monthly* (May 2002) (O.H. Lee letter received about two months before JFK assassination); John Weeks, oral history, Sixth Floor Museum, Dallas, Texas, July 31, 1998 (confirming A.C. Greene conversation with O.H. Lee.)

2. Karen Martin. "Fighters See Return to Cuba in 6 Months." *Dallas Morning News*, October 13, 1963: 7. *NewsBank: America's News—Historical and Current*. https://infoweb.newsbank.com/apps/news/document-view?p=AMNEWS&docref=image/v2%3A0F99DDB671832188%40EANX-0FFE5DD6FB081A04%402438316-0FFE5DD7205D2350%406-0FFE5DD9594F6330.

3. Newman at p. 446.

4. Newman at p. 446.

5. Newman at p. 68.

6. Minutaglio and Davis at p. 237.

7. Paul Edward Trejo, *A Brief History of Ex-General Edwin Walker* (2012) at p. 209. (Trejo Academic Research, Inc. submitted to Dr. H.W. Brands, University of Texas, Austin).

8. Mike Quinn. "Walker Says U.S. Main Battleground." *Dallas Morning News*, October 24, 1963: 1. *NewsBank: America's News—Historical and Current*. https://infoweb.newsbank.com/apps/news/document-view?p=AMNEWS&docref=image/v2%3A0F99DDB671832188%40EANX-0FFE5BB888C19283%402438327-0FFE5BB9232D37A2%4044-0FFE5BBC6329B054; see also, Cravens (1991) at p. 141.

9. Minutaglio and Davis at p. 241.

10. Trejo at p. 209.

11. Cravens at p. 141.

12. WCR at p. 738; 2 WCH at p. 408 (Michael Paine testimony).

13. These were the same handbills that were distributed in Dallas on November 22 before and during President Kennedy's motorcade. 5 WCH at pp. 535–540 (Robert G. Klause testimony).

14. Trejo at p. 208.

15. Trejo at p. 210.

16. Schmidt had wanted the Young Americans for Freedom to picket the Stevenson speech. Its president refused. Schmidt resigned from the organization. Bill Minutaglio and Steven L. Davis, *Dallas 1963* (2013) at p. 237.

17. 5 WCH at p. 493 (Bernard Weissman testimony).

18. Minutaglio and Davis at p. 244.

19. Minutaglio and Davis at p. 243.

20. Minutaglio and Davis at pp. 243–244.

21. Minutaglio and Davis at p. 244.

22. Minutaglio and Davis at pp. 244–245.

23. Minutaglio and Davis at p. 245.

24. Minutaglio and Davis at p. 245.

25. Cravens at p. 142.

26. Minutaglio and Davis at p. 246.

27. Minutaglio and Davis at p. 246.

28. Minutaglio and Davis at p. 247.

29. Minutaglio and Davis at p. 249.

30. 5 WCH at p. 491 (Bernard Weissman testimony).

31. 18 WCH at pp. 837 (CE 1033).

32. 18 WCH at p. 836 (CE 1032).

33. Minutaglio and Davis at p. 251.

34. *Dallas Times Herald*, October 25, 1963.

35. "Our Apologies." *Dallas Morning News*, October 26, 1963, Section 4, p. 2.

36. "Cabell Appeals for Sanity." *Dallas Morning News*, October 27, 1963: 21. *NewsBank: America's News—Historical and Current*. https://infoweb.newsbank.com/apps/news/document-view?p=AMNEWS&docref=image/v2%3A0F99DDB671832188%40EANX-0FFE5B61C92CC812%402438330-0FFE5B62039FA274%4020-0FFE5B64ED0FEB77.

37. Minutaglio and Davis at p. 256.

38. Minutaglio and Davis at p. 252.

39. Minutaglio and Davis at p. 250; Mike Quinn. "Civic Leaders Wire Apologies to Adlai." *Dallas Morning News*, October 26, 1963: 1. *NewsBank: America's News—Historical and Current*. https://infoweb.newsbank.com/apps/news/document-view?p=AMNEWS&docref=image/

v2%3A0F99DDB671832188%40EANX-0FFE5B5BA1E9633D%402438329-0FFE5B5BAB38C981%400-0FFE5B5CB9FA758D.

40. Minutaglio and Davis at p. 260; Leslie (1964) at p. 203; Cf., Manchester (1967) at p. 40.

41. Minutaglio and Davis at pp. 250–251; Cravens at p. 145.

42. Cravens at pp. 146, 150.

43. Darwin Payne, *Big D: Triumphs and Troubles in an American Supercity in the 20th Century* (2000) at p. 314.

44. WCR at p. 441. 5 WCH at pp. 34–39 (Jack Revill testimony); 17 WCH at p. 49. 4 WCH at pp. 463–464 (James Hosty testimony); 17 WCH at pp. 778–784 (CE 831); 16 WC at pp.ahH at p. 496;HH at p. 496 (CE 711); 5 WCH at pp. 47–58 (V.T. Brian testimony).

45. Newman at pp. 88–89.

46. 20 WCH at pp. 271–275 (Arnold Johnson Exhibit No. 7).

47. 2 WCH at p. 407 (Michael Paine testimony).

48. 2 WCH at p. 408 (Michael Paine testimony).

49. 2 WCH at p. 409 (Michael Paine testimony).

50. Bugliosi at p. 773; WCR at pp. 312, 739, 745; 7 WCH at pp. 292–293 (Harry D. Holmes testimony); 20 WCH at p. 172 (Holmes Ex. No. 1).

51. 20 WCH at pp. 271–275 (Arnold Johnson Exhibit No. 7).

52. 25 WCH at p. 901 (CE 2642).

53. www.britannica.com/topic/The-shark-and-the-Sardines.

54. www.questia.com/library/78689/the-shark-and-the-sardines.

55. The book, due for return on November 13, 1963, had not been listed as returned to the Dallas Library when the Warren Commission did its investigation. It was later found at the library by author Albert Newman. Newman at p. 108. Newman speculated that his ultimate finding of the book after Oswald's death suggested that Oswald may have loaned it to a friend (a possible conspirator) and the friend returned it. Author Vincent Bugliosi noted that the library's listing it as an unreturned overdue book may simply have been an error in the library's record keeping. Bugliosi at p. 777, footnote.

56. Newman at p. 482.

Chapter 35

1. Bugliosi at p, 761; Hosty at pp. 47–48.
2. Hosty at pp. 43–44.
3. Hosty at p. 48.
4. Hosty at pp. 48–49.
5. Bugliosi at pp. 774–75.
6. Hosty at p. 49.
7. Hosty at p. 49.
8. Hosty at p. 50; McMillan at pp. 493.
9. Hosty at p. 50; McMillan at p. 493.
10. For security reasons, FBI agents did not carry business cards.
11. Hosty at p. 50.
12. McMillan at p. 494.
13. McMillan at p. 494.
14. McMillan at p. 494.
15. McMillan at p. 495.
16. McMillan at p. 495.
17. McMillan at p. 495.
18. Many researchers believe that Oswald delivered the Hosty note on November 12. See, e.g., Mailer at p. 660; McMillan at pp. 505–506. However, Ruth Paine testified that on the weekend of November 9, Lee told her that he had already gone to the FBI to see an agent and that, as Hosty was not there, he left a note telling Hosty to cease bothering Marina. 3 WCH at p. 18 (Ruth Paine testimony). In 1975, Hosty told the House Select Committee on Assassinations that Oswald left the note on November 6, 7, or 8, 1963. Bugliosi pp. 124–125, footnote. Twenty one years later, Hosty believed it was "about November 12." James P. Hosty, *Assignment Oswald* (1996) at p. 30.
19. McMillan at pp. 496–497.
20. McMillan at p. 497.
21. McMillan at p. 498.
22. 17 WCH at p. 777 (CE 830, Report of FBI Special Agent James Hosty).
23. McMillan at p. 498; Hosty at p. 51; 3 WCH at pp. 99–100 (Ruth Paine testimony). Hosty said he never went inside on November 5. 4 WCH at p. 453.
24. McMillan at p. 498.
25. 16 WCH at pp. 443–444 (CE 103).
26. See Commission Exhibit 103, 16 WCH pp. 443–444. Since the handwritten draft refers only to Hosty's November 1 visit, and Oswald did not learn of the November 5 visit until he arrived in Irving on November 8, one can infer that he began drafting the letter while he was in Dallas.
27. 3 WCH at pp. 14–17 (Ruth Paine testimony); McMillan at pp. 501–503.
28. McMillan at p. 499.
29. McMillan at p. 500.
30. This final version was voluntarily supplied to the Commission by the Soviet Embassy in Washington, D.C., House Select Committee on Assassinations, Testimony of W. David Slawson. November 15, 1977.
31. Conspiracy theorists cite Oswald's knowledge that the Cuban consul had been replaced as evidence that someone from the Cuban embassy communicated with Oswald after he returned to Dallas; however, the replacement was already at the embassy, learning from the Cuban consul, when Oswald was there in late September. The change of responsibilities did not occur until November 18, 1963; therefore Oswald could only be assuming that the change had occurred when he was drafting this letter on November 9. Warren Commission Exhibit 2121 at p. 37.
32. 16 WCH at p. 33.
33. CE 16, 16 WCH at p. 34 (CE 15).
34. Personal communication from Ruth Paine to this author on March 21, 2017.
35. McMillan at pp. 503–504.
36. WCR at p. 740.
37. 2 WCH at p. 412 (Michael Paine testimony).

Chapter 36

1. McMillan (1977) at p. 513; 1 WCH at pp. 54, 63 (Marina Oswald testimony); 3 WCH at pp. 41, 43 (Ruth Paine testimony).
2. 10 WCH at pp. 297–298 (Gladys J. Johnson testimony).
3. After Oswald was arrested on November 22, 1963, a copy of an uncompleted form was found in his Beckley Street room. Bugliosi at p. 782. Author Albert Newman believed it unlikely that Oswald would have sought a driver's license application form on November 16 if, at that time, he had been planning to assassinate the president on November 22. Newman at p. 503.
4. McMillan at pp. 513–514.
5. If true and it occurred on Saturday, November 16, Oswald looking for a car on that day would reenforce an argument that he was not thinking then of shooting the president.
6. 2 WCH a p. 413 (Michael Paine testimony).
7. 2 WCH at p. 221 (Buell Wesley Frazier testimony).
8. 10 WCH at p. 345 (Frank Pizzo testimony); Bugliosi at pp. 1030–1035.
9. 10 WCH at p. 352 (Albert Bogard testimony).
10. Bugliosi at p. 1032.
11. 10 WCH at p. 346.
12. In the Warren Commission's investigation, it was unusual to subject a witness to a polygraph investigation. Neither the FBI nor the Commission regarded polygraph tests as probative. The test was not conducted at the Commission's initiative. The Commission's exhibits do not show why the test was administered. See, CE 3078, 26 WCH at pp. 682–686.
13. Bugliosi at pp. 1031–1032.
14. 10 WCH at pp. 353–354 (Albert Bogard testimony).
15. WCR at p. 321.
16. WCR at pp. 320–321.
17. WCR at pp. 320–321. Bugliosi at p. 1031.
18. Conversation of author with Ruth Paine.
19. Mallon at pp. 70–91.
20. Mallon at pp. 10–11, 149; interview of Ruth Paine by author.
21. Mallon at p. 98.
22. Mallon at p. 105.
23. Mallon at pp. 105–106.
24. Mallon at p. 106.
25. Mallon at p. 107.
26. WCR at pp. 320–321.
27. WCR at pp. 316–318.
28. Mallon at pp. 8–9.
29. Interview of Ruth Paine by author, February 22, 2017.
30. 10 WCH at pp. 310–318 (Clifton Shateen testimony); CE 3130 (Bert Glover interview).
31. WCR at pp. 331–332.
32. Bugliosi at Endnotes pp. 588–589.
33. Warren Commission CD 385 at p. 142 (FBI interview of Garrett Claud Hallmark, January 27, 1964). https://www.maryferrell.org/showDoc.html?docld=10786#relPageId=146&search=Hallmark. When shown a photograph of Lee Harvey Oswald, Hallmark said he had never seen Oswald other than seeing news and TV photos of him after the president's assassination. 20 WCH at p. 72 (FBI Hallmark Exhibit 1, interview of Hallmark on December 11, 1963).
34. Russo (1998) at p. 266.
35. Russo (1998) at p. 267.
36. FBI report of February 2, 1964, in HSCA Administrative Folder V-3. See, https://www.maryferrell.org/showDoc.html?docld=10100#PageId=29&tab=page.
37. WCR at pp. 318–320.
38. WCR at pp. 318–320.
39. 10 WCH at pp. 385–389 (Homer Wood testimony); 10 WCH 391–397 (Sterling Wood testimony).
40. 10 WCH at p. 390 (Homer Wood testimony); 10 WCH at p. 397 (Sterling Wood testimony). For twenty-nine years, the Woods did not give further published information. In 1993, however, Sterling Wood agreed to be interviewed for the *Frontline* program, "Who Was Lee Harvey Oswald?" He told the show that they had seen Oswald on another occasion at the shooting range, had driven him to his Beckley street rooming house, and had talked to him about Minsk. Gus Russo, *Live by the Sword* (1998) at p. 263. One must wonder why this information had been provided neither to the Warren Commission nor the House Select Committee on Assassinations. Sterling said he feared violence against himself.
41. WCR at p. 320.
42. Some examples of identifications the Commission deemed false are discussed at pages 315–317 of the Warren Commission Report. David Kaiser relies on them in pages 349–350 of *The Road to Dallas* (2008) to suggest that Oswald either had a second rifle or borrowed a rifle from a friend (a possible coconspirator). Without giving reasons, Kaiser calls the Woods "highly credible." Kaiser at p. 355. Vincent Bugliosi discusses their unreliability in *Reclaiming History: The Assassination of President John F. Kennedy* (2007) at pp. 1028–1030.
43. Newman at pp. 482–485.
44. Newman at pp. 499, 501, 503.
45. Newman at p. 500.
46. McMillan at p. 514.
47. McMillan at p. 514.
48. 22 WCH at p. 631 (CE 1379).
49. 22 WCH at p. 631 (CE 1380).
50. 22 WCH at p. 630 (CE 1378).

Chapter 37

1. 4 WCH at pp. 344–345 (Winston Lawson testimony); 7 WCH 335 (Forrest Sorrels testimony).
2. Minutaglio and Davis at p. 274.
3. Minutaglio and Davis at pp. 279 and 281; Caufield at pp. 458–459.
4. Minutaglio and Davis at p. 266.
5. Minutaglio and Davis at p. 266; D. Payne (2000) at p. 362.

6. 5 WCH at p. 489 (Bernard Weissman testimony).

7. 5 WCH at p. 505 (Bernard Weissman testimony).

8. 5 WCH at p. 505 (Bernard Weissman testimony).

9. 5 WCH at pp. 504–505, 509 (Bernard Weissman testimony); D. Payne (2000) at p. 361.

10. 5 WCH at p. 506 (Bernard Weissman testimony).

11. T. Clarke at pp. 279–280.

12. WCR at p. 294; 18 WCH 835 (CE 1031).

13. 5 WCH at p. 508 (Bernard Weissman testimony).

14. T. Clarke at p. 210.

15. Minutaglio and Davis at p. 262; Cravens at p. 151; see also, Merle Miller, *Lyndon* (1980) at p. 310.

16. T. Clarke at pp. 211–212.

17. T. Clarke at p. 76.

18. T. Clarke at p. 213.

19. T. Clarke at p. 213.

20. T. Clarke at p. 224.

21. T. Clarke at pp. 239–241.

22. T. Clarke at p. 248.

23. T. Clarke at p. 248.

24. T. Clarke at p. 250.

25. T. Clarke at p. 251.

26. T. Clarke at p. 252.

27. T. Clarke at p. 252.

28. T. Clarke at p. 252.

29. T. Clarke at p. 253.

30. T. Clarke at p. 253.

31. Manchester (1967) at p. 38.

32. Manchester (1967) at p. 38.

33. T. Clarke at pp. 256–258. The entire speech is preserved on video at https://www.aptonline.org/catalogJFK--THE-LAST-SPEECH.

34. T. Clarke at pp. 268–269.

35. T. Clarke at pp. 269–279.

36. T. Clarke at p. 279.

37. 5 WCH at pp. 422–431 (Robert Alan Surrey testimony); 18 WCH 646 (CE 996).

38. T. Clarke at p. 283.

39. Jack Crichton, *The Republican-Democratic Campaigns in Texas in 1964* (self-published, 2004) at p. 11 (paperback); D. Payne at pp. 349–350.

40. Manchester at pp. 34–35.

41. T. Clarke at p. 283; LeoGrande and Kornbluh at p. 74.

42. T. Clarke at p. 283.

43. LeoGrande and Kornbluh at p. 76.

44. T. Clarke at p. 291.

45. After President Kennedy's death, some have speculated that Cubela was, in reality, a double agent—pretending to be working with the CIA while, in fact, securing information for Castro about CIA plots against him. Gus Russo and Stephen Molton, *Brothers in Arms: The Kennedys, The Castros and the Politics of Murder (2008),* at pp. 270, 295.

46. T. Clarke at p. 312; Caufield at p. 103 (transcript of conversation of Joseph Milteer with informant at pages 98–104, copied from Harold Weisberg, *Oswald in New Orleans: Case for a Conspiracy with the CIA*, 1967).

47. T. Clarke at p. 312.

48. T. Clarke at p. 314. William Manchester gives the statement as "Keep those Ivy League charlatans off the back of the car." Manchester at p. 37.

49. T. Clarke at p. 316; LeoGrande and Kornbluh at p. 76.

50. Bugliosi at pp. 783–84.

51. T. Clarke at p. 321.

52. LeoGrande and Kornbluh at p. 78.

53. T. Clarke at pp. 321–322 (referencing "When Castro Heard the News," an article by Jean Daniel in *New Republic*, December 7, 1963).

54. Caufield at p. 246.

55. T. Clarke at p. 325.

56. T. Clarke at p. 327; Manchester (1967) at p. 18–19.

57. Manchester (1967) at p. 18.

Chapter 38

1. 3 WCH 43–44 (Ruth Paine testimony); McMillan at pp. 514–515.

2. 3 WCH at p. 44 (Ruth Paine testimony). When I reviewed the transcript of Ms. Paine's testimony with her in 2019, she asked that I delete the transcript's language, "Is this a rooming house?" and, "I thanked him and hung up." She was not certain that the answerer was a man, nor was she certain that she had said those words. At her request, I replaced the first *he* and decided to include, "As best as I can recall." I decided to retain, "I thanked him and hung up." In a note to me, Ms. Paine wrote, "I thought this person who answered was female, but I really don't remember. I don't remember asking if it was a rooming house." There may be no better reflection of Ms. Paine's concern and determination to be accurate—for the Commission and for history—than her communications to me in that note.

3. 3 WCH at p. 45 (Ruth Paine testimony); 1 WCH 63 (Marina Oswald testimony).

4. McMillan at p. 515.

5. McMillan at p. 515. The Warren Commission's transcript of Ruth Paine's testimony was that Marina said, "twenty two fires." 3 WCH at p. 45. Either the transcript is incorrect or Ruth's recollection was wrong. McMillan's recitation of what Marina told her and the meaning of the phrase are more likely correct.

6. McMillan at pp. 515–516.

7. 1WCH at p. 65 (Marina Oswald testimony).

8. 22 WCH at p. 631 (CE 1379).

9. WCR at p. 2; Newman at p. 507.

10. Minutaglio and Davis at pp. 278–279.

11. Bugliosi at p. 785.

12. Posner at p. 220.

13. Bugliosi, p. 784.

14. Newman at p. 512.

15. 7 WCH at pp. 387–388 (Warren Caster testimony); 7 WCH at pp. 381–382 (Roy Truly testimony). Mrs. C.L. Connell told the FBI that a man known as

"Col. Caster" was a close associate of Edwin Walker and an anti-Kennedy activist. CE 3108, 26 WCH at 738 (FBI interview of Mrs. C.L. Connell). One might speculate that, if Oswald were aware of Warren Caster's last name and associated it with the Walker supporter named Caster, he might attempt, at trial, to link the Caster name and the gun purchase in a defense that someone else at the School Book Depository was the assassin of President Kennedy.

16. Bugliosi, Endnotes p. 67, note to p.125. Bugliosi quotes a dialogue between Dallas Police Captain Will Fritz and Oswald in which Oswald says, in response to whether he owned a rifle, "I saw Mr. Truly, my supervisor at work, he had one at the Depository on Wednesday, I think it was, showing it to some people in his office on the first floor." Bugliosi improperly reports the owner of the rifle as Warren Carter. The correct name is Caster. 7 WCH at pp. 386–388.

17. McMillan at p. 518.
18. McMillan at p. 519.
19. Bugliosi at p. 785.
20. McMillan at pp. 519–520.
21. Bugliosi at p. 785.
22. 2 WCH 222 (Buell Wesley Frazier testimony).
23. 2 WCH 222 (Buell Wesley Frazier testimony).
24. WCR at p. 130.
25. WCR at p. 130.
26. 2 WCH at p. 237 (Buell Wesley Frazier testimony).

Chapter 39

1. 5 WCH at pp. 505, 507, 510–511 (Bernard Weissman testimony)
2. WCR at pp. 298–299.
3. Manchester (1967) at p. 57.
4. Minutaglio and Davis at p. 283.
5. Manchester (1967) at p. 127.
6. Minutaglio and Davis at pp. 283–284.
7. Manchester (1967) at p. 65.
8. Manchester (1967) at pp. 67–86.
9. Manchester (1967) at pp. 73–74, 79, 116, 122.
10. McMillan at p. 520.
11. McMillan at p. 520.
12. McMillan at pp. 520–521.
13. Bugliosi at p. 786.
14. McMillan at p. 521.
15. McMillan at p. 521.
16. McMillan at pp. 521–522.
17. McMillan at 522; Posner at p. 222.
18. HSCA, volume II at pp. 268–269 (Marina Oswald testimony).
19. McMillan at p. 522.
20. McMillan at pp. 522–523.
21. 3 WCH at p. 47 (Ruth Paine testimony); McMillan at p. 523.
22. McMillan at pp. 523–524.

Chapter 40

1. McMillan at p. 524.
2. The exact amount that Lee left on the dresser that morning is unclear. However, the total amount available for Marina was $170, which was placed in a wallet in the dresser. The wallet with $170 was later taken by a Secret Service agent to Marina when she was staying at a Dallas hotel after the assassination. 22 WCH at pp. 194–195 (CE 1155).
3. WCR at p. 745 (Appendix XIV Analysis of Lee Harvey Oswald's Finances). Oswald had $13.87 on him at the time of arrest. He is known to have paid $1.00 for a taxi (WCR at p. 162) and also paid for a Coke and a Dallas bus. The estimate of the bus fare to Mexico is based on Oswald's travel expenses to Mexico in September 1963.
4. WCR at pp. 131–133; 2 WCH at pp. 248–251 (Linnie Mae Randle testimony).
5. 2 WCH at pp. 225–226 (Buell Wesley Frazier testimony).
6. 2 WCH at p. 220 (Buell Wesley Frazier testimony).
7. 2 WCH at p. 227 (Buell Wesley Frazier testimony).
8. Minutaglio and Davis at p. 292.
9. 2 WCH at pp. 228–229 (Buell Wesley Frazier testimony).
10. Manchester (1967) at p. 106.
11. Manchester (1967) at p. 113; Minutaglio and Davis at p. 292.
12. Manchester at p. 121.
13. Manchester at p. 121.
14. Manchester at p. 121; Minutaglio and Davis at pp. 301–302.
15. Manchester at pp. 122–127.
16. Democrats from the South who opposed many liberal programs of northern Democrats.
17. Manchester at pp. 128–129.
18. Manchester at p. 128.

Chapter 41

1. Vol. 57, pp. 7826–8077, National Archives, Warren Commission Documents (transcript of July 9, 1964, conference involving Allen H. Dulles, John J. McCloy, J. Lee Rankin, Norman Redlich, Wesley J. Liebeler, Albert E. Jenner, W. David Slawson, Howard Willens, Dr. Dale C Cameron, Dr. Howard P. Rome, and Dr. David A. Rothstein).
2. Oswald at p. 228.
3. Oswald at pp. 240–241.
4. Belin (1973) at p. 414.
5. Belin (1973) at p. 425.
6. Belin (1973) at p. 425
7. Belin (1973) at p. 426.
8. Belin (1973) at pp. 425–428.
9. Caufield at p. 542 (citing letter of Walker dated September 18, 1989, on file in Edwin A. Walker Papers, University of Texas library, Austin, Texas).
10. Leslie at p. 208.
11. Robert A. Fein and Bryan Vossekuil, *Preventing Assassination—Secret Service—Exceptional Case Study Project,* United States Secret Service (A project supported by the National Institute of Justice) (May 1997). Author Mel Ayton

elaborated that shooting the President of the United States brought the most notoriety and satisfaction to psychologically needy persons. Mel Ayton, *Hunting The President: Threats, Plots, and Assassinations—from FDR to Obama* (2014) at pp. 243–250.

12. 1 WCH at p. 123 (Marina Oswald testimony).

13. Erik H. Erikson, *Identity: Youth and Crisis* (1968).

14. Mailer at p. 786.

Chapter 42

1. McMillan at p. 536.
2. McMillan at p. 537.
3. 9 WCH at pp. 432–433 (Ruth Paine testimony).
4. McMillan at p. 537.
5. WCR at p. 131; McMillan at pp. 539–540.
6. McMillan at p. 543.
7. McMillan at p. 553.
8. When a mock trial of Lee Harvey Oswald was conducted in London in 1986, Marina declined to testify for either side. Vincent Bugliosi, *Reclaiming History: The Assassination of President John F. Kennedy* (2007) at p. xxiv. The mock jury convicted Oswald without Marina's testimony.
9. McMillan at pp. 546, 555–557.
10. Hosty at pp. 90–93.
11. WCR at p. 183; 1 WCH at p. 18 (Marina Oswald testimony).
12. 5 WCH at p. 388 (Marina Oswald testimony).
13. For assessments by Commissioners Ford and Russell, see Gerald R. Ford and John R. Stiles, *Portrait of the Assassin* (1965) at pp. 271–272, 495–503.
14. WCR at pp. 183–187.
15. Marina's statements on November 27, 1963, when Hosty was present for his first interview of Marina. Hosty believed that deportation steps would not be initiated. Hosty, Jr. at pp. 87–92.
16. 18 WCH at p. 642 (CE 994). By April 1964, Marina had received $68,000 in cash contributions. Ford (1965) at p. 500. Contracts with publishing companies exceeded $130,000. 2 WCH at pp. 23–29 (James Herbert Martin testimony); 16 WCH at p. 917 (CE 325). Her lawyer estimated her total income by February 27, 1964, as more than $200,000. 2 WCH at p. 29 (James Herbert Martin testimony).
17. Interview of Priscilla McMillan by author, July 25, 2017.
18. Willens (2013) at pp. 61–63; Howard Willens and Richard M. Mosk, "The Truth About Dallas," *The American Scholar,* Vol. 85, No. 3 (Summer 2016).
19. 1 WCH at p. 2 (Marina Oswald testimony).
20. 1 WCH at p. 125 (Marina Oswald testimony). After her testimony, Marina assured Ruth Paine—to Ruth's recollection—that the Warren Commission "were nice people, and they would be kind and thoughtful, that I shouldn't be worried about going to testify." Thomas Mallon, "Marina and Ruth," *The New Yorker* (December 3, 2001) at p. 85.
21. "Oswald didn't act alone, widow says," *Dallas Times Herald,* September 28, 1988, at p. A-3.
22. For interviews of Marina Oswald, see *Fort Worth Press*, December 26, 1963 ("Mrs. Oswald Visits Grave"); ("Mrs. Oswald Grateful to Many For Most Abundant Christmas" *Fort Worth Star Telegram*, December 27, 1963. Morning Edition, Section 1 at page 1. https://www.newspapers.com/image/640291581/; "Oswald Paraffin Tests Disputed by Attorney. 'Lee Shot Kennedy,' Wife Says." *Fort Worth Star-Telegram,* January 28, 1964, Evening Chaser Edition, Section 1at page 1. ["I don't want to believe but I have too much facts, and facts tell me that Lee shot Kennedy."]; https://www.youtube.com/watch?v=LRi0z#swQ (1964, "I don't want to go back to Russia. I want to be an American citizen"); http://jfk-archives.blogspot.cmc/2010/09marina-oswald.html#HSCA-Testimony-Audio [1977: six-hour testimony of Marian Oswald to HSCA. "When I gave testimony to the Warren Commission it was all the truth." "I do believe (Lee) was capable of (killing the president)." "I do not believe that Lee will trust and confide in anyone." "All the facts in the book (*Marina and Lee)* are true."]; *Dallas Times Herald,* October 13, 1977, at p. A-27 ["My regret through the years has ... been immense." "I can never forget nor forgive what Lee did to me and to my children, to the President and to his family, to the whole world." "For a while after the assassination I hated him ... now I no longer hate him." "He acted alone." "... the events of November 22, 1963, had to happen, the final act of a slow painful tragedy which was our life together."]; *Dallas Times Herald,* January 20, 1980, *Parade* ["I spoke to Lee in Dallas jail ... I saw guilt in his eyes even though he tried to hide it... Lee was too much of a loner to conspire with anybody about anything ... No government would have trusted him with anything important. He was too ... unstable.]; *Dallas Times Herald,* September 28, 1988, p. A-3 ["I think he was caught between two powers—the government and organized crime ... Lee was killed to keep his mouth shut.]; *Ladies Home Journal,* May 1993, p. 158 ["although she once believed her husband was guilty, she had now come to doubt the Warren Commission's findings "I'm all crumbled inside ... Lee was buried but I was (buried) even deeper by (the weight of my) humiliation.... Lee never fired a shot. He was a patsy.... I don't want to live in the past. I want to live right now, but it's not in my power."]; television interview by Tom Brokaw; August 19, 1993, https://www.youtube.com/watch?v=2GcivWUViRc ["I have been used ... People have betrayed me. People from government have 'lied to me.'" Marina asks President Clinton to pardon Lee.]; Interview by Oprah Winfrey, June 17, 1996, https.www.youtube.com/watch?v=01zvds9Vz0 [Marina says that by 1988 she became convinced that Lee was innocent. She believes that documents are being withheld. She says "33 years is too long for me to wait."]
23. Mailer at p. 785.

24. 5 WCH at p. 604 (Marina Oswald testimony).
25. Conversation of author with Priscilla McMillan, July 24, 2017.
26. John Harrison Pollack. "Marina Oswald Talks. From widow to housewife." *San Francisco Examiner,* January 5, 1979. Section 1 at pp. 19, 21. https://www.newspapers.com/image/460973520; *New York Times Magazine,* https://www.nytimes.com/1995/04/30/magazine/lee-harveys-oldest-june-oswald.html; see also, Mailer at p. 771.
27. McMillan at pp. 567–568; John Harrison Pollack. "Marina Oswald Talks. From widow to housewife." *San Francisco Examiner,* January 5, 1979. Section 1 at pp. 19, 21, 28. https://www.newspapers.com/image/460973520
28. Mailer at p. 774; Eric Aasen, *Whatever Happened to Marina Oswald,* www.kera.org/listen (2013); http://www.texasmonthly.com/story/lee-harvey%E2%99s-legacy.
29. Conversations of author with Ruth Paine and Priscilla McMillan.
30. Conversations of author with Ruth Paine.
31. https://web.archive.org/*http://jfkresearch.com/marina/marsha.htm (Interview of Marina by Oprah Winfrey, Nov. 22, 1996); Mallon at pp. 90–91.

Chapter 43

1. 5 WCH at p. 505 (Bernard Weissman testimony).
2. 5 WCH at pp. 515–516 (Bernard Weissman testimony).
3. 23 WCH at pp. 471–473 (CE 1815) (FBI interview of Larrie Schmidt).
4. 5 WCH at p. 516 (Bernard Weissman testimony).
5. 5 WCH at p. 516 (Bernard Weissman testimony).
6. 5 WCH at p. 532 (Bernard Weissman testimony).
7. 23 WCH at p. 473 (CE 1815) (FBI interview of Larrie Schmidt).
8. 5 WCH at p. 517 (Bernard Weissman testimony).
9. 18 WCH at p. 891 (CE 1052) (FBI Interview of Bernard Weissman).
10. 23 WCH 471–473 (CE 1815) (FBI interview of Larrie Schmidt).
11. Interview by author with Bernard Weissman, August 3, 2017.
12. Interview by author with Bernard Weissman, August 3, 2017. For information on demise of CUSA see, *Look Magazine,* January 1965, "CUSA: Conspiracy Plot That Failed."
13. Caufield at p. 543. It should be noted that Dr. Caufield does not believe this claim was true, although he does not dispute that such an incident was reported to the FBI. Even if untrue, the claim is relevant to whether Walker was receiving reports of hostility toward him.
14. Caufield at p. 549.
15. Caufield at p. 543.
16. 11 WCH at p. 428 (Edwin A. Walker testimony).
17. Caufield at p. 556.
18. Caufield at p. 557.
19. Caufield at p. 558.
20. Howard L. Brennan with J. Edward Cherryholme, *Eyewitness to History: the Kennedy Assassination: as seen by Howard Brennan* (1987) at pp. 1–44.
21. Brennan at p. 8
22. Brennan at pp. 19–20, 23.
23. Brennan at p. 25.
24. Brennan at pp. 17–18.
25. Brennan at p. 18. However sincere, Brennan's evaluation on this is probably erroneous because Oswald so quickly left the building after the shooting.
26. LeoGrande and Kornbluh, at p. 78.
27. "Excerpts from Castro's Talk," *New York Times,* November 25, 1963. https://www.archives.gov/files/research/jfk/releases/docid-32401329.pdf A transcript of the speech can be found at https://www.kennedysandking.com/john-f-kennedy-articles/fidel-castro-s-first-speech-on-the-jfk-assassination-11-23-1963; see also, Bugliosi at p. 304.
28. Bugliosi at p. 1294.
29. Warren Commission document CD 1135 in subsection headed "Developments on the Cuba Scene, A. Kennedy Assassination Shakes Cuba" at pp. 2–6. (Documents bearing the prefix CDare, not the exhibits bearing the prefix CE that are published in the Warren Commission hearing volumes.) http://www.maryferrell.org/showDoclhtml?docId=11531&relPageId=215 to 226.
30. Russo (1998) at p. 290.
31. Cubela's statements were not sworn testimony but responses to questioning by the HSCA staff. HSCA. JFK Document No. 012208. It is not clear whether they are statements under oath. https://www.maryferrell.org/showDoc.html?docId=800#relPageId=640. W. David Slawson, interview for documentary film *Truth Is the Only Client,* transcript p. 20.
32. https://history.state.gov/historicaldocuments/frus1964-68/v32/d315. *Foreign Relations of the United States 1964–1968,* Volume xxxii, Dominican Republic, Cuba, Haiti, Guyana, 315. Editorial Note.
33. HSCA Report at p. 126; Louis Stokes with David Chanoff, *The Gentleman from Ohio* (2016) at pp. 166–167.
34. HSCA Report at p. 127. [***=ellipses in the HSCA Report. "..."=author's ellipses.]
35. Sergei Khrushchev, *Khrushchev on Khrushchev* (1990) at pp. 53–54 (edited and translated by William Taubman).
36. William Taubman, *Khrushchev: The Man, His Era* (2003) at p. 604. Taubman and Sergei Khrushchev give different accounts Nikita Khrushchev's location in the Kremlin when the call about Kennedy was received. See Khrushchev at pp. 53–54.

37. Khrushchev at p. 54.
38. Khrushchev at pp. 50–51.
39. Taubman at pp. 10–18.
40. Oswald's friend, Ernst Titovets, feels differently. Titovets at p. 348. He offers no evidence, however.
41. Posner at pp. 35, 54–55; aarclibrary.org/publib/jfk/hsca/secclass/pdf/nosenko5-30-18 (p. 18–19 of 43).
42. Posner at p. 37; see also HSCA Report at pp. 101–102.
43. Posner at p. 35.
44. Posner at pp. 36–44.
45. Email from Howard Willens to author, March 31, 2019.
46. Email from Howard Willens to the author, February 3, 2019. See also, Posner, at p. 39; Willens at pp. 111 and 321.
47. HSCA Report at p. 102.
48. https://www.washingtondecoded.com/site/2007/03/how_moscow_unde_1.html (Article by Max Holland, dated 30 March 2007 entitled "How Moscow Undermined the Warren Commission.") Holland Emailed the author on April 10, 2019, that he believed that this information was provided to President Bill Clinton in 1991 by Vladimir Putin when the United States was experiencing good relations with Russia. The KGB's specific argument was that U.S. oil magnates had paid Ruby to kill Oswald and that Oswald had been selected to assassinate Kennedy in order to make that death appear as a communist plot. Christopher Andrew and Vasili Mitrokhin, *The Sword and the Shield: The Mitrokhin Archive and the Secret History of the KGB* (1999) at pp. 225–227. See also Boris Yeltsin, *The View from the Kremlin* (1994) at pp. 306–309, Appendix B.
49. washingtondecoded.com/site/2007/05/the_power_of_disinf. (Article by Max Holland entitled "The Power of Disinformation: The Lie That Linked CIA to the Kennedy Assassination").
50. Christopher Andrew and Vasili Mitrokhin, *The Sword and the Shield: The Mitrokhin Archive and the Secret History of the KGB* (1999) at pp. 226–227.
51. Andrew and Mitrokhin, *The Sword and the Shield: The Mitrokhin Archive and the Secret History of the KGB* (1999) at pp. 227–231.
52. Fred Litwin, *On the Trail of Delusion* (2020) at p. 263; Patricia Lambert, *False Witness: The Real Story of Jim Garrison's Investigation and Oliver Stone's Film JFK* (1998) at pp. xiii–xvii.
53. washingtondecoded.com/site/2007/05/the power of disinf. (Article by Max Holland entitled "The Power of Disinformation: The Lie That Linked CIA to the Kennedy Assassination").
54. Caro at pp. 324–329.
55. Caro at pp. 320–321.
56. Doris Kearns Goodwin, *Lyndon Johnson and the American Dream* (1976, 1991) at p. 170.
57. Caro at pp. 313.
58. Caro at p. 320.
59. Danger to Johnson did not abate. On November 14, 1965, the FBI arrested 31 year-old Billy Ray Pursley for threatening President Johnson. Pursley believed Johnson had brought about Kennedy's murder. Mentally ill, he was placed on probation. In March of 1966, the FBI arrested Oswald S. Pick for threatening and taking steps to kill Johnson. He was sentenced to five years prison. Mel Ayton, *Hunting the President: Threats, Plots, and Assassination Attempts—from FDR to Obama* (2014) at p. 83.
60. Doris Kearns Goodwin at p. 178.
61. Bugliosi at p. 989, footnote.
62. Bugliosi at p. 995.
63. Art Swift, "Majority in U.S. Still Believe JFK Killed in Conspiracy" (Gallup Polls, 1963–2013), gallup.com/poll/165893/majority-believe-jfk-killed_cons piracy.
64. https://fivethirtyeight.com/features/the-one-thing-in-politics-most-americans-believe-in-jfk-conspiracies?
65. A partial exception to this was Gerald R Ford's book, *Portrait of the Assassin*, which was published in 1965.
66. William Coleman and Arlen Specter described their own work on the Commission in their autobiographies but did not address the other analyses of the Commission's report. William Coleman, *Counsel for the Situation* (2010); Arlen Specter, *Passion for the Truth* (2000).
67. Edward Kennedy at p. 210.
68. Willens at p. 288.
69. Edward Kennedy at p. 211. One should be aware that Robert Kennedy's son, Robert, Jr., has expressed his own belief that there was a conspiracy and that his father concurred. https://youtu.be/5quAg6thaEc?t=81. Robert, Jr., was 14 at the time his father died, leaving some question as to what Robert, Sr., actually said to his son.
70. Edward M. Kennedy, *True Compass* (2009) at pp. 211–212, 339. A few days after the Commission's report was issued, President Johnson told Senator Kennedy that he believed the FBI was negligent in not warning the Secret Service that Lee Oswald was dangerous. Id. at p. 224.
71. Willens at pp. 23–24.
72. In 1975, Walter Sheridan, former head of the FBI's Hoffa team in the Criminal Division of the Justice Department, provided a different take in telling a Senate committee, "Hoover did not want the Warren Commission to conduct an exhaustive investigation for fear it would discover important and relevant facts that we in the FBI had not discovered … [since] it would be greatly embarrassing to him … and the FBI as a whole." 11 HSCA at p. 53.
73. Willens at p. 24.
74. Report, HSCA, Vol. III, at pp. 513–525 (James H. Gale testimony and JFK Exhibit F-460).
75. Report, HSCA, Vol. III, at p. 514 (JFK Exhibit F-460); Bugliosi at pp. 1246 citing FBI Report 124-10182-104 (December 10, 1963).
76. Bugliosi at p. 1246.
77. Bugliosi Endnotes pp. 121–122, note top 328 quoting Assistant FBI Director Alan Belmont. House Select Committee on Assassinations, Record 180-10099-10282 (1978) at pp. 1, 6, and 11.

78. Report, HSCA, Vol. III, pp. 513–525 (JFK Exhibit F-460).
79. Willens at pp. 257–258.
80. Cartha D. "Deke" DeLoach, *Hoover's FBI: The Inside Story by Hoover's Trusted Lieutenant* (1995) at p. 150.
81. DeLoach at pp. 150–151.
82. WCR at pp. 443–444. Agent Hosty believed that to interview Oswald at that time would have been counterproductive. He does not mention in his justification that Oswald had left him a threatening note, an action that might have made contacting him promptly even more necessary. Hosty at pp. 161–163. The Commission's rebuke was to the "Bureau," not to a particular agent. Criticism by the Commission of a particular agent would have been a form of public accusation that the agent bore responsibility for the president's death. In that respect, Hoover keeping his discipline secret protected Hosty and other agents from public shame.
83. Bugliosi at pp. 1246; Bugliosi, Endnotes pages 121–123, note top 328. See also FBI memo of J. H. Gale dated September 30, 1964, headed "Shortcomings of Handling Lee Harvey Oswald Matter by FBI Personnel," https://maryferrell.org/showDoc.html?docld=10100#relPageld=14.
84. Willens at p. 296.
85. Willens at pp. 119–120, 258, 295–296.
86. DeLoach at p. 150.
87. Hosty at pp. 163–166.
88. Hosty at pp. 159–160.
89. Hosty at pp. 173–174.
90. Willens at pp. 155–158.
91. Willens at pp. 66–70.
92. WCR at p. 429.
93. WCR at pp. 24.
94. WCR at p. 429.
95. WCR at p. 26.
96. WCR at p. 429.
97. 4 WCH at p. 302 (Testimony of Robert Bouck).
98. WCR at pp. 461–462.
99. WCR at p. 462; 18 WCH at pp. 720 (CE No. 1023).
100. WCR at p. 463.
101. WCR at p. 429.
102. Robert A. Fein and Bryan Vossekuil, 44 *Journal of Forensic Sciences* (1999) at p. 321. The Fein/Vossekuil study was preceded by *Behavioral Science and the Secret Service: Toward the Prevention of Assassination,* Jane Takeuchi, Fredric Solomon, W. Walter Meninger, editors (National Academy Press, 1981).
103. Takeuchi et al. at p. 2.
104. Takeuchi et al. at p. 26.
105. *Protective Intelligence and Threat Assessment Investigations: A Guide for State and Local Law Enforcement Officials* by Robert A. Fein and Bryan Vossekuil (January 2000) (National Institute of Justice). Selected incidents of presidential protection, threatened assassinations, motivations, and prosecutions from 1932 to 2014 are also described in Mel Ayton, *Hunting the President: Threats, Plots, and Assassination Attempts from FDR to Obama (2014).*
106. Fein and Vossekuil (January 2000) (National Institute of Justice).
107. Fein and Vossekuil (1999) at p. 323.
108. Fein and Vossekuil (1999) at p. 321.
109. Fein and Vossekuil (1999) at pp. 324–325.
110. Fein and Vossekuil (2000) at pp. 14–15.
111. Fein and Vossekuil (2000) at p.13.
112. Fein and Vossekuil (2000) at p. 17.
113. Fein and Vossekuil (2000) at p. 19.
114. Fein and Vossekuil (2000) at p. 19.
115. Fein and Vossekuil (2000) at p. 41.
116. Fein and Vossekuil (2000) at p. 16.
117. E.g., Robert T. M. Phillips, "Assessing Presidential Stalkers and Assassins," 34 *Journal of the American Academy of Psychiatry and the Law,* Issue 2 (2006) at pp. 154–164.
118. In a telephone conference with the author on December 9, 2019, Bryan Vossekuil explained that the ECSP study had not discussed Oswald's life in great detail because the events were so many years before that study.
119. David Robarge, *John McCone: Director of Central Intelligence* (1961–1965) at p. 95, https://www.cia.gov/library/readingroom/doc/DOC_000126720.pdf.
120. Robarge at pp. 86, 95–99.
121. D. Payne (1994) at pp. 320–321.
122. D. Payne (1994) at p. 318.
123. D. Payne (1994) at p. 321.
124. D. Payne (1994) at p. 321.
125. Diane Holloway, editor, *Dallas and the Jack Ruby Trial* (2001) at p. 5.
126. D. Payne (1994) at pp. 322–324.
127. D. Payne (1994) at pp. 322–324.
128. Paul H. Santa Cruz, *Making JFK Matter* (2015) at pp. 29–56.
129. Stephen Fagin, *Assassination and Commemoration* (2013) at p. 35.
130. Fagin at pp. 33–34; Lacie Ballinger, et. al., *The Rededication of the John Fitzgerald Kennedy Memorial: June 24, 2000* [The Sixth Floor Museum at Dealey Plaza, 2000].
131. Fagin at p. 36.
132. Fagin at pp. 75–76.
133. Fagin at p. 37.
134. Fagin at pp. 37–38.
135. Fagin at p. 40.
136. Fagin at p. 41.
137. Fagin at p. 43.
138. Fagin at pp. 54–58.
139. Fagin at p. 43.
140. Fagin at pp. 45, 53.
141. Fagin at p. 59.
142. Fagin at p. 48.
143. Fagin at p. 109.
144. Fagin at pp. 99–100.
145. Fagin at p. 73.
146. Fagin at pp. 61–62.
147. Fagin at pp. 123–137.

Chapter 44

1. HSCA, Vol. XI, Attachment E, at p. 261 (Wesley J. Liebeler testimony).
2. See Warren Commission memo, August 17, 1964, Burt W. Griffin to Howard Willens, National Archives, John F. Kennedy assassination files.
3. Howard Willens and Richard Most, "The Truth About Dallas," *The American Scholar*, Vol. 85, No. 3 (Summer 2016).
4. See, e.g., James Buchanan, *Who Killed Kennedy?* (1964); Joachim Joesten, *Oswald: Assassin or Fall Guy?* (1964); Harold Weisberg, *Whitewash* (1965); Mark Lane, *Rush to Judgment* (1966).
5. Edward Jay Epstein, *Inquest* (1966); Mark Lane, *Rush to Judgment* (1966); Richard Popkin, *The Second Oswald* (1966); Leo Sauvage, *The Oswald Affair* (1966); Harold Weisberg, *Whitewash* (1966).
6. Jim Moore, *Conspiracy of One* (1990) at pp. 79, 81.
7. Author Philip Shenon said, "*Inquest* would be remembered as the book that gave credibility to the conspiracy-theory movement." Philip Shenon, *A Cruel and Shocking Act: The Secret History of the Kennedy Assassination* (2013) at p. 501.
8. Senator John Sherman Cooper, Congressman Hale Boggs, Congressman Gerald Ford, Commission member Allen Dulles, Commission member John McCloy, General Counsel J. Lee Rankin, Assistant Counsel Norman Redlich, Howard Willens, Joseph Ball, Melvin Eisenberg, Wesley J. Liebeler, Arlen Specter, and Samuel Stern, and Commission historian Alfred Goldberg.
9. Epstein (1966) at pp. 41–61, 115–126.
10. Epstein (1966) at p. 153.
11. Some of the outrage is quoted by author Vincent Bugliosi in *Reclaiming History: The Assassination of President John F. Kennedy* (2007) at p. 348 footnote. See also, Willens at pp. 298–299; House Select Committee on Assassinations, Appendix. Vol XI, pp. 442–443 (Howard Willens testimony).
12. Confirmed by author through conversations and emails with Howard Willens and David Slawson and letter from Norman Redlich to Andrew Hacker dated June 2, 1966.
13. I was never interviewed by Epstein. He mentions my work only twice. Epstein (1966) at pp. 96–97, 101. In both, his statements are inaccurate and misleading. In one he states, "the staff was explicitly prohibited from controverting the testimony of witnesses." To the contrary, we constantly engaged in attempting to determine witness credibility. Epstein (1966) at p. 98. The statement that Epstein quotes from Chief Justice Warren was that it was improper for staff lawyers to tell a witness he was lying. None of us would disagree. None of us was ever "prohibited from controverting the testimony of witnesses." The second misleading statement is that in June 1964, I was "ordered to proceed with other areas of investigation," suggesting that I was told to cease pursuing how Ruby entered the police department basement. Epstein (1966) at p. 101. The issue never left our agenda, and we were able to conduct all of the investigation we believed necessary.
14. Epstein (1966) at pp. 96–97.
15. Bugliosi at pp. 348–350.
16. Bugliosi at pp. 348–350.
17. HSCA, Vol. XI, Attachment E. at pp. 217–218 (Wesley J. Liebeler testimony).
18. Willens at pp. 277–280.
19. HSCA, Vol. XI, Attachment E. at p. 220 (Wesley J. Liebeler testimony).
20. HSCA, Vol. XI, Attachment E. at pp. 260–261 (Wesley J. Liebeler testimony).
21. The author has a copy of the letter. Other copies were sent to Chief Justice Warren and Howard Willens. Willens at p. 299. Willens has informed the author that all of his records were sent to the National Archives.
22. Shenon at p. 501.
23. Bugliosi at p. 994.
24. Willens at p. 302.
25. Willens at p. 303.
26. Posner at p. 455.
27. Rockefeller Commission, Final Report, *The Investigation of the Assassination of President John F. Kennedy: Performance of the Intelligence Agencies*, Book V, Select Committee to Study Governmental Operations With Respect to Intelligence Activities (1976).
28. Congressman Louis Stokes characterized Warren Commission critics as "piggybacking" on the efforts of the Congressional Black Caucus to secure an investigation of the King assassination. Stokes (2016) at pp. 157–158; see also Blakey and Billings (1992) at p. 70.
29. Stokes (2016) at pp. 157–158.
30. HSCA Report, Part 2, Findings and Recommendations (1979) at p. 47.
31. HSCA Report at pp. 41–63.
32. HSCA Report at p. 63.
33. HSCA, Report Part 2, Findings and Recommendations (1979) at pp. 65–95, 483–491.
34. HSCA Report at p. 487.
35. Bugliosi at pp. 380–381; see also Endnotes pp. 196–218 for a discussion of the National Academy's efforts.
36. Bugliosi at pp. 1350–1352.
37. Bugliosi at p. 1349.
38. See, Max Holland, *How the KGB Duped Oliver Stone*, https://www.thedailybeast.com/was-russia-behind-cia-killed-jfk . Max Holland, "The Lie that Linked the CIA to the Kennedy Assassination: The Power of Disinformation," Central Intelligence Agency (2001), https://www.cia.gov/library/center-for-the-study-of-intelligence/CSI-publications/CSI-studies/studies/fall_winter_2001/article.
39. Bugliosi at pp. 1351–1352.
40. Stokes at p. 169. Newspaper columnist George Will wrote, "Stone falsifies so much he may be an intellectual sociopath, indifferent to the truth." Fred Litwin, *On the Trail of Delusion* (2020)

at p. 277. For a detailed analysis of the movie *JFK*, see Bugliosi at pp. 1347–1436.

41. These were the younger members. After 28 years, many of the older members had died or were unable to make the trip.

42. "Ex-Warren Staffers Urge JFK Data Release," *Washington Post*, January 31, 1992, p. A-7.

43. Email from Howard Willens to author, March 30, 2019.

44. Public Law 102–526, 44 USC Section 2107 (1992).

45. John R. Tunnheim, "The Assassination Records Review Board: Unlocking the Government's Secret Files on the Murder of a President," *The Public Lawyer*, Vol 8, No. 1, Winter 2000.

46. Willens at pp. 336–337. These records remained subject to litigation at the time this book went to press. Presidents Obama, Trump, and Biden had upheld agency requests for privacy.

Chapter 45

1. 18 U.S.C. Sections 1961–1968; see also, https// wikipedia//wiki/Racketeer_Influenced_and_Corrupt_Organizations_Act.

2. Blakey Tr. at pp. 2–3.

3. Blakey Tr. at p. 96.

4. Blakey and Billings (1992) at pp. 277–279.

5. Author Gus Russo has told this author that the reputed cellmate has admitted to Russo that he never heard Marcello make the statement.

6. For analyses of the credibility of witnesses claiming that Carlos Marcello or other members of organized crime orchestrated the assassination of President Kennedy, the reader should consider Gerald Posner, *Cased Closed: Lee Harvey Oswald and the Assassination of JFK* (1993) pp. 460–466, and Vincent Bugliosi, *Reclaiming History: The Assassination of President John F. Kennedy* (2007) pp. 1167–1187. The view of the House Select Committee on Assassinations with respect to those witnesses may be found in Part 2, pages 159–176 of its report. Blakey gives his view at G. Robert Blakey and Billings (1992) at pp. 205–295, 397–424.

7. This sentence and some others were requested by Blakey after he read a first draft of this chapter. He did not say it at the time of our interview, but it provides a more complete view of his reasoning.

8. Blakey and Billings (1992) at p. 279.

9. For a cursory history of FBI placing "bugs" (sound devices) in rooms used by organized crime leaders beginning in 1959, see Gerald Posner, *Case Closed: Lee Harvey Oswald and the Assassination of JFK* (1993) at pp. 463–464; Blakey and Billings (1992) at pp. 238–240. There is no evidence that Carlos Marcello was the subject of FBI bugging at any relevant time before or after November 22, 1963.

10. In retrospect, this point may have been exaggerated. Nelson Delgado suggests that Oswald acquired at least functional (though not fluent) Spanish.

11. HSCA Report at pp. 156–160.

12. See Bugliosi, Endnotes, pp. 676–690. Bugliosi gives his analysis of what he believes Joannides knew about the anti-Castro group, Student Revolutionary Directorate (DRE), and its relationship to the CIA, Oswald, and the assassination of President Kennedy. Bugliosi outlines the suspicion of the House Select Committee staffer, Gaeton Fonzi, that the CIA utilized the DRE to assassinate Kennedy. Bugliosi, Endnotes, pp. 685–687. A line of questioning by Blakey for Joannides would have been what Joannides knew, prior to November 22, 1963, about Oswald's relationship with DRE. Bugliosi, Endnotes, p. 689. Although failure of the CIA to communicate knowledge about Oswald's relationship to the FBI and Secret Service might have been negligence, Bugliosi concludes that there is no evidence that the DRE murdered Kennedy or that Joannides "was involved with the DRE, or anyone else in the murder of Kennedy." Bugliosi Endnotes, p. 690.

13. Blakey Tr. at pp. 96–97.

14. Blakey Tr. at pp. 96–97.

15. Blakey Tr. at p. 97.

16. Blakey Tr. at p. 100.

Chapter 46

1. Wikipedia. Mark Lane (author), Section 2.4. A poster advertising the movie said, "Based on Novel by Mark Lane and Donald Freed." The novel was entitled *Executive Action*, copyrighted 1973. The co-author, Donald Freed, was a journalist. http//Spartacus-eductional.com/JFKfreed.htm. The novel and movie apparently were written at the same time and were intended to reinforce sales for each. Available for viewing on Amazon.com Prime Video.

2. HSCA Report at p. 9.

3. Belin, *Final Disclosure* at pp. 98–99.

4. Hosty at pp. 181–182.

5. Belin, *Final Disclosure* at pp. 183–185.

6. HSCA Report at p. 9.

Postscript

1. For Mary Ferrell Foundation: www.maryferrell.org/php/showlist.php?docset=1000. Instructions on its use are at https://www.maryferrell.org/search.html. For the National Archives, use the JFK Assassination Reference System at https://www.archives.gov/research/jfk.

Bibliography

Books and Articles

Abrahamsen, David. "A Study of Lee Harvey Oswald: Psychological Capability of Murder," *Bulletin of the New York Academy of Medicine* Vol. 43, No. 10 (October 1967).

Abrams, Dan and David Fisher. *Kennedy's Avenger: Assassination, Conspiracy, and the Forgotten Trial of Jack Ruby.* Toronto: Hanover Square Press, 2021.

Adelson, Alan. *The Ruby Oswald Affair.* Seattle: Romar Books, 1988.

Anderson, Susan. *The Past on Trial: The Sixteenth Street Baptist Church Bombing, Civil Rights Memory and the Remaking of Birmingham.* Dissertation, University of North Carolina at Chapel Hill, 2008.

Andrew, Christopher and Vasili Mitrokhin. *The Sword and the Shield: The Mitrokhin Archive and the Secret History of the KGB.* New York: Basic Books, 1999.

Aynsworth, Hugh with Michaud, Steve. *JFK: Breaking the News.* Richardson, TX: International Focus Press, 2003.

Ayton, Mel. *Hunting the President: Threats, Plots, and Assassination Attempts from FDR to Obama.* New York: MJF Books, 2015.

Baker, Judyth Vary. "Lee Harvey Oswald, the Reader: Oswald's Reading Habits in New Orleans, and Evidence Manipulation," April 10, 2015. https://fdocuments.net/document/lee-harvey-oswald-his-reading-habits-in-new-orleans-and-evidence-manipulation.html?page=1.

Ballinger, Lacie, et al. *The Rededication of the John Fitzgerald Kennedy Memorial: June 24, 2000.* Dallas, TX: The Sixth Floor Museum at Dealey Plaza, 2000.

Beale, E.E., J.C. Overholser, and J. Ridley. "Reasons for living: blocking passive suicidal ideation from becoming active suicide plans," pp. 99–132 in Patty Terri and Ron Price (eds), *Understanding Suicide: Perspectives, Risk Factors, and Gender Differences*; New York: Nova Science, 2018.

Beckemeier, Eric. *Traitors Beware: A History of Robert DePugh's Minutemen.* Hardin, MO: Eric C. Beckemeier, 2007.

Belin, David. *Final Disclosure: The Full Truth About the Assassination of President Kennedy.* New York: Charles Scribner's Sons, 1988.

Belin, David. *November 22, 1963: You Are the Jury.* New York: Quadrangle, 1973.

Belli, Melvin M. with Maurice C. Carroll. *Dallas Justice: The Real Story of Jack Ruby and His Trial.* New York: David McKay Company, Inc., 1964.

Beschloss, Michael R. *The Crisis Years.* New York: HarperCollins, 1991.

Beschloss, Michael R. *Taking Charge: The Johnson White House Tapes, 1963–1964.* New York: Simon & Schuster, 1997.

Blakey, G. Robert and Richard N. Billings. *The Plot to Kill the President.* Times Books, 1981. Reprinted as *Fatal Hour: The Assassination of President Kennedy by Organized Crime, the Contract. The Cover-Up. Including Startling New Information.* New York: Berkley Books, 1992.

Blanton, Thomas. "Annals of Brinksmanship," *The Wilson Quarterly* (Summer, 1997).

Bohning, Don. *The Castro Obsession: U.S. Covert Operations Against Cuba, 1959–1965.* Washington, DC: Potomac Books, Inc., 2005.

Brennan, Howard L. with J. Edward Cherryholme. *Eyewitness to History: The Kennedy Assassination: as Seen by Howard Brennan.* Waco, TX: Texian Press, 1987.

Buchanan, James. *Who Killed Kennedy?* New York: G.P. Putnam's, 1964.

Bugliosi, Vincent. *Reclaiming History: The Assassination of President John F. Kennedy.* New York: W.W. Norton & Company, 2007.

Caro, Robert A. *The Years of Lyndon Johnson: The Passage of Power.* New York: Alfred A. Knopf, 2012.

Caufield, Jeffrey H. *General Walker and the Murder of President Kennedy: The Extensive New Evidence of a Radical-Right Conspiracy.* Clearwater: Moreland Press, 2015.

Clarke, Thurston. *JFK's Last Hundred Days: The Transformation of a Man and the Emergence of a Great President.* New York: The Penguin Press, 2013.

Coleman, William T. with Donald T. Bliss. *Counsel for the Situation: Shaping the Law to Realize America's Promise.* Washington, DC: The Brookings Institution, 2010.

Cravens, Chris. "Edwin A. Walker and the Right Wing in Dallas, 1960–1966." Master's Thesis, Texas State University—San Marcos, 1991.

Cray, G. Edward. *Chief Justice: A Biography of Earl Warren.* New York: Simon & Schuster, 1997.

Crichton, Jack. *The Republican-Democratic Campaigns in Texas in 1964.* Self-Published, 2004.

David, Lester and Irene David. *Bobby Kennedy: The Making of a Folk Hero.* New York: Dodd, Mead, 1986.

Davison, Jean. *Oswald's Game.* New York: W.W. Norton & Company, 1983.

DeLoach, Cartha D. *Hoover's FBI: The Inside Story by Hoover's Trusted Lieutenant.* Washington, DC: Regnery Publ., 1995.

de Mohrenschildt, George. "I Am a Patsy! I Am a Patsy!" (unpublished manuscript, March 1977), https://www.jfk-assassination.net/russ/jfkinfo4/jfk12/hscapatsy.htm.

Dempsey, John Mark (ed.) *The Jack Ruby Trial Revisited: The Diary of Jury Foreman Max Causey.* Denton, TX: University of North Texas Press, 2000.

DeRonja, Frank S. and Max Holland. "A Technical Investigation Pertaining to the First Shot Fired in the JFK Assassination." *Journal of the Association for Crime Scene Reconstruction.* Vol. 20 (2016).

Deutsch, Hermann B. *The Huey Long Murder Case.* Garden City, NY: Doubleday, 1963.

Deutscher, Isaac. *The Prophet Outcast, Leon Trotsky: 1929–1940.* London; New York: Oxford University Press, 1963.

Enten, Harry. "Most People Believe in JFK Conspiracy Theories." *FiveThirtyEight,* October 23, 2017, https://fivethirtyeight.com/features/the-one-thing-in-politics-most-americans-believe-in-jfk-conspiracies?.

Epstein, Edward Jay. *Counterplot.* New York: Viking Press, 1968.

Epstein, Edward Jay. *Inquest: The Warren Commission and the Establishment of Truth.* New York: The Viking Press, 1966.

Epstein, Edward Jay. *Legend: The Secret World of Lee Harvey Oswald.* New York: McGraw-Hill Book Company, 1978.

Erikson, Erik H. *Identity: Youth and Crisis.* New York: W.W. Norton Company, 1968.

Fagin, Stephen. *Assassination and Commemoration.* Norman, OK: University of Oklahoma Press, 2013.

Fein, Robert A., and Bryan Vossekuil. "Assassinations in the United States: An Operational Study of Recent Assassinations, Attacks, and Near Lethal Approaches," *Journal of Forensic Sciences* Vol. 44 (1999).

Fein, Robert A. and Bryan Vossekuil. *Protective Intelligence and Threat Assessment Investigations: A Guide for State and Local Law Enforcement Officials.* Washington, DC: U.S. Department of Justice, Office of Justice Programs, National Institute of Justice, 2000.

Ford, Gerald R. and John R. Stiles. *Portrait of the Assassin.* New York: Ballantine Books, Inc., 1965.

Freed, Donald, and Mark Lane. *Executive Action.* New York: Dell Publishing Co, 1973.

Garrison, Jim. *On the Trail of the Assassins.* New York: Warner Books, 1988.

Goodwin, Doris Kearns. *Lyndon Johnson and the American Dream.* New York: St. Martin's Press, 1976, 1991.

Goodwin, Richard. *Remembering America: A Voice from the Sixties.* Boston, MA: Little, Brown and Company, 1988.

Haig, Jr., Alexander M. with Charles McCarry. *Inner Circles: How America Changed the World* New York: Warner Books, 1992.

Heller, Deane, and David Heller. *The Berlin Wall.* New York: Walker, 1962.

Holland, Max. "The Assassination Tapes," *The Atlantic Monthly* (June 2004).

Holland, Max. *The Kennedy Assassination Tapes.* New York: Alfred A. Knopf, 2004.

Holland, Max. "The Power of Disinformation: The Lie That Linked CIA to the Kennedy Assassination"; CIA Report Information. Vol 44, No. 5. (2001). https://www.cia.gov/static/9a38d5a70e38c768763718c45d98a092/Lie-That-Linked-CIA.pdf.

Holland, Max. "The Truth Was Out There," *Newsweek* (November 28, 2014).

Holloway, Diane. *The Mind of Oswald.* Victoria, BC: Trafford Publishing, 2000.

Holloway, Diane (ed.) *Dallas and the Jack Ruby Trial: Memoir of Judge Joe B. Brown, Sr.* San Jose: Authors Choice Press, 2001.

Hosty, James P., Jr. with Thomas Hosty. *Assignment Oswald.* New York: Arcade Publishing, Inc., 1996.

Howe, Irving. *The Basic Writings of Trotsky.* New York: Vintage Books, A Division of Random House, 1963.

Jennings, Peter. *Peter Jennings Reporting, the Kennedy Assassination—Beyond Conspiracy,* Springs Media Inc., ABC-News (2003).

JFK Assassination Debate: Mark Lane vs. Wesley Liebeler (January 25, 1967) UCLA Communications Studies Archives, YouTube, https://www.youtube.com/watch?v=47fu1NQ-wls.

Joesten, Joachim. *Oswald: Assassin or Fall Guy?* New York: Marzani & Munsell, 1964.

Kaiser, David. *The Road to Dallas: The Assassination of John F. Kennedy.* Cambridge, MA: The Belknap Press of Harvard University, 2008.

Kantor, Seth. *The Ruby Cover-Up.* New York: Kensington Publishing Co., 1978.

Kantor, Seth. *Who Was Jack Ruby?* New York: Everest House, 1978.

Kaplan, John and Jon R. Waltz. *The Trial of Jack Ruby: A Classic Study of Courtroom Strategies.* New York: The Macmillan Company, 1965.

Kaplan, Robert M. "Jack Ruby's Complex: The Factors Driving the Assassination of Lee Harvey Oswald," *Forensic Res. In.t J.* 1(6): 00032. D01 (2015); http://medcraveonline.com/FRCIJ-FRCLJ-01-0032.php.

Kelleher, James. *He Was Expendable: National Security, Political and Bureaucratic Cover-Ups in the Murder of President John F. Kennedy.* Lexington, KY: Lulu Publishing Service, 2014.

Kennedy, Edward M. *True Compass: A Memoir.* New York: Hachette Book Group, 2009.

Kennedy, John F. *Profiles in Courage*. New York: HarperCollins, 1956.

Kennedy, Robert F. *Thirteen Days*. New York: W.W. Norton, 1969.

Khrushchev, Sergei. *Khrushchev on Khrushchev: An Inside Account of the Man and His Era by His Son, Sergei Khrushchev*. Boston: Little, Brown and Company, 1990.

King, Martin Luther, Jr. *Letter from a Birmingham Jail* (1963). http://okra.stanford.edu/transcription/document_images/undecided/630416-019.pdf.

Klobuchar, Lisa. *1963 Birmingham Church Bombing; The Ku Klux Klan's History of Terror*. Minneapolis, MN: Compass Point Books, 2009.

Lambert, Patricia. *False Witness: The Real Story of Jim Garrison's Investigation and Oliver Stone's Film JFK*. New York: M. Evans and Company, Inc., 1998.

Lane, Mark. *A Citizen's Dissent*. New York: Holt, Rinehart and Winston, 1968.

Lane, Mark. *Rush to Judgment*. New York: Holt, Rinehart and Winston, 1966.

Lane, Mark and Robert K. Tannenbaum. *Last Word: My Indictment of the CIA in the Murder of JFK*. New York: Skyhorse Publishing, 2011.

LeoGrande, William and Peter Kornbluh. *Back Channel to Cuba: The Hidden History of Negotiations Between Washington and Havana*. Chapel Hill: University of North Carolina Press, 2014.

Leonnig, Carol. *Zero Fail: The Rise and Fall of the Secret Service*. New York: Penguin Random House, LLC, 2021.

Leslie, Warren. *Dallas: Public and Private*. New York: Avon, 1964.

Levitas, Daniel, *The Terrorist Next Door: The Militia Movement and the Radical Right*. New York: Thomas Dunne Books/St. Martin's Press, 2002.

Litwin, Fred. *I Was a Teenage Conspiracy Freak*. NorthernBlues Books, 2018.

Litwin, Fred. *On the Trail of Delusion*. NorthernBlues Books, 2020.

Long, Alecia. *Cruising for Conspirators: How a New Orleans DA Prosecuted the Kennedy Assassination*. Chapel Hill: The University of North Carolina Press, 2021.

Mailer, Norman. *Oswald's Tale: An American Mystery*. New York: Random House, 1995.

Mallon, Thomas. "Marina and Ruth," *The New Yorker* (December 3, 2001).

Mallon, Thomas. *Mrs. Paine's Garage and the Murder of John F. Kennedy*. New York: Vintage Books, 2002.

Manchester, William. *Death of a President*. New York: Hachette Book Group, 1967.

Manchester, William. *Portrait of a President*. New York: Macfadden-Bartell Books, 1962.

McAdams, John. *JFK Assassination Logic: How to Think About Claims of Conspiracy*. Washington, DC: Potomac Books, 2011.

McFadyen, Chris. "Sixties Flashback: Lee Harvey Oswald Visits Spring Hill," *Mobile Bay Magazine* (January 2014).

McMillan, Priscilla Johnson. *Marina and Lee: The Tormented Love and Fatal Obsession Behind Lee Harvey Oswald's Assassination of John F. Kennedy*. Lebanon, NH: Steerford Press, 2013. [Originally published as *Marina and Lee* by Harper and Row, 1977; all citations are from the 2013 edition unless otherwise indicated.]

Miller, Merle. *Lyndon, an Oral Biography*. New York: Putnam, 1980.

Minutaglio, Bill and Steven L. Davis. *Dallas 1963*. New York: Hachette Book Group, 2013.

Moore, Jim. *Conspiracy of One: The Definitive Book on the Kennedy Assassination*. Fort Worth, TX: The Summit Group, 1990.

Myers, Dale K. *With Malice—Lee Harvey Oswald and the Murder of Officer J.D. Tippit*. Milford, MI: Oak Cliff Press, 1998.

Myers, Dale K. and Todd W. Vaughan. "Mr. Holland's Opus: Max Holland and National Geographic Channel's 'The Lost Bullet,'" January 5, 2012. http://jfkfiles.blogspot.com/2012/01/mr-hollands-opus-max-holland-and.html.

Nechiporenko, Oleg Maximovich. *Passport to Assassination: The Never Told Story of Lee Harvey Oswald by the KGB Colonel Who Knew Him*. New York: Carol Publishing Group, 1993.

Newman, Albert H. *The Assassination of John F. Kennedy: The Reasons Why*. New York: Clarkson N. Potter, Inc., 1970.

O'Brien, Gary W. *Oswald's Politics*. Victoria, B.C.: Trofford Publishing, 2010.

Olsen, Charles and Scott Martin (Sonalysts, Inc.). "Analysis of the Dallas Police Department Tape Recording Relating to the Assassination of President John F. Kennedy" (October 15, 2013). https://www.washingtondecoded.com/files/sonalysts.pdf.

Olsen, Charles, Mark Bamforth, and Jonathan Grant (Sonalysts, Inc.). "Observations on Properties of Impulses Attributed to Gunfire." (June 11, 2013). Appended report in https://www.washingtondecoded.com/files/sonalysts.pdf

Oswald, Robert. *Lee: A Portrait of Lee Harvey Oswald*. New York: Coward-McCann, 1967.

Parker, Greg. "Oswald and Albert Schweitzer College," *Covert History* (July 4, 2005). http://coverthistory.blogspot.com/2005/07/oswald-and-albert-schweitzer-college.html

Parsch, Andreas. "Jupiter IRBM." http://www.astronautix.com/j/jupiterirbm.html.

Payne, Darwin. *Big D: Triumphs and Troubles in an American Supercity in the 20th Century* Dallas, TX: Three Forks Press, 1994, revised ed., 2000.

Payne, Robert. *Portrait of a Revolutionary: Mao Tse Tung*. London; New York: Abelard-Schuman, 1961.

Phillips, Robert T.M. "Assessing Presidential Stalkers and Assassins," *Journal of the American Academy of Psychiatry and the Law*. Vol. 34 (2006).

Pierson, James. *Camelot and the Cultural Revolution: How the Assassination of John F. Kennedy Shattered American Liberalism*. New York: Encounter Books, 2007.

Popkin, Richard Henry. *The Second Oswald.* New York: Avon Books, 1966.

Posner, Gerald, *Case Closed: Lee Harvey Oswald and the Assassination of JFK.* New York: Random House, 1993.

Redekop, John H. *The American Far Right: Billy James Hargis and the Christian Crusade.* Grand Rapids, MI: W.B. Eerdmans Pub. Co., 1968.

Reiman, Richard A. "Six 'Shots' in Dallas: 'Framing' the Perpetrator of the Kennedy Assassination through the Zapruder Film, 1963–2012. *Journal of Perpetrator Research.* Vol. 2, No. 2 (October 5, 2019).

Robarge, David. *John McCone: Director of Central Intelligence* (1961–1965), Washington, DC: Center for the Study of Intelligence, January 1, 2005. https://www.cia.gov/library/readingroom/doc/DOC_000126720.pdf.

Russo, Gus. *Live by the Sword: Lee Harvey Oswald and the Assassination of JFK.* Baltimore, MD: Bancroft Press, 1998.

Russo, Gus and Stephen Molton. *Brothers in Arms: The Kennedys, the Castros, and the Politics of Murder.* New York: Bloomsbury USA, 2008.

Sabato, Larry J. *The Kennedy Half-Century: The Presidency, Assassination, and Lasting Legacy of John F. Kennedy.* New York: Bloomsbury USA, 2013.

Santa Cruz, Paul H. *Making JFK Matter,* Denton, TX: University of North Texas Press, 2015.

Sauvage, Leo. *The Oswald Affair.* New York: World Pub., 1966.

Scearce, Kenneth. "The Girl in the Red Skirt, a Micro-Study of the Zapruder Film." *Washington Decoded,* December 11, 2013. https://www.washingtondecoded.com/site/2013/12/redskirt.html.

Schlesinger, Jr., Arthur M. *A Thousand Days: John F. Kennedy in the White House.* New York: A Fawcett Crest Book, 1967.

Shenon, Philip *A Cruel and Shocking Act: The Secret History of the Kennedy Assassination.* New York: Henry Holt and Company, 2013.

Silverman, Hillel E. *The Time of My Life: Sixty Fulfilling Years as a Congregational Rabbi.* Jersey City, N.J: Ktav Publishing House, Inc. 2009.

Singleton, M.K. *H.L. Mencken and the "American Mercury" Adventure.* Durham, NC: Duke University Press, 1962.

Sorensen, Theodore. *Kennedy.* New York: Harper & Row, Publishers, 1965.

Specter, Arlen, with Charles Robbins. *A Passion for Truth: From Finding JFK's Single Bullet to Questioning Anita Hill to Impeaching Clinton.* New York: HarperCollins Publishers, Inc., 2000.

Stanton, Mary. *Freedom Walk: Mississippi or Bust.* Jackson, MS: University Press of Mississippi, 2003.

Stokes, Louis, with David Chanoff. *The Gentleman From Ohio.* Columbus, OH: Ohio State University Press, 2016.

Summers, Anthony. *Not in Your Lifetime: The Defining Book on the J.F.K. Assassination.* New York: Open Road, 2013.

Swift, Art. "Majority in U.S. Still Believe JFK Killed in Conspiracy" Gallup, November 15, 2013. https://news.gallup.com/poll/165893/majority-believe-jfk-killed-conspiracy.aspx.

Takeuchi, Jane, Fredric Solomon, and W. Walter Menninger, eds. *Behavioral Science and the Secret Service: Toward the Prevention of Assassination.* Washington, D.C.: National Academy Press, 1981.

Taubman, William. *Khrushchev: The Man, His Era.* New York: W.W. Norton & Co., 2003.

Thornley, Kerry. *Oswald.* Chicago: New Classics House, 1965.

Titovets, Ernst. *Oswald: Russian Episode.* Washington, DC: Eagle View Books, 2010.

Trejo, Paul Edward. *A Brief History of Ex-General Edwin Walker (Part One).* Paul Trejo at Smashwords (2012). https://www.smashwords.com/extreader/read/501625/1/a-brief-history-of-ex-general-edwin-walker-part-one.

Trotsky, Leon. *The Death Agony of Capitalism and the Task of the Fourth International.* (1938) as published at https://www.marxists.org/archive/trotsky/1938/tp/transprogram.pdf.

Trotsky, Leon. *Marxism and Terrorism.* New York, NY: Pathfinder Press, Second Printing, 1995.

Tunnheim, John R. "The Assassination Records Review Board: Unlocking the Government's Secret Files on the Murder of a President," *The Public Lawyer,* Vol 8. No. 1 (Winter, 2000).

Weisberg, Harold. *Oswald in New Orleans: Case for a Conspiracy with the CIA, 1967.* New York: Skyhorse, 2013.

Weisberg, Harold. *Whitewash.* Hyattstown, MS: H. Weisberg, 1965.

White, G. Edward. *Earl Warren: A Public Life.* New York: Oxford University Press, 1982.

Whitney, Peter R. "A Little Logic Please," no date. https://www.jfk-assassination.net/crawford.txt.

Willens, Howard. "The Imaginary Conspiracy: Unmasking JFK Invisible Second Shooter on the Grassy Knoll," February 1, 2019. https://drive.google.com/file/d/1MsnGP0mEFFYugQUntp9GyyPWtd6YhHFj/view.

Willens, Howard and Richard M. Mosk. "The Truth About Dallas," *The American Scholar,* Vol. 85, No. 3 (Summer, 2016).

Willens, Howard P. *History Will Prove Us Right: Inside the Warren Commission Report of the Assassination of John F. Kennedy.* New York: The Overlook Press, 2013.

Wills, Garry, and Demaris, Ovid. *Jack Ruby.* New York: The New American Library, Inc., 1968.

Wise, David and Thomas B. Ross. *The Espionage Establishment.* New York: Random House, 1967.

Yeltsin, Boris. *The View from the Kremlin.* London: HarperCollins, 1994.

Zapruder, Alexandra. *Twenty-Six Seconds: A Personal History of the Zapruder Film.* New York: Hachette Book Group, 2016.

Zinman, David. *The Day Huey Long Was Shot, September 8, 1935.* Jackson, MS: University Press of Mississippi, 1963.

Government Publications

The Investigation of the Assassination of President John F. Kennedy: Performance of the Intelligence Agencies, Book V, Final Report of the Select Committee to Study Governmental Operations with Respect to Intelligence Activities. 94th Congress, 2d Session. Report no. 94–755 (April 23, 1976).

Report, President's Commission on the Assassination of President John F. Kennedy (September 24, 1964)

Report, Select Committee on Assassinations, U.S. House of Representatives, 85th Congress, 2d Session (March 29, 1979)

Senate Select Committee to Study Government Operations with respect to Intelligence Activities, 94th Congress, 1st Session, Interim Report on Alleged Assassination Plots Involving Foreign Leaders (November 20, 1975); *Alleged Assassination Plots Involving Foreign Leaders: An Interim Report of the Select Committee to Study Government Operations* (W.W. Norton, 1976)

Interviews and Personal Communications

Blakey, Robert. Transcript of interview by author February 21, 2017. Cited herein as Blakey Tr. Transcript available from Rev, 222 Kearney Street, 8th Floor, San Francisco, California, 99108 (Rev.com) tel, 888-369-0701; ref: Warren Commission, Order# TC0887728893.

Index

Bold italic numbers refer to photographs.